CHRONOLOGY
OF THE EXPANDING WORLD

Also by Neville Williams

Chronology of the Modern World

NEVILLE WILLIAMS

M.A., D.Phil., F.S.A., F.R. Hist. Soc.

Chronology
of the Expanding World

1492 to 1762

BARRIE AND ROCKLIFF
THE CRESSET PRESS
LONDON

© 1969 by Neville Williams
SBN 214.66784.7
First published 1969 by
Barrie & Rockliff, The Cresset Press
2 Clement's Inn, London WC 2
Set in Monotype Ehrhardt
and printed in Great Britain by
William Clowes and Sons Ltd
London and Beccles

To
P. J-S.

Contents

Introduction

Chronology of the Expanding World, 1492 to 1762 has been prepared as a companion volume to *Chronology of the Modern World, 1763 to 1965* and is a guide to the events and achievements in every walk of life during the formative centuries from the discovery of America down to the conclusion of the long series of dynastic wars in Europe in 1762. As in the published volume, the information is given chronologically, yet a large-scale index is provided which readily supplies specific references. Political events appear throughout on left-hand pages, in quarterly paragraphs, under precise calendar dates wherever these are known. The corresponding right-hand pages for each year are devoted to achievements in the Arts and Sciences arranged under classified headings. Both the quarterly paragraphs of the left-hand pages and the subject paragraphs of the right-hand pages bear individual letters to enable speedy reference to be made from the index (A to E on the left, F to M on the right.)

The theme of expansion is sounded by Christopher Columbus' first westward voyage and is developed in the discoveries in Africa, India and the Far East during the next twenty years, leading in the fullness of time to permanent colonies of European powers which were to reach their apogee in the mid-eighteenth century as the volume closes. In the years around 1500 man's intellectual horizons, too, were being extended and a new dimension was given to scholarship and government by the rapid development of printing. In the full tide of the humanist Renaissance came the Reformation, to challenge the unity of the old order. Christendom was rent asunder. The new monarchies in France, Spain, England and the German states hastened the growth from medieval realms to national states. Freed at last from clerical control, art and science, philosophy and learning came of age. The many strands of history are unravelled year by year in these pages as the modern world gradually formed, and the contributions of men of renown are set in their true context as we move steadily forward from the age of Erasmus, Leonardo and Macchiavelli to the age of Voltaire, Rousseau and Franklin.

Although the general arrangement of material is similar to that followed in *Chronology of the Modern World*, to avoid wasting space there are various modifications; the left-hand paragraphs are set by quarters (instead of by months) and there are no longer separate paragraphs for 'Entertainment', 'The Press', 'Sport' and 'Statistics'. Entries on each side of the page have been provided with explanatory detail where necessary, though conciseness has been the aim. All facts have been checked to achieve a high standard of accuracy.

LEFT-HAND PAGES: One or more of the chief events of the year have been selected to form headlines. Events are placed by date order in five paragraphs: 'A' for the months January, February and March; 'B' for April, May and June; 'C' for July, August and September; 'D' for October, November and December. Paragraph 'E' contains those events which cannot be assigned to a particular month. Cross-references to the same, or another, year are given where appropriate. Each entry appears on a fresh line to assist clarity and quick reference.

RIGHT-HAND PAGES: Here, too, headlines show the chief achievements of the year. The paragraphs are classified under these headings:

F Politics, Economics, Law and Education (occasional entries for the press and statistical information are included)
G Science, Technology and Discovery
H Philosophy, Religion and Scholarship (including Archaeology)
J Art, Sculpture, the Fine Arts and Architecture
K Music
L Literature, including Drama
M Births and Deaths of notabilities. As before exact calendar dates are given wherever these are known; the death date is included within brackets in the birth entry and the individual's age is shown at death. The corresponding paragraph in *Chronology of the Modern World* aroused considerable interest, and in response to requests these entries have been provided on a more generous scale. All individuals are fully identified in the index.

OLD AND NEW STYLE DATES: By the third quarter of the sixteenth century astronomers found that January 1st was getting further and further from the shortest day owing to the length of the year having been slightly underestimated. The accumulated error by then amounted to ten days and to correct this Pope Gregory XIII in 1582 introduced his New Style of reckoning, or the 'Gregorian Calendar'. In Italy, France, Portugal, Spain and the other Catholic states which adopted this new chronology, 4 October 1582 was followed by 15 October. Gradually other countries abandoned the Julian for the Gregorian Calendar; for instance Austria in 1584, Holland in 1700 and Great Britain in 1752 (the last to conform was Russia, though not until after the Revolution). The dates at which different countries adopted the Gregorian Calendar are noted in the appropriate left-hand pages. The gap between British and Continental chronology had increased from ten to eleven days as the eighteenth century opened so that, when Britain and her colonies at last made the changeover in 1752, 2 September was followed by 14 September.

All events after 1582 relating to countries which adopted the Gregorian Calendar are given as New Style dates, while those for countries which retained the Julian Calendar are given as Old Style dates. Where an event concerns two or more countries following different styles the dates for both styles are shown, *e.g.* the general peace treaty of Utrecht of 171**3** is given as Mar. 31/ Apr. 11.

The dates of births and deaths of individuals recorded in paragraph M are shown according to the style of the country of the individual; *e.g.* both Shakespeare and Cervantes are noted as dying on Apr. 23rd 1611, though in fact Shakespeare lived on in Stratford-upon-Avon for ten days after Cervantes had died in Madrid.

OTHER EDITORIAL CONVENTIONS: The titles of foreign works are given in general in translation only when they have been subsequently translated into the English language; for most works retaining a title in Latin a descriptive comment in English is given. Where a work was published anonymously the author's name, if known, is placed within square brackets. Pseudonyms are noted and also works which appeared posthumously.

Sometimes an item might equally well have appeared in a different paragraph from the one in which it is placed. This is particularly the case with the overlapping of political and religious issues during the Reformation; some of the entries for the Reformation which have been classed as political events for inclusion on the left-hand page might equally well have been printed in paragraph H opposite. Any difficulties caused to readers by the choice of paragraphs and any unintentional oddities of arrangement that remain uncorrected will be readily solved through the index.

THE INDEX

Entries for Persons, Places and Subjects and titles of books are listed in a single alphabetical sequence. Prefixes to surnames have been disregarded. There are ample cross-references. A table of abbreviations used and a list of principal subject entries precedes the index.

PERSONS: The entries include full names and titles, dates of birth and death, nationality and a brief description of the individual's claim to fame, *e.g.* dramatist, Lutheran bishop, soldier. For the most important persons there are classified sub-entries, which show at a glance his career and achievement and, taken together, form a biographical dictionary for the period. Because of the part played by sovereigns in the era of personal monarchies, the principal events of a reign will often be summarised under the King or Queen concerned.

PLACES: All places are assigned their country according to the current world map. Entries for major cities are divided into series of sub-entries for events there, listed in date order, followed by a series for buildings and institutions in alphabetical order. There is a single chronological arrangement for less important places. Prefixes such as 'New' or 'South' are taken as part of the place-name proper. The entries for countries are of two kinds, as in the published volume. For minor states, such as Bavaria or Tuscany, there is one chronological sequence of sub-entries, which show at a glance the main features of the country's history during these 271 years. For major countries, where a similar practice would lead to a mass of entries, only information relating to alterations in frontiers or a change of dynasty is given. The political events of a major country will be found indexed in the series of classified Subject Entries.

SUBJECT ENTRIES: The most important is the series in which political events are classified. These include entries for Assassinations, Civil Wars, Legislation, Marriages, notable, Monarchies, Parliaments and other Assemblies, Revolutions, Treaties and Wars. In each case the sub-entries are arranged by countries alphabetically and, within countries, chronologically.

OTHER SUBJECT ENTRIES include—Dictionaries, Machines, Maps, the Reformation, Religious Denominations and Universities. In the case of long entries these are subdivided by countries, otherwise the arrangement is alphabetical.

TITLES OF WORKS: All books and plays are indexed individually in the main alphabetical sequence; the definite or indefinite article in the language of the title has been disregarded, *e.g. Midsummer Night's Dream, A*. There are, however, general entries for Newspapers, Operas and Oratorios, within which these works are listed alphabetically.

*   *   *

Many have played a part in the preparation of this volume and I cannot possibly name them all. I owe most to Leopold Ullstein. In an earlier preface I described him as 'the friendliest of publishers', and our friendship has been further enriched through working closely together in this series of chronologies. Rosemary Proctor has provided me with detailed information for the entries for painting, sculpture, architecture and music, while Frank Seymour Smith has given me the benefit of his extensive knowledge of literature, drama and scholarship. Adrian Yendel undertook a great deal of preliminary compilation and assisted with the preparation of the Index. Diana Steer typed a difficult manuscript with skill and in the final stages of production I have leaned heavily on David Sharp. My wife, as always, helped me to retain a sense of proportion when the going was difficult. But for some of the questions my children asked, the book would be far less complete. To all of these, then, I return my warmest thanks.

As my literary agent, Peter Janson-Smith has been closely connected with all my published work and, since I would like his name to be associated in print with a book of mine that I hope will stand the test of time, I have dedicated this to him in token of his friendship over the years.

Hampstead Garden Suburb   N.W.
Twelfth Night 1969

CHRONOLOGY

A **Jan:** 2nd, the Spanish complete the conquest of Granada, extinguishing the Moorish Kingdom and consolidating the Spanish monarchy of Ferdinand of Aragon and Isabella of Castille.
   Feb: Charles VIII of France, under the influence of Étienne de Vesc, abandons the former regent Anne of Beaujeu and himself takes control of affairs.
   Mar: 31st, Jews in Spain are given three months in which to accept Christianity or to leave; many subsequently cross to North Africa.

B **Apr:** 8th, Piero de' Medici succeeds as ruler of Florence (–1495) on the death of his father, Lorenzo the Magnificent;
   17th, Ferdinand of Spain agrees to finance Christopher Columbus's voyage of discovery.
   May: 3rd, Alfonso Fernández de Lugo conquers the island of Palma for Spain.
   Jun: 7th, on the death of Casimir IV, John Albert succeeds as King of Poland (–1501) while Alexander succeeds as ruler of Lithuania (–1506).

C **Jul:** 25th, Pope Innocent VIII dies.
   Aug: 3rd, Christopher Columbus sails from Palos;
   10th, Roderigo Borgia is elected Pope Alexander VI (–1503); vast sums are spent in bribes to secure his defeat of Cardinals Ascanio Sforza and Guiliano della Rovere.
   Sep: Perkin Warbeck, a Fleming claiming to be Richard, Duke of York (the second son of Edward IV), is accepted at the French court as rightful claimant to the English throne.

D **Oct:** 2nd, Henry VII of England invades France, concerned at the power of Charles VIII following the union with Brittany in *Dec.* 1491 and French support for Perkin Warbeck;
   12th, Christopher Columbus reaches the Bahamas;
   22nd, Henry VII begins the siege of Boulogne but
   30th, sends ambassadors to treat for terms.
   Nov: 3rd, by Peace of Étaples, Charles VIII undertakes to expel Perkin Warbeck from France and to pay Henry VII an indemnity of £159,000 by instalments.
   Dec: Florence and Naples sign secret alliance to despoil Milan.

E Duke Albert of Bavaria, whose designs on the Tyrol had led to the formation of the Swabian League in 1487, to maintain the authority of the Holy Roman Empire, yields to the Emperor Frederick III and joins the League.
   A peasants' revolt in Kempten is crushed.

F **Politics, Economics, Law and Education**

G **Science, Technology and Discovery**
Martin Behaim constructs a terrestrial globe at Nuremberg.
Christopher Columbus on a voyage from Palos, Spain, in search of a western route to India, discovers the New World. He reaches Cuba (*Oct.* 12th), which he names San Salvador.
Mont Aiguille in the Alps is ascended by a party of Frenchmen on the orders of Charles VIII of France, to destroy the peak's reputation for inaccessibility.

H **Philosophy, Religion and Scholarship**
Elio Antonio Lebrija, *Arte de la Lingua Castellana.*

J **Art, Sculpture, Fine Arts and Architecture**
Painting:
Carlo Crivelli, *The Immaculate Conception.*
Architecture:
Bramante starts building the choir and cupola of S. Maria delle Grazie, Milan (–1498).
Da Vinci draws a flying machine.

K **Music**
Anicius Manlius Severinus Boethius, *Opera* (posth., Venice. Contains the first discussion written in Europe in the Christian era, relating to theory of music).

L **Literature (including Drama)**
Diego de San Pedro, *La Cárcel de amor* (first Spanish novel of courtly love to be widely read in English, French and Italian translations of 1540).
Morten Borup, *Carmen vernale* (Danish topographical poem in Latin).
Bernardo Bellincioni, *Sonetti, canzoni e capitoli* (posth.).

M **Births and Deaths**
Jan. 12th Andrea Alicati b. (–1550).
Mar. 6th Juan Luis Vives b. (–1540).
Apr. 20th Pietro Aretino b. (–1557).
Sept. 7th Giacomo Aconcio b. (–1566).
— Romano Giulio b. (1546).
— Henry the Minstrel d.
— Marguerite d'Angoulême (Margaret of Navarre), b. (–1549).
— Ludwig Senfl b. (–*c.* 1556).
— Lorenzo de' Medici d. (*c.* 43).
— William Tyndale b. (–1536).
— Diaz del Castillo b. (–1576).

A Jan: 19th, by Treaty of Barcelona France cedes Roussillon and Cerdágne to Spain, as an assurance for French annexation of Brittany (in 1491) which had provoked Spanish and Imperial alarm, and to bid for Spanish support for French designs on Naples; Maximilian, King of the Romans, saves West Germany from French invasion at the battle of Salins.

Feb: Ludovico Sforza of Milan, alarmed at his isolation among the Italian States, appeals to Charles VIII of France to claim the Kingdom of Naples.

Mar: 15th, Christopher Columbus returns to Palos.

B Apr: 25th, Pope Alexander VI forms a league against Naples to counter Ferdinand of Naples' alliance with Florence, Milan and Verona. Ferdinand appeals unsuccessfully for Spanish aid. Alfonso Fernández de Lugo begins Spanish conquest of Teneriffe (–1496).

May: 3rd and 4th, Pope Alexander VI publishes first bull *Inter cetera* dividing New World between Spain and Portugal (revised in *July*);

23rd, by Treaty of Senlis with the Empire, Charles VIII of France restores Artois and Franche Comté.

Jun: Lucretia Borgia marries Giovanni Sforza of Pesano (annulled in 1497);

28th, Pope Alexander VI's second bull is issued at Ferdinand of Spain's request, to guard against Portuguese counter claims to Spanish dominion in the New World; Spain is assigned all territory west of a line drawn north to south, 100 leagues west of the Azores—confirmed *Sept.* 26th (Spain and Portugal make their own Concordat, *June* 1494).

C Jul: Alexander VI makes peace with Naples;

Henry VII denounces Perkin Warbeck to Margaret, Duchess of Burgundy, at whose court the Pretender had settled and this provokes stoppage of trade between England and the Netherlands;

Statute of Piotrkow in Poland grants land-owning gentry privileges at the expense of burghers and the movement of peasants is severely curtailed.

Aug: 19th, on Ferdinand III's death, Maximilian I assumes the title of Holy Roman Emperor elect (–1519).

Sep: 18th, Henry VII banishes Flemings from England and the Merchants' Adventurers move their staple from Antwerp to Calais.

D Oct:
Nov:
Dec:

E Peasants' revolt in Alsace.
Turks invade Dalmatia and Croatia.

F **Politics, Economics, Law and Education**

G **Science, Technology and Discovery**

Christopher Columbus returns to Lisbon from the West Indies (*Mar.* 4th); his announcement that he has discovered 'the Indies' is rapidly reported in the capitals of Europe. He leaves Spain on a second voyage (*Sept.* 25th–*June* 11th, 1496), on which he discovers Dominica, Puerto Rico, Antigua and Jamaica, and circumnavigates Hispaniola, where he founds a settlement at Isabella.

H **Philosophy, Religion and Scholarship**

Jacques Lefèvre d'Étaples, *Paraphrasis in Aristotelis octo physicos libros*.
Hartmann Schedel, *The Nuremburg Chronicle* (a world history from the Creation to the accession of the Emperor Maximilian I, with illustrations).

J **Art, Sculpture, Fine Arts and Architecture**

K **Music**

L **Literature (including Drama)**

M **Births and Deaths**

— Stephen Gardiner b. (–1555).

A Jan: 25th, Alfonso II succeeds to the throne of Naples on the death of Ferdinand I; he is recognised by Pope Alexander VI, but Charles VIII of France decides to press his claims, derived from the house of Anjou.

Feb:

Mar: 16th, Emperor Maximilian I marries Bianca Sforza.

B Apr:

May: Maximilian I recognises Perkin Warbeck as King of England.

Jun: 7th, by Treaty of Tordesillas, Spain and Portugal agree to divide the New World between themselves: Portugal to have all lands east of a line north and south drawn 370 leagues west of Cape Verde, Spain to have the rest.

C Jul:

Aug:

Sep: 1st, Charles VIII of France invades Italy to claim his inheritance to the throne of Naples (Naples remains under foreign rulers until 1870);

8th, Charles VIII enters Turin.

D Oct: 13th, Henry VII sends Edward Poynings as deputy for Ireland to reduce Carlow and end support for Perkin Warbeck;

22nd, Charles VIII recognises Ludovico Sforza as Duke of Milan.

Nov: 8th, Charles VIII enters Lucca and 17th, Florence, where the Republican Party, influenced by Savonarola, expels Piero de' Medici;

revolt in Pisa, which throws off its yoke with Florence;

Alfonso Fernández de Lugo lands at Santa Cruz to reduce Teneriffe.

Dec: 1st, Poynings opens a Parliament at Droghedra which passes legislation ('Poynings Law') making Irish legislature dependent on England;

de Lugo wins battle of La Laguna in Teneriffe, securing the island for Spain (though guerilla warfare continues to *Sept.* 1496);

31st, Charles VIII enters Rome; the Pope takes refuge in the Castle of St. Angelo.

E

F **Politics, Economics, Law and Education**
King's College, Aberdeen, is founded.

G **Science, Technology and Discovery**
Luca Pacioli's *Algebra*, includes a study of the problems of cubic equations.

H **Philosophy, Religion and Scholarship**
Cardinal Cajetano holds a disputation with Pico della Mirandola.
Walter Hylton (or Hilton), *The Scale (or Ladder) of Perfection* (popular devotional and mystical work) printed.
Johann Reuchlin, *De Verbo mirifico* (a study of cabbalism; –1517).
Johannes Tritheim (pseud. of J. von Heidenberg), *Liber de scriptoribus ecclesiasticis* (first chronological bibliography of church writers and books, listing nearly 1,000 items, with an index).
Charles VIII of France appoints Aemilius Paulus of Verona as Historiographer Royal.

J **Art, Sculpture, Fine Arts and Architecture**
Painting:
Sandro Botticelli, *Calumny*.
Francesco Francia, *Felicini Madonna*.
Leonardo da Vinci, *Madonna of the Rocks*.

K **Music**
Jean Mauburnus, *Rosetum exercitiarum spiritualium* (first systematic study of musical instruments; extra chapter with illustrations added in 1510).

L **Literature (including Drama)**
Sebastian Brandt, *Das Narrenschiff* (*The Ship of Fools*; trans. –1509).
John Lydgate, *The Falls of Princes* (posth.).

M **Births and Deaths**
Aug. 11th Hans Memling d. (*c.* 64).
Sept. 12th Francis I b. (–1547).
Sept. 24th Politian (Angelo Ambrogini) d. (40).
Nov. 5th Hans Sachs b. (–1576).
Nov. 17th Giovanni, Count Pico Della Mirandola, d. (31).
Nov. — Melozzo da Forli d. (*c.* 56).
Dec. 21st Matteo, Count Boiardo, d. (60).
— David Beaton b. (–1546).
— Correggio (Antonio Allegri) b. (–1534).
— Johann Friis b. (–1570).
— Domenico Ghirlandaio d. (*c.* 45).
— Jacopo Pontormo b. (–1556).
— Suleiman the Magnificent b. (–1566).
— François Rabelais b. (–1553).

A Jan: 28th, Charles VIII leaves Rome for Naples, Pope Alexander VI having agreed to
surrender Civita Vecchia and to give his son Cesare Borgia as a hostage but 30th,
Cesare escapes. Alfonso II of Naples flees to Sicily, leaving his kingdom to his son
Ferrante, who takes the title Ferdinand II and who has to face a revolt.

Feb: 6th, trial of Sir William Stanley, Henry VII's Lord Chamberlain, for complicity in
Perkin Warbeck's conspiracy;
10th, Stanley is executed;
22nd, Charles VIII enters Naples.

Mar: 26th, Maximilian appeals to the German princes at the Diet of Worms to check the
progress of the French in Italy;
31st, Pope Alexander VI forms the Holy League with the Empire, Spain, Venice and
Milan, ostensibly to fight the Turks but aiming at expelling Charles VIII from Italy.

B Apr:
May: 12th, Charles VIII is crowned King of Naples and
20th, retreats towards northern Italy;
the Imperial Diet opens in Worms.
Jun:

C Jul: 3rd, Perkin Warbeck fails to land at Deal in Kent and decides to move to the court of
James IV in Scotland;
5th, Charles VIII defeats forces of the Holy League at the Battle of Fornovo, near
Parma;
Ferdinand II reconquers Naples, with the help of the Spanish fleet under Gonzalo de
Cordova.

Aug: 7th, the Diet of Worms proclaims Perpetual Peace within the Empire, the right of
private warfare is abolished, an Imperial Chamber and Court of Appeal are established
and an imperial tax (the Common Penny) is authorised.

Sep: the French fleet is captured in Rapallo; the Duke of Orleans capitulates at Novara.

D Oct: Charles VIII makes Treaty of Vercelli with Ludovico Sforza of Milan, which ends
the effectiveness of the Holy League;
14th, English Parliament meets at Westminster (–Dec. 22nd) and frames a new statute
of treasons, declaring that service of a de facto king cannot subsequently be construed
as treason, and an Act against vagabonds and beggars;
25th, Manuel the Fortunate succeeds to the throne of Portugal on the death of his
cousin, King John the Perfect (–1521).

Nov: Charles VIII returns from Italy, leaving the Duke of Orleans behind;
27th, James IV of Scotland receives Perkin Warbeck at Stirling.
Dec:

E Jews are expelled from Portugal.

F **Politics, Economics, Law and Education**
An English Act of Parliament permits any pauper having an action at law to sue *in forma pauperis*.

G **Science, Technology and Discovery**

H **Philosophy, Religion and Scholarship**
John de Trevisa translates *De Proprietatibus Rerum* of Bartholomew Anglicus.
Aldine Press (founded by Aldus Manutius at Venice in 1490) begins publication of celebrated editions of the Greek classics, notably with Aristotle: *Opera Omnia*, vol. 1 (5 vols. –1498) thus making available for the first time, through the medium of the printed book, the philosophy of ancient Greece to Western scholars (–1498, 1501, 1597).

J **Art, Sculpture, Fine Arts and Architecture**
Painting:
Hieronymus Bosch, *Adoration of the Magi*; also *Garden of Worldly Delights*.
Andrea Mantegna, *Holy Family with St. Elizabeth and the Young St John* (–1500).
Perugino, *The Entombment*.
Leonardo da Vinci, *The Last Supper* (–1498).

K **Music**
Josquin des Prés appointed music director at Cambrai Cathedral (–1499).

L **Literature (including Drama)**
Matteo Maria Boiardo, *Orlando Innamorato* (posth. romantic epic; sequel by Ariosto –1516).
Elckerlijk (perhaps by Petrus Dorlandus), Dutch morality probably the original of the English *Everyman* (–1520).

M **Births and Deaths**
Jan. 11th Pedro Gonzalez de Mendoza d. (66).
Nov. 21st John Bale b. (–1563).
— Johannes Ockeghem d. (*c.* 75).
— Diego de Siloe b. (–1563).
— John Taverner b. (–1545).

A Jan:
  Feb: 24th, Henry VII ends the commercial dispute with Flanders (since 1493) by the treaty 'Magnus Intercursus', under which the English Merchants Adventurers subsequently return to Antwerp; and Margaret of Burgundy is to lose her dower lands if she gives refuge to English rebels.
  Mar: 5th, Henry VII commissions John and Sebastian Cabot to discover new lands.

B Apr:
  May:
  Jun:

C Jul: 18th, England nominally joins the Holy League against France.
  Aug:
  Sep: James IV of Scotland invades Northumberland in support of Perkin Warbeck's claim to the English throne;
  29th, Teneriffe finally surrenders to the Spanish; de Lugo is appointed Governor of Palma and Teneriffe and *adelantado* of the Canaries;
  Maximilian I leads an army to oust the remaining French from Italy.

D Oct: 6th, Frederick III succeeds as King of Naples on the death of Ferdinand II (–1501); Pope Alexander VI begins to reduce the Orsini with an army led by his son the Duke of Gandia (–*Feb.* 1497);
  21st, Philip the Handsome, Duke of Burgundy, son of the Emperor Maximilian I, marries Joanna, heiress of Spain.
  Nov: The Emperor Maximilian, having failed to take Leghorn, leaves Italy.
  Dec:

E

F **Politics, Economics, Law and Education**
   Marino Sanudo the younger begins his 'diaries' of affairs in Venice (–1535; they are published 1879–1903).
   An Act of the Scottish Parliament requires substantial householders to send their eldest sons to school from the age of eight.
   John Alcock founds Jesus College, Cambridge.
   John Colet begins lecturing in Oxford.

G **Science, Technology and Discovery**
   Treatyse of Fysshynge wyth an Angle is printed by Wynkyn de Worde.

H **Philosophy, Religion and Scholarship**
   Richard Rolle, the Hermit of Hampole, *The Abbaye of the Holy Ghost*.
   George Reisch, *Margarita philosophia*.

J **Art, Sculpture, Fine Arts and Architecture**
   Painting:
   Perugino, Pietà and Crucifix with Saints (frescoes, Florence).

K **Music**
   Franchino Gafori, *Practica Musicae* (treatise on composition).

L **Literature (including Drama)**
   Juan del Encina, *Cancionero* (Easter plays).
   Sir John Mandeville (pseud.), *Travels*.
   Johann Reuchlin, *Sergius* (Latin play, introducing comedy into Germany).

M **Births and Deaths**
   — Clement Marot b. (–1544).

1497   The end of Perkin Warbeck

A   Jan: 16th, English Parliament meets to grant high taxation (two fifteenths and tenths and
a subsidy of equal amount) for war against Scotland.
Feb: Alexander VI makes peace with the Orsini, recovering various papal fiefs.
Mar: 27th, Truce signed between France and Spain at Lyons (leads to treaty of *Aug.*
1498);
severe famine in Florence;
Lucretia Borgia is divorced from Giovanni Sforza and subsequently marries Alfonso of
Naples, to further Pope's alliance with Naples.

B   Apr: 3rd, John the Infante of Spain marries Margaret of Austria;
Ostia, held by a French garrison, is reduced by Spanish troops under Gonzalo de
Cordova.
May: Rising breaks out in Cornwall, provoked by taxation. James Tutchet, Lord Audley,
leads an army of 15,000 from Taunton through the southern counties to attack
London;
Henry VII signs a commercial treaty with France.
Jun: 14th, the Duke of Gandia is murdered, allegedly by his half-brother, Cesare Borgia,
who now acquires a dominant position in papal politics;
Jun: 17th, Henry VII defeats the Cornish rebels under Lord Audley at Blackheath;
18th, Henry VII ratifies the marriage treaty with Spain.

C   Jul: 26th, Perkin Warbeck arrives in Cork from Scotland at the invitation of Sir James
Ormond; finding little support, as a result of Ormond's death, he subsequently sails
for Cornwall (landing there *Sept.* 7th).
Aug: 10th, Scottish army crosses the Border and lays siege to Norham Castle;
Prince Arthur is betrothed to Catherine of Aragon.
Sep: Manuel, King of Portugal marries Isabella of Spain;
17th, rebels under Perkin Warbeck attempt to take Exeter;
30th, Anglo-Scottish truce is signed at Ayton to last for 7 years;
Ferdinand II of Naples dies.

D   Oct: 4th, the Infante John of Spain dies;
5th, Perkin Warbeck is captured and taken to King Henry VII at Taunton; the West
Country submits;
28th, John II of Denmark defeats the Swedes at Brunkeberg and enters Stockholm,
reviving the Scandinavian Union.
Nov. Maximilian I leaves Rome, having failed to take Leghorn from the League.
Dec: 5th, Anglo-Scottish truce is extended to the lives of Henry VII and James IV;
21st, Sheen Palace, Richmond, destroyed by fire.

E

F **Economics, Politics, Law and Education**
    Baccarat is introduced to France from Italy.
G **Science, Technology and Discovery**
    John Cabot, sailing from Bristol (*May* 2nd), under instructions from Henry VII to dis-
    cover and settle new lands across the Atlantic, reaches the American coast at Cape
    Breton Island (*Jun.* 24th) and explores the coast of Newfoundland. He announces he
    has discovered the land of the Great Khan.
    Vasco da Gama leaves Lisbon (*July* 9th) on a voyage to India; he rounds the Cape of
    Good Hope (*Dec.*).

H **Philosophy, Religion and Scholarship**
    John Alcock, *The Hill of Perfection*.
    Aristotle's philosophy is expounded in Padua for the first time in Greek.

J **Art, Sculpture, Fine Arts and Architecture**
    Painting:
    Albrecht Dürer, *The Artist's Father*.
    Filippino Lippi, *Meeting of Joachim and Anne at the Golden Gate*.
    Perugino, murals in Collegio del Cambio, Perugia (–1500).
    Sculpture:
    Michelangelo, *Bacchus*.

K **Music**

L **Literature (including Drama)**
    Johann Reuchlin, *Henno* (a comedy in Latin –1496).

M **Births and Deaths**
    Feb. 16th Philipp Melanchthon b. (–1560).
    — John Heywood b. (–1578).
    — Hans Holbein the younger b. (–1543).

A Jan: Renewed feuds of the Colonna and Orsini families in the papal states (*–June*).
Feb: Ferdinand and Isabella ratify the treaty for marrying Catherine of Aragon to Arthur, Prince of Wales.
Mar:

B Apr: 7th, Louis XII, Duke of Orleans, the last of the direct line of the house of Valois, succeeds as King of France (–1515) on the death of his cousin Charles VIII. The Duchy of Orleans and the Comté of Blois are thus united with the French crown.
May: 22nd, death sentence is pronounced on Savonarola, former Prior of St. Mark's and effective ruler of Florence, who had been excommunicated in *June* 1497, for attempting to seek the deposition of Pope Alexander VI;
English merchants return to Antwerp.
Jun:

C Jul: 14th, Louis XII confirms his predecessor's Treaty of Étaples with Henry VII in 1492, with the article against receiving English rebels strengthened;
15th (and 19th), Perkin Warbeck, who had attempted to flee from Henry VII's court, makes public confession of his treasons in London and Westminster and is imprisoned in the Tower;
Isabella, Infanta of Spain and wife of Manuel the Fortunate of Portugal, dies after giving birth to a prince.
Aug: 2nd, Philip the Handsome of Burgundy confirms the Treaty of Senlis with France;
5th, Louis XII and Ferdinand I sign the treaty of Marcoussis, which ends the effectiveness of the Holy League; they make plans for a Franco-Spanish partition of Naples.
Sep:

D Oct: 1st, Cesare Borgia (who had renounced the priesthood in *Aug.*), leaves Rome as papal legate to Louis XII with a dispensation for Louis' marriage to Jeanne, daughter of Louis XI, to enable him to marry Anne of Brittany.
Nov: Venice sends an ambassador to Istanbul with tribute for the island of Zante and an assurance that the Republic does not seek war with the Turks.
Dec:

E

F Politics, Economics, Law and Education
   The first known cases of syphilis in Europe.

G Science, Technology and Discovery
   Vasco da Gama who rounded the Cape of Good Hope in *Dec.* 1497, explores the
   Mozambique coast and discovers the sea route to India, arriving at Calicut on the
   Malabar coast (*May* 20th).
   Christopher Columbus sails on third voyage of exploration (*May* 30th to *Nov.* 25th,
   1500), on which he discovers Trinidad (*July* 31st), and South America (*Aug.* 1st), near
   the mouth of the R. Orinoco.
   Duarte Pereira is sent on a westward expedition by John of Portugal, and may have
   reached South America.

H Philosophy, Religion and Scholarship
   Joannes Annius of Viterbo exploits the demand for historical works of the ancient
   world by publishing 17 volumes of forgeries of 'lost works' of Cato the elder and
   others.
   The Aldine Press, Venice, begins production of octavo editions of the Greek and Latin
   classics at 'popular' prices. Thus Aldus is pioneer publisher-printer to produce great
   books in cheap series (1495, 1501, 1597).
   The *Comedies* of Aristophanes published at the Aldine Press, Venice.
   Erasmus teaches at Oxford.
   Girolamo Savonarola is strangled, then burnt, at Florence for continuing to preach and
   for sedition and 'religious errors'.

J Art, Sculpture, Fine Arts and Architecture
   Painting:
      Albrecht Dürer, *Self-Portrait; The Knight, Death and the Devil; Apocalypse;* and
      Great Passion (–1510).
      Gerard David, *Examples of Justice.*
   Sculpture:
      Michelangelo, Pietà, St. Peter's, Rome (–1500).

K Music

L Literature (including Drama)

M Births and Deaths
   Apr. 8th Charles VIII d. (28).
   May 23rd Girolamo Savonarola d. (45).
   June — Julius Pomponius Laetus (or Laebo) d. (73).
   Sept. 16th Tomás de Torquemada d. (78).
   — John Cabot d. (48).

A   Jan: 8th, Louis XII of France, having obtained a divorce from Joanna, daughter of Louis
         XI, marries Anne, Duchess of Brittany, widow of Charles VIII, to keep the Duchy of
         Brittany for the crown.
     Feb: Florence joins the French alliance for the partition of Milan;
         Plot for a Yorkist rising in Kent is discovered by Henry VII;
         War between the Swabian League and the Swiss Cantons flares up in the Rhine;
         Maximilian I is aided by an army from Nuremberg.
     Mar: Louis XII signs agreement with the Swiss League for supplying mercenaries for his
         Italian campaign in return for an annual pension of 20,000 florins;
         Ximenes increases repressive policy against the Moors in Granada.

B   Apr: Louis XII gives the hand of Charlotte d'Albret to Cesare Borgia and assigns him the
         Duchy of Valentinois.
     May:
     Jun:

C   Jul: Edmund de la Pole, Earl of Suffolk, fearful for his life, flees to the Continent;
         outbreak of war between the Turks and Venice; Turkish raids on Venetian possessions
         in Albania and Dalmatia;
         22nd, decisive victory of the Swiss over the Swabian League, led by Albert of Bavaria,
         at Dornach near Basle.
     Aug: 2nd, conspiracy of the Earl of Warwick and Perkin Warbeck to escape from the
         Tower is discovered;
         12th, Turks defeat Venetian fleet at Sapienza;
         29th, Lepanto surrenders to the Sultan.
     Sep: 2nd, Ludovico Sforza flees from Milan to the Tirol to raise an army;
         11th, the French take Milan, meeting with little opposition;
         22nd, the Peace of Basle ends the Swabian War of Maximilian I against the Swiss
         League; the Swiss establish their independence from imperial jurisdiction and taxa-
         tion;
         the Turks ravage Vicenza.

D   Oct: 6th, Louis XII's solemn entry to Milan.
     Nov: 21st, Perkin Warbeck is tried for treason and
         23rd, executed;
         28th, Edward, Earl of Warwick, is executed for treason.
     Dec:

E   Cesare Borgia begins conquest of the Romagna (–1501), reducing the papal estates to
         central control.
     Philip the Handsome cedes his rights in Friesland to Albert of Saxony to satisfy a debt.

F **Politics, Economics, Law and Education**
  Alcalá University is founded.

G **Science, Technology and Discovery**
  Alonso de Ojeda and Amerigo Vespucci leave Spain (*May* to *June* 1500) on a voyage of discovery in South America on which they discover the mouth of the R. Amazon.

  Vincente Yanèz Pinzon makes a similar voyage of discovery (*Sept.* to *Dec.* 1500) and explores the Brazilian coast.

H **Philosophy, Religion and Scholarship**
  Francesco Colonna, *Hypnerotomachia Poliphili* (an allegorical and architectural romance-fantasy; probably written about 1475; printed by Aldus Manutius at his Aldine Press, Venice, embellished with 172 woodcuts and floriated initials; one of the great achievements of the Italian renaissance).

J **Art, Sculpture, Fine Arts and Architecture**
  Painting:
    Albrecht Dürer, portraits of *Oswald Krell* and of *Hans Felicites and Elzabeth Tucher*.
    Luca Signorelli, fresco cycle at Orvieto Cathedral (begun by Fra Angelico in 1447).
  First known political cartoon (on the subject of Louis XII of France and the Italian war).

K **Music**
  Oxford University institutes a degree in music.

L **Literature (including Drama)**

M **Births and Deaths**
  Mar. 31st Giovanni Angelo Medici (Pope Pius IV) b. (–1565).
  Aug. 29th Alessio Baldovinetti d. (71).
  Sept. 3rd Diane de Poitiers b. (–1566).
  — Marsilio Ficino d. (66).
  — Thomas Elyot b. (–1546).

A Jan: 12th, Forli, held by Caterina Sforza, surrenders to Cesare Borgia.
   Feb: 5th, Ludovico Sforza with the aid of German and Swiss mercenaries recovers Milan
   from the French;
   24th, Joanna, wife of Philip of Austria, Duke of Burgundy, gives birth to the future
   Emperor Charles V.
   Mar: 21st, the French garrison in Novara capitulates to Ludovico Sforza.

B Apr: 8th, a French army under Louis de la Trémouille, aided by Swiss mercenaries commanded by Trivulzio, reconquer Milan; Ludovico Sforza is sent as a prisoner to
   France (–1508);
   10th, at the Diet of Augsburg, Maximilian I, bent on creating a strong monarchy with
   a standing army, is forced to agree to the scheme of Berthold of Henneberg, Archbishop of Mainz and arch-chancellor of the Empire, for a representative supreme
   executive council (Edict *July* 2nd);
   21st, Pedro Alvarez Cabral lands in Brazil, which he claims for Portugal, naming it
   Tierra de Vera Cruz;
   the death of Dom Miguel, heir to the thrones of Spain and Portugal, dashes Ferdinand
   of Aragon's hopes for a union of the Kingdoms and leaves Joanna and Philip of
   Burgundy heirs to Spain.
   May: Louis XII sends Georges d'Amboise, Cardinal of Rouen, to govern Milan. The
   Italian states come to terms with France;
   Ferdinand of Aragon suppresses a Moorish revolt in Granada.
   Jun: 1st, Pope Alexander VI proclaims a Year of Jubilee and calls on all princes to support
   a crusade against the Turks, for which he imposes a tithe;
   9th, Henry VII of England confers at St. Omer with Philip the Handsome of Burgundy
   about matrimonial alliances between Tudors and Hapsburgs and commercial interests.

C Jul: 2nd, Edict of the Diet of Augsburg recognises the Holy Roman Empire on the scheme
   of Berthold of Henneberg by establishing a Council of Regency, with representatives
   from the three colleges of electors, princes and cities; it divides Germany into six
   'circles', or administrative provinces (the number of 'circles' is increased in 1512);
   Louis XII makes treaty of alliance with John Albert, King of Poland.
   Aug: Alfonso of Naples, Lucretia Borgia's husband, is murdered.
   Sep:

D Oct: 1st, Cesare Borgia, with French aid, resumes operations in the Romagna, taking
   Rimini and Pesaro;
   Manuel the Fortunate, King of Portugal, marries Maria, the Infanta of Spain.
   Nov: 11th, Louis XII of France and Ferdinand of Aragon sign secret treaty of Granada
   for the conquest and partition of Naples; France is to have the Abruzzi, the Terra di
   Luvoro, Naples and Gaeta, while Spain is to have Apulia and Calabria (Pope Alexander
   ratifies the treaty *June* 1501).
   Dec:

E

F **Politics, Economics, Law and Education**

G **Science, Technology and Discovery**
Diego Diaz discovers Madagascar (*Aug.* 10th).
Pedro Álvarez Cabral discovers Brazil (*Apr.* 21st).
Gaspar de Corte Real explores the east coast of Greenland and Labrador.
Juan de la Cosa's map of the new world.
Jerome Brunschwig, *Liber de arte distillandi*.
Italian version of the *trompe* (forcing air by the suction of a water chute) replaces bellows in the forging of iron.

H **Philosophy, Religion and Scholarship**
Desiderius Erasmus, *Adagia* (one of the most widely-read books of the century. It consisted of Greek and Latin proverbs, with comments, opinions, quotations and long disquisitions by Erasmus, who enlarged his original compilation from time to time).

J **Art, Sculpture, Fine Arts and Architecture**
Painting:
Hieronymus Bosch, *Ship of Fools*.
Sandro Botticelli, *Mystic Nativity;* also *The Miracles of St. Zenobius*.
Albrecht Dürer, *The Nativity*.
Lucas Cranach, *The Crucifixion*.
Luca Signorelli, *Lawyer in a Red Cap*.
Sculpture:
Michelangelo, *Madonna and Child* (Bruges).

K **Music**

L **Literature (including Drama)**
The first edition of the oldest German *Schwank* (–1509) collection of tales known as *Till Eulenspiegel* published about this time in Lübeck (extant edition in High German –1515).
Mariken van Nieumeghen (Dutch miracle play; trans. into English *c.* 1519).

M **Births and Deaths**
Apr. 23rd Alexander Ales b. (–1565).
May 8th Peter Martyr (Pieto Martire Vermigli) b. (–1562).
May 29th Bartholomew Diaz de Novaes d. (70).
Nov. 1st Benvenuto Cellini b. (–1571).
— Richard Cox b. (–1581).
— Edward Seymour, Duke of Somerset, b. (–1552).

A Jan: 17th, Cesare Borgia returns to Rome in triumph from his campaign in the Romagna, in which he succeeds in bringing the States of the Church under direct rule.
Feb:
Mar: Moorish rebels in western Granada offer stiff resistance to Spanish army.

B Apr: Faenza surrenders to Cesare Borgia, who murders Astorre Manfredi, Lord of Faenza, despite promises to spare his life.
May: French army masses in Lombardy.
Jun: French enter Rome and, 25th, Pope Alexander VI confirms the Franco-Spanish Treaty of Granada (*Nov.* 1500) for the partition of Naples and declares Louis XII King of Naples. The Pope creates Cesare Borgia Duke of Romagna and is assured that the French will not interfere with his policy of aggrandisement.

C Jul: In the conquest of Naples (–1503), the French, with the help of Cesare Borgia, take Capua, while the Spanish take Apulia and Calabria;
Ferdinand I of Spain declares the Kingdom of Granada to be Christian; repressive policy against the Moors is intensified.
Aug: 4th, the castles of Naples fall to the French; Louis XII offers Frederick of Naples honourable asylum in France and appoints Louis' d'Armagnac, Duke of Nemours, Viceroy of Naples;
10th, treaty for the marriage between Charles of Austria, infant son of Philip, Duke of Burgundy, with Claude, infant daughter of Louis XII.

Sep: discussions begin in Antwerp for the expulsion of English rebels from imperial territory;
Lucretia Borgia is betrothed to the Duke of Ferrara (marriage takes place *Jan.* 1502).

D Oct:
Nov: 7th, Edmund, Earl of Suffolk, who had escaped abroad in August to raise forces for an invasion of England to support his Yorkist claims to the throne, is denounced by Henry VII as a traitor (Suffolk is attainted in 1504 and executed in 1513);
15th, Arthur, Prince of Wales, marries Catherine of Aragon;
Henry VII declines Pope Alexander's request to lead a crusade against the Turks, but permits a collection for the crusade to be made in England.
Dec:

E Ivan the Great of Russia invades Polish Lithuania.
The south German states of Basle and Schaftenhausen are admitted as members of the Swiss Confederation.
Ismail the Sofi, Shiekh of Ardabil, conquers Persia at the Battle of Shurnur and founds the Safavid dynasty (–1736).

F **Politics, Economics, Law and Education**

G **Science, Technology and Discovery**

Amerigo Vespucci leaves Portugal (*May–Sept.* 1502) to explore the South American coast. He is convinced that the continent is a new world.

De Bastidas traces the coast from Panama to Port Manzanilla (–1502).

H **Philosophy, Religion and Scholarship**

Desiderius Erasmus, *Enchiridion Militis Christiani*.

Giorgio Valla, *De expetendis fugiendis rebus* (Venice, posth.).

Aldus Manutius first uses italic type at his Aldine Press, Venice.

J **Art, Sculpture, Fine Arts and Architecture**

Painting:

Albrecht Dürer, *Life of the Virgin*.

Filippino Lippi, *St. Catherine*.

Sculpture:

Michelangelo, Statue of *David* (–1504, Florence).

K **Music**

Ottaviano dei Petrucci publishes in Venice *Harmonice Musices Odhécaton*, the first book of music printed with movable type.

L **Literature (including Drama)**

Fernando de Rojas, *La Celestina* (a romance, part tragi-comedy, part novel) in racy dialogue; of great importance in the development of realistic comedy in European literature (trans. 1631).

M **Births and Deaths**

Jan. 17th Leonhard Fuchs b. (–1566).

May 6th Marcello Cervini (Pope Marcellus II) b. (–1555).

Sept. 24th Girolamo Cardan b. (–1576).

1502   France and Spain fall out over Naples

A   Jan: Marriage treaty is signed to cement Anglo-Scottish relations (see *Aug.* 7th).
    Feb: Maximilian I summons the German princes to join him on a crusade on *June* 1st.
    Mar: 2nd, Maximilian I demands the resignation of Berthold of Henneberg from the
        arch-chancellorship of the Empire for maintaining the Emperor elect has acted con-
        trary to the Edicts of Worms and Augsburg; his dismissal ends the effectiveness of the
        Executive Council of the Empire;
        Gonzalo de Cordova compels Taranto to surrender to the Spanish after a siege; Prince
        Ferrante of Naples is sent as prisoner to Spain.

B   Apr: 2nd, Arthur, Prince of Wales dies.   Henry VII subsequently refuses the demands of
        Ferdinand and Isabella of Spain to restore her dowry.
    May:
    Jun: 19th, by Treaty of Antwerp between England and the Empire, Henry VII agrees to
        pay Maximilian I £10,000 towards his proposed crusade in return for an undertaking
        to banish English rebels, notably the Earl of Suffolk who had taken refuge in Aachen
        (confirmed *July* 28th).

C   Jul: Open warfare breaks out between the French and Spanish in Italy over the partition
        of Naples (–1503);
        Louis XII purchases the neutrality of Cesare Borgia;
        the Spaniards are driven from Cepignola.
    Aug: 7th, James IV of Scotland marries Margaret Tudor;
        the French drive the Spaniards from Canosa.
    Sep:

D   Oct: Gonzalo de Cordova is besieged in Barletta;
        conspiracy of La Magione against Cesare Borgia.
    Nov:
    Dec: French troops aid Cesare Borgia in putting down a revolt of the Orsini and his
        condottieri and
        31st, Borgia takes Urbino, murdering Vitellozzo Vitelli and Oliverotti da Fermo, who
        had plotted against him.

E   The Venetians seize Santa Maura from the Turks;
    Rising of peasants at Speyer in Germany.

F   **Politics, Economics, Law and Education**
Vasco da Gama founds a Portuguese Colony at Cochin, Malabar, in India.
Henry VII's mother, the Lady Margaret, founds professorships of Divinity at Oxford and Cambridge Universities.
Maximilian I founds Wittenberg University (*July* 6th).

G   **Science, Technology and Discovery**
Christopher Columbus sails on his final voyage of exploration (*May* 11th–*Nov.* 7th, 1504), visiting Honduras and Panama. He plants a short-lived colony at Nombre de Dios (*Nov.*).
João de Nova discovers St. Helena (*May* 21st).

H   **Philosophy, Religion and Scholarship**
Arnold's *Chronicle* ('of the baylifs, Custos mairs and sherefs of the cite of London'; published about now in Antwerp).
Ambrogio Calepino, *Cornucopiae* (a polyglot dictionary).
Thucydides, *The Peloponnesian War*, first printed edition, published by Aldus in Venice.

J   **Art, Sculpture, Fine Arts and Architecture**
Painting:
    Giovanni Bellini, *Baptism of Christ*.
    Sandro Botticelli, *The Last Communion of St. Jerome*.
    Gerard David, St. John the Baptist triptych, Bruges (–1507).
    Albrecht Dürer, *Bunch of Violets;* and *Young Hare*.
    Raphael, *Coronation of the Virgin*.

K   **Music**
The Eton Choirbook completed (begun 1490).
First book of Masses by Josquin, published by Petrucci.

L   **Literature (including Drama)**

M   **Births and Deaths**
Jan. 7th Ugo Buoncompagno (Pope Gregory XIII) b. (–1585).
Apr. 2nd Arthur, Prince of Wales, d. (16).
Dec. 31st Vitellozzo Vitelli d. (*c.* 45).
— John Dudley, Duke of Northumberland, b. (–1553).

A   Jan: 20th, the Casa Contratacion (or Board of Trade) is founded in Spain for dealing with the affairs of America.
Feb: 4th, Queen Elizabeth, consort of Henry VII of England, dies in childbed;
18th, Henry Tudor is created Prince of Wales.
Mar: Venice signs peace treaty with the Turks, abandoning Lepanto, but retaining certain of the Ionian Islands.

B   Apr: 16th, Margaret, Duchess of Burgundy, widow of Charles the Bold, dies;
28th, Spaniards destroy the French fleet at Cerignola.
May: 13th, Gonzalo de Cordova defeats French army and enters Naples.
Jun: 23rd, Henry, Prince of Wales, is betrothed to Catherine of Aragon.

C   Jul:
Aug: 18th, Pope Alexander VI dies.
Sep: 3rd, Ferdinand I sends an army to North Africa against the Moors; Mers-el-Kebir falls to the Spanish;
22nd, Francesco Todeschini is elected Pope Pius III, as successor to Alexander VI. The princes in the Romagna and other States of the Church deposed by Cesare Borgia rise against him and the Orsini return to Rome.

D   Oct: Guidobaldo, Duke of Urbino returns to his duchy with the help of Venice.
Nov: 1st, Giuliana della Rovere is elected Pope Julius II (–1513) on the death of Pius III. Cesare Borgia is imprisoned for refusing to surrender his castles in the Romagna to the new Pope; he is freed on restoring his conquests;
5th, Revolt of Imola against the Duke of Valentinois;
29th, William Warham, is appointed Archbishop of Canterbury (–1532) on Archbishop Deane's death;
Venice invades the Romagna.
Dec: 1st, war of succession between Bavaria and the Palatinate, on the death of George, Duke of Bavaria-Landshut;
26th, Pope Julius II grants dispensation for the marriage of Henry, Prince of Wales and Catherine of Aragon (married in 1509);
29th, Gonzalo de Cordova defeats the French at the battle of Garigliano, completing the Spanish conquest of Naples and assuring Spanish control in south Italy.

E   Poland surrenders the left bank of the R. Dnieper to Russia.

F **Politics, Economics, Law and Education**
The Portuguese send African slaves to South America.

G **Science, Technology and Discovery**
Pedro di Navarro first uses explosive mines, during the siege of Naples.
Gregor Reisch, *Margarita Philosophia*, a scientific text book.

H **Philosophy, Religion and Scholarship**
The first English translation (*Anon.*) of Thomas à Kempis, *The Imitation of Christ.*

J **Art, Sculpture, Fine Arts and Architecture**
Painting:
 Filippino Lippi, *Virgin and Saints.*
 Leonardo da Vinci, *Mona Lisa.*
Architecture:
 Henry VII's chapel, Westminster Abbey, is begun (–1519).
 Bramante, plans the Vatican and St. Peter's, Rome.

K **Music**

L **Literature (including Drama)**

M **Births and Deaths**
Dec. 13th Nostradamus (Michel de Notredame) b. (–1566).
— Angelo Bronzino b. (–1572).
— Thomas Wyatt b. (–1542).

A   Jan: 1st, Gaeta, the last French garrison in Naples, surrenders to Spanish troops;
    25th, English Parliament meets (–*Apr.* 1st) and passes statutes against retainers and
    liveries, to curb private warfare among over-mighty subjects, and to place guilds and
    companies under state supervision. Parliament also attaints the Yorkist Edmund,
    Earl of Suffolk, who is subsequently imprisoned in Guelderland;
    31st, by Treaty of Lyons, Louis XII of France finally cedes Naples to Ferdinand of
    Aragon (confirmed *Mar.* 31st; Naples remains under Spanish control until 1713).
    Feb:
    Mar:

B   Apr: 23rd, Maximilian I pronounces the ban of the Holy Roman Empire on Rupert, son
    of the Elector Palatine (who had married the daughter of the late Duke George of
    Bavaria-Landshut), for seizing Landshut which he claimed under George's will.
    Campaigns in South Germany are fought to preserve the succession of the Dukes of
    Bavaria-Munich to Landshut.
    May:
    Jun:

C   Jul:
    Aug: Albert of Bavaria-Munich defeats Rupert of the Palatinate.
    Sep: Pope Julius II forces Venice to restore Ravenna and Cervia to his control;
    12th, Maximilian I defeats the mercenaries engaged by Rupert of the Palatinate near
    Regensberg;
    22nd, Treaty of Blois is signed by Louis XII of France with Maximilian I and his son,
    Philip the Handsome of Burgundy. Louis affiances his daughter Claude to Philip's
    son Charles, the future Emperor Charles V; if Louis dies without a son, Charles and
    Claude are to succeed to Milan, Blois and Brittany. By a secret treaty Louis is allowed
    to retain Milan for 100,000 ducats, and agrees with Maximilian for a joint attack on
    Naples.

D   Oct: Maximilian takes Kufstein in the Tyrol, which had declared for Rupert. The Duke
    of Bavaria-Munich acquires the Landshut dominions;
    Pope Julius II restores the Colonna and Orsini to their castles.
    Nov: 26th, the death of Isabella of Castille leaves Joanna, wife of Philip the Handsome,
    heir to Castille. Ferdinand of Aragon secures from the Cortes authority to govern
    Castille in her name.
    Dec:

E   Venice sends an ambassador to the Sultan of Turkey, proposing the construction of a Suez
    Canal;
    The Constitution of Radom makes the Diet the legislative organ of Poland;
    Accession of Basil III in Russia (–1533).

F Politics, Economics, Law and Education
English trade guilds and companies are placed under the supervision of the Crown.
University of Santiago de Compostela, in Spain, is founded by bull of Pope Julius II.

G Science, Technology and Discovery

H Philosophy, Religion and Scholarship

J Art, Sculpture, Fine Arts and Architecture
Painting:
Lucas Cranach, *Rest on the Flight to Egypt.*
Giorgione, *Madonna*, Castelfranco.
Albrecht Dürer, *Nativity;* and *Adam and Eve* (etching).
Raphael, *Marriage of the Virgin.*
Sculpture:
Michelangelo, *Madonna and Child* (Florence); *Little St. John.*

K Music

L Literature (including Drama)
Jacopo Sannazzaro, *L'Arcadia* (pastoral romance in prose and verse).

M Births and Deaths
Jan. 11th Francesco Parmigianino b. (–1540).
Jan. 17th Michele Ghislieri (Pope Pius V) b. (–1572).
July 18th Heinrich Bullinger b. (–1575).
Aug. 6th Matthew Parker b. (–1575).
Nov. 24th Isabella of Castille d. (53).
— Nicholas Udall b. (–1556).

A   Jan:
    Feb:
    Mar:
B   Apr: Maximilian I, assured of his position with the settlement of the Bavarian settlement
        and the death of his enemy Berthold of Henneberg, Archbishop of Mainz, is in a
        position to face his critics at the Diet of Cologne. He obtains support from the German
        princes for an expedition to Hungary to assist Ladislas II against his factious nobility
        and begins to reform the Empire according to his own plans, which are coloured by a
        dream of a universal Hapsburg monarchy.
    May:
    Jun: 27th, Henry, Prince of Wales, denounces his marriage contract with Catherine of
        Aragon.

C   Jul:
    Aug:
    Sep:
D   Oct: 12th, by the Treaty of Blois with Louis XII, Ferdinand I of Aragon contracts to
        marry Germaine de Foix, strengthening his claim to Navarre. Louis resigns his rights
        in Naples to Germaine, but if Ferdinand dies without issue France is to recover those
        portions assigned to Spain by the Treaty of Granada (of 1500).
    Nov: Following the death of Isabella of Castille (in *Nov.* 1504), Ferdinand I of Aragon
        signs Treaty of Salamanca, undertaking to rule jointly with his daughter Joanna and
        her husband Philip the Handsome.
    Dec:

E   Basil IV succeeds as Grand Duke of Moscow (–1533).

F **Politics, Economics, Law and Education**
   The Portuguese establish a fort at Sofala in East Africa.
   A regular mail service is established between Brussels and Vienna.
   Christ's College, Cambridge, is founded by Lady Margaret Beaufort.

G **Science, Technology and Discovery**
   Scipio Ferro solves a form of cubic equation.

H **Philosophy, Religion and Scholarship**
   John Colet is appointed Dean of St. Paul's, where he lectures on the Scriptures.
   Martin Luther enters the Augustinian monastery, Erfurt (*July* 17th).
   Jakob Wimpfeling, *Epitome rerum Germanicarum* (the first history of Germany based on
   original sources).

J **Art, Sculpture, Fine Arts and Architecture**
   Painting:
   Giovanni Bellini, altar-piece, San Zaccaria.
   Lucas Cranach, woodcuts (–1509).
   Albrecht Dürer, *Virgin and Child and Animals*.
   Lorenzo Lotto, *The Maiden's Dream*.
   Raphael, *Madonna del Granduca*.

K **Music**

L **Literature (including Drama)**

M **Births and Deaths**
   — John Knox b. (–1572).
   — Thomas Tallis b. (–1585).

1506   The Treaty of Windsor between England and the Netherlands—
Death of Philip the Handsome

A **Jan:** 16th, Joanna and Philip the Handsome, on passage from the Netherlands to Castille to claim their inheritance, are driven by storms to the English coast and, 31st, are received by Henry VII at Windsor.

Feb: 9th, by the Treaty of Windsor, Philip promises to effect the extradition of the Yorkist pretender, the Earl of Suffolk, and affiances his sister, Margaret of Austria, to Henry. By a secret treaty Henry agrees to guard the Netherlands during Philip's absence in Spain and to aid him, if necessary, in conquering Castille.

Mar: 18th, Ferdinand I of Aragon marries Germaine de Foix;

24th, Edmund, Earl of Suffolk, is returned to England and lodged in the Tower of London;

Maximilian I secures the betrothal of the infant princess Anne of Hungary to his grandson, the Archduke Ferdinand, younger son of Philip the Handsome, which guarantees Hapsburg succession to Hungary and Bohemia.

B **Apr:** 30th, commercial treaty between England and the Netherlands is signed which is so unfavourable to the latter that it is dubbed 'Malus intercursus'; Philip the Handsome, who leaves England with Joanna for Spain, never ratifies the treaty.

May: Louis XII of France throws over the Burgundian alliance by betrothing Princess Claude to Francis of Angoulême (she had previously been affianced to Charles, the elder son of Philip the Handsome). The States-General of France had declared in favour of this marriage and stated that the duchies of Brittany and Burgundy were inalienable.

Jun: Popular movement against the nobility in Genoa; the people appoint a doge.

C **Jul:** Philip the Handsome meets the Cortes of Castille at Valladolid. Ferdinand I gives way to the demands of his son-in-law, Philip, for ruling Castille and signs a treaty with him.

Aug: Pope Julius II leaves Rome at the head of an army to reduce Perugia.

Sep: 25th, Philip the Handsome dies at Burgos. Because of the insanity of his widow, Joanna (who is confined until her death in 1555), the grandees of Castille nominate a council of regency under Cardinal Ximenéz de Cisnéros.

D **Oct:** 7th, Julius II deposes the Duke of Bologna and with French help takes Bologna, bringing the territorial power of the papacy to a new height.

Nov:

Dec:

E Sigismund I accedes to the throne of Poland (−1548) on the death of Alexander I.

F Politics, Economics, Law and Education
> N. Machiavelli forms the Florentine militia, which is the first national army in Italy. Frankfort-on-Oder University is founded.

G Science, Technology and Discovery
> Tritão da Cunha discovers the island named after him.

H Philosophy, Religion and Scholarship
> Johann Reuchlin, *Rudimenta linguae hebraicae* (epoch-making grammar, with a lexicon).

J Art, Sculpture, Fine Arts and Architecture
> Painting:
>> Lucas Cranach, St. Catherine altar-piece.
>> Raphael, *Madonna di Casa*, Colonna; also *Ansidei Madonna* and *Tempi Madonna*.
> Sculpture:
>> Laocoon group (2 B.C.) is unearthed at Rome.
> Architecture:
>> Bramante begins to rebuild St. Peter's, Rome.

K Music

L Literature (including Drama)

M Births and Deaths
> Feb. — George Buchanan b. (–1582).
> Apr. 7th St. Francis Xavier b. (–1552).
> May 20th Christopher Columbus d. (55).
> Sept. 13th Andrea Mantegna d. (75).
> Sept. 13th John Leland b. (–1552).
> Sept. 25th Philip I (the Handsome) of Spain d. (28).

1507 The Diet of Constance—Margaret of Austria becomes Regent in the Netherlands

A Jan:
Feb:
Mar: 12th, Cesare Borgia dies;
   25th, Louis XII attacks Genoa with a Swiss army to restore order;
   28th, Genoa falls.

B Apr: Henry VII throws over his projected match with Margaret of Austria and begins intriguing for the hand of the mad Joanna of Castille;
   the Diet of Constance restores the imperial chamber and places imperial taxation and armed levies on a permanent basis. The unity of the Holy Roman Empire is recognised;
   the States-General of the Netherlands appoint Margaret of Austria as Regent during the minority of the Archduke Charles.
May: 11th, France annexes Genoa.
Jun: Ferdinand I and Louis XII meet at Savonna and agree to sell Pisa to Florence (effected in 1509).

C Jul: Julius II celebrates his military successes in enlarging the Papal States with triumphal processions in Rome and forms plans for a league against Venice;
   Ferdinand I, returning to Spain from Italy, suppresses the pro-Hapsburg party.
Aug:
Sep:

D Oct:
Nov:
Dec: 21st, marriage treaty for the Archduke Charles to marry Henry VII's daughter, Mary;
   the chief Flemish grievances in the commercial treaty of 1506 with England ('Malus intercursus') are alleviated.

E

F Politics, Economics, Law and Education

G Science, Technology and Discovery
   Alvise Cadamosto publishes an account of his exploration of Gambia, *La Prima Navigazione per l'Oceano alle terre de' Negri della Bassa Ethiopia*.
   Martin Waldseemüller in *Cosmographie introductio* proposes the new world should be called 'America' after Amerigo Vespucci, the first navigator to be convinced this was a new continent, not an outlying part of Asia.

H Philosophy, Religion and Scholarship
   Henry VII, King of England, appoints Polydore Vergil, Historiographer Royal.
   Pope Julius II proclaims an indulgence for aiding the rebuilding of St. Peter's, Rome.

J Art, Sculpture, Fine Arts and Architecture
   Painting:
   Albrecht Dürer, *Adam and Eve*.
   Lorenzo Lotto, *Madonna and Child and Four Saints*.
   Raphael, *Holy Family with a Palm*.

K Music

L Literature (including Drama)

M Births and Deaths
   Feb. 20th Gentile Bellini d. (77).
   Mar. 12th Cesare Borgia d. (33).

A   Jan:
   Feb: 4th, Maximilian I issues Proclamation of Trent, assuming the imperial title without
      being crowned;
      Pope Julius II subsequently confirms that the German King automatically becomes
      Holy Roman Emperor;
      Maximilian I attacks Venice for refusing to give him a free passage to Rome. Louis XII
      of France secretly aids the Venetians.
   Mar:

B   Apr:
   May: Ludovico Sforza of Milan dies.
   Jun: Maximilian I, defeated by Venice, is forced to sign a three-year truce with the
      Republic.

C   Jul:
   Aug:
   Sep:

D   Oct:
   Nov:
   Dec: 10th, Margaret of Austria and the Cardinal of Rouen form the League of Cambrai
      with Ferdinand I, for despoiling Venice; the papacy and other Italian states subse-
      quently join. War is to be declared on Venice *Apr.* 1st, 1509;
   Dec: 17th, Margaret of Austria confirms marriage treaty for the Archduke Charles to
      marry Mary Tudor.

E   Pedro Navarro leads Spanish expedition to North Africa in which Penon de la Gomera is
      captured.

F **Politics, Economics, Law and Education**
   Maximilian I creates the financier Jacob Fugger of Augsburg, a Knight of the Holy
   Roman Empire.
   Guillaume Budé, *Annotationes in Pandectas*, a criticism of medieval interpretations of
   Roman law.

G **Science, Technology and Discovery**
   Ocampo circumnavigates Cuba.

H **Philosophy, Religion and Scholarship**
   [Dirc Coelde van Münster], *Suverlijc Boecxken* (authorship doubtful; but these
   spiritual songs were the first printed in the Dutch language).
   Regular courses in Greek under Girolamo Aleandro begin at Paris University.

J **Art, Sculpture, Fine Arts and Architecture**
   Painting:
   Albrecht Dürer, *Hands of an Apostle*.
   Lorenzo Lotto, *Sacra Conversazione*
   Giorgione, *The Tempest*.
   Raphael, *Esterházy Madonna*.
   Michelangelo begins to paint the roof of the Sistine Chapel, Rome (–1512), and
   Raphael enters the service of Pope Julius II.
   Architecture:
   Peruzzi, Villa Farnesina, Rome (–1511).

K **Music**

L **Literature (including Drama)**
   The Maying or Disport of Chaucer (first book printed in Scotland).
   William Dunbar, *Lament for Makaris; The Thrissil and the Rois* (a political allegory)
   and five other poems, printed at Edinburgh by Chepman and Myllar (earliest extant
   example of Scottish typography).
   Garci Rodriguez de Montalvo, *Amadis de Gaula* in 4 bks. (revision of a much earlier,
   probably 14th-century, narrative of chivalry; trans. –1590).

M **Births and Deaths**
   Feb. 4th Konrad Celtes d. (49).
   — Isaac Abrabanel d. (71).
   — Fernando Alvarez de Toledo, Duke of Alva, b. (–1583).
   — Pietro Carnuesecchi b. (–1567).
   — Thomas, Lord Seymour of Sudeley, b. (–1549).
   — Andrea Palladio b. (–1580).

1509   Venice is despoiled following Battle of Agnadello—Accession of
Henry VIII

A Jan:
Feb:
Mar: 18th, Maximilian I formally appoints Margaret of Austria Regent in the Netherlands during the minority of the Archduke Charles (see *Apr.*, 1507);
23rd, Pope Julius II joins the League of Cambrai.

B Apr: 7th, France declares war on Venice;
Venice offers to deliver Faenza and Rimini to the papacy as an attempt to divide the
League of Cambrai; Pope Julius II refuses and, 27th, excommunicates the Venetian
Republic;
21st, Henry VIII succeeds as King of England (–1547) on the death of Henry VII;
25th, Henry VIII's offers of reparation to those injured by fiscal extortion produces
demands for the punishment of his father's finance ministers Richard Empson and
Edmund Dudley.
May: 14th, the French defeat the Venetians at Agnadello and become masters of north
Italy. As a result, Pope Julius II annexes Faenza, Rimini and Ravenna and overruns
the Romagna; Ferdinand I takes Otranto and Brindisi, and Maximilian I annexes
Verona, Vicenza and Padua;
Spanish troops under Cardinal Ximénez de Cisnéros take Oran from the Moors.
Jun: 11th, Henry VIII marries Catherine of Aragon;
Florence takes Pisa.

C Jul: 17th, Venetians again take control of Padua, which Maximilian I tries in vain to reduce by siege;
18th, Richard Empson is found guilty of constructive treason.
Aug: 8th, Edmund Dudley is found guilty of constructive treason (Dudley and Empson
are both attainted by Parliament in 1510 and executed).
Sep: rift between Pope Julius II and Louis XII of France widens (leading to the Pope's
desertion of the League of Cambrai in 1510).

D Oct: 12th, Maximilian I, unable to reduce Padua, leaves Italy for the Tyrol.
Nov:
Dec:

E Francisco d'Almeida, the Portuguese viceroy of the Indies, defeats the Moslem princes of
north-west India;
Earthquake destroys Constantinople;
Almeida defeats the combined Indian and Egyptian fleets at the battle of Diu (Gujarat),
establishing Portuguese supremacy in the Indian Ocean.

F **Politics, Economics, Law and Education**
Edmund Dudley writes *The Tree of Commonwealth* (published in 1859).
Brasenose College, Oxford, and St. John's College, Cambridge, are founded.

G **Science, Technology and Discovery**
Peter Henle of Nuremberg invents the watch (the 'Nuremberg Egg').

H **Philosophy, Religion and Scholarship**
Alexander Barclay translates Sebastian Brandt's *The Ship of Fools* (printed by Richard Pynson, London).
John Fisher, *The Seven Penitential Psalms* (is printed and published, *June* 12th, by Wynkyn de Worde, London).
Desiderius Erasmus visits England and lectures at Cambridge (–1511).

J **Art, Sculpture, Fine Arts and Architecture**
Painting:
Albrecht Dürer, *Little Passion* (–1511).
Gerard David, *Virgin among Virgins*.
Quentin Massys, *St. Anne triptych*.
Andrea del Sarto, *Miracles of St. Fillipo, Benizzi* (–1510).
Matthias Grünewald paints the Isenheim triptych.
Architecture:
Raphael, St. Eligio degli Orefixi, Rome (–1526).

K **Music**

L **Literature (including Drama)**
Fortunatus (anon. example of German story form known as *Schwank* –1555).

M **Births and Deaths**
May 20th Caterina Sforza, Countess of Forli, d. (46).
June 29th Margaret, Countess of Richmond (The Lady Margaret), d. (68).
July 10th John Calvin b. (–1564).
Aug. 3rd Étienne Dolet b. (–1546).
— Nicholas Bacon b. (–1579).

A   Jan: 21st, Parliament meets (*–Feb*. 23rd) to attaint Empson and Dudley and pass sumptuary legislation.

Feb: Pope Julius II detaches himself from the League of Cambria and, 24th, absolves Venice from excommunication. The Venetians grant free navigation in the Gulf of Venice to subjects of the papal states and restore to the Pope all ecclesiastical rights in the Republic.

Mar: Julius II declares war on Ferrara, Louis XII's ally.

B   Apr:

May: Julius II engages 15,000 Swiss mercenaries, accepting terms which Louis XII could not afford, and reduces Modena.

Jun:

C   Jul: Julius II secures Ferdinand's alliance against France by investing him with Naples.

Aug: 17th, Richard Empson and Edmund Dudley are beheaded;

Pedro Navarro, having taken Algiers and Tripoli for Spain, is killed in an ambush in North Africa.

Sep: Louis XII summons a synod of French bishops at Tours to condemn the conduct of Pope Julius II; the synod recommends the calling of a general council of the church and declares Louis is justified in making war on the Pope and his allies.

D   Oct: the Swiss desert Julius II on the grounds that they had undertaken not to fight against France.

Nov:

Dec: Papal troops defend Bologna from French attack.

E   Shah Ismail of Persia drives the Usbeks from Khorasan;

Politics, Economics, Law and Education
Desiderius Erasmus, *Institutio Christiani Principis*, a tract on politics.
The Portuguese acquire Goa.
John Colet founds St. Paul's School, London.

G Science, Technology and Discovery

H Philosophy, Religion and Scholarship
Sir Thomas More, *The lyfe of Johan Picus Erle of Mirandula*, trans. from the Italian life of Pico Della Mirandola by his nephew.

J Art, Sculpture, Fine Arts and Architecture
Painting:
Sebastiano del Piombo, *Salome*.
Titian, *The Gipsy Madonna*.

K Music

L Literature (including Drama)
Everyman (morality play; based probably on a Dutch morality of 1495).

M Births and Deaths
Mar. 1st Dom Francisco de Almeida d. (60).
Mar. 10th Johann Geiler von Kaisersberg d. (65).
May 17th Sandro Botticelli d. (66).
May 25th Georges D'Amboise d. (50).
Oct. 6th John Caius b. (–1573).
Oct. 25th Giorgione d. (*c.* 32).
— Louis Bourgeois b. (–1561).
— Ambrose Paré b. (–1590).

1511 The Holy League formed to expel the French from Italy—the Portuguese capture Malacca

A Jan: Pope Julius II takes Mirandola.
Feb: Gian Trivulzio recaptures Mirandola; Julius II fails to take Ferrara.
Mar:

B Apr:
May: French under Gian Trivulzio capture Bologna and expel the papal troops—Michelangelo's statue of Julius II is hurled from its pedestal;
16th, French ecclesiastics call for a general council of the church to meet at Pisa.
Jun:

C Jul:
Aug: 21st, Julius II is seriously ill, but recovers.
Sep: 1st, a general council of dissident ecclesiastics hostile to Julius II meets, but subsequently transfers to Milan because of Florentine hostility to them.

D Oct: 5th, Pope Julius II forms the Holy League of Ferdinand I of Aragon, Venice and the Papacy, ostensibly to defend the unity of the Church, but in reality to drive the French out of Italy; Ferdinand is to acquire Navarre and the Pope to recover Bologna and Ferrara.
Nov: 13th, Henry VIII joins the Holy League and thus enters European politics;
17th, offensive alliance between England and Spain for a joint attack on Guienne and Navarre in *Apr.* 1512;
English troops aiding Margaret of Austria against Guelders are forced to raise the siege of Venlo.
Dec:

E The Portuguese capture Malacca;
Ships of the Lübeck Hansa capture a Netherlands trading fleet for infringing the Hansa monopoly in the Baltic.

F **Politics, Economics, Law and Education**
   Diego de Velazquez occupies Cuba.
   Henry VIII begins to reform the Royal Navy.

G **Science, Technology and Discovery**
   The Portuguese discover Amboyna and conquer Malacca.

H **Philosophy, Religion and Scholarship**
   Desiderius Erasmus, *Encomium Moriae* (*In Praise of Folly*) published in Paris (written in England 1509).
   Erasmus is appointed as Professor of Greek at Cambridge (–1514).
   Martin Luther is sent by his Order to Rome.
   A Patriarch of Moscow is appointed by Vassili III.

J **Art, Sculpture, Fine Arts and Architecture**
   Painting:
   A. Dürer, *Adoration of the Trinity*.
   Andrea del Sarto, Grisailles at the Church of the Scalzi (–1526).
   Leonardo da Vinci, Studies for the Trivulzio monument.

K **Music**
   Arnold Schlick, *Spiegel der Orgelmacher und Organisten* (on organ building; includes lute songs and lute solos).

L **Literature (including Drama)**
   Gil Vicente, *Four Seasons* (Portuguese *auto*—sacred play).

M **Births and Deaths**
   July 30th Giorgio Vasari b. (–1574).
   Oct. 18th Philippe de Comines d. (66).

1512 Spanish conquest of Navarre—the Medici return to Florence

A Jan:
Feb: 4th, English Parliament meets (*–Mar*. 30th) to vote supplies for the French war; Gaston de Foix, Duke of Nemours, defeats the Holy League and takes Brescia.
Mar:

B Apr: Maximilian I and the Swiss join the Holy League against France; Gaston de Foix defeats the Spanish and Papal forces at Ravenna with the help of German mercenaries, but Gaston's death in battle checks the French advance into Italy;
English burn villages on Breton coast;
Bayazid II, Sultan of Turkey, abdicates in favour of his youngest son, Selim, Governor of Trebizond, who becomes Selim I (–1520), following a civil war in which he defeats his brothers Ahmad and Corcud;
10th, Pope Julius II holds Fifth Lateran Council (–1517).
May: Swiss descend on the Milanese.
Jun: French troops withdraw from Milan;
Florence is left at the mercy of the Holy League;
English force under the Marquess of Dorset undertakes expedition to Guienne, which fails through lack of support from Ferdinand I.

C Jul: Spanish army under the Duke of Alva invades Navarre;
Pope Julius II recovers Bologna.
Aug: 10th, indecisive Anglo-French naval action off Brest, but, 12th, English fleet under Sir Edward Howard destroys 25 French vessels in the harbour;
at Congress of Mantua held by the cities of the Holy League, Parma and Piacenza are conceded to the Papacy; the Swiss restore the duchy of Milan to Maximilian Sforza, but acquire Lugano, Locarno and Ossola; and the rule of the Medici is restored in Florence (–1527).
Sep:

D Oct: The German diet assembles in Cologne, after an abortive meeting at Trier in Apr., to undertake further imperial reorganisation. The number of administrative 'circles' of the empire, established in 1500, is increased, and one Aulic Council is formed which remains under the Emperor's control;
the German Swabian League is renewed for a further 10 years, but the Duke of Württemberg, the Elector Palatine and the Margrave of Baden stay aloof to form a rival union (which Frederick the Wise of Saxony joins in 1515).
Nov: 4th, English Parliament meets for a second session (*–Dec*. 20th).
Dec:

E Polish war with Russia over White Russian region (–1522);
By Peace of Malmoe, Netherlands vessels are permitted by the German Hanseatic League to trade in the Baltic provided they carry no contraband of war.

F Politics, Economics, Law and Education

G Science, Technology and Discovery
    Stobnicza, *Introductio in Ptolemaei Cosmographiam*.
    Portuguese navigators discover Celebes.

H Philosophy, Religion and Scholarship
    Girolamo Aleandro (Hieronymus Aleander), *Lexicon: Graeco-Latinum*.
    The Fifth Lateran Council (*Apr.* 10th–*Mar.* 16th, 1517), at which the Immortality
    of the Soul is pronounced a dogma of the Church.
    Martin Luther lectures on the Epistle to the Romans.

J Art, Sculpture, Fine Arts and Architecture
    Painting:
        Hans Baldung, *A Mystic Pietà*; also altar-piece, Fribourg Cathedral (–1516).
        Albrecht Dürer, *Squirells*.
        Vecchio Palma, *Portrait of a Man*.
        Andrea del Sarto, *The Annunciation*.
        Raphael, fresco of Galatea, Rome.
    Sculpture:
        P. Torrigiano, Henry VII's tomb, Westminster Abbey (–1518).

K Music
    Second book of Masses by Josquin, published by Petrucci.

L Literature (including Drama)
    First use of the word *masque*, to denote a poetic form of dramatic art, used in an entry
    for the year 1512 in Edward Halle's *Chronicle* (first published in 1550).

M Births and Deaths
    Feb. 22nd Amerigo Vespucci d. (61).
    Mar. 5th Gerardus Mercator (Gerhard Kremer) b. (–1594).
    Apr. 10th James V of Scotland b. (–1542).
    Apr. 25th Bayazid II, Sultan of Turkey, d. (65).
    Aug. 2nd Alessandro Achillini d. (49).

A Jan: 20th, Christian II succeeds as King of Denmark and Norway (–1523) on the death of
   John I.
   Feb: 21st, Pope Julius II dies.
   Mar: 9th, Giovanni de' Medici elected Pope Leo X (–1521);
      Louis XII of France renews alliance with Venice to facilitate his recovery of Milan; this
      alliance turns the Emperor Maximilian I towards the Holy League;
      Henry VIII's ambassador to Edinburgh attempts to renew the Anglo-Scottish 'per-
      petual peace' without success.

B Apr: 5th, by the Treaty of Mechlin Maximilian I, Henry VIII, Ferdinand I and Pope
      Leo X form alliance for a joint invasion of France; the Netherlands are declared
      neutral.
   May: 4th, Edmund de la Pole, Earl of Suffolk, is executed;
      French and Venetian troops invade Milan.
   Jun: 6th, French army is defeated at Novara by the Swiss and returns to France;
      30th (–Oct. 22nd), Henry VIII commands his army in France.

C Jul: James IV of Scotland declares war against England.
   Aug: Henry VIII and Maximilian I rout the French at the Battle of the Spurs (or
      Guineagate);
      22nd, Thérouenne, on the Netherlands frontier, surrenders to the English and is de-
      livered to Maximilian;
      James IV crosses the Tweed to attack Norham Castle, which surrenders to him, 29th;
      the Swiss occupy Franche-Comté, but Louis XII buys them off.
   Sep: 9th, the Earl of Surrey defeats the Scots at the Battle of Flodden; heavy casualties
      include King James IV;
      James V, an infant of 17 months, succeeds as King of Scotland (–1542); his mother,
      Margaret Tudor, assumes the Regency;
      24th, Tournai surrenders to the English;
      the Swiss attack Dijon.

D Oct: 12th, Henry VIII and Maximilian I sign a further offensive alliance against France.
   Nov:
   Dec: Louis XII makes peace with Pope Leo X.

E Peasants' Revolts in the Black Forest and Württemberg (–1514).

F **Politics, Economics, Law and Education**
Niccolò Machiavelli begins writing *The Prince* (published 1532).

G **Science, Technology and Discovery**
Vasco Nuñez de Balboa crosses the Panama Isthmus to discover the Pacific Ocean, which he sights from Darien (*Sept.* 26th).
A Portuguese expedition under Jorge Alvarez reaches Canton.
Juan Ponce de Leon discovers Florida (*Apr.*)

H **Philosophy, Religion and Scholarship**
The Aldine Press, Venice, edition of Plato.
A Greek printing press is established in Rome.
Raphael makes plans for the excavation of ancient Rome.

J **Art, Sculpture, Fine Arts and Architecture**
Painting:
Hans Baldung, *Count von Löwenstein.*
Giovanni Bellini, altar-piece, St. John Chrysostom.
Hans Holbein the younger begins painting in Basle.
Sculpture:
Michelangelo, *Moses* (Rome); also *Dying Captive* and *Heroic Captive* (Paris, –1516).
Pope Leo X begins forming a sculpture gallery at the Vatican.
Architecture:
Michelangelo, façade, S. Lorenziana, Florence.
Pope Julius II halts work on St. Peter's, Rome.

K **Music**

L **Literature (including Drama)**
Cardinal Bernardo Dovizi (*Il Bibbiena*), *La Calandria* (produced at Urbino; at the Vatican –1514).
Niccolò Machiavelli, *La Mandragola* (comedy).

M **Births and Deaths**
Feb. 28th Robert Fabyan d. (53).
Dec. 23rd Thomas Smith b. (–1577).
— Henry Bradshaw d. (63).

A Jan: 9th, Anne of Brittany, Queen of France, dies.
Feb:
Mar:

B Apr: Maximilian I and Ferdinand I sign truce with Louis XII of France;
  24th, Selim I, Sultan of Turkey, begins to march his army through Erzinjan and
  Erzerum to Persia.
  May: Princess Claude of France, daughter of Louis XII, marries Francis, Duke of
  Angoulême.
  Jun: Basil III of Moscow takes Smolensk.

C Jul: Anglo-French truce.
  Aug: 6th, Margaret Tudor, Regent of Scotland, marries Archibald Douglas, Earl of
  Angus;
  23rd, Selim I defeats Shah Ismail of Persia at Tchadiran.
  Sep: 5th, Selim I of Turkey enters Tabriz;
  8th, Polish-Lithuanian armies crush Russians at Orsza;
  15th, Thomas Wolsey is appointed Archbishop of York (–1530).

D Oct: Louis XII of France marries Mary Tudor, sister of Henry VIII.
  Nov: Albert of Brandenburg, appointed Archbishop of Magdeburg in 1513, is elected
  Archbishop of Mainz through bribery.
  Dec: 4th, Richard Hunne dies in the Tower of London; subsequent enquiries into his
  death provoke widespread anticlericalism in London.

E Peasants' revolt in Hungary, led by George Dózsa, is suppressed by John Zápolya;
  By the *decretum tripartitum juris* drawn up by Stephen Verböczy in Hungary the King is
  to be independent of Pope and Emperor, the powers of the nobility are increased and
  serfdom is fixed.

F **Politics, Economics, Law and Education**

Santiago is founded by Diego Valazquez and becomes the capital of Cuba, in place of Baracoa.

Johann von Eck defends usury.

The Corporation of Trinity House, London, is founded to control pilotage and provide navigational aids for the R. Thames and its approaches.

G **Science, Technology and Discovery**

H **Philosophy, Religion and Scholarship**

Nicolaus Cusanus, *Opera*, 3 vols., published in Paris ('Nicolaus of Cusa', Cardinal, initiates philosophical speculation concerning the limitations of human knowledge and man's intuitive understanding of God).

The first book to be printed in Arabic type, *septem horae canonicae*, is published at Fano in Italy.

The first *Polyglot Bible* started. Known as *The Complutensian Bible*, having been edited and printed at Alcala de Henares, near Madrid (*Complutum* in Latinised form). O.T.—in Hebrew, Aramaic, Greek, Latin; N.T.—in Greek and Latin. N.T. completed *Jan.* 10th, 1514; final (fourth) volume of O.T. completed 1517. Not published until 1522. This great achievement was directed and paid for by Cardinal Francisco Jimenez de Cisneros.

J **Art, Sculpture, Fine Arts and Architecture**

Painting:

Antonio Allegri da Correggio discovers chiaroscuro; and Correggio paints *Madonna of St. Francis* (–1516).

Lucas Cranch, *Henry the Pious of Saxony*.

Vecchio Palma, *Sacra Conversazione, with a female donor* (–1518).

Quentin Massys, *The Banker and his wife*.

Raphael, *Nymph Galatea* (fresco).

Andrea del Sarto, Cloister of Chiesa dello Scazio (–1517, 1522–6); and *Birth of the Virgin*.

Titian, *The Tribute Money*.

Architecture:

Michelangelo, Chapel Castel, St. Angelo, Rome.

K **Music**

L **Literature (including Drama)**

Lucas Fernández, *Farsas y églogas* (six plays).

M **Births and Deaths**

Mar. 11th Donato d'Augnolo Bramante d. (70).

June 16th John Cheke b. (–1557).

Oct. 25th William Elphinstone d. (83).

— Christophe Plantin b. (–1589).

1515   Accession of Francis I—Cardinal Wolsey becomes Lord Chancellor
—Hapsburg marriage treaties with Bohemia–Hungary

A Jan: 1st, Francis, Duke of Angoulême succeeds as Francis I of France (–1547), on the
death of his uncle Louis XII;
the Infante Charles of Austria takes over as Governor of the Netherlands.

Feb: Mary Tudor, widow of Louis XII of France, secretly marries Charles Brandon,
Duke of Suffolk (they are pardoned by Henry VIII on making over to him Mary's
dowry from Louis and paying a fine of £24,000 by instalments, and publicly re-marry
May 13th).

Mar:

B Apr: Anglo-French peace treaty is signed.

May: 1st, Duke of Albany, nephew of James III, lands in Scotland as an agent of Francis
I to exploit divisions at the Scottish court.

Jun:

C Jul: Scottish Parliament names Duke of Albany as Protector of Scotland; Margaret
Tudor, the Queen Regent, escapes to England;
22nd, at the Congress of Vienna Maximilian I, Sigismund I of Poland and Ladislas II
of Hungary settle points at issue between Poland and the Empire and the succession to
the throne of Hungary. Maximilian's grand-daughter Mary is to marry Louis, Prince
of Hungary, Ladislas's son, and his grandson Ferdinand to marry Anne Jagiello,
heiress to Bohemia and Hungary (as a result of this compact on Louis's death, the
Hapsburgs acquire Bohemia and Hungary).

Aug: Francis I sets out for Italy with an army of 110,000;
Spanish Navarre is incorporated with Castille.

Sep: 10th, Thomas Wolsey, Archbishop of York, is appointed a cardinal;
13th, at the battle of Marignano, Francis I defeats the Swiss and Venetian armies and
conquers Milan; the supremacy of the Swiss mercenaries is ended.

D Oct: 10th, Anglo-Spanish commercial treaty.

Nov: 7th, by Treaty of Geneva the Swiss sign a peace with France.

Dec: 11th, by Treaty of Bologna Pope Leo X surrenders Parma and Piacenza to France;
24th, Thomas Wolsey is appointed Lord Chancellor of England.

E The Sultan Selim I conquers eastern Anatolia and Kurdistan;
Frederick the Wise of Saxony joins the Elector Palatine, the Duke of Württemberg and
the Margrave of Baden in their rival union (of 1512) to the Swabian League.

F **Politics, Economics, Law and Education**

G **Science, Technology and Discovery**

H **Philosophy, Religion and Scholarship**
   Epistolae Obscurorum Virorum (vol. 2 –1517), a collective satire of scholarship, ridiculing the 'schoolmen' who oppose humanism. Written in dog-Latin, in support of the Hebrew scholar, Reuchlin (–1494, 1517).
   The Lateran Council's decree (*De impressione librorum*), by which no work could be printed without previous examination by the relevant ecclesiastical authority.

J **Art, Sculpture, Fine Arts and Architecture**
   Painting:
   Hans Baldung, *Death and the Woman* series (–1517); also *The Margrave of Baden*.
   Albrecht Dürer, marginal drawings in the Emperor Maximilian I's prayer book.
   Lorenzo Lotto, *Giovanni Agostino*; also *Niccolo della Torre*.
   J. G. Mabuse, *A Man*.
   Raphael, tapestry cartoons for the Sistine Chapel, Rome (–1516; now at Hampton Court).
   Titian, *Flora*.
   Architecture:
   Hampton Court Palace is completed for Cardinal Wolsey.
   Raphael, Palazzo Vidoni Caffarelli, Rome; Raphael also works on St. Peter's, Rome (–1519).

K **Music**

L **Literature (including Drama)**
   Till Eulenspiegel (*Master Tyll Owlglass*; published in Strasbourg, anon.; see 1500).

M **Births and Deaths**
   July 21st Philip Neri b. (–1595).
   Sept. 22nd Anne of Cleves b. (–1557).
   Dec. 2nd Gonzalo Ferdinandez de Córdoba d. (62).
   Dec. 16th Alphonso d'Albuquerque d. (62).
   — Aldus Manutius (Aldo Manuzio) d. (65).
   — Roger Ascham b. (–1568).
   — Nicholas Throckmorton b. (–1571).

A   Jan: Archduke Charles (later Emperor Charles V) succeeds as King of Spain on the death of Ferdinand I of Aragon (–1556), founding the Hapsburg dynasty in Spain; Cardinal Jimenez de Cisnéros is appointed Regent.
Feb:
Mar: Louis II, aged 10, succeeds as King of Bohemia and Hungary (–1526) on the death of Ladislas II.

B   Apr: Maximilian I undertakes expedition to north Italy which fails through the Swiss refusing their support.
May: Margaret, Queen Mother of Scotland, remains at the English court (–1515). Henry VIII schemes to remove the Duke of Albany as Protector of Scotland.
Jun:

C   Jul:
Aug: 13th, by the Peace of Noyon between France and Spain, Francis I retains Milan but renounces his claim to Naples; Charles of Spain agrees to marry Louise, daughter of Francis I; both kings pledge themselves to force Maximilian I to renounce his claims to Brescia and Verona;
18th, by Concordat of Bologna between France and the Papacy, Francis I secures the right to appoint to French bishoprics and abbacies and restores annates to the Pope; he also declares that the Pope is not subject to a general council;
24th, the Sultan Selim I, having conquered north Mesopotamia, moves to face the Mameluke Sultan of Egypt, Kansu-al-Guari, whom he defeats near Aleppo and, as a result, annexes Syria.
Sep:

D   Oct: 29th, Maximilian I signs a treaty with England to prevent Verona falling into Venetian hands.
Nov: 29th, Francis I signs the Treaty of Freiburg of perpetual peace with the Swiss (this remains in force to 1789).
Dec: 13th, by the Peace of Brussels with Francis I, Maximilian accedes to the Peace of Noyon (of *Aug.*), overturning his treaty with England (of *Oct.*). He waives his claims in Italy for 200,000 ducats and hands over Verona to Venice.

E

F **Politics, Economics, Law and Education**

Sir Thomas More, *Libellus . . . Insula Utopiae* (original Latin text of *Utopia*, printed at Louvain; trans. 1551).

Sir Anthony Fitzherbert, *Abridgement of the Year Books*.

G **Science, Technology and Discovery**

Juan Diaz de Solis, searching for a passage to the Pacific Ocean, explores the coast of Argentina and is killed near the Rio de la Plata.

Peter Martyr's *Decades* discusses the discoveries in the New World.

H **Philosophy, Religion and Scholarship**

Robert Fabyan, *The New Chronicles of England and France* (posth.).

Pietro Pomponazzi, *De immortalitate animae* (challenged, but influential up to the age of Kant).

The *New Testament* in Greek and Latin (the first published Greek text, with the annotations of Erasmus; Basle).

Concordat between Pope Leo X and Francis I; in return for the restoration of Annates to the Papacy, the King of France acquires internal independence in ecclesiastical appointments, and appeals to Rome from France are restricted.

J **Art, Sculpture, Fine Arts and Architecture**

Painting:

Titian, *The Assumption*, Frari Church, Venice (–1518).

Architecture:

Raphael, Villa Madama, Rome.

K **Music**

Third book of Masses by Josquin, published by Petrucci.

L **Literature (including Drama)**

Ludovico Ariosto, *Orlando Furioso* (romantic epic; sequel to Boiardo's work of 1495).

Garcia de Resende, *Cancioneiro Geral* (a Portuguese songbook, anthologising the work of more than 250 Portuguese and Spanish poets).

M **Births and Deaths**

Feb. 18th Queen Mary I b. (–1558).

Mar. 26th Konrad von Gesner b. (–1565).

Nov. 29th Giovanni Bellini d. (86).

— Hieronymus Bosch d. (*c.* 66).

— John Foxe b. (–1587).

A Jan: 22nd, the Turks take Cairo. The Sherif of Mecca subsequently surrenders to Selim I and Arabia comes under Turkish suzerainty.
  Feb:
  Mar: Pope Leo X publishes a bull for a 5-year peace in Christendom and calls for a crusade against the Turks.

B Apr: Thomas Wolsey begins secret negotiations for a peace with France.
  May: 1st, in 'Evil May Day' riots in London apprentices attack foreign residents. Wolsey suppresses the rioters of whom 60 are hanged.
  Jun: the Duke of Albany leaves Scotland for France, where he is later confined.

C Jul:
  Aug:
  Sep: Archduke Charles arrives in Spain from the Netherlands.

D Oct: 31st, Martin Luther nails his 95 theses at Wittenberg Palace church, denouncing the sale of papal indulgences by Johann Tetzel and others; this marks the beginning of the Reformation in Germany.
  Nov: 8th, on the death of Cardinal Ximenes, the effective government of Spain passes into Hapsburg hands; Charles appoints his former tutor, de Chièvres, as chief minister in Spain;
  Charles's triumphal entry into Valladolid.
  Dec:

E

F Politics, Economics, Law and Education

Royal Commission on enclosure of common lands in England.
The Portuguese establish a factory at Colombo, Ceylon.
Coffee is first brought to Europe.
Corpus Christi College, Oxford, is founded by Richard Fox, Bishop of Winchester.
Collège de Trois Langues, Louvain, is established.

G Science, Technology and Discovery

Francisco Hernández de Cordoba discovers Yucatan.
The wheel-lock musket is invented by a Nuremberg gunsmith.

H Philosophy, Religion and Scholarship

Richard Pace, *De fructu*.
Johann Reuchlin, *De arte cabbalistica*.
Pope Leo X closes the Lateran Council, declaring that all reforms of the Church have been accomplished.
In protest against the sale of Indulgences, Martin Luther, *Oct.* 31st, posts on the door of the Palace Church in Wittenberg, his *Ninety-Five Theses*, following the usual custom for giving notice of disputations.

J Art, Sculpture, Fine Arts and Architecture

Painting:
Quentin Massys, *Erasmus*.
Sebastiano del Piombo, *Raising of Lazarus* (–1519).
Andrea del Sarto, *Madonna della Arpie*.

K Music

L Literature (including Drama)

Bartolomé de Torres Naharro, *Propalladia* (collection of seven plays by the first Spanish dramatist to write *comedias*).
Teofilo Folengo, *Liber Macaronices* (*La Macaronea; or Il Baldus*, a satirical parody of the contemporary romantic epic).

M Births and Deaths

Jan. 6th Francia d. (*c.* 67).
Aug. 20th Antoine Perrenot, Cardinal de Granvella, b. (–1586).
Nov. 8th Francisco Ximenes d. (81).
— Vasco Nuñez de Balboa d. (42).
— Henry Howard, Earl of Surrey, b. (–1547).
— Heinrich Isaac d. (*c.* 67).

A   Jan:
Feb: 28th, a Dauphin of France is born.
Mar:

B   Apr:
May:
Jun: 1st, new agreement is signed between the Merchants Adventurers of England and
the city of Antwerp.

C   Jul: 12th, decree in England that enclosures made since 1488 are to be destroyed;
Cardinal Wolsey signs protocol with the French ambassador for the detention of the
Duke of Albany in France.
Aug:
Sep:

D   Oct: 2nd, Cardinal Wolsey devises the Peace of London between England, France, the
Emperor Maximilian I, Spain and the Papacy;
4th, Anglo-French marriage treaty for Mary Tudor to marry the Dauphin;
8th, Henry VIII and Francis I agree to meet in *Apr.* near Calais to arrange for the sale
of Tournai to France;
12th, Martin Luther, summoned by Cardinal Cajetan (de Vio) to the Diet of Augsburg,
refuses to recant. The Diet of Augsburg refuses to provide the Emperor with a subsidy for fighting the Turks.
Nov:
Dec:

E   Foundation of the Barbary States of Algiers and Tunis.

F Politics, Economics, Law and Education

The Emperor Charles V grants Lorens de Gominot the first licence (or *asiento*) to import 4,000 African slaves into the Spanish American colonies during eight years.

G Science, Technology and Discovery

Juan de Grijalva explores the coast from Yucatan northwards to the Panuco River.
Through Thomas Linacre's efforts the Royal College of Physicians, London, is founded.
Pynson uses Roman type for a book set in London.

H Philosophy, Religion and Scholarship

John Trithemius, *Polygraphia* (a treatise on code systems or cryptography).
P. Melanchthon is appointed Professor of Greek at Wittenberg University.

J Art, Sculpture, Fine Arts and Architecture

Painting:
Albrecht Altdorfer, St. Florian altar-piece.
Antonio Correggio, frescoes for the Convent of St. Paul, Palma (–1524).
Albrecht Dürer, *The Emperor Maximilian I.*
Jacopo Pontormo, *Madonna.*
Raphael, *Pope Leo X with Two Cardinals.*
Architecture:
Notre Dame, Antwerp, is completed.

K Music

L Literature (including Drama)

M Births and Deaths

Sept. 29th Tintoretto b. (–1594).
— Hubert Waelrant b. (–1595).

1519　Charles V is elected Holy Roman Emperor

A　Jan: 12th, the Emperor Maximilian I dies. Charles I of Spain, Maximilian's grandson, and Francis I of France prepare to contest the coming imperial election, spending vast sums in Germany. Pope Leo X and Henry VIII pledge support to Francis I;

27th, Martin Luther has private discussions with Charles von Militz, the papal chamberlain, who advises him to write a letter of submission to Leo X, which Luther agrees to do.

Feb:

Mar: Ulrich, Duke of Württemburg attacks the free city of Reutlingen and defies his nobility. The Swabian League, under Franz von Sickingen, expels Ulrich from his duchy, which is taken under imperial control.

B　Apr:

May: Henry VIII decides to stand as a candidate for the imperial election and sends his secretary, Richard Pace, to Germany.

Jun: 26th (–*July* 16th), Martin Luther's public disputation with Johann Eck at Leipzig on doctrine;

28th, Charles I of Spain, Sicily and Sardinia, is elected Holy Roman Emperor as Charles V (–1556), thanks to the money of the Fuggers of Augsburg and the concern of the German electors to exclude Francis I, and at the last moment Leo X abandons his opposition. His election brings to a head the conflict between Hapsburg and Valois.

C　Jul:
Aug:
Sep:

D　Oct:
Nov: 8th, Hernando Cortes enters Tenochtitlán, Mexico, and is received by Montezuma, the Aztec ruler.
Dec:

E　The Portuguese secure trading privileges at Martaban in Burma.

F **Politics, Economics, Law and Education**
The Sherifs found the Moorish Empire of Morocco.
A settlement for paupers is established in Augsburg.

G **Science, Technology and Discovery**
Alvárez Pineda explores the Gulf of Mexico from Florida to Vera Cruz.
Ferdinand Magellan, a Portuguese in the service of Spain, leaves Europe (*Sept.* 20th), on a westward expedition in search of a strait to the Moluccas. He explores the Rio de la Plata estuary and, in 1520, rounds Cape Horn. Though Magellan is killed in the Philippines, the expedition continues under Sebastien del Cano, completing the circumnavigation of the globe.

H **Philosophy, Religion and Scholarship**
Bild aus Rheinau (known as 'Beatus Rhenanus') edits, with a commentary, the *Germania* of Tacitus.
Desiderius Erasmus, *Colloquia* (–1524).
The Leipzig Disputation, in which Martin Luther gives evidence of his determination to questions such fundamental ideas as the infallibility of papal decisions, and even the General Council of the Church.

J **Art, Sculpture, Fine Arts and Architecture**
Painting:
Andrea del Sarto, *Assumption of the Virgin*.
Sculpture:
Michelangelo, *The Victory* (Florence); also *The Risen Christ*.
Architecture:
Diego de Siloe, Escalera Dorada, Burgos Cathedral (–1523).
St. George's Chapel, Windsor, completed (begun 1473).

K **Music**

L **Literature (including Drama)**

M **Births and Deaths**
Feb. 15th Pedro Menédez de Avilés b. (–1574).
Feb. 16th Gaspard de Coligny b. (–1572).
Mar. 31st Henry II of France b. (–1559).
May 2nd Leonardo da Vinci d. (67).
June 24th Lucretia Borgia d. (39).
June 24th Theodore Beza b. (–1605).
July 4th Johann Tetzel d. (*c.* 79).
Sept. 16th John Colet d. (52).
— Catherine de' Medici b. (–1589).
— Cosimo de' Medici b. (–1574).
— Giovanni Antonio Fachinetti (Pope Innocent IX) b. (–1591).
— Thomas Gresham b. (–1579).

A Jan: 18th, Christian II of Denmark and Norway with an army of mercenaries defeats the Swedes under Sten Sture at Lake Asunden and subsequently conquers Sweden.
Feb:
Mar:

B Apr:
May: Charles V, Holy Roman Emperor elect, leaves Spain for north Europe; he appoints Adrian of Utrecht as Regent of Castille;
26th (–31st), Charles V visits Henry VIII at Dover and Canterbury.
June: 4th (–24th), Henry VIII and Francis I meet at the Field of Cloth of Gold, between Gravelines and Ardres, and, 6th, sign a treaty confirming the marriage contract of Mary Tudor with the Dauphin and for ending French interference in Scotland;
15th, Pope Leo X excommunicates Martin Luther by the bull *Exsurge*.

C Jul: 10th, Henry VIII meets Charles V at Gravelines; by the Treaty of Calais they bind each other to make no further arrangements with France to effect the respective treaties for Mary Tudor to marry the Dauphin and for Charles to marry Charlotte of Valois;
14th, England signs a further commercial treaty with the Empire;
during Charles's absence the Spanish *communeros* in Toledo and Castille revolt; led by Juan de la Padrilla they form a Holy League at Avila in protest against abolition of ancient privileges under Hapsburg rule.
Aug:
Sep: 20th, Suleiman I (the Magnificent) succeeds as Sultan of Turkey (–1566) on the death of his father Selim I.

D Oct: 23rd, Charles V is crowned Holy Roman Emperor at Aachen and grants a capitulation to preserve the rights of the Estates, to reside in Germany and to restore the Council of Regency.
Nov: 1st, Charles V summons a diet to meet at Worms in *Jan.* 1521;
4th, Christian II of Denmark is crowned King of Sweden in Stockholm and grants an amnesty to his opponents;
8th, in the Stockholm Bloodbath, Christian II massacres Eric Vasa and leading Swedish bishops and nobles, in spite of his grant of an amnesty, provoking a national revolt under Gustavus Vasa (–1523).
Dec: 10th, Martin Luther publicly burns the bull *Exsurge*.

E Portuguese traders settle in China (–1523).

F **Politics, Economics, Law and Education**

Martin Luther urges German princes and nobles to nationalise the Church in his *Address 'to the most Serene and Mighty Imperial Majesty and to the Christian Nobility of the German Nation.'*

Chocolate in slab form is on sale in Spain.

G **Science, Technology and Discovery**

Ferdinand Magellan passes through the Magellan Straits into the Pacific (*Nov.* 28th) and sails for the Philippines, which he reaches in 110 days.

A. Achillini, *Anatomicae Annotationes* (posth.).

Gaspard Koller invents rifling on fire-arms.

H **Philosophy, Religion and Scholarship**

Alexander Barclay translates Sallust, his *Chronicle of the War . . . against Jugurtha.*

The Royal Library of France is founded by Francis I in the Palace of Fontainebleu, with Guillaume Budé, the scholar and humanist, as his Librarian.

The Scots New Testament.

Martin Luther is declared a heretic (*June* 15th).

Luther burns the Papal Bull of Excommunication (*Dec.* 10th). He attacks all sacraments except Baptism and the Lord's Supper in his Latin thesis on 'The Babylonish Captivity of the Church' (–1521). Luther's works are burned at Paul's Cross, London.

Cambridge Protestants meet in secret.

J **Art, Sculpture, Fine Arts and Architecture**

Painting:

Hans Baldung, *Nativity.*

Lucas Cranach, woodcuts for edition of the Bible.

Matthias Grünewald, *St. Erasmus and Maurice* (–1525).

Quentin Massys, *Madonna and Child enthroned.*

Sebastione del Piombo, *Martyrdom of St. Agatha.*

Andrea del Sarto, *The Story of Joseph.*

Architecture:

Michelangelo, Medici Chapel, St. Lorenziana, Florence.

Raphael, Pallazzo Pandolfini, Florence.

K **Music**

Robert Fairfax organises music for Henry VIII at the Field of Cloth of Gold.

L **Literature (including Drama)**

M **Births and Deaths**

Apr. 6th Raphael Sanzio d. (37).

Sept. 13th William Cecil, Lord Burghley, b. (–1598).

— Andrea Amati b. (–1578).

— William Dunbar d. (*c.* 60).

— Elizabeth Talbot (Bess of Hardwick, b. (–1608).

A Jan:
Feb: Rising of Gustaf Eriksson (Gustavus Vasa) in Sweden against Danish rule begins
   with the capture of Vesterås and is consolidated by the surrender of Upsala.
Mar:

B Apr: 17th (–18th), Martin Luther appears before the Diet of Worms and is cross-
   examined by the papal nuncio, Cardinal Aleander;
   23rd (–24th), the Spanish *communeros* are defeated at Villalar and the leaders of the
   anti-Hapsburg movement are executed;
   28th, Charles V grants his brother, the Archduke Ferdinand, the Hapsburg possessions
   in Lower Austria, Carinthia, Styria and Carinola.
May: 17th, Edward Stafford, Duke of Buckingham, a claimant to the English throne,
   is executed for constructive treason;
   26th, the Edict of Worms imposes on Martin Luther the ban of the Empire;
   28th, Emperor Charles V and Pope Leo X conclude a secret treaty to expel the French
   from Milan and to extirpate heresy;
   Archduke Ferdinand marries Anne of Hungary.
Jun: Henri d'Albret invades Navarre, then under Spanish control.

C Jul:
Aug: Cardinal Wolsey presides over a conference at Calais to arbitrate between Francis I
   and Charles V on their disputed claims to Milan, Burgundy and Navarre. To strengthen
   his hand against England Francis I allows the Duke of Albany to return to Scotland.
Sep: 13th, Spanish force under Cortes takes Tenochtitlan, the Aztec capital, after 8-week
   siege, assuming his control of Mexico;
   25th, Charles V and Wolsey sign the secret Treaty of Bruges for a joint declaration of
   war against France in *Mar.* 1523 and for Charles to marry Mary Tudor;
   29th, Suleiman I conquers Belgrade and begins his advance into Hungary.

D Oct: 11th, Pope Leo X confers the title 'Defender of the Faith' on Henry VIII.
Nov: 19th, war between Hapsburg and Valois (–1526) breaks out in Italy with the in-
   vasion of French-occupied Milan by imperial and papal armies under Prospero
   Colonna.
Dec: 1st, Pope Leo X dies;
   Mary of Austria marries Louis, King of Hungary;
   13th, John III (the Pious) succeeds as King of Portugal (–1557) on the death of his
   father Manuel I.

E Peasants in Majorca massacre the nobility.

F Politics, Economics, Law and Education

Niccolò Machiavelli, *Dell 'arte della Guerra* (trans. 1560 as *Seven Books on the Art of War*).

Eberlin of Günzberg, *The Fifteen Allies*, a programme of social reform, dedicated to Charles V.

Silk manufacture is introduced to France.

The Portuguese establish a trading post in Amboyna.

G Science, Technology and Discovery

Francisco de Gordillo explores the American Atlantic coast northwards to South Carolina.

H Philosophy, Religion and Scholarship

Henry Bradshaw, *The Holy Lyfe and Chronicon of Saynt Werburge* (posth.).

John Fisher, *Sermon* (Against the Doctrine of Luther).

Henry VIII, King of England, *Assertio Septem Sacramentorum* ('The Assertion of the Seven Sacraments' in opposition to Martin Luther; see 1520, 1522).

Niccolò Machiavelli's *Discourses* on the First Decade of Titus Livius read before Accademia degli Orti Oricellari, Florence, between 1513 and 1521.

John Major (or Mair), *Historia Majoris Britanniae* (published in Paris).

Philipp Melanchthon (i.e. Schwarzerd), *Loci Communes* (the earliest notable work on Lutheran dogma).

Charles V convenes the first Diet of Worms (*Mar.* 26th); order proclaimed for the destruction of Luther's books in the Empire.

J Art, Sculpture, Fine Arts and Architecture

Painting:

Lorenzo Lotto, *Virgin and Child with Saints*.

J. G. Mabuse, *Venus and Cupid*.

Jacopo Pontormo, frescoes in the Medici Palace.

Andrea del Sarto, Villa Poggio a Cajano.

Sculpture:

Michelangelo, tombs of Guiliamo de' Medici and of Lorenzo de' Medici, Florence (–1534).

K Music

L Literature (including Drama)

M Births and Deaths

Mar. 21st Maurice, Elector of Saxony, b. (–1553).

Apr. 27th Ferdinand Magellan d. (*c.* 41).

Aug. 4th Giovanni Battista Castagna (Pope Urban VII) b. (–1590).

Aug. 27th Josquin des Prés d. (76).

Dec. 13th Felice Peretti (Pope Sixtus V) b. (–1590).

— Tamás Bakócz d. (79).

— Edward Poynings d. (62).

1522　The French are driven from Milan—Turks take Rhodes

A Jan: 9th, Adrian of Utrecht, Regent of Spain, is elected Pope Adrian VI (–*Sept.* 1523), the last non-Italian pope;
Henry VIII declines to continue the truce with Scotland while the Duke of Albany remains north of the border;
30th, by the Treaty of Brussels Charles V grants his brother, the Archduke Ferdinand of Austria, the Hapsburg possessions in south-west Germany and the Tyrol and confirms the grant of *Apr.* 1521;
Lübeck declares war on Denmark and lays waste Bornholm.
Feb:
Mar: Martin Luther returns to Wittenberg and condemns the religious riots in Saxony.

B Apr: 4th, Francesco Sforza, son of Ludovico, enters French-occupied Milan;
27th, Spanish and imperial troops defeat the French and Swiss at Bicocca, three miles from Milan; Francesco Sforza is restored to the duchy and the French retreat from Lombardy.
May: England declares war against France and Scotland;
30th, the imperialists drive the French from Genoa.
Jun: 19th, Charles V visits England and signs the Treaty of Windsor with Henry VIII, by which both sovereigns undertake to invade France in *May* 1524.

C Jul: Charles V arrives in Spain;
English force under the Duke of Suffolk ravages Normandy and Picardy (–*Oct.*).
Aug: War of the German Knights under Ulrich von Hutten and Franz von Sickingen against the bishoprics and other spiritual principalities begins; von Sickingen lays siege to Trier (which he is forced to raise *Sept.* 14th);
24th, Gustavus Vasa accepts the office of Administrator of Sweden from an assembly at Vadstena and pledges himself to free the rest of Sweden from Danish control;
by the Treaty of Bordesholm, Christian II abandons claim to Schleswig-Holstein to his uncle Frederick.
Sep: 11th, the Duke of Albany, who had laid siege to Carlisle, agrees to a truce with Lord Dacre, warden of the West March.

D Oct: Albany leaves Scotland for France;
15th, Charles V appoints Cortes Governor of New Spain (Mexico).
Nov: rising of nobles in Denmark against Christian II for misrule.
Dec: the Turks under Suleiman I take Rhodes from the Knights of St. John (the knights are re-established in Malta by Charles V in 1530).

E Shih Tsung becomes Emperor of China (–1566);
Spanish force under Pedro de Alvarado conquers Guatemala (–1524).

F **Politics, Economics, Law and Education**
Cuthbert Tunstall, *De arte supputandi*, a manual for calculation.
Alessandro Alessandri, *Dies Geniales*.

G **Science, Technology and Discovery**
Pascual de Andagoya leads an expedition by land from Panama to discover Peru (Biru).
Francisco Montaño ascends Mount Popocatepetl, Mexico.
Portuguese ships reach Brunei, North-West Borneo.
Sebastien del Cano discovers New Amsterdam Island.

H **Philosophy, Religion and Scholarship**
Martin Luther's translation of the *New Testament* (*Sept.*) ('The Bible of the Reformation'; his complete Bible is available in 1534).
Martin Luther introduces a liturgy in German and communion in both kinds for the laity at Wittenberg.
Zwingli condemns fasting and the celibacy of priests, at Zurich.
Adrian VI, the last non-Italian pope, is elected (–1523).
A Polyglot Bible (Greek, Latin, Hebrew, Aramaic) is published by Alcalá University in Spain.

J **Art, Sculpture, Fine Arts and Architecture**
Painting:
Francesco Parmigianino, frescoes in Palma Cathedral (–1523).
Jacopo Pontormo, frescoes of the Passion, Ceritosa (–1525).

K **Music**
Martin Luther reforms the church service.

L **Literature (including Drama)**
Jacopo Sannazzaro, *De partu Virginis* (religious poem, fusing classical myth with the Christian story).

M **Births and Deaths**
Feb. 25th William Lilye d. (54).
May 24th John Jewel b. (–1571).
June 30th Johann Reuchlin d. (67).
Sept. 11th Ulissi Aldrovandi b. (–1605).
— François Clouet b. (–1572).
— John Day b. (–1584).
— Gavin Douglas d. (*c.* 48).
— Lamoral, Count of Egmont, b. (–1568).
— Margaret of Austria, Duchess of Parma, b. (–1586).

1523 Accession of Gustavus Vasa in Sweden—failure of English expedition to France

A **Jan:** 3rd, at the Diet of Nuremberg the papal nuncio promises that the reform of the Church will be undertaken by Adrian VI, but the German princes demand the summoning of a general council in Germany.

Feb:

Mar: In the civil war in Denmark an assembly of nobles at Viborg deposes Christian II; his uncle Frederick of Schleswig-Holstein becomes Frederick I of Denmark and Norway (–1533).

B **Apr:** 13th, the deposed Christian II, realising there is insufficient support for him in Norway, goes into exile;

English Parliament meets at Blackfriars; Sir Thomas More is elected Speaker of the Commons. Cardinal Wolsey's attempts to secure high taxation for the French war are stoutly resisted;

the Earl of Surrey harries the Scottish border (*–Sept.*);

the Elector Palatine, the Landgrave of Hesse and the Archbishop of Trier storm Landstuhl in the War of the German Knights; Franz von Sickingen is killed and Ulrich von Hutten goes into exile and dies in Zurich.

May:

Jun: 7th, Gustavus Vasa is elected Gustavus I of Sweden (–1560).

C **Jul:**

Aug: Charles V forces the Castillian Cortes to vote supplies for the war before presenting petitions for the redress of grievances;

Venice joins Charles V's league against France. Charles of Bourbon, Constable of France, defects to Charles V.

Sep: an English army under the Duke of Suffolk lands in France for a joint attack with imperialist forces against Boulogne but, 19th, Wolsey agrees to Charles V's design for an advance on Compiègne;

14th, Pope Adrian VI dies;

—, the French army under Admiral Bonnivet crosses the R. Ticino;

25th, the Earl of Surrey burns Jedburgh;

—, the Duke of Albany lands at Dumbarton from France and begins to rally the Scots.

D **Oct:** A Spanish force crosses the Pyrenees to threaten Bayonne;

27th, Suffolk takes Montalidier, but with the disbanding of the imperial troops he retires to Valenciennes, marking the failure of the English expedition to France.

Nov: 19th, Guilio de' Medici is elected Pope Clement VII (–1534);

the French under Admiral Bonnivet are forced to abandon the siege of Milan.

Dec: The imperialist general Prospero Colonna dies.

E The Portuguese are expelled from China, where they formed a settlement in 1520.

F **Politics, Economics, Law and Education**

Martin Luther expounds his political views in *Von Weltlicher Oberkeyt* (Wittenberg).

Spanish Town, Jamaica, is founded.

Marine insurance policies are first issued in Florence.

G **Science, Technology and Discovery**

[Anthony] Fitzherbert, *Book of Husbandry*, the first manual of agricultural practice.

H **Philosophy, Religion and Scholarship**

John Bourchier, Lord Berners, translates Froissart's *Chronicles*, pt. 1 (pt. 2, 1525), both published for him by Pynson.

Hans Sachs, *Die Wittenbergische Nachtigall* (an allegory in verse, *The Nightingale of Wittenberg*, in praise of Luther and his doctrines).

The first Hebrew concordance, based on the work of Rabbi Isaac Nathan.

J **Art, Sculpture, Fine Arts and Architecture**

Painting:

  Romano Giulio, *Stoning of St. Stephen*.

  Hans Holbein the younger, *Erasmus*; also illustrations for *The Dance of Death* (–1524).

  Titian, *Bacchus and Ariadne*.

K **Music**

Keyboard music printed in Italy with right- and left-hand staves of five lines each and divided into measures by means of bar lines.

L **Literature (including Drama)**

John Skelton, *A Goodly Garland; or Chapelet of Laurell* (a poem in celebration of a wreath of laurel bestowed on the poet by noble ladies. The poet lists his own works).

M **Births and Deaths**

Aug. 29th Ulrich von Hutten d. (35).

Oct. 2nd Alessandro Alessandri d. (72).

— John Merbecke b. (–1585).

A Jan: The French army in Lombardy under Admiral Bonnivet is driven from Vigevano and retreats to Novara to await Swiss reinforcements;

Lorenzo Campeggio, the papal legate, at the Diet of Nuremberg orders the Edict of Worms (of *May* 1521) to be carried out as far as possible. The 'Lutheran' Party, led by the Elector Frederick the Wise of Saxony, and Philip, Landgrave of Hesse, the pupil of Philip Melanchthon, demand that a national synod should meet to discuss church reform at Speyer in *Nov.* Lutheranism is also adopted during the year by the rulers of Silesia, Pomerania, Brandenburg-Culmbach, Brunswick-Luneburg, Schleswig and Holstein;

at the Diet of Nuremberg the imperial cities and Duke George of Saxony attack the *Reichsregiment*, on the grounds of its financial levies, and this experiment at political reorganisation in the empire is effectively buried.

Feb: Imperial troops recover Fuentarrabia (captured by the French in *Oct.* 1521).

Mar: Pope Clement VII sends the Archbishop of Capua to France, Spain and England to propose peace negotiations should be opened, but conditions are unfavourable;

Bonnivet withdraws from Novara and is defeated on the Sesia by the imperialists.

B Apr: 24th, the exiled Duke of Bourbon, in the service of the Emperor Charles V, expels Admiral Bonnivet from Milan;

30th, the Chevalier Bayard, who has taken over Bonnivet's command, is killed, and the French are driven from Lombardy.

May: 20th, the Duke of Albany, discredited in Scotland as a leader, leaves the Kingdom for the last time;

25th, Henry VIII and Charles V form a new league to support the Duke of Bourbon in a fresh attack on France.

Jun: The Peasants' Revolt in southern Germany (–*May* 1525) begins at Stühlingen on the estates of Count von Lupfen. The rebels demand the abolition of enclosures and feudal services;

28th, the Duke of Bourbon, with the Marquis of Pesara, invades Provence with a huge army of Spaniards and Germans;

the Archduke Ferdinand of Austria, the dukes of Bavaria and the bishops of southern Germany meet at Ratisbon to plan the reform of the Church from within.

C Jul: 15th, the Emperor Charles V prohibits the holding of the proposed German synod at Spires;

26th, James V of Scotland, aged 12, is 'erected' King at Edinburgh, a triumph for the English party under the Queen Mother and the Earl of Arran;

Archbishop Beaton, leader of the pro-French party, is imprisoned.

Aug: 8th, the Duke of Bourbon takes Aix-en-Provence and, 19th, lays siege to Marseilles;

the Peasants' Revolt, led by Thomas Müntzer, extends to Swabia, Franconia, Bavaria, the Tyrol, Carinthia, Thuringia and Alsace.

Sep: 10th, Henry VIII orders preparations for an expedition to aid Bourbon in France, but no army is in fact sent;

29th, Bourbon retires from Provence, having abandoned the siege of Marseilles, which is able to resist through the help of the galleys of Andrea Doria;

the Spanish attack on Roussillon fails.

D Oct: Francis I, collecting an army at Avignon, crosses the Mount Cenis Pass, to attack the retreating imperialists;

26th, the Spanish surrender Milan, stricken by the plague, to the French. Bourbon and Pesara withdraw to Lodi;

the Protestant Princes of Germany meet at Ulm (and in *Dec.* at Speyer) to concert a campaign against the Emperor.

(*Continued opposite*)

F   Politics, Economics, Law and Education
> Grenada, Nicaragua, is founded.

G   Science, Technology and Discovery
> Giovanni de Verrazano, sent on an expedition to the New World by Francis I, explores the coast from Cape Fear to Newfoundland, and discovers New York Bay and the Hudson River.
>
> Esteban Gómez traces the American coast from Nova Scotia to Florida (–1525).
>
> Peter Apian, *Cosmographicus liber*, the first text book of general theoretical geography.

H   Philosophy, Religion and Scholarship
> Philippe de Comines (or Commynes), *Memoirs* (first French historical narrative to depart from the 'Chronicle' form.
>
> Desiderius Erasmus, *Colloquies* (final edition of the humanist's masterpiece—Conversations displaying his liberal philosophy).
>
> The *Gesta Romanorum* translated anon; printed by Wynkyn de Worde (popular collection of stories of the deeds of the Romans, written in Latin, perhaps by English scholars).
>
> Wynkyn de Worde's printing of Wakefield's *Oratio*, in which for the first time in English typography the italic type is used.

J   Art, Sculpture, Fine Arts and Architecture
> Painting:
> Lucas Cranach, *Judgement of Paris*; also *Luther and his wife* (roundels).
> Hans Holbein the younger, illustrations for *The Alphabet of Death*.
> Architecture:
> Michelangelo, Biblotheca Laurenziana, Florence (–1525).

K   Music
> Martin Luther, *Geistliche Leider* (a German hymnal, expanded 1549).

L   Literature (including Drama)
> Giangiorgio Trissino, *La Sophonisba* (tragedy—the first to be written in blank verse).

M   Births and Deaths
> Apr. 30th Pierre, Chevalier de Bayard, d. (51).
> Aug. 23rd François Hotman b. (–1590).
> Sept. 7th Thomas Erastus b. (–1583).
> Sept. 11th Pierre de Ronsard b. (–1585).
> Oct. 20th Thomas Linacre d. (*c.* 64).
> Dec. 24th Vasco da Gama d. (*c.* 64).
> — Luis Vaz de Camoens b. (–1580).
> — Hans Holbein the elder d. (*c.* 64).

Nov: 6th, Francis I lays siege to Pavia; he tries unsuccessfully to divert the course of the River Ticino to gain access to the south side of the town.

Dec: 12th, Venice, Florence and the Papacy sign a secret treaty undertaking they will not aid Francis I's allies.

E   Zwingli establishes control over Zurich, and Bucer over Strassburg.
> By the Treaty of Malmö, Denmark confirms the independence of Sweden under Gustavus Vasa, thus ending the Union of Calmar (since 1397).

1525   Charles V becomes Master of Italy by the Battle of Pavia—The Catholic League is formed at Dessau

A **Jan:** The Duke of Albany takes Naples from Francis I, but the detachment of his force from the main army weakens the French position in Italy.

Feb: 24th, the Duke of Bourbon and the Marquis of Pesara lead an imperialist-Spanish army to rout the French and Swiss at the battle of Pavia. Francis I of France is taken prisoner to Spain; 14,000 men are slain in battle, including Richard de la Pole, self-styled Earl of Suffolk and pretender to the English throne. Charles V becomes master of Italy, since he soon regains Milan and Genoa. In the battle the Spanish infantry first use muskets.

Mar: 20th, Louise of Savoy, Queen Mother of France, requires the *Parlement* of Paris to appoint a commission for the trial of Lutherans. Proceedings are subsequently brought against the preachers of Meaux, and Jacques Le Sèvres's translation of the New Testament is burnt.

B **Apr:** 10th, Albert of Brandenburg, Grand Master of the Teutonic Knights, surrenders the lands of his order to the King of Poland to form a secular, Protestant duchy of Brandenburg, with Albert as duke, under Polish suzerainty.

May: 5th, John the Steadfast, succeeds as Elector of Saxony (–1532) on the death of his brother, Frederick the Wise;

the Peasants' Revolt in south Germany is suppressed and Thomas Müntzer is executed.

Jun: 18th, Henry VIII creates his natural son, Henry Fitzroy, Duke of Richmond;

Cardinal Wolsey is forced to abandon the Amicable Loan, a tax without Parliamentary sanction which he has required from all with goods worth £50 a year, to meet the expenses of a proposed invasion of France. Opposition to Wolsey is unrelenting.

C **Jul:** Girolamo Morone, Chancellor of Milan, betrays to Charles V a plot of the Pope, Venice and various Italian princes against him. Francesco Sforza is subsequently deprived of his rule in the Milanese;

George Duke of Saxony (of the Albertine branch), cousin of the Elector, John of Saxony, the Elector Joachim of Brandenburg and Archbishop Albrecht of Mainz meet with other Catholic princes at Dessau to consider the formation of a Catholic League.

Aug: 14th, the failure of the Amicable Loan leads Wolsey to seek a truce with France, and, 30th, the Peace is signed. France is to pay Henry VIII a pension of 100,000 crowns a year for the rest of his life. The Peace is a severe setback for the Emperor Charles V and is an attempt by Wolsey to restore in some measure the 'balance of power', overturned by the imperialists' victory at Pavia.

Sep:

D **Oct:** In retaliation to the Catholic League of Dessau, the Protestant Philip, Landgrave of Hesse, proposes a defensive alliance with the Elector John of Saxony (concluded *Feb.* 1526).

Nov:

Dec: The Imperial Diet is summoned to Augsburg for a discussion of the religious situation; the discussion proves fruitless.

E Cardinal Wolsey, to sustain himself in power, presents Henry VIII with Hampton Court;

Sultan Suleiman I of Turkey signs a 7-year truce with Sigismund of Hungary, and is urged by France to attack Germany;

the Mogul Emperor Barbar invades the Punjab.

F **Politics, Economics, Law and Education**

Roderigo de Bastidas founds Santa Marta, the first settlement of the future New Granada.

Thomas Wolsey endows Cardinal College, Oxford, on the site of St. Frideswide's Monastery (the college is refounded by Henry VIII as Christ Church in 1546).

G **Science, Technology and Discovery**

Hops are introduced to England from Artois.

H **Philosophy, Religion and Scholarship**

Pietro Bembo, *Prose della volgar lingua* (influential argument in favour of the use of Italian as a literary and scholarly language instead of Latin).

Niccolò Machiavelli presents his *Istorie Fiorentine* (*The Annals of Florence*) to Clement VII (trans. 1595).

Polydore Vergil's edition of Gildas: *De Excidio Britanniae*; the first attempt in England at a critical edition of historical source material.

Zacharie Ferreri prepares a revised hymnal at the direction of Pope Leo X.

William Tyndale's translation of *The New Testament* published by Peter Schoeffer at Worms (–1536).

Ulrich Zwingli, *Commentarius* ('de vera et falsa religione').

J **Art, Sculpture, Fine Arts and Architecture**

Painting:

Hans Baldung, *Adam and Eve*.

Angelo Bronzino, frescoes in Palma Cathedral (–1530).

Lorenzo Lotto, *Portrait of a Young Man*.

Vecchio Palma, *Three Sisters*.

Jacopo Pontormo, *Christ at Emmaus*; also *Charity*.

Andrea del Sarto, fresco, *Madonna del Sacco*.

K **Music**

L **Literature (including Drama)**

M **Births and Deaths**

May 18th Pietro Pomponazzi d. (63).

— Pieter Breughel b. (–1569).

— Jacob Fugger d. (66).

— George Gascoigne b. (–1577).

— Charles, Cardinal of Lorraine, b. (–1574).

— John Stow b. (–1605).

A Jan: 14th, Francis I of France and the Emperor Charles V sign the Peace of Madrid, by which Francis promises to surrender the Duchy of Burgundy and his claims to Naples, Milan, Asti, Genoa, Flanders and Artois; he undertakes to render no aid to Navarre or Gelders and to leave two sons in Spain as hostages;
—, Anglo-Scottish Peace is signed.
Feb: 27th, Elector John of Saxony and Philip, Landgrave of Hesse, sign the League of Gotha, as an association of Protestant princes (extended in *May* at Torgau).
Mar: 17th, Francis I of France is released from Spanish captivity;
a peasants' revolt in Austria is suppressed with great cruelty;
the Emperor Charles V marries Isabella of Portugal;
23rd, Charles V forbids religious innovations in the empire, but offers the Protestant princes his services in persuading the Pope to summon a general council of the Church.

B Apr: 27th, Barbar, Mogul Emperor of India, defeats Ibrahim at the battle of Panipat and establishes the Mogul dynasty in Delhi (–1761);
29th, Henry VIII confirms his alliance with Francis I at Greenwich.
May: 2nd, The Protestant League or Torgau is formed under Elector John of Saxony, Philip, Landgrave of Hesse, the princes of Brunswick-Lüneburg, Anhalt and Mecklenberg and the city of Magdeburg;
23rd, Pope Clement VII forms the League of Cognac as an offensive league against the Emperor Charles V; signatories include Venice, Florence, Milan and France (thus overturning the Peace of Madrid of *Jan.*). It aims at compelling the Emperor to restore the French princes, kept as hostages in Spain, to give Francesco Sforza independent sovereignty over Milan and the other Italian States their ancient liberties; Cardinal Wolsey, while supporting the principle of the League, refuses to commit England.
Jun: 1st, the First Diet of Speyer advises every member of the Empire so to conduct himself with reference to the Edict of Worms as he should answer to God and his Imperial Majesty. Charles V's subsequent quarrel with the Pope prevents him from enforcing the Edict.

C Jul: 6th, the Duke of Bourbon defeats the Duke of Urbino and, 25th, takes Milan for Charles V, compelling Francesco Sforza to surrender.
Aug: 20th, Cardinal Pompeo Colonna plunders Rome, forcing Pope Clement VII to take refuge in the Castle of St. Angelo. Cosimo de' Medici with papal troops still carries on the fight for the League;
29th (–30th), Suleiman I defeats the Hungarian army at the battle of Mohacs, at which Louis II of Hungary is killed.
Sep: 10th, Suleiman I takes Buda;
23rd, Cremona surrenders to the Duke of Urbino, leading an army of Swiss mercenaries, Venetians and soldiers from the Papal States, but the Duke fails to take strategic advantage of this.

D Oct: The Duke of Urbino begins the blockade of Milan, and is joined by Alfonso, Duke of Ferrara; later in the year the arrival of Charles V's German levies forces them to abandon the siege.
Nov: 10th, John Zápolya is crowned King of Hungary, but
Dec: 17th, Ferdinand of Austria is elected King of Bohemia; the birth of the Austro-Hungarian state (–1920).

E Russo-Polish Twenty Years' War is concluded; Russia retains Smolensk (conquered in 1514);
The Turkish fleet attacks the Arab corsairs of the Red Sea.

F **Politics, Economics, Law and Education**
Lucas Vasquez de Ayllon founds a settlement of San Miguel in Carolinas, later abandoned.
Piquet is first played.

G **Science, Technology and Discovery**
Sebastian Cabot undertakes an expedition to the Moluccas for Spanish merchants, but
decides to explore the Rio de la Plata in search of a passage to the east, and sails up the
Paraná and Paraguay rivers.
Portuguese vessels visit New Guinea.

H **Philosophy, Religion and Scholarship**
Hector Boece, *Historiae Gentis Scotorum* (*History of Scotland*; trans. by John Bellenden,
or Ballantyne with additions, –1535).
Martin Luther's *German Mass* and *Order of Service*.

J **Art, Sculpture, Fine Arts and Architecture**
Painting:
Albrecht Dürer, *Four Apostles*.
Hans Holbein the younger first visits England.
Architecture:
Michelangelo, vestibule, Laurenziana, Florence.

K **Music**

L **Literature (including Drama)**

M **Births and Deaths**
July 31st Augustus I, Elector of Saxony, b. (–1586).
Dec. 12th Alvaro de Baza, Marquis of Santa Cruz, b. (–1588).
— Giovanni Pierluigi da Palestrina b. (–1594).

A Jan: 1st, the Hapsburg administration of Austria is reorganised (the system remains basically unchanged to 1848).
   Feb: 24th, Archduke Ferdinand of Austria is crowned King of Bohemia in Prague. John Zápolya subsequently musters his forces to invade Bohemia.
   Mar: 16th, the Mogul Emperor Barbar defeats a Hindu Confederacy at Kanwanha.

B Apr: 30th, an Anglo-French alliance is signed at Westminster (confirmed in *Aug.* at Amiens). Cardinal Wolsey, architect of the alliance, aims at achieving a lasting peace. Francis I is to pay Henry VIII a substantial tribute; Princess Mary Tudor is to marry into the house of Valois.
   May: 6th, the Sack of Rome, when imperialist troops under Charles, Duke of Bourbon (who is killed), mutiny, pillage the city and kill some 4,000 of the inhabitants. Valuable art treasures are looted. Philibert Prince of Orange succeeds Bourbon but is soon forced to relinquish his command. Law is not restored until *Feb.* 1528;
      subsequently the imperialists occupy Civita Vecchia; the Duke of Ferrara besieges Modena and Reggio, Venice takes Ravenna, and Italy again falls under Charles V's sway;
      16th, the Medici nephews of the Pope are expelled from Florence, which reverts to a republic;
      17th (–31st), Archbishop Warham holds a secret inquiry at Greenwich into Henry VIII's marriage with Catherine of Aragon, the first step in divorce proceedings;
      the Elector Joachim of Brandenburg, Duke George of Saxony and the Archduke Ferdinand meet at Breslau. The meeting gives rise to rumours of a Catholic conspiracy, which particularly alarms Philip, Landgrave of Hesse.
   Jun: 7th, Pope Clement VII is obliged to surrender to the imperialists;
      24th, the Swedish Diet of Västerås bows to the demands of Gustavus Vasa in effecting a Reformation, under which most of the property of the Church passes to the Crown.

C Jul: A French army under Vicomte de Lautrec invades the Milanese and turns south, aiming at rescuing the Pope.
   Aug: 10th, Ferdinand of Bohemia defeats John Zápolya of Hungary at Tokay;
      18th, Cardinal Wolsey meets Francis I at Amiens to ratify the treaty of *Apr.*;
      the French take Pavia and Genoa; but Naples resists, owing to the defection of Andrea Doria to the imperialists.
   Sep: Dissolution of the monasteries in Berne.

D Oct:
   Nov: 3rd, Ferdinand is recognised King of Hungary by the Diet at Buda;
      26th, Pope Clement VII is forced to sign a treaty with Charles V, granting him ecclesiastical privileges and paying considerable sums; he also undertakes to call a general council of the Church.
   Dec: 6th, Clement VII is allowed to escape to Orvieto;
      16th, Francis I calls an assembly of Notables to vote supplies;
      23rd, Clement VII agrees to issue a dispensation to Henry VIII for his remarriage if his marriage with Catherine of Aragon should prove to be invalid.

E

F **Politics, Economics, Law and Education**
Sebastian Cabot builds a fort at Santo Espiritu in Paraguay.
Philip, Elector of Hesse, founds Marburg University (*May* 30th).

G **Science, Technology and Discovery**
Paracelsus lectures in medicine at Basle University.

H **Philosophy, Religion and Scholarship**
A Baptist sect is founded in Zurich.
The Sack of Rome, led by the Constable of Bourbon (*May*), ends the Revival of Learning in Italy.
Pope Clement VII is imprisoned in the Castle of S. Angelo.

J **Art, Sculpture, Fine Arts and Architecture**
Painting:
Hans Holbein the younger, *The More Family Portraits*; also *Lady with a Squirell*.
Francesco Parmigianino, *St. Jerome*; also *The Madonna of St. Zachariah* (–1530).

K **Music**
Adrian Willaert founds a singing school in Venice.
The first *chansons* are printed in Paris by Attaignant.

L **Literature (including Drama)**

M **Births and Deaths**
May 5th Charles, Duke of Bourbon, d. (37).
May 21st Philip II of Spain b. (–1598).
June 22nd Niccolò Machiavelli d. (58).
— Giuseppe Arcimboldi b. (–1593).
— John Lesley b. (–1596).
— Jane Shore d. (*c.* 80).

A Jan: 22nd, England and France declare war on the Emperor Charles V at Burgos.
Feb: 11th, the imperial army leaves Rome to meet the Vicomte Lautrec's advance from Bologna;
24th, John Zápolya makes a treaty with Suleiman I, recognising the Sultan's suzerainty; Henry VIII sends Stephen Gardiner and Edward Fox to Rome, to persuade Pope Clement VII to hasten proceedings in the King's suit for divorce, but the Pope, reluctant to cause offence to Charles V, Catherine's uncle, plays for time.
Mar: Philip, Landgrave of Hesse, and the Elector John of Saxony form the defensive alliance of Weimar and mobilise troops for withstanding a Catholic attack;
the arrest of English merchants in Spain and Flanders provokes a commercial crisis. The English staple town for wool is moved from Antwerp to Calais. Widespread distress among weavers in the eastern counties, and, in *May*, riots in Kent against Wolsey's policy.

B Apr: 13th, Pope Clement VII issues a commission to Cardinals Wolsey and Campeggio to try the question of the validity of Henry VIII's marriage to Catherine of Aragon;
20th, Vicomte Lautrec lays siege to Naples, where he is aided by Fillipino Doria;
a truce is signed between England and the Netherlands (*–Feb.* 1529), to ease the commercial crisis.
May: 31st, A statue of the Virgin Mary is defaced in Paris, while a Synod is being held before the Archbishop of Sens to enquire into heresies.
Jun: 1st, Pope Clement VII removes from Orvieto to Viterbo.

C Jul: 4th, Andrea and Fillipino Doria defect from France to the Emperor;
England experiences the first severe outbreak of the plague.
Aug: 16th, Vicomte Lautrec dies of the plague in Italy;
30th, the French army capitulate at Aversa and is subsequently expelled from Naples and Genoa.
Sep: 12th, Andrea Doria enters Genoa which regains its independence, under the protection of the Emperor, as a republic (–1796).

D Oct: 7th, Cardinal Lorenzo Campeggio arrives in England to find that Charles V has once more become the master of Italy, and Pope Clement VII has to make his peace with the Emperor to save the fortunes of the Medici family;
25th, the Genoese occupy Savona;
28th, surrender of the French brigade which had taken refuge in Castellelto.
Nov: 8th, at a gathering of nobles and leading citizens of London at Bridewell Henry VIII explains his motives for seeking a divorce from Catherine of Aragon.
Dec:

E Cardinal Wolsey dissolves 22 religious houses with less than 7 members to provide funds for the foundation of colleges at Ipswich and Oxford.

F **Politics, Economics, Law and Education**
  Baldassare, Count Castiglione, *Il Cortegiano*, a manual of polite conduct, inspired by the court of Urbino (Eng. translation by Thomas Moby, *The Courtier*, 1561).
  Juan de Valdez, *Dialogo de Mercurio y Caron*, a discussion of current political questions.
  P. Melanchthon proposes thoroughgoing educational reforms in Germany.

G **Science, Technology and Discovery**
  P. Paracelsus, *Die Kleine Chirugie*, the first manual proper of surgery.

H **Philosophy, Religion and Scholarship**
  William Copland translates *Till Eulenspiegel* (see –1500, 1515).
  Desiderius Erasmus, *Ciceronianus* (a satire on the devotees of Cicero in scholarship).
  William Tyndale, *Obedience of a Christian Man*.
  Order of the Capuchins is organised, as a branch of the Observants, to enforce the strict monastic rule as instituted by St. Francis.
  The Reformation begins to take root in Scotland (–1560).

J **Art, Sculpture, Fine Arts and Architecture**
  Painting:
    Hans Holbein the younger, *The Artist's Wife and Two elder Children*; also *The Virgin with the family of Burgomaster Meyer*.
  Architecture:
    Michelangelo, Fortifications, Florence (–1529).
    Diego de Siloe, Granada Cathedral.

K **Music**
  Agricola's *Musica Instrumentalis* is published.

L **Literature (including Drama)**
  Ulrich von Hutten, *Arminius* (posth.; a romantic dialogue in glorification of a national, heroic German figure of the Reformation).

M **Births and Deaths**
  Apr. 6th Albrecht Dürer d. (57).
  July 8th Emanuel Philibert, Duke of Saxony, b. (–1580).
  — Theodorus Dirk de Bry b. (–1598).
  — William Maitland of Lethington b. (–1573).
  — Paul Veronese (Paoli Caliari) b. (–1588).

1529   The term 'Protestant' is born at the Diet of Spires—Siege of
        Vienna—Fall of Wolsey

A Jan: 6th, Pope Clement VII is taken ill; on learning this, Cardinal Wolsey orders his
       agents in Rome to lay plans for his election in the event of Clement's death, but he
       recovers.
   Feb:
   Mar: The Second Diet of Speyer opens.

B Apr: 19th, the Diet votes to quash the Edict of *June* 1526 and put in force the Edict of
       Worms (of 1521), as the Archduke Ferdinand refuses to make any concessions to the
       Lutherans;
         the minority, led by the Elector John of Saxony, the Margrave George of Branden-
         burg and Philip, Landgrave of Hesse, read their 'Protest' against the decision of the
         Catholic majority in religious affairs, giving rise to the term 'Protestant'. Other sig-
         natories of the Protest are the princes of Brunswick-Lüneburg and Anhalt, Nurem-
         berg, Strassburg and 12 other cities;
       the Turkish attack on Austria subsequently averts civil war in Germany;
       22nd, the Treaty of Saragossa defines the interests of Spain and Portugal in the Pacific;
       Spain gives up its claim to the Moluccas;
       —, the Catholic Forest Cantons of Switzerland sign a Christian Union with Austria in
       opposition to the Protestant Civic League formed by Zurich, Berne, Strassburg and
       Constance.
   May: 31st, Cardinals Campeggio and Wolsey open their legatine court at the Blackfriars
       (–*July* 30th).
   Jun: 9th, on Zwingli's advice Zurich declares war on the Catholic Forest Cantons,
       following a dispute over the election of the Abbot of St. Gallen;
       18th, Henry VIII and Catherine of Aragon appear before the legatine court;
       21st, Count St. Pol, commander of the French army in Lombardy, is captured at
       Landriano, near Pavia;
       24th, the first Peace of Kappel ends the civil war in Switzerland. The defeated Catholic
       Cantons agree to break off their alliance with Austria; neither side is to attack the other
       for the future;
       29th, Pope Clement VII agrees to the Emperor Charles V's terms by the Treaty of
       Barcelona. Charles grants Milan to Francesco Sforza for his life and undertakes to
       establish the Medici in Florence and to encourage various towns in the papal states to
       return to the Pope's allegiance. Clement is to crown Charles V and invest him with the
       Kingdom of Naples. Alessandro de' Medici is to marry Charles's natural daughter,
       Margaret.

C Jul: 13th, Pope Clement VII removes Henry VIII's divorce suit to Rome.
   Aug: 5th, Francis I of France and the Emperor Charles V sign the Treaty of Cambrai, by
       which France renounces all claims to Italy and sovereignty over Flanders and Artois;
       Charles renounces his claim to Burgundy. Francis undertakes to marry Eleanor of
       Portugal, recognises Charles's right to the succession in Gelders, surrenders Tournai
       and pays 2 million crowns. This, 'The Ladies Peace', confirms Spanish rule in Italy;
       9th, writs are issued for a Parliament in England;
       12th, Charles V arrives at Genoa;
       27th, England accedes to the Treaty of Cambrai;
       Henry VIII, on progress with Anne Boleyn, is persuaded by Thomas Cranmer to seek
       the opinion of universities on the question of his proposed divorce.
   Sep: 21st (–*Oct.* 15th), the Turks under Suleiman I lay siege to Vienna, arousing con-
       siderable national sentiment in the empire;
       a defensive league of the powers of Italy is formed by the Pope, Venice, Florence,
       Mantua and Savoy;

F **Politics, Economics, Law and Education**
   Simon Fish, *A Supplicacyon for the Beggars*, exhorts Henry VIII to rescue the people of England from papal tyranny and to despoil the monasteries.
   Sir Thomas More, a common lawyer, is appointed Lord Chancellor, as Cardinal Wolsey's successor.
   The Diet of Speyer imposes censorship of the Press in Germany.
   Francis I of France, influenced by Margaret of Navarre and Guillaume Budé, founds the Collège de France, initially as an academy for the study of Greek and Hebrew.

G **Science, Technology and Discovery**
   Emperor Charles V begins the Imperial Canal of Aragon.

H **Philosophy, Religion and Scholarship**
   Guillaume Budé, *Commentaries on the Greek Language* (*Commentarii Linguae Graecae*).
   Geoffrey Tory designs and publishes in Paris his book *Champfleury*, being instructions for the design of the Roman alphabet, intermingled with stories and anecdotes (a landmark in the history of printing and book design).
   Bernardino de Sahagún starts his Franciscan mission in Mexico. (From 1569 he is to write—sometimes in the Aztec language—about his discoveries of their history and on the cultural life of ancient Mexico.)
   The Library at Hamburg, Germany, is founded.
   The Short Catechism is published, with preface by Luther, known as 'Luther's Catechism', and adopted in the churches of Southern Germany.
   Luther and Zwingli hold disputation on the Eucharist at Marburg (*Oct.*).

J **Art, Sculpture, Fine Arts and Architecture**
   Painting:
      Albrecht Altdorfer, *Battle of Alexander*.
      Lorenzo Lotto, *Christ and the Woman taken in Adultery*.
   Architecture:
      Sanmicheli, Palazzo Canossa, Verona.

K **Music**

L **Literature (including Drama)**
   Antonio de Guevara, *El Relox de principes* (translated as the *Golden Boke of Marcus Aurelius* –1535, 1557).
   Antonio Telesia, *Imber aureus* (a mythological tragedy).

M **Births and Deaths**
   May 5th Paolo Emilio d. (*c.* 55).
   June 21st John Skelton d. (69).

30th (–*Oct*. 4th), Luther and Zwingli hold a disputation at Marburg, to attempt a re-conciliation of their beliefs, which Philip of Hesse has promoted to ease political strains in Germany; the disputation reveals their differences.

D Oct: 9th, The King's attorney prefers an indictment against Cardinal Wolsey in the Court of King's Bench for receiving bulls from Rome in contravention of the Statute of Provisors;

15th, Suleiman I is forced to raise the siege of Vienna, but Ferdinand, hampered by a mutiny, fails to recapture Buda, leaving the greater part of Hungary under John Zápolya;

18th, Cardinal Wolsey falls from power; as a desperate gesture to save himself he pre-sents Henry VIII with York Place (soon to be renamed Whitehall Palace);

26th, Sir Thomas More is appointed Lord Chancellor in succession to Wolsey;

opposition to the restoration of the Medici in Florence, to which the imperialists are forced to lay siege (–*Aug*. 1530).

Nov: 4th (–*Dec*. 17th), English Parliament meets, the first session of the 'Reformation Parliament' (–1536). An address is made to the King charging Wolsey with great offences, but the Cardinal is ably defended by his solicitor, Thomas Cromwell, and Henry VIII refuses the address. The Commons attack mortuary dues and other clerical abuses;

Henry VIII is released from his debts by statute.

Dec:

E

A   Jan: 26th, Thomas Boleyn, Earl of Wiltshire, is appointed Lord Privy Seal and sent by
Henry on a mission with Stokesley, bishop elect of London, to Pope Clement VII at
Bologna to press the King's case for a divorce from Catherine of Aragon.
Feb: 6th, Charles Brandon, Duke of Suffolk, is appointed Lord President of the Council
(–1545);
14th, Cardinal Wolsey is restored to the archbishopric of York;
24th, Charles V is crowned Holy Roman Emperor and King of Italy by Pope Clement
VII at Bologna—the last imperial coronation by a pope. Charles V influences Clement
to refuse Henry VIII's petition for divorce.
Mar: 21st, Clement VII issues a bull forbidding all ecclesiastical judges and lawyers
from speaking or writing on the question of Henry VIII's marriage and suspends proceedings in the case until *Sept.*

B   Apr: Oxford University narrowly votes in favour of the King's divorce.
May: 24th, a list of heretical books is drawn up in London: Tyndale's Bible is burnt;
Charles V crosses the Alps for Germany.
Jun: 20th, the Diet of Augsburg meets in the presence of Charles V, who is determined on
exterminating heresy; Philip Melanchthon states the Lutheran case, since Martin
Luther is under the ban of the Empire;
25th, the Confession of Augsburg, prepared by Melanchthon, is signed by the Protes-
tant princes; hopes of an agreement with Zwinglians fade.

C   Jul: 3rd, Zwingli's Confession is presented to Charles V;
13th, the opinions of the universities favouring Henry VIII's divorce are taken by
Thomas Cranmer to Pope Clement VII.
Aug: 12th, Florence is restored to the Medicis by imperial troops after a siege of 10
months;
20th, rising in Geneva.
Sep: 20th, Martin Luther advises the Protestant princes to prepare for war, rather than
accept a compromise with the Emperor;
22nd, the Diet of Augsburg rules that the Protestant princes must conform by *Apr.* 15th
1531.

D   Oct: 28th, Alessandro de' Medici is appointed Governor of Florence.
Nov: 4th, Cardinal Wolsey is arrested as a traitor and travels towards London, dying at
Leicester, 29th;
the Diet of Augsburg decrees the execution of the Edict of Worms of 1521, the restitu-
tution of Church property and the maintenance of episcopal jurisdiction;
Charles V reforms the Imperial Chamber.
Dec: 1st, Margaret of Savoy, Governor of the Netherlands, dies;
proceedings are initiated in the Court of King's Bench against the entire clergy of
England for violating the statutes of provisors and *praemunire* in recognising the
legatine authority of Cardinal Wolsey;
22nd, the Protestant princes of Germany deliberate at Schmalkalden, and
31st, form the Schmalkaldic League in self-defence against the Emperor Charles V
and his Catholic allies. The original signatories include the Elector of Saxony, the
Landgrave of Hesse, Prince Wolfgang of Anhalt, the Counts Mansfeld and the cities
of Magdeburg and Bremen.

E   Francis I of France marries Eleanor of Portugal, widow of Emmanuel I and sister of
Charles V, in accordance with the Treaty of Madrid of *Jan.* 1526;
the Knights Hospitallers are established in Malta;

(*Continued opposite*)

F Politics, Economics, Law and Education
William Tyndale in *Practyse of Prelates* attacks Henry VIII's proceedings for divorce.
Peter Martyr, *Decades de Orbe Nova* (posth.; written from 1493), a survey of the impact of the Discoveries on Europe.
The Antwerp Exchange is built.
English merchants trading to Spain are formed into a company.

G Science, Technology and Discovery
Regnier Gemma Frisius suggests longitude can be found by means of difference of times.
C. Rudolff uses decimals to extend whole-number rules to fractions.

H Philosophy, Religion and Scholarship
P. Melanchthon, *Apologia*.
The English Parliament forbids the procurement from Rome of licences for clerks to hold benefices in plurality.
The Confession of Augsburg (*June* 25th) of the German Reformers is presented to Charles V and signed by the German princes at the Diet of Augsburg, and accepted as the Creed of the Lutheran Church (the *Confession* probably drafted by Philipp Melanchthon).
Claude Garamond, typographer, sets up his own foundry in Paris. In recognition of the typographical art of Geoffrey Tory, Francis I creates for him the post of *Imprimeur du roi*.

J Art, Sculpture, Fine Arts and Architecture
Painting:
Angelo Bronzino, *Guidobaldo di Montefeltro*.
Antonio Allegri da Correggio, *Adoration of the Shepherds*; also *Love of the Gods*; and *Leda and the Swan* (–1532).
Franceso Parmigianino, further frescoes in Palma Cathedral (–1540).
Titian, *Woman in a fur*; also *Cardinal Ippolito de' Medici*.
Architecture:
Sanmicheli, Fortifications and Palazzo Bevilacqua, Verona.

K Music
First extant book of printed songs (printed by Wynkyn de Worde).

L Literature (including Drama)

M Births and Deaths
Aug. 25th Ivan IV ('The Terrible') b. (–1584).
Nov. 29th Thomas Wolsey d. (55).
Dec. 26th Barbar, Mogul Emperor, d. (48).
— Jean Bodin b. (–1596).
— Orlando de Lassus b. (–1594).

---

a Protestant rising occurs in Bremen;
Martin Affonso de Souza leads a Portuguese expedition to establish a colony in South America and founds São Vincente;
Antonio de Sedeño attempts to occupy Trinidad.

1531   Henry VIII becomes Supreme Head of the Church in England— Civil War in Switzerland

A   Jan: 5th, Ferdinand of Bohemia is elected King of the Romans;
—, Pope Clement VII forbids Henry VIII to re-marry until his case is decided and prohibits secular courts, parliaments and universities from interference;
16th, English Parliament meets (*–Mar.* 31st)—the second session of the 'Reformation Parliament';
31st, Ferdinand of Bohemia and John Zápolya sign a truce;
Charles V appoints his sister, Mary of Hungary, Regent of the Netherlands (–1552). She issues a decree establishing councils for justice, finance and foreign affairs.
Feb: 11th, Henry VIII is recognised as Supreme Head of the Church in England;
the English clergy, led by Archbishop Warham, sue for pardon for the offence of *praemunire*, and pay a total fine to the King of £118,840;
the Schmalkaldic League holds a second meeting at which the Dukes of Brunswick and the city of Lübeck join;
the Swiss cities refuse to join the League; Zwingli attacks the quasi-Catholic ceremonial of Lutheran churches;
Henry VIII sends bishops Stephen Gardiner and Edmund Bonner to press his case with Clement VII.
Mar: Francis I signs an alliance with John Zápolya of Hungary.

B   Apr: 15th, the period set by the Diet of Augsburg (of *Sept.* 1530) during which Lutherans are to conform expires, yet Charles V delays action;
21st, Charles V awards Reggio and Modena to the Duke of Ferrara.
May:
Jun: Henry VIII sends a deputation to Catherine of Aragon to try and persuade her to withdraw her appeal;
9th, Clement VII agrees to the marriage of Catherine de' Medici to Henry, Duke of Orleans. A secret article binds the Pope to assist Francis in the recovery of Milan and Genoa from the imperialists.

C   Jul: Queen Catherine of Aragon is established in a separate household from Henry VIII, who does not see her again.
Aug:
Sep: War breaks out in Switzerland between Zurich, dominated by Zwingli, and the Catholic Forest Cantons.

D   Oct: 11th, Zwingli is killed at the battle of Kappel, where the Forest Cantons defeat Zurich. The end of the Zwinglian cause in Germany;
24th, Bavaria, though a Catholic state, joins the Schmalkaldic League, to oppose Charles V;
Henry Duke of Orleans marries Catherine de' Medici.
Nov: 5th, Christian II of Denmark attempts to invade Norway;
23rd, the Peace of Kappel ends the second civil war in Switzerland; by its terms each canton and each district have the right to worship as they choose. The peace ensures that the Swiss Confederation will be divided between Protestant areas, notably Zurich, Berne, Geneva and Basle, and Catholic areas, notably Lucerne, Zug and Freiburg;
conferences of the Schmalkaldic League are held at Nordhausen (and in *Dec.* at Frankfurt), to plan a military campaign against Charles V. Most of the north German principalities and cities accede to the League.
Dec: 17th, Pope Clement VII founds the Inquisition in Lisbon, Portugal, by the bull *Cum ad nihil*;
Zurich is forced to confirm the terms of the Peace of Kappel.

E

F **Politics, Economics, Law and Education**

Sir Thomas Elyot, *The Boke Named the Governour*, a treatise on education for statesmen (this contains the first use of the word 'encyclopaedia' in an English book).

An act is passed by the English Parliament for sentencing convicted poisoners to be boiled to death (repealed 1547).

Charles V founds Granada University.

Luis Vives, *De Tradendis Disciplinis*, advocates the serious study of cooking, building, navigation, agriculture and clothmaking, and warns the scholar against despising the manual worker.

G **Science, Technology and Discovery**

Martin Affonso de Souza explores the coastline of Brazil.

Diego de Ordaz explores the R. Orinoco.

H **Philosophy, Religion and Scholarship**

Bild aus Rheinau (known as 'Beatus Rhenanus'), *Rerum germanicarum libri tres* (the first German history of its kind).

Michael Servetus, *De Trinitatis Erroribus* (denying the Trinity, influences the development of the Unitarian doctrine, *see* 1553).

Henry VIII is recognised Supreme Head of the Church in England (*Feb.*).

J **Art, Sculpture, Fine Arts and Architecture**

Painting:

Francesco Parmigianino, *Cupid Carving his Bow*.

Titian, *The Magdalen*.

K **Music**

L **Literature (including Drama)**

M **Births and Deaths**

Jan. 22nd Andrea del Sarto d. (43).

Oct. 11th Ulrich Zwingli d. (47).

Nov. 18th Robert di Ridolfi b. (−1612).

A Jan: 15th, English Parliament meets (–*Mar.* 28th), the third session of the 'Reformation Parliament'.

Feb:

Mar: Parliamentary attack on ecclesiastical legislation and jurisdiction culminates in, 18th, the Supplication of the Ordinaries, a petition to Henry VIII, complaining of the severity of the church courts in heresy cases;

19th, Henry VIII confiscates annates (or first fruits of benefices) as an attempt to force Pope Clement VII to pronounce his divorce suit in his favour;

Charles V meets the German Diet at Regensburg, demanding supplies for the campaign against the Turks.

B Apr: 10th, English Parliament meets (–*May* 14th), the fourth session of the 'Reformation Parliament';

13th, the last convocation of the clergy to be independent of the crown is held in England;

15th, the Submission of the Clergy is made to Henry VIII;

26th, Suleiman I invades Hungary and advances towards Vienna.

May: 16th, Sir Thomas More resigns as Lord Chancellor;

20th, Sir Thomas Audley is appointed Lord Keeper of the Great Seal (–1544);

26th, alliance of Kloster-Severn is signed between Francis I of France, Bavaria, Saxony and Hesse, to oppose the recognition of Ferdinand as King of the Romans.

Jun: 23rd, Henry VIII signs a secret alliance with Francis I of France for mutual aid against the Emperor Charles V.

C Jul: 23rd, the Turkish invasion forces Charles V to agree to the peace of Nuremberg with the German Protestants; the Edict of Augsburg is revoked and no one is to be molested for his religion until a general council should meet. The peace is to be kept secret from the Catholic powers.

Aug: John Frederick succeeds as Elector of Saxony (–1554) on the death of his father, Elector John;

7th (–28th), Suleiman I fails to take Güns and retires, ravaging Carinthia and Croatia (*Sept.*), but subsequently has to face a threat from Persia.

Sep: 1st, Anne Boleyn is created Marchioness of Pembroke;

the Emperor Charles V invades Italy (–*Apr.* 1533).

D Oct: Henry VIII, accompanied by Anne Boleyn, visits Francis I to sign the Treaty of Boulogne for an Anglo-French alliance.

Nov: The Electors of Trier and the Palatinate and Philip, Landgrave of Hesse, refuse to renew membership of the Schmalkaldic League;

15th, Pope Clement VII's brief, warning Henry VIII to put away Anne Boleyn on pain of excommunication;

Francisco Pizarro leads expedition from Panama for the conquest of Peru (–1534), and, 16th, takes the Inca Atahualpa prisoner.

Dec: The Earl of Northumberland harries the Scottish border;

Charles V and Clement VII hold a conference at Bologna at which a defensive league is renewed between the Pope, Milan, Ferrara, Mantua, Genoa, Lucca and Siena. The Republic of Venice refuses to join.

E

F **Politics, Economics, Law and Education**

Christopher St. German in *Treatise concerning the division between the spirituality and the temporalty*, attacks the English clergy and pleads for a national church under royal supremacy.

The Diet of Ratisbon approves the Caroline Code, compiled from Roman, German and Christian sources, for reforming the criminal law in Germany.

G **Science, Technology and Discovery**

F. Rabelais recommends an educational curriculum based on the study of the sciences in *Pantagruel*.

Sugar-cane is first cultivated in Brazil.

H **Philosophy, Religion and Scholarship**

Robert Estienne (Stephens), *Thesaurus linguae Latinae* (the first Latin/English dictionary).

The political Reformation in England begins with the Submission of the Clergy under Henry VIII (–1535).

Jean Calvin lays the foundation of the French Reformation in Paris.

The Library at Augsburg, Bavaria, is founded.

J **Art, Sculpture, Fine Arts and Architecture**

Painting:

Lucas Cranach, *The Payment*.

Hans Holbein the younger settles in England, and paints the *Merchants of the Steelyard* (–1536).

Romano Giulio, frescoes, Palazzo del Tè.

Architecture:

Peruzzi, Palazzo Massimo alle Colonne, Rome (–1536).

K **Music**

Henry VIII founds the gentlemen and choristers of the Chapel Royal, at St. James's Palace.

L **Literature (including Drama)**

Geoffrey Chaucer, *Works* (posth.—the first collected edition, issued by W. Thynne; contains a number of items then wrongly attributed).

Robert Henryson, *The Testament of Cresseid* (posth. included in Chaucer's Works in error) (–1593).

M **Births and Deaths**

June 24th Robert Dudley, Earl of Leicester, b. (–1588).

Aug. 22nd William Warham d. (*c.* 82).

Oct. 1st Jean Mabuse d. (63).

— William Allen b. (–1594).

— Jean-Antoine de Baïff b. (–1589).

— John Hawkins b. (–1595).

— Tutsī Dās b. (–1623).

1533   Henry VIII's marriage to Catherine of Aragon is declared void

A   Jan: Henry VIII secretly marries Anne Boleyn.

Feb: 4th, English Parliament meets (*–Apr*. 7th), the fifth session of the 'Reformation Parliament'; an Act is passed restraining appeals to Rome.

Mar: A revolutionary movement in Lübeck places Jürgen Wullenwever as burgomaster; 30th, Thomas Cranmer is consecrated Archbishop of Canterbury, in succession to William Warham (who died *Aug*. 1532).

B   Apr: 9th, the Emperor Charles V leaves Italy for Spain;

10th, Archbishop Cranmer begins holding his court of enquiry into Catherine of Aragon at Dunstable and, 23rd, declares her marriage with Henry VIII void;

death of Frederick I of Denmark leads to a civil war ('The War of the Counts'; Christian III succeeds in 1534).

May: 28th, Archbishop Cranmer pronounces Anne Boleyn's marriage to Henry VIII lawful;

the cities of Ulm, Nuremberg and Augsburg form a league for the defence of freedom of conscience.

Jun: 1st, coronation of Queen Anne Boleyn;

22nd, Ferdinand of Austria and Suleiman I of Turkey sign a peace treaty. Ferdinand is to retain the portion of Hungary in his hands, while Zápolya is to remain King of the rest of the territory; both are to pay tribute to the Porte. Suleiman is to have the right to sanction future arrangements about Hungary. The peace does not include the Emperor Charles V, who continues warfare against the Turks in the Mediterranean.

C   Jul: 11th, Pope Clement VII excommunicates Henry VIII (publication to be deferred until *Oct*.);

a revolt of peasants is suppressed in Barcelona.

Aug:

Sep: 7th, Queen Anne Boleyn gives birth to Princess Elizabeth.

D   Oct: Francis I of France and Pope Clement VII meet at Marseilles.

Nov: 7th, Henry VIII appeals from the Pope to a general council;

the Catholic League of Halle is formed under Elector Joachim I of Brandenburg and George, Duke of Saxony.

Dec:

E   Accession of Ivan IV (The Terrible) of Russia, aged three, on the death of Basil III; Ivan's mother Helen Glinski becomes Regent (–1538);

Charles V enfeoffs the Duke of Mantua with Montferrat;

Lithuanian-Russo War (–1536);

Bernard Rottman, reforming divine, invites Dutch Anabaptists to Münster in Westphalia;

Pizarro executes the Inca of Peru, Atahualpa, and occupies Cuzco;

Cortes attempts to found a colony in Lower California (–1535);

Spanish colonisation of La Plata by Pedro de Mendoza;

Spanish conquest of Yucatan.

F **Politics, Economics, Law and Education**
Pedro de Heredia founds Cartagena.
The King of Portugal creates hereditary captaincies in Brazil.
Sir Thomas Smith is appointed lecturer on Greek and philosophy at Cambridge.

G **Science, Technology and Discovery**

H **Philosophy, Religion and Scholarship**
Nicholas Udall, *Floures for Latine speaking* ('gathered out of Terence and translated . . .').
John Leland, chaplain to Henry VIII, is appointed 'king's antiquary', empowered to search for and collect from cathedral libraries, abbeys, priories and colleges of England records and books.
Henry VIII is excommunicated by Pope Clement VII (*July* 11th).
Protestantism gains ground at the French court through the influence of Madame d'Étampes, Francis I's mistress.
Juan Valdez and his circle in Naples, including Vittoria Colonna and Peter Martyr, propagate the need for doctrinal reform.

J **Art, Sculpture, Fine Arts and Architecture**
Painting:
Hans Holbein the younger, *The Ambassadors*.
Giorgio Vasari, *Lorenzo the Magnificent*.

K **Music**
Earliest published madrigals, including works by Philippe Verdelot and Jacob Arcadelt, printed in Rome.

L **Literature (including Drama)**
John Heywood, *The Pardoner, the Frere, the Curate and Neighbour Pratte* (interlude); *The Play of the Wether*.
John Skelton, *Magnificence:* a goodly interlude (posth.).

M **Births and Deaths**
Feb. 28th Michel de Montaigne b. (–1592).
Apr. 25th William the Silent b. (–1584).
July 6th Lodovico Ariosto d. (58).
July 6th Bernardino Baldi b. (–1617).
Sept. 7th Queen Elizabeth I b. (–1603).

A Jan: 15th, English Parliament meets (*–Mar.* 30th), the sixth session of the 'Reformation Parliament', and regulates the succession to the throne to the heirs of Henry and Anne Boleyn;

24th, Francis I of France signs a secret treaty with the German Protestant princes;

John of Leyden joins the Anabaptists at Münster, Westphalia, where a 'Communist state' is established (–1535), following an insurrection on *Feb.* 9th.

Feb: Thomas, Earl of Kildare, Lord Deputy in Ireland, is summoned to England and imprisoned for alleged treasons in Ireland.

Mar: 16th, final severance of England from Rome; Acts are passed forbidding the payment of annates (confiscated by Henry VIII in 1533) and Peter's Pence to the Pope and forbidding the introduction of papal bulls or briefs. The Act of Succession to the Crown (embodying the resolutions of Convocation in 1532) requires an oath to the succession to the Crown to be taken by members of both Houses of Parliament as well as by all clergy and officials;

23rd, Pope Clement VII declares Henry VIII's marriage to Catherine of Aragon valid.

B Apr: 13th, Sir Thomas More refuses to take the oath to the succession;

20th, Elizabeth Barton, the Maid of Kent, is executed with five of her associates for treason.

May: 11th, Henry VIII makes peace with his nephew, James V of Scotland;

12th (–13th), Philip, Landgrave of Hesse, with French support, defeats the army of Ferdinand of Austria at Laufen, to restore Ulrich, Duke of Württemberg, to his duchy;

30th, Charles V leaves Barcelona to join Andrea Doria, with support from the Papacy and the Italian states, in an expedition against the Turks; they land at Carthage in North Africa, defeat the troops of Barbarossa and rescue Christian slaves.

Jun: 29th, the Peace of Cardan confirms the restoration of Ulrich of Württemberg to his duchy. The Lutherans demand that Ferdinand of Austria should quash all proceedings against the Schmalkaldic League in the imperial chamber;

'The Count's War' (–1535) between Count Christopher of Oldenberg, allied with Lübeck and Holstein against Denmark and Sweden, for the succession to Gotland and Helsingborg.

C Jul: 9th, William, Lord Dacre, Warden of the West March, is acquitted of the charge of treasonable communications with the Scots;

28th, Lord Thomas Fitzgerald, Kildare's son, who has rebelled against Henry VIII, assassinates Archbishop Allen of Dublin, the Chancellor of Ireland.

Aug: 30th, John of Leyden, leader of the Münster Anabaptists, crushes an attempted *coup* of Burgomaster Knipperdollinck to replace him, shedding much blood.

Sep: 25th, Pope Clement VII dies. Alessandro Farnese is subsequently elected Pope Paul III (–1550), and appoints a number of reforming cardinals.

D Oct: 18th, 'Placards' appear in Paris describing the Mass in offensive terms, which provokes a rigorous persecution of heretics in the city.

Nov: 3rd, English Parliament meets (*–Dec.* 18th), the seventh session of the 'Reformation Parliament', and passes a new Act of Supremacy, confirming Henry VIII in all judicial and political powers formerly exercised by the Pope in England, and a new Treasons Act. First fruits and tenths of all benefices are granted to the Crown, and the King is authorised to appoint suffragan bishops. Acts of Attainder are brought against Sir Thomas More and Bishop Fisher of Rochester for misprision and against the Earl of Kildare for treason.

Dec:

E Pomerania becomes a Protestant state.

F **Politics, Economics, Law and Education**
To attempt to prevent further enclosures of common land and the loss of arable, English farmers are forbidden to own more than 2,000 sheep.

G **Science, Technology and Discovery**
Jacques Cartier, on his first voyage to North America, sights the coast of Labrador (*May* 10th), and explores the Gulf of St. Lawrence.

H **Philosophy, Religion and Scholarship**
John Bourchier, Lord Berners, trans. *Huon of Bordeaux*.
Polydore Vergil, *Anglicae Historiae* (Libri XXVI –1570; –1582).
Martin Luther completes his translation of the Holy Bible (based on the Greek version of Erasmus and the Hebrew version by Johann Reuchlin, 1522).
Jesuit Order is founded in Paris by Ignatius Loyola (*Aug.* 15th).
The Anabaptists, under John of Leyden occupy Münster, in Germany, for a year, creating a communist society in which polygamy is practised, until expelled by Lutherans and Catholics.
Oswald Myconius drafts the first Confession of Basle.

J **Art, Sculpture, Fine Arts and Architecture**
Architecture:
Sangallo, Palazzo Farnese, Rome (completed 1546 by Michelangelo).
Sansovino, St. Francesco della Vigna, Venice.

K **Music**

L **Literature (including Drama)**
François Rabelais, *Gargantua* (i.e. *Pantagruel*, pt. 2, *see* –1532).
John Heywood, *A Play of Love* (interlude).

M **Births and Deaths**
Jan. 9th Johann Turmair (or Aventinus) d. (67).
Apr. 18th William Harrison b. (–1593).
Apr. 20th Elizabeth Barton ('The Maid of Kent') d. (28).
— Correggio (Antonio Allegri) d. (40).
— Wynkyn de Worde (Jan van Wynkyn) d. (*c*. 66).

1535   End of Manseatic sea-power—Executions of Fisher and More— Charles V's North African campaign

A Jan: 15th, Henry VIII assumes the title 'Supreme Head of the Church', and the English clergy abjure the authority of the Pope;

21st, Thomas Cromwell is appointed Vicar General to hold visitations of religious houses in England and Wales.

Feb: France and Turkey sign an offensive and defensive alliance, aimed at the Emperor Charles V, and also a commercial treaty.

Mar:

B Apr: 29th, John Houghton, Prior of the London Charterhouse, and other Carthusians are found guilty of treason in refusing to acknowledge the royal supremacy (they are executed at Tyburn, *May* 4th);

a joint expedition from German states is made against Münster; Hessian troops lay siege to the city (*–June* 24th).

May: 12th, Anglo-Scottish peace treaty is signed.

Jun: 7th, John Fisher, Bishop of Rochester, is tried for treason (he is executed, 22nd);

11th, a Danish-Swedish army defeats the troops of Lübeck near Assens in Fünen; subsequently Christian's navy defeats the ships of Lübeck off Bornholm, ending the era of Hanseatic sea-power. Fünen and Seeland surrender to the Scandinavian allies;

24th, Münster capitulates to the Hessian army; the Anabaptist leaders John of Leyden and Burgomaster Knipperdollinck are tortured to death, and the city is restored to the bishop, who re-establishes Catholicism;

Charles V leads an expedition to conquer Tunis from Barbarossa, with a fleet commanded by Andrea Doria (*–Aug.*). Charles restores the Bey, Mulai Hassan (deposed by the Turks in 1534) and completes the Spanish conquest of the North African coast (begun in 1494).

C Jul: 1st, Sir Thomas More is tried for treason in refusing the oath of Supremacy;

6th, More is executed;

11th, accession of Joachim II of Brandenburg, a moderate Catholic, on the death of his father, Joachim I; the Elector's youngest brother, John of Brandenburg-Neumark becomes a Protestant;

Richard Layton and Thomas Leigh begin visitations of the English and Welsh monasteries.

Aug: 17th, Charles V lands in Sicily, which he leaves under the command of Ferrante di Gonzaga.

Sep:

D Oct:

Nov: 1st, on the death of Francesco Sforza II of Milan, the last of the House of Sforza, the duchy is occupied by Charles V who subsequently offers the lands to Charles, Duke of Angoulême, with the hand of Christina of Denmark, on condition that France supports his demands for a general council of the Church, recognises Ferdinand as King of the Romans and ends the alliance with the Turks;

25th, Charles V enters Naples, under the government of Pedro di Toledo; the city readily supplies him with money.

Dec: 15th, at the Diet of Schmalkalden, English envoys press for an alliance between Henry VIII with the Protestant princes in Germany.

E James V of Scotland reduces the clans of Galloway to obedience.

F **Politics, Economics, Law and Education**
  The Statute of Uses in England is passed to curb the power of landowners in devising
  lands by testament.
  The last English legal 'Year Book' to be (later) printed; henceforth the year books are
  superseded by authoritative legal reporting.
  Thomas Cromwell's injunctions encourage the New Learning and forbid the study of
  Canon Law in Cambridge.
  Angela Merici founds the Order of Ursulines at Brescia (*Nov.*), for the education of
  girls and care of the sick and needy.
  Anon, *La Noble Science des jouers d'épée.*

G **Science, Technology and Discovery**
  Jacques Cartier, on his second voyage to North America, sails up the St. Lawrence
  River and visits the sites of Quebec and Montreal (–1536).

H **Philosophy, Religion and Scholarship**
  John Bourchier, Lord Berners, trans. *The Golden Book of Marcus Aurelius* from the
  Spanish of Antonio de Guevara (*see* 1529, 1557).
  Miles Coverdale's translation of the *Holy Bible* (dedicated to Henry VIII; but printed
  abroad, –1537).
  Marino Sanudo's *Diarii* ended (started *c.* 1496–8; unique source for the history and
  daily life of Venice, the diarist having access to official documents).

J **Art, Sculpture, Fine Arts and Architecture**
  Painting:
    Hans Holbein the younger, *Henry VIII.*
    Francesco Parmigiano, *La Madonna dal Collo Longo* (–1540).
  Architecture:
    Sanmicheli, Fortifications, Venice.

K **Music**

L **Literature (including Drama)**

M **Births and Deaths**
  Feb. 11th Nicolo Sfondrato (Pope Gregory XIV) b. (–1591).
  June 22nd John Fisher d. (*c.* 66).
  July 6th Sir Thomas More d. (57).
  Oct. 24th Francesco Sforza d. (53).
  — Ippolito Aldobrandini (Pope Clement VIII) b. (–1605).
  — Thomas Este b. (–1608).
  — Sir Thomas North b. (–1601).
  — Thomás Vittoria b. (–1611).

A Jan: 7th, Catherine of Aragon dies at Kimbolton;

30th, Pope Paul III's bull for the reform of many papal offices is read in the papal Consistory.

Feb: 4th, English Parliament meets (*–Apr.* 14th), the eighth and last session of the 'Reformation Parliament'. This is the last occasion on which mitred abbots sit in the House of Lords;

Francis I of France conquers Savoy, occupies Turin and by *Apr.* completes conquest of Piedmont, seeking to gain the duchy of Milan for his third son;

Francis I signs a fresh alliance with the Sultan Suleiman I.

Mar:

B Apr: 2nd, Malmö surrenders to Christian III of Denmark;

14th, Henry VIII dissolves the 'Reformation Parliament'. The royal assent is given to an Act for the dissolution of the lesser monasteries, with property worth under £200 a year, under which 376 religious houses are dissolved, with lands worth a total of £32,000 a year. The Court of Augmentations is established to administer former monastic property and soon takes over many of the financial responsibilities of the ancient Exchequer;

Parliament also passes Acts for the relief of paupers, authorising parochial collections, and for the incorporation of Wales with England; all suits to be in the English language and land is to descend according to English law.

May: 2nd, Queen Anne Boleyn is sent to the Tower of London;

12th, Sir Francis Weston, Mark Smeaton and other alleged paramours of Anne are tried for treason (executed, 17th);

15th, Anne Boleyn and her brother, Lord Rochford, are tried and found guilty of adultery and incest;

17th, Archbishop Cranmer declares Henry VIII's marriage to Anne Boleyn invalid, and, 19th, Anne is executed;

30th, Henry VIII marries Jane Seymour;

the Edict of Courcy in France promises freedom of conscience.

Jun: 8th, English Parliament meets (*–July* 18th) and settles the succession on the future children of Henry by Jane Seymour; the Princesses Mary and Elizabeth are declared illegitimate;

Henry VIII's natural son, the Duke of Richmond, dies;

29th, Thomas Cromwell is appointed Lord Privy Seal in succession to the Earl of Wiltshire, father of Anne Boleyn;

Margaret, natural daughter of Charles V, marries Alessandro de' Medici.

C Jul: 11th, the Ten Articles, embodying a Profession of Faith for the Church of England, are presented to Parliament (–1539); the Latin Mass is preserved;

14th, France signs the Treaty of Lyons with Portugal, for an attack on Spain;

18th, the authority of the Pope is declared void in England by Act of Parliament;

25th, Spain invades Provence, but the French under Montmorency lay the country waste to hinder Charles V's advance;

29th, Copenhagen surrenders to Christian III, who subsequently establishes his authority in Denmark and Norway.

Aug: 10th, the Dauphin Francis dies;

the Count of Nassau occupies Guise;

Sep: 13th, Charles V abandons the siege of Marseilles after a disastrous campaign and sails from Genoa to Barcelona;

F **Politics, Economics, Law and Education**
  Guicciardini begins writing his *History of Florence*, covering the years 1494–1534.
  Reginald Pole, *Pro Ecclesiasticae Unitatis Defensione*.
  Spain founds Asunción on the Paraguay River, the first permanent settlement in the
  interior of South America.

G **Science, Technology and Discovery**
  Pedro de Mendoza founds Buenos Aires on the La Plata estuary (*Feb*. 2nd) and sends
  expeditions to explore the Parana and Paraguay rivers in search of a route to Peru.
  Alvar Núñez Cabeza de Vaca reaches Sonora in Arizona.

H **Philosophy, Religion and Scholarship**
  John Calvin, *Christianae Religionis Institutio* (first edition of six chapters, with a preface
  addressed to Francis I, King of France, and persecutor of the Protestants –1542).
  Calvin settles in Geneva (*July*).
  Bullinger and others prepare First Helvetic Confession.
  Revised edition of Tyndale's trans. of the New Testament reprinted in England by T.
  Godfray (first printing of the New Testament in England).
  Dissolution of the English monasteries (–1539).
  William Tyndale is strangled and burnt (*Oct*. 6th).
  The Ten Articles are authorised by Henry VIII, and approved by Convocation. As
  supreme head of the Church in England, he published through his Vicar-General,
  Thomas Cromwell, the Royal Injunctions.

J **Art, Sculpture, Fine Arts and Architecture**
  Painting:
    Michelangelo, *Last Judgement* on altar wall of Sistine Chapel (–1541).
    Titian, *La Bella*.
  Architecture:
    Sansovino, St. Mark's Library, Venice (–1553).

K **Music**
  First book of songs with lute accompaniment is printed, in Spain.

L **Literature (including Drama)**

M **Births and Deaths**
  May 19th Anne Boleyn d. (26).
  July 12th Desiderius Erasmus d. (70).
  Oct. 6th William Tyndale d. (44)
  — Charles Howard, Earl of Nottingham, b. (–1624).
  — Baldassare Peruzzi d. (55).
  — Robert Smythson b. (–1614).

21st, rising in Lincolnshire in protest at the dissolution of the monasteries begins at Louth Park;

the Count of Nassau is forced to abandon the siege of Peronne.

D   Oct: 9th, the Pilgrimage of Grace, a popular rising in the north country against the dissolution of the monasteries and religious innovations, begins under Robert Aske of Doncaster (*–Feb.* 1537);

18th, the Duke of Suffolk arrives at Lincoln to suppress the Lincolnshire rising;

27th, the Duke of Norfolk signs a truce with the Yorkshire rebels who have captured York and Hull and the rising spreads to Durham, Cumberland and Westmorland;

30th, episcopacy is ended in Denmark.

Nov:

Dec: 5th, the Duke of Norfolk at Doncaster promises a pardon to the Yorkshire rebels and undertakes to move the King to summon a Parliament to York;

Henry VIII summons Robert Aske to court to discover the origins of the rebellion;

Reginald Pole is created a cardinal;

James V of Scotland arrives in France.

E

A **Jan:** 1st, James V of Scotland marries Madeleine, daughter of Francis I of France (she dies, *July* 7th);

7th, Alessandro de' Medici is assassinated; Cosmo de' Medici succeeds him in Florence;

8th, Robert Aske returns to Yorkshire from court to attempt to pacify those who had risen in the Pilgrimage of Greece;

Francis I, reviving French claims to the sovereignty of Artois and Flanders in violation of the Treaty of Cambrai, summons Charles V before the *Parlement* of Paris, to do homage for those duchies, which the Emperor ignores. Francis secures an agreement with Suleiman I of Turkey for a joint attack on Charles V.

Feb: 9th, Cardinal Pole is appointed a legate by Pope Paul III to bring about Henry VIII's return to the obedience of Rome; Pole returns to Rome in *Aug.*, having failed to enter England;

10th, the Pilgrimage of Grace in Yorkshire is effectively ended with the capture of Sir Francis Bigod. Risings later in the month in Cumberland and Westmorland are soon put down.

Mar: 10th, the French invade Italy and advance as far as Rivoli. A truce is subsequently signed through the mediation of Pope Paul III;

17th, Francis I invades Artois;

Ghent refuses to pay a subsidy, demanded by Mary, Regent of Hungary, for Charles V's war with France;

a Turkish fleet fails to take Corfu.

B **Apr:**

May: German Lutherans refuse to accept Pope Paul III's invitation to attend a general council;

17th, Robert Aske, leader of the Pilgrimage of Grace, is sentenced to death for treason, despite Henry VIII's promise of a pardon in *Dec.* 1536 (he is executed at York in *July*).

Jun:

C **Jul:** Thomas Lord Darcy, Sir Robert Constable, the Abbots of Fountains and Jervaulx and other leaders of the Pilgrimage of Grace are executed.

Sep: 2nd, Christian III issues Ordinance for the Danish Church, with Luther's approval;

24th, Wullenwever, Burgomaster of Lübeck, is executed, following the suppression of the revolutionary movement;

Henry VIII creates the Council of the North as a permanent body to govern the northern counties, following the suppression of the Pilgrimage of Grace, with Cuthbert Tunstall, Bishop of Durham, as president.

D **Oct:** 18th, Joachim II, Elector of Brandenburg, and the Duke of Liegnitz sign a treaty for mutual succession on failure of heirs;

24th, Queen Jane Seymour dies, following the birth of Prince Edward, 12th.

Nov:

Dec:

E

F **Politics, Economics, Law and Education**
The Portuguese obtain Macao as a trading settlement (permanently settled in 1557).
Francisco de Orellana makes a permanent settlement of Guayaquil.
Lisbon University is transferred to Coimbra.
Robert Recorde, *Introductions for to lerne to recken with the Pen.*

G **Science, Technology and Discovery**
Mercator's Map of Flanders (–1540).
Nūnez realises that the course of a ship cutting meridians at a constant angle (the loxodrome) is a spiral, not a curve.
Niccolò Tartaglia explains the trajectory of bullets in *La Nova Scientia* (Venice).

H **Philosophy, Religion and Scholarship**
Marcus Tullius Cicero, *Opera Omnia*, 4 vols., ed. with notes by Pietro Victorius (published in Venice; a landmark in classical scholarship).
Miles Coverdale's translation of the *Bible*, revised and published in England (this is the first complete *Bible* printed in England –1535).
Calvin founds his system of government in Church and State for Geneva ('the perfect school of Christ').
M. Vete compiles first Roman Catholic hymnal.

J **Art, Sculpture, Fine Arts and Architecture**
Painting:
Hans Holbein the younger, *Jane Seymour.*
Architecture:
Sansovino, Mint, Venice (–1554) and façade, Doge's Palazzo Loggietta, Venice (–1540).
Serlio publishes *D'Architettura* (in six parts).

K **Music**
Conservatories of music are founded for boys at Naples, and for girls at Venice.

L **Literature (including Drama)**

M **Births and Deaths**
Oct. 12th Edward VI b. (–1553).
Dec. 10th Giovanni Battista Guarini b. (–1612).

1538   Hapsburg and Valois sign a ten-year truce—The Catholic League
        of Nuremberg—Iconoclasm in England

A Jan: The visitation of the greater monasteries in England is begun (they are dissolved
       1539).
   Feb: 24th, Ferdinand of Austria and John Zápolya of Hungary sign the Peace of Gross-
       wardein, by which Zápolya, at this time childless, agrees that Ferdinand shall acquire
       the whole of Hungary on his death.
   Mar:

B Apr:
   May: 26th, Jean Calvin is expelled from Geneva and settles in Strassburg (–1541).
   Jun: 10th, the Catholic princes of Germany sign the defensive League of Nuremberg, a
       counterpart to the Protestant Schmalkaldic League; the principal signatories are the
       Emperor Charles V, Ferdinand of Austria, Duke George of Saxony, the Elector of
       Bavaria and the Archbishops of Mainz and Salzburg;
       18th, Francis I of France and the Emperor Charles V sign the Truce of Nice, to suspend
       hostilities for 10 years. By its terms Francis and Charles retain their conquests, the
       Duke of Savoy losing all his territories except Nice; Francis recovers Hesdin and gains
       Mirandola; the Swiss retain the Pays de Vaud;
       James V of Scotland marries Mary of Guise.

C Jul: 14th (–16th), through the mediation of Queen Eleanor of France, Charles V and
       Francis I meet at Aigues Mortes to discuss the repression of Protestant heresies and a
       crusade against the Turks. The *rapprochement* of Hapsburg and Valois leaves England
       isolated and Henry VIII subsequently negotiates for an alliance with the German
       Protestant princes.
   Aug:
   Sep: Thomas Cromwell issues injunctions for registers to be maintained in English
       parishes for recording baptisms, marriages and burials and for providing English
       Bibles; mutinies of Spanish troops in Galetta and Sicily delay Charles V's proposed
       expedition against the Turks.

D Oct:
   Nov: Death of Duke Charles of Gelders; the estates of the duchy subsequently elect
       William de la Marck (heir to the duchy of Cleves, Jülich and Berg) his successor.
   Dec: 3rd, Cardinal Pole's brothers, Henry Courtenay, Marquess of Exeter (next in suc-
       cession to the English throne, if Henry VIII should die without an heir) and Henry
       Pole, Lord Montague, are sentenced to death for treason;
       16th, Francis I issues an edict, at the Parlement of Toulouse, for the persecution of
       French Protestants;
       17th, Pope Paul III issues a further bull excommunicating and deposing Henry VIII;
       20th, David Beaton, Archbishop of St. Andrews, is created a Cardinal.

E Destruction of relics, images and shrines in churches and abbeys in southern England in a
       wave of anti-papal iconoclasm, notably of Thomas à Beckett's shrine at Canterbury;
       The nobility and clergy withdraw from the Cortes of Castille;
       Barbarossa takes the Morea from Venice.

F **Politics, Economics, Law and Education**
Philip Melanchthon, *Ethica Doctrinae Elementa*, stating the Protestant theory of Natural Right.
Bogotá is founded by Gonzalo Jiminéz de Quesada.

G **Science, Technology and Discovery**

H **Philosophy, Religion and Scholarship**
Sir Thomas Elyot, *Latin-English Dictionary*.
A professorship of Oriental languages is established at the Collège de France.

J **Art, Sculpture, Fine Arts and Architecture**
Painting:
Hans Holbein the younger, *The Duchess of Milan*; also *The 3rd Duke of Norfolk*.
Titian, *The Urbino Venus*.
Architecture:
Palladio, Villa Godi, Loredo (–1542).

K **Music**
Cristóbal de Morales, Cantatas for Peace Conference at Nice.

L **Literature (including Drama)**

M **Births and Deaths**
Oct. 2nd Carlo Borromeo b. (–1584).
— Louis, Count of Nassau, b. (–1574).

1539   Spread of the Reformation in North Germany—Fall of the greater monasteries and the Act of Six Articles in England— Spain annexes Cuba

A **Jan:** Cardinal David Beaton, Archbishop of St. Andrews, enemy of the pro-English faction, becomes chief adviser to James V of Scotland.

Feb: 1st, the Emperor Charles V and Francis I of France sign the Treaty of Toledo, binding themselves to make no new alliance with England without mutual consent; and further marriages are arranged between the houses of Hapsburg and Valois;

15th, Cardinal Reginald Pole, papal legate to reduce Henry VIII to obedience, is received by the Emperor Charles V at Toledo, but fails to win his support for an expedition to England;

Joachim II, Elector of Brandenburg, becomes a Protestant, and with the accession later in the year of Henry, Duke of Saxony (–1541), a Lutheran, on the death of his elder brother, Duke George, a Catholic, all the states of northern Germany, except Brunswick, accept the Reformation;

the estates of Gelders admit the claim of William of Cleves, a Lutheran, to the duchy, which further embarrasses Charles V.

Mar: Following the new accord between Hapsburg and Valois, Henry VIII fears an invasion and orders preparations for the defence of the realm. The scare of invasion evaporates by *May*, since Francis I will not act without the Emperor, whose difficulties in Germany increase with the establishment of Protestantism in Saxony and Brandenburg.

B **Apr:** 19th, Charles V signs the Truce of Frankfurt with the Protestant princes, who have demanded a permanent religious settlement, but the Emperor will only agree to a 6-months truce;

the surrender of the greater monasteries in England and Wales to the King's visitors proceeds (*–Dec.*);

28th, English Parliament meets (*–May* 23rd), and passes an Act for enforcement of royal proclamations and attaints Margaret Pole, Countess of Salisbury, without trial.

May: Royal assent is given to an Act (the Six Articles of Religion) 'abolishing diversity of opinions' in England, after Henry VIII has personally intervened in the Lords' debate to argue with the Reforming bishops. Transubstantiation, communion in one kind, the vow of chastity, private masses, the celibacy of the clergy and auricular confession are declared to be agreeable to the law of God. Denial of transubstantiation is declared a heresy. This reactionary measure, repealing the Ten Articles of 1536, is nicknamed 'the Whip with Six Strings'.

Jun:

C **Jul:** 1st, Nicholas Shaxton, Bishop of Salisbury, and Hugh Latimer, Bishop of Worcester, resign their sees, unable to subscribe to the Six Articles.

Aug: Ghent breaks into open rebellion against Mary of Hungary, Regent of the Netherlands, refusing to contribute a subsidy to the Emperor. The militia is levied in Alost, Oudenarde and Courtrai, towns subject to Ghent, which join the revolutionary movement.

Sep:

D **Oct:** 4th, a marriage treaty is signed at Hampton Court for Henry VIII to marry Anne of Cleves, elder sister of William Duke of Cleves. The marriage is part of Thomas Cromwell's design for an alliance between England and the Protestant princes of Germany;

20th, Edmund Bonner, a reactionary, is elected Bishop of London.

(*Continued opposite*)

F **Politics, Economics, Law and Education**
   A public lottery is held in France.

G **Science, Technology and Discovery**
   Hernando de Soto begins the exploration of Florida (−1542).
   Olaus Magnus, Map of the World.

H **Philosophy, Religion and Scholarship**
   Philipp Melanchthon in *De officio principum* declares that princes are bound to use force
   to extirpate heresy.
   Henry Nicholas (or Niclaes) founds the sect 'The Family of Love'.
   The Great Bible (or *Cranmer's Bible*), a revision of Tyndale's and Coverdale's versions,
   is issued in England.
   Henry VIII founds six new bishoprics.
   Jean Calvin, *Commentary on the Epistle to the Romans*, an enlarged edition of *The
   Institutes* in Latin.
   Damiano de Goes writes a history of Portuguese India (*Commentarius rerum gestatum
   in India citra Gangeum*).
   Richard Taverner translates the *Adagia* of Erasmus (*Proverbs and Adagies, with New
   Addicions*).

J **Art, Sculpture, Fine Arts and Architecture**
   Painting:
   Hans Holbein the younger, portrait and miniature of *Anne of Cleves*.
   Architecture:
   Michelangelo replans the Capitol and Marcus Aurelius statue, Rome.

K **Music**
   George Förster, *Frische Teutsche Liedlein* (a song book collection).

L **Literature (including Drama)**
   Gentse Spelen (allegorical plays performed at Ghent at Chambers of Rhetoric com-
   petitions).

M **Births and Deaths**

Nov: The Abbots of Reading and Colchester are executed for treason in denying the
   King's supremacy and (*Dec.*) the Abbot of Glastonbury for felony. These executions
   spur the remaining abbots to surrender their property to the Crown.
Dec: 12th, Charles V, *en route* for Flanders to suppress the revolt in Ghent, meets
   Francis I of France at Loches.

E Spain annexes Cuba.

A   Jan: 1st, Francis I and Charles V enter Paris;

6th, Henry VIII marries Anne of Cleves (*–July* 9th);

21st, Charles V meets Mary of Hungary, Regent of the Netherlands, at Valenciennes.

Feb: 14th, Charles V enters Ghent without resistance, executes the leaders of the revolt and abrogates the city's liberties for the refusal to pay a subsidy in 1536 and for offering allegiance to Francis I of France.

Mar: 4th, Philip, Landgrave of Hesse, contracts a bigamous marriage, which discredits the Lutheran cause in Germany;

office of principal secretary in England first divided among two men, the first officials being Sir Thomas Wriothesley and Sir Ralph Sadler.

B   Apr: 12th, English Parliament meets (*July* 24th); a heavy subsidy is voted and the Military Order of St. John of Jerusalem is suppressed;

17th, Thomas Cromwell is created Earl of Essex.

May: 4th, treaty between Venice and Turkey is signed at Constantinople (confirmed *Oct.* 2nd); the Republic surrenders Upana, other places on the Dalmatian coast, and the isles of Skyros and Patmos in the Aegean and agrees to pay Turkey an indemnity;

18th, Lord Lisle is arrested on the charge of betraying Calais to Cardinal Pole;

Charles V appoints René of Chalons *stadtholder* in Holland, Zeeland and Utrecht, bringing the House of Orange into public affairs in the Netherlands.

Jun: 1st, Francis I issues the Edict of Fontainebleau for a new procedure for the trial of heretics;

18th, Thomas Cromwell, Earl of Essex, is arrested at the Council table for treason, largely on the grounds of his advocacy of Henry's marriage to Anne of Cleves (he is executed *July* 28th). Lord Treasurer Norfolk becomes Henry VIII's principal minister and attempts to secure his position by the King's marriage (in *July*) to his niece, Katherine Howard.

C   Jul: 9th, Henry VIII's marriage to Anne of Cleves is annulled by the convocations of Canterbury and York;

17th, Francis I of France betroths his niece Jeanne d'Albret to Duke William of Cleves;

23rd, the infant John Sigismund Zápolya succeeds as King of Hungary (–1571) on the death of his father, John Zápolya, in defiance of the treaty of 1538, stating that the Archduke Ferdinand should succeed. Ferdinand subsequently sends troops into Hungary to claim the whole country and lays siege to Buda, provoking the intervention of Suleiman I of Turkey;

28th, Henry VIII marries Katherine Howard.

Aug:

Sep: 27th, by the bull *Regimini militantis ecclesiae* Pope Paul III confirms the Jesuit Order.

D   Oct: 11th, Charles V invests his son Philip with the duchy of Milan.

Nov:

Dec:

E   Massacre of the Vaudois in Provence;

Hamayun is expelled from India by Afghans under Sher Shat, who becomes Emperor of Delhi.

F **Politics, Economics, Law and Education**
Henry VIII founds Regius Professorships of divinity, Greek, Hebrew, civil law and physics at Oxford and Cambridge.

G **Science, Technology and Discovery**
G. L. de Cardenas discovers the Grand Canyon, Arizona.
Francisco Alvarez, *Verdadera Informacam das terras do Preste Joam*.
Biringuccio, *Pirotechnia*.

H **Philosophy, Religion and Scholarship**
John Bourchier, Lord Berners, translates *La Cárcel de amor* from the Spanish of Diego de San Pedro (*The Castel of Love* –1492).
Clément Marot prepares a metrical translation of the Psalms for the Reformed Churches in France and Switzerland (completed 1553 by Théodore de Bèze).
Augustinus Steuchus, *De perenni philosophia*.
Fathers of the Oratory formed in Rome.

J **Art, Sculpture, Fine Arts and Architecture**
Painting:
Titian, *Young Englishman*.
Sculpture:
Michelangelo, *Brutus*.
Architecture:
Villa Pisani, Bagnolo (–1560), also Casa Civena, Vicenza (–1546).

K **Music**

L **Literature (including Drama)**
Sir David Lyndsay, *Ane Satyre of the Thrie Estaits* (morality play, acted; published in 1602).

M **Births and Deaths**
Jan. 25th Edmund Campion b. (–1581).
May 6th Juan Luis Vives d. (56).
— 22nd Francesco Guicciardini d. (53).
June 11th Barnabe Googe b. (–1594).
July 28th Thomas Cromwell, Earl of Essex, d. (*c.* 55).
Aug. 23rd Guillaume Budé (Budaeus) d. (73).
Aug. 24th Francesco Parmigianino d. (36).
— Arthur Agarde b. (–1615).
— Ralph Agas b. (–1621).
— Pierre de Chastelard b. (–1563).
— Christopher Hatton b. (–1591).
— Joseph Justus Scaliger b. (–1609).

Hungary becomes a Turkish Province—Fall of Queen Katherine Howard

A Jan:

Feb:

Mar: Anne, Duke of Montmorency, Constable of France, is disgraced and retires into private life (–1547), the victim of intrigues of Madame d'Étampes.

B Apr: 5th, the Diet of Ratisbon meets (–*July*) in the presence of the Emperor Charles V, who attempts a reconciliation of rival creeds in Germany. He is forced to admit Protestants to the Imperial Chamber and also to renew the Catholic League (of 1538);

9th, a conspiracy is discovered for assassinating Bishop Holgate, President of the Council in the North.

May: 27th, Margaret Countess of Salisbury, daughter of the Duke of Clarence, is executed for conspiracy in corresponding with her exiled son, Cardinal Pole;

Francis I of France, to embarrass Charles V, reaches an undertaking with Suleiman I, Sultan of Turkey; he subsequently makes a treaty with the Duke of Cleves, claimant to Gelderland.

Jun: 13th, Philip of Hesse comes to terms with the Emperor Charles V, undertaking to recognise the Archduke Ferdinand, Charles's brother, as next emperor, and to abandon his allies in France and Cleves;

the accession of Maurice Duke of Saxony, son-in-law of Philip of Hesse, on the death of Duke Henry, strengthens Philip's position among the German princes;

28th, Leonard Lord Grey is executed for treasonable dealings with the Geraldines when Lieutenant of Ireland.

C Jul: The Scots harry Northumberland and the border country of England;

Henry VIII leaves London for a progress to the north (–*Nov.* 2nd).

Aug: 26th, Suleiman I, Sultan of Turkey, having invaded Hungary to dispute the Archduke Ferdinand's claim to that kingdom, takes Buda and annexes Hungary, which remains a Turkish province (–1668).

Sep: 16th, Henry VIII at York receives the submission of those who had taken part in the Pilgrimage of Grace (in 1537), including Archbishop Lee.

D Oct: The expedition of Charles V to Algiers fails, largely as a result of storms. The Turks remain in command of the seas.

Nov: 9th, Queen Katherine Howard is sent to the Tower of London on suspicion of immoral conduct;

Francis I of France signs a treaty of alliance with Denmark.

Dec: 18th, Culpeper and Dereham, alleged paramours of Queen Katherine Howard, are executed;

29th, by the Treaty of Gyalu, John Zápolya's widow cedes Hungary to Ferdinand.

E The Spanish begin the conquest of Peru (–1542);

Roberval is appointed Viceroy of Canada by Francis I, who makes an unsuccessful attempt to establish a French colony at Quebec (–1543).

F   **Politics, Economics, Law and Education**
Martin Luther, *Wider Hans Worst*.
English Act of Parliament for the maintenance of archery and debarring of unlawful games, such as slide thrift.

G   **Science, Technology and Discovery**
Hernando de Soto discovers the Mississippi River and crosses Arkansas and Oklahoma.
Francisco de Coronada leads an expedition from New Mexico across the buffalo plains of Texas, Oklahoma and Eastern Kansas in search of the reputedly wealthy Gran Quivira region.
Francisco de Orellana first descends the R. Amazon.
Pedro de Valdivia founds Santiago.
Mercator's terrestrial globe.

H   **Philosophy, Religion and Scholarship**
Olaus Petri and others, *Gustav Vasas Bibel* (a complete translation of the Bible into Swedish).

J. D. van Ringelberg, *Lucubrationes vel potius absolutissima* κυκλοπαιδεια.
Jean Calvin returns to Geneva.

J   **Art, Sculpture, Fine Arts and Architecture**

K   **Music**
First villanelle published in Italy.

L   **Literature (including Drama)**
Giambattista Cinzio Giraldi, *Orbeche* (the first tragedy on classical models to be performed in Italy).

M   **Births and Deaths**
June 26th Francisco Pizarro d. (70).
Sept. 24th Paracelsus d. (48).
Oct. 18th Margaret Queen of Scotland d. (52).
— Jean Clouet ('Janet') d. (c. 60).
— El Greco b. (–1614).
— Jan Zanoyski b. (–1605).

1542   War between France and the Empire—Scots defeated at Solway
         Moss

A Jan: 16th (*–Apr.* 1st), English Parliament meets and
       21st, a bill of attainder is brought against Queen Katherine Howard;
       23rd, Henry VIII takes the title King (instead of 'Lord') of Ireland.
   Feb: 13th, Queen Katherine Howard is executed;
       Francis I proposes a meeting with Henry VIII and James V of Scotland, which never
       takes place.
   Mar:

B Apr:
   May: Joachim of Brandenburg attacks Turkey.
   Jun:

C Jul: 21st, Pope Paul III establishes the Inquisition in Rome;
       further war breaks out between Francis I of France and the Emperor Charles V (–1544),
       in retaliation to the Emperor's investiture of his son Philip with Milan (in *Oct.* 1540),
       with campaigns in Rousillon, Piedmont and the Netherlands;
       border warfare between England and Scotland is intensified;
       Francis I signs a treaty of alliance with Sweden.
   Aug: John Frederick, Elector of Saxony and Philip of Hesse invade Brunswick since the
       Catholic Duke Henry of Brunswick has disregarded the Recess of the Diet of Ratisbon;
       the Duke's lands are sequestered by the Schmalkaldic League;
       24th, Sir Robert Bowes, Warden of the East March, on a punitive raid into Teviotdale
       is captured by the Scots at Hadden Rigg.
   Sep: The imperial campaign against the Turks in Hungary fails.

D Oct: 6th (–12th), the Duke of Norfolk invades Scotland and burns Kelso. James V pre-
       pares to retaliate by invading Cumberland.
   Nov: 25th, the Scots under James V are routed at the battle of Solway Moss, with 1,200
       slain, against 7 English lives lost.
   Dec: 3rd, John Lord Russell is appointed Lord Privy Seal by Henry VIII (–1553);
       14th, accession of Mary Queen of Scots, born on *Dec.* 8th, following the death of James V
       at Falkland. Cardinal Beaton claims the regency.

E

F **Politics, Economics, Law and Education**
Magdalene College, Cambridge, is founded.
Castellio, *Dialogues Sacrés*, a Latin text book.

G **Science, Technology and Discovery**
Antonio da Mota is the first European to reach Japan.
Andreas Vesalius, *De Fabrica Corporis Humani*, founds the modern study of anatomy.

H **Philosophy, Religion and Scholarship**
Martin Luther consecrates a bishop.
Parlement of Paris orders the suppression of Calvin's *Institutes* (of 1536).
St. Francis Xavier arrives at Goa as a Jesuit missionary.

J **Art, Sculpture, Fine Arts and Architecture**
Art:
Titian, altarpiece in the church of Le Gracie, Milan.
Sculpture:
Michelangelo, *Active and Contemplative Life* (Rome).

K **Music**
Sylvestre Ganassi publishes his *Regola Rubertina*, which includes what is probably the first *ricercari* for viol (the first for organ appeared in 1523).

L **Literature (including Drama)**

M **Births and Deaths**
June 24th St. John of the Cross (Juan de Yepez y Alvarez) b. (–1591).
Oct. 4th Roberto Bellarmine b. (–1621).
Oct. 11th Sir Thomas Wyatt d. (39).
Nov. — Hans Holbein the younger d. (46).
Dec. 8th Mary Queen of Scots b. (–1587).
— Hernando de Soto d. (*c.* 50).

A   Jan: 10th, Scottish lords depose Cardinal Beaton from the regency and subsequently
       imprison him (–*Apr.* 10th); they approve the appointment as Regent of the Earl of
       Arran, heir presumptive to the throne and leader of the pro-English party, which is
       anxious for peace;
       22nd, Parliament meets (–*May* 12th); it dispenses Henry VIII from repaying a forced
       loan contributed in 1542, and provides for the administration of Wales in 12 counties.
       A Council for Wales and the Marches is also established.
     Feb: 11th, Henry VIII signs a treaty of alliance with the Emperor Charles V against
       France (confirmed *May* 20th).
     Mar: 12th, the Scottish Parliament meets.

B   Apr: 23rd, Henry VIII appoints Sir William Paget Principal Secretary of State in place of
       Sir Ralph Sadler;
       Hermann von Wied, Archbishop of Cologne, is deposed for favouring Protestantism.
     May: Charles V arrives in Genoa from Spain, for campaigning against Francis I of France.
     Jun: 22nd, Henry VIII's ultimatum to France, serving as a declaration of war. An army
       under Sir John Wallop joins with the imperial army in Flanders.

C   Jul: 1st, England and Scotland sign the Treaties of Greenwich, to secure peace and pro-
       vide for the betrothal of Mary Queen of Scots to Prince Edward Tudor (repudiated by
       the Scots in *Dec.*);
       7th, Francis I invades Luxemburg;
       12th, Henry VIII marries Catherine Parr, widow of Lord Latimer;
       24th, Cardinal Beaton marches on Linlithgow with 600 men.
     Aug: 5th, the French and Turkish combined fleets capture Nice;
       24th, Charles V begins the siege of Duren in Gelderland.
     Sep: 3rd, the Earl of Arran submits to Cardinal Beaton, who assumes the regency and
       with the Queen Mother, Mary of Guise, plans to set aside the Treaties of Greenwich;
       7th, Charles V forces the Duke of Cleves, ally of Francis I, to yield Gelderland and
       Zutphen to the Netherlands and to break off his alliances with France, Denmark and
       Sweden.

D   Oct: 20th, English and imperial armies attempt the siege of Landrecies, but the French
       refuse to do battle and retire.
     Nov:
     Dec: 11th, Scottish Parliament repudiates the Treaties of Greenwich (of *July* 1st).

E   Portuguese seamen land on the island of Tanegashima, Japan.

F **Politics, Economics, Law and Education**

G **Science, Technology and Discovery**

Nicolaus Copernicus, *De Revolutionibus Orbium Coelestium* explains the heliocentric theory for the movement of the planets (which he formed 1506–12).

H **Philosophy, Religion and Scholarship**

A Necessary Doctrine and Erudition for a Christian Man, commonly called 'King Henry's Book'.

Index Librorum Prohibitorum is issued by Pope Paul III for the Catholic Churches (–1557, 1559, 1564).

John Calvin publishes a revised Latin edition of the *Institutes* (–1536).

The Sorbonne condemns *Animadversiones Aristotelicae*, by Pierre de la Ramée (Ramus).

The first Protestant is burned in Spain.

J **Art, Sculpture, Fine Arts and Architecture**

Fine Arts:

Benvenuto Cellini, salt-cellar for Francis I of France, and *Nymph of Fontainebleau*.

K **Music**

L **Literature (including Drama)**

Garcilaso de la Vega and Juan Boscán, posth. volume of poems.

[Sir Thomas More] History of *Richard the Third* (notable in the development of a narrative prose style in English.

M **Births and Deaths**

Jan. 9th Guillaume du Bellay d. (52).

Jan. 19th Francis II of France b. (–1558).

Feb. 10th Johann Maier Eck d. (56).

May 24th Nicolaus Copernicus d. (70).

— William Byrd b. (–1623).

A Jan: 13th, an Act in Sweden recognises hereditary succession to the Crown in the male line;

14th, Parliament meets (–Mar. 28th), and recognises the Princesses Mary and Elizabeth as heirs to the English throne after Prince Edward.

Feb: Diet of Speyer meets (–Apr.); the Lutheran princes vote supplies for the Emperor's wars with France and Turkey and Charles V is forced to leave open the question of a national settlement of religion in Germany, instead of leaving it to the Pope's general council.

Mar:

B Apr: 14th, François, Count d'Enghien defeats the imperialists and Swiss mercenaries at Cerisolo, to recover Carignano;

Denmark repudiates its alliance with France;

Barbarossa sails from Toulon for Constantinople;

Charles V invades Champagne.

May: 1st, the Turks again invade Hungary, take Wischegrad and seize the Hungarian crown jewels. Suleiman I subsequently organises the country into 12 sanjaks, with Buda as the administrative centre;

3rd, an English military and naval expedition is sent to Scotland under Edward Seymour, Earl of Hertford, and John Dudley, Lord Lisle, which captures Leith and burns Edinburgh;

17th, Matthew, Earl of Lennox, signs a secret treaty with England at Carlisle; Henry VIII promises to appoint him Governor of Scotland in the event of a Scottish defeat, and agrees that Lennox shall marry Lady Margaret Douglas, Henry's niece (the marriage takes place June 1545).

Jun: Charles V and the Archduke Ferdinand persuade the Pasha in Buda to agree to an amnesty.

C Jul: 14th, Henry VIII crosses to Calais to join with the Emperor in the campaign against Francis I in Picardy.

Aug: 17th, the imperial and English armies take St. Dizier, and Paris is threatened;

Pope Paul III denounces Charles V's attitude to the Lutheran princes at the Diet of Spires (in Feb.).

Sep: 12th, Charles V attacks Soissons;

14th, Henry VIII captures Boulogne and orders the siege of Montreuil (abandoned in Oct.);

18th, Peace of Crépy is signed between Francis I and Charles V, who has not consulted his ally, Henry VIII. By its terms conquests since the Truce of Nice (1538) are restored; Francis surrenders his claims to Naples, Flanders, Artois, Gelderland and Zutphen; Charles surrenders his claim to Burgundy; Charles promises the hand of (i) his daughter Mary or of (ii) his niece, the daughter of the Archduke Ferdinand to Francis's second son, the Duke of Orleans, with dowry of (i) Milan or (ii) the Netherlands and Franche-Comté (this is abandoned with the death of Orleans in 1545); and Piedmont and Savoy are to be restored to the rightful ruler;

Gustavus of Sweden makes an alliance with France, to counter Denmark's alliance with the Emperor;

30th, Henry VIII returns to England and campaigning in France ends for the year.

D Oct:

Nov: 19th, Pope Paul III's bull summoning a general council to meet at Trent in 1545.

Dec:

E

F **Politics, Economics, Law and Education**
   St. Bartholomew's Hospital, London, is re-founded.
   Albert I, Duke of Prussia, founds Königsberg University.

G **Science, Technology and Discovery**
   Lourenço Marques and Antonio Calderia explore the rivers in the region of Delagoa
   Bay, East Africa.
   Sebastien Münster, *Cosmographia Universalis*.
   Georg Agricola (or Bauer), *De ortu et causis subterraneis*, founds the study of physical
   geology.

H **Philosophy, Religion and Scholarship**
   Filippo Neri founds the Congregation of the Oratory.

J **Art, Sculpture, Fine Arts and Architecture**

K **Music**

L **Literature (including Drama)**
   Margaret of Navarre, *Heptameron*.
   Matteo Bandello, *Il Canzoniere* (lyric poetry).
   Maurice Scève, *Délie*.
   Jan Roelans prints at Antwerp a collection (the oldest extant anthology in the language)
   of 221 Dutch Songs: *Antwerps Liedboek—Een school Liedekens Boeck*.

M **Births and Deaths**
   Mar. 11th Torquato Tasso b. (–1595).
   Apr. 30th Thomas, Lord Audley, d. (56).
   May 24th William Gilbert b. (–1603).
   Sept. 8th Clément Marot d. (48).
   Dec. 9th Teofilo Folengo d. (53).

A Jan: The French under Marshal du Biez attempt to recover Boulogne (–*Sept.*).

Feb: 25th, after an English force under Sir Ralph Evers had raided the Border country as far as Melrose, the Scots, led by the Earls of Angus and Arran, inflict a defeat at Ancrum Moor;

Henry VIII attempts to forge an alliance with the Landgrave of Hesse, Denmark and the Duke of Holstein for a defensive league, which fails.

Mar: 24th, the Diet of Worms opens. The Protestant princes voice their dissatisfaction with the terms of the general council summoned by Paul III and demand a permanent religious settlement for Germany to be made independent of the Council's edicts, which Charles V refuses.

B Apr: 12th, Francis I authorises a further massacre of the Vaudois Protestants (by the end of *June* some 3,000 had been put to death).

May:

Jun:

C Jul: A French fleet under Admiral d'Annebault enters the Solent; the *Mary Rose*, England's finest warship, heels over in Portsmouth harbour and sinks;

19th, a French force lands on the Isle of Wight;

24th, the French fleet leaves the Solent unscathed.

Aug: 15th (–16th), Admiral d'Annebault attempts to force the English fleet under Lord Lisle to give battle off Shoreham; he retires after a skirmish and the English resume command of the English Channel;

26th, Pope Paul III creates his son, Pier Luigi Farnese, Duke of Parma, without imperial sanction.

Sep: 8th (–23rd), the Earl of Hertford leads a further punitive raid into Scotland, destroying Kelso, Melrose and five other abbeys and sixteen castles;

the Duke of Orleans, Francis I's second son, dies;

English fleet under Lord Lisle burns Tréport, Normandy.

D Oct: 1st, Matthew Earl of Lennox forfeits his Scottish estates, following his marriage to Lady Margaret Douglas (restored 1564).

Nov: Charles V and Ferdinand make the Truce of Adrianople with Suleiman I, Sultan of Turkey; the Emperor is thus free to turn to German affairs;

23rd, English Parliament meets (–*Dec.* 24th) and is required to vote a benevolence of 20d. in the £ on lands and of 10d. in the £ on goods, to finance the Scottish war; it dissolves colleges, chantries and hospitals, whose possessions pass to the Crown.

Dec: 13th, the Council of Trent opens;

the Diet of the Schmalkaldic League of Protestant princes opposing the Emperor Charles V meets at Frankfurt (–*Feb.* 1546).

E The Palatinate becomes Protestant;

John de Castro is appointed Viceroy of Portuguese India;

Humayun takes Kandahar.

F **Politics, Economics, Law and Education**

The opening of the silver mines at Potosi, Peru, leads to the Price Revolution in Europe, spreading from Spain.

Sleidan begins writing *Commentaries on the state of Religion and Politics in the reign of the Emperor Charles V*, an impartial survey of contemporary events in 26 books (-1555).

Henry VIII refounds Wolsey's College as Christ Church, Oxford.

G **Science, Technology and Discovery**

The earliest botannical garden is established in Padua.

Jerome Cardan in *Ars Magna* puts forward Tartaglia's system of solving quadratic equations.

Ambrose Paré, *Manière de traitez les Plaies*, founds the study of modern surgery by his treatment of gunshot wounds.

H **Philosophy, Religion and Scholarship**

Konrad von Gesner, *Bibliotheca Universalis*, vol. 1 (completed 1549; this bibliography of Latin, Greek and Hebrew writers, classified and indexed, entitles Gesner to be called 'the father of bibliography').

The Council of Trent meets to determine the policy of the Roman Catholic Church in the Reformation era and inaugurates the Counter-Reformation (-1551, 1562, 1564).

J **Art, Sculpture, Fine Arts and Architecture**

Painting:

Bronzino, frescoes for the chapel of Eleanor of Toledo (-1564).

Lorenzo Lotto, *Apollo Sleeping*.

Titian, *Pietro Aretino*.

Sculpture:

Benvenuto Cellini, *Perseus* (Florence; -1554).

Architecture:

Palladio, Palazzo Thiene, Vicenza (-1550).

Fine Arts:

Benvenuto Cellini writes his *Autobiography*.

K **Music**

Tylman Susato publishes 24 chansons by Josquin in his seventh book of chansons, printed in Antwerp.

L **Literature (including Drama)**

Roger Ascham, *Toxophilus* (a treatise in English prose, on archery).

Philippe de Commines, *Mémoires* (-1548; posth.).

John Heywood, *The Four P's* ('A new and a very mery enterlude of A palmer, A pardoner, A potycary, A pedler').

M **Births and Deaths**

Feb. 24th Don John of Austria b. (-1578).

Mar. 2nd Thomas Bodley b. (-1613).

July 8th Don Carlos b. (-1568).

Aug. 1st Andrew Melville b. (-1622).

Aug. 27th Alessandro Farnese, Duke of Parma, b. (-1592).

Dec. 7th Henry Stuart, Lord Darnley, b. (-1567).

— John Taverner d. (50).

1546 War of Schmalkaldic League in Germany—Peace of Ardres between France and England

A Jan: An English force under the Earl of Surrey is defeated at St. Étienne.

Feb: Following Martin Luther's death, 18th, the Schmalkaldic League prepares for civil war in Germany.

Mar: 2nd, George Wishart is burnt for heresy by Cardinal Beaton, which inflames the Protestant Party in Scotland;

25th, Edward Seymour, Earl of Hertford, replaces the Earl of Surrey as commander of the English army in France.

B Apr:

May: 29th, Cardinal Beaton is assassinated at St. Andrews by Leslie and Kirkcaldy of Grange, leaders of the pro-English party.

Jun: 7th, the Peace of Ardres ends England's war with France and Scotland: Boulogne is to remain in English hands for 8 years and then be restored to France for 2 million crowns (England restores it in *Mar.* 1550); Francis I undertakes to pay Henry VIII the customary pensions;

13th, the Protestant princes at Ratisbon denounce the Council of Trent;

19th, Maurice, Elector of Saxony, signs a secret treaty to aid Charles V against the Schmalkaldic League;

23rd, Pope Paul III undertakes to supply 12,000 men to aid Charles V.

C Jul: 16th, Anne Askew is burnt at Smithfield for denying the doctrine of transubstantiation;

20th, John Frederick of Saxony and Philip, Landgrave of Hesse, leaders of the Schmalkaldic League, receive the ban of the Empire;

Schärtlin occupies the imperial city of Donauwörth on behalf of the League.

Aug: Stephen Dolet is burnt as a heretic in France.

Sep: 17th, Van Buren with an imperial force from the Netherlands makes juncture with Charles V's main army at Ingoldstadt, enabling the Emperor to take the offensive.

D Oct: 7th, execution of 'the Fourteen of Meaux', a Protestant congregation, for heresy;

27th, Charles V formally assigns the Saxon electorate from John Frederick to Maurice of Saxony;

30th, Bohemian troops invade Saxony; Maurice offers to defend the towns in the duchy on condition they pay homage to him, and (*Nov.*) completes his occupation of Ernestine Saxony.

Nov: Henry VIII's health rapidly deteriorates; a feud develops between Lord Lisle and Bishop Stephen Gardiner, and the Earl of Hertford intrigues to secure the downfall of the Duke of Norfolk and his son, the Earl of Surrey;

the Schmalkaldic League begins to disintegrate.

Dec: 12th, as a result of Hertford's intrigues, Norfolk and Surrey are sent to the Tower for alleged treason;

John Frederick of Saxony recovers his Ernestine Saxon lands and invades the Albertine lands of Duke Maurice;

23rd, Ulm and, 29th, Frankfurt, formerly strongholds of the Schmalkaldic League, submit to Charles V.

E The Turks occupy Moldavia;

In Mexico the Spaniards put down a serious Maya rising.

F **Politics, Economics, Law and Education**
Henry VIII founds Trinity College, Cambridge.

G **Science, Technology and Discovery**
G. Mercator states the earth has a magnetic pole.

H **Philosophy, Religion and Scholarship**
Sixt Birck, a Lutheran, compiles the first Greek Concordance to the New Testament.
Étienne de la Boétie, *Le Discours de la servitude volontaire.*
Yny Lhyvyr hwnn, the first Welsh book printed.
Étienne Dolet, scholar and printer of learned books, charged with publishing heretical books (i.e. Protestant translations of the Scriptures). Pardoned by the King; re-arrested, convicted, hanged and burnt in the Place Maubert, Paris (*Aug.*).

J **Art, Sculpture, Fine Arts and Architecture**
Painting:
Jacopo Pontormo, frescoes at St. Lorenzo (destroyed).
Titian, *Pope Paul III and his Nephews.*
Architecture:
Michelangelo, Palazzo Farnese, begun by Sangallo, 1534, completed, with re-designed façade.
Michelangelo designs the Dome and undertakes the completion of St. Peter's, Rome, begun by Bramante (–1564).
Pierre Lescot begins constructing the Louvre, Paris.

K **Music**

L **Literature (including Drama)**
Hans Sachs, *Lisabetha* (tragedy).

M **Births and Deaths**
Feb. 18th Martin Luther d. (62).
Mar. 20th Thomas Elyot d. (56).
May 29th David Beaton d. (52).
Aug. 3rd Étienne Dolet d. (37).
Nov. 1st Giulio Romano d. (*c.* 54).
Dec. 14th Tycho Brahe b. (–1601).

1547   Battles of Mühleberg and Pinkie—Deaths of Henry VIII and Francis I—Charles V at the height of his power

A Jan: 2nd, Gianluigi Fiesco stages an unsuccessful *coup d'état* against Andrea Doria in Genoa;

16th, Ivan IV (the Terrible), who had ascended the throne in 1533 at the age of three, is crowned Tsar of Russia in Moscow, the first tsar to assume the crown formally;

24th, Earl of Surrey is executed for treason;

28th, Edward VI, aged nine, succeeds as King of England (–1553) on the death of Henry VIII;

31st, Edward Seymour, Earl of Hertford, who had seized power on the demise of the Crown, is appointed Lord Protector, in defiance of the arrangements for a regency in Henry VIII's will;

the cities of Augsburg and Strasbourg submit to the emperor Charles V;

the Council of Trent's decrees on justification by faith end Charles V's chances of reconciliation with the German Protestant princes.

Feb: 16th, the Earl of Hertford, Lord Protector, is created Duke of Somerset;

25th, Archbishop Hermann von Wied of Cologne resigns his see and Catholicism is re-established;

Duke Henry of Brunswick takes Minden;

Cosimo de' Medici counsels the Emperor Charles V to undertake a complete reform of the Church through the Council of Trent.

Mar: 31st, Henry II succeeds as King of France (–1559) on the death of his father, Francis I. A bigoted Catholic, Henry is dominated by Francis, Duke of Guise, and by his mistress, Diana of Poitiers. Guise subsequently arranges for Mary Queen of Scots to marry the Dauphin, instead of Edward VI;

the Council of Trent is transferred to Bologna, on the pretext of avoiding the plague, against the wishes of the Emperor Charles V.

B Apr: 13th, Charles V invades Saxony and

24th, defeats the army of the Schmalkaldic League at Mühlberg, where the Elector John Frederick of Saxony is taken prisoner.

May: 19th, by the capitulation of Wittenberg, the Saxon electorate is given by the Emperor to Duke Maurice.

Jun: 13th, a truce between Hungary and Turkey is signed for five years: the Sultan Suleiman I restores most of western Hungary to the Archduke Ferdinand and pays him annual tribute for his eastern share;

20th, Philip, Landgrave of Hesse, is taken prisoner at Halle, but is assured of his life;

a rebellion breaks out in Naples.

C Jul: Duke Henry of Brunswick is restored to his duchy.

Aug: The French capture St. Andrews Castle, Scotland.

Sep: 1st, Charles V, at the height of his power, meets the Diet of Augsburg and proposes constitutional reforms to strengthen the executive of the Empire. He offers Pope Paul III the submission of all Germany if the general council is removed from Bologna to Trent;

10th, Protector Somerset, who has invaded Scotland to enforce the marriage treaty of 1543 (for Mary's betrothal to Edward VI), defeats the Scots army at Pinkie, near Musselburgh. He subsequently captures Edinburgh and places English garrisons in Roxburgh and other castles;

—, Pierluigi Farnese, the Pope's son, is murdered by Ferrante di Gonzaga, Governor of Milan.

D Oct: *La Chambre Ardente* is created in Paris as a criminal court for the trial of heretics. Persecution of Protestants in France becomes more severe.

(*Continued opposite*)

F **Politics, Economics, Law and Education**
Guillaume Budé, *De l'Institution du Prince*.
Benefit of clergy is extended to English peers, even if they are illiterate.
Moscow is destroyed by fire.
Torquemada publishes a treatise on draughts.

G **Science, Technology and Discovery**

H **Philosophy, Religion and Scholarship**
William Baldwin, *A Treatise of Morall Phylosophie*: contayning the sayinges of the wyse, two parts (an anthology).
John Wilkinson makes the first English translation of the *Ethics* of Aristotle.
Peter Martyr lectures in theology at Oxford University.

J **Art, Sculpture, Fine Arts and Architecture**
Architecture:
Edward Seymour, Duke of Somerset, begins building Somerset Place in the Strand, London.

K **Music**
L. Bourgeois, *Psalter*.

L **Literature (including Drama)**
Giovanni Giorgio Trissino, *L'Italia Liberata da' Goti* (epic poem).

M **Births and Deaths**
Jan. 21st Henry Howard, Earl of Surrey, d. (*c.* 29).
Feb. 25th Vittoria Colonna d. (57).
Mar. 31st Francis I of France d. (53).
June. 21st Sebastiano del Piombo d. (62).
Sept. 14th Johan van Oldenbarneveldt b. (–1619).
Oct. 5th Miguel de Cervantes Saavedra b. (–1616).
Dec. 2nd Hernando Cortes d. (62).
— Nicholas Hilliarde b. (–1619).
— Jacopo Sadoleto d. (70).

Nov: 4th, English Parliament meets (*–Apr.* 15th, 1552) and repeals the Henrican Act of Six Articles (of 1539) as the first stage of a Protestant Reformation. The treason laws of Henry's reign are repealed;
the Bohemian Crown is proclaimed hereditary in the house of Hapsburg.
Dec:

E A poor rate is levied in the city of London;
Final union of the Crown of Brittany with the Crown of France;
The Inquisition is finally established at Lisbon;
Humayun captures Kabul.

A Jan: Protector Somerset explores the possibility of a Union of England and Scotland.
Feb:
Mar:

B Apr: 17th, Sir Thomas Smith is appointed a principal Secretary of State as successor to
William Paget;
English troops seize Haddington, Scotland, which they occupy (*–Sept.* 1549).
May: 15th, the Augsburg Interim is proclaimed as an attempt at compromise settlement
of religious differences in Germany. Clerical marriage is permitted, the laity are to
receive communion in both kinds and the doctrine of justification by faith is modified;
all seven sacraments are retained and the dogma of transubstantiation is reaffirmed.
The terms of the acceptance of the Interim by the German Diet are, however, vague;
the city of Magdeburg, centre of opposition, is placed under the ban of the Empire;
the Turks occupy Tabriz, Persia.
Jun: Henry II of France visits Turin, but is summoned home to face a revolt against the
imposition of the *gabelle* in Guienne, which claims exemption on the grounds of its
liberties under English rule.

C Jul: The Emperor Charles V annexes the 17 provinces of the Netherlands to the Burgun-
dian Circle of the Empire (*–June* 1549).
Aug: Sigismund II Augustus succeeds as King of Poland (–1572) on the death of
Sigismund I;
15th, Mary Queen of Scots, aged six, betrothed to the Dauphin, lands in France.
Protector Somerset in retaliation renews English feudal claims to Scotland.
Sep:

D Oct:
Nov. 24th, English Parliament meets (*–Mar.* 14th, 1549) and passes the Chantries Act;
John Hales introduces a bill to reform abuses in the enclosure of common land in
England, which is quashed.
Dec:

E Pedro de la Gasca defeats Gonzalo Pizarro at the battle of Xaquixaguana to end the separatist movement in Peru.

F **Politics, Economics, Law and Education**
Avila y Zuniga, *Commentarios de la guerra de Alemana*, a Spanish survey of the Schmalkaldic War in Germany.
Fourquevaux, *Instructions sur le Faict de la Guerre*.
The silver mines of Zaatecar, Mexico, are exploited by the Spanish.
Messina University is founded.

G **Science, Technology and Discovery**
The Guinea pepper plant is first grown in England.

H **Philosophy, Religion and Scholarship**
John Bale, *Illustrium maioris Britanniae Scriptorum, hoc est Angliae, Cambriae ac Scotiae summarium* (–1557; a bibliography of British writers arranged in chronological order: the first reference book of its kind).
St. Ignatius Loyola, *Spiritual Exercises* printed (*Ejercicios espirituales*, written in 1522).
Hugh Latimer preaches his sermon 'of the plough'.
St. Francis Xavier founds a Jesuit mission in Japan.

J **Art, Sculpture, Fine Arts and Architecture**
Painting:
Titian, *Charles V on horseback*.
Tintoretto, *St. Mark rescuing a slave* (Venice).

K **Music**

L **Literature (including Drama)**
John Bale, *Kynge Johan* (acted interlude, and the first historical drama in English literature).
The first Paris theatre, Hôtel de Bourgogne, opened (a roofed building).
Edict forbidding performance of *Mystères* in Paris.

M **Births and Deaths**
Sept. 5th Catherine Parr d. (36).

1549   The Netherlands Circle is formed—First Prayer Book of Edward
        VI—Fall of Protector Somerset

A Jan:
   Feb: Maximilian, son of the Archduke Ferdinand, is recognised as the next King of
        Bohemia.
   Mar: 14th, English Parliament is prorogued; royal assent is given to the Act of Uni-
        formity; from *May* 20th only the new Book of Common Prayer to be used;
        20th, Thomas Lord Seymour of Sudeley, the Protector's brother, is executed for
        treason.

B Apr: Protector Somerset offers to restore Boulogne to France if Henry II will further
        the marriage of Mary Queen of Scots to Edward VI.
   May:
   Jun: 26th, the seventeen provinces of the Netherlands are made independent of the
        Empire, to form a Circle of their own. The Emperor Charles V remains in the Nether-
        lands for the entire year;
        risings in the West Country under Humphrey Arundel, aimed at the restoration of the
        Catholic liturgy (*–Aug.*).

C Jul: Robert Kett leads a revolt in Norfolk in protest at the enclosure movement. The
        rebels capture Norwich and establish a 'commonwealth' on Mousehold Heath.
   Aug: 8th, France declares war on England;
        9th, Lord Russell relieves Exeter to end the Prayer Book rising in the West Country;
        12th, the French capture Ambleteuse and begin the siege of Boulogne;
        26th, John Dudley, Earl of Warwick, defeats Robert Kett's Norfolk rebels at the Battle
        of Dussindale, near Norwich.
   Sep: 13th, Pope Paul III closes the Council of Bologna;
        14th, the English abandon Haddington to the Scots.

D Oct: 10th, fall of Protector Somerset, who is sent,
        12th, to the Tower by John Dudley, Earl of Warwick, and Thomas Wriothesley, Earl of
        Southampton; Warwick, though he does not accept the title of Lord Protector, con-
        centrates offices and power in his hands, including, 28th, the office of Lord Admiral;
        —, Sir Thomas Smith is deprived of the secretaryship for siding with Somerset.
   Nov: 1st, Pope Paul III dies (Julius III is elected *Feb.* 1550, after a prolonged conclave);
        4th, Parliament meets (*–Feb.* 1550) and passes Acts against unlawful assemblies and
        making the destruction of enclosures a felony.
   Dec: 23rd, the Duke of Somerset makes formal submission to Edward VI and his council.

E Tsar Ivan IV calls the first national assembly in Russia (*Zemski Sobor*);
   Thomé de Souza founds São Salvador;
   The Audiencia of New Grenada is created, with Santa Fé (now Bogotá) the provincial
   capital.

F Politics, Economics, Law and Education
   The Complaint of Scotland, an attack on English policy.

G Science, Technology and Discovery
   The first Anatomical Theatre is established in Padua.

H Philosophy, Religion and Scholarship
   Joachim Du Bellay, *La Déffense et illustration de la langue française* (the first statement
   of the theory of the poetic group known as *La Pléiade*, based on the classical works of
   the Greeks and Romans, and rejecting mediaevelism).
   Act of Uniformity orders the use of the Common Prayer Book (*Jan.* 15th; repealed
   –1553; restored –1559, 1662).
   First Prayer Book of Edward VI (The Book of Common Prayer –1552, 1559, 1662).
   In this year a Prayer Book (unbound) cost 2/2d.; bound, 3/8d.

J Art, Sculpture, Fine Arts and Architecture
   Painting:
      Hans Eworth, *A Turk on Horseback.*
   Architecture:
      Palladio, Basilica, Vicenza.

K Music
   Martin Luther, *Geistliche Lieder mit einer newen Vorrhede* (101 hymns, some by Hans
   Sachs; posth.).

L Literature (including Drama)
   Joachim Du Bellay, *L'Olive* (the first sonnet-sequence in the French language. *Vers
   Lyriques*).
   Juan de Pedraza, Easter Play (*La Aparicion que hizo Jesu Christo . . .*).

M Births and Deaths
   Mar. 20th Thomas Lord Seymour of Sudeley d. (*c.* 41).
   Sept. 21st Marguerite d'Angoulême d. (57).
   Nov. 5th Philippe de Plessis-Mornay b. (–1623).
   Dec. 7th Robert Ket d. (*c.* 35).

A **Jan:**
Feb: 1st, English Parliament is dissolved;
   3rd, William Paulet, Marquess of Winchester, is appointed Lord Treasurer of England (–1572).
   7th, Giovanni Maria del Monte is elected Pope Julius III (–1555);
   a defensive league is agreed at Königsberg between Johann Albrecht of Mecklenburg, Albrecht Duke of Prussia and Hans of Cüstria, against the Emperor Charles V; they put out feelers for an alliance with France.
Mar: 24th, the Peace of Boulogne ends the war between England with France and Scotland: England returns Boulogne to France on payment of 400,000 crowns. Henry II is now free to oppose the Emperor Charles V.

B **Apr:**
May:
Jun:

C **Jul:** Mary Tudor attempts to flee to Flanders.
Aug:
Sep: 5th, Sir William Cecil is appointed principal Secretary of State;
   22nd, the troops engaged by the city of Magdeburg, under the ban of the Empire, are defeated by Duke George of Mecklenburg, but the citizens refuse to submit;
   the imperial fleet captures the 'Port of Africa' at Mehedia in Tunis, naval headquarters of the corsair Dragut.

D **Oct:** Maurice of Saxony besieges Magdeburg.
Nov: 14th, Papal bull summons the general council to meet at Trent in *May* 1551.
Dec: Ottavio Farnese, restored to the duchy of Parma, seeks the aid of Henry II of France in facing the opposition of Ferrante di Gonzaga of Milan.

E

F **Politics, Economics, Law and Education**
Robert Crowley, *Way to Wealth* laments the failure of Somerset's policy.
Accademia degli Innominati is founded in Padua.

G **Science, Technology and Discovery**
Siegmund von Herberstein, *De Natura Fossilium.*

H **Philosophy, Religion and Scholarship**
Thomas Cranmer, *A Defence of the Catholic Doctrine of the Sacrament.*
Robert Estienne (Stephens) prints a notable edition of the Greek New Testament.
Antonio Francesco Doni, *La Libraria* (*La Seconda Libraria* –1551).
Edward Halle, *Chronicles* (2nd edn. of 'The Union of the Noble and Illustre Families of Lancastre and York').
John Harington (the elder) translates Cicero's *De Amicita* (*The Booke of Freendeship*).

J **Art, Sculpture, Fine Arts and Architecture**
Painting:
Hans Eworth, *Sir John Lutterell* and *Captain Thomas Wyndham.*
Lorenzo Lotto, *A Nobleman in his study.*
Giorgio Vasari, *Lives of the Artists* (*Lives of Most Excellent Architects, Painters and Sculptors of Italy*; enlarged edn., 1568), and Vasari founds the Fine Arts Academy, Florence.
Sculpture:
Michelangelo, deposition from the Cross, containing a self-portrait (Florence).
Architecture:
Palladio, Palazzo Chiericati, Vicenza; Villa Rotunda, Vicenza (–1551), and Villa Thiene, Quinto.

K **Music**
Jean Calvin compiles a complete psalter, including 'The Old Hundredth', for developing metrical pointing for congregational singing.
Jambe de Fer, *Épitome Musicale* published at Lyons.
John Marbeck compiles and publishes *The Booke of Common Praier noted*, first musical setting of English liturgy.

L **Literature (including Drama)**
Olaus Petri, *Tobie Commedia* (earliest extant Swedish drama).
Pierre de Ronsard, *Odes* (bks. I–IV). *Les Bocages.*
Nicholas Udall, *Ralph Roister Doister* (comedy—the earliest known English comedy; licensed 1566).

M **Births and Deaths**
Sept. 10th Don Alonso de Guzman, Duke of Medina Sidonia, b. (–1615).
— Andrea Alciati d. (58).
— John Napier b. (–1617).

A Jan:
   Feb: 14th, Stephen Gardiner is deprived of the see of Winchester.
   Mar: 9th, a family compact is agreed, for the Archduke Ferdinand to succeed to the imperial title and the Hapsburg lands on the death of Charles V, with Philip to succeed him (abrogated *Sept.* 1555).

B Apr:
   May: Pope Julius III deprives Ottavio Farnese of the duchy of Parma; second session of the Council of Trent (–1552).
   Jun: Henry II of France begins campaigning in Italy against Charles V.

C Jul: 19th, the Treaty of Kalsburg re-affirms the Archduke Ferdinand's right to the Crown of Hungary and Transylvania; the Turkish fleet fails to capture Malta.
   Aug: 14th, the Turks capture Tripoli.
   Sep: The French under François de Brissac begin campaigning in Saxony against Charles V; rising in Transylvania on behalf of the Archduke Ferdinand, against John Sigismund and Isabel, the son and daughter-in-law of Zápolya, and the rule of Cardinal Martinuzzi.

D Oct: 11th, John Dudley, Earl of Warwick, is created Duke of Northumberland.
   Nov: 3rd, Magdeburg capitulates to Maurice of Saxony.
   Dec: Cardinal George Martinuzzi, the effective ruler of Transylvania, is assassinated by the imperialists.

E

F **Politics, Economics, Law and Education**
The English currency is further debased.
First licensing of alehouses and taverns in England and Wales.
Printing is introduced to Ireland.

G **Science, Technology and Discovery**
G. Mercator's celestial fire.
Pierre Belon, *Histoire naturelle des estranges poissons.*
Konrad von Gesner, *Historia Animalium*, a pioneer study of zoology (–1558).
Robert Record, *The Castle of Knowledge*, the first English work to mention the astronomical theory of Copernicus.

H **Philosophy, Religion and Scholarship**
Jerome Cardan, *De subtilitate rerum.*
Sir Thomas More, *Utopia*, translated from the Latin original into English, by Raphe Robynson.
Edict of Châteaubriant is issued (*June* 27th) by Henry II of France, to combat Calvinism.
The Council of Trent resumes meetings (–1552).
The Jesuits found the Collegio Romano.
John Hopkins makes additions to Thomas Sternhold's 'Old Version' of metrical psalms (–1562).

J **Art, Sculpture, Fine Arts and Architecture**
Painting:
Titian, *St. Jerome* and portrait of *Philip II.*

K **Music**
Giovanni Pierluigi da Palestrina is appointed director of music at St. Peter's, Rome.

L **Literature (including Drama)**

M **Births and Deaths**
Feb. 27th Martin Bucer d. (60).
May 2nd William Camden b. (–1623).
Sept. 19th Henry III of France b. (–1589).

1552   Henry II of France signs Alliance with Protestant Princes of Germany—Lutherans are assured of the free exercise of their religion in Germany

A   Jan: Treaty of Friedewalde between Maurice of Saxony, Albrecht of Brandenburg, the Landgrave William of Hesse, Duke Johann Albrecht of Mecklenburg and other German princes with Henry II of France, who is to support the princes against Charles V in return for the bishoprics of Metz, Toul and Verdun, and Cambrai;

15th, the Treaty of Chambard confirms the above;

22nd, Edward Seymour, Duke of Somerset, is beheaded for treason;

23rd, Parliament meets (*–Apr.* 15th) and passes a second Uniformity Act authorising the more radical Second Prayer Book of Edward VI.

Feb: 24th, the privileges of the Hanseatic League in England are abrogated.

Mar: 13th, Henry II invades Lorraine with 35,000 men to occupy the bishoprics of Metz, Toul and Verdun;

the Turks invade Hungary to win the battle of Szegedin, but fail to capture Erlau.

B   Apr: Maurice of Saxony secedes from Charles V and

4th, takes Augsburg;

10th, Henry II takes Metz and declares his alliance with the German Protestants (of *Jan.*);

18th, Maurice of Saxony captures Linz;

19th, Maurice fails to capture Charles V at Innsbruck and the Emperor escapes across the Brenner Pass to take refuge in Villach in Carinthia;

Henry II of France and Pope Julius III sign a two-year truce, allowing Ottavio Farnese to return to the duchy of Parma.

May: Albrecht Alcibiades, Margrave of Brandenburg-Culmbach, deserts his Protestant allies for a private war in Franconia.

Jun: 12th, Henry II returns to Verdun after being threatened by Mary of Hungary, Regent of the Netherlands, and Count Mansfeld.

C   Jul: 17th, Siena revolts against the imperial garrison (*–Apr.* 1555);

the Conference of Passau at which German Protestant princes meet with Maurice of Saxony.

Aug: 2nd, by the Treaty of Passau John Frederick of Saxony and Philip of Hesse are released from imprisonment; the Augsburg Interim of 1548 is annulled; Lutherans are assured of the free exercise of their religion in Germany and a diet is to be called to make a permanent settlement;

Charles V marches his army through southern Germany.

Sep:

D   Oct: 31st, Charles V attempts to lay siege to Metz (*–Jan.* 1553) which has been fortified by Francis, Duke of Guise. The Emperor is aided by an army of Albrecht Alcibiades, Margrave of Brandenburg-Culmbach.

Nov:

Dec:

E   Ivan IV of Russia begins the conquest of Kazan and Astrakhan from the Tartars.

F **Politics, Economics, Law and Education**

Antonio Francesco Doni, *I Mondi*, advocates a 'Utopia', based on Socialist ideas.
The privileges of the Hansa in England are curtailed.
Christ's Hospital and some 35 grammar schools are founded in the name of King
Edward VI.

G **Science, Technology and Discovery**

Bartolomeo Eustachio, in *Tabulae Anatomicae*, makes known his discoveries of the
Eustachian tube and valve.

H **Philosophy, Religion and Scholarship**

João de Barros, *Asia* (*Decades of the Portuguese in Asia*, 1) (3rd and his last decade,
1563; 4th, ed. by Lavanha, 1615).
Thomas Cranmer, *The Second Prayer Book* of Edward VI (–1549).
Friedrich Dedekind, *Grobianus* (satire against the moral coarseness of the age).
Robert Estienne (i.e. Stephens), *Censures des théologians de Paris*.
Francesco López de Gómara (secretary to Cortéz), *Historia general de las Indias* (–1553;
banned in 1553; trans. 1578 as *The pleasant historie of the conquest of the West India*).
The *Forty-Two Articles* issued (without consent of Parliament) (–1562).
Treaty of Passau (*July* 16th–*Aug.* 2nd), between the Elector of Saxony and King
Ferdinand (for Charles V) granting freedom of religion to the Lutherans.
Collegium Germanicum, Rome, is founded.

J **Art, Sculpture, Fine Arts and Architecture**

Architecture:
Philibert Delorme, Anet Château (–1559).

K **Music**

L **Literature (including Drama)**

Étienne Jodelle, *Cléopâtre captive* (tragedy, the first French drama of its kind). *Eugène*
(comedy in verse).
Pierre de Ronsard, *Amours*, vol. 1 (*Amours de Marie* –1555–6).

M **Births and Deaths**

Jan. 14th Alberico Gentili b. (–1608).
Jan. 22nd Edward Seymour, Duke of Somerset, d. (51).
Feb. 1st Edward Coke b. (–1634).
Apr. 18th John Leland d. (46).
June — Alexander Barclay d. (76).
July 18th Emperor Rudolph II b. (–1612).
Aug. 14th Paolo Sarpi b. (–1623).
Sept. 17th Camillo Borghese (Pope Paul V) b. (–1621).
Oct. 7th Matteo Ricci b. (–1610).
— Gabriello Chiabrera b. (–1637).
— Henry, Prince of Condé, b. (–1588).
— Walter Raleigh, b. (–1618).
— John Speed b. (–1629).
— Edmund Spenser b. (–1599).

1553   Warfare in Germany—Northumberland's plot for the Crown to pass to Lady Jane Grey fails

A Jan: 1st, Charles V retires from Metz and returns to Brussels, leaving Germany to its own fate. The bishoprics of Metz, Toul and Verdun pass to the French Crown; attempts to restore imperial control to Siena, with a force from Naples, fail (the city holds out until *Apr.* 1555).
Feb:
Mar: 1st, English Parliament meets (*–Mar.* 31st);
the League of Heidelberg is formed by both Catholic and Protestant princes in Germany to preserve peace and prevent the election of Philip of Spain as Holy Roman Emperor.

B Apr: 11th, Albrecht Alcibiades of Brandenburg-Culmbach defeats an army of the Heidelberg League at Pommersfelden.
May: 21st, Lady Jane Grey marries Lord Guildford Dudley.
Jun: Charles V captures Térouanne from the French after a two-month siege;
21st, Edward VI is prevailed upon by the Duke of Northumberland to bestow the succession on Lady Jane Grey (daughter of Henry Grey, Marquess of Dorset and Duke of Suffolk, and Frances, daughter of Mary, younger sister of Henry VIII), eldest claimant in the Suffolk line to the succession.

C Jul: 6th, on the death of Edward VI, Lady Jane Grey is unwillingly proclaimed Queen of England by Northumberland, 10th;
9th, Maurice of Saxony is killed defeating Albrecht Alcibiades, Margrave of Brandenburg-Culmbach at the Battle of Sievershausen. The Saxon electorate is united in the Albertine branch, descending to Maurice's brother, Augustus;
14th, Northumberland leaves London to face Mary's (daughter of Henry VIII) supporters who are gathering around her in East Anglia;
19th, Lady Jane Grey is deposed and Mary proclaimed Queen of England (–1558);
20th, Northumberland surrenders at Cambridge.
Aug: 3rd, Queen Mary I enters London. The Roman Mass is celebrated at Court;
22nd, the Duke of Northumberland is executed;
23rd, Stephen Gardiner, Bishop of Winchester, is appointed Lord Chancellor.
Sep: 12th, Henry Duke of Brunswick defeats Albrecht Alcibiades at Steterburg;
13th, Bishop Latimer is sent to the Tower of London;
Protestants begin to leave England for Geneva and Zurich.

D Oct:
Nov: 13th, Lady Jane Grey, Lord Guildford Dudley, Archbishop Cranmer and others are tried for treason;
a marriage treaty is signed between Mary I and Philip of Spain;
Emmanuel Philibert accedes as Duke of Savoy (–1580).
Dec: 1st, Albrecht Alcibiades of Brandenburg-Culmbach receives the ban of the Empire;
20th, the form of service as at Henry VIII's death is prescribed for general use in place of the 1552 Prayer Book.

E A Turkish fleet, aided by the French, ravages the Mediterranean, provoking a rebellion in Corsica, which is put down by the Genoese, with Spanish help;
Sultan Suleiman I makes peace with Persia.

F **Politics, Economics, Law and Education**
Domingo de Soto, *De Justicia et Jure*.
Lima University, Peru, is founded.

G **Science, Technology and Discovery**
Hugh Willoughby and Richard Chancellor set out to discover a north-east passage to
China. Willoughby reaches the Russian coast near the Pechora mouth and dies while
wintering on the Kola Peninsula. Chancellor reaches the site of Archangel and travels
to Moscow (–1554).
P. Belon, *De aquatilibus*, a study of ichthyology.
Michael Servetus in *Christianismi Restitutio* relates his discovery of the pulmonary
circulation of the blood.

H **Philosophy, Religion and Scholarship**
Gavin Douglas translates Virgil's *Aeneid*, with original prologues written for each book,
being the first translation of a Latin poet to be published in Britain.
Sir Thomas More, *A Dialogue of Comfort Against Tribulation* (posth.).
Polydore Vergil, *Anglica Historia*.
Thomas Wilson, *The Arte of Rhetorique*.
Michael Servetus, *Christianismi Restitutio* (denying the belief that Christ is the eternal
Son of God); he is burnt at the stake in Geneva.
The Roman Catholic bishops are restored in England (*Aug.*), after the accession of
Mary I.
The Act of Uniformity of 1549 is repealed (restored, 1559).

J **Art, Sculpture, Fine Arts and Architecture**
Painting:
Titian, *Danae*.
Veronese, ceilings for the palace of the Doge, Venice.
Architecture:
Palladio, Villa Pisana, Montagnana (–1555).

K **Music**
Christopher Tye, *The Acts of the Apostles* (includes the hymn tunes 'Dundee' and
'Winchester Old').

L **Literature (including Drama)**
Gavin Douglas, *The Palyse of Honour*: an allegorical poem.
[Diego Hurtado de Mendoza], *Lazarillo de Tormes* (the first Spanish picaresque novel.
Attributed to Mendoza).
Pierre de Ronsard, *Les Folastries*.
Hans Sachs, *Tristran und Isolde*.

M **Births and Deaths**
Apr. 9th François Rabelais d. (*c.* 63).
May 14th Marguérite de Valois b. (–1615).
July 9th Maurice, Elector of Saxony, d. (32).
Aug. 22nd John Dudley, Duke of Northumberland, d. (51).
Oct. 16th Lucas Cranach d. (81).
Oct. 27th Michael Servetus d. (42).
Dec. 14th Henry IV b. (–1610).
— Richard Hakluyt b. (–1616).
— Thomas Morley b. (–1603).
— Jacques Auguste de Thou b. (–1617).

A Jan: 25th, Sir Thomas Wyatt gathers an army of 2,000 at Rochester, in Kent, to raise rebellion, in opposition to Mary I's projected Spanish marriage.

Feb: 3rd, Wyatt reaches Southwark, but is unable to force a passage over London Bridge;

7th, Wyatt crosses Kingston Bridge, marches on London, and

9th, is defeated;

12th, Lady Jane Grey is executed;

—, Edward Courtenay, Earl of Devon, is sent to the Tower of London for complicity in Wyatt's rebellion;

23rd, Henry Grey, Duke of Suffolk, Lady Jane Grey's father, is executed.

Mar: 3rd, John Frederick, the Ernestine Elector of Saxony, dies;

15th, Wyatt is tried (executed *Apr.* 11th);

18th, Princess Elizabeth is sent to the Tower for suspected complicity in Wyatt's rebellion.

B Apr: 2nd, English Parliament meets (*–May* 5th);

12th, Mary of Guise, the Queen Mother, succeeds the Earl of Arran as Regent of Scotland (–1560);

16th (–18th), Archbishop Cranmer, Bishop Ridley and others take part in a public disputation at Oxford on the doctrines of the Mass.

May: 19th, Princess Elizabeth is removed from the Tower to Woodstock;

Henry II of France invades the Netherlands, capturing Marienburg and other towns in the Meuse valley.

Jun: Duke Henry of Brunswick defeats Albrecht Alcibiades, Margrave of Brandenburg-Culmbach, at Schwarzart, and the Margrave takes refuge in France.

C Jul: 25th, Queen Mary I marries Philip of Spain, son of the Emperor Charles V, at Winchester.

Aug: 2nd, Piero Strozzi, the ally of Henry II is defeated at Marciano, enabling the Spanish blockade of Siena to be completed;

the Emperor Charles V empowers the Archduke Ferdinand to settle the religious question with the German diet.

Sep:

D Oct:

Nov: 12th, Parliament meets (*–Jan.* 1555) and re-establishes Roman Catholicism;

30th, England is reconciled with Pope Julius II.

Dec:

E The Turkish corsair Dragut recaptures Mehedia, Tunisia, from the Spanish.

F **Politics, Economics, Law and Education**
São Paulo, Brazil, is founded.
Dilligen University is founded in Bavaria.
First known autograph album is begun.
David Lyndsay, *The Monarchie* (Ane dialog betwix Experience and ane Courtier of the miserabill estait of the World).

G **Science, Technology and Discovery**
Jean Fernel, *Universa Medicina*.
Jerome Cardan produces pure alcohol.

H **Philosophy, Religion and Scholarship**
Jerome Cardan, *De Varietate Rerum* (discussion of psychic experiences).
Roman Catholicism restored in England (*Nov.* 30th).
John Knox flees to Dieppe and thence to Geneva, where he meets John Calvin.
Calvin (*Feb.*) defends the action of Geneva in executing Servetus (in 1553); but Sebastian Castellion and others publish a tract (*Mar.*) in favour of religious toleration.

J **Art, Sculpture, Fine Arts and Architecture**
Painting:
Titian, *La Gloria* and *Venus and Adonis*.
Antonio Moro, a Fleming, is appointed court painter to Philip and Mary.
Architecture:
Palladio, *L'Antichita di Roma*, a guidebook to Roman antiquities.

K **Music**
Palestrina writes his first book of Masses.

L **Literature (including Drama)**
Matteo Bandello, *Le Novelle* (214 short stories and tales, –1573, one of which was *Giulietta e Romeo*).
Durich Chiampel, *Judit e Holofernes* (biblical drama in the Romansch language of the Lower Engadine).
Jörg Wickram, *Der Goldfaden* (the first German romance novel).

M **Births and Deaths**
Jan. 9th Alessandro Ludovisi (Pope Gregory XV) b. (–1623).
Feb. 12th Lady Jane Grey d. (17).
May — Richard Hooker b. (—1600).
Nov. 30th Philip Sidney b. (–1586).
— Fulke Greville, Lord Brooke, b. (–1628).
— John Lyly b. (–1606).

1555   **The Peace of Augsburg in Germany—Charles V resigns the government of the Netherlands, Milan and Naples to Philip of Spain**

A Jan:
   Feb: 5th, the Archduke Ferdinand opens the Diet of Augsburg (*–Oct.*);
   9th, Hooper, the deprived Bishop of Gloucester, is burnt at Smithfield for heresy.
   Mar: 23rd, Pope Julius III dies.

B Apr: 9th, Pope Marcellus II is elected (dies *Apr.* 30th);
   17th, the Spanish regain Siena, which surrenders after a famine (Philip subsequently sells the city to Cosimo de' Medici);
   Princess Elizabeth returns to Mary's court and is subsequently reconciled to her sister.
   May: 23rd, Giovanni Pietro Caraffa is elected Pope Paul IV (*–1559*);
   John Knox returns to Scotland.
   Jun:

C Jul:
   Aug: 26th, Philip of Spain leaves England for the Low Countries.
   Sep: Trial of Archbishop Cranmer and Bishops Ridley and Latimer;
   25th, by the Peace of Augsburg, the princes and free cities of the Empire who acknowledge the Confession of Augsburg are free to worship and introduce Lutheranism within their territories. Lutheran states are to enjoy equal rights with Catholic, including membership of the Imperial Chamber. By imperial decree, those bishops and abbots who become Protestant are to lose their positions and income; the Diet of Augsburg comes to no agreement about this 'ecclesiastical reservation', which in effect buttressed the power of the Hapsburgs and helped cause the Thirty Years War; at the Diet of Augsburg, Philip of Spain renounces his claim to the Imperial Crown in favour of Maximilian, son of the Archduke Ferdinand.

D Oct: 21st, Parliament meets (*–Dec.* 9th) and opposes the idea that Philip be crowned King;
   25th, the Emperor Charles V resigns the government of the Netherlands, Milan, and Naples to Philip of Spain at a ceremony in Brussels.
   Nov: 12th, Bishop Stephen Gardiner, Chancellor, dies (succeeded by Nicholas Heath, Archbishop of York, *Jan.* 1556).
   Dec:

E In Geneva an anti-Calvinist rising is ruthlessly put down;
   a French colony is established on the Bay of Rio de Janeiro, as the first stage of 'Atlantic France';
   Japanese pirates besiege Nanking.

F **Politics, Economics, Law and Education**
Foundation of the English Muscovy Company for trade with Russia.
Tobacco is first brought to Spain from America.
Sir Thomas Pope founds Trinity College, Oxford.

G **Science, Technology and Discovery**
Zeno of Venice publishes a map of the northern seas.
Eden, *Decades of the New World*, the first account in English of the discoveries.
Pierre Belon, *L'Histoire de la nature des oyseaux*.
John Caius publishes his observations on the sweating sickness.
Walter Rippon makes the first coach in England, for the Earl of Rutland.

H **Philosophy, Religion and Scholarship**
Christophe Plantin settles in Antwerp where he sets up his printing press.
John Knox returns to preach in Scotland (returning to Geneva in *July* 1556).
Johannes Sleidanus, *De Statu Religionis et Reipublicae Carlo V, Caesare*.
An Aztec dictionary is published.

J **Art, Sculpture, Fine Arts and Architecture**
Painting:
Hans Eworth, *Lady Dacre* and *Mary Tudor*.
Tintoretto, *St. George's fight with the Dragon* and *Christ Washing the Disciples' feet*.
Titian, *The Martyrdom of St. Lawrence*.
Sculpture:
Michelangelo, *Pietà Palestrina* (Florence) and *Pietà Rondanini* (Rome, –1564).
Architecture:
Gray's Inn Hall, London (–1560).

K **Music**

L **Literature (including Drama)**
John Bourchier, Lord Berners, *Arthur of Lytell Brytayne*.
Lewis Brecht, *Euripus sive de inanitate rerum omnium* (first Jesuit play produced in Vienna).
Pierre de Ronsard, *Hymnes* (–1556).
Jörg Wickram, *Das Rollwagenbüchlein* (example of the collection of anecdotal facetiae known as *Schwanke*; see 1500, 1509).

M **Births and Deaths**
Oct. 16th Bishops Hugh Latimer (*c.* 65) and Ridley d. (*c.* 55).
Feb. 9th John Hooper, Bishop of Gloucester, d. (*c.* 60).
Nov. 12th Stephen Gardiner d. (*c.* 62).
Nov. 21st Georg Agricola (or Bauer) d. (65).
— Lancelot Andrewes b. (–1626).
— Henry Garnett b. (–1606).
— François de Malherbe b. (–1628).

1556   Charles V resigns Spain to Philip II and the Holy Roman Empire
to Ferdinand I

A Jan: 1st, Nicholas Heath, Archbishop of York, is appointed Lord Chancellor of England
(–1558);
16th, Charles V resigns Spain to Philip II (–1598);
20th, English Parliament meets (–*Mar.* 7th).
Feb: 5th, a truce is signed at Vaucelles between Henry II and Philip II.
Mar: 22nd, Cardinal Pole is consecrated Archbishop of Canterbury, following Thomas
Cranmer's deposition and execution, 21st;
28th, Pole assumes the functions of Papal Legate in England.

B Apr:
May:
Jun:

C Jul: Cardinal Carlo Caraffa persuades Henry II of France to renew the war against the
Hapsburgs in Italy;
the secretary of the Spanish ambassador is seized in Naples and the Duke of Alva sends
an ultimatum to Pope Paul IV.
Aug:
Sep: 4th, Spanish troops occupy the Campagna;
7th, Charles V resigns the Holy Roman Empire to his brother, Ferdinand I (–1564);
9th, Pope Paul IV, claiming the disposal of the Empire, refuses to acknowledge
Ferdinand I.

D Oct. 17th, Charles V leaves the Low Countries for Spain, to retire into the monastery of
Yuste.
Nov: 5th, Akbar, who has succeeded as Mogul Emperor of India (–1605) on the death of
Humayun, defeats the Afghans at Panipat;
17th, Ferdinand I forms a council of military affairs for the German territories of the
House of Hapsburg.
Dec: The French under François, Duke of Guise, invade Italy;
Pope Paul IV signs an armistice with Spain and calls for French aid.

E

F **Politics, Economics, Law and Education**
John Ponet, a refugee from Marian England, allows the right of resistance to an evil ruler in *A Shorte Treatise of Politicke Power*.
The Stationers' Company of London are granted the monopoly of printing in England.

G **Science, Technology and Discovery**
Stephen Burrough discovers Novaya Zemlya and the Kara Strait.
Georg Agricola (or Bauer), *De Re Metallica*, a pioneer study of minerology (posth.).

H **Philosophy, Religion and Scholarship**
Juan de Ávila (the Blessed), *Audi filia* (translated by Sir Tobie Matthew, –1620, as *A Rich Cabinet full of Spiritual Jewels*).
George Colvile translates *The Consolation of Philosophy* of Boethius.
The Jesuit Order is established in Prague.

J **Art, Sculpture, Fine Arts and Architecture**
Architecture:
Palladio, Villa Emo, Fanzola.
Palladio provides illustrations for Barbaro's *Vitruvius*.
San Micheli, Palazzo Grimalani, Venice.

K **Music**
De Lassus writes his first book of Masses.

L **Literature (including Drama)**

M Births and Deaths
Mar. 21st Thomas Cranmer d. (67).
July 31st Ignatius de Loyola d. (64).
Nov. 10th Richard Chancellor d. (*c.* 43).
Dec. — Nicholas Udall d. (52).
— Pietro Aretino d. (64).
— Lorenzo Lotto d. (76).
— Jacopo Pontormo d. (62).

A   Jan:
     Feb: 28th, an Anglo-Russian commercial treaty is signed in London, with Osep Napea, first envoy from Moscow.
     Mar: Philip II returns briefly to England, to ensure that England joins Spain in the war with France.

B   Apr: 25th, the Cardinals of Lorraine, Bourbon and Châtillon are appointed Inquisitors-General in France.
     May:
     Jun: 6th, Sebastian I succeeds to the throne of Portugal (–1578) on the death of his grand-father, John III; Sebastian's mother, Joanna of Austria, daughter of Charles V, acts as Regent (–1562);
     7th, England declares war on France, as ally of Spain;
     the Scots invade England.

C   Jul:
     Aug: 10th, the French under Gaspard de Coligny are defeated by a Spanish force under Philibert Emmanuel of Savoy, aided by English troops, at St. Quentin. Panic in Paris results in the Duke of Guise being summoned from Italy to command the French army in the north-east.
     Sep: 11th, a religious disputation is held at Worms (–Nov. 28th)—the final effort at conciliation between Catholics and Protestants in the Empire;
     Siena is incorporated in Tuscany;
     Pope Paul IV makes peace with Philip II of Spain.

D   Oct:
     Nov:
     Dec: 3rd, the First Covenant is signed in Scotland.

E   Bankruptcy in France and Spain, caused by the influx of American silver;
     The continual burnings of Protestants at Smithfield provoke disillusionment with Mary's reign;
     Russians invade Livonia in a war of succession to the Baltic lands of the German knights (–1571); Poland, Russia, Sweden and Denmark make conflicting claims;
     The Portuguese settle at Macao.

F **Politics, Economics, Law and Education**
National bankruptcies in France and Spain.
The Portuguese establish trading factories at Macao.
Gonville and Caius College, Cambridge, is refounded.
Repton School, Derbyshire, is founded.
Serious influenza epidemic in Europe.

G **Science, Technology and Discovery**
Robert Record, *Whetstone of Wit*, the first English treatise on algebra. Record invents the 'equal' sign (=) and explains the method of obtaining a square root.
Thomas Tusser, *A hundredth good pointes of husbandrie* (–1573).

H **Philosophy, Religion and Scholarship**
George Cavendish completes his *Life of Cardinal Wolsey* (not printed until 1641).
The Geneva *Testament*, probably translated by William Whittingham (the earliest English *Testament* printed in Roman type, and with verse divisions; –1560).
Sir Thomas More, *Works* written in English (posth. collection).
Sir Thomas North translates *El Relox de Principes* of Antonio de Guevara, as *The Diall of Princes* (*see* 1529).
Henry Howard, Earl of Surrey, translates Books I and IV of Virgil's *Aeneid* (posth.); he was the first poet to use blank verse in English.
First Covenant is signed in Scotland.
Pope Paul IV, through the Inquisition at Rome, issues the first Roman *Index Librorum Prohibitorum* (reissued 1559, 1564).

J **Art, Sculpture, Fine Arts and Architecture**

K **Music**

L **Literature (including Drama)**
The Sack-Full of Newes, burlesque produced at the Boar's Head Inn, Aldgate (anon. suppressed—the first play to be subjected to complete censorship in Tudor England).
Tottel's Miscellany (of Songs and Sonnets by Wyatt, Surrey and other courtly poets, compiled by Richard Tottel and Nicholas Grimald, publishers, and one of the first English anthologies).

M **Births and Deaths**
June 28th Philip Howard, Earl of Arundel, b. (–1595).
July 28th Anne of Cleves d. (41).
Sept. 1st Jacques Cartier d. (66).
Sept. 13th John Cheke d. (43).
— Vittoria Accoramboni d. (72).

A   Jan: 7th, The French under François, Duke of Guise, capture Calais from England. The loss of Calais is regarded as a national disaster and provokes widespread distrust of Mary's Spanish marriage, so that all hopes of Philip II succeeding to the throne on Mary's death are dashed;
9th, Geneva becomes independent from Berne Canton.
Feb:
Mar: 14th, Ferdinand I assumes the title of Holy Roman Emperor without being crowned by the Pope.

B   Apr: 24th, Mary Queen of Scots marries the Dauphin, the future Francis II.
May:
Jun: 22nd, the French take Thionville from the English.

C   Jul: 13th, a Flemish army under the Duke of Egmont in the service of Philip II of Spain, aided by an English fleet, defeats the French at Gravelines;
29th, Lord Clinton leads an English expedition to Brittany and burns Conquet, but makes no attempt to attack Brest.
Aug:
Sep: 21st, the ex-Emperor Charles V dies.

D   Oct: Peace conference between England, France and Spain opens at Cambrai (leads to the Treaty of Cateau-Cambrésis of *Apr.* 1559).
Nov: 5th, English Parliament meets (–17th);
17th, accession of Elizabeth I, Queen of England (–1603), on the death of Mary I;
20th, Sir William Cecil is appointed a principal Secretary of State.
Dec: 22nd, Nicholas Bacon is appointed Lord Keeper of the great Seal of England (–1579);
great numbers of English Protestant exiles return from Zurich and Geneva.

E   Akbar, Mogul Emperor of India, conquers Gwalior.

F **Politics, Economics, Law and Education**

Thomas Gresham formulates 'Gresham's Law' in his suggestions for reforming English currency.

Jean Nicot, French Ambassador in Spain, sends samples of tobacco ('Nicotine') to Paris. The Portuguese introduce the habit of taking snuff to Europe.

Jena University is founded (*Feb.* 2nd) on the scheme devised by the late Elector, John Frederick, of Saxony.

G **Science, Technology and Discovery**

Anthony Jenkinson journeys to Bokhara (–1559).

H **Philosophy, Religion and Scholarship**

G. Acontio (or Jacopo Aconzio), *De Methodo, hoc est, de recte investigandarum tradendarumque scientiarium ratione* (Basle)—an attempt to introduce Unitarian doctrines into England (*Dec.*).

John Knox, *The first blast of the trumpet against the monstrous regiment of women.*

Thomas Phaer translates Virgil's *Aeneid*, bks. I–VII (completed –1562; 1584 by Thomas Twyne).

The Bavarian Royal Library, Munich, founded by Albert V of Bavaria.

J **Art, Sculpture, Fine Arts and Architecture**

K **Music**

L **Literature (including Drama)**

Joachim du Bellay, *Les Antiquités de Rome* and *Les Regrets* (sonnet sequences).

Marguérite de Navarre, *Heptaméron* (in imitation of Boccaccio).

M **Births and Deaths**

July — Robert Greene b. (–1592).
Oct. 21st Julius Caesar Scaliger d. (74).
Nov. — Thomas Kyd b. (–1595).
— Thomas Lodge b. (–1625).
— George Peele b. (–1598).

A Jan: 1st, accession of Frederick II of Denmark and Norway (–1588) on the death of
      Christian II;
      13th, coronation of Elizabeth I;
      23rd (–May 8th), Parliament meets and passes the Acts of Supremacy and Uniformity;
      Count de Feria, Spanish ambassador in London, presses Philip II's suit for Elizabeth's
      hand.
   Feb: 16th, Pope Paul IV issues the bull Cum Ex Apostolatus, advocating that all sovereigns
      who support heresy be deposed.
   Mar: Peace conference between England, France and Spain reassembles at Cateau-
      Cambrésis;
      the Elector of Trier, Archbishop John of Leyen, is forced by Calvinists to leave his
      See.

B Apr: 2nd, peace treaty is signed at Cateau-Cambrésis between England and France:
      Calais to remain in French hands for 8 years and then be restored to England under
      a penalty of 500,000 crowns; both countries undertake to restrain from acts of
      aggression in Scotland and any such act by England to nullify France's obligation to
      return Calais;
      3rd, by the terms of the peace between France and Spain, France restores Piedmont
      and Savoy to Emmanuel Philibert of Savoy, but retains Saluzzo and the bishoprics of
      Metz, Toul and Verdun. Spanish possession of Franche-Comté is reaffirmed;
      Robert, Lord Dudley, Master of the Horse, establishes himself as chief favourite of
      Elizabeth I.
   May: 2nd, John Knox returns to Scotland and
      10th, preaches a defiant sermon at Perth, inciting the Protestant Lords of the Congre-
      gation to rise. They seize Edinburgh and destroy religious houses at Stirling, Scone
      and St. Andrews, and subsequently approach Elizabeth I for aid;
      Selim and Bayazid, sons of Suleiman I, Sultan of Turkey, fight for the future succession
      at Konia in Asia Minor; the defeated Bayazid flees to Persia, where he is murdered.
   Jun: 24th, the Elizabethan Prayer Book is first used;
      27th, Margaret of France marries Emmanuel Philibert, Duke of Savoy;
      the new Elector Frederick III of the Palatinate (–1576) attempts, at the Diet of Augs-
      burg, to delay supplies for the Turkish war until the religious grievances are settled.

C Jul: 10th, accession of Francis II of France (–1560) on the death of his father Henry II in
      a tournament; François, Duke of Guise, and his brother, the Cardinal of Lorraine,
      seize power. Francis's wife, Mary Queen of Scots, assumes the title Queen of England.
   Aug: 18th, Pope Paul IV dies.
   Sep:

D Oct: 21st, the Scottish Lords of the Congregation depose the Regent, Mary of Guise for
      refusing to prevent the French from fortifying Leith;
      the Swedes take Estonia from Livonia.
   Nov:
   Dec: 17th, Matthew Parker is consecrated Archbishop of Canterbury (–1575);
      18th, Elizabeth I sends to the Scottish Lords of the Congregation aid by land and sea
      for driving the French from Scotland (–1560);
      25th, Giovanni Medici elected Pope Pius IV (–1565).

E

F **Politics, Economics, Law and Education**
An Edict of Henry II makes printing without authority punishable by death in France.
Ferdinand I attempts to standardise the coinage in the Holy Roman Empire.
Geneva Academy is founded (it acquires University status in 1873).

G **Science, Technology and Discovery**

H **Philosophy, Religion and Scholarship**
Matthias Flacius, *Ecclesiastica Historica* (–1574).
Count Paul Scalich de Lika, *Encyclopaedia seu orbis* . . . (first use of the word 'encyclopaedia' in the title of a printed book; *see* 1531 F).
James Amyot's translation of Plutarch's *Parallel Lives* from the Greek into French (–1579).
Elizabeth's *Act of Supremacy* passed (*May* 8th); and *Act of Uniformity* ordains the Elizabethan *Prayer Book*.
Bishop John Jewel's Sermon at Paul's Cross (*Nov.* 26th), starts the 'Apology for the Church of England' controversy (–1562).
Index Librorum Prohibitorum (List of Prohibited books) drawn up (*Jan.*) under the authority of Paul IV.
Final Latin version of Calvin's *Institutes*.

J **Art, Sculpture, Fine Arts and Architecture**
Painting:
Pieter Breughel, *Proverbs* and *Battle of Carnival*.
Hans Eworth, portraits of the *Duchess of Suffolk* and *Adrian Stokes*.
Titian, *The Entombment of Christ* and *Diana and Calliste*.

K **Music**
Adrien Le Roy of Paris publishes a collection of music by Clément Jannequin.

L **Literature (including Drama)**
William Baldwin's edition of *Mirror for Magistrates* ('wherein may be seen by example of other, howe grevous plages vices are punished') (19 tragedies in verse; enlarged –1578, to include Thomas Sackville's *Induction*, which introduced a new age of Elizabethan verse).
Jorge de Montemayor, *La Diana* (Castilian pastoral romance).

M **Births and Deaths**
Jan. 29th Thomas Pope d. (*c.* 52).
Feb. 18th Isaac Casaubon b. (–1614).
— George Chapman b. (–1634).
— Johann Tzerclaes, Count of Tilly, b. (–1632).

1560   Conspiracy at Amboise—Treaty of Edinburgh ends the 'Auld Alliance'

A   **Jan:** Margaret of Parma, Regent of the Netherlands, recalls Spanish troops to maintain order after Protestant incidents in Holland and Zeeland following establishment of new Catholic bishoprics.
   Feb: Turkish galleys rout Spanish fleet under Duke of Medina Celi off Tripoli;
   27th, Treaty of Berwick between England and the Lords of the Scottish Congregation for expelling French from Scotland.
   Mar: 15th, Huguenot conspiracy at Amboise fails to rescue King Francis II of France from the Guise faction. The Prince of Condé is subsequently imprisoned by the Duke of Guise;
   Protestant immigrants are expelled from the imperial city of Aachen (*–May*).

B   **Apr:** Alarmed at Huguenot threat, Francis II appoints Michel de L'Hôpital, Constable of France, as chief minister, who promises liberty of worship.
   May:
   Jun: 10th, Mary of Guise, Queen Dowager of Scotland dies.

C   **Jul:** 6th, by Treaty of Edinburgh between England and Scotland, French troops are evacuated, a Protestant Council of Regents is appointed, Queen Elizabeth's sovereignty to England is recognised and the claims of Mary Queen of Scots to the English throne are annulled. The 'Auld Alliance' between Scotland and France is thus ended; but Mary refuses to ratify the treaty.
   Aug: The Scottish Parliament abolishes papal jurisdiction and approves a Calvinistic Confession of Faith, drawn up by John Knox and others, thus founding the Church of Scotland.
   Sep: 29th, Eric XIV succeeds as King of Sweden (–1568) on death of Gustavus I.

D   **Oct:** Vaudois attack Savoy in defence of their Protestant Confession (*–June* 1561).
   Nov:
   Dec: 5th, Charles IX succeeds as King of France (–1574), on death of Francis II, with Catherine de' Medici as Regent; Mary Queen of Scots, widow of Francis, plans to return to Scotland;
   General Assembly meets in Scotland to approve Calvinistic *First Book of Discipline*, compiled largely by John Knox, as basis of doctrine and government of Church of Scotland.

E   Madrid becomes the capital of Spain;
   Treaty of Luzen between Savoy and six Catholic Swiss Cantons for mutual defence;
   In India the Mogul Emperor Akbar conquers the Rajput kingdom and Lower Bengal and establishes a new capital at Agra.

F **Politics, Economics, Law and Education**
William Cecil reforms the English currency.
Westminster School is founded.

G **Science, Technology and Discovery**
The first scientific society, Academia Secretorum Naturae, is founded in Naples.
Battista Porta in *Magia Naturalis* discusses the structure of the eye and invents the Camera Obscura.

H **Philosophy, Religion and Scholarship**
Matthias Flacius and others, *The Magdeburg Centuries* (church history compiled by a number of Lutheran theologians, up to 1574).
John Knox, ... *Gods eternal Predestination* ... (Geneva).
Jean Calvin's final French edition of *The Institutes*.
Étienne Pasquier, *Recherches de la France*, bk. 1 (completed later, published posth. 1621).
Francesco Patrizi, *Della historia* (early work on the philosophy and methodology of history).
Peter Whitehorne translates Machiavelli's *The Art of War* (of 1521).
William Whittingham publishes *Geneva Bible* and the first 'family' Bible, with Roman type, numbered verses and maps (known as the *Breeches Bible*).
A papal Nuncio is appointed at Vienna.
Parliament in Scotland adopts the Calvinistic Confession; and (*Aug.*) abolishes papal jurisdiction.

J **Art, Sculpture, Fine Arts and Architecture**
Painting:
 Pieter Breughel, *Adoration of the Magi* (I).
 Jacopo Tintoretto, *Man in Armour; Susannah and the Elders;* and *Descent from the Cross* (–1570).
 Titian, *Venus with a Mirror*.
 Paolo Veronese, frescoes, Villa Maser.
Architecture:
 Palladio, Refectory, St. Giorgio Magiore, Venice.

K **Music**

L **Literature (including Drama)**
Hsü Wei, *Ching P'Ing Mei* (the first classic Chinese novel of social realism).
Pierre de Ronsard, *Les Discours* (poems about the wars of religion).

M **Births and Deaths**
Jan. 1st Joachim du Bellay d. (*c*. 38).
Apr. 19th Philipp Melanchthon d. (63).
Oct. 18th Jacobus Arminius b. (–1609).
Nov. 25th Andrea Doria d. (*c*. 94).
— Annibale Carracci b. (–1609).
— Hugh Myddleton b. (–1631).
— Robert Greene b. (–1592).

A Jan: The triumvirate of Montmorency, Guise and St. André in France provokes militant opposition of Condé and Coligny, but at the meeting of the States-General at Orleans, Michel de L'Hôpital appeals to moderates to rally to the Crown;

28th, by the Edict of Orleans persecution of the Huguenots is suspended; the Prince of Condé presses for liberty of conscience.

Feb:

Mar: Emmanuel Philibert, Duke of Savoy, is forced to grant religious toleration to the Vaudois, whom he is unable to subdue.

B Apr:

May: St. Paul's Cathedral, London, is badly damaged by fire.

Jun:

C Jul: 16th, German engineers begin mining operations for copper and lead in England.

Aug: 19th, Mary Queen of Scots, denied a passage through England on returning from France, lands at Leith in Scotland.

Sep: At the Poissy Conference the Cardinal of Lorraine and Theodore Beza discuss the problem of the Hugenots.

D Oct:

Nov:

Dec:

E The Baltic states of the Order of the Teutonic Knights are secularised. Livonia, fearing Russian attack, transfers its allegiance from the Teutonic Knights to Poland.

Eric XIV of Sweden annexes Reval.

F **Politics, Economics, Law and Education**
An ordinance in France permits craft guilds to revise their statutes under Crown supervision.
The first Calvinist refugees from Flanders settle in England, at Sandwich, as cloth-workers.
Merchant Taylors' School, London, is founded.

G **Science, Technology and Discovery**
Gabriello Fallopius, *Observationes anatomicae*, a pioneer study.

H **Philosophy, Religion and Scholarship**
Sir Thomas Hoby translates *The Courtier* (*Il Cortegiano* of 1528) by Baldassare, Count Castiglione.
Thomas Norton translates John Calvin's *Institution of Christian Religion* (of 1536).
Julius Caesar Scaliger, *Poetics* (*Poetices libri septem*) interpreting the literary theories of Aristotle.
Scottish Church Ministers draw up the *Confession of Faith*, for the establishment of Protestantism (largely the work of John Knox).
Portuguese monks at Goa introduce printing into India.

J **Art, Sculpture, Fine Arts and Architecture**
Painting:
François Clouet, *Charles IX of France*.
Architecture:
Cornelius Floris, Antwerp town hall (–1565).
Michelangelo, St. Maria degli Angeli, Rome; also Porta Pia, Rome (–1565).
Palladio, Monastery of S. Maria della Carita, Venice.

K **Music**

L **Literature (including Drama)**
William Baldwin, *A Marvellous Hystory intituled Beware the Cat* (early example of fiction).

M **Births and Deaths**
Jan. 22nd Francis Bacon b. (–1626).
Oct. — Anthony Babington b. (–1586).
Dec. 9th Edwin Sandys b. (–1629).
— Louis Bourgeois d. (51).

A Jan: 6th, Shane O'Neill, Earl of Tyrone, ends his first rebellion by surrendering to Queen Elizabeth;

15th, the third session of the Council of Trent opens (*–Dec.* 1563);

17th, Michel de l'Hôpital promulgates the Edict of St. Germain, which recognises the Huguenots in France. The Duke of Guise, the Cardinal of Lorraine and Montmorency form a militant league to prevent the edict from being enforced.

Feb:

Mar: 1st, 1,200 French Huguenots are slain by order of the Guises at the Massacre of Vassy, which provokes the First War of Religion.

B Apr:

May: 26th, Shane O'Neill leads a second rebellion in Ireland (–1567).

Jun: 1st, the Emperor Ferdinand I and Suleiman I, Sultan of Turkey, sign an eight-year truce.

C Jul: Cardinal Henry of Portugal succeeds Joanna of Austria as Regent for Sebastian I of Portugal.

Aug:

Sep: 22nd, Queen Elizabeth signs the Treaty of Hampton Court with the Huguenot leader, Louis I de Bourbon, Prince of Condé, for English troops to occupy Le Havre and Dieppe and to assist in the defence of Rouen;

22nd, Maximilian, son of the Emperor Ferdinand I, succeeds as King of Bohemia (he is elected King of the Romans *Nov.* 20th).

D Oct: 4th, English troops under the Earl of Warwick occupy Le Havre;

Queen Elizabeth is dangerously ill from smallpox;

John Hawkins leaves Plymouth for Sierra Leone to begin operating the slave trade between Africa and Hispaniola.

Nov: 5th, the rebellion of George Gordon, Earl of Huntly, in Scotland is crushed by the Earl of Moray at Corrichie.

Dec: 19th, at the Battle of Dreux in the French Civil War, the Duke of Guise bars the progress of German allies of the Huguenots and marches towards Orleans; Condé and Montmorency are taken prisoners;

Catherine de' Medici pays Emmanuel Philibert of Savoy 100,000 scudi to retain French garrisons at Pinerolo and Savigliano and undertakes to remove other troops; Turin again becomes the capital of Savoy.

E Ribault establishes a Huguenot colony at Charlesfort, at Coligny's instigation, and claims Florida.

F   **Politics, Economics, Law and Education**
Milled coins are introduced to England.
Earliest English slave-trading expedition under John Hawkins, between Guinea and the West Indies.

G   **Science, Technology and Discovery**
William Turner publishes a survey of European spas and watering-places.

H   **Philosophy, Religion and Scholarship**
Richard Grafton, *An Abridgement of the Chronicles of England.*
John Jewel, *Apology for the Church of England* (*Apologia Ecclesiae Anglicanae*), a defence of the Elizabethan settlement of 1559.
The Articles of Religion of 1552 in England are reduced to the *Thirty-Nine Articles.*
Thomas Sternhold and John Hopkins translate *The Whole Book of Psalms* (old version; new version –1696).
Jan. 15th. The third session of the Council of Trent meets (–1563).
The Elector Palatine, Frederick III, the first Calvinist elector in Germany, orders the Heidelberg Catechism to be drawn up.

J   **Art, Sculpture, Fine Arts and Architecture**
Painting:
Pieter Breughel, *Two Chained Monkeys; Death of Saul;* and *Fall of the Rebel Angels.*
François Clouet, *Pierre Quthe.*
Hans Eworth, *Thomas, 4th Duke of Norfolk.*
Paul Veronese, *Marriage of Cana.*

K   **Music**
Gasparo Bertolotti (Gasparo da Salo) moves to Brescia to become the first famous violin-maker.

L   **Literature (including Drama)**
Thomas Norton and Thomas Sackville, Lord Buckhurst, *Gorboduc,* earliest English tragedy in blank verse (printed as *Ferrex and Porrex,* 1571).
Rabelais, *Pantagruel* continued (bk. v; posth.; begun 1532).

M   **Births and Deaths**
Nov. 12th Peter Martyr d. (62).
Nov. 25th Lope de Vega b. (–1635).
— Adrian Willaert d. (*c.* 82).

1563   The Council of Trent ends—The Plague comes to England

A   Jan: 11th, the English Parliament meets and presses Queen Elizabeth to marry and settle the succession.
Feb: 24th, Francis, Duke of Guise, is killed before Orleans.
Mar: 19th, the Peace of Amboise ends the First War of Religion in France; under its terms the Huguenots are granted limited toleration, being permitted to exercise their religion in all places where it was established, except Paris, before the war. The factions in France unite to expel the English troops.

B   Apr: 10th, the English Parliament is prorogued; legislation passed includes the Statute of Apprentices.
May: Ivan IV of Russia conquers Polotski in Eastern Livonia, taking it from Poland (intermittent warfare between Russia and Poland continues to 1582).
Jun:

C   Jul: 27th, French army regains Le Havre, where the English garrison is stricken with plague; soldiers returning to England introduce the plague;
the Turks fail to capture Oran in North Africa.
Aug: 17th, Charles IX of France, now 13, is declared to be of age.
Sep: 8th, Maximilian, King of the Romans, is elected King of Hungary.

D   Oct: Brandenburg and Poland sign a treaty for the ultimate succession of the Elector of Brandenburg in Prussia.
Nov: The English Merchants Adventurers Company, finding their activities in Antwerp curtailed by the Spanish embargo on trade, leave for Emden (–1564).
Dec: 6th, the Council of Trent ends.

E

F Politics, Economics, Law and Education

Acts for the relief of the poor (–1597) and for regulating apprentices (–1814) are passed by the English Parliament. The latter Act empowers local justices of the peace to settle the level of wages.

General outbreak of plague in Europe, spreading to England, kills over 20,000 inhabitants of London.

G Science, Technology and Discovery

The Portuguese navigator Juan Fernandez discovers the island in the S. Pacific named after him.

Gerardus Mercator surveys Lorraine at the request of the Duke of Lorraine to make the first detailed, accurate map.

H Philosophy, Religion and Scholarship

John Foxe, *Actes and Monuments* (popularly known as *Foxe's Book of Martyrs;* first English edition; illustrated).

Ivan IV orders the foundation of the first printing press in Russia.

The Counter-Reformation begins in Bavaria, with Jesuit control of Ingoldstadt University.

J Art, Sculpture, Fine Arts and Architecture

Painting:

Pieter Breughel, *Tower of Babel.*

Hans Eworth, *Lord Darnley and his Brothers.*

Sculpture:

Giovanni da Bologna, Neptune fountain, Bologna (–1567).

Architecture:

Herrera begins to build the Escorial for Philip II of Spain.

John Shute, *First and Chief Grounds of Architecture.*

K Music

Byrd is appointed organist at Lincoln Cathedral (*Feb.* 27th).

L Literature (including Drama)

Thomas Sackville, Lord Buckhurst, *Induction*, intended as the first item in a new collection of verse stories on the lines of *A Mirror for Magistrates.*

M Births and Deaths

Nov. — John Bale d. (68).

— John Bull b. (–1628).

— Pierre de Chastelard d. (23).

— John Dowland b. (–1626).

— Michael Drayton b. (–1631).

— Diego de Siloe d. (68).

A Jan: 24th, Pope Pius IV publishes decrees confirming the work of the Council of Trent in
settling questions of dogma;
24th (*–May* 1st, 1566), Catherine de' Medici makes a tour of France to present her son
Charles IX to his subjects.
Feb:
Mar: 13th, Philip II recalls Cardinal Granvelle from the Netherlands at the request of the
Regent Margaret of Parma and of the Nationalist Party led by Count Egmont.

B Apr: 11th, the Peace of Troyes ends the war between England and France; England re-
nounces her claim to Calais on payment by France of 222,000 crowns.
May: 31st, Lübeck and Denmark defeat Swedes off Gotland.
Jun: Ivan IV of Russia in the course of a struggle for power against the boyars, led by
Prince Kurbsky, is forced to withdraw from Moscow.

C Jul: 18th, the English Merchants Adventurers Company is granted a new royal charter;
25th, Maximilian II succeeds as Holy Roman Emperor and as King in Austria, Bohemia
and Hungary (–1576) on the death of Ferdinand I; the rest of the Hapsburg dominions
pass to the Archduke Charles.
Aug: Berne restores Gex and Chablais to Savoy;
18th, Philip II orders that the decrees of the Council of Trent are to be enforced
throughout his dominions.
Sep: 29th, Lord Robert Dudley is created Earl of Leicester.

D Oct: 18th, John Hawkins leaves Plymouth on his second voyage to the New World
(*–Sept.* 1565).
Nov: 13th, Pius IV promulgates *professio fidei*, a final definition of Roman Catholicism.
Dec:

E Cosimo de' Medici resigns the government of Tuscany to his son, Francesco.

F **Politics, Economics, Law and Education**

G **Science, Technology and Discovery**
   Bartholomes Eustachio, *Opuscula Anatomica*.

H **Philosophy, Religion and Scholarship**
   Wierus attacks belief in witchcraft.
   The *Scots Psalter*.
   Index Librorum Prohibitorum is published (*Nov.* 24th) after receiving papal approval as
   the list of prohibited books (1543, 1557, 1559).
   The Council of Trent's *Professio Fidei* is confirmed by Pope Pius IV, together with Rules
   De Libris Prohibitis (–1545, 1551, 1562).
   The term 'Puritan' is first used in England.
   Counter Reformation begins in Poland.
   Philip Neri founds the *Congregation of the Oratory* in Rome (*May* 25th).

J **Art, Sculpture, Fine Arts and Architecture**
   Painting:
      Pieter Breughel, *Christ Carrying the Cross;* and *Adoration of the Magi* (II).
      Jacopo Tintoretto, Paintings for the Scuolo Grande di San Rocco (–1587).
   Architecture:
      Philibert Delorme designs the Tuileries, Paris.

K **Music**
   One of earliest extant violins made by Andrea Amati is dated to this year.

L **Literature (including Drama)**

M **Births and Deaths**
   Feb. 6th Christopher Marlowe b. (–1593).
   Feb. 15th Galilei Galileo b. (–1642).
   Feb. 18th Michelangelo d. (89).
   Apr. 23rd William Shakespeare b. (–1616).
   May 27th John Calvin d. (54).
   — Bernadino Ochino d. (77).

1565　The Turks attack Malta—The Bayonne Meeting

A Jan: Count Egmont is sent to Philip II to seek concessions to Calvinists in Holland and
Zeeland.
Feb:
Mar:

B Apr:
May: 2nd, Shane O'Neill, Earl of Tyrone, Irish rebel, defeats the MacDonnells at
Ballycastle;
(–*Sept*.) the Knights of St. John, under La Valette, defend Malta from the Turks.
Jun: 14th (*July* 2nd), Queen Catherine de' Medici and the Duke of Alva meet at Bayonne
to discuss measures for eradicating Protestantism.

C Jul: 29th, Mary Queen of Scots marries Henry, Lord Darnley, in Edinburgh.
Aug:
Sep: With the arrival of Spanish troops from Sicily the Turks are obliged to abandon the
siege of Malta.

D Oct:
Nov:
Dec: 9th, Pope Pius IV dies.

E

F Politics, Economics, Law and Education
Pierre de la Place, *Histoire de nostre temps*.
Regnier de la Planche, *Le Livre des marchands*, a tract against the House of Lorraine.
Sir Thomas Gresham founds the Royal Exchange, London.

G Science, Technology and Discovery
The Royal College of Physicians, London, is empowered to carry out human dissections.
Pencils are first manufactured in England.
Sir John Hawkins introduces tobacco to England.

H Philosophy, Religion and Scholarship
G. Aconcio, *Stratagemata Satanae*, advocates religious toleration.
Thomas Cooper, *Thesaurus Linguae Romanae et Britannicae*.
Arthur Golding translates Ovid's *Metamorphoses*, bks. 1–4 (completed 1567).
John Stow, *A Summarie of English Chronicles*.
Bernardino Telesio, *De rerum natura* (enlarged edition –1586) (foreshadows the empirical method).

J Art, Sculpture, Fine Arts and Architecture
Painting:
Pieter Breughel, *A Country Wedding; Hunters in the Snow;* and *Stormy Days.*
Sculpture:
Giovanni da Bologna, *Samson* (–1566).
Architecture:
Palladio, St. Giorgio Maggiore Church, Venice; also St. Francesco della Vigna, Venice.

K Music
Palestrina, *Missa Papae Marcelli.*

L Literature (including Drama)
Giambattista Cinzio Giraldi, *Ecatommiti* (collection of moral and love tales—probably the source of Shakespeare's *Othello* and *Measure for Measure*).
El Abencerraje y de la Hermosa Jarifa (anon.; revised version of this 16th-century Spanish *novella* published in Villegas: *Inventario*).
Pierre de Ronsard, *Élegies, Mascarades at Bergeries.*

M Births and Deaths
Mar. 17th Alexander Ales d. (64).
May 14th Nicolaus von Amsdorf d. (71).
— Jean Grolier d. (86).

A Jan: 7th, Michaele Ghislieri is elected Pope Pius V (–1572).
Feb:
Mar: 9th, David Rizzio, Mary Queen of Scots' confidential secretary, is murdered in Holyrood House on Darnley's orders.

B Apr: 5th, by the Compromise of Breda, Louis of Nassau, Philip de Marnix and Henry, Count of Brederode organise resistance to Spanish persecution in the Netherlands in a confederacy of lesser nobility, nicknamed *Les Gueux*, and present the Regent in Brussels with a petition for the withdrawal of the Inquisition and liberty of conscience.
May: Despite the truce (of 1562), the Turko-Hungarian war is renewed (–1569).
Jun: 19th, James VI of Scotland is born.

C Jul:
Aug: 10th (–18th), iconoclastic riots in the Netherlands by fanatical Calvinists in Hond-schoote, Valenciennes, Amsterdam and (16th–17th) Antwerp; the Regent Margaret abolishes the Inquisition.
Sep: 5th, Selim II (The Sot) succeeds as Sultan of Turkey (–1574) on the death of Suleiman I; henceforward the Janissaries become a hereditary caste;
30th, English Parliament re-assembles.

D Oct: Catherine de' Medici issues the Moulins Ordinances for extending the power of the French Crown in legislation.
Nov:
Dec:

E The Turks take the island of Chios from Genoa.

F **Politics, Economics, Law and Education**

G **Science, Technology and Discovery**
>   G. Blundeville, *Foure Chiefest Offices belonging to Horsemanship*, a manual of veterinary science.

H **Philosophy, Religion and Scholarship**
>   William Adlington translates *The Golden Ass* of Apuleius.
>   Johannes Aventius (Thurmair), *Bayerische Chronik*.
>   Jean Bodin, *Methodus ad facilem historiarum cognitionem* (on the philosophy of history).
>   Archbishop Matthew Parker's 'Advertisements', laying down the practice of the Anglican Clergy in matters of ritual, provoke the Vestarian Controversy.
>   Heinrich Bullinger in his *Second Helvetian Confession* combines Calvinism with Zwinglianism.
>   The Calvinist Synod of Antwerp's *Confessio Belgica*.

J **Art, Sculpture, Fine Arts and Architecture**
>   Painting:
>   Pieter Breughel, *St. John the Baptist*; *Numbering the People*; and *Wedding Dance*.

K **Music**

L **Literature (including Drama)**
>   George Gascoigne, *The Supposes* (adapted and translated from Ariosto's *Suppositi*, and the earliest prose comedy extant in English dramatic literature) acted at Gray's Inn.
>   *Jocasta*, adapted and translated from Euripides acted (–1575).
>   William Painter, *The Palace of Pleasure Beautified ... with Pleasaunt Histories and excellent Novelles selected out of divers ... authors* (especially Boccaccio and Bandello).
>   Nicholas Udall, *Ralph Roister Doister* (the first original native comedy in English literature—written for Eton College, St. Andrew's Day celebrations).
>   Lewis Wager, *A New Enterlude ... the Life and Repentaunce of Marie Magdalene*.

M **Births and Deaths**
>   Apr. 22nd Diane de Poitiers d. (66).
>   May 10th Leonhard Fuchs d. (65).
>   June 19th James VI and I b. (–1625).
>   July 2nd Nostradamus d. (62).
>   July — Bartolomé de Las Casas d. (91).
>   Sept. 1st Edward Alleyn b. (–1626).
>   Sept. 6th Suleiman I ('The Magnificent') d. (72).
>   Oct. 13th Richard Boyle, Earl of Cork, b. (–1643).
>   Nov. 19th Robert Devereux, Earl of Essex, b. (–1601).
>   — Giacomo Aconcio d. (74).

1567 Mary Queen of Scots Abdicates—Alva's Reign of Terror in the Netherlands

A Jan: 2nd, English Parliament is dissolved; Elizabeth has refused Parliament's request to name her successor but undertakes to pursue marriage negotiations with Charles, Archduke of Austria.

Feb: 10th, Darnley is murdered at Kirk o'Field, Edinburgh, on the orders of James Hepburn, Earl of Bothwell.

Mar: 13th, Margaret of Parma, Regent of the Netherlands, with German mercenaries, annihilates 2,000 Calvinist sectaries led by John de Marnix at Austruweel.

B Apr: 19th, Bothwell carries off Mary Queen of Scots to Dunbar;

Valenciennes, the centre for Calvinist disturbances in the southern Netherlands, surrenders to the Governor of Hainault, who inflicts savage punishment.

May: 15th, Mary Queen of Scots marries Bothwell in Edinburgh.

Jun: 2nd, Shane O'Neill, Earl of Tyrone, the Irish rebel, is assassinated following his invasion of Tyrconnel;

15th, at the battle of Carberry Hill, the Lords of the Covenant rout Bothwell's supporters; the Earl escapes to Norway but Mary is taken captive, and, 17th, is imprisoned in Lochleven Castle;

20th, the Earl of Morton discovers the Casket Letters.

C Jul: 24th, Mary Queen of Scots is forced to abdicate and appoint her step-brother, the Earl of Moray, as Regent for the infant James.

Aug: 8th, the Duke of Alva arrives in the Netherlands as military governor with 10,000 veteran Spanish and Italian troops;

22nd, the Duke of Alva establishes the Council of Blood, and begins a reign of terror.

Sep: 9th, the Duke of Alva arrests Counts Egmont and Hoorn;

the Emperor Maximilian II establishes a Monastic Council to superintend the clergy in the Hapsburg dominions;

29th, the Huguenot Conspiracy of Meaux, to capture Charles IX, provokes the Second War of Religion in France; the court repairs to Paris, to which Condé lays siege.

D Oct: 6th, Margaret of Parma resigns the regency of the Netherlands, and the Duke of Alva takes complete command. Calvinist refugees from the Netherlands land in England.

Nov: John Casimir leads an army of German Protestants to fight for the French Huguenots.

Dec:

E In Japan Nobunaga deposes the Shogun and acquires dictatorial powers, to bring an era of peace.

F   **Politics, Economics, Law and Education**

Philip II establishes the archives at Simancas, appointing as curator Jeronimo de Zurita, who gathers material for his *Anales de la Corona de Aragon* (to 1576).

Helmstedt University, Brunswick, is founded.

Laurence Sheriff founds Rugby School.

G   **Science, Technology and Discovery**

H   **Philosophy, Religion and Scholarship**

Francesco Guicciardini, *L'Historia d'Italia* (*Storia d'Italia*) (posth. complete edition).

Edward Hake translates Thomas à Kempis, *The Imitation of Christ*.

John Day cuts an Anglo-Saxon type for Archbishop Parker's edition of Asser's *Life of Alfred*.

Separatist congregations meet secretly in London.

Lay patronage is adopted for the Church of Scotland.

Martin Chemnitz, a Lutheran, draws up *Corpus doctrinae Prutenicum*.

J   **Art, Sculpture, Fine Arts and Architecture**

Painting:

Pieter Breughel, *Adoration of the Magi* (III; snow scene); *Fools' Paradise;* and *Conversion of St. Paul.*

Titian, *Jacopo de Strada* (–1568).

Sculpture:

Giovanni de Bologna, *Mercury.*

K   **Music**

L   **Literature (including Drama)**

George Turberville, *Epitaphs, Epigrams, Songs, and Sonets.*

M   **Births and Deaths**

Feb. 12th Thomas Campion b. (–1620).

May — Claudio Monteverdi b. (–1643).

June 2nd Shane O'Neill d. (*c.* 34).

Aug. 21st St. Francis de Sales b. (–1622).

Sept. 21st Pietro Carnesecchi d. (59).

Nov. 1st Diego, Count Gondomar, b. (–1626).

— Richard Burbage b. (–1619).

— Thomas Nashe b. (–1601).

A Jan: 24th, the Duke of Alva declares William of Orange (the Silent) an outlaw.
Feb: 17th, Sultan Selim II makes peace with the Emperor Maximilian II; in return for nominal territorial concessions the Emperor undertakes to pay the Sultan an annual tribute of 30,000 ducats;
Michel de L'Hôpital is dismissed from the Chancellorship of France;
Prince of Condé raises the siege of Orléans.
Mar: 23rd, the Treaty of Longjumean ends the Second War of Religion in France, confirming the concessions to the Huguenots of the Treaty of Amboise (1563).

B Apr:
May: 2nd, Mary Queen of Scots escapes from Lochleven;
13th, her supporters are defeated at Langside by Moray, and, 16th, Mary takes refuge in England;
23rd, William of Orange with German mercenaries defeats a Spanish force under Count Aremberg at Heiligerlee; this action makes the beginning proper of the Revolt of the Netherlands;
28th, the Duke of Alva confiscates the properties of William of Orange and other nobles opposing Spanish rule.
Jun: 2nd, Counts Egmont and Hoorn are pronounced guilty of high treason and, 6th, are beheaded in Brussels.

C Jul: Nobles in Sweden rally to Duke John, declaring Eric XIV unfit through insanity to reign;
21st, the Duke of Alva defeats Louis of Nassau at Jemmingen and returns in triumph to Utrecht while his army plunders;
23rd, Don Carlos, son of Philip II of Spain, dies.
Aug: The nobility in Lower Austria wring from the Emperor Maximilian II the right to exercise the Augsburg Confession freely in their lands.
Sep: the Electors of the Rhine appeal to Maximilian II to intervene in the Netherlands to check the Duke of Alva's advance;
24th, Spaniards capture English ships and booty at San Juan from the fleet under Sir John Hawkins, marauding west of The Line;
30th, John III is proclaimed King of Sweden (–1592) by the Army and nobility on the deposition of Eric XIV.

D Oct: 5th, William of Orange leads an army from Römersdorf into Brabant and is joined by a force of French Huguenots, but the Duke of Alva avoids a battle and (in *Nov.*) Orange withdraws;
—, the York Conference into the conduct of Mary Queen of Scots opens.
Nov: The Moors in Spain revolt against oppressive treatment, desecrating churches in Granada. In retaliation Philip II orders the slaughter of the Moorish population which is carried out by the Marquis de los Velez and Bishop Deza. Philip later calls his half-brother, Don John of Austria, to subdue the Moors;
25th, the enquiry into the conduct of Mary Queen of Scots reopens at Westminster and the commissioners of James VI declare the Casket Letters, showing Mary's guilt in Darnley's murder, as authentic.
Dec: Three Spanish treasure ships with pay for the Duke of Alva's troops, driven by storm into Plymouth, are impounded by Elizabeth; commercial relations between England and Philip II's dominions are severed (until 1574).

E

F **Politics, Economics, Law and Education**

The first Eisteddfod, for Welsh music and literature, is held at Caerwys.

G **Science, Technology and Discovery**

Gerardus Mercator devises his cylindrical projection for charts.

Alexander Nowell, Dean of St. Paul's, invents bottled beer.

H **Philosophy, Religion and Scholarship**

The Bishops' Bible (under the general direction of Archbishop Matthew Parker, wishing to discourage the growing popularity of the Genevan Calvinistic Bible).

Seminary (the English College) founded at Douai by William Allen to train Jesuit missionaries for work in England (−1580).

Pope Pius V issues the *Brevarium Romanum*, a revision as ordered by the Council of Trent in 1563.

Brunswick becomes a Protestant state.

William Lambarde, *Archaionomia*, a study of Anglo-Saxon documents.

J **Art, Sculpture, Fine Arts and Architecture**

Painting:

Pieter Breughel, *Parable of the Blind*; and *Faithlessness of the World*.

Fernandez de Navarrete is appointed court painter to Philip II of Spain.

Architecture:

Smythson works at Longleat House, Wiltshire (−1574).

K **Music**

Marnix de Ste. Aldegonde composes the 'Wilhelmuslied', which is soon regarded as a 'national anthem' by the Dutch Provinces in revolt against Spain.

L **Literature (including Drama)**

John Skelton, *Works* . . . newly collected ('Pithy, pleasaunt and profitable workes of maister Skelton, Poete Laureate . . .').

A Spanish 'yard play', known as a *Corral*, is presented in Madrid; perhaps the first public theatre presentation in the city (*May* 5th).

M **Births and Deaths**

Feb. — Miles Coverdale d. (80).

June 6th Lamorel, Count of Egmont, d. (46).

July 23rd Don Carlos d. (23).

Dec. 23rd Roger Ascham d. (53).

— Maffeo Barberini (Pope Urban VIII) b. (−1644).

— Jan Bruegel b. (−1725).

— Tommaso Campanella b. (−1639).

— Henry Wotton b. (−1639).

A Jan: Desultory fighting in Périgord leads to the Third War of Religion in France; Charles IX and Catherine de' Medici retire to Metz.
Feb:
Mar: The Duke of Anjou defeats the Huguenots at Jarnac, where the Prince of Condé is killed. The principal Huguenots subsequently meet at Cognac to elect the Duke of Vendôme, son of the Queen of Navarre, as their leader and to appoint Admiral de Coligny Commander-in-chief;
20th, the Duke of Alva requires the States-General at Brussels to grant burdensome taxes, including the Tenth Penny;
the Earl of Leicester and the Duke of Norfolk fail to secure William Cecil's dismissal as Secretary of State.

B Apr:
May: 10th, Wolfgang, Duke of Zweibrücken, leading an army to support the French Huguenots, secures the passage of the R. Loire.
Jun: 23rd, German mercenaries join forces with Admiral Coligny's army at Saint Yrieix.

C Jul: 1st, Sigismund II of Poland achieves the Union of Lithuania with Poland and Lublin; the Kingdom to be a single state with a unified diet;
24th (–Sept. 8th), Huguenot forces attempt the siege of Poitiers;
William of Orange begins issuing letters of marque to the 'Beggars of the Sea' for plundering Spanish shipping.
Aug: Pius V creates Cosimo de' Medici, who had resigned the government of Tuscany to his son Francesco in 1564, Grand Duke of Tuscany in recognition of his services to the Papacy in exterminating heresy.
Sep:

D Oct: 1st, the Duke of Norfolk is imprisoned by Queen Elizabeth for attempting to marry Mary Queen of Scots;
3rd, Admiral Coligny is defeated at Montcoutour by the Duke of Anjou, who thus prevents the Huguenot army from moving south to Poitou.

Nov: 9th, the Northern Rebellion breaks out in England under the Roman Catholic Earls of Northumberland and Westmorland; they sack Durham Cathedral, and, 16th, issue a proclamation at Ripon, but, 25th, retreat north, as Hunsdon's army approaches.
Dec: 15th, the Earls of Northumberland and Westmorland flee to Scotland and their army fades away.

E Don John of Austria subdues the Morisco rebellion in Granada.

F **Politics, Economics, Law and Education**
    A public lottery is held in England to finance repairs to harbours.
    An epidemic of carbunculous fever carries off 50,000 inhabitants of Lisbon.

G **Science, Technology and Discovery**
    Tycho Brahe begins the construction of a 19 ft. quadrant and a celestial globe, 5 ft. in
    diameter, at Augsburg.
    Gerardus Mercator's Map of the World for navigational use, on 'Mercator's' projec-
    tion, with parallels and meridians at right angles. Mercator also publishes *Chronologia*,
    a study of eclipses and astronomical observations.

H **Philosophy, Religion and Scholarship**
    Richard Tottel's translation of Henry de Bracton, *On the Laws and Customs of England*.
    Thomas Underdowne translates the *Aethiopian History* of Heliodorus.

J **Art, Sculpture, Fine Arts and Architecture**
    Painting:
    Hans Eworth, *Queen Elizabeth Confounding Juno, Minerva and Venus*.

K **Music**

L **Literature (including Drama)**
    Alonso de Ercilla, *La Araucana* (epic on Spanish conquest of Chile).

M **Births and Deaths**
    Apr. 16th John Davies b. (–1626).
    Sept. 5th Edmund Bonner d. (*c.* 69).
    Sept. 5th Pieter Breughel the elder d. (*c.* 44).

A Jan: 23rd, assassination of the Earl of Moray, Regent of Scotland, by the Hamiltons at Linlithgow leads to civil war with the Marians, led by William Maitland of Lethington and Kirkcaldy in Edinburgh, opposing the Lords of the Congregation.

Feb: 20th, Lord Hunsdon defeats Leonard Dacre's rebel army near Naworth, Cumberland, ending the Northern Rebellion; Dacre flees to Scotland;

25th, Pope Pius V issues the bull *Regnans in Excelsis*, excommunicating Elizabeth I and absolving her subjects from their allegiance (the bull is published in London in *May* by John Felton, and provokes severe anti-Catholic legislation).

Mar: Thomas Earl of Sussex harries the Scottish border (*–July*) as reprisal for Scottish attacks during the Northern Rebellion and his presence aids the succession of Lennox to the regency.

B Apr: 14th, Calvinists, Lutherans and the Moravian Brethren in Poland ally themselves against the Jesuits by the Consensus of Sendomir;

the Dutch 'Beggars of the Sea' redouble their attack on Spanish shipping in the English Channel, cutting off the Duke of Alva's supplies.

May: Turkey declares war on Venice for refusing to surrender Cyprus; Spain comes to the aid of Venice.

Jun:

C Jul: The Earl of Lennox, father of Lord Darnley, becomes Regent of Scotland (–1571); Imperial diet meets at Speyer;

25th, Huguenot army under Admiral Coligny fights an indecisive battle against Marshal Cossé at Arnay le Duc in Burgundy.

Aug: 8th, the Peace of St. Germain-en-Laye ends the Third Civil War in France. The Huguenots gain greater concessions, including liberty of conscience and an amnesty, and are granted the strongholds of La Rochelle, Montauban, Cognac and La Charité as places of refuge. Admiral Coligny becomes all-powerful at the French court, supplanting the influence of the Duke of Guise (–1572);

—, the Turks sack Nicosia, Cyprus;

16th, John Sigismund Zápolya of Transylvania signs a secret treaty with the Emperor Maximilian II at Speyer, to achieve independence from the Sultan of Turkey; he renounces much of Hungary.

Sep:

D Oct: 16th, Baron Montigny, younger brother of Count Hoorn, is assassinated in Spain on Philip II's orders;

Philip II marries as his fourth wife Anne of Austria, daughter of the Emperor Maximilian II.

Nov: Charles IX marries Elizabeth, daughter of the Emperor Maximilian II; Margaret of Valois is betrothed to Henry of Navarre.

Dec: 13th, by the Peace of Stettin Denmark recognises the independence of Sweden, confirming the Treaty of Brömsebro (1541); Sweden surrenders her claim to Norway.

E Don John of Austria clears the Moriscos from Andalusia; The Japanese open the port of Nagasaki to overseas trade.

F **Politics, Economics, Law and Education**
Blaise de Monluc, French Catholic soldier, writes his *Commentaries* on French politics and civil warfare.
A postal service is organised in Nuremberg.
Roger Ascham, *The Scholemaster*.

G **Science, Technology and Discovery**
Abraham Ortelius of Antwerp publishes *Theatrum Orbis Terrarum*, with 53 maps, the first modern atlas.
The potato is introduced to Europe from Spanish America.

H **Philosophy, Religion and Scholarship**
Barnabe Googe translates *The Polish Kingdom* by Thomas Kirchmeyer.
Matthew Parker's edition of the chronicle, *Flores Historiarum*.
Pope Pius V issues the *Missale Romanum*.
Unification of the Lutherans, Calvinists and Moravians in Poland (*Apr.* 14th).
De Baïf's Académie de Poésie et de Musique, Paris, founded (*see* 1576).

J **Art, Sculpture, Fine Arts and Architecture**
Painting:
Nicholas Hilliarde, portrait of *Queen Elizabeth I*.
Tintoretto, *Leda* and *Moses Striking the Rock*.
Titian, *Crowning with Thorns*.
Architecture:
Palladio, façade of Palazzio Barbarano, Vincenza (begun by Sansovino, 1534).
Palladio publishes *Quottro Libri dell'Architettura*.

K **Music**
A study of Greek writers on music begins in Italy.

L **Literature (including Drama)**
John Barbour, *The Brus* (posth. publication of a national epic poem on Bruce, by the father of Scottish poetry, d. 1395).
Robert Henryson, *The Moral Fables of Aesop* ('Compylit in Eloquent, and Ornate Scottis Meter').

M **Births and Deaths**
Jan. 8th Philibert de' Lorme d. (60).
Jan. 23rd James Stuart, Earl of Moray, d. (*c.* 40).
Apr. — Guy Fawkes b. (–1605).
Oct. 20th Joãno de Barros d. (74).
Dec. 5th Johan Friis d. (76).
— Thomas Dekker b. (–1632).
— Thomas Middleton b. (–1627).

1571 The Turks take Cyprus but are defeated at Lepanto by Don John of Austria

A Jan: 2nd, negotiations for a marriage between Elizabeth I and Henry Duke of Anjou are opened (abandoned *Jan.* 1572 for a match between the Queen of England and Anjou's younger brother, François, Duke of Alençon).

Feb: 25th, Sir William Cecil is created Lord Burghley.

Mar: 14th, on the death of John Sigismund Zápolya of Transylvania, the Emperor Maximilian II acquires the prince's possessions in Hungary, but the estates of Transylvania elect Stephen Báthory as their Voivode;

25th, Roberto Ridolfi leaves England to concert his designs for a Spanish invasion of England to rescue Mary Queen of Scots, depose Elizabeth I and restore Catholicism, with the Duke of Alva, the Pope and Philip II; Alva refuses his support unless a rising of English rebels succeeds.

B Apr: 2nd (–*May* 29th), Parliament meets. Acts are passed making the bringing of papal bulls into England treason and forbidding the export of wool to protect the domestic clothing industry. Subscription to the 39 Articles of Religion is statutorily enforced on the clergy.

May: 20th, Pope Pius V signs a league with Spain and Venice to combat the Turks.

Jun:

C Jul: 30th, a treaty for mutual succession is signed between the Elector of Brandenburg and the Duke of Pomerania.

Aug: 3rd, the Turks take Famagusta, Cyprus, after a siege of eleven months; they massacre many of the inhabitants;

the Duke of Alva introduces additional taxation in the Netherlands.

Sep: 4th, the Marian Party in Scotland, led by the Hamiltons and William Maitland, makes a successful *coup d'état* at Stirling, where the Regent Lennox is killed;

5th, John, Earl of Mar, succeeds as Regent (–1572);

7th, Thomas, Duke of Norfolk, is sent back to the Tower on suspicion of treason (which is confirmed, 28th, with the dénouement of the Ridolfi Conspiracy);

12th, reconciliation between Charles IX of France and the Huguenot leader Admiral Coligny;

The Turkish fleet harry shipping in the Adriatic; a fleet to oppose them is assembled by John of Austria.

D Oct: 7th, Don John of Austria decisively defeats the Turkish fleet off Lepanto; the Turks lose 117 ships.

Nov: The confession of John Leslie, Bishop of Ross, reveals the ramifications of the Ridolfi Conspiracy.

Dec:

E The embargo is enforced in the Netherlands on English trade.

F **Politics, Economics, Law and Education**
The Royal Exchange, London, is opened.
A royal edict in France imposes uniform prices, sizes and qualities for cloth.
Harrow School is founded by John Lyon.

G **Science, Technology and Discovery**

H **Philosophy, Religion and Scholarship**
Hugh Latimer, *Frutefull Sermons* (posth. 3 parts –1575).
Francesco Patrizi, *Discussiones peripateticae* (enlarged edn. –1581).
Matthew Parker's edition of the *Historia Major of Matthew Paris*.
Bibliotheca Laurenziana, Florence, is opened to the public.

J **Art, Sculpture, Fine Arts and Architecture**
Painting:
Veronese, Justinian altarpiece in Church of San Sebastiano.
Architecture:
Palladio, Loggia del Capitaniato, Vicenza.

K **Music**
Giovanni Pierluigi da Palestrina, five-part Mass.

L **Literature (including Drama)**
Richard Edwards, *Damon and Pithias* ('excellent Comedie of two of the most faith-
fullest Freendes').

M **Births and Deaths**
Jan. 22nd Robert Bruce Cotton b. (–1631).
Feb. 12th Nicholas Throckmorton d. (56).
June. 27th Giorgio Vasari d. (59).
Sept. 23rd John Jewel d. (49).
Dec. 27th Johann Kepler b. (–1630).
— Benvenuto Cellini d. (71).
— Gabrielle d'Estrées b. (–1599).

1572　Dutch rebels capture Brill—Massacre of St. Bartholomew

A Jan: 16th, the Duke of Norfolk is tried for treason for complicity in the Ridolfi plot
(executed *June* 2nd).
Feb:
Mar:

B Apr: 1st, the Dutch 'Beggars of the Sea', who had been plundering Spanish shipping,
capture Brill, following their expulsion from English ports: the effective beginning of
the Dutch War of Independence;
21st, Anglo-French defensive treaty signed at Blois, ends England's isolation. Elizabeth I proceeds to negotiate for a marriage with François, Duke of Alençon (–1583).
May: 1st, Pope Pius V dies;
8th (–*June* 30th) Parliament meets, demanding the execution of Mary Queen of Scots,
which Elizabeth I resists;
13th, Ugo Buoncompagni is elected Pope Gregory XIII (–1585);
15th, Lewis of Nassau takes Valenciennes from the Spanish (it is recaptured by the
Duke of Alva in *July*);
23rd, Lewis of Nassau seizes Mons and prepares to withstand the Duke of Alva's
siege.
Jun: 9th, William of Orange invades Gelderland from Germany;
a new Turkish fleet puts to sea against Don John of Austria to complete the capture of
Cyprus.

C Jul: 7th, the Estates of Poland declare the monarchy elective on the death of Sigismund
II, the last of the Jagellon dynasty (since 1386); the Duke of Anjou is elected King of
Poland in *May* 1573);
11th, Sir Humphrey Gilbert lands in the Netherlands with a band of English volun-
teers to fight against the Spanish;
18th, William of Orange is elected Stadtholder by Holland, Friesland, Zeeland and
Utrecht at the Dort Assembly; de la Marck is appointed Admiral and Paul Buys,
Advocate. William awaits the arrival of a French force under the Huguenot leader
Coligny to press his attack against the Duke of Alva;
Lord Burghley is appointed Lord Treasurer (–1598).

Aug: 18th, Henry of Navarre marries Margaret of Valois, sister of Charles IX of France;
22nd, the Earl of Northumberland is executed at York for treason;
22nd (–24th), Catherine de' Medici's plot for the assassination of Admiral Coligny
fails but provokes the Massacre of St. Bartholomew's Day in Paris where Coligny
and many Huguenots are killed, though Navarre and Condé are spared. The massacre
spreads to the provinces and provokes the fourth War of Religion (–*July* 1573). The
Huguenots, deprived of their leading soldiers, withdraw to La Rochelle, Nîmes and
Montauban. The massacre drives the centre party 'politiques', such as L'Hôpital, to
support the Huguenots. Huguenot refugees leave France for England and Germany.
Sep: 12th, the Duke of Alva recaptures Mons.

D Oct: 28th, the Earl of Mar, Regent in Scotland, dies (he is succeeded as Regent by
James, Earl of Morton, *Nov.* 24th).
Nov:
Dec: 21st, the Spanish fail to take Haarlem from the Dutch rebels.

E

F Politics, Economics, Law and Education
Jean de Serres, French Huguenot, *Commentariorum de statu religionis et reipublicae*, a survey of the French wars of Religion.

G Science, Technology and Discovery
Artis auriferae quam chemicum vocant, a collection of writings in alchemy, is published at Basle.

H Philosophy, Religion and Scholarship
Henri Estienne, *Thesaurus Linguae Graecae*.
Matthew Parker, *De Antiquitate Britannicae Ecclesiae* (probably the first book privately printed in England).
Society of Antiquaries, London, founded (dissolved 1604; reformed 1707; Royal Charter 1751).
Christian group of the Anabaptists, known as Mennonites, in Holland are accorded toleration.

J Art, Sculpture, Fine Arts and Architecture
Painting:
Nicholas Hilliarde, *Queen Elizabeth I* (miniature).

K Music
Byrd joins Tallis as organist of the Chapel Royal.
Andrea Amati in Cremona makes one of earliest known cellos, known as the 'King' Amati.

L Literature (including Drama)
Luís Vaz de Camoens, *Os Lusíados* (Portuguese epic poem on the discovery by Vasco da Gama of the sea-route to India, and on the heroic achievements of the history of Portugal).
Annibale Caro, *Lettre familiari*.
Pierre de Ronsard, *La Franciade* (unfinished mythological epic on the French kings).

M Births and Deaths
Mar. 10th William Paulet, Marquess of Winchester, d. (89).
June 11th Ben Jonson b. (–1637).
July 6th Sigismund II of Poland d. (52).
Aug. 27th Gaspard de Coligny d. (53).
Nov. 24th John Knox d. (67).
— Angelo Bronzini d. (69).
— François Clouet d. (50).
— John Donne b. (–1631).

1573 Alva is checked in the Netherlands—Anjou is elected King of Poland—Peace of Constantinople

A Jan:
  Feb: 11th, Francis Drake sees the Pacific;
  23rd, James Fitzmaurice surrenders to Sir John Perrot and the Irish rebellion is effectively crushed;
  the Duke of Anjou fails to reduce the Huguenot stronghold of La Rochelle;
  the Pacification of Perth ends the fighting in Scotland between the Regent and the faction supporting Mary Queen of Scots, though Kircaldy and Maitland hold out in Edinburgh Castle (*–May*).
  Mar: 7th, the Peace of Constantinople ends the war between Turkey and Venice. Venice cedes Cyprus and undertakes to pay the Porte an indemnity of 300,000 crowns and to increase the annual tribute;
  13th, Michel de L'Hôpital, Chancellor of France, dies.

B Apr: 17th, Sir William Drury marches an English army into Scotland to capture Edinburgh Castle from the Marians.
  May: 9th, Henry Duke of Anjou is elected King of Poland (–1575), undertaking that he will neither marry nor declare war without the Assembly's consent;
  28th, Edinburgh Castle surrenders to Drury (Maitland, leader of the Marians, dies *June* 9th). Elizabeth I is now free from any threat from north of the border.
  Jun:

C Jul: 6th, the Pacification of Boulogne ends the Fourth War of Religion in France; by its terms the Huguenots are granted an amnesty and freedom of conscience, but they are free to worship only in La Rochelle, Nîmes and Montauban;
  11th, Haarlem falls to the Spanish under Don Frederick of Toledo.
  Aug: The Spanish fail to take Alkmaar.
  Sep: The Duke of Alva, finding his advance checked by the Dutch, asks Philip II to recall him from the Netherlands.

D Oct: 11th, a Spanish fleet is defeated by the Dutch off Enckhuysen.
  Nov:
  Dec: 18th, the Duke of Alva leaves Brussels for Spain; he is succeeded as Governor of the Netherlands by Don Louis Requesens;
  21st, Sir Francis Walsingham is appointed a Principal Secretary of State in England (–1590).

E

F **Politics, Economics, Law and Education**
François Hotman, *Francogallia*, argues in favour of the election and deposition of kings.

G **Science, Technology and Discovery**

H **Philosophy, Religion and Scholarship**
Taurellus attacks the philosophy of Aristotle.

J **Art, Sculpture, Fine Arts and Architecture**
The Inquisition in Rome calls Paolo Veronese to account for painting profane incidents in his religious pictures.

K **Music**
Orlando di Lasso, *Patrocinium Musices* (–1576).

L **Literature (including Drama)**
Johann Fischart, *Der Flöhhaz* (a satire on women).
Torquato Tasso, *Aminta* (pastoral, not published until 1580).

M **Births and Deaths**
Mar. 13th Michel de l'Hôpital d. (*c.* 68).
Apr. 26th Marie de' Medici b. (–1642).
June 9th William Maitland of Lethingdon d. (45).
July 15th Inigo Jones b. (–1651).
July 29th John Caius d. (63).
Oct. 7th William Laud b. (–1645).
Dec. 21st Mathurin Régnier b. (–1613).

1574   Accession of Henry III in France—William of Orange raises the siege of Leyden

A Jan:
Feb: 18th, Zeeland falls to the Dutch rebels;
   23rd, the Fifth War of Religion breaks out in France (–1576).
Mar: Louis of Nassau is defeated at the battle of Mookden Heath.

B Apr: 8th, the 'Plot of Vincennes' for rescuing the Duke of Alençon and Henry of Navarre from the French Courts fails;
   21st, Francis succeeds as Grand Duke of Tuscany on the death of Cosimo de' Medici, who had resigned the government of the duchy to him in 1564.
May: 30th, Henry III succeeds as King of France (–1589) on the death of Charles IX; Catherine de' Medici, the Queen Mother, acts as Regent until Henry arrives from Poland.
Jun: 18th, Henry III secretly leaves Poland for France; en route he meets the Emperor Maximilian II in Vienna, who advocates a policy of toleration. The Polish Assembly subsequently deposes Henry;
   30th, William of Orange persuades the Estates of Holland to open the dykes to hinder the Spanish siege of Leyden.

C Jul: Bernadino de Mendoza arrives in England as Spanish ambassador.
Aug: 28th, the Treaty of Bristol settles the commercial disputes between English and Spanish merchants arising from the mutual confiscations and embargoes following the seizure of the Spanish treasure ships in 1569.
Sep: 5th, Henry III enters France and is met by Henry of Navarre and the Duke of Alençon.

D Oct: 3rd, William of Orange raises the siege of Leyden.
Nov: 3rd, Damville, Marshal of France, issues a manifesto from Languedoc calling for religious toleration, administrative reforms and the expulsion of the Guises.
Dec: 12th, Murad III succeeds as Sultan of Turkey on the death of Selim II;
   26th, Charles de Lorraine, Cardinal of Guise, dies.

E John the Terrible, Prince of Moldavia, is slain during his attack on the Turks; his principality is laid waste;
The Spaniards lose Tunis to the Turks. Tunis becomes a Turkish Regency with an elective bey;
The Portuguese settlement at Angola is begun with the foundation of São Paulo.

F **Politics, Economics, Law and Education**
   Hubert Languet writes *Vindiciae Contra Tyrannos* (published 1579).
   Jean Bodin, *Discours sur les causes de l'extreme cherté qui est aujourdhuy en France.*

G **Science, Technology and Discovery**
   Josias Simler, *De Alpibus commentarius.*
   Ulissi Aldrovardi compiles a treatise on drugs, *Antidotarii Bononiensis Epitome.*
   Jacob Verzellini, a Venetian resident in London, uses soda-ash from seaweed in place
   of crude potash for the manufacture of glass.
   A clock is made in Strasburg, which displays a series of scenes.

H **Philosophy, Religion and Scholarship**
   Justus Lipsius edits *The Histories* and *The Annals* of Tacitus with notes and com-
   mentary (published by Plantin, Antwerp; a landmark in classical scholarship).
   The first *auto-da-fé* (held in Mexico).

J **Art, Sculpture, Fine Arts and Architecture**
   Painting:
      Tintoretto, *Paradise* in the Doge's Palace, Venice.
   Architecture:
      Longleat House, Wiltshire, is completed.
      The Gate of Honour at Caius College, Cambridge, the first entirely classical building
      in England.

K **Music**

L **Literature (including Drama)**

M **Births and Deaths**
      Mar. 6th Henry Pelham d. (58).
      Apr. 21st Cosimo de' Medici d. (55).
      May 6th Giovanni Battista Pamfili (Pope Innocent X) b. (–1655).
      June 13th Richard Barnfield b. (–1627).
      Sept. 17th Pedro Menéndez d. (55).
      Sept. — Louis, Count of Nassau, d. (36).
      Dec. 12th Queen Anne of Denmark b. (–1619).
      Dec. 26th Charles of Lorraine d. (49).

1575   John Casimir aids the Huguenots—Financial Crisis in Spain

A **Jan:**
   Feb: 13th, Henry III of France is crowned at Rheims, and
   14th, marries Louise de Vaudémont of Lorraine, thus allying himself with the House of Guise.
   Mar: Don Louis Requesens, Governor of the Netherlands, signs an agreement with Elizabeth I, to banish all English political refugees from the Low Countries and to permit English merchants to trade with Antwerp. Elizabeth undertakes to prevent the Dutch rebels from using English ports and English volunteers from serving with William of Orange.

B **Apr:** Peace negotiations in France founder.
   May: (*–July*) a series of conferences is held at Breda between Requesens and William of Orange to reach an accommodation, but Philip II refuses to grant any concessions to the rebels.
   Jun: 24th, William of Orange marries Charlotte de Bourbon, daughter of the Duke of Montpensier, though his insane second wife is still alive.

C **Jul:** 22nd, two Dutch Anabaptists are burnt at Smithfield on Elizabeth's orders;
   Queen Elizabeth visits the Earl of Leicester at Kenilworth on her summer progress.
   Aug: 15th, François Duke of Anjou (formerly Alençon) escapes from the French court to join Henri I de Bourbon, Prince of Condé, the Huguenot leader;
   Don Louis Requesens captures Schoonhoven.
   Sep: 15th, John Casimir, son of the Elector Palatine, aided by an English subsidy, signs a treaty with the French Huguenot leaders for bringing an army of 16,000 German and Swiss mercenaries into France;
   27th, Requesens captures the isles of Duiveland and subsequently of Schouwen, except for Zierickzee (which holds out until *July* 1576), to cut communications between Holland and Zeeland.

D **Oct:** 3rd, the Duke of Anjou forces Henry III to release the Duke of Montmorency;
   17th, Rudolf, King of Hungary is elected King of the Romans;
   19th, Henri de Lorraine, Duke of Guise, forces a Huguenot army back across the River Marne.
   Nov: 8th, a truce in the French War is signed at Marigny, permitting the Huguenots to hold certain towns and assigning lands to the Duke of Anjou which Henry III had withheld from him;
   14th, Elizabeth I refuses to accept the sovereignty of the Netherlands, which William of Orange, in desperation at the course of the war, had agreed to have offered to her.
   Dec: 14th, Stephen Báthory is elected King of Poland (–1586) in succession to Henry (now King of France) whom the Estates had deposed in his absence. A minority faction elect the Emperor Maximilian II;
   29th, Edmund Grindal is elected Archbishop of Canterbury (–1583).

E Financial crisis in Spain becomes more acute. In *Sept.* Philip II suspends all payments.
   Requesens, Governor of the Netherlands, has no money to pay his soldiers;
   The Mogul Emperor Akbar conquers Bengal.

F **Politics, Economics, Law and Education**
The plague breaks out in Sicily and spreads to Italy, where casualties are heavy in Milan and Florence.
Leyden University is founded, to commemorate the siege.

G **Science, Technology and Discovery**
Christopher Saxton, *County Atlas of England and Wales.*
Tycho Brahe constructs an observatory for the King of Denmark.
Maucolycus discovers the measurement of the intensity of light.
The first European imitation of Chinese porcelain is made at Florence.

H **Philosophy, Religion and Scholarship**
Archbishop Matthew Parker leaves his collection of manuscripts, rich in Anglo-Saxon documents and mediaeval chronicles, to Corpus Christi College, Cambridge.

J **Art, Sculpture, Fine Arts and Architecture**
Painting:
Veronese, *Moses saved from the Waters.*

K **Music**
William Byrd and Thomas Tallis, *Cantiones Sacrae.*

L **Literature (including Drama)**
Gammer Gurton's Needle (farce; anon).
Johann Fischart, *Geschichtsklitterung* (German satirist's boisterous adaptation of the *Gargantua* of Rabelais of 1534).
George Gascoigne, *Posies* ('corrected and completed'; contains *Jocasta*, the second tragedy in English blank verse, paraphrased from the *Phoenissae* of Euripides; and also 'Certain Notes of Instruction Concerning the Making of Verse', the earliest critical essay of its kind in English literature). *The Glasse of Government* ('a tragicall comedie').

M **Births and Deaths**
Mar. — Lionel Cranfield b. (–1645).
Apr. 10th Anna Bijns d. (*c.* 81).
May 17th Matthew Parker d. (70).
Sept. 17th Heinrich Bullinger d. (71).
Nov. 4th Guido Reni b. (–1642).
— Jakob Boehme b. (–1624).
— Cyril Tourneur b. (–1626).

1576 Accession of Emperor Rudolf II—'Spanish Fury' at Antwerp—Pacification of Ghent

A **Jan:** Louis, Prince of Condé, and John Casimir of the Palatinate invade France near Sedan and march towards Vichy.

Feb: 3rd, Henry of Navarre escapes from Paris and

5th, abjures Catholicism at Tours;

8th (*–Mar.* 15th), English Parliament meets; the attempt of the Puritans to promote a radical reform of the Church of England fails. Peter Wentworth, a Puritan M.P., is imprisoned in the Tower (*Mar.* 12th), for attacking Queen Elizabeth's interference with the Commons claim to freedom of speech.

Mar: 3rd, death of Don Louis Requesens, Governor of the Netherlands (in *Apr.* Philip II appoints his half-brother, Don John of Austria, as Governor);

11th, William of Orange summons the Estates of Holland and Zeeland to Delft to sign an Act of Federation;

—, the Duke of Anjou's army makes juncture with John Casimir's army at Moulins.

B **Apr:**

May: 6th, the Fifth War of Religion in France is ended by the Peace of Monsieur (after the Duke of Anjou), promulgated by the Edict of Beaulieu. By its terms the Huguenots are granted freedom of worship in all places except Paris and are to garrison eight strongholds. The Duke of Anjou gains estates in Anjou and Tourraine, and John Casimir is rewarded with a pension by Henry III. The Edict provokes Henri of Lorraine, Duke of Guise to form a Catholic League to overthrow the Huguenots.

C **Jun:** Lewis VI succeeds as Elector Palatine (–1580) on the death of Frederick III;

25th, at the Diet of Ratisbon the Emperor Maximilian II obtains support for an expedition to Poland to dispute the election of Stephen Báthory as King.

Jul: Ziericksee in the Isle of Schouwen falls to the Spanish, enabling them to cut communications between Walcheren and south Holland.

Aug:

Sep: 4th, members of the Netherlands Council of State suspected of Spanish leanings are imprisoned. Spanish soldiers without pay mutiny and seize Alost.

D **Oct:** 12th, accession of the Emperor Rudolf II (–1612) on the death of his brother Maximilian II. As a result of his patronage of the Jesuits, the Counter-Reformation gathers pace in Austria;

19th, William of Orange calls a Congress to Ghent to discuss the pacification of the Netherlands.

Nov: 4th, the Spanish army mutinies and sacks Antwerp—'the Spanish Fury';

8th, by the Pacification of Ghent all 17 Provinces of the Netherlands are united. They agree to require Philip II to recall Spanish troops, grant religious toleration and summon a representative assembly. The Archduke Matthias is to be invited to become Governor. The Pacification is ratified by the States-General at Antwerp.

Dec: The French Estates-General meet at Blois. Henri of Lorraine, Duke of Guise by controlling the elections secures an assembly opposed to the Huguenots so that the policy of moderation counselled by Jean Bodin and the 'Politiques' is defeated. The Duke of Anjou goes over to the court party.

E

F **Politics, Economics, Law and Education**
Jean Bodin, *Les Six livres de la République*, advocating a limited monarchy, with property and the family as the basis of society (–1577).
Foundation of Warsaw University, Poland.

G **Science, Technology and Discovery**
Martin Frobisher discovers Frobisher Bay.
Robert Norman discovers the magnetic 'dip', or inclination (he publishes his results, 1581).
François Viète introduces decimal fractions.

H **Philosophy, Religion and Scholarship**
Académie du Palais founded by Henry III in Paris (associated with Baïf's Académie, of 1570; Pierre Ronsard is elected a member; he delivers the introductory address on *Les vertus intellectuelles et morales*).
The League of Torgau (between the Elector of Saxony and the Landgrave of Hesse) to support the opinions of the Lutherans, draws up Articles of Faith ('The Torgau Book').
Edict of Beaulieu (*May* 6th) tolerating the reformed religion in France (except in Paris).

J **Art, Sculpture, Fine Arts and Architecture**
Architecture:
Palladio, Il Redentore Church, Venice (–1577).

K **Music**
Tomás Luis de Victoria, *Liber Primus* (Canticles and Masses).

L **Literature (including Drama)**
Johann Fischart, *Das glückhafft Schiff von Zürich* (a voyage by river from Zurich to Strasbourg).
George Gascoigne, *The Steele Glas* (first verse satire).
William Lambarde, *Perambulation of Kent*.
George Pettie, *Petite Pallace of Pettie his Pleasure* (a collection of tales translated from the Latin and Greek originals).
The Paradise of Dainty Devices (an anthology of 99 poems by Richard Edwards and others).
James Burbage obtains a twenty-one year lease of land in Shoreditch, London (*Apr.* 13th), with permission to build a playhouse on part of the site. *The Theatre* opens at the end of the year.

M **Births and Deaths**
Jan. 19th Hans Sachs d. (81).
Apr. 24th St. Vincent de Paul b. (–1660).
Aug. 27th Titian (Tiziano Vecellio) d. (99).
Sept. 21st Girolamo Cardan d. (74).
— John Marston b. (–1634).
— Diaz del Castillo d. (84).

1577   Don John of Austria issues the Perpetual Edict—The Peace of
             Bergerac in France

A Jan: 1st, Henry III announces to the States-General at Blois that the Edict of Beaulieu
       (of *May* 1576), granting toleration to the Huguenots, had been obtained by force.
   Feb: 6th, Henry of Navarre becomes recognised as head of the Huguenot Party;
       12th, Don John of Austria, the new Governor of the Netherlands, issues the Perpetual
       Edict to settle the civil war; by its terms all Spanish troops are to leave within 20 days,
       the States are to provide 600,000 livres as their arrears of pay, and the ancient liberties
       of the provinces are to be restored. William of Orange refuses to publish the Edict.
       Fearing Don John will use his troops for an invasion of England, Queen Elizabeth
       secures that they shall leave the Netherlands by a land route, and grants a further
       subsidy to John Casimir.
   Mar: The Sixth War of Religion breaks out in France (*–Sept.*); operations are mainly in
       the west.

B Apr:
   May: 1st, Don John of Austria enters Brussels. The Duke of Anjou takes La Charité,
       showing great cruelty. The Duke of Mayenne lays siege to Brouage, near La Rochelle
       (which surrenders in *Aug.*).
   Jun: Edward Grindal is sequestered from the Archbishopric of Canterbury for refusing to
       suppress the Puritan 'prophesying' movement in the Church of England.

C Jul: Don John of Austria seizes Namur in desperation, after the failure of his design to
       attempt an invasion of England, where he intended to depose Elizabeth I, rescue Mary
       Queen of Scots and marry her.
   Aug: 17th, the Peace of Bergerac ends the Sixth War of Religion. Huguenots secure im-
       portant concessions for exercising their religion, and a town in each district is ceded to
       them. They retain 9 strongholds and representation in 4 provincial assemblies.
   Sep: 23rd, William of Orange enters Brussels. The States-General depose Don John of
       Austria.

D Oct: 6th, the Archduke Matthias, aged 20, brother of the Emperor Rudolf II, arrives in
       Brussels at the secret invitation of the southern Catholic Provinces.
   Nov: 15th (*Nov.* 30th, 1580) Francis Drake leaves on his voyage round the world, via the
       Cape of Good Hope, to attack Spanish settlements and shipping;
       29th, Cuthbert Maine, the first seminary priest in England, is executed for treason.
   Dec: 16th, Danzig surrenders to Stephen Báthory, King of Poland, and opposition to
       him in the country ends.

E

F **Politics, Economics, Law and Education**

G **Science, Technology and Discovery**
William Harrison, *Description of England*.

H **Philosophy, Religion and Scholarship**
William Allot, *Thesaurus Bibliorum*.
Ralph Holinshed and others, *Chronicles* (of England, Scotlande and Irelande) (2nd edn.
–1587).
Jacob Andreae of Tübingen, Martin Chemnitz and others, draft the Lutheran Book of
Concord.

J **Art, Sculpture, Fine Arts and Architecture**
Painting:
El Greco, altarpiece in church of San Domingo el Antiquo, Toledo.
Nicholas Hilliarde, portrait of his father, Richard, and self-portrait (miniatures).

K **Music**

L **Literature (including Drama)**
Richard Eden, *History of Travel in East and West Indies*.
The Curtain Theatre, Finsbury, London, opened (the second theatre).

M **Births and Deaths**
Feb. 8th Robert Burton b. (–1640).
Mar. 6th Remy Belleau d. (50).
June 29th Peter Paul Rubens b. (–1640).
Aug. 12th Sir Thomas Smith d. (63).
Nov. 10th Jacob Cats b. (–1660).
Nov. 15th George Gascoigne d. (52).
— Beatrice Cenci b. (–1599).
— Thomas Coryat b. (–1617).
— Father Joseph (François Leclerc du Tremblay) b. (–1638).

1578 Battle of Alcazar—Anjou takes Mons—Catholic reaction in South Germany

A Jan: 31st, Don John of Austria, aided by Alexander Duke of Parma, defeats the Dutch federal army at the Battle of Gembloux.

Feb: The Duke of Anjou invades the southern Netherlands with a French army and takes Mons.

Mar: 10th, Elizabeth I pays a subsidy of £20,000 to John Casimir of the Palatinate to aid the Dutch;

12th, the Earl of Morton resigns the regency and James VI takes over the government of Scotland;

31st, Escobedo, secretary to Don John of Austria, is assassinated on the orders of Antonio Perez; Perez had not succeeded in murdering Escobedo in *July* 1577 in Spain on Philip II's orders to restrain Don John from his ambitious schemes of an invasion of England for his personal gain.

B Apr: Elizabeth I offers to mediate between Don John of Austria and the Dutch, hoping for a return to peaceful conditions in the Netherlands.

May:

Jun: Swedish army defeats the Russians at Wenden in the battle for the Baltic.

C Jul:

Aug: 4th, Sebastian, King of Portugal, invades Morocco, but he is killed at Alcazar, together with Sebastian, King of Fez, and the Moorish Pretender—'The Battle of the Three Kings'; Cardinal Henry, aged 67, accedes as King of Portugal (–1580);

13th, in view of the unsatisfactory leadership of the Archduke Matthias, François Duke of Anjou is proclaimed Defender of Liberties in the Netherlands by the States-General, and undertakes to lead an army of 2,000 horses and 10,000 foot against the Spanish.

Sep: The Earl of Leicester secretly marries Lettice Knollys, Viscountess Hereford.

D Oct: 1st, Alessandro Farnese, Duke of Parma, is appointed Governor of the Netherlands by Philip II on the death from a fever of Don John of Austria;

John Casimir holds Ghent with a largely Calvinist army;

the differences between the Flemish southern provinces and the Dutch northern provinces become more marked as a result of religious allegiance.

Nov:

Dec:

E John III of Sweden secretly becomes a Catholic. Catholic reaction in South Germany; Mohammed Khudabanda succeeds as Shah of Persia (–1587) on the death of Ismail II; Ōtomo Yoshishige, one of the chief rulers in Japan, is converted to Christianity.

F **Politics, Economics, Law and Education**

Jacques Cujas, *Commentaries on Roman Law*.

Henri Estienne attacks the use of Italianate words in fashion in France in *Deux dialogues de langage français italianisé* (–1579).

G **Science, Technology and Discovery**

H **Philosophy, Religion and Scholarship**

The English College removed to Rheims from Douai.

Egelantier (Chamber of Rhetoric), Amsterdam, reconstituted (*see* 1584 L, 1587 L).

The Catacombs of Rome discovered by accident (*May* 31st).

J **Art, Sculpture, Fine Arts and Architecture**

Painting:

Nicholas Hilliarde, portrait of his wife, Alice.

K **Music**

L **Literature (including Drama)**

Guillaume de Salluste, Seigneur du Bartas, *La Semaine* (religious epic in seven cantos, on the theme of the Creation; *La Seconde Semaine* –1584, unfinished).

John Lyly, *Euphues, the Anatomy of Wit*, pt. 1 (pt. 2—*Euphues and His England*, 1580; complete 1617).

Pierre de Ronsard, *Sonnets pour Hélène* (addressed to Hélène de Surgères).

M **Births and Deaths**

Apr. 1st William Harvey b. (–1657).

Apr. 14th James Hepburn, Earl of Bothwell, d. (42).

July 9th Emperor Ferdinand II b. (–1637).

Oct. 1st Don John of Austria d. (33).

— Andrea Amati d. (58).

— Thomas, Lord Coventry, b. (–1640).

— John Heywood d. (81).

1579   The Southern Netherlands are reconciled to Spain—Anjou courts
         Elizabeth I

A Jan: 6th, by the Treaty of Arras the deputies of Hainault, Douai and Artois undertake to
      protect the Catholic faith and effect a reconciliation with Philip II;
      7th, England signs an offensive and defensive alliance with the Netherlands;
      25th, the Union of Utrecht is signed by Holland, Zeeland, Utrecht, Gelderland, Fries-
      land, Groningen and Overyssel, to defend their rights and liberties against Spain and
      to establish complete freedom of worship; William of Orange, hoping for a con-
      federacy that would include the southern provinces, withholds his signature until
      May 3rd. The Union marks the foundation of the Dutch Republic.
   Feb:
   Mar:

B Apr:
   May: 17th, by the Peace of Arras the southern provinces of the Netherlands are for-
      mally reconciled to Philip II.
   Jun: 17th, Francis Drake proclaims England's sovereignty over New Albion (California);
      —, a force of Italians, Spaniards and Portuguese sails from Ferrol to aid the rebels in
      Ireland under James Fitzmaurice Fitzgerald.

C Jul: Lord Grey, Lord Deputy of Ireland, massacres the invading force at Smerwick,
      Kerry.
   Aug: 17th (–29th), the Duke of Anjou visits Elizabeth at Greenwich, intent on marrying
      her.
   Sep: Maestricht falls to the Spanish after a siege of four months;
      Esmé Stuart, Seigneur d'Aubigny, Catholic cousin of James VI, arrives at Leith and
      ingratiates himself as a royal favourite.

D Oct: 7th, the Privy Council fails to give Elizabeth I the support she expected in pro-
      ceeding with a marriage treaty with the Duke of Anjou; though a preliminary treaty is
      signed, *Nov.* 24th, negotiations are delayed as a result of Anjou's unpopularity in
      England, especially with Puritans;
      24th, accession of William V, Duke of Bavaria (–1598), on the death of Duke Albert.
   Nov:
   Dec:

E The expedition of Sir Humphrey Gilbert to the West Indies fails.

F **Politics, Economics, Law and Education**
[Hubert Languet], *Vindiciae contra tyrannos*; a 'Counterblast against tyrants', propounding the theory relating to the ruler's 'contract' with his subjects associated with the Huguenots.
Plowden, *Law Reports*.
The English Eastland Company is chartered for trading with Scandinavia and the Baltic States.

G **Science, Technology and Discovery**

H **Philosophy, Religion and Scholarship**
St. John of the Cross, *Dark Night of the Soul* (–1583).
Sir Geoffrey Fenton translates the *History of the Wars of Italy* (*Storia d'Italia*) by Francesco Guicciardini; a work of permanent value as a record of events, politics and policies in Italy from 1494 to 1532 (posth.).
Sir Thomas North translates Plutarch's *Lives* into English from the French of Jacques Amyot (–1559).
Paruta appointed official historian of Venice, and begins his *Storia de Venetia* (bks. 1–4 in Latin; 5–12 in Italian).
English College, Rome, founded.
Faustus Socinus goes to Cracow to teach (in criticism of Luther and Calvin) and helps to found the Polish sect of Socinians.
Father Thomas Stephens settles in Goa, and is the first Englishman known to have settled in India.

J **Art, Sculpture, Fine Arts and Architecture**
Sculpture:
Bologna, *Rape of the Sabines*.
Architecture:
Palladio, Teatro Olimpico, Vicenza (–1580).

K **Music**

L **Literature (including Drama)**
Stephen Gosson, *The Schoole of Abuse* (a pamphlet attacking the theatre on moral and religious grounds).
Thomas Lodge, *A Defence of Poetry, Music and Stage Plays* (an answer to Gosson, above, and against the Puritan view in general).
Edmund Spenser, *The Shepheards Calender* (twelve eclogues).

M **Births and Deaths**
Feb. 20th Nicholas Bacon d. (70).
Nov. 21st Thomas Gresham d. (60).
Dec. — John Fletcher b. (–1625).
— Henri, Duc de Rohan, b. (–1638).
— John Smith b. (–1631).

A Jan: 31st, Cardinal Henry, King of Portugal, dies, leaving five claimants to the throne—
Philip II, as grandson of Manuel the Favourite, Philibert Duke of Savoy, Ranuccio
Duke of Parma, Catherine Duchess of Braganza and Don Antonio, Prior of Crato.
Philip II recalls the Duke of Alva from the Netherlands to command the invasion of
Portugal.
Feb:
Mar:

B Apr: the Seventh War of Religion breaks out in France (–*Nov.*). Henry of Navarre takes
Cahors after four days of heavy street fighting, but is later defeated. The rest of the
campaigning is desultory.
May: Frederick IV, a Calvinist, succeeds Elector Palatine on the death of Lewis VI, a
Lutheran.
Jun:

C Jul: 5th, Proclamation to restrict the growth of London forbids new building;
Robert Parsons and Edmund Campion land in England to begin the Jesuit mission;
they deny that their work of conversion can be construed as treason against Queen
Elizabeth.
Aug: 25th, Spanish invasion of Portugal under the Duke of Alva, who defeats the supporters of Don Antonio at the battle of Alcántana, near Lisbon. As a result of the conquest Spain doubles her colonial empire and gains valuable shipping and harbours in
the peninsula;
30th, Charles Emmanuel I accedes as Duke of Savoy on the death of Emmanuel Philibert.
Sep:

D Oct: John Casimir provokes civil strife in the southern Netherlands.
Nov: 9th, a force of Italians and Spaniards lands in Ireland to aid the rebels;
26th, the Peace of Fleix ends the Seventh War of Religion in France, renewing the
terms of the Peace of Bergerac (of *Aug.* 1577);
30th, Francis Drake returns to England from his voyage of circumnavigation in the
Golden Hind.
Dec:

E England signs a commercial treaty with Turkey.

F **Politics, Economics, Law and Education**

François de la Noue (or 'Bras-de-fer'), Huguenot soldier, writes 24 *Discours politiques et militaires*, including military affairs and political theory during the French Wars of Religion.

Johann Fischart, *Das Jesuiterhütlein*, a harsh attack on the Jesuits.

G **Science, Technology and Discovery**

Sir Francis Drake completes circumnavigation of the globe (begun 1577).

Palissy studies fossils.

H **Philosophy, Religion and Scholarship**

Johannes Aventinus (Thurmair), *Annales ducum Boaiorum*, vol. 7 (completion of an historical work by one of the founders of historiography).

Jean Bodin, *Démonomanie des sorciers* (against witchcraft).

Théodore de Bèze, *Histoire ecclésiastiques des églises réformées au royaume de France*, 1521–1563.

John Stow, *The Chronicles of England* (–1592; in later editions called 'Annals').

A new translation of *De Imitatione Christi* (Thomas à Kempis) is published.

Robert Browne founds the first English Separatist congregation (in Norwich) in defiance of the established church.

The Jesuits Edmund Campion and Robert Parsons land in England (*July*).

J **Art, Sculpture, Fine Arts and Architecture**

Architecture:

Smythson, Wollaton Hall.

K **Music**

'Greensleeves', traditional English tune, is first mentioned.

L **Literature (including Drama)**

Jan Kochanowski, *Threny* (Polish laments).

Michel de Montaigne, *Essais*, 2 vols. (–1588).

M **Births and Deaths**

Apr. — Thomas Middleton b. (–1627).

May 3rd Thomas Turner d. (*c.* 56).

June 10th Luis Vaz de Camoens d. (56).

Aug. 30th Emmanuel Philibert, Duke of Savoy, d. (52).

— Francisco Quevedo Y Villegos b. (–1645).

— Franz Hals b. (–1666).

— John Webster b. (–1625).

— Andrea Palladio d. (72).

1581 Act of Abjuration of the Seven Northern Provinces of the Netherlands—Anti-Catholic Legislation in England

A **Jan:** 16th (*Mar.* 18th), English Parliament meets; severe legislation is framed against Roman Catholics, to retain their obedience to the Queen, with fines of 100 marks for hearing Mass and of £20 per month for recusancy;
28th, James VI signs the second Confession of Faith in Scotland.
Feb:
Mar:

B **Apr:** 1st, the Portuguese Cortes at Thomar submit to Philip II;
4th, Queen Elizabeth knights Francis Drake at Deptford.
May: Stephen Báthory, King of Poland, invades Russia.
Jun: 2nd, the Earl of Morton is executed, having been found guilty of complicity in Darnley's murder (in 1566).

C **Jul:** 17th, Edmund Campion is seized; he subsequently defends his position in disputations, is tried for treason and, *Dec.* 1st, executed;
26th, by the Act of Abjuration the seven northern provinces of the Netherlands renounce their allegiance to Philip II of Spain;
Don Antonio of Portugal escapes to England.
Aug: A French army under the Duke of Anjou enters Cambrai, and the Duke of Parma retreats.
Sep: Secret negotiations between the Jesuits Holt and Creighton with Esmé Stuart, Duke of Lennox and the Catholic peers Huntly and Caithness on behalf of Mary Queen of Scots.

D **Oct:** Marriage negotiations are entered between Elizabeth I and François Duke of Anjou; John Stubbs voices the Puritans' horror of the proposed marriage through mistrust of France.
Nov: 7th(–11th), a marriage treaty is signed between Anjou and Elizabeth I (but further proceedings peter out);
30th, the Duke of Parma takes Tournai.
Dec:

E Sigismund Báthory becomes Prince of Transylvania (–1602);
Beginnings of the Russian Conquest of Siberia (completed 1598);
Peace between Spain and Turkey, based on the *status quo*;
The Mogul Emperor Akbar conquers Afghanistan.

F **Politics, Economics, Law and Education**

The practice of life assurance is forbidden in the Spanish Netherlands.

The English Levant (or Turkey) Company is founded.

Compendious or Brief Examination of Certain Ordinary Complaints of Our Countrymen, a standard work on mercantilism.

Richard Mulcaster, *Positions*, a treatise on education; urges exercise, the education of girls and the training of teachers.

G **Science, Technology and Discovery**

G. Galileo discovers the principle of the pendulum.

William Borough, *A Discourse on the Variation of the Compass or Magneticall Needle*.

Robert Norman, *New Attractive*, a study of magnetism.

H **Philosophy, Religion and Scholarship**

Lancelot Popelinière, *Premier livre de l'idée de l'histoire accomplié*, a pioneer work of contemporary history.

Francisco Sanchez, *Quod Nihil Scitur* (on the limitations of human knowledge).

George Pettie translates *The Civil Conversations of Stefano Guazzo*, bks 1–3 (completed by Bartholomew Young –1586) (a set of four dialogues of courtesy and good behaviour for courtiers and gentlemen).

J **Art, Sculpture, Fine Arts and Architecture**

Painting:

Caravaggio, *Martyrdom of St. Maurice*.

K **Music**

Baltasar de Beaujoyeux's *Balet de la Royne* (earliest ballet with music extant) performed at French court.

Caroso, *Il Ballarino* (on dance technique) published in Venice.

Vincenzo Galilei, *Dialogo della musica antica e della moderna*.

Geuzenliedboek (anthology of Dutch marching, military and historical songs. Includes the national anthem, 'Wilhelmus').

Count Bardi of Vernio founds the Florentine Camerata.

Sieur Juvigny invents the flageolet.

L **Literature (including Drama)**

Torquato Tasso, *Gerusalemme Liberata* (first complete and authorised edition published in Ferrara).

M **Births and Deaths**

Jan. 4th James Ussher b. (–1656).

June 2nd James Douglas, Earl of Morton, d. (*c.* 56).

July 22nd Richard Cox d. (81).

Oct. 21st Zampieri Domenichino b. (–1641).

Dec. 1st Edmund Campion d. (41).

— Thomas Overbury b. (–1613).

A   Jan: 15th, Peace of Jam-Zapolski between Russia and Poland is signed through the mediation of Pope Gregory XIII. Russia abandons Livonia and Estonia to Poland, losing
her access to the Baltic.
Feb: 3rd, the Duke of Anjou leaves England for Flushing, and
19th, is inaugurated as Duke of Brabant in Antwerp.
Mar: 18th, attempted assassination of William of Orange.

B   Apr:
May:
Jun:

C   Jul: The Duke of Parma takes Oudenarde;
the Imperial Diet is summoned by Rudolf II to provide money for repairing forts on
the Turkish frontier. The right of the Protestant Joachim Frederick of Brandenburg
to hold the bishopric of Magdeburg is unsuccessfully contested at the Diet and the
situation in Aachen, where control has passed to Protestants, embitters discussion;
the Duke of Anjou is inaugurated as Lord of Friesland, Duke of Gelderland and Count
of Flanders, through the efforts of William of Nassau, son of William of Orange.
Aug: 22nd, in the Ruthven Raid, the English Party in Scotland, led by Earls of Angus,
Gowrie and Mar, capture James VI while hunting at Ruthven Castle, forcing him to
dismiss his favourites, the Earls of Arran and Lennox, to avenge the former Regent
Morton's death; James remains in captivity until *June* 1583.
Sep:

D   Oct: 4th–15th, the Gregorian Calendar is adopted in the Papal States, Spain and Portugal.
Nov:
Dec: 10th/20th, the Gregorian Calendar is adopted in France, and, 15th/25th, in the
Spanish Netherlands, Denmark and Norway.

E   The Venetian Constitution is amended to restrict the authority of the Council of Ten;
Nobunaga, ruler of Japan, is assassinated by Akechi Mitsuhide, who is subsequently defeated by Hideyoshi.

F **Politics, Economics, Law and Education**
Graduated pay, according to rank, is introduced into the Royal Navy.
Edinburgh University is founded.

G **Science, Technology and Discovery**
Urbain Hémand, *Researches Upon the Anatomy of the Teeth.*
Water-wheels are installed on London Bridge; London's first waterworks is established.

H **Philosophy, Religion and Scholarship**
George Buchanan, *Rerum Scoticarum Historiae.*
Richard Stanyhurst translates bks. 1–4 of the *Aeneid.*
The New Testament (Rheims and Douay Bible) (–1609).
Utrecht Library is founded.
Accademia della Crusca, Florence, is founded (–1612).
Jesuit Mission in China is started.

J **Art, Sculpture, Fine Arts and Architecture**

K **Music**

L **Literature (including Drama)**

M **Births and Deaths**
Jan. 28th John Barclay b. (–1621).
Apr. 8th Phineas Fletcher b. (–1650).
Sept. 28th George Buchanan d. (76).
Oct. 4th St. Teresa d. (67).
Nov. 30th Richard Farrant d. (50).
— William Juxon b. (–1662).

A   Jan: 7th/17th, François, Duke of Anjou intending to conquer a principality for himself in the southern Netherlands, sacks Antwerp, but fails to seize the city—'The French Fury'.

Feb: Archbishop Gebhard of Cologne, having married and changed his religion from Lutheranism to Calvinism, attempts to return to his See but is opposed by the Lutherans—'the Cologne War'.

Mar:

B   Apr: Pope Gregory XIII deposes Archbishop Gebhard of Cologne and appoints Ernest of Bavaria as his successor.

May:

Jun: The Duke of Anjou retires from the Netherlands to France;

James VI of Scotland escapes from the hands of the Ruthven raiders (of *Aug.* 1582), takes refuge in St. Andrews, and recalls the Earl of Arran.

C   Jul: Ivan the Terrible in a fit of rage kills his son Ivan.

Aug: 14th, John Whitgift is elected Archbishop of Canterbury (–1604), following the death of Edmund Grindal;

Sir Humphrey Gilbert makes an unsuccessful attempt to plant an English colony in Newfoundland (and is drowned on the voyage home, *Sept.* 9th);

William of Orange accepts the sovereignty of the northern Netherlands.

Sep: Catholic rising on Languedoc.

D   Oct: The Somerville Plot to assassinate Elizabeth I is discovered (John Somerville is executed *Dec.* 20th).

Nov: 11th, the Earl of Desmond, who had been attainted for treason in Ireland, is killed; his extensive estates are parcelled out among Sir Walter Raleigh and other English adventurers.

Dec: The Throgmorton Plot, for a Spanish invasion of England, is discovered and Francis Throgmorton arrested.

E   Duke William V of Bavaria signs a concordat with Pope Gregory XIII.

F **Politics, Economics, Law and Education**

Sir Thomas Smith, *De Republica Anglorum*, describes the machinery of government in England and discusses the problem of sovereignty.

Francesco Sansovino, *Del Governo et ammistrazione di diversi regni et republiche* (published in Venice).

First-known life insurance policy in England, made *June* 18th, on the life of William Gibbons for one year at eight per cent premium.

G **Science, Technology and Discovery**

Ralph Fitch and John Eldred, English merchants, undertake expeditions to Mesopotamia, the Persian Gulf and India (–1591).

H **Philosophy, Religion and Scholarship**

Giovanni Battista Adriani, *Istoria dei suoi tempi* (–1536–1574; posth.).

Joseph Justus Scaliger, *Opus De Emendatione Temporum* (the foundation of modern chronology).

Giordano Bruno visits England.

J **Art, Sculpture, Fine Arts and Architecture**

K **Music**

L **Literature (including Drama)**

Rembert Dodoens, *Pemptades* (a herbal; basis of Gerard's *Herball* –1597).

Baptista Honwaerd, Dutch didactic poem, *Pegasides Pleyn Amorosity* (or 'The Palace of the Maidens').

Queen's Company of Players (Queen Elizabeth's Men) is formed by Sir Edmund Tilney, Master of the Revels.

M **Births and Deaths**

Jan. — Fernando, Duke of Alva, d. (74).

Mar. 3rd Edward, Lord Herbert of Cherbury, b. (–1648).

Apr. 10th Hugo Grotius b. (–1645).

July 8th Fernão Mendes Pinto d. (74).

Sept. 9th Humphrey Gilbert d. (*c.* 44).

Sept. 15th Albrecht von Wallenstein b. (–1634).

Nov. 11th Gerald, Earl of Desmond, d. (50).

Nov. 24th Philip Massinger b. (–1640).

Dec. 3rd Thomas Erastus d. (59).

— Girolamo Frescobaldi b. (–1644).

— Orlando Gibbons b. (–1625).

1584   Guise forms the Catholic League—Parma's successes— Assassination of William of Orange

A   Jan. 7th/17th, the Gregorian Calendar is adopted in the Catholic states of the Holy Roman Empire and in the Catholic cantons of Switzerland;

     9th, Mendoza, the Spanish ambassador in London, is expelled for his complicity in the Throgmorton Plot.

Feb:

Mar: 18th, Feodore, the last of the Rurik dynasty, succeeds as Tsar of Russia (–1598) on the death of Ivan the Terrible. Feodore is dominated by his brother-in-law, Boris Godunov.

B   Apr: The Duke of Parma recovers Ypres from the Dutch.

May: Parma takes Bruges.

Jun: 15th, François Duke of Anjou (formerly Duke of Alençon) dies at Château-Thiery, leaving the Protestant Henry of Navarre as heir to the French throne. The Duke of Guise consolidates the Catholic factions in France into a Catholic League to oppose Navarre's claim.

C   Jul: 10th, Francis Throgmorton is executed for treason;

     —, William of Orange is assassinated by Balthazar Gérard, at the instigation of Philip II; William is succeeded as Stadtholder by his son, Maurice of Nassau, with Olden-barneveldt as his chief aide.

Aug: Philip II imprisons Antonio Perez for the murder, on his instructions, of Escobedo, secretary to Don John of Austria, in *Mar.* 1578.

Sep: Ghent submits to the Duke of Parma.

D   Oct: The arrest of Fr. Creighton reveals the Catholic Enterprise (of Philip II, Parma and the Duke of Guise) against England, for the deposition of Elizabeth I and the accession of Mary Queen of Scots;

     19th, the Bond of Association, a signed declaration of Englishmen to defend Elizabeth I and to kill the perpetrators of her assassination, is presented to the Queen.

Nov: 23rd (–*Dec.* 21st), Parliament meets and frames legislation for expelling Jesuits and seminary priests within 40 days.

Dec:

E   The Turkish fleet fails to capture the coast of Zanzibar from the Portuguese;

     An alliance is signed between the Protestant cantons of Berne, Geneva and Zurich against Savoy, which is threatening Geneva;

     the Dutch establish a trading post at Archangel on the White Sea.

F Politics, Economics, Law and Education
    Banco di Rialto is established in Venice.
    Sir Walter Mildmay founds Emmanuel College, Cambridge, a bulwark of Puritanism.
    Reginald Scott, *The Discoverie of Witchcraft*, an attack on superstition.
    Uppingham School is founded.

G Science, Technology and Discovery

H Philosophy, Religion and Scholarship
    José de Acosta published a catechism, in Quichua; the first book to be printed in Peru.
    Giordano Bruno, *Spaccio della bestia trionffante* (Banishment of the Triumphant Beast,
      an ethical treatise dedicated to Sir Philip Sidney); *La cena de le ceneri* (Ash Wednesday
      supper, in support of the Copernican system); and *De la causa, principio et uno* (a
      treatise on metaphysics—anti-Aristotelian).
    Nicholas Sanders (Saunder?), *De Origine ac Progressu Schismatis Anglicani* (completed
      by Rishton in 1585).
    Carlo Sigonio completes his history of Italy in the middle ages (284–1268; *de regno
      Italiae*).
    Accademia di Scienze, Lettere ed Art, Lucca, is founded.

J Art, Sculpture, Fine Arts and Architecture
    Painting:
      Annibale Caracci, frescoes in the Fara Palace.

K Music

L Literature (including Drama)
    John Lyly, *Alexander and Campaspe* (play). *Sapho and Phao* acted.
    George Peele, *The Arraignment of Paris* (pastoral masque).
    Twespraack von de Nederd, letterkunst, published by Egelantier, Dutch Chamber of
      Rhetoric, Amsterdam (*see* 1578 H).

M Births and Deaths
    Jan. 24th James Balfour of Pittendreich d. (60).
    Mar. 18th Ivan IV ('The Terrible') d. (53).
    May — André du Chesne b. (–1640).
    June 15th François, Duke of Anjou, d. (30).
    Nov. 4th Carlo Borromeo d. (46).
    Dec. 16th John Selden b. (–1654).
    — William Baffin b. (–1622).
    — Francis Beaumont b. (–1616).
    — John Day d. (62).
    — John Pym b. (–1643).

1585　Raleigh's Roanoke Colony—Parma sacks Antwerp—Elizabeth I aids the Dutch

A　Jan: 2nd, by the Treaty of Joinville the Catholic League in France, under Henry Duke of Guise, gains Spanish support for Henry, Cardinal of Bourbon's candidature to the French throne, excluding the claims of his elder brothers Henry of Navarre and the Prince of Condé; for this support Philip II is to acquire Navarre and Béarn.

Feb: 4th (–*Mar.* 29th), Parliament meets, to pass legislation for the security of the Queen's person;
Henry III of France refuses the sovereignty of the Netherlands.

Mar: 2nd, Dr. William Parry, M.P., is executed for alleged high treason;
the Catholic League declares Henry of Navarre incapable of inheriting the French throne;
Sir Francis Drake leaves for the West Indies as a privateer and attacks Vigo and St. Domingo (–*July* 1586).

B　Apr: 24th, Felice Peretti is elected Pope Sixtus V (–1590), following the death of Pope Gregory XIII, *Apr.* 12th.

May: 19th, English shipping in Spanish ports is confiscated, as a reprisal for depredations across the Line; this serves as a declaration of war on England.

Jun: 29th, Dutch commission offer Queen Elizabeth the sovereignty of the Low Countries, which she declines.

C　Jul: 7th, Henry III is forced to sign the Treaty of Nemours with the Guises, in which he capitulates to their demands for revoking all toleration to Huguenots; this provokes the War of the Three Henries (Henry III, Henry of Navarre and Henry of Guise) for the succession. End of the Anglo-French alliance under the Treaty of Blois of 1572.
7th, An expedition under Grenville and Lane lands at Roanoke, Virginia, to plant Raleigh's first colony.

Aug: 2nd/12th, preliminary treaty of Elizabeth I with the estates-General to aid them in the defence of Antwerp;
7th/17th, the Duke of Parma sacks Antwerp;
14th, Elizabeth I issues Declaration taking the Netherlands under her protection.

Sep: 3rd, Treaty of Nonsuch between England and the States-General: to supply 1,000 horse and 5,100 foot under a proved general, and in return to garrison the towns of Flushing, Brielle and Rammekins, in the Isle of Walcheren, as security;
9th, Pope Sixtus V excommunicates Henry of Navarre;
14th, English Parliament is dissolved.

D　Oct:
Nov:
Dec: The Earl of Leicester takes up his command in the Netherlands.

E　The Mogul Emperor Akbar annexes Afghanistan;
Hideyoshi is appointed Dictator in Japan.

F **Politics, Economics, Law and Education**
   The Sack of Antwerp by Spanish troops (*Aug.* 17th) ends the days of Antwerp as an international port, especially for the spice trade, and as the hub of the international money market.
   A Jesuit University is founded at Graz.

G **Science, Technology and Discovery**
   John Davis visits West Greenland and discovers Davis Strait.
   Lucas Janszon Wagheraen, *Spiegel der Zeevaart* ('The Mariners' Mirror', a book of sailing directions).
   Simon Stevin discovers the law of equilibrium and in *De Thiende* (printed by Plantin at Leyden) argues that a decimal system should be used for calculations instead of common fractions and for coinage, weights and measures.

H **Philosophy, Religion and Scholarship**
   Giordano Bruno, *De gli heroici furori* (dedicated to Sir Philip Sidney).
   Elizabethan Act against the Jesuits and Seminarists (–1568) to depart 'out of the realm of England' within forty days after the end of the parliamentary session.

J **Art, Sculpture, Fine Arts and Architecture**

K **Music**

L **Literature (including Drama)**
   Miguel de Cervantes Saavedra, *Galatea* (pastoral romance).
   Battista Guarini, *Pastor Fido* (pastoral drama).
   Lord Chamberlain's Men; and then Lord Admiral's Company of actors formed, led by Edward Alleyn.
   William Shakespeare leaves Stratford-upon-Avon for London.
   Teatro Olimpico, Vicenza, is opened.

M **Births and Deaths**
   Sept. 9th Armand Jean du Plessis de Richelieu b. (–1642).
   Oct. 28th Cornelius Jansen b. (–1638).
   Nov. 23rd Thomas Tallis d. (*c.* 60).
   Dec. 13th William Drummond of Hawthornden b. (–1649).
   Dec. 22nd Vittoria Accoramboni d. (28).
   Dec. 27th Pierre de Ronsard d. (61).
   — James ('Admirable') Crichton d. (*c.* 25).
   — Heinrich Schütz b. (–1672).

A Jan:
   Feb: 4th, the Earl of Leicester accepts the title of Governor and Captain-General of the Netherlands, but Queen Elizabeth insists on his resigning it.
   Mar: 16th, Christian I succeeds as Elector of Saxony on the death of the Elector Augustus; Nicholas Krell becomes his chief minister.

B Apr: Colonel Pfyffer forms the Borromean League of the Seven Swiss Catholic Cantons.
   May:
   June: Leicester angers Johan van Oldenbarneveldt, the new Advocate of Holland, and other moderates by allowing the exclusive Calvinists to hold a National Synod at Dort;
   Mary Queen of Scots recognises Philip II of Spain as her heir.

C Jul: 1st, by the Treaty of Berwick, Elizabeth I and James VI form a league of amity; James is to receive an annual pension from England;
   the Duke of Parma takes Venlo;
   17th, Sir Francis Walsingham succeeds in unravelling the Babington Plot to murder Elizabeth I, establishing that Mary Queen of Scots was implicated in the plans;
   27th, the English plantation of Munster is attempted.
   Aug:
   Sep: 13th, Anthony Babington and his fellow conspirators are tried, and, 20th, executed; 22nd, Sir Philip Sydney is fatally wounded at the attack on Zutphen (dies *Oct.* 17th).

D Oct: 11th (–14th), Mary Queen of Scots is tried for treason before special commissioners at Fotheringhay;
   25th, sentence is pronounced against Mary Queen of Scots in the Star Chamber;
   29th (–*Dec.* 2nd), English Parliament meets to deal with the problem of Mary Queen of Scots.
   Nov: Leicester returns to England, leaving Sir John Norris in command in the Netherlands;
   the Sixteen establish a revolutionary government in Paris, pledged to support the Duke of Guise and the Catholic League.
   Dec: 4th, Queen Elizabeth confirms the sentence against Mary Queen of Scots (but delays signing the death warrant until *Feb.* 4th, 1587). James VI makes attempts to save his mother;
   Stephen Báthory, King of Poland, dies (Sigismund III is elected his successor *Aug.* 1587);
   Olivarez, Spanish ambassador to the Pope, extracts a pledge from Pope Sixtus V to help finance the sending of an Armada against England;
   Catherine de' Medici and Henry of Navarre meet near Cognac.

E Abbas I accedes as Shah of Persia (–1629).

F Politics, Economics, Law and Education
Pope Sixtus V, by the bull *Detestabilis*, forbids usury.
Severe shortage of corn in England.
The Russians found Voronezh.
Claudius Aquaviva expounds the Jesuit system of education in *Ratis atque institutio studiorum*.

G Science, Technology and Discovery
Thomas Cavendish leaves Plymouth, *July* 21st, on a voyage of circumnavigation, west to east (he returns to Plymouth, *Sept.* 10th, 1588).

H Philosophy, Religion and Scholarship
Robert Francis Romulus, St. Bellamine, *De Controversiis Christianae Fidei adversus huius Temporis Haereticos* (–1593).
William Camden, *Britannia* (Latin text; trans. –1610).
Francesco Patrizi, *Della poetica* (incomplete).
William Webbe, *Discourse of English Poetrie*.
Star Chamber decree, inspired by Archbishop Whitgift, forbids publication of pamphlets and books unless previously approved by the ecclesiastical authorities (*see Martin Marprelate* pamphlets, 1588).
Pope Sixtus V (Felice Peretti) fixes the number of cardinals at 70.

J Art, Sculpture, Fine Arts and Architecture
Painting:
El Greco, *Burial of Count Orgaz*.

K Music

L Literature (including Drama)
Pierre de Ronsard, *Les Oeuvres*, ed. by Jean Galland and Claude Binet (posth.).
William Warner, *Albion's England*, bks. 1–4 (a metrical history, 16 bks. –1606).

M Births and Deaths
Apr. 17th John Ford b. (–1640).
Sept. 20th Anthony Babington d. (24).
Sept. 21st Cardinal Granvella d. (89).
Oct. 17th Philip Sidney d. (31).
— Margaret of Austria, Duchess of Parma, d. (64).
— Théophraste Renaudot b. (–1653).

A Jan:
  Feb: 1st, Elizabeth I signs warrant for the execution of Mary Queen of Scots, and, 8th,
    she is executed at Fotheringhay. Elizabeth heavily fines William Davidson, a Secre-
    tary of State, for his share in sending the death warrant to Fotheringhay and Lord
    Treasurer Burghley remains in disgrace until *July*;
    15th (*–Mar.* 23rd), Parliament meets;
      John Casimir of the Palatinate signs a treaty of alliance with Henry of Navarre.
  Mar: 1st, Peter Wentworth, Puritan, M.P., is imprisoned in the Tower for presenting
    to the Speaker of the House of Commons a paper on freedom of speech in which
    he denied the Queen's ecclesiastical supremacy.

B Apr: 19th, Sir Francis Drake singes the King of Spain's beard by sacking Cadiz; he takes
    many prizes and prevents Philip II from sending an Armada against England during
    the year;
    29th, Sir Christopher Hatton is appointed Lord Chancellor.
  May: Henry of Navarre captures Talmont and Fontenay in Poitou from the Catholic
    League.
  Jun: The Earl of Leicester returns to his command in the Netherlands (*Aug.* 6th; he
    resigns his command *Mar.* 1588).

C Jul: The Duke of Parma captures Neurs.
  Aug: 5th, Parma captures Sluys;
    19th, Sigismund III, son of John of Sweden, is elected King of Poland (–1632),
    following the death of Stephen Báthory (in *Dec.* 1586);
    Pope Sixtus V proclaims a Catholic Crusade for the invasion of England and the de-
    position of Elizabeth I;
    Cardinal William Allen's manifesto justifying a Spanish invasion.
  Sep:

D Oct: 20th, Henry of Navarre defeats Catholic League at Battle of Coultras, the first
    notable Huguenot victory;
    Cardinal Ferdinand de' Medici succeeds as Grand Duke of Tuscany on the death of
    Francis de' Medici.
  Nov: The Duke of Guise defeats the German force under Fabian von Dohna at Auneau,
    near Chartres.
  Dec: Martin von Schenck takes Bonn from the Spaniards (it is recaptured *Sept.* 1588);
    Henry III forbids the Duke of Guise to enter Paris and he retires to Nancy.

E Raleigh's second settlement in Roanoke, Virginia under John White (–1591);
  Queen Elizabeth attempts to sign a treaty of alliance with Turkey against Spain;
  The Catholic cantons of Switzerland sign a treaty of alliance with Spain;
  Portuguese missionaries are banished from Japan.

F **Politics, Economics, Law and Education**
> The second edition of Raphael Holinshed's *Chronicles of England, Scotland and Ireland*, is suppressed by the government for dealing with contemporary affairs and publishing recent documents.
> Agustino, *Dialogo de Medallas y Inscriciones*, a pioneer study of numismatics.

G **Science, Technology and Discovery**
> Rialto Bridge, Venice, is built (–1591).

H **Philosophy, Religion and Scholarship**
> Angel Day translates Amyot's French version of the *Daphnis and Chloe* of Longus.
> John Knox, *History of the Reformation in Scotland* [to 1567] (posth. 1586/7).
> Isaac Casaubon edits Strabo, and writes *Notes on the Four Gospels and the Acts of the Apostles*.
> Bartholomew Young translates the *Amorous Fiametta* of Boccaccio.
> William Allen is created a Cardinal (*Aug.* 7th).

J **Art, Sculpture, Fine Arts and Architecture**

K **Music**

L **Literature (including Drama)**
> Robert Greene, *Euphues, his Censure of Philautus* (continuation of Lyly's work).
> *Historia von D. Johann Fausten* (anon.).
> A company of English players visits Germany for the first time.
> *Rederijckkunst* published by Egelantier, Dutch Chamber of Rhetoric, Amsterdam (*see* 1578 H).

M **Births and Deaths**
> Jan. 6th Gaspar de Guzman, Count of Olivares, b. (–1645).
> Feb. 8th Mary Queen of Scots d. (45).
> Apr. 18th John Foxe d. (71).
> Aug. 18th Virginia Dare b. (–?).
> Nov. 17th Joost van den Vondel b. (–1679).

1588   The Day of the Barricades in Paris—Defeat of the Spanish Armada—Assassination of Guise

A Jan:

Feb: The Catholic League presents a memorial to Henry III of France demanding that he should purge his court and council of Huguenot sympathisers, implement the Tridentine decrees and confiscate Huguenot property;

the Marquis of Santa Cruz, the Spanish admiral, dies.

Mar: The Polish Grand Chancellor defeats the Archduke Maximilian in Silesia and imprisons him. To ransom his brother, the Emperor Rudolf II subsequently agrees to cede the county of Zips to Poland.

B Apr: 4th, Christian IV accedes to the throne of Denmark (–1648) on the death of Frederick II;

Henry III summons Swiss mercenaries under Biron to the suburbs of Paris to defend him against the Catholic League; in alarm the Parisians send for the Duke of Guise.

May: 9th, Guise enters Paris;

12th, at the Day of Barricades, Guise makes himself master of Paris;

13th, Henry III escapes to Chartres;

30th/*June* 9th, the Duke of Medina Sidonia sets sail from Lisbon with the Spanish Armada.

Jun:

C Jul: 11th, Henry III agrees to all the Duke of Guise's demands, including the summoning of the States-General to Blois (in *Oct.*);

19th/29th, the Spanish Armada is sighted off the Cornish coast;

23rd, the English army to repel invasion is summoned to Tilbury under the Earl of Leicester as Lieutenant General of the realm;

27th/*Aug.* 6th, after a running fight up the English Channel the Armada anchors in Calais Roads;

28th/*Aug.* 2nd, Lord Admiral Howard of Effingham sends in fire ships to destroy many of the Spanish galleons off Calais;

29th/*Aug.* 8th, defeat of the Armada at the Battle of Gravelines; the surviving galleons take to the North Sea, and many are subsequently wrecked off the Scottish and Irish coasts.

Aug: 8th, recognition in London that the Duke of Parma's opportunity for invading England from the Netherlands has vanished;

Maurice of Nassau is created Captain-General of the United Provinces by the States-General.

Sep: A Spanish force recaptures Bonn from John Casimir.

D Oct: 16th, the States-General meet at Blois and suggest the surrender of the French Crown to the Duke of Guise.

Nov:

Dec: 23rd, Henry III arranges for the assassination of Henry, Duke of Guise, at Blois;

24th, Louis Cardinal of Guise is also assassinated, and the Cardinal of Bourbon and the Duke of Joinville are arrested. In consequence, the leadership of the Catholic League passes to the Duke of Mayenne.

E

F **Politics, Economics, Law and Education**
Timothy Bright, *An Arte of Shorte, Swifte and Secrete Writing by Character* (shorthand).
The English Guinea Company is founded.

G **Science, Technology and Discovery**
Joachim Camerarius, *Hortus Medicus*.
Thomas Hariot, *Briefe and True Report of the New Found Land of Virginia*, recommends tobacco as a medicine.

H **Philosophy, Religion and Scholarship**
Thomas Stapleton, *Tres Thomae* (collective biographies of St. Thomas the Apostle, St. Thomas of Canterbury, and Sir Thomas More).
Cesare Baronius, *Annales ecclesiastici a Christo nato ad annum* 1198 (12 vols., –1607; completed by Antoine Pagi; the first critical Church History, and written to refute the *Magdeburg Centuries* of the Protestants –1560).
Luis de Molina, *Liberi Arbitrii cum Gratiae Donis . . . Concordia* (leads to a dispute on free will by Jesuits and Dominicans—Molinists and Thomists).
William Morgan's translation of the Bible into Welsh.
The *Martin Marprelate Tracts* (seven extant) are issued from a secret press, in defence of Presbyterianism, and published in defiance of the Star Chamber decree instigated by Archbishop Whitgift (in 1586). Suspected authors John Penry and John Udall are arrested; Penry executed in 1593; Udall dies whilst awaiting punishment in prison).
Thomas Cooper, *Admonition to the People of England* (one of the many anti-tracts and pamphlets resulting from the controversy –1589).

J **Art, Sculpture, Fine Arts and Architecture**
Painting:
Annibale Carracci, frescoes in the Magnani Palace.
Nicholas Hilliarde, *Man clasping a hand* and *A Youth leaning against a tree among Roses* (miniatures).
Isaac Oliver, *A Man Aged* 59 (miniature).
Architecture:
Fontana completes cupola and lantern of St. Peter's, Rome (–1590).

K **Music**
William Byrd, *Psalmes, sonets, and songs*.
Nicholas Yonge, *Musica Transalpina* (collection of 57 madrigals) published in London.

L **Literature (including Drama)**
Robert Greene, *Pandosto, or Dorastus and Fawnia; Perimedes the Blacksmith* (romances).
Michel de Montaigne, *Essais*, vol. 3 (~1580).

M **Births and Deaths**
Jan. 12th John Winthrop b. (–1649).
Feb. 9th Marquis of Santa Cruz d. (61).
Apr. 5th Thomas Hobbes b. (–1679).
Apr. 19th Paolo Veronese d. (*c*. 60).
June 18th Robert Crowley d. (*c*. 70).
Sept. 4th Robert Dudley, Earl of Leicester, d. (56).
— Henry, Prince of Condé, d. (36).
— Catherine de Vivone, Marquise de Rambouillet, b. (–1665).

A   Jan: 5th, Catherine de' Medici, Queen Mother of France, dies.
    Feb: 4th, English Parliament meets (*-Mar.* 29th);
        15th, the Duke of Mayenne enters Paris and is declared Lieutenant-General of the Kingdom by the Catholic League.
    Mar: 9th, by the Peace of Benten, the Archduke Maximilian renounces his claim to the Polish throne.

B   Apr: 3rd, Henry III and Henry of Navarre sign a truce, to oppose the designs of the Catholic League (the two Kings meet outside Tours *Apr.* 30th);
        13th, Sir Francis Drake and Sir John Norris undertake an expedition of 150 ships and 18,000 men to Portugal. They destroy Corunna but fail to take Lisbon, after much loss of life through sickness, and the attempt to place Don Antonio on the Portuguese throne ends in failure (*-July*);
    May: Charles Emmanuel, Duke of Savoy, attacks Geneva, which is deserted by her Bernese allies (–1598).
    Jun:

C   Jul: 29th, Henry III's army forces the bridge at St. Cloud and begins to threaten Paris.
    Aug: 2nd, Henry III is assassinated at St. Cloud by Jacques Clément, a Jacobin monk; on his deathbed the last of the House of Valois recognises Henry of Navarre as his successor, who claims the throne as Henry IV (–1610). Philip II of Spain lays claim to the French throne for his daughter Isabel, by his marriage with Elizabeth Valois, Henry III's sister;
        5th, Henry IV makes Tours his headquarters in his struggle against the Catholic League.
    Sep: 21st, Henry IV repulses the Leaguers under the Duke of Mayenne at the Battle of Arques;
        30th, Lord Willoughby arrives in France with 4,000 English troops to aid Henry.

D   Oct: Maurice of Nassau is elected Stadtholder of Utrecht, Gelderland and Overyssel.
    Nov: 1st, Henry IV captures the faubourgs of St. Jacques and St. Germain, Paris, but is later repulsed.
    Dec: Le Mans and Bayeux surrender to Henry IV.

E   The English Council undertake an enquiry into the state of the plantation of Ulster;
    Gebhard, Archbishop of Cologne, deposed by Gregory XIII in 1583, retires to Strasbourg to end his struggle with the Papacy;
    Antonio Perez, formerly Philip II's private secretary, escapes from prison in Castille to Aragon.

F **Politics, Economics, Law and Education**
   Justus Lipsius, *Politicorum sive Civilis Doctrinae.*
   House of Commons first appoints a Standing Committee for Privileges.
   Sidney Sussex College, Cambridge, is founded.
   Kiev Academy is founded.

G **Science, Technology and Discovery**
   Richard Hakluyt, *The Principall Navigations, Traffiques and Discoveries of the English Nation* (enlarged 1598, 1600).
   G. B. Della Porta, *Magia naturalis.*
   William Lee invents the stocking frame.

H **Philosophy, Religion and Scholarship**
   Amador Arrais, *Diálogues de Dom Frei Amador Arraiz* (ten conversations on moral and religious themes in classical Portuguese prose).
   John Lyly, *Pappe with an Hatchet* (supporting bishops in Marprelate controversy).
   George Puttenham, *The Arte of English Poesie.*
   Metropolitan Patriarch of Moscow asserts independence from Constantinople.
   Henry Barrowe, separatist leader (–1580), writes *A True Description of the Visible Congregation of the Saints.*

J **Art, Sculpture, Fine Arts and Architecture**
   Painting:
      Caravaggio, *Bacchus.*

K **Music**
   William Byrd, *Songes of sundrie natures.*

L **Literature (including Drama)**
   Robert Greene, *Menaphon* (romance; reprinted as *Greene's Arcadia* 1599).

M **Births and Deaths**
   Jan. 5th Catherine de' Medici d. (70).
   July 1st Christophe Plantin d. (75).
   — Jean Antoine de Baïf d. (57).

A   Jan: Philip II of Spain agrees to support the Holy League in France, providing ports and
       other towns are placed under Spanish control;
       the Cardinal of Bourbon is proclaimed Charles X of France by the Leaguers (he dies
       May 10th).
    Feb: the Duke of Mayenne leads a Leaguer army to take Pontoise and lays siege to
       Meulan (which he abandons, 25th).
    Mar: 1st, Henry IV lays siege to Dreux;
       3rd, Dutch army under Prince Maurice of Nassau, takes Breda;
       14th, Henry IV routs Mayenne's Leaguer army of 25,000 troops at Ivry on the River
       Eure and marches to Paris.

B   Apr:
    May: 7th, Henry IV begins to invest Paris from the north, causing famine in the capital.
    June: Charles Emmanuel, Duke of Savoy, sends an army under Martinengo to ravage
       Provence;
       Christian I of Saxony and the Elector John Casimir of the Palatinate present a list of
       grievances of German Protestant princes to the Emperor Rudolf II at Plauen.

C   Jul: 10th, Charles, Archduke of Inner Austria, dies and is succeeded by the future
       Emperor Ferdinand II, then aged 12.
    Aug: 27th, Pope Sixtus V dies.
    Sep: The Duke of Parma, advancing from the Spanish Netherlands, forces Henry IV to
       raise the siege of Paris;
       15th, Giovanni Battista Castagna elected Pope Urban VII (dies *Sept.* 27th).

D   Oct: Maurice of Nassau fails to take Nijmegen from the Spanish, but raids the country-
       side of North Brabant;
       a Spanish force lands at Blavet in Brittany to join forces with the Leaguer army of the
       Duke of Mercoeur.
    Nov: Drake, Hawkins and Frobisher return from an indecisive expedition to the Spanish
       coast;
       Charles Emmanuel I of Savoy enters Aix.
    Dec: 5th, Niccolò Sfondrato elected Pope Gregory XIV (–1591), a forceful supporter of
       the League in France;
       the Huguenot Lesdiguières takes Grenoble for Henry IV.

E   Shah Abbas I of Persia makes peace with the Turks, abandoning Tabriz, Shirva and
       Georgia, to enable him to deal with the Uzbeks under Abdullah II who have advanced
       into Khorasan;
       the Emperor of Morocco annexes Timbuctoo and the Upper Niger;
       Akbar, Mogul Emperor of India, conquers Orissa.

F **Politics, Economics, Law and Education**
Coalmining is begun in the Ruhr.
Alphonso Orozo establishes the College of Dona Maria de Aragon in Madrid (later Madrid University).
Peter Bales, *Writing Schoolemaster*, which includes 'the Arte of Brachygraphie' (a shorthand system).

G **Science, Technology and Discovery**
Zacharias Jansen invents a microscope.

H **Philosophy, Religion and Scholarship**
José de Acosta, *Historia natural y moral de las Indias*.
Henry Holland, *Treatise Against Witchcraft*.
Anthony Munday translates from the French the Spanish (or perhaps Portuguese) romance of chivalry called *Amadis of Gaul* (of 1508).
Critical edition of the Vulgate translation of the Bible issued by order of Sixtus V (-1592).

J **Art, Sculpture, Fine Arts and Architecture**
Painting:
Nicholas Hilliarde, *The Third Earl of Cumberland, Queen's Champion* (miniature).
Isaac Oliver, *A Girl aged five holding a red Carnation, A Girl aged four holding an apple*, and *A man aged 27* (miniatures).
Sculpture:
Giovanni de Bologna, *Mercury* (Florence).

K **Music**

L **Literature (including Drama)**
Robert Greene, *Mourning Garment* and *Never Too Late* (pamphlets).
Thomas Lodge, *Rosalynde. Euphues Golden Legacie* (pastoral romance in style of Euphues -1579).
Christopher Marlowe, *Tamburlaine the Great* (tragedy).
George Peele, *Polyhymnia*.
Sir Philip Sidney, The Countess of Pembroke's *Arcadia* (posth.).
Edmund Spenser, *The Faerie Queene*, bks. 1-3 (-1596, 1609).
Robert Wilson, *Three Lords and Three Ladies of London* (morality).
The *Accesi*, Italian company of *commedia dell'arte*, starts about now; it is taken by Martinelli and Cecchini to France in 1600.

M **Births and Deaths**
Feb. 12th François Hotman d. (65).
Mar. — William Bradford b. (-1657).
Apr. 6th Francis Walsingham d. (c. 60).
Sept. — Robert Blake b. (-1657).
— Ambrose Paré d. (80).

1591   Loss of the *Revenge*—Zutphen and Nijmegen fall to Maurice of Nassau

A **Jan:**
Feb: 3rd, formation of the German Protestant League of Torgau (a predominantly Calvinistic league) under Christian I of Saxony, John Casimir of the Palatinate and Christian of Anhalt.
Mar: 1st, Gregory XIV issues his monitorial excommunicating Henry IV of France.

B **Apr:** 17th, Elizabeth I sends Sir John Norris with 3,000 men to aid Henry IV;
19th, Chartres surrenders to Henry IV.
May: 15th, Dmitri, son of Ivan the Terrible, dies (a false Dmitri appears in Poland in 1601);
20th, Zutphen falls to Maurice and William Lewis of Nassau after a 5-day siege;
Antonio Perez, former private secretary to Philip II, defects to France.
Jun: 20th, Deventer surrenders to the Dutch.

C **Jul:** Sir John Hawkins and Sir Martin Frobisher are sent to intercept the Spanish Plate fleet off the Azores, but Philip II orders the flotilla to remain in America;
Maurice of Nassau routs the Duke of Parma's cavalry at Knodsenburg.
Aug: Robert Earl of Essex is sent with an army to France to aid Henry IV in the siege of Rouen;
19th, Henry IV takes Noyon in Picardy;
the *Revenge* is captured by the Spaniards in an action off the Azores and Sir Richard Grenville is mortally wounded.
Sep: Accession of Christian II of Saxony (–1601), then aged 8, on the death of his father, Christian I; his guardians, John George, Elector of Brandenburg, and the Duke of Saxe-Weimar, uproot Calvinism;
21st, French bishops meeting at Rouen accept Henry IV as King of France, in answer to the papal monitorial (of *Mar.* 1st).

D **Oct:** 16th, Pope Gregory XIV dies;
21st, Maurice of Nassau takes Nijmegen from the Spanish;
29th, Antonio Facchinetti is elected Pope Innocent IX (dies *Dec.* 30th).
Nov: 3rd, Sir Brian O'Rourke is executed at Tyburn for treason in Ireland;
Duke William V of Bavaria, through illness, is forced to admit his son Maximilian to a share in government (William resigns in 1598).
Dec: Philip II sends Alonso de Vergas with an army to Aragon and suppresses the traditional liberties at Tarragona.

E Navarre and the counties of Foix and Albret are annexed to the Crown of France.

F **Politics, Economics, Law and Education**
Trinity College, Dublin, is founded by Queen Elizabeth I.

G **Science, Technology and Discovery**
James Lancaster leaves Plymouth, *Apr.* 10th, on his first voyage to the East Indies.

H **Philosophy, Religion and Scholarship**
Giordano Bruno, *De immenso et innumerabilis seu de universo et mundis.*
Sir John Harington translates Ariosto's *Orlando Furioso* into English heroical verse.
Sir Henry Savile translates the *Histories of Tacitus.*

J **Art, Sculpture, Fine Arts and Architecture**

K **Music**

L **Literature (including Drama)**
Robert Greene, *Conny Catching*, parts 1 and 2. *Farewell to Folly* (pamphlet). *Philomela* (romance).
John Lyly, *Endymion, the Man in the Moon* (allegorical prose comedy).
Sir Philip Sidney, *Astrophel and Stella* (a sonnet sequence, posth.).
Edmund Spenser, *Complaints; Daphnaida* (an elegy).
The Troublesome Raigne of King John of England (anon., attributed to Shakespeare).
The first printed collection of *Danish Ballads* (anon.) appears.

M **Births and Deaths**
Aug. 31st Richard Grenville d. (*c.* 50).
Aug. — Robert Herrick b. (–1674).
Nov. 20th Christopher Hatton d. (51).
— St. John of the Cross (Juan de Yepez y Álvarez) d. (49).
— Guercino b. (–1666).
— Luis Ponce de Leon d. (*c.* 63).

A Jan: 6th, Frederick IV succeeds as the Elector Palatine on the death of John Casimir;
    15th, Queen Elizabeth I recalls Robert Earl of Essex from his command in France to England; he returns later in the year;
    30th, Ippolito Aldobrandini elected Pope Clement VIII (–1605).
   Feb:
   Mar:

B Apr: The Duke of Parma strengthens the Leaguer garrison of Paris with 1,200 Walloons, relieves Rouen and returns to the Netherlands.
   May: Spaniards defeat English force under Sir John Norris at Cranon, Brittany.
   Jun: Emperor Rudolf II makes peace with Poland.

C Jul:
   Aug: Sir John Burrows captures the Portuguese galleon *Madre de Dios* at Flores with a cargo valued at £850,000.
   Sep: Maurice succeeds as Landgrave of Hesse-Cassel on the death of William the Wise. Affairs are directed by Count Mansfeld until 1593, when Maurice, a Calvinist, comes of age.

D Oct: The Archduke Matthias is sent by Rudolf II to govern Hungary.
   Nov: 27th, Sigismund III succeeds as King of Sweden (–1604) on the death of John III.
   Dec: 3rd, on the death of Alessandro Farnese, Prince of Parma, Philip II appoints the Archduke Ernest Governor of the Netherlands (he arrives in Brussels *Jan.* 1594); Philip II plans to place the Infanta Isabel on the throne of France.

E Périgord and Béarn are annexed to the French Crown;
   The Mogul Emperor Akbar takes Sind;
   The Portuguese settle at Mombasa;
   Hideyoshi, Shogun of Japan, plans to invade China; when Korea refuses to allow the passage of Japanese troops it is invaded (–1593).

July — Thomas Cavendish d. (*c.* 37).
Aug. 28th George Villiers, Duke of Buckingham, b. (–1628).
Sept. 3rd Robert Greene d. (*c.* 32).
Sept. 13th Michel de Montaigne d. (59).
Dec. 3rd Alessandro Farnese, Duke of Parma, d. (47).
— Nicholas Ferrar b. (–1637).

F **Politics, Economics, Law and Education**
   The plague kills 15,000 inhabitants of London (–1593).

G **Science, Technology and Discovery**
   A windmill is used to drive a mechanical saw in Holland.
   G. Galileo, *Scienza Mechanica*, discusses the problems of raising weights.
   Sir James Lancaster rounds the Malay Peninsula (*June*).

H **Philosophy, Religion and Scholarship**
   Jean Bodin, *Colloquium Heptaplomeres* (written about now; not published until 1857.
   Consisted of discussions between a Jew, a Mohammedan, a Roman Catholic, a
   Lutheran, a Zwinglian, and a Theist, etc., resulting in the conclusion that it may be
   best for them all to relinquish disputing about religious beliefs).
   Thomas Sanchez, *De Sacramento Matrimonii* (on religious and legal aspects of marriage).
   The Parliament in Edinburgh ratifies the Presbyterian Order of the Church of Scotland.
   The Vulgate (Latin translation of the Bible –1590), issued in a definitive text with the
   approval of Clement VIII.
   The ruined Roman city of Pompeii is discovered.
   Juan de Mariana, *Historiae de Rebus Hispaniae* (later continued to 1605; trans. by the
   author into Spanish, 1601–9).
   Academia de los Nocturnos, Valencia (the earliest Spanish academy is founded about
   1592–3).

J **Art, Sculpture, Fine Arts and Architecture**
   Painting:
      Tintoretto, *The Last Supper* (–1594).

K **Music**

L **Literature (including Drama)**
   Henry Constable, *Diana* (sonnet sequence).
   Samuel Daniel, *Delia* (sonnet sequence); *The Complaint of Rosamond*.
   Robert Greene, *A Groatsworth of Wit Bought with a Million of Repentance* (contains
   in the autobiographical narrative the oft-quoted attack on 'an upstart crow' . . . who
   'is in his owne conceit the only Shake-scene in a Countrey' regarded as a slighting
   reference to Shakespeare's early work).
   Robert Greene, *A Quip for an Upstart Courtier* (with Nashe's pamphlet satire below)
   starts the famous, long-drawn out literary quarrel between these two controversialists
   and others (Gabriel and Richard Harvey; ended in 1597).
   Philip Henslowe, theatrical manager, of the Rose Theatre from about 1692 until 1603,
   begins his *Diary* (–1603).
   Arden of Feversham (anon. tragedy, at one time attributed to Shakespeare).
   Thomas Kyd, *The Spanish Tragedy*.
   John Lyly, *Midas* (play).
   Thomas Nashe, *Pierce Penniless his Supplication to the Devil* (prose satire).

M **Births and Deaths**
   Jan. 22nd Pierre Gassendi b. (–1655).
   Apr. 20th John Eliot b. (–1632).
   May 8th Francis Quarles b. (–1644).
   July 26th Armand de Gontaut, Baron Brion, d. (68).

(*Continued opposite*)

1593   Henry IV of France becomes a Roman Catholic

A **Jan:** The French States-General, meeting in the Louvre, Paris, refuse to entertain Philip II's claim that the Infanta Isabel should be acknowledged Queen of France and agree to support the young Duke of Guise.

Feb: 19th, English Parliament meets (*–Apr.* 12th) and passes an Act, directed against Puritans, for restraining the Queen's subjects in obedience. Other legislation includes the promotion of parish collections as a fund for wounded soldiers and seamen.

Mar: 23rd, Henry Barrow, a Puritan, is convicted of slandering Queen Elizabeth.

B **Apr:** 6th, Henry Barrow is executed.

May: 29th, John Penry, a Brownist, is executed for denying Queen Elizabeth's royal supremacy.

Jun: 2nd, Rudolf II summons the Imperial Diet to Ratisbon for voting supplies for the renewed war against Turkey, in which Sigmund Báthory, Prince of Transylvania, fights for the Emperor. Michael the Brave subsequently becomes Prince of Wallachia, but revolts, to win independence from the Turks.

C **Jul:** 25th, Henry IV becomes a Roman Catholic, hearing Mass at St. Denis. Subsequently many nobles submit to him.

Aug:

Sep: Archduke Albert of Austria is appointed Viceroy of Portugal by Philip II.

D **Oct:** Sigismund III's attempt to restore Roman Catholicism in Sweden is successfully opposed by the Convention of Uppsala.

Nov:

Dec:

E Barent Erikszen leads a voyage to the coast of Guinea.

F **Politics, Economics, Law and Education**

G **Science, Technology and Discovery**
    G. B. Della Porta, *De Refractione, optices parte*, including an account of binocular vision.
    John Norden, *Speculum Britanniae*, a survey of England.
    Purana Pul bridge of 23 arches is built across the R. Musi in Hyderabad.

H **Philosophy, Religion and Scholarship**
    Pierre Charron, *Les Trois Vérités* (i.e. the existence of God; the rightness of Christianity, the supremacy of the Catholic faith).
    Christopher Marlowe's translation of Lucan's *Pharsalia*, bk. 1.
    John Penry (suspected author of *Martin Marprelate Tracts* of 1588) is executed.
    Henry IV of France formally professes himself a member of the Roman Catholic Church.

J **Art, Sculpture, Fine Arts and Architecture**
    Painting:
        Nicholas Hilliarde, *Mrs. Holland* (miniature).

K **Music**

L **Literature (including Drama)**
    Robert Henryson, *The Testament of Cresseid*.
    George Peele, *The Chronicle* (play) *of Edward the First. The Honour of the Garter* (poem).
    William Shakespeare, *Venus and Adonis; The Comedy of Errors* is acted between 1592 and 1594, including a performance at Gray's Inn, *Dec.* 28th, 1594.
    The theatres in London are closed throughout this year until *Dec.* because of the plague (–1594).

M **Births and Deaths**
    Apr. 3rd George Herbert b. (–1633).
    Apr. 6th Henry Barrowe d. (43).
    Apr. 13th Thomas Wentworth, Earl of Strafford, b. (–1641).
    Apr. 24th William Harrison d. (61).
    May 30th Christopher Marlowe d. (29).
    Aug. 9th Isaak Walton b. (–1683).
    — Giuseppe Arcimboldi d. (66).
    — Anthony van Diemen b. (–1645).

A Jan: The Archduke Ernest of Austria arrives in Brussels as Governor of the Netherlands; Lyons declares for Henry IV.
Feb: 27th, Henry IV is crowned King of France at Chartres;
28th, Roger Lopez, a royal physician, is arrested for an alleged conspiracy to poison Queen Elizabeth (he is executed *June* 7th).
Mar: 6th, the Duke of Mayenne, holding Paris for the League, leaves the capital;
22nd, Henry IV enters Paris; the rest of the country gradually submits to him and the League disintegrates. Henry subsequently disburses 32 million livres to Leaguer generals and nobles;
27th, Villars, Governor of Rouen, surrenders Rouen, Havre and Harfleur to Henry IV; the German Protestant princes, led by Frederick IV of the Palatinate, meet at Heilbronn, to oppose the Emperor.

B Apr: Jean Chastel, a pupil of the Jesuits, attempts to assassinate Henry IV.
May: Rudolf II meets the Diet at Ratisbon where supplies are voted for the Turkish war over the heads of the Protestant Party.
Jun: The Duke of Guise surrenders Champagne to Henry IV.

C Jul: Laon, the last stronghold of the Catholic League, is taken; the only remaining opposition to Henry IV is in Brittany where the Duke of Mercoeur is aided by a Spanish force.
Aug: Hugh O'Neill, Earl of Tyrone, in alliance with O'Donnell, Earl of Tyrconnell, leads a rising in Ulster against Queen Elizabeth I and appeals to Philip II for aid.
Sep: Anglo-French expedition to dislodge the Spanish, under Don Juan, from Crojon, Brittany.

D Oct:
Nov: 7th/17th, Anglo-French force recaptures Brest from the Spaniards, but Martin Frobisher is mortally wounded.
Dec: Henry IV expels the Jesuits from certain areas of France (they return in 1603).

E Henry IV issues the Edict of St. Germain-en-Laye granting Huguenots liberty of worship, but at an assembly held at Sainte-Foy the Huguenots demand securities for its observance and full equality with Catholics in public life;
The Turks take Raab from the Austrians;
The Mogul Emperor Akbar takes Kandahar;
The Lisbon spice market is closed to Dutch and English merchants (prompting future voyages to the Far East).

F **Politics, Economics, Law and Education**

Pierre Matthieu, Henry IV's official historiographer, writes *Histoire des derniers troubles de France sous Henri III et Henri IV.*

Crompton, *Authoritie et juridiction des Courts.*

G **Science, Technology and Discovery**

H **Philosophy, Religion and Scholarship**

Richard Carew translates Cantos 1–5 of Tasso's *Jerusalem Delivered*, as *Godfrey of Bulloigne.*

Richard Hooker, *Of the Laws of Ecclesiastical Polity*, bks. 1–4 (8th bk. –1648), a defence of the Church of England under the Elizabethan settlement.

J **Art, Sculpture, Fine Arts and Architecture**

Painting:

Caravaggio, *The Musical Party* (–1595).

Sculpture:

Giovanni de Bologna, equestrian statues of Cosimo I and Ferdinando (Florence).

K **Music**

Queen Elizabeth sends an organ, made by Thomas Dallam, to the Sultan of Turkey.

L **Literature (including Drama)**

Diego Bernades, *Várias rimas ao Bom Jesus* (devotional poems).

Robert Greene, *Friar Bacon and Friar Bongay* (posth.; comedy).

John Lyly, *Mother Bombie* (comedy).

Christopher Marlowe, *Edward the Second* (posth.; tragedy). *The Tragedy of Dido* (with Nashe).

Thomas Nashe, *The Unfortunate Traveller;* or The Life of Jack Wilton (an early picaresque novel).

George Peele, *The Battle of Alcazar.*

William Shakespere, *The Rape of Lucrese ; Titus Andronicus*, the first Shakespeare play to be printed.

London theatres reopen, *May.*

M **Births and Deaths**

Feb. 2nd Giovanni da Palestrina d. (68).

Feb. — Barnabe Googe d. (54).

May 31st Jacopi Tintoretto d. (76).

June 3rd John Aylmer d. (73).

June 14th Orlando di Lasso d. (*c.* 64).

June — Nicolas Poussin b. (–1665).

Oct. 16th Cardinal William Allen d. (62).

Nov. 22nd Martin Frobisher d. (*c.* 59).

Nov. 30th John Cosin b. (–1672).

Dec. 5th Gerardus Mercator d. (82).

Dec. 9th Gustavus Adolphus b. (–1632).

A   Jan: 17th, Henry IV of France, abandoning the fiction of periodic hostilities, declares war
       on Spain.
     Feb: 2nd, Robert Southwell, a Jesuit, is hanged at Tyburn;
       20th, following the death of Archduke Ernest, Philip II appoints the Archduke Albert
       as Governor of the Netherlands; until he arrives in *Jan.* 1596, Fuentes acts for him.
     Mar:

B   Apr: Philip II undertakes to aid the Earl of Tyrone's rebellion in Ireland.
     May: 4th, Sir John Norris is sent to Ireland to put down the rebellion.
     Jun: 24th, the Earl of Tyrone is finally proclaimed a traitor;
       Beaune, Dijon and Autun revolt against Henry IV, who marches east through Burgundy;
       the Duke of Mayenne subsequently signs a truce with Henry.

C   Jul: 23rd, the Spanish land in S.W. Cornwall and burn Mousehole and Penzance before
       taking to their ships.
     Aug: 28th, Sir Francis Drake and Sir John Hawkins leave Plymouth on their last voyage
       to the Spanish Main (–1596).
     Sep: 17th, Pope Clement VIII absolves Henry IV and recognises him as King of France.

D   Oct: 9th, Cambrai falls to the Spanish;
       28th, Sigmund Báthory defeats the Turks at Giurgevo and subdues Wallachia;
       Gustavus Vasa (the future Charles IX) is appointed Lieutenant-General of Sweden.
     Nov: Henry IV begins the siege of La Fère, held by the Spanish;
       rising of peasants in Upper Austria is crowned with a victory at Neumarkt;
       the Treaty of Teusina ends Sweden's war with Lithuania; Sweden acquires Estonia
       and Narva.
     Dec:

E   Mohammed III succeeds as Sultan of Turkey (–1603) on the death of Murad III.
     Sir Walter Raleigh explores 300 miles up the R. Orinoco.

F **Politics, Economics, Law and Education**

Peter Bor, *Oorsprongk, begin vervolgh der Nederlantsche Oorlogen* (–1611), an account of the Revolt of the Netherlands, 1555–1600.

The trial of Francesco Cenci.

The bow is finally abandoned as a weapon by the English army.

G **Science, Technology and Discovery**

Andreas Libavius, *Opera Omnia Medico-chymica*.

H **Philosophy, Religion and Scholarship**

Thomas Beddingfield makes the first English translation of Machiavelli's *Florentine History* (1525).

Andrew Maunsell, *The Catalogue of English Printed Books*.

Sir Philip Sidney, *An Apologie for Poetrie* (sometimes entitled *The Defence of Poetry*).

Robert Southwell, Jesuit priest and poet, is hanged at Tyburn after prolonged torture and imprisonment.

Index librorum prohibitorum is in force in all Roman Catholic States.

J **Art, Sculpture, Fine Arts and Architecture**

Painting:

Carracci, decorations for the Farnese Gallery.

K **Music**

L **Literature (including Drama)**

George Peele, *The Old Wives Tale* ('a pleasant conceited comedie').

Robert Southwell, *St. Peter's Complaint* (with other poems). *The Triumphs over Death* ('a consolatorie epistle'—prose).

Edmund Spenser, *Amoretti. Epithalamion. Colin Clouts Come Home Again* (containing the elegy, entitled *Astrophel*, on the death of the poet's friend, Sir Philip Sidney).

M **Births and Deaths**

Jan. 28th Francis Drake d. (*c.* 50).

Feb. 2nd Robert Southwell d. (*c.* 34).

Apr. 25th Torquato Tasso d. (51).

May 26th Philip Neri d. (79).

Oct. 19th Philip Howard, Earl of Arundel, d. (38).

Nov. 12th John Hawkins d. (63).

Dec. 4th Jean Chapelain b. (–1674).

— Thomas Kyd d. (37).

— Hubert Waelrant d. (74).

The Spanish capture Calais—Sack of Cadiz—Turkish advance in Hungary

A Jan: Archduke Albert of Austria succeeds Fuentes as Governor of the Spanish Netherlands;
   31st, the decrees of Folembray, confirming the submissions to Henry IV of the Dukes of Mayenne, Nemours and Joyeuse, end the war of the Catholic League.
   Feb: 17th, the Duke of Guise prevents the Spanish capture of Marseilles.
   Mar: 24th, d'Epernon submits to Henry IV, and the entire south-east of France is pacified. The only opposition to the Crown within France is in Brittany under the Duke of Mercoeur.

B Apr: 7th/17th, the Archduke Albert captures Calais from the French;
   24th, Pacification of Ireland is signed, but the Earl of Tyrone refuses to abide by this.
   May: 16th, the Spanish stronghold of La Fère capitulates to the French;
   16th/26th, England, France and the United Provinces sign an offensive and defensive league against Spain.
   Jun: 30th (–*July* 5th), English expedition under Lord Howard of Effingham and the Earl of Essex sacks Cadiz, ravages the Spanish coast and captures much booty. Philip II is thus prevented from sending an Armada against England.

C Jul:
   Aug:
   Sep:

D Oct: 23rd (–26th), the Turks under Mohammed III defeat the Imperialist army under the Archduke Maximilian at Keresztes, near Erlau, North Hungary;
   25th, Spanish expedition leaves Lisbon with men and arms to support the Earl of Tyrone in Ireland, but subsequently founders off Cape Finistère;
   Henry IV summons an Assembly of Notables to discuss the public revenue; the assembly adopts the suggestion of a 5 per cent sales tax on all goods except corn.
   Nov:
   Dec:

E The Spanish coinage is further devalued to stave off bankruptcy.

F Politics, Economics, Law and Education
Gresham College, London, is founded for education in seven liberal sciences.

G Science, Technology and Discovery
Willem Barents discovers Spitzbergen.
Ludolph von Ceulen in *Van den Circkel* gives the ratio of the diameter to the circumference of a circle to 20 places.
Rheticus compiles trigonometrical tables.

H Philosophy, Religion and Scholarship
Caesar Baronius, *Martyrologium Romanum.*
Davila y Padilla Augustin ('Chronicler of the Indies') publishes a *History of Mexico.*
Luis de Carvajal, El Mozo, a Mexican Jew, burnt at the stake (*Dec.* 8th) with his mother and sisters in an auto-da-fé in Mexico City.

J Art, Sculpture, Fine Arts and Architecture
Painting:
Isaac Oliver, *Sir Arundell Talbot* (miniature).

K Music

L Literature (including Drama)
Sir John Davies, *Orchestra* (a poem).
Sir John Harington, *The Metamorphosis of Ajax* (a Rabelaisian satire).
Edmund Spenser, *Faerie Queene*, bks. 4–5 (*see* 1590).
The Blackfriars Theatre, London, opened.

M Births and Deaths
Mar. 31st René Descartes b. (–1650).
May 31st John Lesley d. (69).
June 23rd John Banér b. (–1641).
Aug. 19th Elizabeth, 'the Winter Queen' of Bohemia, b. (–1662).
— Nicola Amati b. (–1684).
— Jean Bodin d. (66).
— Henry Lawes b. (–1662).

A **Jan:** Maurice of Nassau, aided by the English contingent under Sir Francis Vere, defeats the Spanish at Turnhout, freeing north Brabant and Zeeland from further attack.

Feb: Henry IV urges the German Protestant princes to join France and the United Provinces in a final attack on the Spanish Netherlands.

Mar: 11th, Archduke Albert of Austria captures Amiens;
12th, the Duke of Biron is sent with a substantial army to lay siege to Amiens.

B **Apr:** 16th, the Earl of Tyrone fails to keep his undertaking to submit to Queen Elizabeth; desultory fighting follows;
Henry IV supervises siege works to cut off Amiens from the north.

May: 21st, Henry IV holds a *lit de justice* in Paris to register the edicts for taxation;
Archduke Albert plans to take Metz, but has to abandon the plan.

Jun: Maurice of Nassau takes Meurs.

C **Jul:** Henry IV's authority is challenged by the *Parlement* of Rouen which delays its support for the edicts;
the Count of Auvergne is restrained from rebellion;
the Earl of Essex and Sir Walter Raleigh undertake a voyage to the Azores ('the Islands Voyage'), which fails (*–Oct.*), despite the capture of Fayal.

Aug: 1st/11th, English merchants are expelled from the Empire in retaliation for the treatment of the Hansa in London.

Sep: 15th, Archduke Albert leads an army of 21,000 from Douai to relieve Amiens, but,
16th, is prevented from crossing the River Somme and retires;
25th, Amiens falls to Henry IV;
the Duke of Mercoeur in Brittany sues for terms from Henry IV.

D **Oct:** Spanish Armada leaves Ferrol for England, but is scattered by storms; reports of its sailing cause alarm in London;
24th, English Parliament meets (*–Feb.* 9th, 1598).

Nov: Philip II opens peace negotiations with Henry IV.

Dec: The Archduke Matthias, representing the Emperor Rudolf II, is opposed at the Diet of Ratisbon by the Protestant princes who are alarmed at the excessive demands for imperial taxation.

E William V, Elector of Bavaria abdicates in favour of his son Maximilian I (–1651);
William retires to a monastery, surviving until 1626;
Persian army defeats the Uzbeks to prevent further invasion of Khorasan;
The Japanese resume the campaign in Korea (–1598).

F **Politics, Economics, Law and Education**
An English Act of Parliament prescribes sentences of transportation to colonies for convicted felons.
Jean de Serres, *Inventaire général de l'histoire de France . . . à present.*

G **Science, Technology and Discovery**
John Gerard, *Herball.*

H **Philosophy, Religion and Scholarship**
James VI of Scotland, *Demonologie* (on witchcraft).
The Aldine Press, Venice, ceases, after the publication of 908 works, since 1494.

J **Art, Sculpture, Fine Arts and Architecture**
Painting:
Caravaggio, *St. Matthew.*
El Greco, *St. Martin and the Beggar* (–1599); *Resurrection of Christ* (–1604).

K **Music**
John Dowland, *First Book of Songs.*
Thomas Morley, *A Plaine and Easie Introduction to Practicall Musick.*
Jacopo Peri's *Dafne* (the first opera) performed in Florence, and Vecchi's *L'Amfiparnasso* in Modena.

L **Literature (including Drama)**
Sir Francis Bacon (Lord Verulam), *Essays: Civil and Moral* (10 essays; increased –1612; and to 58 in 1625, the final edition).
Diego Bernardes, *Rimas várias, flores do Lima.*
John Lyly, *The Woman in the Moone* (play).
Thomas Nashe, *The Isle of Dogs* (satirical comedy; suppressed; text not extant. Nashe sent to the Fleet Prison).
William Shakespeare, *King Richard the Second; Romeo and Juliet; Richard the Third.*
Blackfriars Theatre adapted by James Burbage to provide a roof for his company of actors (which includes Shakespeare –1608). Shakespeare purchases New Place, Stratford-upon-Avon.

M **Births and Deaths**
June 30th William Barents d. (*c.* 50).
Oct. 10th Aldus Manutius the younger, d. (50).
Dec. 23rd Martin Opitz von Boberfeld b. (–1639).

A Jan: 7th, on the death of Feodore I of Russia, last surviving son of Tsar Ivan the Terrible, Boris Godunov seizes the throne (–1605);

8th, Joachim Frederick, a staunch Calvinist, succeeds as Elector of Brandenburg on the death of John George (–1608); by contesting his father's will, the new Elector prevents a division of the electoral lands;

12th, Pope Clement VIII seizes the duchy of Ferrara following the death (in 1597) of the last of the House of Este, Duke Alfonso II.

Feb: 9th, English Parliament is dissolved, having voted further taxation for the war with Spain and having passed an Act to punish vagabonds and establish workhouses (–1834). Queen Elizabeth promises she will reform the system of monopolies;

27th, Boris Godunov is formally elected Tsar of Russia by a national assembly; to strengthen his position he forces the head of the Romanovs to enter a monastery.

Mar: 20th, by the Treaty of Ponts de Cé, the Duke of Mercoeur in Brittany submits to Henry IV, effectively ending the civil war in France;

Henry IV makes peace with the Archduke Albert, Governor of Flanders.

B Apr: 15th, Henry IV publishes the Edict of Nantes (–1685) by which the Huguenots in France are granted freedom of worship in those places where this had been exercised during the past two years, and are admitted to equal political rights as Roman Catholics, notably to public offices, but they are required to abandon alliances with foreign powers and to dissolve their provincial assemblies;

the Ban of the Holy Roman Empire is proclaimed against those of the Protestant minority in the Diet who refuse to accept majority decisions. At this time Catholicism is re-introduced in Aachen by force.

May: By the Peace of Vervins between Henry IV and Philip II, Spain restores Calais, Blavet and all conquests except Cambrai, and Philip resigns his claim to the Crown of France. As a result, France is reunited under a single sovereign;

Philip II assigns the Spanish Netherlands to the Archduke Albert of Austria and the Infanta Isabel, who agree to marry. In the event of a failure of heirs the Netherlands is to revert to the Spanish Crown.

Jun:

C Jul:

Aug: 4th, the Steelyard, London headquarters of the Hanseatic League, is closed by Queen Elizabeth;

14th, the Earl of Tyrone, Irish rebel, annihilates an English force under Sir Henry Bagnal at the Yellow Ford on the Blackwater River. The disaster prompts the appointment of the Earl of Essex as Lord Lieutenant of Ireland (in *Mar.* 1599).

Sep: 13th, Philip III succeeds as King of Spain (–1621) on the death of Philip II; he entrusts the government to his favourite, the Duke of Lerma;

25th, Charles IX of Sweden defeats Sigismund II of Poland at Stangebro.

D Oct:

Nov: 13th, Philip III marries Margaret of Austria, and the Archduke Albert of Austria marries the Infanta Isabel.

Dec: Philip III summons the Cortes to deal with Spain's financial crisis.

E The Dutch take Mauritius; and send traders to Guiana.

On the death of Hideyoshi, Jeyasu Tokugawa restores the Shogunate in Japan (–1868).

F **Politics, Economics, Law and Education**

Juan de Mariana, *De rege et regis institutione*, a treatise on kingship written for the future Philip III of Spain.

John Manwood, *Treatise of the Laws of the Forest*.

Henry IV reorganises the University of Paris; in particular he encourages the study of the classics, the Bible and the natural sciences.

G **Science, Technology and Discovery**

Tycho Brahe in *Astronomiae Instauratae Mechanica* gives an account of his discoveries and describes his instruments.

Lindschoten publishes maps and charts of the Far East.

Carlo Ruini, *Dell'Anatomia e dell'Infirmita de Cavello, e suoi Remedii*, a manual of veterinary science.

G.W., *The cure of the diseased in remote regions*, the earliest treatise on tropical medicine.

H **Philosophy, Religion and Scholarship**

Richard Bernard translates the *Six Comedies* of Terence.

George Chapman translates seven books of the *Iliad*; followed by *Achilles Shield* ('the other seven Bookes of Homer').

John Florio, *A World of wordes, Italian and English* (a dictionary).

Philibert Mareschal, *Le Guide des arts et sciences*.

Francis Meres, *Palladis Tamia, Wit's Treasury* (an anthology of quotations and maxims from 125 English writers from Chaucer onwards, compared and contrasted with Greek and Latin authors: hence making a valuable source book).

John Stow, *A Survey of London* (enlarged eds., 1603, 1633).

Edict of Nantes issued by Henry IV of France (*Apr.* 15th) granting toleration to the Huguenots (this is revoked by Louis XIV, *Oct.* 22nd, 1685).

The Parish Library at Grantham, Lincolnshire, England, is founded.

The Oxford University Library, originally founded by Humphrey, Duke of Gloucester, and destroyed, is refounded and enriched by Sir Thomas Bodley (opened, 1602); henceforth known as The Bodleian Library.

J **Art, Sculpture, Fine Arts and Architecture**

Painting:

El Greco, *Cardinal Don Fernando Niño de Guevara*.

Isaac Oliver, *The Three Brothers Broune and Servant* (miniature).

K **Music**

L **Literature (including Drama)**

Christopher Marlowe, *Hero and Leander* (poem on the classical story completed after Marlowe's death by George Chapman).

John Marston, *The Scourge of Villainy* (a satire in verse). *The Metamorphosis of Pigmalion's Image* (erotic poem).

William Shakespeare, *Henry IV*, part 1. *Love's Labour's Lost*.

M **Births and Deaths**

Mar. 27th Theodorus (Dirk) de Bry d. (70).

Aug. 4th William Cecil, Lord Burghley, d. (77).

Sept. 13th Philip II of Spain d. (70).

— Gianlorenzo Bernini b. (–1680).

— Thomas Carew b. (–1639).

— George Peele d. (39).

— Vincent Voiture b. (–1648).

— François Mansard b. (–1666).

A Jan:
  Feb:
  Mar: 27th, Robert Devereux, Earl of Essex, is appointed Lord Lieutenant of Ireland (he lands at Dublin *Apr.* 15th).

B Apr: 10th, Gabrielle d'Estrées, Henry IV's mistress, dies;
  29th, the Gera agreement is ratified by the House of Hohenzollern, by which the younger branch is to acquire Culmbach, and if either branch fails the other is to inherit the electorship and the margraviate of Brandenburg, with provision for subsequent division for the benefit of younger branches.
  May:
  Jun:

C Jul: Leaders of the Orthodox Church in Poland ally themselves with the Dissentients by the Confederation of Vilna against the Jesuits.
  Aug:
  Sep: 7th, the Earl of Essex, after displaying his lack of strategy, signs a truce with the Irish rebel Tyrone and, 24th, in disobedience to Queen Elizabeth's commands, leaves Ireland, arriving at the court at Nonsuch, 28th, where he is arrested.

D Oct: 2nd, Charles Blount, Lord Mountjoy is appointed Lord Lieutenant of Ireland in succession to Essex.
  Nov: Peace negotiations between Spain and the United Provinces and between Spain and England are opened at Bergen op Zoom and Boulogne respectively (*–May* 1600).
  Dec: Henry IV of France obtains a divorce from Queen Margaret of Valois.

E A final Armada is collected in Spain for sending against England, but is scattered by storms and returns to port;
  Rosnay, Duke of Sully, is appointed Superintendent of Finances in France and pursues a vigorous economic policy, reforming taxation, reducing the *taille*, freeing overseas trade from restrictions and encouraging agriculture and industry;
  Michael the Brave deposes Andrew Báthory in Moldavia and conquers Wallachia, with the encouragement of the Emperor Rudolf II (–1600);
  The Mogul Emperor Akbar begins to campaign in the Deccan.

F **Politics, Economics, Law and Education**

James VI of Scotland, *Basilikon Doron* (instruction for his son, Henry, d. 1612, on the divine right of kings).

Juan de Mariana, *De rege et regis institutione*, on kingship; justifies the killing of a tyrant.

Sir John Hayward's extravagant dedication to Robert, Earl of Essex, of *The Life and Reign of Henry IV*, which casts the earl in the role of a Bolingbroke, encouraging him in his Revolt against Elizabeth I.

Sully creates the office of 'grandvoyer', to begin the reform of the French road system.

Severe outbreak of the plague in Spain (–1600).

Duke of Lerma introduces copper coinage into Spain.

G **Science, Technology and Discovery**

Edward Wright explains the mathematical basis of Mercator's projection.

Ulissi Aldrovandi publishes his studies in ornithology.

H **Philosophy, Religion and Scholarship**

Jean Bodin and Lancelot de la Popelinière, *Histoire des histoires*, founds a critique of history.

J **Art, Sculpture, Fine Arts and Architecture**

Painting:

Nicholas Hilliarde, *Portrait of a Young Man*.

K **Music**

The church of St. Cecilia, Rome, is rebuilt, and the saint's body examined, still intact since martyrdom in 176 A.D. A statue by Stefano Maderno of the Patron Saint of Music is placed at the high altar (first music festival in London of St. Cecilia is held in London, *c*. 1683).

L **Literature (including Drama)**

Mateo Alemán, *Guzmán de Alfarache* (picaresque novel; trans. 1622, as *The Rogue*).

George Peele, *David and Bethsabe* (play).

William Shakespeare's *Julius Caesar* is acted, by the Lord Chamberlain's Men, *Sept.* 21st.

The Globe Theatre, Bankside, Southwark, is built (with timber from *The Theatre*, 1576), and is owned by the actors themselves.

M **Births and Deaths**

Jan. 16th Edmund Spenser d. (*c*. 47).

Feb. 13th Fabio Chigi (Pope Alexander VII) b. (–1667).

Mar. 22nd Anthony van Dyck b. (–1641).

Apr. 10th Gabrielle d'Estrées d. (28).

Apr. 25th Oliver Cromwell b. (–1658).

June 6th Diego y Valasquez b. (–1660).

Sept. 11th Beatrice Cenci d. (22).

Oct. 31st Denzil Holles b. (–1680).

Nov. 11th Octavio Piccolomini b. (–1656).

A **Jan:** The Earl of Tyrone resumes his rebellion against Queen Elizabeth I (*–Mar.* 1603) by invading Munster.
  Feb: Charles IX of Sweden executes leaders of the pro-Polish Party for treason.
  Mar:

B **Apr:**
  May: Peace negotiations between Spain and the United Provinces and between Spain and England at Bergen op Zoom and Boulogne founder;
  Sir Henry Docwra fortifies Derry and Lord Mountjoy, Essex's successor as Lord Deputy in Ireland, advances from Westmeath to Newry, forcing the Earl of Tyrone to retire to Armagh.
  Jun: Robert Earl of Essex is tried for misdemeanours in Ireland and sentenced to lose his offices at court;
  27th, Maurice of Nassau takes Oudenburg from the Spanish.

C **Jul:** 2nd, Maurice of Nassau with an army, including English volunteers led by Sir Francis Vere, defeats the Archduke Albert's Spanish and Italian troops at the battle of Nieuport. Prince Maurice subsequently retires into Holland.
  Aug: 5th, the Gowrie Conspiracy in Scotland when Lord Gowrie and his brother, Alexander Ruthven, seize King James VI, who is subsequently rescued by attendants;
  6th, Henry IV of France invades Savoy on the breakdown of negotiations for the return of Saluzzo, which Charles Emmanuel of Savoy annexed in 1588;
  13th, Henry IV takes Bourg, and, 15th, Chambery surrenders to him.
  Sep:

D **Oct:** 5th, Henry IV of France marries Marie de' Medici.
  Nov: Montmélion falls to the French.
  Dec:

E Ieyasu defeats his rivals in Japan at the Battle of Sekigahara.

F **Politics, Economics, Law and Education**
The English East India Company is founded.
Edward Coke, *Law Reports*.
Approximate populations (in millions): France, 16; German states, etc., 14½; Poland, 11; Spain, 8; Austrian Hapsburg dominions, 5½; England and Ireland, 5½; Holland, 3; Portugal, 2; Sweden, 1½; Scotland, 1.

G **Science, Technology and Discovery**
William Gilbert, *De magnete*, a pioneer study of electricity and magnetism.
Claude Dangou of Lyons makes improvements to the weaving machine.
Kircher invents the magic lantern.
William Adams anchors the *Charity* off Kiushiu Island, Japan.

H **Philosophy, Religion and Scholarship**
Edward Fairfax translates Tasso's *Jerusalem Delivered* (*Godfrey of Bulloigne*; or, The Recoverie of Jerusalem).
Philemon Holland translates Livy's *Roman History*.
Christopher Marlowe's translation of bk. 1 of Lucan's *Pharsalia* published (posth.).
Giordano Bruno burnt for his belief in the plurality of inhabited worlds in Campo di Fiori, Rome (*Feb.* 17th, aged 52).

J **Art, Sculpture, Fine Arts and Architecture**
Painting:
Caravaggio, *Doubting Thomas*.
Nicholas Hilliarde, *Treatise concerning the Art of Limning*.

K **Music**
Emilio de Cavalieri, *La representazione di anima e di corpo* (first extant opera) published; performed two years later.
Thomas Morley, *The First Book of Aires*.

L **Literature (including Drama)**
Thomas Dekker, *Old Fortunatus; The Shoemaker's Holiday* (comedies).
Ben Jonson, *Everyman Out of His Humour* (comedy).
William Kemp's Nine Daies Wonder.
Thomas Nashe, *Summers Last Will and Testament* (satirical masque).
William Shakespeare, *As You Like It; Henry IV*, part 2; *Henry V; The Merchant of Venice; A Midsummer-Night's Dream; Much Ado About Nothing*.
Anthologies: *England's Parnassus. England's Helicon*.
The Fortune Theatre, London, opened.

M **Births and Deaths**
Jan. 17th Pedro Calderón de la Barca b. (−1681).
Feb. 17th Giordano Bruno d. (*c.* 52).
Nov. 2nd Richard Hooker d. (46).
Nov. 19th Charles I b. (−1649).
— Edmund Calamy b. (−1666).
— Claude of Lorraine (Claude Gellée) b. (−1682).
— William Prynne b. (−1669).

A **Jan:** 7th (–8th), Robert Earl of Essex leads a revolt in London against Queen Elizabeth
which is swiftly crushed;

17th, by the Treaty of Lyons between France, Spain and Savoy, Henry IV gains
Bresse, Bugey, Valromey and Gex, connecting France with Switzerland; in return,
Charles Emmanuel of Savoy recovers Saluzzo and undertakes to allow the passage of
Spanish troops for Flanders along a route to Franche-Comté;

the capital of Spain is transferred from Madrid to Valladolid.

Feb: 13th, John Lancaster leads the first East India Company's voyage from London;

19th, the Earl of Essex is tried for treason and, 25th, executed.

Mar: The Earl of Mountjoy opens a campaign to end the rebellion in Munster (Tyrone
submits in *Mar.* 1603).

B **Apr:**
May:
Jun:

C **Jul:** 15th, Archduke Albert of Austria with a Spanish force begins the siege of Ostend
(–*Sept.* 1604);

Mountjoy makes himself the Master of Lough Foyle in Ireland.

Aug: 19th, Michael the Brave, Prince of Moldavia, is assassinated by Hungarian patriots.

Sep: 27th, birth of a Dauphin (the future Louis XIII) to Queen Marie de' Medici of
France;

a force of 3,000 Spaniards lands at Kinsale, Ireland, to support the Earl of Tyrone's
rebellion (it capitulates to Mountjoy in *Jan.* 1602);

a joint expedition of Spaniards and Italians against Algiers, led by Gian Andrea Doria,
fails.

D **Oct:** 19th, Krell, former Chancellor of Saxony, is executed;

26th, Lord Mountjoy lays siege to Kinsale;

27th (–*Dec.* 19th), the last Parliament of Queen Elizabeth meets at Westminster, during
which the Queen is forced to promise to reform the system of monopolies; an Act
forbidding payment of blackmail is passed.

Nov: 20th, Queen Elizabeth's 'Golden Speech' to Parliament, in which she surveys the
history of her reign.

Dec: 23rd, Tyrone and O'Donnell, Irish rebels, make joint attack on Mountjoy's lines
near Kinsale but they are routed.

E The False Dmitri, claiming to be a son of Tsar Ivan IV, appears in Poland where he wins
support for an invasion of Russia;

The Mogul Emperor Akbar annexes Khandest.

F Politics, Economics, Law and Education
   G. de Malynes, *A Treatise of the Cancer of England's Commonwealth*, a commercial tract.

G Science, Technology and Discovery

H Philosophy, Religion and Scholarship
   Pierre Charron, *De la sagesse* (a system of stoic philosophy without a theological basis).
   Philemon Holland translates Pliny (the Elder), *Natural History*.

J Art, Sculpture, Fine Arts and Architecture
   Painting:
      Caravaggio, *Conversion of St. Paul*.

K Music
   Thomas Morley, *Triumphs of Oriana*.

L Literature (including Drama)
   Ben Jonson, *Everyman in His Humour* (comedy).
   Bento Teixeira Pinto, *Prosopopeya* (the first Brazilian epic).
   William Shakespeare, *Twelfth Night*.

M Births and Deaths
   Feb. 25th Robert Devereux, Earl of Essex, d. (34).
   May 2nd Athanasius Kircher b. (−1680).
   Sept. 27th Louis XIII b. (−1643).
   Oct. 24th Tycho Brahe d. (54).
   — Thomas Nashe d. (34).

1602   Execution of Marshal Biron—Repressive Religious policy in Hapsburg Lands

A   **Jan:** 2nd, the Spanish force which landed in Ireland, in *Sept.* 1601, surrenders at Kinsale to the English;
Lord Mountjoy begins the reconquest of Ireland from the rebels (–1603), and a pardon is offered to the Earl of Tyrone (who submits in *Mar.* 1603).
Feb:
Mar: 20th, the United East India Company is chartered by the States-General of Holland.

B   **Apr:** The Counter-Reformation is enforced with repression in the Hapsburg lands of Styria, Carinthia and Carniola. The success of this policy leads the Emperor Rudolf II to persecute Protestants in Bohemia and Hungary, which enflames the nationalist spirit of Bohemian Protestants.
May:
Jun: 12th, the Duke of Biron agrees to appear before Henry IV at Fontainebleu to answer alleged treasons; his ally, the Duke of Bouillon, escapes to Germany.

C   **Jul:** 31st, Marshal Biron is executed for treason.
Aug:
Sep:

D   **Oct:**
Nov: All Jesuits and seminary priests are ordered to leave England within six weeks.
Dec: Charles Emmanuel, Duke of Savoy, fails in his attempt to reduce Geneva.

E   A fresh war between Persia and Turkey breaks out (–1627);
Spanish traders arrive in eastern Japan.

F **Politics, Economics, Law and Education**

John Willis, *Art of Stenographie*.

The Dutch East India Company is founded with a monopoly of trade between the Cape of Good Hope and the Straits of Magellan.

G **Science, Technology and Discovery**

Tycho Brahe, *Astronomia Instauratae Progymnasmata* (–1603 posth. ed. Kepler), gives the plans of 777 fixed stars.

Thomas Blondeville, *Theoriques of the Planets*.

Vincenzio Cascarido discovers barium sulphide.

H **Philosophy, Religion and Scholarship**

Thomas Campion, *Observations on the Art of English Poesie* (against the use of rhyme; for reply *see* 1603).

Richard Carew, *Survey of Cornwall*.

Conrad Kircher, *A Concordance to the Septuagint*.

Sir Thomas Bodley opens the Bodleian Library at Oxford (refounded 1598).

J **Art, Sculpture, Fine Arts and Architecture**

K **Music**

Giulio Caccini writes his treatise *Nuovo Musiche*.

L **Literature (including Drama)**

Thomas Dekker, *Satiromastix* (satirical comedy; Dekker's counterblast to Jonson— *see below*).

Ben Jonson, *The Poetaster;* or *The Arraignment* (satirical comedy).

Sir David Lindsay, *Ane Pleasant Satyre of the Three Estaitis* (morality) (posth. see 1540).

Lope de Vega, *La hermosura de Angélica* (sequel to Ariosto's *Orlando Furioso*).

John Marston, *Antonio and Mellida;* and *Antonio's Revenge* (tragedies).

William Shakespeare, *The Merry Wives of Windsor*. His *Twelfth Night* is performed *Feb.* 2nd, in Middle Temple.

M **Births and Deaths**

Feb. 13th Alexander Nowell d. (*c.* 95).

Apr. 30th William Lilly b. (–1681).

July 14th Jules Mazarin b. (–1661).

Oct. — William Chillingworth b. (–1644).

Dec. 10th John Bradshaw b. (–1659).

— Alessandro Algardi b. (–1654).

— Simonds D'Ewes b. (–1650).

— Edward Montagu, Earl of Manchester, b. (–1671).

A Jan:

Feb:

Mar: 24th, James VI King of Scotland accedes as James I of England and Ireland (–1625) on the death of Queen Elizabeth I. James retains Robert Cecil as Secretary of State;

30th, the Earl of Tyrone, Irish rebel, submits to Lord Mountjoy at Mellifort. A general amnesty follows in Ireland.

B Apr: Some 800 of the English Puritan clergy present James I with the Millenary Petition, urging changes in the established Church.

May: 7th, James I reaches London.

Jun: By the Anglo-French Treaty of Hampton Court, James I permits the recruitment of soldiers in England and Scotland for defending Ostend against the Spanish, to be paid by Henry IV.

C Jul: The Intrigues of Lords Cobham and Grey in 'the Main Plot' for the dethronement of James I and the succession of Arabella Stuart are discovered and

17th, Sir Walter Raleigh is arrested for suspected complicity;

—, James I remits the £20 per month fines levied on Catholic recusants;

25th, coronation of James I;

the Imperial Diet, summoned to Ratisbon to vote supplies for the Turkish war, is prorogued by the Archduke Matthias after acrimonious debates between Catholic and Protestant representatives on the validity of majority decisions;

by the Treaty of Saint Julien, signed through papal mediation, the *status quo* is restored after the attack of Charles Emmanuel of Savoy on the city of Geneva.

Aug:

Sep: Henry IV recalls the Jesuits to France, despite the opposition of the *Parlement* of Paris.

D Oct: Transylvania revolts against the Emperor Rudolf II.

Nov: 12th, Sir Walter Raleigh's trial for high treason at Winchester; he is found guilty and sentenced to imprisonment.

Dec: Ahmad I succeeds as Sultan of Turkey (–1617) on the death of Mahommed III.

E Alliances are signed between Henry IV of France and Venice, and between Venice and the Grisons, the Swiss League controlling the Valtelline Pass into north Italy;

On the death of George of Ansbach, Christian of Anhalt becomes the leading Calvinist prince in Germany.

F **Politics, Economics, Law and Education**

Johannes Althusias, *Politica methodice digesta et exemplis sacris et profanis illustrata*, a grammar of politics, on the foundations of which much subsequent political theory, through Locke and Gierke, is based. Althusias favours a republican form of government.

Thomas Craig, *Jus feudale*.

G **Science, Technology and Discovery**

Samuel de Champlain sails up the River St. Lawrence and takes possession of the Isle St. Jean (Prince Edward Island) for France.

Beneho de Goes sets out for India in search of Cathay, through Eastern Turkestan (reaches Suchou in *Mar.* 1606).

Fabricius of Acquapendente discovers that the veins contain valves.

Cessi founds the Academia dei Lincei, Rome.

H **Philosophy, Religion and Scholarship**

Samuel Daniel, *A Defence of Rhyme* (in reply to Campion, 1602).

John Florio translates the *Essays* of Montaigne.

Jan Gruter, *Inscriptiones antiquiae totius orbis Romanorum*.

Philemon Holland translates the *Morals* of Plutarch.

Richard Knolles, *General Historie of the Turkes*.

J **Art, Sculpture, Fine Arts and Architecture**

Architecture:

Carlo Maderno, church of St. Susanna, Rome.

K **Music**

Jean-Baptiste Besard, *Thesaurus harmonicus* (anthology of lute music) published in Cologne.

Thomas Robinson writes *Schoole of Musicke*.

L **Literature (including Drama)**

Francisco Gomez de Quevedo, *La vida del buscón* (The Sharper's Life; picaresque novel).

William Shakespeare, *Hamlet* (in the 'bad' quarto –1604).

Philip Henslowe, theatrical manager, ends his *Diary* (begun 1592).

M **Births and Deaths**

Mar. 24th Queen Elizabeth I d. (69).

Nov. 11th Kenelm Digby b. (–1665).

Nov. 30th William Gilbert d. (59).

Dec. 27th Thomas Cartwright d. (*c.* 68).

— Pierre Charron d. (58).

— Thomas Morley d. (50).

1604   **Anglo-Spanish Peace Treaty—Ostend falls to Spinola—Revolt in Hungary**

A   Jan: 14th (–16th), the Hampton Court Conference between leading Anglicans and Puritans is held before James I. The King and Archbishop Whitgift, though refusing to entertain doctrinal changes in the Church of England, support the request for a new translation of the Bible;
21st, the False Dmitri (claiming to be the son of Tsar Ivan IV), who has invaded Russia, is defeated by Tsar Boris Godunov.
Feb:
Mar: 19th, the first Parliament of James I meets (–*Feb.* 1611). Parliament opposes the King's plans for a Union with Scotland, but commissioners are appointed to treat with the Scots. During the session, the House of Commons indicates its claim to free elections (in Goodwin's Case, *Apr.* 5th) and to protect members from arrest (in Sherley's Case, *May* 15th);
20th, following the deposition of Sigismund III (1598), Charles IX assumes the title of King of Sweden (he is crowned *Mar.* 1607).

B   Apr: Prince Maurice of Nassau begins the siege of Sluys (–*Aug.*).
May:
Jun:

C   Jul: 7th, James I prorogues English Parliament.
Aug: 18th/28th, peace is signed between England and Spain and the Archdukes. James I undertakes to give no further aid to the Dutch, to work for peace between Spain, Holland and the Archdukes and to secure the return to Spain of the cautionary towns. England receives various trading privileges but undertakes not to trade in the Indies;
Sluys falls to Maurice of Nassau.
Sep: 25th, Ambrogio de Spinola captures Ostend from the Dutch after a siege of 3½ years.

D   Oct: 24th, James VI and I is proclaimed King of 'Great Britain, France and Ireland';
the discovery of plots by the Count of Auvergne and Henry of Entraques, both in league with Spain, against Henry IV of France;
England and France sign a commercial treaty.
Nov:
Dec: 10th, Richard Bancroft, Bishop of London, is elected Archbishop of Canterbury, as John Whitgift's successor.

E   Protestants in Hungary revolt against the Hapsburgs and join forces with Stephen Bocskai, who invades Hungary from Transylvania and is subsequently recognised by the Sultan of Turkey;
Abbas the Great of Persia takes Tabriz from the Turks;
The French East India Company is chartered;
Sir Henry Middleton leads an English East India Company voyage to Java and the Moluccas, while John Mildenhall, another servant of the Company, arrives at Agra, India.

F **Politics, Economics, Law and Education**

Oxford and Cambridge Universities are granted the privilege of Parliamentary representation (–1948).

James VI and I, *Counterblast to Tobacco*.

The Dutch establishing trading posts on the west coast of Borneo.

Samuel de Champlain founds a French settlement at Port Royal in Acadia (later Annapolis Royal, Nova Scotia), the first French colony in North America.

The Cossacks found Tomsk.

G **Science, Technology and Discovery**

Sully begins constructing a canal to link the R. Loire with a tributary of the R. Seine.

J. Kepler, *Optics*.

H **Philosophy, Religion and Scholarship**

Robert Cawdrey, *A Table Alphabetical*.

Jacques August de Thou, *Historiae sui temporis* (11 vols. –1614).

Herzog August Bibliothek, Wolfenbüttel, founded by August, Duke of Brunswick.

Conference of English Clergy at Hampton Court Palace, resulting in the decision to prepare an Authorised Version of the Bible (–1611). With this exception James I resisted requests for reform.

Francis Johnson and Henry Ainsworth, *An Apology or Defence of such True Christians as are commonly but ignorantly called Brownists*.

J **Art, Sculpture, Fine Arts and Architecture**

Karel van Mander, *Het Schilderboeck* (history of art).

K **Music**

Orlando di Lasso, *Magnum Opus Musicum* (posth.).

Negri's book on dance technique is published in Milan.

L **Literature (including Drama)**

Christopher Marlowe, *The Tragicall History of Dr. Faustus* (tragedy; posth.).

Lope de Vega Carpio, *Comedias* (25 vols. –1647).

John Marston, *The Malcontent* (tragi-comedy).

William Shakespeare, *Hamlet* (the 'good' quarto); *Measure for Measure*. *Othello* is acted (–1622).

M **Births and Deaths**

Feb. 29th John Whitgift d. (*c.* 74).

Apr. — Thomas Churchyard d. (*c.* 84).

— Edward Pococke b. (–1691).

1605   The time of the troubles in Russia—Gunpowder Plot—The Dutch
        seize Amboyna

A Jan:
   Feb:
   Mar: 5th, George Weymouth visits the New England court (–*July* 1606).

B Apr: 1st, Alexander de' Medici is elected Pope Leo XI (–*Apr*. 27th) following the death of
        Clement VIII;
        13th, Theodore II succeeds as Tsar of Russia (*June* 20th) on the death of his father
        Boris Godunov;
        Stephen Bocskai is elected Prince of Transylvania by the Diet of Szerenes.
   May: 7th, in the 'Time of the Troubles' in Russia the chief army declines to support the
        False Dmitri;
        16th, Camillo Borghese is elected Pope Paul V (–1621) following the death of Leo XI.
   Jun: 20th, the False Dmitri enters Moscow; in a palace revolution Tsar Theodore II is
        assassinated by the boyars;
        21st, Dmitri is crowned (–*May* 17th, 1606) and begins a programme of reforms.

C Jul: 2nd, a General Assembly of Presbyterian ministers meets at Aberdeen in defiance of
        James VI; the leaders are subsequently imprisoned and a future assembly is forbidden
        by the Council of Scotland;
        26th, French Protestants hold an Assembly at Chatelhérault and in defiance of Henry
        IV take an oath to keep their resolutions secret.
   Aug:
   Sep:

D Oct: Jehangir succeeds as Mogul Emperor of India (–1627) on the death of his father,
        Akbar.
   Nov: 4th, Guy Fawkes is arrested in the cellars of Parliament;
        5th, Gunpowder Plot, to blow up the House of Lords during James I's state opening of
        Parliament, is discovered; Robert Catesby and other conspirators flee but, 8th, are
        captured.
   Dec:

E Henry IV of France faces rebellion from the Count of Auvergne and the Duke of Bouillon
        and marches an army through the south of France;
   The master of the *Olive Blossom* claims Barbados, West Indies as an English colony (first
        settlement made in 1624);
   The Dutch seize Amboyna, Malaysia;
   Hidetada succeeds as Shogun of Japan (–1623) on the retirement of his father, Ieyasu.

F **Politics, Economics, Law and Education**
Justus Lipsius, *Monita et exempla politica*, a tract on political obligation and the organisation of the state.
Pierre Matthieu (historiographer of France), *Histoire de France . . . durant sept années de paix du règne de Henri IV*.
Santa Fé, New Mexico, is founded.
The entire English customs revenue is farmed to a consortium of London merchants for an annual rent (–1671).
University of Geissen, Hesse, is founded by Lutherans who have left Marburg.
Angelo Rocca founds the Biblioteca Anglica, the first library in Rome open to the public.
Nieuwe Tijdinghen, a journal, is issued in Antwerp.

G **Science, Technology and Discovery**

H **Philosophy, Religion and Scholarship**
Sir Francis Bacon, *The Advancement of Learning*.
Joshue Sylvester translates the *Divine Weekes and Workes* (*La Semaine*, etc.) by Du Bartas (1578).
A catechism, largely denied by Socinus, is adopted by the Unitarians in Poland.

J **Art, Sculpture, Fine Arts and Architecture**
Painting:
Nicholas Hilliarde, *A Knight of the Garter* (miniature).

K **Music**
John Dowland, *Lachrymae, or Seaven Teares, in Seaven Passionate Pavans* (for lute, viols and violins).
Tomás Luis de Victoria, *Officium Defunctorum*.

L **Literature (including Drama)**
Miguel de Cervantes Saavedra, *Don Quixote*, part 1 (part 2, –1615).
George Chapman, *All Fooles* (comedy). *Eastward Ho!* (comedy), with Ben Jonson and John Marston.
Samuel Daniel, *Philotas* (Senecan tragedy).
Michael Drayton, *Poems*.
Ben Jonson, *Sejanus His Fall* (tragedy).
John Marston, *The Dutch Courtezan* (comedy).
William Shakespeare, *Macbeth*.
Jean Vauquelin de la Fresnaye, *L'Art poétique* (in verse).

M **Births and Deaths**
Apr. 6th John Stow d. (*c.* 80).
May 10th Ulissi Aldrovendi d. (82).
June 3rd Jan Zamoyski d. (64).
June 15th Thomas Randolph b. (–1635).
Aug. 19th Bulstrode Whitelocke b. (–1675).
Sept. 12th William Dugdale b. (–1686).
Oct. 13th Théodore Beza d. (86).
Oct. 19th Thomas Browne b. (–1682).
— John Gauden b. (–1662).

1606　　The Hapsburg Archdukes rebel against Rudolf II—The Peace of Zsitva-Torok

A　Jan: 21st, English Parliament meets (*–May* 27th) and imposes severer penalties against Roman Catholics; persons convicted of recusancy are disabled from holding public office;

27th, trial of Guy Fawkes and his fellow conspirators.

Feb:

Mar: Henry IV of France occupies Sedan to end the rebellion of the Duke of Bouillon.

B　Apr: 10th, royal charters are granted to the Virginia Companies of London and Plymouth for authorising colonisation;

12th, James VI and I's proclamation for a national flag combining the cross of St. George and the saltire of St. Andrew;

the Hapsburg archdukes rebel against the Emperor Rudolf II and recognise the Archduke Matthias as leader (*see June* 1608).

May: 3rd, the Jesuit Henry Garnett is executed for alleged complicity in the Gunpowder Plot;

17th, the False Dmitri murdered in Russia by Basil Shuisky, with support from the boyars.

Jun: 23rd, by the Peace of Vienna between the Archduke Matthias and Hungary, Stephen Bocskai is recognised as ruler of Transylvania.

C　Jul:

Aug:

Sep:

D　Oct:

Nov: 11th, treaty of peace is signed at Zsitva-Torok between the Turks and the Austrians;

the House of Hapsburg abandons Transylvania to Stephen Bocskai, under Turkish suzerainty, but ceases paying tribute for the Hapsburg part of Hungary;

18th, English Parliament reassembles (*–July* 4th, 1607).

Dec: The London Virginian Company sends three ships with 120 colonists to Virginia under Captain Christopher Newport.

E　Episcopacy is restored in Scotland by Act of the Scottish Parliament which passes severe laws against Roman Catholics; Presbyterian ministers are banned;

Pope Paul V places Venice under an interdict after the Council of Ten had taken proceedings against an ecclesiastic, an action which Fra Paolo Sarpi vigorously defended against papal criticism.

F **Politics, Economics, Law and Education**

In Bates' Case the judges declare the legality of impositions on trade levied by the Crown without Parliamentary sanction.

G **Science, Technology and Discovery**

Completion of the canal linking Eskilstuna with Lake Malar, in Sweden.
The Spanish navigator Torres sails between New Guinea and Australia.

H **Philosophy, Religion and Scholarship**

Johann Arndt, *Wahres Christenthum* (*True Christianity*—A Lutheran mystic's Imitation of Christ).
Philemon Holland translates *The History of the Twelve Caesars* by Suetonius.
Joseph Scaliger, *Thesaurus Temporum* (a chronology of the ancient world).

J **Art, Sculpture, Fine Arts and Architecture**

Painting:
Isaac Oliver (d. 1617) adopts English nationality.

K **Music**

L **Literature (including Drama)**

Thomas Dekker, *The Seuen deadly Sinnes of London ; Newes from Hell* (pamphlets).
John Marston, *The Parasitaster* (comedy). *Sophonisba* (tragedy).

M **Births and Deaths**

Jan. 31st Guy Fawkes d. (36).
Mar. 3rd William Davenant b. (–1668).
Mar. 9th Edmund Waller b. (–1687).
May 3rd Henry Garnett d. (51).
June 6th Pierre Corneille b. (–1684).
July 15th Rembrandt b. (–1669).
Sept. 22nd Richard Busby b. (–1695).
Nov. — John Lyly d. (*c.* 52).

1607   Foundation of Jamestown, Virginia—The flight of the Earls—
        Spanish bankruptcy

A   Jan:
     Feb: The Emperor Rudolf II confirms the English Merchants Adventurers' Company in
        their mart at Stade.
     Mar: 15th, Charles IX, King of Sweden since 1604, is formally crowned.

B   Apr:
     May: 13th, foundation of Jamestown, Virginia, as an English colony under the leadership
        of Captain John Smith;
        riots in Northamptonshire and other Midland counties of England in protest at wide-
        spread enclosure of common land.
     Jun:

C   Jul: 4th, James I prorogues English Parliament, which has rejected the King's proposed
        Treaty of Union with Scotland.
     Aug: The Bank of Genoa fails, following the announcement of national bankruptcy in
        Spain.
     Sep: 14th, the 'Flight of the Earls' when Hugh O'Neill, Earl of Tyrone, and Rory
        O'Donnell, Earl of Tyrconnel, flee from Ireland for Spain with their families and
        retainers, fearing their arrest for attempted insurrection.

D   Oct:
     Nov:
     Dec: 17th, Maximilian of Bavaria occupies the imperial city of Donauwörth, after exe-
        cuting the ban of the Empire as punishment of this predominantly Protestant city
        when a mob had disturbed a Catholic procession.

E   Henry IV of France successfully mediates between Pope Paul V and the Venetians in the
     Sarpi controversy (see 1606 E).

F Politics, Economics, Law and Education

First English settlement is founded on American mainland at Jamestown, Virginia (*May* 13th).

J. Cowell, *The Interpreter*.

G Science, Technology and Discovery

Galileo makes a thermometer.

J. Norden, *The Surveyors Dialogue*, a manual of surveying.

H Philosophy, Religion and Scholarship

Joseph Calasanza organises the brotherhood of Piarists in Rome (fathers of the religious schools) which later (–1622) receive a constitution from Gregory XV.

The Bollandists (followers of Jean Bolland), a congregation of Jesuits in Belgium, plan the *Acta Sanctorum* (–1643).

J Art, Sculpture, Fine Arts and Architecture

K Music

William Byrd, *Gradualia*.

Claudio Monteverdi, *Orfeo*.

L Literature (including Drama)

George Chapman, *Bussy D'Ambois* (tragedy).

Thomas Heywood, *A Woman Killed with Kindness* (tragedy).

Ben Jonson, *Volpone, or The Fox* (comedy).

John Marston, *What you Will* (comedy).

William Shakespeare, *Timon of Athens*.

Cyril Tourneur, *The Revenger's Tragedy*.

Honoré D'Urfé, *Astrée*, part 1 (pastoral romance, completed 1627 by Baro).

M Births and Deaths

Jan. 31st James Stanley, 7th Earl of Derby, b. (–1651).

Mar. 24th Michael de Ruyter b. (–1676).

May 21st John Rainolds d. (58).

Dec. 23rd John Fortescue d. (*c.* 74).

— Archibald Campbell, Marquess of Argyll, b. (–1661).

— Penelope Rich d. (*c.* 45).

— Madeleine de Scudéry b. (–1701).

1608 The Protestant Union of German Princes is formed—Gabriel
Báthory becomes ruler of Transylvania

A Jan:
Feb:
Mar:

B Apr: 18th, Cahir O'Dogherty of Tyrone raises rebellion in Ulster, surprising Culmore
Castle and capturing Derry;
27th, Protestants break up the Diet of Ratisbon, denying the right of the Catholic
majority to bind the minority, after Maximilian of Bavaria had annexed the imperial
city of Donauwörth, where Protestantism was strong, on the orders of the imperial
Aulic council (in *Dec.* 1607).
May: 12th, a Protestant Union of German princes opposing the Catholic *bloc* is formed at
Anhausen under Christian of Anhalt and Frederick IV of the Palatinate;
20th, O'Dogherty's rebellion in Ulster collapses (he is slain *July* 20th).
Jun: 16th/26th, Anglo-Dutch treaty for mutual defence;
25th, the Emperor Rudolf II is compelled by the Archdukes to cede Austria, Hungary
and Moravia to his brother Matthias and to promise him the succession to Bohemia;
judgment in the case of the '*Post Nati*' that a Scot, born after the Union of the Crowns
in 1603, is a natural subject of the King of England.

C Jul: 18th, John Sigismund succeeds as Elector of Brandenburg (–1619) on the death of
Joachim Frederick, and subsequently establishes Calvinism in the electorate.
Aug: Sir Henry Foliot massacres Irish rebels who had taken refuge in Tory Island.
Sep:

D Oct:
Nov:
Dec: 20th, following the escheat to the English Crown of estates in Ulster, a scheme is
prepared for the English settlement of Tyrone leading to the settlement of the entire
six counties.

E Gabriel Báthory becomes ruler of Transylvania under Turkish suzerainty (–1613);
the Dmitri, pretended son of Ivan IV, defeats Tsar Shuisky and advances towards
Moscow; the Tsar agrees to cede Karelia to Sweden in return for aid (confirmed *Feb.*
1609).

F **Politics, Economics, Law and Education**
Samuel de Champlain founds a French settlement at Quebec (*July*).
Captain John Smith, *A True Relation of Virginia*.
In Calvin's Case the judges decide that Scots born after the Union of the Crowns of England and Scotland are to be accounted natural-born subjects of England.

G **Science, Technology and Discovery**
Johann Lippershey of Middleburg constructs a binocular telescope.
Galileo invents the microscope.

H **Philosophy, Religion and Scholarship**
Edward Grimestone, *A General History of the Netherlands*.
Thomas Heywood translates Sallust (*The Catiline Conspiracy*; and the *Jugurthan War*).
William Perkins, *A Discourse of the Damned Art of Witchcraft* (posth.).

J **Art, Sculpture, Fine Arts and Architecture**
Painting:
Domenichino, *Scourging of St. Andrew* (Fresco).
El Greco, *Golgotha*; *View of Toledo*; *Assumption of the Virgin Mary* (–1613).

K **Music**
Claudio Monteverdi, *Arianna*.
Frescobaldi appointed organist at St. Peter's, Rome.

L **Literature (including Drama)**
George Chapman, *The Conspiracy and Tragedy of Charles, Duke of Byron, Marshall of France*.
Joseph Hall, *Characters of Virtues and Vices* (first imitations in English literature of the 'Characters' of Theophrastus, 372–286 B.C.).
Thomas Middleton, *A Mad World my Masters* (satirical comedy).
William Shakespeare, *King Lear*; *Coriolanus*.
Richard West, *A Century of Epigrams*.
The Kings Men, company of actors, play at the Blackfriars Theatre, London (–1597).

M **Births and Deaths**
Jan. 28th Giovanni Alfonso Borelli b. (–1679).
Feb. 6th Antonio Vieira b. (–1697).
Feb. 13th Bess of Hardwick d. (88).
Apr. 19th Thomas Sackville, Earl of Dorset, d. (*c*. 78).
June 19th Alberico Gentili d. (56).
June 19th Thomas Fuller b. (–1661).
July 13th Emperor Ferdinand III b. (–1657).
July 14th George, Lord Goring, b. (–1657).
Oct. 15th Evangelista Torricelli b. (–1647).
Dec. 6th George Monck, Duke of Albemarle, b. (–1670).
Dec. 9th John Milton b. (–1674).
— George Bannantyne d. (63).
— Thomas Este d. (72).
— Richard Fanshawe b. (–1666).

1609 The Succession to the Duchies of Jülich and Cleves—Spain and Holland sign 9-years' Truce

A Jan:
Feb: Charles IX of Sweden signs an alliance at Viborg to aid Tsar Basil Shuisky of Russia against Sigismund III of Poland, who advances to Smolensk.
Mar: 25th, on the death of John William, last Duke of Jülich-Cleves, the Elector of Brandenburg and the Duke of Neuburg each claim succession to the duchy; Henry IV of France supports the claim of Brandenburg.

B Apr: 9th, Spain signs a nine years' truce with Holland, which implies the virtual independence of the seven United Provinces; the truce is guaranteed by the Emperor Rudolf II and by Henry IV of France.
May: 12th, Lord Somers and Captain Newport leave Plymouth, England, for Virginia.
Jun: 17th, the United Provinces sign a twelve years' alliance with England and France.

C Jul: 9th, the Emperor Rudolf II is forced by Zerotin to grant a charter permitting freedom of religion in Bohemia;
10th, a Catholic League of German princes is formed at Munich under Maximilian, Duke of Bavaria, in opposition to the Protestant Union (of *May* 1608).
Aug: Archduke Leopold of Austria lays siege to the fortress of Jülich for the Emperor (*–Feb.* 1610).
Sep: 22nd, the Duke of Zerma expels 500,000 Moors and Moriscoes from Spain.

D Oct: Sir John Elphinstone, Lord Balmerino, leader of the Scottish Catholics, is found guilty of forging a letter from James VI and I to Pope Clement VIII; his life is spared.
Nov:
Dec:

E The Jesuits, given complete control of the Indian missions by Philip III of Spain, establish their first mission at San Ignacio Guazu in Paraguay.

F **Politics, Economics, Law and Education**
> The Bank of Amsterdam is founded.
> Tea from China is first shipped to Europe by the Dutch East India Company.

G **Science, Technology and Discovery**
> Johann Kepler, *De Motibus Stellae Martis.*
> C. Butler, *The feminine monarchie; or a treatise concerning bees.*
> Henry Hudson explores the Delaware Bay and the Hudson River.
> Samuel de Champlain discovers Lake Champlain.

H **Philosophy, Religion and Scholarship**
> André Duchesne, *Les Antiquités et Recherches de la Grandeur et Majesté des Rois de France.*
> G. de la Vega, *History of the Conquest of Peru* (–1617).
> St. Francois de Sales, *Introduction à la vie devoté* (revised –1619).
> Lope de Vega, *El arte nuevo de hacer comedias.*
> English Baptist Church founded in Amsterdam by John Smith and Thomas Helwys (in London –1612).
> *The Old Testament* (Rheims and Douay Bible; *see* 1582).

J **Art, Sculpture, Fine Arts and Architecture**
> Painting:
>> El Greco, *Brother Paravicino.*
>> Rubens, *The Artist and his first wife, Isabella Brant.*

K **Music**
> Orlando Gibbons, *Fantazies of three parts* for viols (first example of engraved music in England; engraved plates used in Italy since about 1516).
> Thomas Ravenscroft, *Pammelia* (first book of catches).

L **Literature (including Drama)**
> Thomas Dekker, *The Guls Horne-booke* (satirical account of the way of life in London of certain Jacobean gallants).
> Ben Jonson, *The Case is Alter'd* (comedy); *Epicœne, or The Silent Woman* (comedy).
> William Shakespeare, *Troilus and Cressida; Pericles;* the *Sonnets* (the original quarto).

M **Births and Deaths**
> Jan. 21st Joseph Justus Scaliger d. (69).
> Feb. 10th John Suckling b. (–1642).
> Feb. 18th Edward Hyde, Earl of Clarendon, b. (–1674).
> Aug. 19th Jean de Rotron b. (–1650).
> Oct. 19th Jacobus Arminius d. (49).
> Nov. 1st Matthew Hale b. (–1676).
> Nov. 25th Henrietta Maria b. (–1666).
> — Michelangelo Caravaggio d. (30).
> — Annibale Caracci d. (49).

1610   Assassination of Henry IV of France—Basil Shuisky of Russia is deposed

A Jan:
Feb: 9th, English Parliament meets (–*July* 23rd), critical of James I's levying of impositions on overseas trade by virtue of his prerogative, following the judicial decision in Bates's case (in 1606);

12th, Henry IV of France signs an alliance with the German Protestant Union (of 1608) and prepares to intervene in German affairs. Henry is credited by the Duke of Sully with a grand design for European federation to secure peace and end Hapsburg dominance;

28th, Thomas West, baron De La Warr, is appointed Governor of Virginia; a further expedition under Captain Newport with 400 colonists shortly leaves England.

Mar: John Cowell is censured by Parliament and Council for enhancing the authority of the Crown in his *The Interpreter*, a law dictionary (1607), and, 26th, the book is burnt by the common hangman.

B Apr:
May: 14th, François Ravaillac, a fanatic, assassinates Henry IV of France, who is succeeded by Louis XIII, then aged 9 (–1643), with Marie de' Medici, the Queen Mother, as Regent (–1617). Concino Concini, her favourite, takes over direction of affairs from the Duke of Sully (who resigns his posts, *Jan.* 26th, 1611) and is created Marquis d'Ancre;

23rd, the House of Commons petitions James I against levying impositions;

24th, the King retracts his remarks about Parliamentary privilege.

Jun: 4th, Prince Henry, eldest son of James I, is created Prince of Wales;

9th, Arabella Stuart, Pretender to the Throne, is imprisoned for marrying William Seymour, Earl of Hertford, claimant of the Suffolk line to the English succession;

Earl of Salisbury veers towards an anti-Spanish policy;

26th, James I accepts the terms of the Great Contract, or an amount of £200,000 in return for the abolition of feudal tenures and wardship, but negotiations founder as a result of disputes about purveyance.

C Jul: 19th, Basil Shuisky, Tsar of Russia, is deposed, after a Swedish army under Jacob de la Gardie, sent against the Polish invaders of Russia, is forced to surrender. The Russian throne is offered to Vladislav, son of Sigismund III of Poland, but the latter, jealous of this offer, advances on Moscow;

23rd, James I prorogues Parliament.

Aug:
Sep: 1st, Archduke Leopold of Austria, who had seized Jülich (in *Feb.*) is expelled by a force of German, Dutch and English troops;

19th, Frederick V becomes Elector Palatine on the death of his father, Frederick IV.

D Oct: 16th, the English Parliament reassembles (–*Dec.* 6th).
Nov:
Dec: Mercenaries of the Archduke Leopold of Austria devastate Upper Austria and advance on Prague.

E First skirmishes between English and Dutch settlers in India.

F **Politics, Economics, Law and Education**

Following the condemnation of Juan de Mariana by the Sorbonne for favouring tyrannicide, the Jesuit General Claudio Aquaviva disclaims the tenet.

The Portuguese found a settlement at Cape Coast, Gold Coast.

G **Science, Technology and Discovery**

Galileo observes Jupiter's satellites (*Jan.* 7th), naming them 'Sidera Medicea', after Cosmo II, Grand Duke of Tuscany. He describes the first-fruits of his other astronomical discoveries with his telescope of 32-fold magnifying power in *Sidereus Nuncius*.

Thomas Harriott and others discover sunspots.

Jean Beguin, *Tyrocinium Chymicum*, the first text-book on chemistry.

Henry Hudson sails through Hudson's Straits (*June*) and discovers Hudson's Bay (*Aug.* 3rd).

John Speed's collection of maps, *Theatrum of Great Britain*.

R. Vaughan, *Most approved and long experienced water works*, a manual on the irrigation of grasslands.

H **Philosophy, Religion and Scholarship**

Cardinal Bellarmine, *De potestate summis pontificio in rebus temporalibus* (replying to tracts written by William Barclay).

John Donne, *Pseudo-martyr* (...' this conclusion ... that those which are of the Romane Religion in this Kingdome, may and ought to take the Oath of Allegiance ').

Philemon Holland translates the Latin original of Camden's *Britannia* (1586).

Guilio Alenio, an Italian Jesuit missionary, lands in Macao.

J **Art, Sculpture, Fine Arts and Architecture**

Painting:

El Greco, *The opening of the Fifth Seal*.

Rubens, *Raising the Cross*.

K **Music**

L **Literature (including Drama)**

John Fletcher, *The Faithful Shepherdess* (pastoral drama).

Robert Jones, *The Muses Garden of Delights*.

Ben Jonson, *The Alchemist* (comedy).

William Shakespeare, *Cymbeline; A Winter's Tale; The Tempest*.

M **Births and Deaths**

Feb. 13th Jean de la Badie b. (–1674).

Apr. 18th Robert Persons d. (65).

May 11th Matteo Ricci d. (57).

July 4th Paul Scarron b. (–1660).

Oct. 19th James Butler, Earl of Ormonde, b. (–1688).

Dec. 18th Charles du Fresne, Sieur du Cange, b. (–1688).

— Adriaen van Ostade b. (–1684).

1611   Resignation of Emperor Rudolf II—Accession of Gustavus Adolphus of Sweden

A Jan: 26th, the Duke of Sully resigns as French Superintendent of Finances;
James I opens negotiations for a marriage between his daughter, Elizabeth, and the Elector Frederick V of the Palatinate (in *Apr*. proposals for a match with the Prince of Piedmont are considered; the marriage with the Elector Palatine takes place in *Feb*. 1613).

Feb: 9th, angered by the Commons' attack on the Court of High Commission, James I dissolves Parliament before 'the Great Contract' is arranged.

Mar: 4th, George Abbot is elected Archbishop of Canterbury (–1633);
24th, the Archduke Matthias, who has marched from Vienna with 10,000 men, enters Prague and receives a patriotic welcome;
25th, James I creates his favourite, Robert Carr, Viscount Rochester;
by the Treaty of Jüterbok the Elector of Saxony is granted a share in the government of the duchies of Jülich, Berg and Cleves.

B Apr: 4th, Christian IV of Denmark declares war on Sweden—the War of Kalmar (–1613)
—and sends troops to Kalmar and the mouth of the Göta;
13th, proclamation for British 'undertakers' for the plantation of Ulster to assemble at Dublin.

May: 10th, William Laud is elected President of St. John's College, Oxford;
23rd, Matthias is crowned King of Bohemia (the Emperor Rudolf does not formally resign the crown until *Aug*. 11th).

Jun: 3rd, Arabella Stuart, imprisoned for contracting a marriage with William Seymour, Earl of Hertford, escapes from the Tower of London to Ostend (she is subsequently recaptured and dies in the Tower *Sept*. 1615). The Countess of Shrewsbury is imprisoned for her alleged share in Arabella's escape;
Sir John Digby, ambassador in Madrid, attempts to secure the hand of the Infanta, Anne of Austria, for Henry, Prince of Wales, but finds she is contracted to Louis XIII.

C Jul: 23rd, George Elector of Saxony succeeds his brother, Christian II, and becomes leader of the Lutheran Party in Germany.

Aug: 11th, the Emperor Rudolf is forced to resign the Bohemian crown to his brother Matthias, but retains private property in the kingdom.

Sep:

D Oct: At a preliminary meeting of the Imperial Electors at Nuremberg to choose a King of the Romans, Matthias of Bohemia is preferred to the Archduke Albert, but the Spiritual Electors aim at supporting the latter;
30th, Charles IX of Sweden dies; the throne is temporarily left unfilled and Queen Christina and Duke John of Östergötland carry on the government.

Nov:

Dec: The Swedish estates meet at Nyköping to elect Gustavus II (Gustavus Adolphus) king (–1632). Duke John of Östergötland abjures the throne. The new King appoints Axel Oxenstjerna as Chancellor;
27th, the archdukes undertake to prevent the imperial crown from leaving the House of Hapsburg.

E Sir Thomas Sherley arrives in England as ambassador from the Shah of Persia and negotiates a commercial treaty.

F Politics, Economics, Law and Education
James VI and I institutes the baronetage.
First English settlement on the east coast of India, at Masulipatam, Madras.

G Science, Technology and Discovery
Burgi makes a table of anti-logarithms of integers (published 1620).
Simon Sturtevant patents the use of mineral coal for smelting iron, but his process is not adopted for many years.

H Philosophy, Religion and Scholarship
The Authorised Version of the Holy Bible.
George Chapman completes his translation of Homer's *Iliad* (*see* 1598).
Randle Cotgrave, *A Dictionary of the French and English Tongues.*
Georg Draud, *Bibliotheca classica.*
John Speed, *A History of Great Britain.*
Étienne Pasquier, *Les Recherches de la France.*

J Art, Sculpture, Fine Arts and Architecture
Painting:
Rubens, *Descent from the Cross* (–1614).

K Music
Orlando Gibbons, *This is the Record of John* (anthem).
Gibbons, William Byrd and John Bull, *Parthenia* (anthology of music for virginals).

L Literature (including Drama)
Thomas Coryate, *Crudities.*
John Donne, *An Anatomy of the World* (elegy on the death of Elizabeth Drury).
Ben Jonson, *Catiline* (tragedy).
Thomas Middleton, *The Roaring Girl* (comedy).
Cyril Tourneur, *The Atheist's Tragedie; or The Honest Man's Revenge.*

M Births and Deaths
Jan 7th James Harrington b. (–1677).
Sept. 11th Henri, Vicomte de Turenne, b. (–1675).
Nov. 3rd Henry Ireton b. (–1651).
Dec. 12th Thomas Sutton d. (*c.* 79).
— Henry Hudson d. (*c.* 50).
— Thomas Urquhart b. (–1660).
— Thomas Vittoria d. (76).
— John Webb b. (–1672).

1612 Election of Emperor Matthias—Dutch settlement on Manhattan Island

A Jan: 20th, Matthias, King of Bohemia succeeds as Holy Roman Emperor (–1619) on the death of Rudolf II (formal election in *Jun*).

   Feb: Gustavus II of Sweden, eager to end the War of Kalmar, reopens operations at Gulberg.

   Mar: 18th, an Arian is burnt for heresy at Smithfield.

B Apr: The Protestant Union of Germany signs a defensive alliance with England.

   May: James I renews negotiations for his daughter Elizabeth to marry the Elector Palatine Frederick V;

   24th, on the death of Robert Earl of Salisbury, the Secretaryship of State nominally passes to Viscount Rochester, the royal favourite, though in effect James I becomes his own Principal Secretary;

   Gustavus II of Sweden loses Elfsborg and Gulberg to the Danes.

   Jun: 13th, formal election of Matthias of Bohemia as Holy Roman Emperor;

   17th, following Salisbury's death, the Treasurership is put in commission for the first time, with Henry Howard, Earl of Nottingham as first lord. Sir Julius Caesar, Chancellor of the Exchequer, reports that the ordinary annual expenditure of the English Crown exceeds the revenue by £160,000 and that the national debt has risen to £500,000.

C Jul: Philip III of Spain, a widower, aspires to the hand of Princess Elizabeth; James I's treatment of his envoy harms relations with Spain.

   Aug: Christian IX of Denmark attacks Sweden by sea;

   marriage treaties are signed for Louis XIII of France to marry Anne of Austria, the Infanta of Spain, and for Philip Prince of Asturias, heir to the Spanish throne, to marry Elizabeth Bourbon (both marriages take place in 1615). Both France and Spain undertake they will not make an alliance with Savoy.

   Sep: The Elector Palatine, Frederick V, arrives in England.

D Oct: Sweden, under Gustavus II, recovers her position in the war with Denmark.

   Nov: 5th, Henry, Prince of Wales, 'the Hope of Protestantism', dies.

   Dec:

E Dutch first use Manhattan Island as a centre for the fur trade (*see* 1624 E);

   Earliest colonisation of the Bermudas ('The Somers Islands') from Virginia, under Sir George Somers.

F **Politics, Economics, Law and Education**
Sir John Davies, *Discoverie of the True Causes Why Ireland Was Not Entirely Subdued.*
R. Fenton, *Treatie of Usurie.*
John Smith, *A Map of Virginia.*
Bartholomew Legate of London and Edward Wightman of Lichfield are the last persons to be burnt for their religious opinions in England.
Tobacco is first planted in Virginia.
Wadham College, Oxford, is founded.
Ratke begins to reform German education.

G **Science, Technology and Discovery**
Bartholomew Pitiscus first uses a decimal point in his trigonometrical tables.
Neri, *L'Arte Vetraria*, a manual on glass-making.

H **Philosophy, Religion and Scholarship**
Jakob Boehme, *Aurora; oder, Morgenröte im Aufgang* (mystical philosophy condemned by the Lutherans).
Thomas Shelton translates part 1 of *Don Quixote* by Cervantes (completed 1620).
The Accademia della Crusca (*see* 1582) publishes the first dictionary of its kind; the Italian *Vocabolario* (the acknowledged model of later French and Spanish dictionaries).

J **Art, Sculpture, Fine Arts and Architecture**
Painting:
El Greco, *Baptism of Christ; Adoration of the Shepherds* (-1614).

K **Music**
Orlando Gibbons, *First set of Madrigals and Motets of five parts, apt for Viols and Voices.*

L **Literature (including Drama)**
Thomas Deloney, *Thomas of Reading.*
Michael Drayton, *Polyolbion*, part 1 (-1622).
Samuel Purchas, *Hakluytus Posthumus; or, Purchas his Pilgrimes.*
John Webster, *The White Devil* (tragedy).

M **Births and Deaths**
Jan. 17th Thomas Fairfax b. (-1671).
Jan. 20th Emperor Rudolph II d. (60).
Feb. 18th Roberto di Ridolfi d. (80).
Feb. — Samuel Butler b. (-1680).
May 24th Robert Cecil, Earl of Salisbury, d. (*c.* 47).
Oct. — George Digby, Earl of Bristol, b. (-1677).
— Anne Bradstreet b. (-1672).
— Giovanni Guarimi d. (74).
— James Graham, Marquess of Montrose, b. (-1650).
— Louis le Vau b. (-1670).

A Jan: 20th, the Peace of Knärod, mediated by James I of England, ends the War of Kalmar between Denmark and Sweden. Sweden gains Kalmar and Denmark retains Elfsborg for six years with 1 million dollars to be paid for its redemption;

scare of a Spanish invasion in England, induced by threats from Madrid of retaliation for the treatment of English Roman Catholics and for the colonisation of Virginia. Philip III, however, abandons his design and sends (*May*) a new ambassador to improve relations and influence James I.

Feb: 14th, Elizabeth, daughter of James I, marries Frederick V of the Palatinate;

21st, Michael Romanov, son of the Patriarch of Moscow, is elected Tsar of Russia (–1645), the founder of the House of Romanov.

Mar:

B Apr:

May: The Count of Gondomar takes up his appointment as Spanish ambassador in England;

16th, the Protestant Union of Germany signs a treaty of alliance with the United Provinces.

Jun:

C Jul:

Aug: 13th, the German Diet meets at Ratisbon. The Catholic princes, with the Elector of Saxony, agree to the Emperor Matthias's demands for aid against the Turks, but the other Protestant princes dissent. Deadlock is reached on the religious issue.

Sep: 4th, the Earl of Essex is divorced from Lady Frances Howard in scandalous circumstances;

14th, Sir Thomas Overbury, sent to the Tower of London, is poisoned;

Francis Bacon becomes Attorney General;

the Turks invade Hungary.

D Oct: 24th, Gabor Bethlen, a protégé of the Porte, becomes Prince of Transylvania (–1629) in place of Gabriel Báthory, a dependent of the Emperor Matthias.

Nov: 3rd, James I creates his favourite, Viscount Rochester, Earl of Somerset.

Dec: 25th, John Sigismund of Brandenburg is converted to Calvinism;

26th, the divorced Lady Frances Howard marries the favourite, Earl of Somerset. The marriage strengthens the position of the pro-Spanish Howard faction and its hold over James I.

E English colonists in Virginia destroy the French settlement at Port Royal, Nova Scotia, and prevent French colonisation of Maryland.

F **Politics, Economics, Law and Education**
   Serra, *Causes of Wealth*.
   Copper coins are introduced to England.
   Belfast is granted a charter of incorporation (*Apr.* 27th).
   Hugh Myddelton constructs the 'New River' cut to bring water to London.

G **Science, Technology and Discovery**
   Samuel de Champlain explores the Ottawa River as far as Allumette Island.
   Antonio Fernandez penetrates the lands south of Shoa.
   John Dennys, *The Secrets of Angling*.

H **Philosophy, Religion and Scholarship**
   Peter Pázmány, *Guide to Truth* (*Isteni igazságra vezérlo Kalauz*: notable Hungarian polemic in vigorous prose style).
   Francisco Suarez, *Defensio catholicae fidei contra anglicanae sectae errores*, written at Pope Paul V's instigation and directed against the oath of allegiance demanded by English subjects.

J **Art, Sculpture, Fine Arts and Architecture**
   Painting:
   Guido Reni, *Aurora* frescoes.
   Architecture:
   Salomon de Brosse, Château Coulommiers.

K **Music**
   Claudio Monteverdi is appointed maestro di capello at St. Mark's, Venice.

L **Literature (including Drama)**
   Francis Beaumont and John Fletcher, *The Knight of the Burning Pestle* (burlesque comedy).
   William Browne, *Britannia's Pastorals*.
   Cervantes Saavedra, *The Exemplary Novels* (*Novelas Ejemplares*).
   George Chapman, *The Revenge of Bussy D'Ambois* (tragedy).
   Drummond of Hawthornden, *Tears on the Death of Moeliades*.
   Don Luis de Góngora y Argote, *Soledades* (–1614).
   William Shakespeare, *Henry VIII*.
   Lope de Vega, *Fuenteovejuna*.
   The Globe Theatre, Southwark, London, destroyed by fire (–1598).

M **Births and Deaths**
   Jan. 28th Thomas Bodley d. (67).
   Mar. 12th André de Nôtre b. (–1700).
   May 26th Henry Vane the younger b. (–1662).
   Aug. 15th Jeremy Taylor b. (–1667).
   Sept. 15th Thomas Overbury d. (32).
   Sept. 15th François de la Rochefoucauld b. (–1680).
   Oct. 22nd Mathurin Régnier d. (39).
   — Sigismund Báthory d. (41).
   — Richard Crashaw b. (–1650).

A Jan: Gustavus II of Sweden holds a Diet at Orebro, gains support for his campaign in
    Russia, and establishes a supreme court;
    the Prince of Neuburg, a converted Catholic, seizes Jülich, which threatens a general
    war in Germany and the renewal of war between the Spanish Netherlands and the
    United Provinces. The Dutch subsequently occupy Jülich and the crisis passes, with
    the signing (*Nov.*) of the Treaty of Xanten.
Feb: 19th, the Prince of Condé, supported by the Dukes of Nevers, Mayenne and Longue-
    ville, rebels against the Queen Mother and Concino Concini; there is widespread
    support for the rebels in view of the unpopularity of the projected Spanish marriage of
    Louis XIII, the evidence of maladministration and the failure to summon the States-
    General (*–May*).
Mar: 29th, Sir Ralph Winwood, an opponent of the Howard faction, is appointed Secre-
    tary of State (–1617) in succession to Somerset.

B Apr: 5th, James I's second Parliament ('The Addled Parliament') meets (*–June* 7th). The
    Commons refuses to vote supplies until the question of royal impositions is settled.
May: 15th, French Civil War ends with the Peace of St. Menehould; Louis XIII under-
    takes to summon the States-General.
Jun: 7th, James I dissolves Parliament; not a single Act is passed. The King subsequently
    imprisons four members of the Commons who had opposed the Crown. The Council
    sends out requests for a Benevolence, which produces a total of £66,000; action is
    taken in the Court of Star Chamber against persons inciting others to refuse this aid to
    the Crown.

C Jul: 11th, Thomas Howard, Earl of Suffolk, is appointed Lord Treasurer (–1618);
    La Gardie leads a Swedish army to defeat the Russians at Bronnitsy.
Aug: The Archduke Albert, Governor of the Spanish Netherlands, sends troops to put
    down religious disturbances at Aix-la-Chapelle and Mülheim;
    representatives of all the Hapsburg Estates (except Bohemia) meet at Linz.
Sep: Gustavus II captures Gdov and returns in triumph to Sweden.

D Oct: The Protestant Union meet at Heilbronn;
    the French States-General assemble at Paris (*–Mar.* 1615).
    The Third Estate attacks the *Taille* and the sale of offices and demands a declaration
    that no person can depose the King.
Nov: 12th, by the Treaty of Xanten, Jülich and Cleves are divided between the Princes of
    Brandenburg and Neuburg, ending the disputed succession to the duchies.
Dec:

E

F **Politics, Economics, Law and Education**
The States-General of France meet for the last time before 1789.
The New Netherlands Company of Amsterdam is granted a three-year monopoly of the fur trade in North America by the Dutch States-General (*Oct.* 11th).
Groningen University, Holland, is founded.

G **Science, Technology and Discovery**
John Napier devises his logarithmic tables (*Mirifici Logarithmorum Canonis Descriptio*).
Adriaen Block explores Long Island Sound.
Cornelius Jacobsen Mey explores the Lower Delaware.

H **Philosophy, Religion and Scholarship**
George Chapman translates Homer's *Odyssey*, books 1-12 (-1615).
Sir Arthur Gorges translates Lucan's *Pharsalia*.
Sir Walter Raleigh, *The History of the World*.
John Selden, *Titles of Honour*.

J **Art, Sculpture, Fine Arts and Architecture**
Painting:
El Greco, *Betrothal of the Virgin*.
Architecture:
Salzburg Cathedral begun (-1680).

K **Music**
Girolamo Frescobaldi, *Toccate di Cembalo*.
Sir William Leighton, *Teares and Lamentacions of a Sorrowful Soule* (54 metrical psalms; published in London).

L **Literature (including Drama)**
Ben Jonson, *Bartholomew Fayre* (comedy) acted (published 1631).
Sir Thomas Overbury, *Characters*.

M **Births and Deaths**
Apr. 7th El Greco d. (73).
July 1st Isaac Casaubon d. (55).
July 10th Arthur Annesley, Earl of Anglesey, b. (-1686).
Oct. 12th Henry More b. (-1687).
— Jean de Gondi, Cardinal de Retz, b. (-1679).
— Gautier de Coste, Sieur de la Calprenède, b. (-1663).
— Robert Smythson d. (78).

A Jan: Sir Thomas Roe is sent from England on an embassy to the Mogul of India (he arrives *Sept.*).

Feb: 21st, new monopoly of Merchants Adventurers under Alderman Cockaine, for the export of English cloth (the old company is restored 1617).

Mar: The French States-General are dismissed with vague promises of reforms. The apparent lack of faith of the Queen Mother and Concino Concini, her adviser, provokes the Prince of Condé to rise a second time, in *Aug*. The States-General do not meet again until 1789.

B Apr: Charles Emmanuel, Duke of Savoy, who has tried to occupy Montferrat, following the death of his son-in-law, the Duke of Mantua and Montferrat, invades Lombardy, with Venice as his ally; but the Savoyards are defeated by the Spanish Viceroy, the Marquis of Hinojosa, and are subsequently forced by France to sign the Peace of Asti.

May: 6th, by the Peace of Tyrnau the Emperor Matthias recognises Gabor Bethlen as Prince of Transylvania;

22nd, the *Parlement* of Paris, in an extraordinary session to which peers and office-holders are invited, calls for the exclusion of foreigners from office, intending to force the removal of Concino Concini, the favourite, now Marshal of France.

Jun:

C Jul: The Emperor Matthias signs a peace treaty with the Turks, confirming the terms of the Peace of Tyrnau.

Aug: 9th, Second Civil War in France (–*May* 1616), in which the Prince of Condé is in league with the Huguenots, led by Henry Duke of Rohan.

Sep: 27th, Lady Arabella Stuart dies in the Tower of London;

the Duke of Rohan gains support in Guienne and Languedoc.

D Oct: The Prince of Condé takes control of Poitou.

Nov: 9th, exchange of Bourbon and Hapsburg brides at Burgos after proxy marriages of Louis XIII to Anne of Austria and of Philip of Asturias to Elizabeth of Bourbon; France henceforth ceases to interfere with Catholic policy in Germany;

examinations of the Earl and Countess of Somerset for their part in Sir Thomas Overbury's murder (–in 1613).

Dec:

E English fleet defeats the Portuguese off the coast of Bombay;

England lays claim to Spitsbergen;

The Dutch seize the Moluccas from the Portuguese.

F **Politics, Economics, Law and Education**
  D. Digges, *The Defence of Trade.*
  Montchrestien, *Traité de l'Économie Politique*, expounds mercantilist principles.
  The use of timber as fuel for glass furnaces is forbidden in England.
  Theodore Agrippa d'Aubigné's *Histoire Universelle*, a survey from 1553–1602 from the Huguenot standpoint, is officially burnt in Paris.
  Egenolph Emmel founds the *Frankfurter Oberpostamtszeitung* (–1866).

G **Science, Technology and Discovery**
  J. Kepler, *Nova Stereometria Doliorum*, an investigation of the capacity of casks, surface areas and conic sections.

H **Philosophy, Religion and Scholarship**
  William Camden, *Annales Rerum Anglicarum* (of the reign of Elizabeth I), part 1 to 1588 (continued 1627).
  George Chapman completes his translation of Homer's *Odyssey* (*see* 1614).

J **Art, Sculpture, Fine Arts and Architecture**
  Painting:
    Domenichino, *Scenes from the Life of St. Cecilia* (frescoes).
  Sculpture:
    Gianlorenzo Bernini, *The Goat Amalthea* (Borghese, Rome).
  Architecture:
    Salomon de Brosse, Palais de Luxembourg, Paris (–1624).

K **Music**

L **Literature (including Drama)**
  Miguel de Cervantes Saavedra, *Don Quixote*, part 2 (part 1, –1605).
  Samuel Coster, *Spel vande Rijcke-Man* (farce).

M **Births and Deaths**
  Jan. 14th John Biddle b. (–1662).
  Feb. 4th Giovanni Della Porta d. (77).
  Mar. 27th Marguérite de Valois d. (62).
  Aug. 22nd Arthur Agarde d. (75).
  Sept. 27th Arabella Stuart d. (40).
  Nov. 12th Richard Baxter b. (–1691)
  Nov. — Ninon de Lenclos b. (–1705).
  — John Denham b. (–1669).

A Jan: 2nd, the Earl of Worcester, a Catholic, is appointed Lord Privy Seal;
   3rd, Sir George Villiers, James I's new favourite, is appointed Master of the Horse;
   13th, Sir Thomas Lake becomes Secretary of State.
   Feb:
   Mar: 20th, as a result of Villiers' intervention with James I, Sir Walter Raleigh is released
   from the Tower to search for gold in Guiana (he sails 1617).

B Apr: 23rd, England returns the cautionary towns of Flushing and Brielle to the United
   Provinces on payment of £215,000.
   May: 3rd, the Second Civil War in France is ended by the Treaty of Loudun, which
   grants an amnesty for the Prince of Condé and the other rebels, but no concessions
   are made to the Huguenots; Concino Concini remains in power;
   24th (–25th), trial of the Earl and Countess of Somerset for their part in poisoning Sir
   Thomas Overbury, in 1613; they are found guilty. James I pardons them but banishes
   them from court.
   Jun:

C Jul: To improve his serious financial position James I begins to sell peerages; the first so
   ennobled are Lords Teynham and Houghton;
   Lord Hay is sent to France to discuss the question of a French bride for Charles,
   Prince of Wales. When the negotiations break down James I renews negotiations with
   Gondomar, the Spanish ambassador, for a Spanish bride.
   Aug:
   Sep: 1st, the Prince of Condé is arrested at the Louvre and imprisoned in the Bastille.
   The other Princes of the Blood escape from Paris.

D Oct: Catholic oppression in Bohemia is intensified and rouses national sentiment against
   the Emperor Matthias.
   Nov: 1st, James I removes Sir Edward Coke, Chief Justice of the Common Pleas, for
   refusing to suspend an action in which the Crown is an interested party; the remaining
   11 judges give way. Coke is succeeded by Sir Henry Montague, a fervid royalist;
   20th, Richelieu, in France, becomes Minister of State for foreign affairs and war.
   Dec: The States of Holland under Prince Maurice of Nassau, anticipating civil war, arm
   to oppose the Advocate Johan van Oldenbarneveldt.

E The Archdukes Maximilian of the Tyrol and Albert, Governor of the Netherlands, re-
   nounce their claims to the Empire in favour of Ferdinand of Styria;
   The Tartars of Manchu invade China (–1620);
   The Dutch found a colony at Essequito, Guiana.

F **Politics, Economics, Law and Education**
John Smith, *A Description of New England*.
John Selden edits Sir John Fortescue's *De laudibus legum Angliae*.

G **Science, Technology and Discovery**
Galileo is threatened by the severest penalties of the Inquisition unless he agrees not to teach the Copernican system.
William Baffin passes through Davis Strait and discovers Baffin Bay in his search for a North West Passage.

H **Philosophy, Religion and Scholarship**
Johann Valentin Andraea, *Chymische Hochzeit Christiani Rosenkreutz* (may have started the formation of the Rosicrucian sect).
Théodore Agrippa D'Aubigné, *Les Tragiques* (religious poem in seven books).
L'Histoire universelle, 1550–1601, 3 vols. (Amsterdam –1629; burnt in Paris by the common hangman).
Paulus Bolduanus, *Bibliotheca Philosophica*.
George Chapman, *The Whole Works of Homer* (the *Odyssey* and the *Iliad* translated –1611, 1615).
St. François de Sales, *On the Love of God*.

J **Art, Sculpture, Fine Arts and Architecture**
Painting:
Isaac Oliver, *The Third Earl of Dorset* (miniature).
Rubens, *The Lion Hunt*.
Architecture:
Inigo Jones, Queen's House, Greenwich (–1618; and 1629–35).
Salomon de Brosse, façade, St. Gervais, Paris.

K **Music**

L **Literature (including Drama)**
William Browne, *Britannia's Pastorals*, part II (–1613).
Ben Jonson, *Works of Benjamin Jonson* (the first folio and the first collected edition of its kind to be published as the collected 'Works' of an English dramatist).

M **Births and Deaths**
Jan. 13th Antoinette Bourignon b. (–1680).
Jan. 30th William Sancroft b. (–1693).
Mar. 6th Francis Beaumont d. (32).
Apr. 23rd William Shakespeare d. (52).
Apr. 23rd Miguel de Cervantes d. (69).
July 30th Hugh O'Neill, Earl of Tyrone, d. (*c.* 76).
Oct. 11th Andreas Gryphius b. (–1664).
Oct. 18th Nicholas Culpeper b. (–1691).
Nov. 23rd Richard Hakluyt d. (63).
Nov. 23rd John Wallis b. (–1703).
Dec. 14th William, Duke of Hamilton, b. (–1651).
— John Owen b. (–1683).
— Isaac Pennington b. (–1679).

A Jan: James I creates his favourite, George Villiers, Earl of Buckingham (elevated to a dukedom *May* 1623).

Feb: 27th, through the mediation of the United Provinces, the Peace of Stolbovo is signed between Russia and Sweden; by its terms Gustavus II recognises Tsar Michael and surrenders his capture of Novgorod; Sweden obtains Karelia and Ingria; Russia surrenders her claims to Estonia and Livonia. Poland remains at war with Sweden (*–Nov.* 1618).

Mar: 7th, Francis Bacon is appointed Lord Keeper (created Lord Chancellor *Jan.* 7th, 1618);

17th, Sir Walter Raleigh leaves England on his expedition to Guiana (–1618).

B Apr: 24th, Concino Concini, Marquis d'Ancre, is assassinated by order of Louis XIII. Charles d'Albret, Duke of Luynes, favourite of Louis XIII, takes charge of the government of France (–1621). The Queen Mother, Marie de' Medici, ordered to withdraw to Blois, gathers round her opponents of Luynes and is joined by Richelieu.

May: 13th, James I (James VI of Scotland) revisits Scotland (*–Aug.* 4th).

Jun: 6th, the Austrian and Spanish Hapsburgs sign a treaty for mutual succession (confirmed *July* 29th);

15th, restoration of Roman Catholicism in Béarn;

17th, James I meets his Scottish Parliament. His proposal that the Scottish lords should surrender to the Crown their hereditable jurisdictions meets with vigorous opposition, but the five Articles of Religion, for introducing Anglican principles to Scottish worship are endorsed (and are approved by the General Assembly of the Church of Scotland in *Aug.* 1618);

29th, the Archduke Ferdinand of Styria, cousin and imperial heir of the Emperor Matthias, is recognised by the Bohemian Estates as heir to the Bohemian throne. The Protestant Opposition under Count Thurn, demand that he guarantee religious liberties, which he refuses. Subsequently the Estates of Moravia and Silesia endorse Ferdinand's right of succession.

C Jul: 9th, Maurice of Nassau declares himself the champion of the Contra-Remonstrants in Holland, in opposition to Johan van Oldenbarneveldt.

Aug: 5th, Oldenbarneveldt, asserting the Particularist sovereignty of Holland, secures the adoption of the 'Scherpe Resolution' by the States of Holland, requiring local levies to be raised for defence and requiring all in the pay of all the provinces to be subject to the authority of the States of Holland, instead of to the usual tribunals;

John George, Elector of Saxony, undertakes to support the Archduke Ferdinand's candidature in the election of a King of the Romans.

Sep: The Peace of Madrid ends the war since 1616 between Venice and Austria, occasioned by the settlement of piratical Uskoks in eastern Carniola and Croatia (confirmed *Feb.* 1618).

D Oct: 9th, the peace Treaty of Pavia is signed between Spain and Savoy, leaving the Duke of Savoy unpunished for his depredations;

the Duke of Osuna, with the connivance of Philip III of Spain, plunders Venice with the aid of Pedro de Toledo, Viceroy of Milan.

Nov:

Dec: 31st, Sir Walter Raleigh reaches the mouth of the R. Orinoco, and begins his search for gold.

E The Dutch purchase the island of Goree, off Cape Verde, from the natives.

F Politics, Economics, Law and Education

Francisco Suarez, *De Legibus ac Deo Legislatore*, a Jesuit tract which refutes the Divine Right of Kings and advocates the deposition of an evil Sovereign.

Francis Bacon is appointed Lord Keeper of the Great Seal of England (elevated to the Lord Chancellorship 1618).

G Science, Technology and Discovery

Willibrord Snell establishes the technique of trigonometrical triangulation for cartography.

H Philosophy, Religion and Scholarship

John Calvin's *Collected Works* published in Geneva, 12 folio volumes (posth.).

John Minsheu, *The Guide to Tongues* (polyglot: eleven languages: English, Welsh, Dutch, German, French, Italian, Spanish, Portuguese, Latin, Greek, Hebrew; said to have been the first privately printed book offered on subscription in London).

Papal Bull of Leo X condemns *Epistolae Obscurorum Vivorum* (*Mar.* 15th), by Ulrich von Hutten (and perhaps others).

Duytsche Academie (Coster's Academy) founded in Amsterdam by Samuel Coster (*Aug.* 1st; closed 1622).

J Art, Sculpture, Fine Arts and Architecture

Painting:

Guido Reni, *Deeds of Hercules* (–1621).

K Music

Heinrich Schütz appointed kapellmeister of electoral chapel at Dresden (–1672).

L Literature (including Drama)

Middleton and Rowley, *A Fair Quarrel* (comedy).

L. Martin Opitz founds Fruchtbringende Gesellschaft, a literary society in Heidelburg.

M Births and Deaths

Mar. — Pocahontas d. (*c.* 22).

Apr. 4th John Napier d. (67).

May 7th Jacques de Thou d. (64).

May 23rd Elias Ashmole b. (–1692).

Oct. 12th Bernardino Baldi d. (84).

Dec. — Thomas Coryat d. (40).

— Ralph Cudworth b. (–1588).

— Louis Elzevir d. (77).

— Peter Lely b. (–1680).

— Esteban Murillo b. (–1682).

— Gerard Ter Borch b. (–1681).

A Jan: 8th, Sir Robert Naunton is appointed a Principal Secretary of State.
   Feb: The Peace of Madrid (of *Sept.* 1617) is ratified, ending the war between Venice and
   Austria;
      28th, Maurice of Nassau succeeds as Prince of Orange on the death of his brother,
      Philip William.
   Mar: 5th, Count Thurn, leader of the anti-Hapsburg Bohemian Protestants calls an
   assembly to Prague to protest to the Regents.

B Apr: Richelieu is ordered into exile in Avignon for intriguing with the Queen Mother of
   France, Marie de' Medici.
   May: Count Thurn leads the Bohemians to revolt against the anti-nationalist, Catholic
   policy of the Regents in Prague;
      23rd, the Defenestration of Prague, when the Regents, Martinitz and Slawata, are
      overthrown by the Bohemian rebels, begins the Thirty Years War (–1648). A pro-
      visional government is formed in Prague under Wenceslas William von Ruppen.
   Jun: Count Thurn leads a Bohemian army to reduce the imperial garrison of Budweis;
      Count Mansfeld is sent to assist the rebels by the Protestant Union;
      John George Duke of Saxony applies for admission to the Protestant Union;
      the conspiracy of the Duke of Osuna and Francisco Quevedo against Venice is dis-
      covered.

C Jul: 1st, Ferdinand of Styria is crowned King of Hungary;
      20th, Cardinal Klesl, Bishop of Vienna, is arrested;
      31st, Maurice Prince of Orange, Stadtholder of Holland, orders the local levies (raised
      under the 'Scherpe Resolution' of *Aug.* 1617) to be disbanded;
      on the fall of Lord Treasurer Suffolk for misappropriating public funds, the Treasury
      is put in commission, with George Abbot, Archbishop of Canterbury as first com-
      missioner, though policy is controlled by Lionel Cranfield;
      the Elector Palatine, Frederick V, refuses to allow imperial troops to pass through his
      territory.
   Aug: 23rd, Johan van Oldenbarneveldt, Advocate of Holland, is arrested on a charge of
   treason;
      27th, James VI's five Articles of Religion, for introducing Anglican principles into the
      Church of Scotland, are approved by the General Assembly of that Church, represent-
      ing a triumph for the Episcopalian Party;
      —, on the death of Albert II, Duke of Prussia, without heirs, his possessions pass to the
      electorate of Brandenburg, though remaining under Polish suzerainty.
   Sep: The Emperor Matthias puts an army in the field under Count de Bucquoy, who
   enters Bohemia to reduce the rebels;
      James I offers to mediate in Bohemia, but is hampered by his negotiations for a Spanish
      bride for Prince Charles.

D Oct: 4th, the Duke of Lerma in Spain retires from office of premier;
      29th, Sir Walter Raleigh, who has returned to England from his expedition to Guiana,
      is executed, as a result of James I's promise to Count Gondomar that any attack on
      Spanish possessions would render Raleigh liable to the sentence passed on him in
      1603.
   Nov: The Archduke Leopold succeeds as ruler of the Tyrol on the death of his elder
   brother, the Archduke Maximilian;
      13th, the Synod of Dort opens (–*Apr.* 23rd, 1619) with 28 representatives attending
      from countries other than the United Provinces;
      Count Mansfeld occupies Pilsen for the Protestant Union.
   (*Continued opposite*)

F **Politics, Economics, Law and Education**
James VI and I issues the 'Book of Sports' permitting a variety of popular sports to be played, which provokes Puritan objections.

G **Science, Technology and Discovery**
The Royal College of Physicians issues *Pharmacopeia Londinensis*.

H **Philosophy, Religion and Scholarship**
R. H. Balfour, *Commentarii in Organum Logicum Aristotelis*.
George Chapman translates the *Georgics* of Hesiod.
Jan van der Meulen, *Bibliotheca Materiarum* (posth.).
John Selden, *The History of Tythes* (suppressed by order of the Privy Council).
John Stow and E. Howes, *A Summarie of Englyshe Chronicles* (–1565).
Synod of Dort on the Arminian heresy (–1619).

J **Art, Sculpture, Fine Arts and Architecture**
Painting:
    Gerard von Honthorst, *Christ before Pilate*.
    Jacob Jordaens, *Adoration of the Shepherds*.
    Daniel Mytens, *Earl of Arundel*.
Sculpture:
    Gianlorezo Bernini, *Aeneas and Anchises*.
Architecture:
    Salomon de Brosse, Palais du Parlement, Rennes.

K **Music**

L **Literature (including Drama)**
Catherine de Vivonne, Marquise de Rambouillet, starts a literary *salon* as a centre of wit and letters in her Hotel Rambouillet, Paris (–1650).
Teatro Farnese, Parma, opened.

M **Births and Deaths**
May 4th James Sharp b. (–1679).
May 9th James Lancaster d. (*c.* 50).
July 6th Alexander Lindsay, Earl of Balcarres, b. (–1659).
Oct. 29th Walter Raleigh d. (*c.* 66).
Nov. — Aurangzeb b. (–1707).
— Henry Bennet, Earl of Arlington, b. (–1685).
— Abraham Cowley b. (–1667).
— Richard Lovelace b. (–1658).

Dec: 24th, Poland signs a two-year truce with Sweden (afterwards extended to *July* 1621) and a fourteen-year truce with Turkey.

E Foundation of the Dutch West African Company.

A   Jan:

Feb: 20th, Johan van Oldenbarneveldt is tried and found guilty of treason;

22nd, Marie de' Medici, Queen Mother of France, allies herself with the Duke d'Épernon to challenge the power of her son;

23rd, the Synod of Dort ends.

Mar: 10th, Louis XIII recalls Richelieu from Avignon to persuade Marie de' Medici to negotiate and prevent a major revolt;

20th, Emperor Matthias dies (the Archduke Ferdinand is elected his successor in *Aug.*). Ferdinand assumes the crown of Bohemia.

B   Apr:

May: 1st, the Netherlands Confession is approved for the United Provinces, an Orthodox Calvinist creed; in consequence 200 Remonstrant preachers are expelled;

13th, the execution of Oldenbarneveldt at the Hague, regarded by some as judicial murder, leaves Maurice Prince of Orange supreme in Holland. Hugo Grotius is imprisoned.

Jun: 2nd, a treaty is signed between England and Holland regulating the trade in the East between the English and Dutch East India Companies; all disputes that cannot be settled by the Council in India or the companies in London and Amsterdam are to be referred to the King of England and the States-General;

5th, Count Thurn leads an army of Bohemian patriots towards Vienna, which prepares to stand a siege but 14th, Thurn withdraws.

C   Jul: 30th, a representative colonial assembly—the first in America—is held at Jamestown, Virginia, under the new governor of the colony, Sir George Yeardley.

Aug: 7th, Louis XIII, who has marched an army into Angers, defeats the troops supporting the Queen Mother at Ponts de Cé;

19th, the Bohemian Diet deposes Ferdinand and

26th, elects Frederick V, the Elector Palatine, King of Bohemia (he is crowned in *Oct.*). Frederick V, son-in-law of James I of England, is the head of the Protestant Union and the leading Calvinist prince;

28th, Ferdinand II is elected Holy Roman Emperor (–1637);

Gabor Bethlen of Transylvania invades Hungary.

Sep: The Treaty of Angoulême ends the dispute between Louis XIII and the Queen Mother, Marie de' Medici. Louis grants an amnesty to his mother's supporters and restores places captured, advantageous terms secured through Richelieu's diplomacy. To cement his own position with the court Richelieu arranges a marriage between his niece and the nephew of the Duke de Luynes;

26th, James I refuses to aid his son-in-law, Frederick V of the Palatinate, to gain his throne in Bohemia, but later undertakes to support him if the Palatinate is invaded;

28th, Frederick V, after much hesitation, accepts the throne of Bohemia.

D   Oct: 8th, the Emperor Ferdinand II signs a treaty at Munich with Duke Maximilian of Bavaria; in return for support in the Empire, Ferdinand agrees that if the Elector Palatine is placed under the ban of the Empire, he will transfer his electoral dignity to the Duke;

12th, Gabor Bethlen, who had signed an alliance with Count Thurn, leader of the Bohemian nationalists, captures Pressburg and

25th, crosses the Danube in his advance on Vienna.

Nov: Frederick V of the Palatinate is crowned King of Bohemia in Prague—'the Winter King';

Gabor Bethlen retreats from Vienna.

(*Continued opposite*)

F **Politics, Economics, Law and Education**
Jan Pieters Coen founds Batavia.
The library of Dulwich College, London, is founded.

G **Science, Technology and Discovery**
J. Kepler, *Harmonia Mundi*.
John Bainbridge, *An Astronomical Description of the Late Comet*.
William Harvey announces his discovery of the circulation of the blood in his lectures
at St. Bartholomew's Hospital (discourse published 1628).

H **Philosophy, Religion and Scholarship**
Johann Valentin Andreae, *Christianopolis* (a Calvinist Utopia).
Jakob Boehme, *Three Principles of Christianity*.
Pietro Sarpi, *Istoria del Concilio Tridentino* (published in London, and later, –1620,
translated by Sir N. Bent).
George Wither, *A Preparation to the Psalter*.
William Ames prepares *Coronis ad Collationem Hagiensem* for the Synod of Dort.

J **Art, Sculpture, Fine Arts and Architecture**
Architecture:
Salomon de Brosse, Château Blérancourt.
Inigo Jones, Banqueting House, Whitehall (–1622).

K **Music**
Francis Tregian compiles the *Fitzwilliam Virginal Book* (begun in prison, 1609).

L **Literature (including Drama)**
Francis Beaumont and John Fletcher, *A King and No King; The Maid's Tragedy* (two
tragedies).
Georg Rudolf Weckherlin, *Oden und Gesange*, 2 vols.

M **Births and Deaths**
Jan. 7th Nicholas Hilliarde d. (72).
Mar. 2nd Queen Anne of Denmark d. (45).
Mar. 13th Richard Burbage d. (52).
May 13th Johan van Oldenbarneveldt d. (71).
May — James Dalrymple, Viscount Stair, b. (–1695).
Aug. 29th Jean Baptiste Colbert b. (–1683).
Oct. — Samuel Daniel d. (57).
Dec. 17th Prince Rupert b. (–1682).
— John Lambert b. (–1694).
— Charles Lebrun b. (–1690).

Dec: 5th, Maximilian of Bavaria induces the German Catholic League, meeting at
Würzburg, to raise a force of 21,000 foot and 4,000 horse to fight for Ferdinand II.

E The first Negroes in North America arrive in Virginia, as indentured servants.

A Jan:
Feb:
Mar: The Catholic League and the Protestant Union in Germany sign an agreement at Mülhausen, by which the League princes promise they will not recover by force the lands of the Protestant administrators of the Empire, nor the secularised lands in north Germany, 'so long as the holders still act as loyal subjects of the Emperor'.

B Apr: 27th/*May* 8th, secret treaty between England and Spain for Charles, Prince of Wales, to marry the Infanta Maria of Spain; under its terms Roman Catholics are to be granted freedom of worship in England (James I abrogates the treaty in *Dec.* 1623).
May: The Dukes of Mayenne, Longueville and Vendôme lead a further rebellion (*–Aug.*) against Louis XIII, aiming that Luynes be overthrown and Marie de' Medici, the Queen Mother, be restored to court.
Jun: War between Sweden and Poland is resumed; Gustavus II of Sweden occupies Livonia;
19th, the Protestants in the Valtelline, a territory subject to the Grisons League, are massacred. With the aid of Austrian and Spanish troops an independent republic is proclaimed.

C Jul: 3rd, through the mediation of Louis XIII, the Catholic League and the Protestant Union of Germany sign an agreement at Ulm;
22nd, English volunteers leave for service with the Elector Palatine's army in Bohemia;
25th, Maximilian of Bavaria occupies Linz. Lower Austria submits to the Emperor Ferdinand II, who is free to attack Bohemia.
Aug: Richelieu negotiates peace in France between the rebellious nobles led by the Duke of Mayenne and the Crown. Marie de' Medici, the Queen Mother, is reconciled to her son. The rebellion at an end, Louis XIII enters Béarn, which is reunited with the French Crown;
Spanish troops from the Netherlands, under Spinola, invade the Palatinate;
an English fleet is sent against the Barbary pirates of Algiers.
Sep: 6th/16th, the Pilgrim Fathers, members of a Separatist Congregation which had emigrated from Scrooby, Nottinghamshire, to Holland, later returned to England before leaving Plymouth in the *Mayflower* for North America;
20th, the Turks defeat the Poles at Jassy.

D Oct:
Nov: 8th, the Catholic League under Count Tilly defeats the army of Frederick of Bohemia, led by Christian of Anhalt, at the Battle of the White Mountain, near Prague. The Bohemian revolt against Emperor Ferdinand II is suppressed, leading rebels are executed and the Protestant clergy are expelled;
the Pilgrim Fathers reach Cape Cod, and sign the 'Mayflower Compact' to establish a government in their proposed settlement.
Dec: 26th, the Pilgrim Fathers land at New Plymouth, Massachusetts, to found Plymouth Colony, with John Carver as Governor, outside the territory assigned to the Plymouth Company of London;
23rd, James I issues a proclamation forbidding the discussion of state affairs;
Huguenots hold an illegal assembly at La Rochelle (*–Feb.* 1621). Fearing fresh persecution, following the re-establishment of Roman Catholicism in Béarn, they decide on war.

E Gustavus II of Sweden marries Marie Eleanor, daughter of John Sigismund, Elector of Brandenburg.

F Politics, Economics, Law and Education

The Pilgrim Fathers leave from Plymouth, England, in the *Mayflower* (*Sept.* 6th/16th), landing at Plymouth, Mass. (*Dec.* 26th).

G Science, Technology and Discovery

Edmund Gunter, *Canon triangulorum*, a discussion of logarithms.
Cornelius Drebbel discovers scarlet 'Bow dye'; he also constructs a thermometer.

H Philosophy, Religion and Scholarship

Johann Heinrich Alsted, *Encyclopaedia septem tomis distincta* (with index).
Sir Francis Bacon, *Instauratio Magna: novum organum.*
Uppsala University, Sweden, library founded and enriched by Gustavus Adolphus.
Thomas Shelton translates *Don Quixote* by Cervantes, part II (–1612).

J Art, Sculpture, Fine Arts and Architecture

Painting:
Gerard van Honthorst, *Evening Meal;* and *The Concert.*
Jacob Jordaens, *Passage to Antwerp* (–1625).
Rubens, *Chapeau de Paille.*
Velazquez, *The Water-Seller.*
Sculpture:
Gianlorenzo Bernini, *Neptune and Triton.*

K Music

Monteverdi's seventh book of madrigals is published.

L Literature (including Drama)

Jacob Cats, *Selfsrijt.*

M Births and Deaths

Feb. 15th François Charpentier b. (–1702).
Feb. 16th Frederick William, the Great Elector, b. (–1688).
Mar. 1st Thomas Campion d. (53).
Mar. 6th Savinien Cyrano de Bergerac b. (–1655).
Oct. 31st John Evelyn b. (–1706).
— Louis, Comte de Frontenac, b. (–1698).
— Henri, Marquis Cinq-Mars, b. (–1642).

A Jan: 22nd, Frederick V, the Elector Palatine, is placed under the ban of the Empire by
Ferdinand II. The Emperor secretly hands over the Upper Palatinate and the
electoral title to Maximilian of Bavaria (confirmed by the Electoral College in *Feb.*
1623). The theatre of war changes from Bohemia to the Palatinate. Christian of
Anhalt is placed under the ban of the Empire;

28th, Pope Paul V dies;

30th, English Parliament meets (*–June* 4th), and the Commons attacks monopolies, a
notable feature of government finance. Sir Francis Mitchell and Sir Giles Mompesson,
leading monopolists, are impeached. Floyd, a Roman Catholic barrister, is branded,
fined and imprisoned by order of the Commons for speaking against the Elector
Palatine and the Bohemian Protestants.

Feb: 9th, Alexander Ludovisi is elected Pope Gregory XV (–1623);

the Huguenot Assembly at La Rochelle, led by Rohan and Soubise, declares for rebellion against Louis XIII.

Mar:

B Apr: 12th, Louis XIII takes the field against the Huguenots;

19th, charges are drawn up in Parliament against Francis Bacon, Lord Verulam, the
Lord Chancellor, for corruption;

23rd, William Bradford becomes Governor of Plymouth Colony, on the death from
sunstroke of John Carver;

the Protestant Union in Germany is dissolved.

May: 3rd, Bacon is impeached, fined £40,000, imprisoned and declared incapable of
holding office (he is pardoned by James I in *Nov.*);

31st, accession of Philip IV of Spain (–1665) on the death of Philip III. He appoints
Zuniga his Chief Minister.

Jun: James I sends Sir John Digby to Vienna to attempt a settlement of the problem of
the Palatinate with the Emperor Ferdinand II; the mission is ineffective and its failure
angers Protestant feeling in England.

C Jul: 16th, John Williams, Bishop of Lincoln, is appointed Lord Keeper, in succession to
Bacon (–1625);

24th, Archbishop Abbot of Canterbury accidentally kills a gamekeeper and withdraws
from public affairs.

Aug: The Twelve Years Truce (of *Apr.* 1609) between the United Provinces and Spain
comes to an end. Overtures for a permanent peace are made by the Archduke Albert,
Governor of the Spanish Netherlands, but as terms are unacceptable to Maurice
Prince of Orange war is resumed;

a Royalist army begins the siege of Montauban, held by the Huguenots.

Sep: 29th, Lionel Cranfield, later Earl of Middlesex, is appointed Lord Treasurer of
England (–1624).

D Oct: Sir Francis Wyatt, the new Governor, arrives in Virginia with fresh regulations for
the administration of the colony by a governor, council of state and an elected assembly.

Nov: 18th, English Parliament meets (*–Dec.* 20th). The Commons petition James I to
declare war on Spain in support of the Elector Palatine and to arrange for Prince
Charles to marry a Protestant princess.

Dec: 15th, the Duke of Luynes dies on campaign in Guienne; the Prince of Condé and
Marie de' Medici, the Queen Mother, dispute for the control of affairs in France and
La Nieuville, a nominee of the Queen Mother, subsequently gains power (–1624);

18th, the House of Commons makes a Protestation, denying the King's claim to the
right to imprison M.P.s, following criticism of James I's pro-Spanish policy;

(Continued opposite)

F **Politics, Economics, Law and Education**

The Dutch West India Company is chartered (*June* 3rd).

T. Mun, *A Discourse of Trade from England unto the East Indies.*

Corante; or newes from Italy, Germany, Hungarie, Spaine and France is issued in London (*Sept.* 24th), the first periodical publication with news.

G **Science, Technology and Discovery**

Willibrord Snell discovers the law of refraction.

Cornelius Vermuyden begins to drain the Fens.

H **Philosophy, Religion and Scholarship**

Robert Burton, *Anatomy of Melancholy.*

Foundation of the French congregation of St. Maur under the Benedictine Rule.

Count Tilly sacks Heidelberg University library.

Pietro della Valle visits Persepolis and sends to Europe the first cuneiform signs.

J **Art, Sculpture, Fine Arts and Architecture**

Painting:

Anthony Van Dyck, *Rest on the Flight to Egypt.*

Sculpture:

Gianlorenzo Bernini, *Rape of Proserpina.*

K **Music**

L **Literature (including Drama)**

John Fletcher, *The Wild Goose Chase* (comedy).

The Fortune Theatre, London, burnt down (reopened, 1623; demolished, 1661).

M **Births and Deaths**

Jan. 5th Paul Van Somer d. (44).

Mar. 23rd John Carver d. (*c.* 46).

Mar. 31st Andrew Marvell b. (–1678).

July 8th Jean de la Fontaine b. (–1695).

July 22nd Anthony Ashley Cooper, Earl of Shaftesbury, b. (–1683).

Aug. 15th John Barclay d. (38).

Sept. 8th Louis, Prince of Condé, b. (–1686).

Sept. 17th Roberto Bellarmine d. (68).

Oct. 16th Jan Sweelinck d. (59).

Nov. 26th Ralph Agas d. (81).

Dec. 23rd Edmund Berry Godfrey b. (–1678).

— Philibert, Comte de Gramont, b. (–1707).

27th, James I imprisons Sir Edward Coke for his share in the Protestation;

30th, James I tears from the Commons *Journal* the page recording the Protestation.

E   The Scots settle at Acadia (Nova Scotia –1632).

A Jan: 1st, the Papal Chancery adopts *Jan.* 1st as the beginning of the New Year (instead of *Mar.* 25th);

7th, the Emperor Ferdinand II and Gabor Bethlen of Transylvania sign a peace treaty;

Richelieu is recalled to the Council of Louis XIII;

James I places John Pym, the Parliamentary leader, under house arrest for criticism of royal policy in the recent Parliamentary session.

Feb: 8th, James I dissolves English Parliament.

Mar: John Digby, Earl of Bristol, is sent by James I to Madrid to complete negotiations for Prince Charles's marriage with the Infanta.

B Apr: Count Mansfeld defeats Count Tilly at the battle of Wiesloch.

May: Count Tilly defeats George Frederick, Margrave of Baden, at the battle of Wimpfen.

Jun: Sigismund of Poland makes an armistice with Gustavus II of Sweden (subsequently renewed until *June* 1625);

Count Tilly defeats Christian of Brunswick, brother of the Duke, at the battle of Höchst, effectively ending the conquest of the Palatinate and Frederick V.

C Jul: Maurice Prince of Orange relieves Bergen-op-Zoom, which Spinola is besieging.

Aug: Count Olivares becomes Chief Minister in Spain (–1643).

Sep: 5th, Richelieu is created a Cardinal;

by the Treaty of Lindau Austrian power in the Grisons and the Valtelline is confirmed;

Heidelberg surrenders to the imperialists. James I sends Endymion Porter to Spain for Philip IV's aid in forcing Ferdinald II to restore Heidelberg to the Elector Palatine within 70 days, but without success;

a plot to assassinate Maurice Prince of Orange, involving two of Oldenbarneveldt's sons, is discovered.

D Oct: 18th, the Treaty of Montpellier ends the rebellion of the Huguenots. The Edict of Nantes (of 1598) is confirmed; La Rochelle and Montauban are left under Huguenot control, but all political meetings are prohibited.

Nov: Mannheim surrenders to the imperialists.

Dec:

E Sir Ferdinando Gorges and John Mason obtain a grant of lands in Maine, North America; An English force captures Ormuz from the Portuguese.

F Politics, Economics, Law and Education

James VI and I grants land in New Hampshire to John Mason (*Mar.* 9th).
First turnpike act in England, for the road between Biggleswade and Baldock.
G. de Malynes, *Consuedo vel Lex Mercatoria*.
Weekeley Newes . . . printed by Nicholas Bourne and Thomas Archer is issued in London (*May* 23rd).
University of Salzburg is founded.

G Science, Technology and Scholarship

Francis Bacon, *Historia Naturalis et Experimentalis*.
Edward Gunter discovers that the magnetic needle does not retain the same declination in the same place all the time.
The Bruges-Dunkirk Canal is completed.

H Philosophy, Religion and Scholarship

Sir Francis Bacon, *History of the Reign of Henry VII*.
Jacob Boehme, *De signatura rerum*.
James Mabbe translates and adopts from the Spanish of Mateo Alemán, *The Rogue*; or, the Life of Guzman de Alfarache.
Pope Gregory XV canonises Philip Neri.

J Art, Sculpture, Fine Arts and Architecture

Painting:
Gerard van Honthorst, *Adoration of the Shepherds*.
Guido Reni, *Job*.
Rubens, *The Medici Cycle of Paintings*; and paintings for the Luxembourg Palais, Paris (–1625).

K Music

Orlando Gibbons, *O Clap Your Hands Together* (anthem).

L Literature (including Drama)

Michael Drayton, *Polyolbion*, part 11 (–1612).
Philip Massinger and John Dekker, *The Virgin Martyr*.
William Shakespeare, *Othello* (posth., but acted since 1604).
Alessandro Tassoni, *Secchia rapita* (mock-heroic poem).

M Births and Deaths

Jan. 15th Molière (Jean-Baptiste Poquelin) b. (–1673).
Jan. 23rd William Baffin d. (38).
Feb. 19th Henry Savile d. (73).
Apr. 17th Henry Vaughan b. (–1695).
Dec. 28th St. Francis de Sales d. (55).
— Andrew Melville d. (77).
— Algernon Sidney b. (–1683).

1623   Massacre of Amboyna—the Bavarian electorate—Charles Prince
of Wales breaks Spanish marriage negotiations

A   Jan: 16th, Sir Edward Conway is appointed a Principal Secretary of State (–1628).
    Feb: 25th, Maximilian Duke of Bavaria is granted the Upper Palatinate by the Emperor
        Ferdinand II, and the electorate, which is confirmed by the Electoral College;
        Catholics thus obtain a majority in the College. Saxony is granted control of Lusatia;
        the Bibliotheca Palatina is removed from Heidelburg to Rome;
    Dutch massacre English colonists at Amboyna;
    Venice and Savoy sign an offensive alliance to take the Valtelline from Austrian control.
    Mar: 7th, Charles, Prince of Wales, and the Duke of Buckingham arrive in Madrid for
        final negotiations which might lead to the Prince's betrothal to the Infanta;
        John George of Brandenburg is placed under the ban of the Empire, for supporting the
        Elector Palatine, and the Emperor Ferdinand II confiscates Jägerndorf.

B   Apr:
    May: Papal troops occupy the Valtelline;
        the *Parlement* of Paris condemns the maladministration of France.
    Jun:

C   Jul: 8th, Pope Gregory XV dies.
    Aug: 6th, Maffeo Barberini is elected Pope Urban VIII (–1644); fearing the growth of
        Hapsburg power he leans towards France;
        30th, Prince Charles and the Duke of Buckingham leave Madrid in disgust at the break-
        down of negotiations. Spain will only send the Infanta to England when religious
        liberty is extended to Roman Catholics in England. Charles is angered by Philip IV's
        refusal to aid the restoration of Frederick V in the Palatinate;
        Christian of Brunswick is defeated at Stadtlohn by Count Tilly;
        Gabor Bethlen again invades the Austrian dominions.
    Sep:

D   Oct: 5th, Prince Charles returns to England, to be greeted with acclaim for breaking off
        negotiations for a Spanish marriage.
    Nov:
    Dec: James I, at Prince Charles's insistence, finally breaks off the Spanish marriage
        treaty, provoking a breach with Spain, leading, in *Mar.* 1624, to war.

E   Gustavus II begins to reform the central administration of Sweden;
    English settlements are made on the coast of New Hampshire and Maine;
    The United Provinces sign a commercial treaty with Persia.

F **Politics, Economics, Law and Education**
New Netherlands in America is formally organised as a province (*June*).
First English settlement at New Hampshire, by David Thomas at Little Harbor, near Rye.
Misselden, *The Circle of Commerce*.
George Heriot makes bequest for a hospital for education in Edinburgh.

G **Science, Technology and Discovery**

H **Philosophy, Religion and Scholarship**
Tommaso Campanella, *La Città de Sole* (*The City of the Sun*) (an Italian Utopia).
William Drummond, *A Cypresse Grove* (thoughts on death).
Owen Felltham, *Resolves: Divine, Moral and Political* (complete edition –1628).
George Wither, *Hymns and Songs of the Church*.
The see of Paris is elevated to an archbishopric.

J **Art, Sculpture, Fine Arts and Architecture**
Painting:
Gerard von Honthorst, *The Merry Fiddler*.
Guido Reni, *Baptism of Christ*.
Anthony van Dyck, *Cardinal Bentiuglio*.
Sculpture:
Gianlorenzo Bernini, *David*.
Architecture:
Inigo Jones, Queen's Chapel, St. James's Palace, Westminster (–1627).
François Mansart, St. Marie de la Visitation, Paris.

K **Music**

L **Literature (including Drama)**
Jacob Cats, and others, *De Zeeuwsche Nachtegaal* (a collection of poetry by Cats and his celebrated circle of Zeeland poets).
William Drummond, *Flowres of Sion*.
Antonio Hurtado de Mendoza, *Querer por sólo querer* (comedy) (*see* 1671).
Giovanni Battista Marino, *Adone*.
Philip Massinger, *The Duke of Milan* (tragedy).
William Shakespeare, *The First Folio* ('Mr. William Shakespeares Comedies, Histories, & Tragedies. Published According to the True Originall Copies'; posth.) (*see* 1632, 1663, 1664, 1685).
Charles Sorel, Sieur de Souvigny, *Histoire comique de Francion*.
John Webster, *The Duchess of Malfi* (tragedy); *The Devil's Law Case* (tragi-comedy).

M **Births and Deaths**
Jan. 15th Paolo Sarpi d. (70).
May 26th William Petty b. (–1687).
June 19th Blaise Pascal b. (–1662).
July 4th William Byrd d. (85).
Nov. 9th William Camden d. (72).
Nov. 11th Philippe du Plessis-Mornay d. (74).
— Tulsī Dās d. (91).

1624   Monopolies declared illegal in England—Occupation of the Valtelline

A   Jan: 31st, Count Mansfeld leaves Dover with 12,000 men to aid the Elector Palatine, Frederick V. Louis XIII forbids the landing of this force in France. It lands in Holland but is prevented by James I from aiding the Dutch in the defence of Breda against the Spanish.
Feb: 12th, James I's last Parliament meets (*–May* 29th). Supplies are voted for an army to aid Frederick V recover the Palatinate, and the House of Commons appropriates money for the Royal Navy. Monopolies are declared illegal;
28th, the House of Lords condemns the Spanish marriage treaty.
Mar: 10th, England declares war on Spain;
sickness among Mansfeld's English troops leads to the failure of his expedition in the Palatinate;
the Dutch send an expedition to Bahia.

B   Apr: 15th, Lionel Cranfield, Earl of Middlesex, Lord Treasurer of England, is impeached for bribery and neglect of duty, at the instigation of the Duke of Buckingham; he is fined £50,000, and suspended from office, 25th (Lord Ley is appointed Treasurer *Dec.* 11th). An attempt to impeach Lord Keeper Williams fails.
May: 11th, the Dukes of Brandenburg and Neuburg sign the Treaty of Düsseldorf for mutual defence.
Jun: 20th, France and the United Provinces sign a treaty of non-aggression at Compiègne; 24th, dissolution of the Virginia Company; Virginia becomes a Crown colony; Sir Francis Wyatt is subsequently re-appointed governor.

C   Jul:
Aug: 13th, Louis XIII dismisses Nieuville and appoints Cardinal Richelieu as First Minister of France (–1642);
Gustavus II of Sweden makes proposals to James I for intervention in the Thirty Years War.
Sep:

D   Oct:
Nov: 1st, France, in alliance with Venice and Savoy, occupies the Valtelline, fearing further Spanish aggression.
Dec: 12th/22nd, Anglo-French treaty for Charles, Prince of Wales to marry Henrietta Maria, daughter of Henry IV and Marie de' Medici.

E   English settlers under Sir Thomas Warner land in St. Christopher's;
the first English settlement is made in East India;
The Dutch West Indies Company begins to operate in South America and West Africa, largely in defiance of the Portuguese.
Dutch settle in New Amsterdam.

F **Politics, Economics, Law and Education**
Captain John Smith, *A General Historie of Virginia, New England and the Summer Isles.*
Pembroke College, Oxford, is founded.

G **Science, Technology and Discovery**
Henry Briggs, *Arithmetica Logarithmica*, containing logarithms of 30,000 numbers to 14 places.
Antonio de Andrade leaves the Jesuit mission at Agra to explore beyond the Himalayas and Tibet.
Philip Cluver, *Introductio in geographiam universam tam veteram quam novam.*

H **Philosophy, Religion and Scholarship**
George Chapman translates Homer's *Batrachomyomachia* (or, *The Battle of the Frogs and the Mice*).
John Donne, *Devotions Upon Emergent Occasions.*
Cappel, *Arcanum Punctationem Revelatum*, discovers that the Old Testament is an Aramaic rescension of ancient Hebrew texts.
Edward, Lord Herbert of Cherbury, *De Veritate* ('Concerning Truth'; published in Paris; regarded as the foundation of the theory of English Deism).
Martin Opitz von Boberfield, *Buch von der deutschen Poeterey.*

J **Art, Sculpture, Fine Arts and Architecture**
Painting:
Frans Hals, *The Laughing Cavalier.*
Nicolas Poussin, *Rape of the Sabine Women.*
Pietro, frescoes, St. Bibiana, Rome.
Sculpture:
Gianlorenzo Bernini, *Apollo and Daphne.*
Architecture:
Bernini, Baldacchino, St. Peter's, Rome.
Campen, Coymans Haus, Amsterdam.
Jacques Le Mercier, extensions to the Louvre, Paris.

K **Music**
Claudio Monteverdi, *Combattimento di Tancredie Clorinda.*

L **Literature (including Drama)**
Philip Massinger, *The Bondman.*
Thomas Middleton's satirical comedy, *A Game at Chess* (–1625) opens at the Globe theatre (*Aug.* 6th) 'on the Bankside', where 'it was acted nine days together' (this being the first 'long run' in English theatrical history).

M **Births and Deaths**
June 2nd John Sobieski b. (–1696).
July — George Fox b. (–1691).
Sept. 10th Thomas Sydenham b. (–1689).
Nov. 10th Henry Wroithesley, 3rd Earl of Southampton, d. (51).
Nov. 17th Jakob Boehme d. (49).
Dec. 14th Charles Howard, Earl of Nottingham, d. (88).
— Margaret Cavendish, Duchess of Newcastle, b. (–1674).

A **Jan:** The princes of Lower Saxony agree to provide an army for Christian IV of Denmark, under Duke of Holstein, the leader of the Protestant Princes in Germany;
the remnant of Count Mansfeld's troops from the campaign in the Palatinate reach Flushing, but few survive to return to England.
Feb:
Mar: 27th, accession of Charles I of England and Scotland (–1649) on the death of James I (James VI of Scotland).

B **Apr:** 7th, Wallenstein is appointed General of the Imperial Forces by Ferdinand II;
23rd, Frederick Henry succeeds as Stadtholder of Holland on the death of Maurice of Nassau.
May: Charles I agrees to subsidise Christian IV of Denmark, who has been elected chief of the Lower Saxon Circle of Germany, with £30,000 per month.
Jun: 13th, Charles I marries Henrietta Maria;
13th, Frederick II creates Wallenstein Duke of Friedland and a Prince of the Holy Roman Empire;
18th, the First Parliament of Charles I meets (*Aug.* 12th). The Commons complain of the mismanagement of affairs, especially by the Duke of Buckingham. Against precedent they vote tonnage and poundage for one year only, instead of for the rest of the King's life, and refuse to vote supplies for the war against Spain, so Charles has to resort to a forced loan;
Ambrogio Spinola takes Breda from the Dutch after a siege of 11 months (it had been captured by Maurice of Nassau in 1598).

C **Jul:** Count Tilly invades Lower Saxony.
Aug: 1st, English Parliament is adjourned to Oxford, because of the plague in Westminster.
Sep: 15th, Soubise, the Huguenot leader, flees to England on the failure of a fresh rising near La Rochelle.

D **Oct:** 8th, an English expedition is sent to Cadiz (but returns with nothing accomplished).
Nov: 1st, Sir Thomas Coventry is appointed Lord Keeper (–1640).
Dec: 9th, by the Treaty of the Hague, England and the United Provinces agree to subsidise Christian IV of Denmark in his campaign in Germany.

E French occupation of the Antilles and Cayenne.

F **Politics, Economics, Law and Education**
Hugo Grotius, *De jure belli et pacis*.
First English settlement on Barbados is made under Sir William Courteen.

G **Science, Technology and Discovery**

H **Philosophy, Religion and Scholarship**
Vincent de Paul founds in Paris a sisterhood of charity: the *Order of Sisters of Mercy*.

J **Art, Sculpture, Fine Arts and Architecture**
Painting:
Daniel Mytens is appointed painter to Charles I.
Nicolas Poussin, *Parnassus* (–1629).
Architecture:
Inigo Jones, Covent Garden Church and Square, Westminister.

K **Music**
Heinrich Schütz, *Cantiones Sacrae*.

L **Literature (including Drama)**
Sir Francis Bacon, *Essays: Counsels Civil and Moral* (58 essays—the 3rd and final edition; *see* 1597).
Thomas Middleton, *A Game at Chess* (satirical comedy) published.
Honorat de Bueil, Marquis de Racan, *Les Bergeries* (pastoral dialogues in five acts).
Joost van den Vondel, *Palamedes* (satirical, political drama).

M **Births and Deaths**
June 5th Orlando Gibbons d. (42).
June 8th Giovanni Cassini b. (–1712).
July 27th Edward Montagu, Earl of Sandwich, b. (–1672).
Aug. — John Fletcher d. (46).
Sept. 23rd John de Witt b. (–1672).
— John Fell b. (–1686).
— John Webster d. (?45).

A Jan: Charles I, in need of revenue, requires all Englishmen with property over £40 a year to undertake the dignity of Knighthood, with fines for exemptions;
a revolt breaks out among Protestant peasants in upper Austria (suppressed *Sept.*).
Feb: 6th, the Peace of La Rochelle is signed between the Huguenot rebels and the French Crown, through the mediation of the English ambassador;
6th, the Second Parliament of Charles I meets (–*June* 15th). The Commons refuse to grant supplies until their grievances are redressed;
23rd, the impeachment of the Duke of Buckingham begins.
Mar: 5th, the Treaty of Monzon between France and Spain confirms the independence of the Grisons, with guarantees for Catholic worship in this Protestant area. Spain is prohibited from sending troops through the Valtelline.

B Apr: 25th, Wallenstein defeats Count Mansfeld at the Bridge of Dessau, proceeds to occupy Pomerania and pursues Mansfeld through Silesia to Hungary, where he joins forces with Gabor Bethlen.
May: 10th, Charles I sends Sir Dudley Digges and Sir John Eliot to the Tower of London for managing the impeachment of Buckingham.
Jun: 6th, Christian of Halberstadt dies;
15th, Charles I dissolves Parliament, refusing to grant the Commons' request for the Duke of Buckingham's dismissal. Without supplies voted, the King orders another forced loan to be collected.

C Jul: The Ordinance of Nantes requires all castles and fortresses to be dismantled in France;
Cardinal Richelieu suppresses a conspiracy against him, led by the Comte de Chalais.
Aug: 5th, Count Tilly takes Göttingen;
14th, Tilly makes juncture with Wallenstein in Brunswick;
27th, Tilly defeats Christian IV of Denmark at Lutter in the Harz mountains; after this rout Christian abandons Brunswick. North Germany is placed at the mercy of the Catholic League.
Sep: Cardinal Richelieu suppresses the offices of Admiral and of Constable of France, concentrating power in his own hands.

D Oct:
Nov: 29th, Ernst von Mansfeld dies.
Dec: 20th, the Emperor Ferdinand II is forced to sign the Treaty of Pressburg with Gabor Bethlen of Transylvania, who is threatening Vienna;
the Notables meet in Paris at Richelieu's instigation and recommend fresh orders to be made against treason and for the maintenance of public order. Seditious libels are to be punished.

E The last of the Rovere family, dying without an heir, bequeaths the duchy of Urbino to the Pope;
Dutch settlement of New Amsterdam on Manhattan Island;
Incorporation of the French 'Company for the Islands of America'.

F **Politics, Economics, Law and Education**

Cardinal Richelieu declares the publication of works against religion or the state a capital offence.

Louis XIII publishes an edict condemning to death anyone who kills his adversary in a duel.

First French settlement on the Senegal River.

Salem, Mass., is first settled by Roger Conant.

G **Science, Technology and Discovery**

Jardin des Plantes, Paris, is established.

H **Philosophy, Religion and Scholarship**

John Donne, *Five Sermons*.

Joseph Hall, *Contemplations*.

William Roper, *The Life of Sir Thomas More* (posth.).

George Sandys makes the first translation of a classic in America: *Ovid's Metamorphosis Englished*.

Sir Henry Spelman, *Glossarium Archaeologicum*.

Congregation of Priests of the Mission founded by Vincent de Paul at the priory of St. Lazarus, Paris (hence the Order is known as The Lazarists).

Port-Royal des Champs transferred to Paris, and henceforth known as *Port-Royal de Paris* (–1709).

The Irish College founded at Rome.

J **Art, Sculpture, Fine Arts and Architecture**

Painting:

Anthony van Dyck, *Marchesa Paola Adorno and her son*.

Architecture:

François Mansart, Château de Balleroy.

Jacques Le Mercier, Le Sorbonne, Paris.

K **Music**

William Heather, a gentleman of the Chapel Royal, founds a Professorship of Music at Oxford University.

L **Literature (including Drama)**

Honorat de Bueil, Marquis de Racan, *Les plus beaux vers*.

M **Births and Deaths**

Jan. 20th/21st John Dowland d. (*c.* 63).

Feb. 5th Marie de Rabutin-Chantal, Marquise de Sévigné, b. (–1696).

Feb. 28th Cyril Tourneur d. (*c.* 51).

Mar. 12th John Aubrey b. (–1697).

Apr. 9th Francis Bacon, Lord Verulam, d. (65).

Apr. — John Dowland d. (64).

Sept. 26th Lancelot Andrewes d. (71).

Oct. 2nd Diego, Count of Gondomar, d. (58).

Oct. 4th Richard Cromwell b. (–1712).

Nov. 29th Ernst Graf von Mansfeld d. (*c.* 46).

Nov. — Edward Alleyn d. (60).

Dec. 8th Sir John Davies d. (57).

Dec. 8th Christina, Queen of Sweden, b. (–1689).

— Jan Steen b. (–1679).

A Jan: Following a commercial dispute England and France drift into war.
Feb: Cardinal Richelieu is appointed Superintendent General of commerce and navigation.
Mar: Huguenots again rise, fearing their freedom of worship will be further curtailed.

B Apr: Cardinal Richelieu signs a treaty of alliance with Spain.
May: 31st, Count Tilly enters Lauenberg.
Jun: 2nd, Charles I grants a charter of incorporation to the Guiana Company;
the Duke of Buckingham sails from Portsmouth with a fleet to aid the Huguenots in the defence of La Rochelle.

C Jul: 2nd, Charles I grants the settlement of the Caribbean Islands to Lord Carlisle;
12th/22nd, Buckingham lands English force on the Isle of Rhé, off La Rochelle.
Aug: 10th, Cardinal Richelieu begins the siege of La Rochelle, which the English fail to relieve;
Silesia submits to Wallenstein.
Sep: The Turks sign a treaty with the Emperor Ferdinand II, which reduces the power of Gabor Bethlen of Transylvania.

D Oct: 12th, the Duke of Buckingham, having failed to relieve the Huguenots, returns from the Isle of Rhé;
Christian IV withdraws to Denmark, in the face of the advance of Tilly and Wallenstein, who by the end of the month subdue Holstein, Schleswig and Jutland;
Gustavus II of Sweden raises the siege of Danzig.
Nov: 28th, five Englishmen, imprisoned for refusing contributions to Charles I's forced loan, unsuccessfully apply to the judges for release (Darnel's Case, or the Case of the Five Knights).
Dec: 14th, Wolfenbüttel surrenders to the imperialists;
26th, on the death of Vincent II of Mantua, the last of the Gonzaga line, Charles Duke of Nevers claims the succession, which is disputed by the Emperor Ferdinand II, who maintains the duchy is an imperial fief.

E Korea becomes a tributary state of China.

F **Politics, Economics, Law and Education**
    Alessandro Tassoni, *Manifesto* (attack on the House of Savoy).

G **Science, Technology and Discovery**
    J. Kepler, employed by Rudolph II, later compiles the 'Rudolphine Tables', giving the places of 1,005 fixed stars, to supersede the 'Prutenic Tables'.
    Francis Bacon in *New Atlantis* (posth.) sketches plans for a national museum of science and art.

H **Philosophy, Religion and Education**
    William Camden, *Annales*, part 11 (–1615).
    Diego Hurtado de Mendoza, *The War of Granada* (the rebellion of the *Moriscos*, 1568–1571) (posth.).
    Thomas May translates Lucan's *Pharsalia*.
    Gabriel Naudé, *Advis pour dresser une bibliothèque* (first French treatise on library economy; trans. 1661).

J **Art, Sculpture, Fine Arts and Architecture**
    Painting:
        Frans Hals, *The Merry Drinker*.
        Daniel Mytens, *George Calvert, Lord Baltimore*.

K **Music**
    Heinrich Schütz, *Dafne* (first German opera; music now lost) produced in Dresden.

L **Literature (including Drama)**
    Michael Drayton, *Nimphidia* (and other poems).
    Francisco Gomez de Quevedo, *Los Sueños*.
    Charles Sorel, Sieur de Souvigny, *Le Berger extravagant* (satirical novel in parody of d'Urfé's *Astrée*; –1610).

M **Births and Deaths**
    Jan. 25th Robert Boyle b. (–1691).
    Mar. — Richard Barnfield d. (51).
    July — Thomas Middleton d. (*c.* 57).
    Sept. 27th Jacques Bossuet b. (–1704).
    — Dorothy Osborne b. (–1695).

1628   The Petition of Right—Assassination of Buckingham—La Rochelle submits to Louis XIII

A   Jan: 2nd, all Englishmen imprisoned for refusing contributions to the forced loan are released;
26th, Wallenstein seizes the duchy of Mecklenburg on the flight of the dukes.
Feb:
Mar: 17th, the Third Parliament of Charles I meets (–*Mar*. 1629), summoned to vote money for a second expedition to La Rochelle. Oliver Cromwell enters Parliament as M.P. for Huntingdon.

B   Apr: 21st, Wallenstein assumes the title of Admiral of the Baltic;
29th, Sir Edward Coke brings in a bill, summing up the principal grievances against Charles I, which leads to the Petition of Right;
Sweden and Denmark sign a treaty for the defence of Stralsund against Wallenstein, which brings Gustavus II into the Thirty Years War.
May: Wallenstein takes Wismar, blockades Rostock harbour and (*June*) begins the siege of Stralsund.
Jun: 7th, Charles I is forced to accept the Petition of Right, drawn up by Sir John Eliot, Sir Edward Coke and John Selden, which declares arbitrary imprisonment, martial law, forced loans and the billeting of troops illegal;
9th, the Emperor Ferdinand II places the Dukes of Mecklenburg under the ban of the Empire;
11th, the House of Commons makes Remonstrances attacking Arminianism and ritualistic practices and demanding the dismissal of the Duke of Buckingham.

C   Jul: 4th, William Laud is appointed Bishop of London;
15th, Richard Weston is appointed Lord Treasurer of England (–1635).
Aug: 23rd, the Duke of Buckingham, about to embark at Portsmouth with a further expedition to La Rochelle, is assassinated by John Felton;
Wallenstein raises the siege of Stralsund, his first reverse.
Sep: 28th, John Endecott leads an English party of colonists to settle at Salem, Massachusetts, later Massachusetts Bay Colony.

D   Oct: 28th, La Rochelle capitulates to the French Crown. Though the Huguenots are assured of the continuation of their religious liberty, the institutions of La Rochelle and other towns is radically changed, to break their political power.
Nov:
Dec: 17th, Sir Dudley Carleton is appointed a Principal Secretary of State (–1632);
Thomas Wentworth is appointed President of the Council in the North.

E   Cardinal Richelieu founds the French companies for Canada and Senegal;
The Dutch seize the Spanish treasure fleet and also occupy Java and Malucca;
English adventurers acquire the Isle of Nevis, one of the Leeward Islands;
Shah Jahan becomes Mogul Emperor of India (–1658).

F Politics, Economics, Law and Education

Edward Coke, *First Institute* (–1644).

Henry Spelman, *Glossary of Law Terms*.

William Prynne, *Healthes sicknesse, or a discourse proving the drinking of healths to be sinfull;* and *The unloveliness of love-locks.*

G Science, Technology and Discovery

William Harvey, *Exercitatio anatomica de motu cordis et sanguinis*, on the circulation of the blood (*see* 1619).

H Philosophy, Religion and Scholarship

Robert Cotton, *Life of King Henry III.*

René Descartes, *Règles pour la direction de l'esprit.*

Sir Simonds D'Ewes, *The Journals of the Parliaments of Queen Elizabeth.*

No Me Mueve, Mi Dios, Para Querete (world-famous and much translated Spanish sonnet on the love of God, sometimes attributed to St. Teresa, and other saints).

Gregory XV canonises Ignatius Loyola.

J Art, Sculpture, Fine Arts and Architecture

Painting:

Frans Hals, *The Gipsy Woman.*

Gerard van Honthorst, *Charles I and Henrietta Maria with the Liberal Arts.*

Nicolas Poussin, *Martyrdom of St. Erasmus.*

Architecture:

Jacques Le Mercier, Hôtel de Liancourt, Paris.

K Music

L Literature (including Drama)

[John Earle], *Microcosmographie* (anon. essays and 'characters').

M Births and Deaths

Jan. 8th François, Duc de Luxemburg, b. (–1695).

Jan. 12th Charles Perrault b. (–1703).

Mar. 13th John Bull d. (66).

Aug. 23rd George Villiers, Duke of Buckingham, d. (35).

Sept. 30th Fulke Greville, Lord Brooke, d. (76).

Oct. 16th François de Malherbe d. (73).

Nov. 28th John Felton d. (*c.* 32).

Nov. 29th John Ray b. (–1705).

Nov. — John Bunyan b. (–1688).

— Sir William Temple b. (–1699).

A Jan: 20th, second session of Charles I's Third Parliament opens (–*Mar.* 2nd). The King is attacked for levying tonnage and poundage without Parliamentary authority;
Count Tilly fails in his attack on Glückstadt.
Feb:
Mar: 2nd, the House of Commons passes resolutions, proposed by Sir John Eliot, against innovators in religion (aimed at the Laudian bishops) and those who recommend the payment and those who pay tonnage and poundage. The Speaker, Sir John Finch, who is ordered by Charles I to dissolve the House, is held down while the Resolutions are read and passed. Charles I dissolves Parliament the same day (Parliament does not meet again until *Apr.* 1640);
5th, Sir John Eliot and eight other M.P.s are imprisoned for their part in the passage of the Resolutions. At his subsequent examination, Eliot refuses to answer the charges against him, relying on Parliamentary privilege;
29th, Edict of Restitution of Church property in Germany, for all property secularised since the Peace of Augsburg, 1555, to be restored to the Catholic Church. This affects the archbishoprics of Magdeburg and Bremen, 12 bishoprics and 120 religious houses. Calvinists, such as the Electors of Saxony and Brandenburg, who were not party to the Peace of Augsburg, are thus excluded from the religious settlement. The Edict of Restitution is rigorously enforced in the ensuing months by Wallenstein and the Catholic League;
Charles I issues a charter to the Company of Massachusetts Bay for the Colony founded in Salem by John Endicott, despite the opposition of Sir Ferdenando Gorges.

B Apr: 14th, the Peace of Susa ends the war between England and France;
Charles I sends John Selden to the Tower of London;
last rising of French Huguenots under Rohan, aided by Spain (–*June*).
May: 22nd, Christian IV of Denmark is forced to sign the Peace of Lübeck with the Emperor Ferdinand, following his defeat by Wallenstein. Christian undertakes that he will not intervene in imperial affairs. The Dukes of Mecklenburg are placed under the ban of the Empire.
Jun: 16th, Wallenstein is created Duke of Mecklenburg;
28th, the Peace of Alais ends the Huguenot revolt. The Huguenots are assured of religious liberty, but are required to end all political organisation. The governments of Nîmes, Montauban and other cities are remodelled.

C Jul:
Aug: French troops support the forces of the United Provinces in taking Bois-le-Duc from the Spanish, and serve against the Spanish in the Palatinate.
Sep: 25th, the Truce of Altmark is signed between Sweden and Poland. By its terms Sweden retains Livonia, Memel, Pillau, Braunsberg and Elbing. Danzig is to pay two-thirds of the customs duties levied in its port to Sweden;
Richelieu, who has mediated the truce, endeavours to unite Sweden and the Catholic League in Germany against the House of Hapsburg.

D Oct:
Nov: 15th, Gabor Bethlen of Transylvania dies;
a Franco-Russian commercial treaty is signed.
Dec:

E In the war of Mantuan Succession the Spanish besiege Casale, controlling the Po Valley, which France relieves. The imperialists lay siege to Mantua;
The Duke of Savoy is won over by Richelieu.

F Politics, Economics, Law and Education
Cardinal Richelieu forms the Company of New France for the monopoly of trade in Canada.

G Science, Technology and Discovery

H Philosophy, Religion and Scholarship
Lancelot Andrewes, *Sermons*, edited by W. Laud and J. Buckeridge.
Thomas Hobbes translates Thucydides: *The Peloponnesian War*.
Cyril Lucaris, *The Eastern Confession of the Orthodox Church* (see 1672).
Gervase Markham, *Markham's faithful farrier*.
The Edict of Restitution promulgated by the Emperor Ferdinand II of Germany, demanding surrender of church lands.

J Art, Sculpture, Fine Arts and Architecture
Painting:
Daniel Mytens, *James, Duke of Hamilton*.
Velazquez, *Los Borrochos*.
Charles I knights Peter Paul Rubens.
Sculpture:
Le Sueur, catafalque figure of James I.

K Music
Heinrich Schütz, *Sinfonia Sacrae*.

L Literature (including Drama)
Pierre Corneille, *Mélite* (comedy).
John Ford, *The Lover's Melancholy* (romantic comedy).
Philip Massinger, *The Roman Actor* (tragedy).

M Births and Deaths
Apr. 14th Christian Huygens b. (–1695).
July 28th John Speed d. (*c.* 77).
Sept. 9th Cornelius van Tromp b. (–1691).
Oct. — Edwin Sandys d. (68).
— 28th Gabriel Metsu b. (–1667).

A Jan: 26th, Sir John Eliot, on trial in the Court of King's Bench for his part in the Com-- mons Protestation (of *Mar.* 1629), denies the jurisdiction of the court to try an M.P. He is fined £2,000 and imprisoned in the Tower at the King's pleasure.
Feb:
Mar:

B Apr:
May: In the War of Mantuan Succession Cardinal Richelieu leads an expedition to Italy, relieving Pinerolo and occupying Saluzzo.
Jun: Richelieu sends Father Joseph to persuade the princes and electors of Germany, meeting at Ratisbon (*-Aug.*) to insist on Wallenstein's dismissal in order to embarrass the Emperor Ferdinand II.

C Jul: 6th, Gustavus II lands in Pomerania and marches his army into Germany;
17th, Mantua falls to the imperialists;
the princes and electors at Ratisbon, stiffened by France, extract from Ferdinand II a promise to dismiss Wallenstein; the Emperor is anxious to achieve his son's election as King of the Romans. Ferdinand subsequently invests the Duke of Nevers with the Duchy of Mantua.
Aug: 13th, Ferdinand II dismisses Wallenstein. Count Tilly assumes command of his army. The Emperor is no longer able to dictate to the Catholic League.
Sep: While Louis XIII is seriously ill at Lyons, Marie de' Medici intrigues with her daughter-in-law, Anne of Austria, to persuade the King to dismiss Cardinal Richelieu, which he promises to do once peace is signed with Spain.

D Oct:
Nov: 5th, the Treaty of Madrid ends the Anglo-Spanish War;
10th, in the 'Day of Dupes', Cardinal Richelieu overthrows the conspiracy of Marie de' Medici and Gaston of Orleans against him. Marillac, the Queen Mother's servant, is executed, and Marie, banished from Paris, takes refuge in Brussels. As a result the Cardinal is in a stronger position than ever before.
Dec:

E Governor John Winthrop arrives in Massachusetts with 1,000 settlers to found Boston. 'The Great Migration' to Massachusetts Bay Colony continues (–1642) with the arrival of 16,000 settlers from England;
Tortuga, off the north-west coast of Hispaniola, is settled by pirates of various nationalities, who become termed 'buccaneers'.

— Isaac Barrow b. (–1677).
— Josiah Child b. (–1699).
— Caius Gabriel Cibber b. (–1700).
— Thomas Clifford b. (–1673).

F Politics, Economics, Law and Education
Théophraste Renaudot founds the Bureau d'Adresse in Paris, a labour bureau, charity organisation and intelligence department.
The last Hanseatic Diet meets at Lübeck.
John Winthrop sails (*Apr.*) with the Plymouth Company's expedition to settle in Massachusetts Bay. Boston, Mass., is laid out (*Sept.* 17th).
Francis Higginson, *New-Englands Plantation*, argues that the Creator has made America most favourable for human life.
John Suckling invents cribbage.

G Science, Technology and Discovery
The flint lock is perfected in France.

H Philosophy, Religion and Scholarship
Anders Christensen Arrebo, *Hexaëmeron* (religious poem in Alexandrines, regarded as the start of the renaissance of Danish literature).
Sir John Hayward, *The Life and Raigne of King Edward VI*.
John Amos Comenius, *The Labyrinth of the World and the Paradise of the Heart*.
Dom Tarisse inaugurates interest in historical scholarship in the Maurist houses in France.

J Art, Sculpture, Fine Arts and Architecture
Painting:
Philippe de Champaigne, *Adoration of the Shepherds*.
Frans Hals, *Daniel van Aken playing the fiddle*.
Georges de la Tour, *Magdalene with the Lamp*.
José Ribera, *Archimedes*.
Rubens, *Blessings of Peace*.
Sculpture:
Gianlorenzo Bernini, *Constanza Buonarelli*.
Le Sueur, *Charles I* (now in Trafalgar Square, London).

K Music
Girolamo Frescobaldi, *Arie Musicale*.

L Literature (including Drama)
Pierre Corneille, *Clitandre* (tragi-comedy).
François de Malherbe, *Oeuvres poétiques*.
Philip Massinger, *The Renegado. The Picture*.
Thomas Middleton, *A Chaste Mayd in Cheapside* (satirical comedy).
John Taylor, *All the Works of John Taylor the Water Poet*, Being 63 in number, Corrected, Revised.
Tirso de Molina, *El Burlador de Sevilla y convidado de Piedra* introduces the story of Don Juan to literature.

M Births and Deaths
Apr. 10th William Herbert, 3rd Earl of Pembroke, d. (50).
May 29th Charles II b. (−1685).
Sept. 29th John Tillotson b. (−1694).
Oct. 14th Sophia, Electress of Hanover, b. (−1714).
Nov. 15th Johann Kepler d. (69).
Nov. 24th Étienne Baluze b. (−1718).
(*Continued opposite*)

A Jan: 23rd, by the Treaty of Bärwalde, France undertakes to subsidise Sweden for six years with an annual one million livres. Gustavus II of Sweden now attempts to win over Saxony and Brandenburg, but the Elector John George of Saxony, bent on neutrality, appeals to the Emperor Ferdinand II to revoke the Edict of Restitution (of *Mar.* 1629) as the basis for a German settlement.

Feb: 20th (*–Apr.* 12th), the German Protestant Princes hold a Convention at Leipzig and decide to form an alliance with Gustavus II.

Mar: 19th/29th, Count Tilly, who has invaded north-east Germany, destroys a Swedish garrison at New Brandenburg and turns back to the R. Elbe to aid Pappenheim in the siege of Magdeburg.

B Apr: 3rd/13th, Gustavus II takes Frankfort-on-Oder, displaying great brutality.

May: 15th, Gustavus II signs a military convention with the Elector of Brandenburg, but is too late to save Magdeburg;
20th, Count Tilly's imperialist army sacks Magdeburg; terrible carnage ensues and the city catches fire, leaving only the cathedral standing. News of the sack heartens the Catholic causes in Germany;
30th, by the Treaty of Fontainebleau between France and Maximilian of Bavaria, leader of the Catholic League, the League undertakes to defend the King of France against all enemies, including Spain, but excepting the Emperor.

Jun: 19th, the Treaty of Cherasco ends the War of Mantuan Succession. By its terms the French and imperialist armies are to leave Italy; the French candidate, Charles Duke of Nevers, is invested by Ferdinand II with the Duchy of Mantua; Savoy is to obtain part of the Duchy of Montferrat. By a secret agreement with Victor Amadeus of Savoy, France is to obtain Pinerolo and the Duke is betrothed to the sister of the French King. France thus gains a foothold in Italy. The Treaty represents a great diplomatic triumph for Cardinal Richelieu;
Count Tilly burns Halle.

C Jul: 23rd and 28th, an imperialist force is twice repulsed by Gustavus II at Werben, at the confluence of the Rivers Elbe and Havel, with heavy losses;
Pope Urban VIII annexes Urbino.

Aug: Count Tilly with 20,000 imperialist troops, freed from Italy with the ending of the Mantuan War, invades Saxony.

Sep: 11th, John George, Elector of Saxony, signs a treaty of alliance with Gustavus II of Sweden;
17th, Gustavus II, supported by the Saxons under Arnim, defeats Count Tilly at the battle of Breitenfeld, near Leipzig, postponing the execution of the Edict of Restitution (of *Mar.* 1629);
France signs the Treaty of Razilly with the Emperor of Morocco.

D Oct: Saxon troops invade Bohemia, while Gustavus II, disregarding advice that he should march on Vienna, crosses Thuringia and Franconia, towards the Rhine, intending to relieve Protestants subject to Maximilian of Bavaria's repression;
the Emperor Ferdinand II empowers Wallenstein to collect an army to oppose Saxony and Sweden.

Nov: 15th, Saxon troops under Arnim take Prague;
Würzburg falls to Gustavus II.

Dec: Gustavus II takes Oppenheim and occupies Mainz.

E Throughout the year Marie de' Medici, Queen Mother of France, and Gaston, Duke of Orleans, heir presumptive to the throne, intrigue against Richelieu from their exile in Brussels;
Agitation grows in England against the harsh sentences inflicted by the Court of High Commission in ecclesiastical affairs;
English settlement of the Leeward Islands is begun from St. Kitts.

F **Politics, Economics, Law and Education**
  The Dutch West India Company makes a settlement on the Delaware River.
  Théophraste Renaudot establishes the *Gazette* in Paris (*May;* from 1752 it takes the title *Gazette de France*).
  Charles I confiscates Sir Robert Cotton's library (now the Cotton MSS in the British Museum) for drawing parallels between the constitutional struggle under Henry III of England with current politics.

G **Science, Technology and Discovery**

H **Philosophy, Religion and Scholarship**
  James Mabbe, *Celestina, the Spanish Bawd*, translated from Fernando de Rojas.

  [Friedrich Spee von Langenfeld], *Cautio Criminalis* (published anonymously. First substantial argument against persecution of supposed witches).
  John Stow, *The Annals of England*, complete edition by E. Howes.

J **Art, Sculpture, Fine Arts and Architecture**
  Painting:
    Rembrandt, *The Artist's Mother*.
  Architecture:
    Jacques Le Mercer, Château Richelieu.

K **Music**

L **Literature (including Drama)**
  Thomas Dekker, *Match Mee in London* (tragi-comedy).
  Thomas Heywood, *The Fair Maid of the West* (comedy).
  Ben Jonson, *Bartholomew Fayre* (*see* 1614); *The Divil is an Asse; The Staple of Newes* (comedies).

M **Births and Deaths**
  Jan. 1st Thomas Hobson d. (86).
  Mar. 31st John Donne d. (59).
  May 6th Robert Cotton d. (60).
  June 21st John Smith d. (52).
  Aug. 9th John Dryden b. (−1700).
  Dec. 10th Hugh Myddelton d. (71).
  Dec. 23rd Michael Drayton d. (68).

A Jan:
   Feb:
   Mar: Gustavus II of Sweden resumes his Palatinate campaign, taking Nuremberg and
   Donauwörth.

B Apr: 13th, Ferdinand II formally reinstates Wallenstein as Supreme Imperial Commander with an army of 50,000 men, with orders to drive the Saxons from Bohemia;
   14th, Gustavus II defeats Count Tilly's imperialist army at the Lech, near the confluence of the Rivers Lenz and Danube. Tilly is mortally wounded (dies, 30th). The
   Swedish army moves on to Ingoldstadt, but is forced to raise the siege;
   Charles I issues a charter for the colony of Maryland, under the control of Lord
   Baltimore, a Roman Catholic, who is to make laws and tax colonists only with the con-
   sent of the adult male population.
   May: 17th, Gustavus II enters Munich and occupies the country south of the R. Danube;
   the Elector John George of Saxony enters Prague, without firing a shot.
   Jun: 15th, Charles I appoints Sir Francis Windebank a Principal Secretary of State.

C Jul: The armies of Gustavus II and of Wallenstein stay camped near Nuremberg, but the
   imperialists decline battle (–Sept.).
   Aug: Maestricht falls to the Dutch. The Infanta Isabella at Brussels puts out feelers for
   peace, but the war is continued.
   Sep: 3rd (–4th), Gustavus II attacks Wallenstein at the Alte Veste, Nuremberg, but is
   repulsed. Wallenstein withdraws to Ingoldstadt and marches into Saxony, plundering.

D Oct: 30th, Montmorency, Governor of Languedoc, is executed for intriguing with
   Gaston, Duke of Orleans, who has joined him from exile, to bring about Cardinal
   Richelieu's fall. Gaston is pardoned and reconciled to his brother, Louis XIII.
   Nov: 6th/16th, Gustavus II, supported by Arnim's Saxon troops, defeats Wallenstein at
   the battle of Lützen, but is killed in action. Bernhard Duke of Saxe-Weimar succeeds
   him as general of the Swedish army;
   6th/16th, accession of Queen Christina of Sweden (–1654): she appoints Axel Oxenstiern as Chancellor and Regent (–1644);
   27th, Sir John Eliot dies in the Tower of London.
   Dec:

E Charles I fines the City of London 1,500 marks for neglect of duty in failing to put down a
   riot in Mar. 1628, during which a servant of the Duke of Buckingham was assaulted;
   Vladislav IV of Poland (–1648) succeeds on the death of Sigismund III;
   English settlements are made in Antigua and Montserrat;
   The Portuguese are forced to leave Bengal.
   The Scottish settlement at Acadia (Nova Scotia) fails.

F **Politics, Economics, Law and Education**

Werdenhagen, *Introductio Universalis in Omnes Respublicas*, originates the study of comparative politics.

John Selden in *Mare Clausum* sets forth England's claim to the sovereignty of the sea.

Famianus Strada writes *De bello belgico* at the request of Alessandro Farnese.

English 'Courants' and political pamphlets cease publication (until 1638), following the complaint of the Spanish ambassador.

G **Science, Technology and Discovery**

Galileo, *Dialogo sopra i due massimi sistemi del mondo*.

Leyden University Observatory is founded.

The Botanic Gardens, Oxford, are established.

H **Philosophy, Religion and Scholarship**

Antonio Bosni, *Roma sotteranea* (posth. account of the excavation of the catacombs of Rome).

Jean Daille, *Traité de l'Emploi des Saints-Pères*.

John Davies, *Welsh Dictionary*.

John Donne, *Death's Duell* (his last sermon).

Philemon Holland translates the *Cyropaedia* of Xenophon.

George Wither, *The Psalms of David* translated.

J **Art, Sculpture, Fine Arts and Architecture**

Painting:

Rembrandt, *The Anatomy Lesson of Dr. Tulp*.

Sculpture:

Gianlorenzo Bernini, portrait bust of Cardinal Scipione Borghese.

K **Music**

Claudio Monteverdi, Great Mass, to mark the end of the plague in Venice.

L **Literature (including Drama)**

Philip Massinger, *The City Madam* (comedy; printed 1658); *The Maid of Honour* (tragi-comedy); *The Emperor of the East*; *The Fatal Dowry* (tragedy).

William Shakespeare, *The Second Folio* (see 1623).

M **Births and Deaths**

Jan. 8th Samuel Pufendorf b. (−1694).

Feb. 20th Thomas Osborne, Earl of Danby, b. (−1712).

Apr. 30th John, Count of Tilly, d. (73).

June 10th Esprit Fléchier b. (−1710).

Aug. 29th John Locke b. (−1704).

Oct. 20th Christopher Wren b. (−1723).

Oct. 31st Jan Vermeer b. (−1675).

Nov. 6th Gustavus Adolphus d. (37).

Nov. 24th Baruch Spinoza b. (−1677).

Nov. 27th John Eliot d. (40).

Dec. 17th Anthony à Wood b. (−1695).

— Thomas Dekker d. (?62).

— Luca Giodano b. (−1705).

— Jean-Baptiste Lully b. (−1687).

— Jean Mabillon b. (−1707).

1633   French occupy Lorraine—Wallenstein's intrigues—the Lancashire witches

A Jan:

Feb: Wallenstein invades Silesia.

Mar: 8th, Charles I fines the City of London £50,000 and seizes its plantation in Ulster for alleged neglect of its undertakings;

the Swedish army under Bernhard of Saxe-Weimar returns to the Palatinate.

B Apr: 23rd, the south German Protestants in the Circles of Swabia, Franconia and the Upper and Lower Rhine, form the League of Heilbronn with Sweden and France for mutual support against the imperialists and the Catholic League.

May: Charles I revives the forest eyre to raise money by fines;

the French occupy Lorraine (–1659).

Jun: 18th, Charles I is crowned King of Scotland at Edinburgh. He orders the Scottish Parliament to prepare a liturgy on Anglican lines. The Scottish Church demands in vain the revival of General Assemblies;

Wallenstein opens negotiations with John George, Elector of Saxony, for a peace on the basis of the repeal of the Edict of Restitution (of *Mar.* 1629); but the Emperor Ferdinand II refuses to consider its repeal.

C Jul: 3rd, Thomas Lord Wentworth, later Earl of Strafford, is appointed Deputy of Ireland. On landing in Dublin he begins administrative reforms and subsequently introduces the cultivation of flax.

Aug: 6th, William Laud is elected Archbishop of Canterbury (–1645), following the death of George Abbot. He begins to enforce ritualistic practices through visitations and the Court of High Commission, and is suspected by Puritans of intending a reconciliation with the Church of Rome;

Wallenstein, who intends establishing himself in the Palatinate to impose his own solution on the German problem, opens negotiations with Axel Oxenstiern of Sweden; relations between Wallenstein and the Emperor Ferdinand II deteriorate.

Sep:

D Oct: 11th, Wallenstein defeats the Swedish army at Steinau in Silesia;

18th, Charles I reissues his father's 'Book of Sports' which may be indulged in on Sundays, angering the Puritans;

23rd, William Juxon is elected Bishop of London.

Nov: 14th, Bernhard of Saxe-Weimar leads a Swedish army to take Regensburg from Maximillian of Bavaria;

Wallenstein, unable to assist Maximilian, goes into winter quarters in Bohemia;

the Infanta Isabella dies in Brussels;

henceforth the Spanish Netherlands are governed direct from Spain. A rising in Brussels is easily suppressed. The States-General there do not meet again until 1790.

Dec: The Emperor Ferdinand II, suspecting Wallenstein of treachery, detaches his chief lieutenants from him.

E Trial of the Lancashire witches;

An English trading post is founded in Bengal.

F **Politics, Economics, Law and Education**
The Dutch settle in Connecticut.
Thomas Witherings begins to reform the postal system in England.

G **Science, Technology and Discovery**
Galileo is condemned at Liège (*Sept.* 20th).
Robert Fludd, *Clavis Philosophiae et Alchymiae* (published at Frankfurt).
Théophraste Renaudot establishes a series of lectures and debates on scientific subjects in Paris (–1642; select papers are published in 1651).

H **Philosophy, Religion and Scholarship**
William Prynne, *Histriomastix: the Players Scourge or Actors Tragedie* (for which the author was fined £5,000, pilloried and mutilated).
Francis Quarles, *Divine Poems*.
Edmund Spenser, *A View of the Present State of Ireland* (posth.).
First Particular Baptist Church (Calvinist) formed (in Southwark, London; –1644).

J **Art, Sculpture, Fine Arts and Architecture**
Painting:
Jacques Callot, *Les Grandes Misères de la Guerre;*
Daniel Mytens, *Charles I.*
Pietro, frescoes and ceiling, Barberini Palace (–1639).
Architecture:
Jacob von Campen, The Mauritshuis, The Hague (–1635).
Jacques Le Mercier, Palais Cardinal (now Palais Royal), Paris.

K **Music**

L **Literature (including Drama)**
Abraham Cowley, *Poetical Blossoms*.
John Donne, *Poems* (posth.).
Phineas Fletcher, *The Purple Island; or The Isle of Man* (an allegorical poem on the human body, the mind, and the virtues and vices).
John Ford, *The Broken Heart* (tragedy); *'Tis Pity She's a Whore* (tragedy).
George Herbert, *The Temple; or Sacred Poems* (posth.).
Christopher Marlowe, *The Rich Jew of Malta* (tragedy) (posth.).
Philip Massinger, *A New Way to Pay Old Debts* (comedy).
William Rowley, *All's Lost By Lust* (tragedy).
James Shirley, *The Bird in a Cage; The Wittie Faire One* (comedies).

M **Births and Deaths**
Jan. 31st Nathaniel Crew b. (–1721).
Feb. 23rd Samuel Pepys b. (–1703).
Mar. 3rd George Herbert d. (39).
Aug. 5th George Abbot d. (70).
Oct. 14th James II b. (–1701).
Oct. — Robert Browne d. (83).
Nov. 11th George Saville, Marquess of Halifax, b. (–1695).
— Sébastien Vaubon b. (–1707).
— Willem van de Velde the younger b. (–1707).

1634 Battle of Nordlingen leads to recovery of the Catholic cause—Prynne's trial

A Jan: 12th, Wallenstein requires lieutenants to sign a declaration of loyalty to him;
24th, the Emperor Ferdinand II secretly deprives Wallenstein of his command for a second time, and declares him a traitor. The Emperor nominates his son Ferdinand as Supreme Commander of Imperial Forces but the effective general is Matthias Gallas, Count of Campo.

Feb: 17th, William Prynne is tried in the Court of Star Chamber for publishing (in 1633) *Histrio-mastix*, an attack on stage plays, which libels Queen Henrietta Maria.

Mar: Cardinal Richelieu arranges to pay a secret subsidy to Bernhard of Saxe-Weimar.

B Apr:
May: 7th, as part of his sentence in the Star Chamber, William Prynne loses both his ears.

Jun: The Duke of Lorraine calls in Spanish and imperialist forces to open the route to the Spanish Netherlands from Franche-Comté.

C Jul:
Aug:
Sep: 5th (–6th), the Swedes under Bernhard of Saxe-Weimar are defeated by Matthias Gallas at the battle of Nördlingen; 17,000 Swedes are slain. The battle leads to the recovery of the Catholic cause in south Germany;
a French army enters the Palatinate and garrisons various fortresses.

D Oct: 20th, Charles I issues first writs for the collection of Ship Money from London and the ports, ostensibly to provide a fleet for the protection of merchant shipping, which is being plundered by pirates off the English and Irish coasts. £104,000 is subsequently collected, which encourages the King to extend Ship Money to inland areas.

Nov: Württemberg and Franconia are reconquered by imperialists from the Swedes.

Dec: A French army compels the imperialists to raise the siege of Heidelberg.

E Cardinal Richelieu reforms the office of Intendant to centralise French administration. Intendants are now representatives of the Crown; the independent power of governors of provinces is consequently weakened;
Dutch fishing vessels persist in fishing in English territorial waters;
The Dutch capture the Island of Curaçao.

F **Politics, Economics, Law and Education**
Forgery in England is made a capital offence, without benefit of clergy.
An English settlement is made at Cochin, Malabar (–1663).
Utrecht University is founded.

G **Science, Technology and Discovery**

H **Philosophy, Religion and Scholarship**
Meric Casaubon translates the *Meditations* of Marcus Aurelius Antoninus, the Roman
Emperor.

J **Art, Sculpture, Fine Arts and Architecture**
Painting:
Rembrandt, *Artemisia*.
Francisco de Zurbarán, *The Siege of Cadiz*.

K **Music**

L **Literature (including Drama)**
Pierre Corneille, *La Veuve* (comedy –1631 ?); *La Suivante* (comedy –1632 ?).
John Fletcher, *The Two Noble Kinsman* (included in the *Shakespeare Apocrypha*)
(posth.).
John Ford, *Perkin Warbeck* (chronicle history drama).
Jean Mairet, *Sophonisbe* (tragedy based on three unities).
The Oberammergau Passion Play is inaugurated (–1662).

M **Births and Deaths**
Feb. 25th Albrecht von Wallenstein d. (50).
May 12th George Chapman d. (74).
June 25th John Marston d. (c. 59).
July 14th Pasquier Quesnel b. (–1719).
Sept. 3rd Edward Coke d. (82).
— Marie-Madeleine de La Fayette b. (–1693).
— Nicolaes Maes b. (–1693).

1635   Charles I extends Ship Money—the Elector of Saxony comes to terms with Ferdinand II

A Jan: The imperialists take Phillipsburg from the French.
Feb:
Mar: 15th, Archbishop Laud becomes First Lord of the Treasury (*–Mar.* 1636).

B Apr: 28th, France signs a further treaty of alliance with Sweden during Axel Oxenstjerna's visit to Louis XIII.
May: 19th, France declares war on Spain on the pretext of Spaniards carrying off the Elector of Trèves, and sends armies against the Spanish Netherlands and against Franche-Comté;
30th, the Peace of Prague is signed between the Emperor Ferdinand II and the Elector John George of Saxony. Saxony obtains Lusatia, and the Elector's second son is to be given the archbishopric of Magdeburg. The Holy Roman Empire is to be placed in the state it was in the year 1627 (prior to the Edict of Restitution of *Mar.* 1629). The Lutheran religion acquires privileged status. The treaty is subsequently accepted by Brandenburg and most Lutheran states. Henceforward the Thirty Years War becomes a conflict of France and Sweden against the House of Hapsburg.
Jun: Cardinal Richelieu forms the League of Rivoli, between France, the United Provinces, Parma and Savoy, though Victor Amadeus of Savoy proves a dubious ally;
a French army is sent to aid Frederick Henry, Prince of Orange.

C Jul: The Duke of Rohan expels the Spanish from the Valtelline.
Aug: 4th, Charles I issues the second writs for the collection of Ship Money, which are extended to inland areas, contrary to precedent; he aims at collecting £208,000.
Sep: 12th, Sweden and Poland sign the twenty-year truce of Stuhmsdorf.

D Oct: 27th, by the Treaty of Saint Germain-en-Laye, Cardinal Richelieu purchases the army of Bernhard of Saxe-Weimar by a regular subsidy.
Nov: Lord Wentworth, Deputy of Ireland, claims the province of Connaught for Charles I and invites settlers.
Dec:

E The colonisation of Connecticut begins with the foundation of Windsor by religious refugees from Dorchester, Massachusetts, and by the settlement of Fort Saybrook by colonists from England, led by John Winthrop the younger;
The French occupy Martinique and Guadeloupe;
The Dutch take Pernambuco from the Portuguese and occupy Formosa.

F **Politics, Economics, Law and Education**

Cornelius Jansen in *Mars gallicus* attacks Cardinal Richelieu's indifference to international Catholic interests.

Charles I extends the incidence of Ship Money from coastal towns to the entire realm.

The sale of tobacco in France is limited to apothecaries, who may supply only on a doctor's prescription.

Académie Française is founded in Paris (*Feb.* 10th).

University of Budapest is established at Tyrnau (moves to Buda in 1777).

The English High and Latin School is founded in Boston, Mass., the oldest secondary school in North America.

G **Science, Technology and Discovery**

H **Philosophy, Religion and Scholarship**

Giulio Alenio publishes a Life of Christ in Chinese (8 vols. –1637).

Vitzentzos Kornaros, *Thysia tou Avraam* ('The Sacrifice of Abraham'; modern Greek mystery drama by the Cretan poet).

The discovery of the tomb of the Merovingian king, Childeric, in the Spanish Netherlands starts an interest in archaeology.

A *New Book of Canons* authorised by Charles I for the Church in Scotland.

J **Art, Sculpture, Fine Arts and Architecture**

Painting:

Philippe de Champaigne, portrait of Cardinal Richelieu.

Pietro, frescoes in the Pitti Palace.

Nicolas Poussin, *The Kingdom of Flora*.

Rembrandt, *Self-portrait with Saskia*; and *Saskia in Arcadian costume*.

Rubens, ceiling of Banqueting Hall, Whitehall; and *Infanta Isabella*.

Van Dyck, *Charles I*.

Velazquez, *Surrender of Breda*.

Francisco de Zurbarán, *St. Veronica's Kerchief*.

Architecture:

Cortona, SS. Martina e Luca, Rome (–1650).

Jacques Le Mercier, Sorbonne Church, Paris.

François Mansart, Château Blois (–1638).

Sculpture:

Bernini, portrait bust of Constanza Bonarelli.

L **Literature (including Drama)**

Pedro Calderòn de la Barca, *La Vida es sueño*.

Pierre Corneille, *Medée* (tragedy).

Thomas Heywood, *The Hierarchie of the Blessed Angells*.

Francis Quarles, *Divine Emblems*.

M **Births and Deaths**

Mar. 17th Thomas Randolph d. (29).

June 3rd Philippe Quinault b. (–1688).

Aug. 24th Count Peter Griffenfeldt ('Peder Schumacher') b. (–1699).

Aug. 27th Lope Félix de Vega Carpio d. (73).

Nov. 14th Thomas Parr d. (52).

Nov. 27th Françoise D'Aubigné, Marquise de Maintenon, b. (–1719).

— George Etherege b. (–1691).

A Jan:
    Feb: John George, Elector of Saxony, gathers an army to fight for Emperor Ferdinand II against the Swedes.
    Mar: 6th, Bishop John Juxon is appointed Lord Treasurer of England (–1641), an appointment which increases control of affairs by the Laudian High Church Party and alarms Puritans.

B Apr: Axel Oxenstjerna, Chancellor of Sweden, signs a further alliance with France at Wismar and returns to Sweden.
    May: Cardinal Ferdinand, Infante of Spain, supported by troops from Bavaria and Cologne invades north-east France from the Spanish Netherlands, advancing through Compiègne;
    the Prince of Condé, Governor of Burgundy, invades Franche-Comté and lays siege to Dôle.
    Jun: Roger Williams, banished from Massachusetts Bay Colony, founds Providence, Rhode Island, a colony with complete religious freedom;
    22nd, the French and Savoyards defeat the Spanish at Tornavento, but Victor Amadeus of Savoy refuses to march on Milan and the strategic advantage is lost.

C Jul: Prince Octavio Piccolomini invades France with a Spanish army and reaches as far as Corbie before he is repulsed. His advance creates alarm in Paris.
    Aug:
    Sep:

D Oct: 4th, Johan Banér leads a Swedish army to defeat the Saxons, under the Elector John George, at the battle of Wittstock. The influence of Sweden in Germany is restored;
    9th, Charles I issues the third writs for the collection of Ship Money. Payment is subsequently refused by Lord Saye and John Hampden.
    Nov: Austrian troops under Matthias Gallas abandon Burgundy following the stout defence by the French of St. Jean-de-Losne.
    Dec: 22nd, the Archduke Ferdinand, son of the Emperor, is elected King of the Romans; to secure this election, Ferdinand II has to make concessions to the Imperial Electors.

E Ceylon is settled by the Dutch.
    The Manchus proclaim the Ch'ing dynasty at Mukden.

F **Politics, Economics, Law and Education**
Roger Williams and other refugees from Massachusetts settle at Providence, Rhode Island (*June*). Dutch colonists settle in Brooklyn by the shore of Gowanns Bay.
R. Powell, *Depopulation arraigned, convicted and condemned by the lawes of God and Man*, a tract against enclosure.
Harvard College (so called from 1639) is founded at Newe Towne, Cambridge, Mass., with Nathaniel Eaton as first president; in 1639 it is endowed by a legacy bequeathed by John Harvard, together with his library.
Utrecht University is founded.
John Davies of Hereford, *The Writing Schoole-Master*.

G **Science, Technology and Discovery**

H **Philosophy, Religion and Scholarship**
Peter Heylyn, *The History of the Sabbath*.
George Sandys, *A Paraphrase Upon the Psalmes* (later, 1638, entitled *A Paraphrase Upon the Divine Poems*).
George Wither, *The Nature of Man* (written in Greek by Nemesius, Englished).

J **Art, Sculpture, Fine Arts and Architecture**
Painting:
Van Dyck, *Charles I on Horseback*.
Rembrandt, *Danae*; and *Portrait of an 83 year-old Woman*.
Velazquez, *Prince Baltasar Carlos as a hunter*.

K **Music**
Martin Rinckhart, *Nun danket alle Gott* (hymn).

L **Literature (including Drama)**
Pedro Calderón de la Barca, *Comedias*, vol. 1 (–1691).
Pierre Corneille, *Le Cid* (tragedy).
Philip Massinger, *The Great Duke of Florence* (comedy).
The Italian Fedeli Company play *Harlequin*: pantomime, at the French court.

M **Births and Deaths**
Nov. 1st Nicolas Boileau-Despréaux b. (–1711).
— Joseph Glanvill b. (–1680).

A Jan:
  Feb: 15th, Ferdinand III succeeds as Holy Roman Emperor (–1657) on the death of
      Ferdinand II;
    the subsequent deaths of Victor Amadeus, Duke of Savoy, the Duke of Mantua and the
      Landgrave of Hesse-Cassel alter the political situation. The Duchess of Mantua goes
      over to the imperialists.
  Mar: 20th, the last Duke of Pomerania, Bogislav XIV, dies.

B Apr: A Spanish army from Catalan invades Languedoc.
  May: A French army begins the conquest of Artois from the Spanish (–1640).
  Jun: 17th, troops raised by the Duke of Rohan in the Valtelline mutiny and Rohan is
      forced to retire;
    30th, William Prynne is tried in the Court of Star Chamber for publishing criticism of
      Laud's ecclesiastical policy. The sentences of mutilation against Prynne and also
      against the Puritans Henry Burton and John Bastwick provoke a public outcry;
    a revolt in Guienne leads to Louis XIII abolishing the privileges of that province.

C Jul: 23rd, Jenny Geddes leads a riot when the new Laudian Prayer Book is first used in
      St. Giles' Cathedral, Edinburgh.
  Aug: The Dutch expel the Portuguese from the Gold Coast.
  Sep:

D Oct: 10th, the Dutch recapture Breda.
  Nov:
  Dec:

E English traders establish a factory at Canton;
  French traders from Dieppe found a settlement at St. Louis at the mouth of the Senegal
    River.

F **Politics, Economics, Law and Education**

Ten of the 12 judges to whom Charles I referred the legality of Ship Money give judgment for the Crown (*June* 11th), but John Hampden still refuses to pay his levy, grounding his action on the Petition of Right.

Prynne, Burton and Bastwick are condemned in the Court of Star Chamber for seditious writings (*June* 14th) and are sentenced to be pilloried and mutilated (*June* 30th).

A proclamation restricts emigration from England to North America (*Apr.* 30th); no propertied persons are to leave the realm or others unless they subscribe the oath of allegiance and furnish a certificate from Justices of the Peace.

G **Science, Technology and Discovery**

René Descartes issues his *Géométrie* as an appendix to the *Discours;* through adopting the analytical method he inaugurates the modern study of mathematics. A second appendix states the law of refraction, as formulated by Snell, and a third partially explains the phenomenon of the rainbow.

H **Philosophy, Religion and Scholarship**

Pierre Corneille's *Le Cid* (1636) translated by Joseph Rutter.

René Descartes, *Discours de la méthode.*

Brian Duppa edits *Jonsonus Virbius; or, The Memory of Ben Jonson Revived by the Friends of the Muses.*

Thomas Hobbes, *A Briefe of the Art of Rhetorique*, from Aristotle.

[W. Prynne], *A breviate of the prelates intolerable usurpations.*

Prayer Book of the Church of Scotland approved.

J **Art, Sculpture, Fine Arts and Architecture**

Painting:

Van Dyck, *Children of Charles I.*

K **Music**

Ancient Society of College Youths founded in London for bell-ringing at St. Martin's Church, College Hill.

Teatro di San Cassiano, the first public opera house, opens in Venice.

L **Literature (including Drama)**

Thomas Deloney, *The Gentle Craft* (in praise of shoemakers and containing the story of Simon Eyre, used by Dekker in 1600).

Jean Desmarets de Saint-Sorlin, *Les Visionnaires* (comedy).

Marin le Roy, Sieur du Gomberville, *Polexandre* (a romance of chivalry).

John Milton, *A Masque* (that is, *Comus*), presented at Ludlow Castle, 1634.

James Shirley, *The Lady of Pleasure* (comedy).

M **Births and Deaths**

Feb. 3rd Gervase Markham d. (69).

Feb. 9th Philemon Holland d. (85).

Feb. 15th Ferdinand II d. (58).

Aug. 6th Ben Jonson d. (65).

Oct. 3rd George Gordon, Earl of Aberdeen, b. (–1720).

Dec. 4th Nicholas Ferrar d. (45).

Dec. 23rd Georg von Schönborn d. (65).

— Dietrich Buxtehude b. (–1707).

— Gabrielle Chiabrera d. (85).

A Jan:

Feb: 19th, Charles I's proclamation, defending the Scottish Prayer Book, is tantamount to a declaration of war. A body of representative commissioners, the Tables, assumes power in Scotland.

Mar: 1st, the Scottish National Covenant is signed by the clergy of Edinburgh, and, 2nd, by the people, and is circulated throughout the northern Kingdom for signatures; 3rd, Bernhard of Saxe-Weimar takes Rheinfelden from the imperialists; the Franco-Swedish alliance is renewed for three years.

B Apr: The Spanish take Vercelli; the Prince of Condé invades Spain from Bayonne, but is checked at Fontarabia.

May: French army joins Bernhard of Saxe-Weimar at Rheinfelden. Bernhard takes Freiburg, defeats the Bavarians at Wittenweiher and frees Breisgar.

Jun: Charles I sends the Marquis of Hamilton as his special commissioner to Scotland, but he fails to secure the renunciation of the Covenant.

C Jul: George William, Elector of Brandenburg, moves his capital from Brandenburg to Königsberg.

Aug: The Emperor refuses to agree to the proposals of the Calvinist princes to accede to the Treaty of Prague.

Sep: 9th, Charles I's declaration withdrawing the canons and liturgy for Scotland and promising to call a General Assembly and a Parliament.

16th, the birth of the Dauphin (the future Louis XIV) dashes the hopes of the Orleanist party in France;

D Oct: 14th, Bernhard of Saxe-Weimar defeats the Duke of Lorraine at Sennheim; peace negotiations are renewed in Cologne and Hamburg.

Nov: 21st, the General Assembly of the Church of Scotland meets at Glasgow, with both clerical and lay representatives, without Charles I's specific permission;

28th, the Marquis of Hamilton dissolves the Assembly in King Charles's name, but it continues to sit until *Dec.* 20th, and abolishes episcopacy;

29th, Count von Götz, with an imperialist army, fails to take Laufenburg.

Dec: 17th, Bernhard of Saxe-Weimar takes Breisach, the key to Alsace, which he aims to rule as a personal kingdom. The fall of Breisach is a turning-point in the struggle between Bourbon and Hapsburg;

Père Joseph (François du Tremblay), Richelieu's secret agent, dies.

E Murad IV of Turkey recovers Baghdad from Shah Abbas I of Persia.

F Politics, Economics, Law and Education
Duc de Rohan, *De l'Interest des Princes et Estats de la Chestienté.*
Charles I grants a monopoly for printing foreign news to Nathaniel Butter and Nicholas Bourne.

G Science, Technology and Discovery
Galileo investigates the motion of falling bodies and publishes *Discorsi e Dimostrazioni Matematiche.*

H Philosophy, Religion and Scholarship
William Chillingworth, *The Religion of Protestants a Safe Way to Salvation.*
Mrs. Anne Hutchinson, leader of the New England Antinomians is banished from Boston, Mass., and sets up a community amongst the Indians of Rhode Island.

J Art, Sculpture, Fine Arts and Architecture
Painting:
Van Dyck, *Lord John and Lord Bernhard Steuart.*
Nicolas Poussin, *Et in Arcadia Ego.*
Architecture:
Francesco Borromini, S. Carlo alle Quattro Fontane, Rome (–1646).

K Music

L Literature (including Drama)
John Ford, *The Ladies Triall.*
John Milton, *Lycidas.*
Niccolò Sabbatini, *Practica di fabricar scene e machine ne' teatri* (published at Ravenna).
The Schouwburg Theatre (the first) opened in Amsterdam (*Jan.* 3rd).
Joost van den Vondel, *Gijsbrecht van Amstel* (historical drama).

M Births and Deaths
Feb. 28th Henri, Duc de Rohan, d. (59).
Mar. — Robert Aytoun d. (68).
May 6th Cornelius Jansen d. (52).
Sept. 16th Louis XIV b. (–1715).
Nov. 25th Catherine of Braganza b. (–1705).
— Jean Bérain b. (–1711).
— Father Joseph d. (61).
— John Harvard d. (31).
— Meindert Hobbema b. (–1709).

A Jan: 24th, the Grisons leader, George Jenatsch, is assassinated.
   Feb: 15th, the Scots appoint Alexander Leslie their commander-in-chief in the First
      Bishops' War;
      27th, Charles I's declaration against the Scots, charging them with seeking to over-
      throw the royal power under pretence of religion.
   Mar: The Scottish Covenanters take Edinburgh, Dumbarton, Stirling and other princi-
      pal towns.

B Apr: 14th, Johan Banér leads a Swedish army to defeat the Archduke Leopold William
      near Chemnitz and subsequently lays siege to Prague;
      Charles I joins his army at York.
   May: 24th, the Skirmish of Turriff opens the First Bishops' War.
   Jun: 7th, the Spanish raise the siege of Thionville;
      18th, since Charles I dare not give battle against the superior Scottish army, he signs
      the Pacification of Berwick to end the war and returns to London. Under the terms of
      the treaty the Scots are to disband their army, while Charles undertakes to refer
      ecclesiastical and civil affairs to a General Assembly and Parliament respectively;
      29th, Hesdin surrenders to the French.

C Jul: 18th, Bernhard of Saxe-Weimar dies, aged 35, of a fever, as he prepares to face
      Banér's army;
      Catalans defend Roussillon against the French.
   Aug: Episcopacy is abolished in Scotland;
      punishment of Puritans in the Church Courts in London provokes a further outcry
      against Archbishop Laud.
   Sep: 22nd, Thomas Lord Wentworth arrives in London from Ireland and becomes
      Charles I's principal adviser;
      by the Peace of Milan the Valtelline is returned to the Grisons; under its terms passage
      is to be provided for Spanish troops.

D Oct: 11th/21st, the Dutch fleet, under Van Tromp, violates English territorial waters by
      defeating the Spanish fleet, carrying troops for Flanders, that had taken refuge in the
      Downs;
      20th, Cardinal Richelieu secures the arrest of Charles, Pretender to the Palatinate, at
      Moulins;
      30th, 'The Directors' of the Bernardine Army (following the death of Bernard of
      Saxe-Weimar), swear fidelity to France at Colmar, and agree to serve under the com-
      mand of the Duke of Longueville;
      31st, the Scottish Parliament is dissolved.
   Nov: 10th, further writs for the collection of Ship Money are issued by Charles I;
      29th, Turenne, in danger of being cut off in North Italy, defeats the Savoyards and
      imperialists.
   Dec: 28th, the army under the Duke of Longueville crosses the Rhine from the east and
      occupies Alsace.

E

F **Politics, Economics, Law and Education**
First printing press in North America operates at Cambridge, Mass.

G **Science, Technology and Discovery**
Jeremiah Horrocks observes the transit of Venus (*Nov.* 24th), as he had predicted.
William Gascoigne invents the micrometer.
Quinine is increasingly used for medicinal purposes following the cure of the Countess of Chinchou in Peru.

H **Philosophy, Religion and Scholarship**
Thomas Fuller, *The Historie of the Holy Warre* (that is, the Crusades).
Sir Henry Spelman, *Concilia, Decreta, Leges, Constitutiones in Re Ecclesiarum orbis Britannici*, vol. 1 (4 vols. –1664).
Académie Française begins the Dictionary of the French Language (*Feb.* 7th; –1694).
Episcopacy is abolished in Scotland by the General Assembly (*Aug.*).

J **Art, Sculpture, Fine Arts and Architecture**
Painting:
Francisco Herrera the elder, *St. Basil dictating his Rule.*
Rubens, *Judgment of Paris;* and *Self-Portrait with a Sword.*
Francisco de Zurbarán, *St. Francis in Meditation.*
Architecture:
Jacob van Campen, Marekerk, Leyden.
Le Nau, Hôtel Lambert, Paris.

K **Music**
Monteverdi's opera *Adone* is performed at the Teatro di San Cassiano.
Chi soffre, speri, the first comic opera, is produced at the Barberini Theatre. The text is by Giulio Respigliosi and the music by Marco Marazzoli and Vergilio Mazzochi.

L **Literature (including Drama)**
William Cartwright, *The Royal Slave* (drama).
Pierre Corneille, *Cinna; Horace* (tragedies).
Philip Massinger, *The Unnatural Combat.*

M **Births and Deaths**
Jan. 19th Noël Alexandre b. (–1724).
Mar. 22nd Thomas Carew d. (41).
May 21st Tomaso Campanella d. (71).
June 21st Increase Mather b. (–1723).
Aug. 4th Juan Ruiz de Alarcón d. (58).
Aug. 20th Martin Opitz von Boberfeld d. (41).
Sept. 29th Lord William Russell b. (–1683).
Dec. 22nd Jean Racine b. (–1699).
Dec. — Henry Wotton d. (71).

A   Jan: 12th, Thomas Wentworth is created Earl of Strafford.
Feb: 3rd, Sir Harry Vane is appointed Secretary of State.
Mar: French complete the occupation of Alsace.

B   Apr: 13th (–*May* 5th), Short Parliament, Charles I's fourth, meets but is dissolved when it refuses to vote money and attacks Charles's Church policy.
May: 12th, revolts break out in Barcelona and spread throughout Catalonia.
Jun:

C   Jul: The Swedes withdraw from Bohemia.
Aug: 20th, Scots at Coldstream cross the Tweed into England in the Second Bishops' War;
—, Charles I leaves London for York to face threatened invasion from Scotland;
27th, Charles I leads troops out of York to relieve Newcastle but
28th, Scots defeat a separate force at Newburn-on-Tyne and
30th, enter Newcastle.
Sep: 13th, Charles I bestows Order of the Garter on Strafford;
24th, Charles I, having heeded petition from 12 peers to call a new Parliament, opens a Great Council at York (–end *Oct.*).

D   Oct: By the Treaty of Ripon, Charles I agrees to pay Scots army £860 per day until a settlement is made.
Nov: 3rd, the Long Parliament meets (–*Apr.* 20th, 1653);
11th, John Pym leads attack on Strafford who is subsequently impeached and sent to the Tower of London.
Dec: 1st, revolt in Portugal which becomes independent under John IV of the Braganzas;
7th, Commons proclaim Ship Money to be an illegal tax;
11th, 'Root and Branch' petition to abolish Episcopacy;
18th, Archbishop Laud is impeached;
21st, Lord Finch, the Lord Keeper, answers accusations before the Commons but
22nd, flees to Netherlands and is impeached in his absence;
Elector George William of Brandenburg dies and is succeeded by Frederick William ('the Great Elector'—1688).

E   Foundation of Fort St. George in Bengal marks end of first stage of British settlements (which began 1633);
Dutch destroy Malacca;
Sultan Ibrahim succeeds Murad IV of Turkey (–1649).

Sept. 29th Charles Antoine Coysevox b. (–1720).
Oct. 20th John Bull d. (55).
— André Du Chesne d. (56).
— John Ford d. (54?).
— Robert Spencer, Earl of Sunderland, b. (–1702).
— William Wycherley b. (–1716).

F **Politics, Economics, Law and Education**

[John Selden], *De jure Naturali et Gentium*, a discourse on the powers of the peers and the commons.

English settlers found a fort which later develops into Madras City.

Åbo University (now Turku, Finland) is founded.

G **Science, Technology and Discovery**

H **Philosophy, Religion and Scholarship**

John Donne, *LXXX Sermons* (posth.).

John Eliot, *Bay Psalm Book* ('The Whole Booke of Psalmes . . . trans. into English metre'—the hymnal of the Massachusetts Bay Colony; printed by Stephen Day at Cambridge, Mass., the oldest surviving book printed in North America).

Joseph Hall, *Episcopacie by Divine Right* (the *Smectymnuus Controversy* –1641).

James Howell, *Dodona's Grove; or, The Vocall Forrest* (Dendrology).

Cornelius Jansen, *Augustinus* (posth.), 4 vols. (opposed to Jesuit thought, and against certain teachings of St. Augustine on such topics as Grace, Free-Will, Predestination, –1642).

James Mabbe translates the *Exemplary Novels* of Cervantes.

Edward Dacres translates *The Prince* of Machiavelli (–1532).

John Milton, *Of Reformation Touching Church Discipline in England*.

John Parkinson, *Theatrum Botanicum* (a herbal).

Francisco Gomez de Quevedo, *Providencia de Dios*.

Sir Henry Spelman founds a lectureship at Cambridge University to promote the study of Saxon antiquities.

Bronze tablet of 186 B.C. discovered in Calabria, portraying the Bacchanalian Festivals.

J **Art, Sculpture, Fine Arts and Architecture**

Painting:

Carel Fabritius, *Abraham de Potter*.

Adriaen Van Ostade, *Barrel-organ-player by a Cottage*.

Pietro, frescoes, Chiesa Nova, Rome (–1667).

Nicolas Poussin, *The Inspiration of the Poet*.

Rembrandt, *Self-portrait at the age of 34*.

K **Music**

L **Literature (including Drama)**

Richard Brome, *The Antipodes* (comedy).

Thomas Carew, *Poems*.

Pierre Corneille, *Polyeucte* (tragedy).

Pierre Du Ryer, *Alcionee* (romantic tragedy).

Ben Jonson, *Works* (2nd volume of the folio collection, *see* –1616).

Joost van den Vondel, *Joseph in Dothan; Joseph in Egypten* (religious dramas).

Izaak Walton, *The Life of Donne*.

M **Births and Deaths**

Jan. 25th Robert Burton d. (63).

Mar. 18th Philip Massinger d. (57).

May 30th Peter Paul Rubens d. (62).

July — Aphra Behn b. (–1689).

(Continued opposite)

A Jan: 30th, the Earl of Strafford is formally accused by Commons;
     Portuguese finally surrender Malacca to Dutch;
     Johan Banér attacks Regensburg and almost captures the Emperor Ferdinand III.
   Feb: 16th, Charles I consents to Triennial Bill in order to obtain loan from Commons,
     and this ultimately becomes Act of Parliament.
   Mar: 22nd, trial of Strafford opens.

B Apr: 21st, Commons votes Bill of Attainder for execution of Strafford.
   May: 2nd, Mary, Charles I's daughter, marries William, son of the Prince of Orange;
     10th, Charles agrees to accept Bill of Attainder;
     12th, Strafford is beheaded;
     the Swedish general Banér dies, and is succeeded by Lennart Torstensson.
   Jun: Portugal concludes treaties of alliance with France and United Provinces against
     Spain;
     Guébriant defeats the Imperialists at Wolfenbüttel.

C Jul: 5th, Courts of Star Chamber and High Commission are abolished;
     Brandenburg concludes two-year treaty of neutrality with Sweden.
   Aug: 9th, English Parliament is prorogued;
     20th, English Treaty of Pacification with Scotland ratifies agreement of 1640;
     21st, extension of 1638 treaty of alliance between France and Sweden who also con-
     cludes treaty of friendship and commerce with Portugal.
   Sep: The conspiracy of the Comte de Soissons against Louis XIII fails.

D Oct: 20th, English Parliament reassembles;
     23rd, outbreaks of Catholic Irish rebellion; Ulster Protestants are massacred.
   Nov: 23rd, Grand Remonstance is carried in Parliament by 11 votes; this rallies Charles
     I's opponents.
   Dec: Peace conference opens at Hamburg;
     Jules Mazarin is elected a Cardinal.

E Body of Liberties codifying 100 laws is set up by General Court of Massachusetts Bay
   Company.

F **Politics, Economics, Law and Education**
   The abolition of the Star Chamber (*Feb.*) clears the way for reporting domestic political events in England, and *Diurnall Occurrences in Parliament* appears (*Nov.*).
   George Thomason begins making his collection of tracts and pamphlets (1662; printed 1762).
   Lewis Roberts, *The Treasure of Traffic*.
   Sheppard, *Touchstone of Common Assurances*.
   Théophraste Renaudot's plan for free medical treatment of the needy in Paris (leads in 1644 to the Faculty of Medicine forbidding him to practise).
   Henry Dunster becomes president of Harvard College (–1659).

G **Science, Technology and Discovery**
   Vincenzio Galileo makes a clock with a pendulum and a pin-wheel escapement.
   The preparation of arsenic is first described.

H **Philosophy, Religion and Scholarship**
   René Descartes, *Méditations métaphysiques*.
   William Habington, *Observations Upon Historie*.
   Sir Robert Naunton, *Fragmenta Regalia* (posth. an account of Queen Elizabeth's court).
   George Sandys, *Paraphrase upon the Song of Solomon*.
   George Wither, *Hallelujah; or, Britain's Second Remembrancer* (hymns).

J **Art, Sculpture, Fine Arts and Architecture**
   Painting:
   Anthony van Dyck, *Prince William of Orange*.
   Claude, *Embarkation of St. Ursula*.
   Jan van Goyen, *Landscape with Two Oaks*.
   Frans Hals, *The Governors of St. Elizabeth Hospital*.
   Nicholas Poussin, *Seven Sacraments* (1st set); and *Bacchanalian Revels before a Term of Pan*.
   José Ribena, *St. Agnes in Prison*.
   David Teniers, *Country Fair*.

K **Music**
   John Barnard, *First Booke of Selected Church Musick* (dedicated to Charles I; includes 60 anthems by Byrd).

L **Literature (including Drama)**
   Pierre Corneille, *La Mort de Pompée* (tragedy).
   Luis Vélez de Guevara, *El Diablo cojuelo* (picaresque novel).
   Ben Jonson, *Timber; or, Discoveries* (posth.).
   Madeleine de Scudéry, *Ibraham; ou, L'Illustre Bassa*, 4 vols.
   John Evelyn begins his *Diary* (–1706).

M **Births and Deaths**
   Jan. 18th François Michel le Tellier, Marquis de Louvois, b. (–1691).
   Apr. 15th Zampieri Domenichino d. (60).
   May 10th John Bauér d. (43).
   May 12th Thomas Wentworth, Earl of Strafford, d. (43).
   Oct. — Henry Spelman d. (*c.* 77).
   Dec. 9th Anthony Van Dyck d. (42).
   — Françoise de Pardaillau, Marquise de Montespan, b. (–1707).
   — Thomas Rymer b. (–1713).

A Jan: 4th, Charles I marches to Westminster to arrest 5 members of the Commons, Pym,
   Hampden, Haselrig, Holles, and Strode, for communicating with the Scots, but they
   seek refuge in the City of London at the Guildhall, and his attempt fails;
   10th, Charles and his family flee from London to Hampton Court;
   Guébriant defeats Imperialists at Kempten.
   Feb: 23rd, Queen Henrietta Maria sails from Dover for Holland.
   Mar: Turks renew peace with Emperor Ferdinand III.

B Apr:
   May: Tortensson defeats Imperialists at Schweidnitz.
   Jun: 1st, 19 Propositions agreed on by both the Houses are presented to Charles who
   subsequently rejects them.

C Jul: 4th, Parliament forms Committee of Public Safety to conduct impending war;
   15th, Lord Strange reaches Manchester for the King and in the ensuing fighting the
   first fatal victim of the war is claimed.
   Aug: 22nd, Royal Standard is raised at Nottingham, and Civil War begins with the King
   calling Parliament and its soldiers traitors.
   Sep: 9th, Earl of Essex, in command of Parliamentary armies, leaves London for the
   Midlands;
   23rd, Prince Rupert defeats Parliamentary army under Essex at Powicke Bridge,
   Worcester;
   conspiracy in France, by Henry, Marquis de Cinq-Mars, who signs secret treaty with
   Spain but is discovered by Cardinal Richelieu and subsequently executed;
   Spanish currency is deflated.

D Oct: 23rd, indecisive battle of Edgehill at which the Earl of Essex claims victory, although
   Prince Rupert distinguishes himself.
   Nov: 2nd, Swedes, under Tortensson, defeat Imperial army at second battle of Breitenfeld;
   7th, Essex returns to London but
   11th, leaves to meet Charles I;
   12th, Charles I, marching on London, turns back at Brentford when faced by Essex.
   Dec: 4th, on death of Cardinal Richelieu, Mazarin becomes Chief Minister;
   5th, Cavaliers take Marlborough;
   13th, Roundheads take Winchester;
   22nd, Pope Urban VIII reduces number of annual feast days and, at instigation of
   Jesuits, condemns Jansen's *Augustinus*.

E Tasman discovers Tasmania (van Dieman's land) and New Zealand;
   Dutch obtain monopoly of foreign trade in Japan on final exclusion of Portuguese (since
   1637) but severe limitations are imposed on their activities;
   French occupy Rousillon;
   Accession of Shah Abbas II (–1667).

F **Politics, Economics, Law and Education**
Thomas Hobbes, *De Cive* (translated edition, 1651).
The Court of Requests ceases hearing causes (not revived in 1660).
Thomas Lechford *Plain Dealing; or Newes from New-England* (a political survey).
Samuel Hartlib translates J. A. Comenius (Komensky), *A Reformation of Schooles*.

G **Science, Technology and Discovery**
E. Torricelli invents the barometer (the 'Torricellian tube').
Blaise Pascal devises an adding machine.
The Loire-Seine canal (begun 1604) is completed.
Van Dieman, governor of the Dutch East India Company sends Tasman on a voyage from Batavia, in which he discovers Tasmania and New Zealand.

H **Philosophy, Religion and Scholarship**
Thomas Fuller, *The Holy State; The Profane State*.
James Howell, *Instructions for Foreign Travel*.
John Milton, *The Reason of Church-Government Urg'd Against Prelaty. An Apology . . . against Smectymnuus* (–1640, 1641).
Jeremy Taylor, *The Sacred Order and Offices of Episcopacy*.
Cornelius Jansen's *Augustinus* is condemned by Urban VIII (–1640).

J **Art, Sculpture, Fine Arts and Architecture**
Painting:
William Dobson, *Endymion Porter*.
Rembrandt, *The Night Watch*.
Architecture:
Francesco Borromini, S. Ivo della Sapienza, Rome (–1660).
François Mansart, Maisons Lafitte, near Paris.

K **Music**
Monteverdi's opera *L'incoronazione di Poppea* is performed in Venice at Santi Giovanni e Paolo, Europe's second public opera house.

L **Literature (including Drama)**
Pierre Corneille, *Le Menteur* (comedy).
Sir John Denham, *Cooper's Hill* (first version of a pastoral-descriptive poem: the first of its kind in English literature).
La Calprenède, *Cassandre* (10 vols. –1645).
Joost van den Vondel, *Brieven der Heilighe Maeghden* (early Dutch fictional sketches).
Theatres in England are closed by order (reopened, 1660).

M **Births and Deaths**
Jan. 8th Galilei Galileo d. (77).
June— John Suckling d. (33).
July 3rd Marie de' Medici d. (69).
Aug. 18th Guido Reni d. (66).
Sept. 12th Henri, Marquis de Cinq-Mars, d. (22).
Dec. 4th Cardinal Richelieu d. (57).
Dec. 25th Isaac Newton b. (–1727).
Dec. 30th John Holt b. (–1710).
— André Boulle b. (–1732).
— Marie Champmeslé b. (–1698).
— Francis Child b. (–1713).

A   Jan: 18th, Cavaliers lose Bradford;
    23rd, Sir Thomas Fairfax takes Leeds for Parliamentarians;
    Cavalier newsheet *Mercurius Aulicus* is published in Oxford and regularly smuggled to London.
Feb:
Mar: Parliamentary Commissioners meet Charles I at Oxford for unsuccessful peace negotiations (*–Apr.* 15th).

B   Apr: 15th, Commissioners recalled by Parliament;
    16th, Earl of Essex lays siege to, and subsequently takes, Reading.
May: 13th, Oliver Cromwell defeats Royalists at Grantham;
    14th, Louis XIII dies, and is succeeded by Louis XIV (–1715);
    16th, Parliament's western forces under Stamford are defeated at Stratton;
    18th, Anne of Austria, the Queen Mother, is invested with supreme power in France at a *Lit de Justice*; she confirms Mazarin as First Minister and appoints the Duke of Orleans as Lieutenant-General;
    19th, French under Enghien defeat Spanish at Rocroi which marks end of supremacy of Spanish forces;
    —, Confederation of New England by Connecticut, New Haven, Plymouth and Massachusetts Bay;
    20th, Fairfax takes Wakefield from Royalists;
    31st, Royalists plotters arrested in London.
Jun: 18th, John Hampden defeated and killed at Chalgrove Field;
    30th, Fairfax loses West Riding to Royalists after battle of Atherton Moor.

C   Jul: 13th, Royalist victory at Roundway Down;
    26th, Prince Rupert takes Bristol but with heavy losses;
    Peace Conference is opened at Münster and Osnabrück by the Imperial envoys;
    28th, Oliver Cromwell takes Gainsborough.
Aug:
Sep: 5th, Earl of Essex relieves Gloucester, under siege since Aug. 3rd.
    15th, 'First Cessation' ends Irish rebellion enabling royalists to bring troops to England;
    20th, first battle of Newbury ends in Royalists' defeat;
    25th, Assembly of Westminster, meeting since *July*, adopts Presbyterianism by the Solemn League and Covenant between Parliament and Scotland. Subsequently a joint committee of the two Kingdoms is formed;
    the *Importants* in France are suppressed;
    Charles I negotiates for aid from Ireland.

D   Oct:
Nov: 23rd, Parliamentary alliance with Scotland confirmed in Edinburgh;
    24th, Austro-Bavarian army defeat French at Duttlingen; Turenne takes command the remnant of the French army;
    Spanish army forces the French invaders to retire into Catalonia.
Dec: 8th, John Pym dies.

E   Fall of Olivares in Spain.

F **Politics, Economics, Law and Education**
  John Milton, *The Doctrine and Discipline of Divorce*.
  William Prynne, *The Soveraigne Power of Parliaments and Kingdomes*.
  The Royalist newspaper *Mercurius Aulicus* (edited in Oxford by John Berkenhead and Peter Heylin) appears every Sunday (–1645).
  The Parliamentarian rejoinder, *Mercurius Britanicus*, is founded by Thomas Audley in London.
  Herman Conring founds the study of German law on an historical basis in *De origine juris Germanici*.
  Coffee is first drunk in Paris.
  A system of parcel post is established in France.

G **Science, Technology and Discovery**

H **Philosophy, Religion and Scholarship**
  Antoine Arnauld, *La Fréquente Communion*.
  Sir Richard Baker, *A Chronicle of the Kings of England* ('. . . unto the Raigne of King Charles II, continued to George I' –1730).
  John Bolland begins the edition of *Acta Sanctorum* (still in progress as a series of critical editions of versions of the lives of the saints, in order of commemoration in the Christian calendar).
  François Eudes de Mézeray, *Histoire de France* (up to 1598; a very popular work, reprinted frequently up to 1830).
  Roger Williams, *Key into the Language of America*.
  The Assembly of Westminster, summoned by the Long Parliament (*Sept.* 25th) adopts the *Solemn League and Covenant* (–1638) and inaugurates a Presbyterian establishment for England and Wales.
  Cardinal Mazarin's Library, Paris, is opened to the public (during *La Fronde*, 1651, it is closed by the Paris *Parlement*).

J **Art, Sculpture, Fine Arts and Architecture**
  Painting:
  Adriaen Ostade, *Slaughtered Pig*.

K **Music**

L **Literature (including Drama)**
  Sir Thomas Browne, *Religio Medici* (preceded in 1642 by an unauthorised edition).
  Johann Michael Moscherosch, *Gesichte Philanders von Sittewald*.

M **Births and Deaths**
  Mar. 1st Girolamo Frescobaldi d. (58).
  June 18th John Hampden d. (*c.* 48).
  Aug. — Anne Hutchinson d. (*c.* 43).
  Sept. 18th Gilbert Burnet b. (–1715).
  Sept. 20th Lucius Cary, Viscount Falkland, d. (*c.* 33).
  Nov. 1st John Strype b. (–1737).
  Nov. 29th Claudio Monteverdi d. (76).
  Dec. 8th John Pym d. (59).
  — Richard Boyle, Earl of Cork, d. (77).

A Jan: 22nd, Charles I's Parliament meets at Oxford;
    24th, Battle of Nantwich at which Fairfax defeats Irish Royalists;
    the Scots invade England;
    the Swedes, having decided on war with Denmark in previous year, cross border into
    Jutland.
Feb:
Mar: 31st, the Peace of Ferrara ends the war of Castro (since 1641) between Pope Urban
    VIII and the Duke of Parma, aided by Venice, Modena and Tuscany.

B Apr: French envoys arrive at the Congress of Münster.
May: 16th, French troops take Gravelines.
Jun: 29th, battle of Copredy Bridge results in Royalist defeat of Waller.

C Jul: 2nd, Royalists under Prince Rupert are defeated by Oliver Cromwell at Marston
    Moor;
    14th, Queen Henrietta Maria flees to France;
    16th, York surrenders to the Parliamentarians;
    Pope Urban VIII dies.
Aug: Montrose enters Scotland to raise help for Charles I and subsequently defeats
    Covenanters at Tibbermore;
    3rd (–5th), Enghien's successes at Freiburg lead to French occupation of the Rhineland.
Sep: 2nd, the Earl of Essex's army surrenders to Charles near Fowey after Essex has
    managed to escape by sea;
    12th, French capture Phillipsburg;
    15th, Giovanni Battista Pamfili is elected Pope Innocent X (–1655);
    17th, French take Mainz and subsequently capture Mannheim, Speyer, Worms and
    Oppenheim.

D Oct: 22nd, Newcastle formally surrenders, having been occupied by Scots since 19th;
    27th, indecisive second battle of Newbury, fought between the Earl of Manchester and
    Waller.
Nov:
Dec: 18th, Queen Christina begins to govern Sweden.

E Series of risings of French peasants in Dauphiné, Languedoc, Normandy and Armagnac.
    In Poitou and Saintonge nobles hatch a conspiracy to oppose Mazarin, who is forced
    to reduce taxation;
Spanish forces manage to drive French from Aragon;
Ming dynasty in China ends and is succeeded by the Ch'ing dynasty.
Dutch establish settlement in Mauritius;
Providence is united by Charter with Newport and Portsmouth, Rhode Island;
Connecticut unites with colony at Saybrook.

F Politics, Economics, Law and Education

John Milton pleads for uncensored printing in *Areopagitica ;* and in a *Letter on Education* proposes the reform of English schools on the lines advocated by Comenius.

Samuel Rutherford, *Lex Rex*, stresses the elective nature of monarchy and that kings may be deposed.

G Science, Technology and Discovery

René Descartes, *Principia Philosophicae*, includes a discussion of the laws of motion and the theory of vortices.

Sir Henry Manwayring, *The Sea-mans Dictionary*.

H Philosophy, Religion and Scholarship

Antonio Escobar Y Mendoza, *Liber Theologiae Moralis* (7 vols. –1663; later publicly burnt, Paris; attacked for its casuistry by Pascal in *Lettres Provinciales* –1656).

Henry Hammond, *A Practical Catechism*.

Roger Williams, *Queries of Highest Consideration* (argument for separation of Church and state).

Roger Williams, *The Bloudy Tenent of Persecution for Cause of Conscience. Mr Cotton's Letter Lately Printed, Examined and Answered.*

Confession of Faith by the Particular Baptists (Calvinists), London (–1633).

English Parliament forbids merriment or religious festivities at Christmas.

J Art, Sculpture, Fine Arts and Architecture

Painting:

Claude, *Landscape—Narcissus;* and *A Seaport.*

Nicolas Poussin, *Seven Sacraments* (2nd set).

Rembrandt, *The Woman taken in Adultery.*

José Ribera, *St. Paul the Hermit* (I).

David Teniers, *Kitchen of the Archduke Leopold Wilelm.*

Velazquez, *The Praga Phillip.*

Sculpture:

G. Bernini, Vision of St. Teresa, Rome.

Architecture:

Jacques Le Mercier, Val-de-Grâce, Paris.

K Music

L Literature (including Drama)

M Births and Deaths

Jan. 10th Louis Boufflers b. (–1711).

Jan. 30th William Chillingworth d. (42).

Apr. 10th William Brewster d. (78).

July — Abraham Sancta Clara b. (–1709).

Sept. 8th Francis Quarles d. (52).

Oct. 14th William Penn b. (–1718).

A Jan: 10th, Archbishop Laud is beheaded;
13th, Lords reject Self-Denying Ordinance excluding members of both Commons and Lords from military office, but Commons immediately appoint Fairfax Commander-in-Chief which deprives Essex of office.
Feb: 2nd, the royalist Montrose is victorious over Argyll's Covenanters at Inverlochy; 22nd, armistice ends when peace negotiations between Royalists and Parliamentarians at Uxbridge (begun *Jan.* 29th) fail.
Mar: 5th, Imperial army is defeated by Swedes under Torstensson at Jankowitz; leading members of the Paris *Parlement* are imprisoned.

B Apr: 3rd, Self-Denying Ordinance is passed by the House of Lords; beginning of New Model Army.
May: 5th, Turenne is defeated at Herbsthausen near Mergentheim; 9th, Montrose is victorious at Auldearn; the French fail to take Orbetello.
Jun: 1st, peace negotiations finally open between Empire and France at Münster and Empire and Sweden at Osnabrück (culminating in Treaty of Westphalia, 1648); 10th, Oliver Cromwell re-appointed Lieutenant-General of the New Model Army; 14th, Cromwell defeats Royalists at Naseby, who flee to Leicester, which falls 17th, and then to Ashby-de-la-Zouche; 23rd, Harcourt leads French victory over Spaniards; 28th, Royalists lose Carlisle; Montrose defeats the Scottish Covenanters at Alford.

C Jul: 10th, Oliver Cromwell is victorious at Langport, near Bridgewater, which is also subsequently taken; Alexis succeeds as Tsar of Russia (–1676);
Aug: 3rd, Turenne defeats Bavarians at Nördlingen, but the French are forced to retire; Torstensson and Ragotsky abandon plans for an attack on Vienna; Sweden and Denmark conclude peace at Brömsebro, the Danes losing much territory.
Sep: 10th, General Fairfax forces Prince Rupert to surrender Bristol and the Prince is subsequently arrested on the King's orders, but is later reconciled with Charles I; 13th, Montrose is defeated at Philiphaugh and flees to Continent; Mazarin, following the French victory at Nördlingen, is in a strong enough position to force the Paris *Parlement* to yield.

D Oct: 5th, Royalists lose Winchester; 8th, Basing House falls to Parliamentarians after a seige.
Nov: Turenne captures Trèves.
Dec:

E Turkish-Venetian war breaks out when former attempts to take Crete; Portuguese in Brazil rebel against Dutch; Capucin monks ascend River Congo; The Dutch occupy St. Helena.

F **Politics, Economics, Law and Education**
John Lilburne founds the Leveller movement in Southwark.
Ordinarie Post-Tidende is issued in Stockholm.

G **Science, Technology and Discovery**
Boyle, Wilkins, Watts, Petty, Seth Ward and others begin regular scientific discussions at Gresham College, London, and in Oxford.

H **Philosophy, Religion and Scholarship**
Sir Kenelm Digby, *A Treatise on Bodies and of Man's Soul.*
Lord Herbert of Cherbury, *De Causis Errorum.*
James Howell, *Epistolae Ho-elianae.*
Ménard's edition of *the Epistle of St. Barnabas,* the first volume of the works of the Early Christian Fathers, edited by Maurists.
John Sparrow and others translate the *Two Theosophical Epistles* of Jakob Boehme (followed by other works –1650).

J **Art, Sculpture, Fine Arts and Architecture**
Painting:
Jacob Jordaens, *Wife of Candaules.*
David Teniers, *Tavern Scene.*
Architecture:
Jacob van Campen, Niewe Kerk, Haarlem.

K **Music**
Lully is appointed violinist and kitchen boy at the French court.
Heinrich Schütz, *Die Sieben Worte Christi am Kreuz* (oratorio).

L **Literature (including Drama)**
Pierre Corneille, *Théodore vierge et martyre* (tragedy).
Vitzentzos Kornaros, *Rotokritos* (romance in verse by the Cretan epic poet).
John Milton, *On the Morning of Christ's Nativity; L'Allegro; Il Penseroso; Sonnets* and other poems, both English and Latin.
Paul Scarron, *Jodelet; ou, Le Maître Valet* (comedy).
Edmund Waller, *Poems.*
Philip von Zesen, *Die Adriatische Rosemund* (autobiographical novel).

M **Births and Deaths**
Jan. 10th William Laud d. (71).
Feb. 18th Richard Baker d. (77).
Apr. 19th Anthony van Diemen d. (52).
July 12th Michael, Tsar of Russia, d. (49).
July 22nd Gaspar, Count of Olivares, d. (58).
Aug. 6th Lionel Cranfield, Earl of Middlesex, d. (70).
Aug. 16th Jean de la Bruyère b. (–1696).
Aug. 29th Hugo Grotius d. (63).
Sept. 8th Francisco Quevedo y Villegas d. (65).

1646   Surrender of Charles I to the Scots

A Jan: 16th, Parliament learns of Glamorgan's Irish treaty of 1645, pledging Charles to Rome in return for 10,000 Catholic Irish troops;
   Courtrai falls to French army under Enghien.
   Feb:
   Mar:

B Apr: The Swedes take Prague.
   May: 5th, Charles surrenders to Scots at Newark.
   Jun: 5th, Irish Catholics defeat Scots at Benburb;
   25th, surrender of Oxford to Roundheads virtually signifies end of Civil War.

C Jul: 7th, Levellers publish *Remonstrance of Many Thousand Citizens* proclaiming the sovereignty of the people, advocating abolition of monarchy and of the House of Lords' veto;
   30th, Parliamentary Commissioners present Charles I at Newcastle with the Newcastle Propositions, demanding that he accept the Covenant, abolish Episcopacy, consent to demands for other religious reforms, agree to restrictions on Catholics and to surrender control of armed forces for 20 years;
   French troops under Turenne, together with Swedes, under Wrangel, invade Bavaria.
   Aug: French fail to take Orbetello.
   Sep: The Elector of Bavaria agrees to a truce.

D Oct: 17th, Charles offers to Scots that he will give up control of militia for 10 years and to accept Presbyterianism for 5 years provided there can be a controlled return to Episcopacy, but this is unacceptable;
   Enghien and the Duke of Orleans take Dunkirk; Piombino falls to French;
   the French under Harcourt are compelled to raise the siege of Lerida.
   Nov: The Great Elector of Brandenburg marries Louise, daughter of Frederick Henry of Orange.
   Dec: 24th, Charles I attempts to escape but plan fails;
   Henry, Prince of Condé, dies.

E Frederick Henry, Prince of Orange, becomes deranged;
   English occupy Bahamas.

F **Politics, Economics, Law and Education**
The schools at Port Royal, France, are fully organised, with special series of text books on logic, grammar and mathematics.

G **Science, Technology and Discovery**

H **Philosophy, Religion and Scholarship**
Jeremy Taylor, *A Discourse Concerning Prayer Ex Tempore; or, By Pretence of the Spirit* (anon.).
John Wilkins, *Ecclesiastes*: a discourse concerning the Gift of Preaching As it Falls Under the Rules of art.

J **Art, Sculpture, Fine Arts and Architecture**
Painting:
Jan van Goyen, *Village Church in the Sand Dunes*.
Murillo, *The Angel's Kitchen; The Miracle of San Diego*.
Rembrandt, *Adoration of the Shepherds*.
José Ribera, *St. Jerome*.

K **Music**

L **Literature (including Drama)**
Sir Thomas Browne, *Pseudodoxia Epidemica;* or, Enquiries into received tenets, and commonly presumed Truths (in the posthumous editions known as *Vulgar Errors*).
Pierre Corneille, *Rodogune* (tragedy).
Richard Crashaw, *Steps to the Temple*.
Jean de Rotrou, *Le Véritable Saint Genest* (religious tragedy).
James Shirley, *Poems* (containing *Narcissus*, and *The Triumph of Beautie* : a masque).
John Suckling, *Fragmenta Aurea* (including *Ballad upon a Wedding*).
Henry Vaughan, *Poems*.
Vida y hechos de Estebanillo González (anon. autobiographical picaresque novel).

M **Births and Deaths**
July 1st Gottfried Wilhelm von Leibniz b. (–1716).
Aug. 8th Godfrey Kneller b. (–1723).
Aug. 19th John Flamsteed b. (–1719).
— Jules Mansart b. (–1708).

A Jan: 30th, Scots agree to sell Charles I to Parliament for £400,000, the amount of their army's back-pay.
Feb:
Mar: 14th, by the Treaty of Ulm with France and Sweden the Elector of Bavaria and his brother, the Elector of Cologne, undertake to remain neutral until the end of the war;
—, William II succeeds in Holland on death of Frederick Henry, the Stadtholder.

B Apr: The Elector of Mainz and the Landgrave of Hesse withdraw from the war.
May: 18th, Commons vote to keep Fairfax as Commander-in-Chief but to disband most of the army, which causes conflict with the army.
Jun: 3rd, Oliver Cromwell flees from Parliament to the army at Triploe Heath and
4th, Cornet Joyce seizes Charles I at Holmby House as prisoner for the army;
14th, 'Representation of Army' setting out grievances and opposition to 11 Presbyterian members of Parliament, among them Holles.

C Jul: 7th, Naples revolts against Spain under Mananiello but, 16th, he is assassinated.
Aug: 2nd, English army presents proposals to the King which are rejected;
7th, army marches into London;
8th, Irish defeated by Parliamentary forces at Dangan Hill.
Sep: 1st, Cardinal Mazarin signs treaty with the Duke of Modena for the invasion of the Milanese;
by Treaty of Pilsen, Bavaria renounces Treaty of Ulm and renews alliance with Empire;
the French campaign in the Netherlands fails.

D Oct: 1st, Don John of Austria enters Naples Bay with Spanish forces;
Maximilian of Bavaria and the Elector of Cologne, breaking the Treaty of Ulm (*Mar.*), again intervene in the war on the Emperor Ferdinand III's side.
Nov: 11th, Charles I escapes but is captured and, 14th, imprisoned at Carisbrooke Castle;
a second revolution in Naples leads to the election of Guise as Duke of Naples.
Dec: 24th, 'Four Bills' are presented to King by Parliament but rejected (28th);
26th, Charles I concludes 'Engagement' with Scots to abolish Episcopacy and restore Presbyterianism. On the other hand, Scots agree to control militia, abolish army, call new Parliament, and restore the King by force if necessary.

E Alexis is faced with revolt in Moscow;
Swedish Africa Company is formed.

F **Politics, Economics, Law and Education**

Thomas Hobbes, *Elementa Philosophica de Cive*.

John Lilburne and others draft the Levellers' Manifesto (*Oct.*).

Chemnitz, *De Ratione Status in Imperio*, argues that the German constitution is German, not Roman, and attacks the leadership of the empire by the House of Hapsburg.

Thomas May, *The History of the Long Parliament* (to 1643).

Parliament appoints a commission to visit Oxford University, which leads to the dismissal of Anglican heads of colleges and professors.

The first newspaper advertisment, being an advertisement for the book *Divine Right of Church Government*, appears in issue no. 13 of *Perfect Occurrences of Every Daie journall in Parliament, and other Moderate Intelligence* (*Apr.*).

G **Science, Technology and Discovery**

Johann Hevel in *Selenographia* describes his discovery of the moon's libration in longitude and first charts the lunar surface.

Pecquet discovers the thoracic duct of the human body.

H **Philosophy, Religion and Scholarship**

Nathaniel Bacon, *An Historical Discourse of the Uniformity of the Government of England*, part 1 (completed –1651).

Sir Richard Fanshawe translates the pastoral play *Il Pastor Fido*, by Giovanni Battista Guarini (–1585).

Baltasar Gracián y Morales, *El Oráculo manual*.

Calvinists are acknowledged by the Lutherans.

J **Art, Sculpture, Fine Arts and Architecture**

Painting:

Peter Lely, *The young children of Charles I*; and *Double Portrait of Charles I and the Duke of York*.

Adriaen van Ostade, *Peasant family in an Interior*.

Paulus Potter, *Cattle and Sheep in a Stormy Landscape*.

José Ribera, *St. Paul the Hermit* (II).

K **Music**

L **Literature (including Drama)**

Francis Beaumont and John Fletcher, *Comedies and Tragedies* (a collection of 34 plays all previously unpublished).

Abraham Cowley, *The Mistress; or Several Copies of Love-Verses*.

Gautier des Costes, Sieur de La Calprenède, *Cléopâtre*, 12 vols. (completed –1657).

Henry More, *Philosophical Poems*.

Jean Rotrou, *Vencelas* (political drama).

M **Births and Deaths**

Apr. 10th John Wilmot, Earl of Rochester, b. (–1680).

June 12th Thomas Farnaby d. (*c.* 72).

July 22nd Marguerite-Marie Alacoque b. (–1690).

Oct. 25th Evangelista Torricelli d. (39).

Nov. 10th Pierre Bayle b. (–1706).

1648   Peace of Westphalia—Outbreak of Second Civil War—Beginning of Fronde

A **Jan:** Oliver Cromwell's speech demanding no allegiance to Charles I;
   30th, Peace between Spain and Netherlands at Münster, defeating Cardinal Mazarin's plan of securing the Spanish Netherlands.
Feb: 11th, Parliamentary 'Declaration' sets out Charles I's misdeeds;
   21st, Frederick III succeeds in Denmark on death of Christian IV (–1670).
Mar:

B **Apr:** Naples is restored to Spanish rule by Don John.
May: 1st, Scots begin Second Civil War;
   2nd, Blasphemy Act is passed at Westminster;
   Cossacks defeat the Poles;
   17th, Turenne defeats the Elector of Bavaria at Zusmarshausen.
Jun:

C **Jul:** 13th, the French take Tortosa.
Aug: 17th–20th, Oliver Cromwell defeats Scots at Preston;
   20th, Condé's victory at Lens hastens the peace negotiations;
   26th–27th, Paris mob rises, which signifies outbreak of Fronde (–*Apr.* 1649);
   27th, Fairfax takes Colchester.
Sep: 18th, Parliament opens negotiations with Charles I at so-called Treaty of Newport and
   28th, Charles I offers some concessions regarding control of armed forces and Presbyterianism.

D **Oct:** 2nd, Parliament rejects Charles I's concessions (*Sept.* 28th);
   24th, Peace of Westphalia ends 30 Years War: by its terms: (1) Sweden obtains Hither Pomerania, part of Farther Pomerania, Rügen, Wismar, and gains access to mouths of Rivers Elbe, Weser and Oder as well as an indemnity of six million rix dollars, and the bishoprics of Bremen and Verden; (2) France obtains Alsace, Breisach and absolute sovereignty over Metz, Toul and Verdun; (3) Brandenburg receives Halberstadt, Minden, Kammin and Magdeburg in return for losses in Pomerania; (4) independence of Netherlands, German states and the Swiss cantons is guaranteed; (5) problems of ecclesiastical estates to be settled in accordance with conditions existing on *Jan.* 1st, 1624; (6) Bavaria retains the electoral dignity; (7) the independence of the States of Germany is recognised by the Emperor; their rulers can make treaties with foreign powers provided they are not directed against the Empire. France and Sweden acquire rights of interference in the Empire;
   27th, English Parliament rejects offer of further concessions by Charles I.
Nov: 26th, Pope Innocent X condemns Peace of Westphalia in the bull *Zelo Domus Dei*;
   27th, Parliamentary Commissioners leave Newport.
Dec: 6th, Colonel Pride's Purge of the House of Commons, removing many Presbyterian members; the remainder is known as the 'Rump' (of the Long Parliament), which subsequently votes to discontinue negotiations with Charles I;
   23rd, Parliament votes to bring Charles I to trial.

E   John II (John Casimir) succeeds his brother, Ladislaus IV, in Poland;
   Charles Louis, son of Frederick V of Palatinate, is created eighth Elector after Peace of Westphalia;
   Rioting in Moscow occasioned by heavy taxation;
   Arabs take Muscat from Portuguese.

F **Politics, Economics, Law and Education**
John Lilburne, *The Foundations of Freedom.*
The Book of the General Lawes and Libertyes of Massachusetts.

G **Science, Technology and Discovery**
J. R. Glauber obtains hydrochloric acid.
J. B. van Helmont in *Ortus medicinae* (posth.) invents the term 'gas', for describing carbon monoxide.
John Wilkins, *Mathematical Magic.*
Roilau studies skin diseases.

H **Philosophy, Religion and Scholarship**
Richard Hooker, *Of the Lawes of Ecclesiasticall Politie*, books VI and VIII (posth.) (–1594).
John Stearne, *Confirmation and Discovery of Witchcraft.*
Jeremy Taylor, *Of the Liberty of Prophesying* (i.e. of Preaching).
George Fox starts his Society of Friends.
Parliament approves the Longer and Shorter Westminster Catechisms.
Thomas Hooker, *Survey of the Summe of Church Discipline.*
The Treaty of Westphalia extends recognition to the Calvinists, but Innocent X declares it is not binding.

J **Art, Sculpture, Fine Arts and Architecture**
Painting:
Claude, *Embarcation of the Queen of Sheba.*
Paulus Potter, *Cow Reflected in the Water.*
José Ribera, *The Holy Family with St. Catherine.*
Ter Borch, *The Swearing of the Oath of Ratification of The Treaty of Münster.*
Architecture:
Jacob Van Campen, Town Hall, Amsterdam (–1655).

K **Music**
Heinrich Schütz, *Musicalia ad Chorum Sacrum.*

L **Literature (including Drama)**
Robert Herrick, *Hesperides;* or, The Workes Both Humane and Divine (with *Noble Numbers*).

M **Births and Deaths**
Feb. 21st Christian IV of Denmark and Norway d. (71).
Apr. 4th Grinling Gibbons b. (–1721).
Aug. 20th Edward, Lord Herbert of Cherbury, d. (64).
Sept. 10th Nicholas Desmaretz b. (–1721).
— John Blow b. (–1708).
— George Jeffreys b. (–1689).

A Jan: 15th, the French Court leaves Paris; opening of the 12-weeks war in the Fronde;
19th, trial of Charles I opens and
30th, he is beheaded. The Prince of Wales, in exile at The Hague, takes the title
Charles II.

Feb: 5th, Scots proclaim Charles II as King in Edinburgh and later in year Irish rise in
his favour under Ormonde.

Mar: 11th, Treaty of Ruel ends first Fronde after the rebels have been forced to treat;
17th, English Parliament abolishes House of Lords and, 19th, abolishes the monarchy;
28th, Leveller leaders are arrested.

B Apr:
May: 15th, the Levellers are defeated at Burford;
19th, England is declared to be a Commonwealth.
Jun:

C Jul:
Aug: 18th, the French Court returns to Paris;
Sultan Ibrahim is deposed and murdered; he is succeeded by Mohammed IV (–1687).
Sep: 11th, Oliver Cromwell sacks Drogheda and

D Oct: 11th, sacks Wexford.
Nov:
Dec: Unrest in France with riots in Paris signify outbreak of second Fronde; Condé
charges leaders of old Fronde with attempted murder.

E Russia abolishes privileges of English traders;
The Holy Roman Empire establishes standing army;
The Persians capture Kandahar.

F **Politics, Economics, Law and Education**

John Milton, *The Tenure of Kings and Magistrates*, a defence of the execution of Charles I.

John Gauden, *Eikon Basilike*, compiled partly from Charles I's notes, defends monarchy and the image of the late King, but is answered by Milton, *Eikonoklastes*.

The Diggers begin to work at St. George's Hill, Surrey, and on being prosecuted denounce the institution of private property.

John Lilburne, *An Agreement of the Free People of England* and *The Legall, Fundamental Liberties of the People of England Revived, Asserted and Vindicated*.

An outcry of the Young Men and Apprentices of London (tract).

English becomes the language of all legal documents in place of Latin (until 1660; reintroduced 1733).

Lay patronage is abolished in Scotland.

Providence (later Annapolis, Maryland) is settled by Puritan exiles from Virginia. The Maryland Assembly passes a Toleration Act for Christians professing belief in the Trinity.

P. Chamberlen, *The Poore Man's Advocate*, proposals for the employment of the poor.

G **Science, Technology and Discovery**

Isbrand de Diemerbroek, *De Peste*, a study of the plague.

Blith, *Treatise on Drainage*.

H **Philosophy, Religion and Scholarship**

René Descartes, *Les Passiones de l'âme*.

John Donne, *Fifty Sermons* (posth.).

James Howell, *A Description of the Country of Scotland*.

William Prynne, *An Historical Collection of the Ancient Parliaments of England*.

J **Art, Sculpture, Fine Arts and Architecture**

Painting:

Ter Borch, *Philip IV of Spain*.

K **Music**

L **Literature (including Drama)**

Andreas Gryphius, *Carolus Stuardus* (tragedy).

Richard Lovelace, *Lucasta*.

Madeleine de Scudéry, *Le Grand Cyrus*, vol. 1 (–1653).

Friedrich Spee von Langenfeld, *Trutznachtigall* (posth.) (lyrical religious poems).

M **Births and Deaths**

Mar. 26th John Winthrop d. (61).

Apr. 9th James Scott, Duke of Monmouth, b. (–1685).

Aug. 21st Richard Crashaw d. (?36).

Aug. — Endymion Porter d. (62).

Nov. 6th Owen Roe O'Neill d. (*c*. 59).

Dec. 4th William Drummond of Hawthornden d. (63).

— John Graham of Claverhouse b. (–1689).

— Louise de Kéroualle, Duchess of Portsmouth, b. (–1734).

— Titus Oates b. (–1705).

1650   Second Fronde

A Jan: 18th, Fronde leaders, including Condé, are imprisoned, and Cardinal Mazarin
allies with leaders of old Fronde.
Feb:
Mar:

B Apr: 27th, Montrose is defeated at Carbisdale and is subsequently executed;
30th, Turenne concludes treaty for French rebels with Spain.
May: 21st, Montrose is executed.
Jun: 23rd, Charles II's vessel arrives at Speymouth and, 24th, he lands;
peace Treaty of Nuremberg between Emperor and Sweden amplifies Peace of Westphalia.

C Jul:
Aug: 1st, Cromwell forms a permanent economic council.
Sep: Cromwell defeats Scots at Dunbar;
29th, French *Parlement* imposes peace on Bordeaux which virtually ends the second
Fronde.

D Oct:
Nov: 6th, the Stadtholder William II dies in Holland.
Dec: 15th, Royalist army defeats Vicomte Turenne and the Archduke Leopold at
Rethel;
24th, Edinburgh Castle surrenders to Cromwell.

E Dutch and English define frontiers of their respective North American colonies.

June 24th John Churchill, Duke of Marlborough, b. (–1722).
June 28th Jean de Rotron d. (50).
Sept. 23rd Jeremy Collier b. (–1726).
Nov. 4th William III b. (–1702).
— Leonardo de Figueroa b. (–1730).
— Phineas Fletcher d. (68).
— George Rooke b. (–1709).

F Politics, Economics, Law and Education
Thomas Hobbes, *The Elements of Law, Moral and Political* (written 1640).
Matthew Hale, *Analysis of the Civil Law*, proposes a system of codification of the laws of England.
H. Halhead, *Inclosures thrown open; or depopulation depopulated.*
Jean Loret's rhymed *Gazette* is issued in Paris (–1665).
Harvard College receives a charter.

G Science, Technology and Discovery
Maria Cunitz, *Urana propitia.*
Jean Brauhin, *Historia plantarum nova et absolutissima* (–1651; posth.).
Otto von Guericke invents the air pump and proves that the air presses with equal force in all directions.
Glisson, *Treatise on Rickets.*
Bernhard Varenius, *Geographia generalis.*
Sir R. Weston, *A Discours of Husbandrie Used in Brabant and Flanders . . . serving as a Pattern for this Commonwealth* (ed. S. Hartlib), draws attention to the cultivation of turnips.

H Philosophy, Religion and Scholarship
Richard Baxter, *The Saints' Everlasting Rest.*
René Descartes, *Traité des Passions de L'ame.*
Gilles Ménage, *Dictionnaire étymologique; ou, Les Origines de la langue française* (completed –1694).
Jeremy Taylor, *Rule and Exercises of Holy Living* (–1651).
James Usher, *Annales Veteris et Novi Testamenti* (–1654; fixes Creation at 4004 B.C., in a scriptural chronology).
Joost van den Vondel, *Manual of Dutch Poetry.*
Mr. Justice Bennet, at Derby, uses the term *Quakers*, of George Fox and his followers, because, said Fox, 'I bid them Tremble at the word of the Lord'.

J Art, Sculpture, Fine Arts and Architecture
Painting:
Philippe de Champaigne, *Portrait of an Unknown Man.*
Jan van Goyen, *View of Dordrecht.*
Murillo, *The Holy Family with the Little Bird.*
Ter Borch, *The Visitors.*
Architecture:
Bernini, Palazzo di Montecirorio.

K Music

L Literature (including Drama)
Pierre Corneille, *Andromède* (tragi-comedy).
Andreas Gryphius, *Leo Arminius* (tragedy).
Henry Vaughan, *Silex Scintillans* (containing *The Retreat* and *Beyond the Veil*).
Anne Bradstreet, *The Tenth Muse Lately Sprung Up in America* (poems).

M Births and Deaths
Feb. 11th René Descartes d. (53).
Apr. 18th Simon D'Ewes d. (48).
May 21st James, Marquess of Montrose, d. (38).
(Continued opposite)

A Jan: 1st, Scots crown Charles II at Scone.
   Feb: 6th–7th, Cardinal Mazarin is forced to flee from Paris during night after *Parlement*
   votes for release of Condé and other Fronde leaders, and, 13th, despite agreeing to
   release them, Mazarin fails to regain support.
   Mar: Beginning of formation of Catholic and Protestant Leagues in German States to
   carry out terms of Peace of Westphalia. The Catholic League of Frankfort is composed
   of the three ecclesiastical electors, the Count Palatine and the Bishop of Münster;
   later it is joined by the Circles of Swabia, Franconia and Lower Saxony. The Protestant League is formed by Queen Christina of Sweden, the Landgravine of Hesse and
   the Dukes of Brunswick and Luxemburg.

B Apr:
   May:
   Jun: 3rd, Ireton lays siege to Limerick;
   the Cossacks make a treaty with Tsar Alexis.

C Jul: The Poles defeat the Cossacks and their allies, the Tartars.
   Aug: 2nd, Oliver Cromwell takes Perth;
   17th, Queen of France allies with the new Fronde against Condé.
   Sep: 3rd, Oliver Cromwell defeats Charles at Worcester and Charles flees to France
   (*Oct.* 17th);
   7th, Louis XIV attains majority and at the same time charges against Condé are withdrawn; but he leaves Paris and subsequently allies with Spain, although Turenne
   refuses to fight the King now that the regency is over.

D Oct: first English Navigation Act, designed to give English Ships monopoly of foreign
   trade, is passed, aimed especially at the Dutch;
   27th, surrender of Limerick after long siege.
   Nov:
   Dec: Condé is attainted of treason in the Paris *Parlement*.

E St. Helena is occupied by East India Company and is established as a station;
   Ietsuna becomes Shogun of Japan and subsequently overcomes two revolts in Edo.

F **Politics, Economics, Law and Education**

Thomas Hobbes, *Leviathan;* and *Philosophical Rudiments Concerning Government and Society* (a translation of *De Cive*, 1642).

John Milton, *Defensio Pro Populo Anglicano*, a reply to Salmasius, who attacked the execution of Charles I.

The East India Company occupies St. Helena.

G **Science, Technology and Discovery**

William Harvey, *Exercitationes de generatione animalium*, a treatise on generation, which founds the study of embryology.

H **Philosophy, Religion and Scholarship**

John Donne, *Essays in Divinity; Letters* (to Several Persons of Honour) (posth.).

William Laud, *Sermons*.

Honorat de Bueil, Sire de Racan, *Psaumes et poésies chrétiennes*.

Jeremy Taylor, *Rule and Exercises of Holy Dying* (–1650).

Roger Williams, *The Bloudy Tenent Yet More Bloudy*.

Sir Henry Wotton, *Reliquiae Wottonianae*.

Cardinal Mazarin's Library, Paris, is closed, and books ordered to be sold, by *Parlement*, under *La Fronde*.

J **Art, Sculpture, Fine Arts and Architecture**

Painting:

Paulus Potter, *Landscape with cows, sheep and horses by a barn*.

David Teniers, *Village Feast*.

Sculpture:

Bernini, portrait bust of Duke Francis I d'Este.

K **Music**

Louis XIV, aged 12, dances in his first court ballet.

L **Literature (including Drama)**

William Cartwright, *Comedies*, *Tragi-Comedies* (containing *The Royal Slave* and *The Siege*).

John Cleveland, *Poems*.

Sir William D'Avenant, *Gondibert*.

Baltasar Gracián y Morales, *El Criticon* (–1657; allegorical novel).

Paul Scarron, *Le Roman comique*.

Thomas Stanley, *Collected Poems* (with translations).

Izaak Walton, *The Life of Wotton*.

M **Births and Deaths**

Feb. 2nd Nell Gwyn b. (–1687).

July 5th Inigo Jones d. (77).

Aug. 6th François de la Mothe-Fénelon b. (–1715).

Oct. 15th James Stanley, Earl of Derby, d. (44).

Nov. 26th Henry Ireton d. (40).

— William, Duke of Hamilton, d. (35).

A Jan: 24th, Duke of Orleans joins French rebels on news of Cardinal Mazarin's recall, but his defection is counteracted by Turenne's subsequent arrival at Court.
Feb: English Parliament passes Act of Pardon and Oblivion to reconcile Royalists;
  Treaty of Hildesheim between Sweden and north German Protestant States.
Mar: 29th, Turenne's victory over Frondeurs at Jargeau.

B Apr: 7th, Condé defeats Royalist army at Bléneau;
  Dutch, under Van Riebeeck found Capetown.
May: 4th, rebels, aided by Condé's Spanish mercenaries, in France are defeated at Etampes by Royalist forces under Turenne;
  19th–29th, English defeat Dutch at battle of the Downs off Folkestone before war is actually declared;
  the Spanish take Gravelines.
Jun: 30th/*July* 10th, English declare war on Dutch.

C Jul: 2nd, Turenne defeats Condé in the Faubourg St. Antoine, Paris, but has to withdraw. Provisional Fronde government is set up in Paris after rising of *June*.
Aug: 2nd, Army rejects Perpetuation Bill and petitions for a new Parliament and for reforms;
  12th, Act of Settlement for Ireland;
  19th, Mazarin leaves France and offers general amnesty.
Sep: The Spanish take Dunkirk;
  28th–*Oct*. 8th, English victory off Kentish Knock.

D Oct: 21st, King Louis XIV returns to Paris and government is re-established. Leading Frondeurs are exiled. Cardinal Mazarin is recalled.
Nov: 30th/*Dec*. 10th, Dutch under Van Tromp defeat English off Dungeness;
  Condé signs alliances with Philip of Spain and the Duke of Lorraine.
Dec:

E Don John of Austria suppresses revolt in Catalonia;
  Governor of Maryland suspends government and assumes control.

F **Politics, Economics, Law and Education**

Gerrard Winstanley, *The Law of Freedom in a Platform*, expounds a system of communism, with the prohibition of buying and selling and the institution of civil marriage.

Maine is joined to Massachusetts Colony.

The Dutch found Cape Town.

Christopher Bowman opens the first Coffee House in London (later known as the 'Pasqua Rosee') in St. Michael's Alley, Cornhill.

G **Science, Technology and Discovery**

The German Scientific Academy, Naturae Curiosi is founded.

H **Philosophy, Religion and Scholarship**

Jean-Louis Guez de Balzac, *Socrate chrétien* (religious dialogues and essays).

Nathanael Culverwell, *Of the Light of Nature*.

John Donne, *Paradoxes, Problems, Essays, Characters* (posth.).

Henry Vaughan, *The Mount of Olives* (devotions).

Roger Williams, *The Hireling Ministry None of Christ's*.

J **Art, Sculpture, Fine Arts and Architecture**

Painting:

Carel Fabritius, *View of Delft*.

Adriaen van Ostade, *Cottage Dancers*.

Rembrandt, *Hendrickje Stoffels*.

José Ribera, *St. Jerome listening to the celestial trumpet*.

K **Music**

John Hilton, *Catch as Catch Can: A Choice Collection of Catches, Rounds and Canons for Three or Four Voyces*.

L **Literature (including Drama)**

Pierre Corneille, *Nicomède* (tragedy).

Sir Fulke Greville (Lord Brooke), *The Life of Sir Philip Sidney*.

George Herbert, *Remains* (posth.), edited by Barnabas Oley (includes the prose work *A Priest To The Temple*).

Johann Lauremberg, *Veer Schertz-Gedichte* (comic poems in the Low-German dialect).

Arte de Furtar (anon. satire on Portuguese society and official corruption; spurious author António Vieira; probable author Manuel de Melo).

M **Births and Deaths**

Mar. 3rd Thomas Otway b. (–1685).

June — William Dampier b. (–1715).

July 17th Edward Sackville, Earl of Dorset, d. (61).

Dec. 23rd John Cotton d. (67).

— Nahum Tate b. (–1715).

A Jan:
   Feb: 3rd, Cardinal Mazarin returns to Paris;
      7th, Fouquet is appointed Superintendent of Finances;
      18th/28th, English defeat Dutch off Portland.
   Mar:

B Apr: 20th, Cromwell expels Long Parliament for trying to pass Perpetuation Bill;
      29th, Cromwell sets up small council of 10 members.
   May: 24th, Ferdinand III elected Emperor (dies *July* 9th, 1654).
   Jun: 2nd–3rd/12th–13th, Dutch are defeated off North Foreland.

C Jul: 4th, Little, or Barebones, Parliament meets (–*Dec.* 12th);
      31st, Fronde surrenders in Bordeaux;
      31st/*Aug.* 9th, English are victorious against Dutch fleet off Texel.
   Aug: 5th, Brandenburg establishes standing army; the Great Elector suppresses his Diet.
   Sep: 26th, 'Act of Satisfaction' for distribution of forfeited lands in Ireland.

D Oct:
   Nov: The French capture Saint Menehould from the Spanish.
   Dec: 16th, by the Instrument of Government a Protectorate is set up in England with a
      Council of State and Oliver Cromwell as Protector, following the resignation of
      Parliament (12th).

E John de Witt becomes Grand Pensionary in Holland;
   Peasant's Revolt in Bern under Leuenberg.

F **Politics, Economics, Law and Education**

R. Filmer, *Quaestio quod libetica, or a discourse whether it be lawfull to take use for money*, an examination of R. Fenton's *Treatie of Usurie* (1612).

G **Science, Technology and Discovery**

H **Philosophy, Religion and Scholarship**

Rabelais, bks. 1 and 2, translated by Sir Thomas Urquhart (complete work –1708).
Chetham's Library, Manchester, founded.
James Naylor is recognised by his English followers as the Messiah. The rise of the 'Fifth Monarchy' men.

J **Art, Sculpture, Fine Arts and Architecture**

Painting:

Jan van Goyen, *View of the Rhine.*
Peter Lely, *Cromwell.*
Ter Borch, *The Dispatch.*
Willem van de Velde, *Dutch men of war and small vessels in a strong breeze.*

Architecture:

Francesco Borromini, St. Agnese, Rome; and St. Andrea della Fratte (–1665).

K **Music**

Matthew Locke, music for the masque *Cupid and Death.*
Lully, music for Bensarade's ballet *La Nuit*, in which Louis XIV dances the part of 'Le Roi Soleil'.
Lully is appointed director of *Les Petits-violons.*

L **Literature (including Drama)**

Thomas Middleton, *The Changeling; The Spanish Gipsie* (tragi-comedies written with William Rowley).
Jean Baptiste Poquelin Molière, *L'Étourdi* (comedy).
Madeleine de Scudéry, *Artamène ou Le Grand Cyrus* (completed in 10 vols. English translation started).
James Shirley, *Six New Playes* (including *The Cardinall*, a tragedy).
Isaak Walton, *The Compleat Angler* (–1676).

M **Births and Deaths**

Feb. 12th Archangelo Corelli b. (–1713).
Mar. 10th John Benbow b. (–1702).
May 8th Claude de Villars b. (–1734).
June 22nd André-Hercule de Fleury b. (–1743).
Oct. 25th Théophraste Renandot d. (67).
— Robert Filmer d. (*c.* 51).

**1654   Union of England, Scotland and Ireland—Queen Christina
         abdicates**

A Jan:
   Feb: Ferdinand III presides at the Diet of Ratisbon to confirm the provisions of the
       Peace of Westphalia of 1648.
   Mar: Surrender of Breisach signifies end of Fronde.

B Apr: 5th/15th, peace Treaty of Westminster ends first Anglo-Dutch War. The Dutch
       agree to recognise Navigation Acts;
       11th/21st, Treaty of Commerce between England and Sweden;
       12th, Union of Ireland and Scotland with England, promising free trade and representa-
       tion in Parliament at Westminster.
   May: The Cossacks place themselves under the protection of Tsar John Alexis.
   Jun: 6th, Christina of Sweden abdicates and subsequently becomes a Catholic; she is
       succeeded by Charles X (–1660);
       7th, coronation of Louis XIV at Rheims;
       9th, death of Ferdinand IV, King of Romans (who was to have succeeded his father as
       Emperor).

C Jul: 10th/20th, Anglo-Portuguese treaty placing Portugal under English control, follows
       commercial treaty of 1653.
   Aug: 5th, French take Stenay;
       24th, Condé raises the siege of Arras.
   Sep: 3rd, meeting of first Protectorate Parliament;
       10th, Tsar Alexis takes Smolensk after outbreak of war with Poland (–1667);
       12th, 100 irreconcilable republicans excluded from Parliament, but, 15th, Oliver
       Cromwell readmits them after they agree to his proposals;
       15th/25th, Anglo-Danish treaty of commerce.

D Oct: The Province of Holland passes an Act of exclusion against William III.
   Nov:
   Dec:

E Dutch are finally driven out of Brazil by Portuguese;
   Gambia becomes a colony of James, Duke of Courland.

F **Politics, Economics, Law and Education**

John Milton, *Defensio Secunda*, a reply to Peter Dumoulin, who had written in protest of Milton's *Defensio Pro Populo Anglicano*, defending the execution of Charles I in 1651.

Conring, *De Finibus Imperii Germanici* discusses the relations between the German States and the Holy Roman Empire.

Duisburg University is founded.

John Amos Comenius (Komensky) publishes in Nuremberg the first picture-book for children, *Orbis Sensualium Pictus*, the world in pictures with a Latin-German text.

G **Science, Technology and Discovery**

Otto von Guericke makes further experiments with the Magdeburg hemispheres to demonstrate the law of air pressures (see 1650).

Pascal and Fermat found the theory of probabilities.

Glisson discovers 'Glisson's Capsules', the fibrous sheath of the human liver.

The professors of Astronomy and Mathematics at Oxford expose Thomas Hobbes's ignorance of science.

H **Philosophy, Religion and Scholarship**

François Hedelin, Abbé d'Aubignac, *Histoire du temps ou relation du royaume de Coquetterie* (first use of the critical term *précieuse*).

[Edward Johnson], *A History of New-England* (i.e. *The Wonder-Working of Providence of Sions Saviour in New-England* (published in London).

Brian Walton, *London Polyglott Bible* (–1657).

Blaise Pascal retires to Port-Royal.

Cromwell's 'Triers' and 'Ejectors' secure the appointment of Puritan ministers to English parish churches.

J **Art, Sculpture, Fine Arts and Architecture**

Painting:

Carel Fabritius, *The Linnet;* and *Young man in a fur cap.*

Pieter de Hooch, *Delft after the Explosion.*

Lely, *The Duet.*

Rembrandt, *Jan Six.*

Architecture:

Webb, Lamport Hall, Northamptonshire; and The Vyne, near Basingstoke, Hampshire (–1657).

K **Music**

L **Literature (including Drama)**

Savinien Cyrano de Bergerac, *Le Pedant joué* (comedy).

George Chapman, *Revenge for Honour* (tragedy).

Friedrich von Logau, *Epigrams.*

Molière, *Le Dépit amoureux* (comedy).

Madeleine de Scudéry, *Clélie : histoire romaine* (10 vols. –1660).

Joost van den Vondel, *Lucifer* (drama).

John Webster, *Appius and Virginia* (tragedy).

M **Births and Deaths**

June 10th Alessandro Algardi d. (52).

Aug. 28th Axel Gustafsson (Oxenstjerna) d. (69).

Nov. 30th William Habington d. (49).

Nov. 30th John Selden d. (69).

Dec. 27th Jacques Bernoulli b. (–1705).

— Louis Joseph, Duke of Vendôme, b. (–1712).

1655   Opening of the First Northern War—English occupy Jamaica—
Vaudois Massacres

A Jan: 22nd, Oliver Cromwell dissolves Parliament.
Feb:
Mar: 11th (–14th), rising in Wiltshire led by Colonel John Penruddock, who is subsequently executed.

B Apr: 28th, Blake destroys pirate fleet from Bey of Tunis and releases prisoners in Algiers;
Protestants in the Vaudois district of Savoy are massacred.
May: 4th, English force under Penn and Venables in San Domingo leaves and embarks for Jamaica, which is soon captured.
Jun:

C Jul: 27th, the Great Elector of Brandenburg concludes treaty of defence with Dutch;
outbreak of First Northern War when Charles X invades Poland;
the Great Elector invades Prussia, to resist Swedish advance.
Aug: 9th, Cromwell divides England into 11 districts, each with a major-general as governor;
23rd, Charles X defeats John Casimir of Poland and, 30th, takes Warsaw;
French win victories in Spanish Netherlands, with help of troops from Lorraine (after arrest of Duke Charles by Spaniards, *Feb.* 1654).
Sep:

D Oct: 8th, Charles X takes Cracow;
24th/*Nov.* 3rd, Anglo-French treaty against Spain; for expulsion of Charles II from France; for end of persecution of Vaudois by Savoy, and also commercial terms.
Nov: 24th, Cromwell prohibits Anglican services.
Dec: The Great Elector, attacked by Charles X of Sweden, is forced to submit.

E Dutch annex New Sweden;
Pope Alexander VII elected in succession to Innocent X;
Plan by Zurich for centralised Swiss State is rejected by Catholic Cantons;
Russia builds forts on R. Amur.

F **Politics, Economics, Law and Education**

G **Science, Technology and Discovery**

John Wallis, *Arithmetica Infinitorum*, a treatise on conic sections, in which he treats curves by the Cartesian method.

H **Philosophy, Religion and Scholarship**

Lieuwe van Aitzema, *Saken van Staet in Oorlogh in ende omtrent de Vereenigte Nederlanden* (14 vols. –1671).

Pierre Borel, *Dictionnaire des termes du vieux françois; ou, Trésor des recherches et antiquites gauloises et françoises.*

William Drummond, *A History of the Five Jameses* (the Kings of Scotland from 1423 to 1524).

François Dujon (Franciscus Junius) edits the scriptural verses attributed to Caedmon (from Bodleian mss. *c.* 1000).

Sir William Dugdale and Roger Dodsworth, *Monasticon Anglicanum* (–1673).

Sir Richard Fanshawe translates the *Lusiads* from the Portuguese of Camoens.

Thomas Fuller, *Church History of Britain* (to 1648), book 12 being *A History of the University of Cambridge.*

Thomas Hobbes, *Elementorum Philosophiae* (*De Corpore*) (–1658).

Sir William Lower translates the *Polyeucte* of Pierre Corneille (classical tragedy).

John Spottiswoode, *A History of the Church and State of Scotland.*

Thomas Stanley, *A History of Philosophy* (–1662; collected –1687).

Jeremy Taylor, *The Golden Grove; or A Manual of Daily Prayers. . . .*

The Jews readmitted into England by Cromwell (*Dec.* 14th; –1656).

J **Art, Sculpture, Fine Arts and Architecture**

Painting:

Jacob Jordaens, *Presentation at the Temple.*

Nicholaes Maes, *Woman Scraping Parsnips;* and *The Idle Servant.*

Rembrandt, *Woman Bathing in a Stream.*

Architecture:

Francesco Borromini, St. Maria dei Sette Dolori (–1665).

K **Music**

Lully bans shawms in favour of oboes for indoor performances at the French court.

L **Literature (including Drama)**

John Cotgrave, *The English Treasury of Literature and Language; The Wit's Interpreter.*

Philip Massinger, *Three New Plays* ('never printed before', posth.; containing tragicomedies: *The Bashful Lover; A Very Woman;* and a comedy *The Guardian*).

James Shirley, *The Gentleman of Venice* (tragi-comedy); *The Politician* (tragedy).

William Strode, *The Floating Island* (a political drama).

Henry Vaughan, *Silex Scintillans* (parts 1 and 2).

M **Births and Deaths**

Sept. — Savinien Cyrano de Bergerac d. (36).

Oct. 24th Pierre Gassendi d. (63).

— Fletcher of Saltoun (Andrew Fletcher) b. (–1716).

A Jan: 17th, Treaty of Königsberg between Brandenburg and Sweden, where Prussia becomes a fief of Charles X;

24th, Protestant cantons of Zurich and Bern are defeated by Catholics at Villmergen (first Villmergen War).

Feb: 24th, alliance of Brandenburg and France;

Spain declares war on England and subsequently signs treaty with Charles II.

Mar: Swedish armies overrun Poland.

B Apr:

May:

Jun: 15th/25th, Swedish-Brandenburg alliance at Marienberg;

further treaty of commerce between England and Sweden;

Sweden's Baltic regions are invaded by Russians.

C Jul: 29th (–31st), Poles under John Casimir are defeated at Warsaw by combined Swedish-Brandenburg force.

Aug: Cardinal Mazarin and the Duke of Orleans are reconciled.

Sep: 5th/15th, Treaty of Amity between England and France after failure of Mazarin's negotiations with Spain;

9th/19th, Spanish treasure ships are captured off Cadiz by Robert Blake;

17th, second Protectorate Parliament meets (–*June* 1657);

Turenne takes La Capelle from the Spanish.

D Oct:

Nov: 3rd, Treaty of Vilna between Russia and Poland;

20th, by the Treaty of Labiau, Sweden cedes Prussia to the Great Elector of Brandenburg.

Dec: 1st, Empire agrees to help Poland by Treaty of Alliance.

E Alfonso VI succeeds as King of Portugal on the death of John IV;

Mohammed Kiuprili becomes Grand Vizier of Mohammed IV in Turkey;

Dutch enter Chinese trade and also take Colombo from Portuguese.

F **Politics, Economics, Law and Education**
M. Nedham, *The Excellency of a Free State*.
James Harrington, *Commonwealth of Oceana* expounds a system of republicanism on the lines of the Venetian oligarchy, suggests reforms in education and in Parliamentary representation and advocates votes by ballot and public service by rotation.
Riksbank, Stockholm, is established by Palmstruck.

G **Science, Technology and Discovery**
C. Huygens observes the satellites of Saturn.

H **Philosophy, Religion and Scholarship**
John Bunyan, *Some Gospel Truths Opened*.
John Davies translation of *Clélie* by Scudéry (concluded 1661, with George Havers).
Sir John Denham, *Destruction of Troy* (a verse paraphrase from Virgil, with an essay on translation; anon.).
Sir William Dugdale, *Antiquities of Warwickshire*.
Thomas Hobbes, *Elementorum Philosophiae* (*De Corpore*) translated.
Manasseh ben Israel, *Vindiciae Judaeorum* (replying to Prynne's and other attacks, on the readmission of Jews –1655).
[Blaise Pascal] *Lettres Provinciales* (–1657, 1660).
Cardinal Pallavicino's *Istoria del Concilio di Trento*.

J **Art, Sculpture, Fine Arts and Architecture**
Painting:
Rembrandt, *Titus Reading*.
Velazquez, *Las Meninas*.
Vermeer, *The Procuress*.
Architecture:
Bernini, Piazza, St. Peter's, Rome; also façade St. Maria della Pace, Rome (–1657).
Landscape Gardening:
André le Nôtre, Gardens, Vaux-le-Viscomte (–1661).

K **Music**
Davenant's *The Siege of Rhodes*, music by Locke, Lawes, Crooke, Colman and Hudson, is first English opera performed in London.

L **Literature (including Drama)**
Jean Chapelain, *La Pucelle* (12 cantos; the completion, in 12 additional cantos, published posthumously, 1882).
Abraham Cowley, *Poems*.
John Ford, *The Sun's Darling* (dramatic masque; posth.).

M **Births and Deaths**
Mar. 20th Archbishop James Ussher d. (75).
Aug. 11th Octavio Piccolomini d. (56).
Sept. 6th Guillaume Dubois b. (–1723).
Sept. 8th Joseph Hall d. (82).
Oct. 29th Edmund Halley b. (–1742).
— Charles Davenant b. (–1714).
— Jacob Tonson b. (–1736).

A Jan:
   Feb:
   Mar: 13th/23rd, Treaty of Paris between England and France against Spain, for a joint attack on Gravelines and Dunkirk;
   31st, Humble Petition and Advice, offers title of King to Oliver Cromwell who subsequently rejects offer (*Apr.* 3rd).

B Apr: 2nd, Emperor Ferdinand III dies (Leopold I is elected his successor in *July* 1658);
   20th/30th, English navy under Robert Blake defeats Spanish fleet off Santa Cruz.
   May: 25th, New Humble Petition and Advice creates new House of Lords, and increases Cromwell's power;
   Louis XIV puts forward his name as a candidate for the Holy Roman Empire.
   Jun: 26th, Additional Petition and Advice enhances power of Parliament, and Cromwell is installed as Protector for the second time;
   Condé forces Turenne to raise the siege of Cambrai.

C Jul: Denmark attacks Charles X of Sweden, who is already campaigning against Russia, Poland and Austria.
   Aug:
   the French take Montmidi in Luxemburg.
   Sep: 19th, by Treaty of Wehlau, Poland renounces sovereignty of Prussia on behalf of Brandenburg.

D Oct: 3rd, French under Turenne capture Mardyke which becomes an English garrison town under the terms of the Treaty of Paris (of *Mar.*).
   Nov: 6th, by Treaty of Bromberg, Brandenburg allies with Poland against Sweden;
   10th, Brandenburg makes an offensive alliance with Denmark.
   Dec:

E Dutch war against Portuguese in Brazil;
   The Turks capture Tenedos and Lemnos from the Venetians.

F **Politics, Economics, Law and Education**
   John Amos Comenius (Komensky), *Didactica*, an educational treatise.
   Oliver Cromwell founds Durham College (dissolved in 1660).
   Drinking chocolate is first sold in London.

G **Science, Technology and Discovery**
   Academia del Cimento is founded in Florence at the instigation of Vincenzo Viviani and Torricelli.

H **Philosophy, Religion and Scholarship**
   'Angelus Silesius' (i.e. Johann Scheffler), *Sinn- und Schlussreime* (–1674, with additions, under title of *Cherubinischer Wandersmann*).
   Richard Baxter, *A Call To the Unconverted*.
   Claude Lancelot, *Le Jardin des racines grecques*.
   Le sieur Saunier, *L'encyclopédie des beaux esprits* ('contenant les moyens de parvenir à la connaissance des belles sciences'; said to be the first reference book to have *encyclopédie* in the title).
   George Thornley's translation of *Daphnis and Chloe*, attributed to Longus.
   Brian Walton's *Polyglott Bible* completed (Hebrew, Chaldee, Samaritan, Syriac, Arabic, Persian, Ethiopic, Greek and Latin).

J **Art, Sculpture, Fine Arts and Architecture**
   Painting:
      Velazquez, *Las Hilanderas*.
      Willem van de Velde, *Dutch men of war and small vessels in a calm sea*.
   Architecture:
      Le Vau, Vaux-le-Viscomte, Château.

K **Music**

L **Literature (including Drama)**
   François Hédelin, Abbé d'Aubignac, *Pratique du théâtre*.
   Andreas Gryphius, *Cardenio und Celinde* (religious drama); *Herr Peter Squentz* (comedy).
   Henry King, *Poems*.
   Thomas Middleton, *No Wit Like a Woman* (comedy). *Two New Plays*, containing the tragedy *Women Beware Women* (posth.).

M **Births and Deaths**
   Jan. 26th William Wake b. (–1737).
   Feb. 11th Bernard de Fontenelle b. (–1757).
   Mar. 19th Jean Le Clerk b. (–1736).
   Apr. 2nd Emperor Ferdinand III d. (48).
   May 9th William Bradford d. (67).
   June 3rd William Harvey d. (79).
   July 11th Frederick I of Prussia b. (–1713).
   July — George, Lord Goring, d. (49).
   Aug. 17th Robert Blake d. (67).
   — Menasseh Ben Israel d. (*c.* 53).
   — John Dennis b. (–1734).

A Jan: 20th, English Parliament meets but
Feb: 4th, is dissolved when Cromwell learns of intrigues between republicans in Commons and the army;
26th/*Mar.* 8th, Treaty of Roskild between Sweden and Denmark.
Mar: 17th, a Royalist conspiracy is discovered in England.

B Apr:
May:
Jun: 4th/14th, Anglo-French army defeats Spaniards at the battle of the Dunes;
15th/25th, Spaniards lose Dunkirk;
Aurangzeb imprisons his father the Shah, after winning battle at Samgarh.

C Jul: 18th, Leopold I is elected Emperor (−1705);
31st, Aurangzeb is proclaimed Mogul Emperor.
Aug: 14th/24th, Spanish are defeated at Gravelines;
15th, Rhenish League established under Protectorate of French, after Louis XIV fails to be elected Emperor. The League comprises the King of France, the three spiritual Electors, Münster, Neuburg, Brunswick, Hesse-Cassel, Sweden and Bavaria. Its formation is a triumph of diplomacy for Lionne;
—, Charles X begins second war with Denmark and besieges Copenhagen (−*Sept.*).
Sep: 3rd, Oliver Cromwell dies and is succeeded as Lord Protector by his son, Richard (−*May* 1659);
the Great Elector of Brandenburg marches to the aid of the Danes and Charles X of Sweden is blockaded.

D Oct:
Nov:
Dec:

E Dutch take Jaffnapatam, the last Portuguese possession in Ceylon.

F Politics, Economics, Law and Education

James Harrington, *The Prerogative of Popular Government*.
Palmstruck devises the first banknote, for issue by the Riksbank, Stockholm.
Sir Thomas Browne advocates cremation.

G Science, Technology and Discovery

J. R. Glauber in *De natura salium* describes 'Glauber's salts', prepared from the action of oil of vitriol (or sulphuric acid) on common salt.
Blaise Pascal uses the method of indivisibles to solve problems of the cycloid.
C. Huygens invents the cycloidal pendulum and makes a pendulum clock.
Sylvius becomes professor of medicine at Leyden.

H Philosophy, Religion and Scholarship

Sir William Dugdale, *History of St. Paul's Cathedral*.
Thomas Hobbes *Elementorum Philosophiae* (*De Homine*; –1655).
William London, *Catalogue* (of Most Vendible Books in England).
Edward Phillips, *A New World of Words*.
James Ussher, *Annals of the World* (translation of his *Annales* of 1650).
Expulsion of the Socinian Sect from Poland.
Société des Missions Étrangères (Roman Catholic) founded in Paris.

J Art, Sculpture, Fine Arts and Architecture

Painting:
 Pieter de Hooch, *Courtyard of a house in Delft*.
 Peter Lely, *The family of the Earl of Carnarvon*.
 Adriaen van de Velde, *Farm with a dead tree*; and *Edge of a wood, with sleeping Shepherd, sheep and goats*.
Architecture:
 Bernini, façade, St. Maria, Via Lata, Rome (–1662); and Castel Gandolfo Church (–1661).

K Music

L Literature (including Drama)

Sir Thomas Browne, *Hydriotaphia; or, Urne-Buriall; The Garden of Cyrus*.
Philip Massinger, *The City-Madam* (comedy).
William Rowley, *The Witch of Edmonton* (tragi-comedy) ('A known true story' written with Thomas Dekker and John Ford).
Georg Stiernhielm, *Hercules* (Swedish epic).
Molière forms the company of actors at the *Théâtre du Petit-Bourbon* which eventually becomes the company to be known as *La Comédie-Française* (–1680).

M Births and Deaths

Sept. 3rd Oliver Cromwell d. (59).
Oct. 3rd Miles Standish d. (72).
Oct. 5th Mary of Modena b. (–1718).
Oct. 23rd Thomas Pride d. (*c.* 50).
— Richard Lovelace d. (40).
— Henry Purcell b. (–1695).
— Alessandro Scarlatti b. (–1725).

A Jan: 14th, Portuguese defeat Spanish at Elvas;
    27th, English Parliament meets (–*Apr*. 22nd).
  Feb:
  Mar:

B Apr: 22nd, Richard Cromwell dissolves Parliament after peaceful army *coup d'état* to
    prevent Parliament gaining command over it.
  May: 7th, Restoration of the Rump Parliament;
    12th, Derby Petition, framed by John Lambert, for a permanent settlement of the
    constitutional crisis between the army and Parliament;
    21st/31st, Dutch, English and French make Treaty at Hague to force Sweden and
    Denmark to make peace, which is followed by two further treaties;
    25th, Richard Cromwell resigns; the Rump Parliament re-establishes the Common-
    wealth;
    26th, Aurangzeb formally becomes Mogul Emperor.
  Jun:

C Jul:
  Aug: Major-General Lambert suppresses a Royalist rising in Cheshire, led by Sir
    George Booth.
  Sep:

D Oct: 12th, army expels the Rump Parliament.
  Nov: 7th, Peace of the Pyrenees, between Spain and France; France obtains Rousillon,
    Cerdagne, Artois and fortresses in Hainault, Flanders and Luxemburg. Spain resigns
    her claims to Alsace; Louis XIV is to marry Maria-Theresa, Philip IV's eldest
    daughter on condition she renounces claim to Spanish throne in return for a dowry.
    Prince of Condé is reinstated to the governorship of Burgundy and the Duke of
    Lorraine obtains partial reinstatement, but on terms he cannot accept.
  Dec: 16th, General Monck in Scotland calls for a free Parliament;
    26th, the Long Parliament meets again, excluding those expelled by Pride's Purge in
    1648.

E The Great Elector drives out the Swedes from Pomerania and Prussia;

F Politics, Economics, Law and Education
  John Milton, *A Treatise of Civil Power in Ecclesiastical Causes.*

G Science, Technology and Discovery
  R. Boyle's observations on the elastic pressure of the air in all directions, with the combination of his 'pneumatical engine'.

H Philosophy, Religion and Scholarship
  John Hales, *Golden Remains* (posth.).
  Henry More, *The Immortality of the Soul.*
  John Rushworth, *Collection of State Papers, 1618–1648* (–1701).
  Charles de Saint-Denis, Sieur de Saint-Évremond, *Lettre sur le Traité des Pyrénées.*
  William Somner, *Dictionarium Saxonico-Latino-Anglicum.*
  Preussische Staats-bibliothek, Berlin, founded (*see* 1661).

J Art, Sculpture, Fine Arts and Architecture
  Painting:
    Jan van Goyen, *View of Nimegen.*
    Velazquez, *The Infante Phillip Prosper; and The Infanta Margarita Teresa, in blue.*

K Music

L Literature (including Drama)
  Richard Brome, *Five New Plays* (posth.).
  Pierre Corneille, *Oedipe* (tragedy).
  John Day, *The Blind Beggar of Bednal Green* (drama).
  Richard Lovelace, *Lucasta* (Posthume Poems).
  Molière, *Les Précieuses ridicules* (comedy).
  James Shirley, *The Contention of Ajax and Ulysses* (masque containing the poem *The Glories of Our Blood and State*).
  Joost van den Vondel, *Jephta* (tragedy).

M Births and Deaths
  July 20th Hyacinthe Rigaud b. (–1743).
  Aug. — Alexander Lindsay, Earl of Balcarres, d. (41).
  Oct. 28th Nicholas Brady b. (–1726).
  Oct. 31st John Bradshaw d. (56).
  — Henry Dunster d. (47).

1660   Restoration of Charles II—Peace of Oliva ends Northern War

A **Jan:** 1st, General George Monck crosses R. Tweed, and, *Feb.* 3rd, leads his army into London.

Feb: 16th, Monck declares for a free Parliament.

21st, the Rump of the Long Parliament recalls the Presbyterian members (excluded since Pride's Purge in 1648);

23rd, Charles XI succeeds as King of Sweden (–1697) on death of Charles X.

Mar: 16th, Long Parliament dissolves itself (elected *Nov.* 1640, restored *May* 1659).

Virginia proclaims Charles II King and restores governor Sir William Berkeley.

B **Apr:** 4th, Charles II issues Declaration of Breda, promising amnesty and religious toleration;

25th, Convention Parliament meets at Westminster (–*Dec.* 29th), and invites Charles II to return to England.

May: 3rd, through French mediation, the Peace of Oliva is signed, ending war between Brandenburg, Poland, Austria and Sweden; by its terms the Elector of Brandenburg's sovereignty in East Prussia is recognised, John Casimir II of Poland renounces claims to Swedish throne and to Estonia and Livonia, and Sweden and Poland recognise the sovereignty of Russia.

29th, Charles II enters London; Edward Hyde, lord keeper, directs affairs; death of George Rákóczy II, Prince of Transylvania, in battle with Turks.

Jun: 6th, Peace of Copenhagen ends war between Sweden and Denmark (after preliminaries signed *May* 27th); the Baltic is reopened to foreign warships;

Louis XIV of France marries Maria Teresa, Infanta of Spain (following Treaty of the Pyrenees of *Nov.* 1659).

C **Jul:**

Aug: Grosswardern, Transylvania, surrenders to the Turks. Subsequently the Emperor Leopold I agrees to send army to check the Turkish advance.

Sep:

D **Oct:** 8th (–13th), Frederick III's *coup d'état* in Denmark strengthens the monarchy and the crown becomes hereditary;

English Parliament rejects concessions to Nonconformists which Charles II had promised in Breda Declaration (*Apr.*).

Nov: 30th, Charles II's Declaration for Settling Affairs of Ireland.

Dec:

E

F **Politics, Economics, Law and Education**
James Harrington, *Political Discourses.*
John Milton, *The Readie and Easie Way to Establish a free Commonwealth* (a tract in favour of Republicanism).
Parliament passes the Navy Discipline Act and strengthens the Navigation Act (of 1651) to protect English shipping and trade, principally from Dutch competition.

G **Science, Technology and Discovery**

H **Philosophy, Religion and Scholarship**
John Donne, *Sermons* (vol 3) (–1640) (posth.).
James Howell, *Lexicon Tetraglotten:* an English-French-Italian-Spanish dictionary.
Henry More, *Grand Mystery of Godliness.*
John Ogilby's translation of the *Iliad.*
Antoine Baudeau, Sieur de Somaize, *Le Grand Dictionnaire des Prétieuses; ou, La Clef de la langue des ruelles.*
Blaise Pascal's *Lettres provinciales* are placed on the Index; ordered to be burnt by the Royal Council in France.

J **Art, Sculpture, Fine Arts and Architecture**
Painting:
Peter Lely begins painting the series 'Windsor Beauties'.
Gabriel Metsu, *The Sick Child.*
Jan Steen, *The Poultry Yard.*
Jan Vermeer, *Head of a Young Girl;* also *The Cook.*
Francisco de Zubarán, *The Young Virgin.*
Architecture:
The Great Elector begins to build Potsdam Palace (–1682).
Borromini, Collegio di Propaganda Fide, Rome.

K **Music**
Francesco Cavalli produces his opera *Serse* for the marriage celebrations of Louis XIV.

L **Literature (including Drama)**
Pierre Corneille, *La Toison d'or* (tragedy).
John Dryden, *Astraea Redux.*
Molière, *Sganarelle* (comedy).
Mme. de Scudéry, *Clélie* (a novel, begun 1654).
Samuel Pepys begins his *Diary* (*Jan.* 1st; –1669).
Patents are granted for re-opening theatres in London (closed since 1642).

M **Births and Deaths**
Apr. 16th Hans Sloane b. (–1753).
May 28th George I b. (–1727).
June 5th Sarah Jennings, Duchess of Marlborough, b. (–1744).
Aug. 6th Velazquez d. (61).
Sept. 12th Jacob Cats d. (82).
Sept. 27th St. Vincent de Paul d. (84).
Oct. 13th Thomas Harrison d. (54).
Oct. 16th Paul Scarron d. (50).
— Johann Joseph Fux b. (–1741).
— Peter Anthony Motteux b. (–1718).
— Thomas Urquhart d. (49).

A **Jan:** 7th, Council for Foreign Plantations first meets.
Feb:
Mar: 9th, Cardinal Mazarin dies and Louis XIV begins his personal rule.

B **Apr:** 1st, Philip Duke of Orleans marries Henrietta, sister of Charles II;
20th, Edward Hyde, Lord Chancellor is created Earl of Clarendon;
23rd, coronation of Charles II.
May: 8th, the 'Cavalier Parliament', Charles II's second Parliament, meets (–1678) and is predominantly Royalist; sometimes known as the Pensionary Parliament or Long Parliament of the Restoration.
Jun: 21st, the Peace of Kardis is signed between Russia and Sweden, ending the northern war; Russia abandons all claims to Livonia;
23rd/*July* 3rd, Portugal cedes Tangier and Bombay to Charles II as dowry of his Queen, and Charles undertakes to try to effect peace between the Portuguese and the Dutch.

C **Jul:** The Great Elector summons a Diet in Prussia, which attacks his authority and is dismissed.
Aug: 6th, by treaty with the Dutch, due to mediation of Charles II, the Portuguese retain Brazil, the Dutch keep Ceylon.
Sep: 5th, on the disgrace of Fouquet in France, Colbert becomes principal financial minister (–1683).

D **Oct:**
Nov: Ahmad Kiuprili becomes Grand Vizier of Turkey, on the death of his father Mohammed.
Dec: 20th, Royal Assent is given to Corporation Act by which all magistrates in England and Wales are to take sacrament according to the Church of England, to swear an oath of allegiance, to renounce the Covenant, and to declare it treason to carry arms against the King.

E Famine in India, where no rain has fallen for two years.

F Politics, Economics, Law and Education

John Graunt, *National and Political Observations on the Bills of Mortality*, provides statistical information for life insurance in England.

Praetorius, *Ludicrum chiromanticum*, a treatise on palmistry.

G Science, Technology and Discovery

Christian Huyghens invents a manometer for ascertaining the elastic force of gases.

H Philosophy, Religion and Scholarship

Leone Allacci appointed Librarian to the Vatican, Rome.

John Eliot, Translation of the Holy Bible into Algonquin (the language of a large Group of Indians): *New Testament* (–1663 *Old Testament*; the first complete Bible to be printed in the American colonies).

Clement Walker, *History of Independency*.

Joseph Glanvill, *The Vanity of Dogmatizing; or Confidence in Opinions*.

The Great Elector opens the Royal Library, Berlin (–1659).

Kongelige Bibliothek, Denmark, is founded.

J Art, Sculpture, Fine Arts and Architecture

Painting:

Charles II appoints Peter Lely his court painter.

Rembrandt, *Two Negroes;* and *Self-portrait as St. Paul*.

Jan Steen, *Easy Come, Easy Go*.

Velazquez, *The Rokeby Venus*.

Willem van de Velde, *Dutch Vessels inshore with men bathing*.

Architecture:

Le Vau, Galerie d'Apollon, Louvre (–1662) and Collège des Quatre Nations, Paris.

K Music

Matthew Locke is appointed composer to Charles II.

The Académie Royale de Danse (consisting of 13 French dancing-masters) is founded by Louis XIV (enlarged, 1672).

L Literature (including Drama)

Gauthier de Costes de La Calprènede, *Pharamond*, 12 vols. (–1670).

Molière, *L'École des maris* (comedy); and *Les Fâcheux* (comedy-ballet).

Lincoln's Inn Fields Theatre, Portugal Street, London, is opened for Sir William Davenant (the first London playhouse to have a proscenium arch) and *Hamlet* is produced (*Aug.* 28th; the first production with scenery).

M Births and Deaths

Mar. 9th Jules Mazarin d. (58).

Apr. 16th Charles Montague, Earl of Halifax, b. (–1715).

May 25th Claude Buffier b. (–1737).

May 27th Archibald Campbell, Marquess of Argyll, d. (54).

Aug. 16th Thomas Fuller d. (53).

Dec. 5th Robert Harley, Earl of Oxford, b. (–1724).

— Daniel Defoe b. (–1731).

— Nicholas Hawksmoor b. (–1736).

— Alexander Leslie, Earl of Leven, d. (*c.* 81).

A Jan:
Feb:
Mar: A Bill is introduced in the House of Commons for the introdution of a Hearth Tax
at the rate of two shillings on each fireplace or stove.

B Apr: 23rd, Connecticut is granted a liberal charter;
27th, Louis XIV agrees by a treaty of alliance, signed at Paris, to help the Dutch if they
are attacked by a third party.
May: 19th, Act of Uniformity gives consent to the revised English Prayer Book and
denies right to take up arms against the King; Presbyterianism in the Church is
destroyed and many ministers who do not conform are ejected. A Licensing Act
forbids imports of literature contrary to Christian faith;
21st, Charles II marries Catherine de Braganza, daughter of John IV of Portugal.
Jun: Alfonso VI assumes the government of Portugal.

C Jul:
Aug:
Sep:

D Oct: 27th, Charles II sells Dunkirk to France for $2\frac{1}{2}$ million livres (£400,000);
Louis XIV's negotiations with Spain for the possession of Franche-Comté and Luxem-
burg are broken off.
Nov:
Dec:

E Pirates attack the southern coast of France;
The County of East Frisia becomes a hereditary principality;
Accession of K'ang-hsi, Emperor of China, aged 8 years. He begins personal rule at the
age of 15 (–1722);
Chinese wrest Formosa from Dutch, Fort Zelandia falls, and Formosa becomes autono-
mous (–1683).

F **Politics, Economics, Law and Education**
William Petty, *A Treatise of Taxes and Contributions* approves of the export of money and states that the division of labour reduces costs of production.
The last silver pennies are minted in England.
A ballot is first used in Britain, by the Scottish Parliament in proceedings in the Billeting Act, to secure the ostracism of Lauderdale and other opponents of Middleton.

G **Science, Technology and Discovery**
The Royal Society receives its charter (*July* 15th).
Robert Boyle, *The Sceptical Chemist.*
William Dugdale, *The History of Imbanking and Drayning of Divers Fens and Marshes.*

H **Philosophy, Religion and Scholarship**
Thomas Fuller, *The Worthies of England.*
Christopher Packe translates *Ortus Medicinae* by Johannes Baptista van Helmont.
Edward Stillingfleet, *Origines Sacrae*, asserts that bishops in the Early Church were the equal of Presbyters.
Michael Wigglesworth, *The Day of Doom* (a poetical description in ballad metre 'of the Great and Last Judgment').
The Book of Common Prayer of the Church of England; final text is approved; it is enforced by the Act of Uniformity.
Episcopal Ordination Act of Scotland, where Presbyterian assemblies are forbidden; 400 ministers are ejected.

J **Art, Sculpture, Fine Arts and Architecture**
Painting:
Rembrandt, *De Staal Meesters.*
Philippe de Champaigne, *Ex Voto, 1662.*
Louis XIV begins to build Versailles Palace and appoints Le Brun his principal painter and director of the Gobelins tapestries.
Architecture:
Christopher Wren, Pembroke College, Cambridge, the Chapel.
Le Nôtre, gardens and park, Versailles.

K **Music**

L **Literature (including Drama)**
Samuel Butler, *Hudibras*, part 1 (–1663, 1678).
Molière, *L'École des femmes* (comedy).
The Passion Play at Oberammergau, earliest extant text (see 1634 L).
Poor Robin's Almanac is started.

M **Births and Deaths**
Jan. 27th Richard Bentley b. (–1742).
Feb. 8th Elizabeth of Bohemia ('the Winter Queen') d. (66).
Apr. 30th Mary II b. (–1692).
May 23rd John Gauden d. (57).
June 14th Henry Vane the younger d. (39).
Aug. 19th Blaise Pascal d. (39).
Sept. 22nd John Biddle d. (47).

A   Jan: 10th, Charles II grants a charter to the Royal African Company;
     23rd, Louis XIV continues his alliance with the League of the Rhine.
   Feb:
   Mar: 24th, grant of Carolina to the eight proprietors.

B   Apr: 18th, Turks declare war against Emperor Leopold I.
   May: 28th/*June* 8th, British and Portuguese defeat the Spaniards at Amegial.
   Jun:

C   Jul: 8th, a Charter is granted by Charles II to Rhode Island;
     26th, French declare Venaissin united with France after quarrel with the Pope, and
     they also seize Avignon.
   Aug:
   Sep: 25th, Neuhäusel surrenders to Turks, who now threaten to invade Germany.

D   Oct:
   Nov:
   Dec: 23rd, sessions of the German Imperial Diet at Ratisbon are made permanent.

E   Colbert forms the colony of New France into a province, with Quebec as its capital, and
     undertakes further reforms in the financial and commercial system of France.

F **Politics, Economics, Law and Education**
The gold guinea-piece is first coined in England.
Turnpike tolls are first levied in England.
Europaische Zeitung, Copenhagen, is issued.
Roger L'Estrange is appointed licenser of the English press.

G **Science, Technology and Discovery**
John Newton discovers the Binomial Theorem.
B. Pascal, *L'Équilibre des Liquers* (posth.).
Otto von Guericke makes a frictional electrical machine consisting of a globe of sulphur
fixed on an axis and rotated by a winch.
A. Yarranton, *The great improvement of lands by Clover*.

H **Philosophy, Religion and Scholarship**
Robert Boyle, *Concerning the Usefulness of Experimental Philosophy*.
Gottfried von Leibniz, *De principio individui*, a defence of nominalistic philosophy.
Lord Herbert of Cherbury, *De Religione Gentilium* (posth.).
Charles de Saint-Denis, Sieur de Saint-Evremond, *Réflexions sur les divers génies du
peuple romain*.
William Shakespeare: *The Third Folio* (contains *Pericles*, and the spurious plays; *see*
1623, 1632).
Académie des Inscriptions et Belles Lettres founded in Paris by Jean Baptiste Colbert.

J **Art, Sculpture, Fine Arts and Architecture**
Painting:
Pieter de Hooch, *At the Linen Closet*.
Adriaen van de Velde, *Cattle near a building*.
Architecture:
Bernini, Scala Regia, Vatican, Rome (–1666).
Borromini, St. Andrea (–1665).

K **Music**
Giovanni Battista Lully, *Le Ballet des Arts*.
James Clifford edits a collection of 393 anthems and services.

L **Literature (including Drama)**
Samuel Butler, *Hudibras*, part 2 (–1662, 1678).
Abraham Cowley, *The Cutter of Coleman Street* (comedy). *Verses Upon Several Occasions*.
Sir William Davenant, *The Siege of Rhodes*, parts 1 and 2 (–1656).
Andreas Gryphius, *Horribilicribrifax* (satirical comedy on the Thirty Years War).
The Theatre Royal, London, opened (*May* 7th; destroyed by fire 1672; reopened
1674).

M **Births and Deaths**
Feb. 12th Cotton Mather b. (–1728).
June 4th William Juxton d. (81).
Oct. 18th Prince Eugène of Savoy b. (–1736).
— Thomas Newcomen b. (–1729).

1664   England annexes New York

A Jan:
Feb: Pope Alexander VII yields to Louis XIV's demands.
Mar: 6th, Alliance of France and Brandenburg.

B Apr: 5th, Triennial Act is repealed;
6th, Alliance between Saxony and France is signed at Ratisbon.
May: Conventicle Act is directed against meetings of Nonconformists, by preventing meetings of more than 5 people unless in a private household.
Jun: War breaks out between England and Holland in the colonies and at sea.

C Jul:
Aug: 1st, Turks are defeated at St. Gotthard-on-the Raab by the imperialists;
10th, Truce of Vasvar ends war between Turkey and Emperor: the rival armies are to retire from Transylvania, and Apasi is to pay a tribute to the Porte;
29th, British annexe New Netherlands from Connecticut to Delaware, and rename New Amsterdam, surrendered 2 days earlier by Peter Stuyvesant as New York.
Sep: 24th, Fort Orange surrenders to British and is renamed Albany.

D Oct:
Nov:
Dec: 15th, union of Connecticut and New Haven (formal Act of Submission, *Jan.* 5th, 1665).

E The Dutch purchase Swedish colonies on Gold Coast.

F **Politics, Economics, Law and Education**
Lord Chancellor Clarendon and Archbishop Sheldon agree that Convocation should waive its rights of voting subsidies from the clergy, which are henceforth voted by the House of Commons together with lay taxes.
Thomas Mun, England's *Treasure by Forraign Trade* (posth.).
Colbert abolishes many internal tariff-duties in France.
The French Compagnie des Indes Occidentales is formed to control French trade in Canada, West Africa, South America and the West Indies.

G **Science, Technology and Discovery**
Thomas Willis, *Anatome Cerebri nervorumque descriptio et usus*, a study of the brain.
J. Forster, *England's happiness increased . . . by a plantation of the roots called potatoes.*

H **Philosophy, Religion and Scholarship**
John Evelyn, *Sylva*.
Armand de Rancé founds the Trappist Order (*La Trappe*) at La Trappe, Normandy.
Conventicle Act forbids general meetings of Nonconformists in England.

J **Art, Sculpture, Fine Arts and Architecture**
Painting:
  Pieter de Hooch, *Young woman weighing gold ;* and *Woman at a window reading a letter.*
  Jan Steen, *The Christening Feast.*
  Jan Vermeer, *The Lace-maker.*
Architecture:
  Christopher Wren, Sheldonian Theatre, Oxford (–1669).

K **Music**

L **Literature (including Drama)**
John Dryden, *The Rival Ladies* (tragi-comedy).
Sir George Etherege, *The Comical Revenge ;* or *Love In a Tub* (comedy).
Jean de La Fontaine, first book of *Contes et Nouvelles.*
Molière, *Le Tartuffe* (comedy; Acts 1–3 first performed).
Joachim Rachel, *Satirische Gedichte.*
Jean Racine, *La Thébaide* (his first tragedy, produced by Molière).

M **Births and Deaths**
Jan. 24th John Vanbrugh b. (–1726).
May 31st Guilio Alberoni b. (–1752).
July 16th Andreas Gryphius d. (47).
July 21st Matthew Prior b. (–1721).

A Jan:
Feb: 22nd, outbreak of second Anglo-Dutch naval war.
Mar:

B Apr:
May:
Jun: 6th/17th, Spanish are defeated by the Portuguese and British at Montes Claros. A
further victory at Villa Viciosa secures Portugal's independence. Charles II signs
treaty of alliance with the Bishop of Münster.

C Jul: 3rd, Dutch are defeated off Lowestoft, at Southwold Bay.
Aug: British military expedition takes St. Eustatius from the Dutch;
the French send an expedition against the Barbary pirates of Tunis and Algiers.
Sep: 17th, Philip IV of Spain dies and is succeeded by Charles II, his son (–1700);
Great Plague of London, bubonic in nature, (–*Sept*. 1666).

D Oct: 9th (–31st), the fifth session of the Cavalier Parliament is held at Oxford on account
of the plague in Westminster;
Five Mile Act imposes further restrictions on Nonconformist ministers; all who refuse
to accept Act of Uniformity are forbidden to come within 5 miles of any Corporate
town or place where they had been a minister.
Nov:
Dec:

E Maine is restored to the heirs of Sir Ferdinando Gorges.

F **Politics, Economics, Law and Education**

English law and administration are introduced into New York.

A census is taken in Quebec, the first of modern times; further censuses are regularly taken there (–1754).

The *London Gazette* is first issued, *Nov.* 16th, from Oxford, to which the court had moved on account of the plague of London; the first issue from London was no. 24, *Feb.* 1st, 1666.

An Indian, Caleb Cheeshateaumuck, takes an A.B. degree at Harvard.

G **Science, Technology and Discovery**

Giovanni Cassini determines the rotations and periods of Jupiter, Mars and Venus (–1667).

Francis Grimaldi in *Physico-Mathesis de Lumine* (posth.) announces his discovery of the diffraction of light.

Robert Boyle proves that air is necessary for candles to burn and for animals to live.

Robert Hooke investigates the vesicular nature of cork and similar substances, naming their cavities 'cells', and describes the microscope in his *Micrographia*.

H **Philosophy, Religion and Scholarship**

John Bunyan, *The Holy City*.

John Eliot, *Communion of Churches* (Harvard, Mass.; the first privately printed work produced in America).

Pope Alexander VII orders the Jansenists to submit to the Bull of 1653.

Jacques Godefroy edits *Codex Theodosianus*, a prime source for the legal systems of the Western Roman Empire.

Philosophical Transactions, vol. 1 (dedicated to the Royal Society, London).

J **Art, Sculpture, Fine Arts and Architecture**

Painting:

    Murillo, *The Rest on the Flight to Egypt* (–1670); and *The Foundation of St. Maria Maggiore*.

    Adriaen van Ostade, *The Physician in his Study*.

    Rembrandt, *The Jewish Bride*.

    Jan Steen, *Garden of an Inn*.

    Ter Borch, *The Gallant*.

    Vermeer, *The Artist's Studio* (–1670).

Architecture:

    Claude Perrault begins to construct the colonnade of the Louvre, Paris (–1670).

K **Music**

L **Literature (including Drama)**

Roger de Bussy-Rabutin, *Histoire amoureuse des Gaules*.

Richard Head, *The English Rogue* (a picaresque novel).

Edward, Lord Herbert of Cherbury, *Occasional Poems* (posth.).

Jean de La Fontaine, *Contes et nouvelles en vers* (–1669).

La Rochefoucauld, *Maximes* (first Paris edition).

Molière, *Don Juan* (comedy).

Jean Racine, *Alexandre le Grand*.

Izaak Walton, *The Life of Richard Hooker*.

Journal des Savants (the first literary periodical is started in Paris –*Jan.* 5th).

M **Births and Deaths**

Feb. 6th Queen Anne b. (–1714).

June 11th Kenelm Digby d. (61).

Nov. 19th Nicholas Poussin d. (71).

Dec. 2nd Catherine de Vivonne, Marquise de Rambrouillet, d. (77).

A   Jan: 16th/26th, France, in alliance with Holland, declares war against England and sends
     an army against the Bishop of Münster, England's sole ally;
     English privateers take Tobago.
   Feb: 16th, Holland signs a treaty of alliance with the Great Elector of Brandenburg.
   Mar:

B   Apr: A French force captures St. Kitts from the English.
   May: The Bishop of Münster is forced to sue for peace.
   Jun: 1st (–4th), English fleet under Lord Albemarle fights an inconclusive battle with the
     Dutch off the Dunes of Dunkirk.

C   Jul: 25th/*Aug.* 4th, Albemarle defeats the Dutch fleet at battle of St. James' Fight, off
     Foreland.
   Aug:
   Sep: 2nd–6th, Great Fire of London virtually destroys the city, including St. Paul's
     Cathedral.

D   Oct: 25th, Quadruple Alliance is signed between Holland, Brandenburg, Brunswick and
     Denmark to ensure the independence of Holland from French aggression.
   Nov: 18th, Scottish Covenanters, revolting against restrictions imposed by the Episco-
     palians, are crushed at the battle of Pentland Hills;
     the French capture Antigua from the English.
   Dec: The Great Elector of Brandenburg and the Duke of Neuburg sign the Treaty of
     Cleves for the partition of Jülich-Cleves; Brandenburg is to receive Cleves, Mark and
     Ravensburg, while Neuburg retains Jülich and Berg.

E   Louvois becomes French Minister of War.

F **Politics, Economics, Law and Education**

The Great Plague of London is at its height (*May–Sept.*), killing 68,596 persons.

The Great Fire of London (*Sept.* 2nd–6th), destroying St. Paul's Cathedral, many city churches, livery halls and other buildings.

Newark, New Jersey, is settled by Puritans from Connecticut.

G **Science, Technology and Discovery**

Académie des Sciences, Paris, is founded by Colbert.

Gottfried von Leibniz, *De arte combinatoria*, an arithmetical tract.

Isaac Newton uses the infinitesimal calculus ('the notation of Fluxions') and measures the moon's orbit.

H **Philosophy, Religion and Scholarship**

John Bunyan, *Grace Abounding to the Chief of Sinners*.

Joseph Glanvill, *Philosophical Considerations concerning Witches and Witchcraft*.

John Tillotson, *The Rule of Faith*.

The Bible is printed in Armenian.

J **Art, Sculpture, Fine Arts and Architecture**

Painting:

Peter Lely begins series of 'Flagmen' at Greenwich.

Nicolaes Maes, *Elderly man in a black Robe*.

Rembrandt, *Portrait of Titus*.

Fine Arts:

Colbert establishes the Gobelin Tapestry workshops in Paris.

André Félibien, *Entretiens sur les vies et sur les ouvrages des plus excellents peintres anciens et modernes*.

K **Music**

L **Literature (including Drama)**

Nicholas Boileau-Despréaux, *Satires*.

Molière, *Le Médecin malgré lui* and *Le Misanthrope* (comedies).

Joachim Rachel, *Der Poet* and *Der Freund*.

Jakob Bidermann, *Ludi theatrales sacri* (posth. collection of Latin plays by the great Jesuit dramatist, whose dramas were based on the *Spiritual Exercises* of St. Ignatius Loyola).

M **Births and Deaths**

June 26th Richard Fanshawe d. (58).

Aug. 26th Frans Hals d. (86).

Aug. 31st Henrietta Maria d. (56).

Sept. 23rd François Mansard d. (68).

Oct. 29th James Shirley d. (70), and Edmund Calamy d. (66).

Dec. 22nd Guercino d. (75).

— George Thomason d. (*c.* 60).

A Jan: 20th, the Truce of Andrussov between Russia and Poland ends the Thirteen Years War; Poland cedes Smolensk and Kiev to Russia;

—, Anne of Austria, Queen-Mother of France, dies.

Feb: The French take Monserrat from the English.

Mar: 21st/31st, Louis XIV signs a secret treaty with Charles II of England, by which England will not oppose a French invasion of the Spanish Netherlands provided France does not aid the Dutch at sea.

B Apr: Louis XIV signs the defensive League of the Rhine with Münster, Neuburg, Brunswick, Hesse-Cassel, Bavaria and Sweden.

May: 22nd, Pope Alexander VII dies (Guilio Raspigliosi is elected Pope Clement IX (–1670) on *June* 20th);

24th, French troops invade the Spanish Netherlands to begin the War of Devolution (–*May* 1668), since Louis XIV, after the death of his father-in-law Philip IV of Spain in 1665, claims Brabant, Flanders and other territories in the Netherlands on the grounds that these personal estates of the Spanish crown should descend by right of devolution; the Turks begin the siege of Candia (–*Sept.* 1669).

Jun: The Electress of Brandenburg dies;

12th/13th, the Dutch fleet under Admiral de Ruyter burns Sheerness, sails up the R. Medway, raids Chatham dockyard and escapes with the royal barge, the '*Royal Charles*'; the nadir of English naval power.

C Jul: 21st/31st, Peace of Breda between Holland and France with England, which obtains Antigua, Monserrat, St. Kitts, Cape Coast Castle and New Netherlands; France retains Acadia; Holland retains Guiana and Surinam, but abandons claims to New Amsterdam;

Turenne completes the French conquest of Flanders and Hainault and threatens the Dutch Republic;

the League of the Rhine (of *Apr.*) is dissolved by France's allies.

Aug: 30th, the fall of the Earl of Clarendon, who resigns as Lord Chancellor; his influence is replaced by that of the cabal of Lords Clifford, Arlington, Buckingham, Ashley and Lauderdale.

Sep:

D Oct:

Nov: 29th, the Earl of Clarendon is banished, following his impeachment.

Dec:

E Revolt in Portugal when Alfonso VI is banished to the Azores by his brother, Pedro, who had acted as Regent during the King's illness;

Shah Suleiman succeeds his father, Shah Abbas II, in Persia.

F **Politics, Economics, Law and Education**

Samuel Freiherr von Puffendorf in *De statu Reipublicae Germanicae* attacks both the house of Hapsburg and the ecclesiastical princes and proposes a Germanic Confederation, with a federal army, and the expulsion of the Jesuits.

Guillaume Lamoignon compiles the Code Louis, as an attempt to simplify French laws.

Colbert extends the state manufacturing of fine arts in France (Manufacture Royale des Meubles de la Couronne).

G **Science, Technology and Discovery**

The National Observatory, Paris, is founded (in 1671 Giovanni Cassini accepts Louis XIV's invitation to direct it).

H **Philosophy, Religion and Scholarship**

François Eudes de Mézeray, *Abrégé chronologique*.

Paul Gerhardt, *Geistliche Andachten*, 10 vols.

Gottfried von Leibniz, *Nova Methodus discendique juris*, discusses man's obedience to the laws of God.

Henry More, *Enchiridion Ethicum*.

Thomas Sprat, *The Early History of the Royal Society*.

J **Art, Sculpture, Fine Arts and Architecture**

K **Music**

L **Literature (including Drama)**

John Dryden, *Annus Mirabilis* (1666).

John Milton, *Paradise Lost* (–1674 enlarged edn.).

Molière, *Le Tartuffe* (comedy; in part performed in 1664).

Margaret, Duchess of Newcastle, *The Life of William Cavendish, Duke of Newcastle*.

Jean Racine, *Andromaque* (tragedy).

M **Births and Deaths**

Apr. 29th John Arbuthnot b. (–1745).

May 2nd George Wither d. (79).

July 28th Abraham Cowley d. (49).

Aug. 13th Jeremy Taylor d. (54).

Nov. 30th Jonathan Swift b. (–1745).

— Gabriel Boffrand b. (–1754).

— Gabriel Metson d. (38).

— Edward (Ned) Ward b. (–1731).

A Jan: 13th/23rd, through the initiative of John de Witt, Pensionary of Holland, and Sir
    William Temple, English ambassador at the Hague, the two countries sign the Alliance
    of the Hague, whereby each comes to the aid of the other if attacked, and both under-
    take to bring about a peace between France and Spain. Sweden subsequently joins
    England and Holland, thus forming a Triple Alliance;
    19th, Louis XIV signs a treaty with the Emperor Leopold I for the future partition of
    the Spanish Empire in the event of the death of the 8-year-old Charles II of Spain,
    without heirs; France is to acquire the Spanish Netherlands, Franche-Comté, Naples,
    Sicily, Navarre and the Spanish possessions in Africa and in the East Philippines,
    while Austria is to have Spain and the rest of the empire.
    Feb: 13th, by the Treaty of Lisbon, Spain recognises the independence of Portugal;
    the French under Condé occupy Franche-Comté.
    Mar: 27th, Bombay passes to the control of the English East India Company.

B Apr:
    May: 2nd, the Peace of Aix-la-Chapelle is signed between France and Spain, ending the
    War of Devolution. France restores Franche-Comté but obtains Lille, Tournai,
    Oudenarde and 9 other towns in Flanders from Spain; the succession to the Spanish
    Netherlands is left undecided.

C Jul:
    Aug:
    Sep: 19th, John II (John Casimir), King of Poland, abdicates.

D Oct:
    Nov:
    Dec:

E The Great Elector of Brandenburg marries the widowed Duchess Dorothea of Bruns-
    wick;
    The government of Maine again passes to the control of Massachusetts.

F Politics, Economics, Law and Education

Josiah Child, *Brief Observations concerning Trade and the Interest of Money*; and *A New Discourse on Trade*.

The Oder-Spree Canal is completed.

Lund University, Sweden, is founded.

G Science, Technology and Discovery

Isaac Newton constructs the first reflecting telescope.

Robert Hooke, *Discourse on Earthquakes*.

Anthony van Leeuwenhoek first describes red corpuscles accurately.

H Philosophy, Religion and Scholarship

Joseph Glanvill, *Plus Ultra; or, Progress of Knowledge Since Aristotle*.

Peter Heylyn, *Cyprianus Anglicanus* (Archbishop Laud).

Sir Roger L'Estrange translates the *Visions* of Quevedo.

Henry More, *Divine Dialogues*.

William Penn, *Sandy Foundation Shaken*.

John Wilkins, *Essay Towards a Real Character and a Philosophical Language*.

J Art, Sculpture, Fine Arts and Architecture

Painting:

Gabriel van de Velde, *Golfers on the ice near Haarlem*.

Architecture:

Cortona, dome of S. Carlo al Corso, Rome.

K Music

Thomas Tomkins, *Music Deo Sacra*.

L Literature (including Drama)

Mrs. Aphra Behn, *Oroonoko* (novel).

Roger Boyle, First Earl of Orrery, *History of Henry V* (drama). *The Tragedy of Mustapha*.

Abraham Cowley, *Works* (posth.), ed. by Thomas Sprat.

Sir John Denham, *Collected Poems*.

John Dryden, *An Essay of Dramatick Poesie*; and *Sir Martin Mar-all* (comedy).

Sir George Etherege, *She Wou'd If She Cou'd* (comedy).

Jean de La Fontaine, *Fables choisies mises en vers*.

Molière, *Amphitryon*, *George Dandin* and *L'Avare* (comedies).

Jean Racine, *Les Plaideurs* (satirical comedy).

Giornale de Letterati (the first Italian magazine, is issued by Francesco Nazzarini, later a cardinal).

M Births and Deaths

Apr. 7th William Davenant d. (62).

May 8th Alain René Lesage b. (−1747).

June 23rd Giovanni Battista Vico b. (−1744).

Nov. 10th François Couperin ('Le Grand') b. (−1733).

— Pieter Burmann the elder b. (−1741).

— Thomas Archer b. (−1743).

A Jan:
   Feb:
   Mar:

B Apr:
   May:
   Jun: 19th, Michael Wisniowiecki, a Lithuanian, is elected King of Poland (–1673) after 9
        months of struggle over the succession, and prevents French attempts to extend
        influence in that country.

C Jul: 21st, John Locke's Constitution for Carolina is approved.
   Aug: South Carolina is founded.
   Sep: The Venetians surrender Crete to the Turks, after a siege begun in 1648.

D Oct:
   Nov: 9th, Pope Clement IX dies.
   Dec: 31st, secret treaty of alliance between Brandenburg and France.

E The Hindu religion is banned in India by Aurangzeb;
   Huguenots from Picardy settle in England.

F **Politics, Economics, Law and Education**
Gottfried von Leibniz writes a tract supporting a German candidate for the vacant Polish throne, but a Lithuanian is elected.
Vauban, *La Conduite des Siéges*.
Bombay becomes under the control of the East India Company.
Earliest French trading station in India.

G **Science, Technology and Discovery**
Nicolaus Steno determines the interfacial angles of quartz crystals.
Phosphorus is first prepared.
Marcello Malpighi's treatise on the silkworm.
Jan Swammerdam writes a History of Insects.
J. W[orlidge], *Systema agriculturae, being the mystery of Husbandry discovered* . . . the first thorough, systematic treatise.

H **Philosophy, Religion and Scholarship**
[? Mariana Alcoforado], *Lettres Portugaises traduites en François*, being letters of a Portuguese nun to a French officer, of doubtful authorship and authenticity.
Jacques-Bénigne Bossuet, *Oraison funèbre de la reine Angleterre*, the first of his series of funeral orations.
Edmund Castell, *Lexicon Heptaglotten; Hebraicum, Chaldaicum, Syriacum, Samaritanum, Aethiopicum, Arabicum conjunctim et Persicum separatim*.
William Penn, *Innocency With Her Open Face; and No Cross, No Crown*.
Labadie, a convert to Calvinism, refuses to sign the Confessio Belgica; on being deposed from his pastorate he forms a Quietist congregation at Amsterdam (which survives to 1725).
Abraham a Santa Clara, court preacher at Vienna, inaugurates a religious revival.
Nil Volentibus Arduum, Amsterdam, founded by Lodewijk Meyer as an academy to promote the study of the arts, grammar and philosophy (inspired by Coster's Academy of 1617; closed –1681).

J **Art, Sculpture, Fine Arts and Architecture**
Architecture:
Le Vau begins remodelling Versailles.

K **Music**
Pierre Perrin receives a patent for founding the Académie Royale des Opéra, Paris, first home of the Paris Opéra (he founds the Académie in 1671).
Matthew Locke, *The Treasury of Musick*.

L **Literature (including Drama)**
John Dryden, *The Wild Gallant* (comedy).
Hans Jakob Christoph von Grimmelshausen, *Simplicius Simplicissimus* (*Der abenteurliche Simplicissimus Teutsch*, 'Description of the Life of a Strange Vagabond').
Molière, *Monsieur de Pourceaugnac* (comédie-ballet).
Jean Racine, *Britannicus* (tragedy).
The last entry in the *Diary* of Samuel Pepys (*May* 31st; –1660).

M **Births and Deaths**
Mar. 10th John Denham d. (54).
Oct. 4th Rembrandt d. (63).
Oct. 24th William Prynne d. (69).

A Jan: The Duke of Monmouth becomes Captain-General of army.

Feb: 17th, France signs a defensive alliance with Bavaria by which Louis XIV promises a subsidy and undertakes that the Dauphin shall marry the Elector's daughter; if the Emperor Leopold I dies or the Spanish Empire is partitioned, King and Elector shall act together.

Mar:

B Apr: 29th, Clement X is elected Pope as successor to Clement IX (–1676);

beginnings of conspiracy of Hungarian magnates, against Hapsburgs, subsequently suppressed.

May: 22nd/*June* 1st, secret Treaty of Dover between England and France; Louis XIV is given free hand in Holland and Spain; England is to receive subsidies of £150,000 (and also of £225,000 so long as the war with Holland lasts) and Charles II will declare himself a Catholic (James, Duke of York, has already openly discussed his own conversion). Louis XIV is to choose the moment for a declaration of war against the Dutch and England is to join in the war. On failure of the Spanish male line Charles is to support Louis' claims to the Spanish Crown;

France forms a treaty alliance with Sweden for three years;

the United Provinces appoint William of Orange as Captain-General.

Jun:

C Jul:

Aug: France occupies Lorraine, as a result of the intrigues of the Duke of Lorraine with the United Provinces.

D Oct:

Nov:

Dec: 21st/31st, Boyne treaty between France and England makes public the secret Treaty of Dover, but Charles's conversion to Catholicism is omitted.

E Christian V succeeds Frederick III in Denmark;

Charleston, Carolina, is founded;

The Bahamas are granted to the proprietors of Carolina.

F **Politics, Economics, Law and Education**
An English settlement is made at Charles Town (Charleston), South Carolina (moved to a new site in 1672).
Uniforms are introduced to the French Army by Louvois.

G **Science, Technology and Discovery**
Paul Amman, *Medicina Critica*.
Francis Lana makes proposals for aerial navigation.

H **Philosophy, Religion and Scholarship**
Peter Heylyn, *Aerius Redivivus;* or The History of Presbyterianism.
John Milton, *The Historie of Britain*.
Blaise Pascal, *Pensées* (posth.).
John Ray, *A Collection of English Proverbs*.
Benedict de Spinoza, *Tractatus Theologico-Politicus*.
John Dryden is appointed Historiographer Royal and Poet Laureate.

J **Art, Sculpture, Fine Arts and Architecture**
Painting:
Vermeer, *The Pearl Necklace*.

K **Music**
Académie Royale des Opéra (original home of the Paris Opéra) is founded.
John Blow is appointed organist of Westminster Abbey (–1680).

L **Literature (including Drama)**
Pierre Corneille, *Tite et Bérénice* (tragedy).
Marie-Madeleine de La Fayette, *Zaïde*.
Molière, *Les Amants magnifiques* (comedy). *Le Bourgeois gentilhomme* (comedy).
Jean Racine, *Bérénice*.
Izaak Walton, *The Life of George Herbert. The Lives of Donne, Hooker, Wotton and Herbert* (collected edition).

M **Births and Deaths**
Jan. 3rd George Monck, Duke of Albemarle, d. (61).
Jan. 21st Claude Duval d. (27).
Feb. 10th William Congreve b. (–1729).
May 12th Augustus II of Poland and Elector of Saxony b. (–1733).
Aug. 21st James Fitzjames, Duke of Berwick, b. (–1734).
— Louis le Vau d. (58).

1671   Morgan destroys Panama

A   Jan: English buccaneers under Sir Henry Morgan destroy Panama.
Feb: Treaty of Assistance between Brandenburg and the Netherlands (to become effective *May* 6th, 1672).
Mar:

B   Apr: Leaders of revolt in Hungary are executed;
22nd, English Parliament is prorogued by Charles II (until *Feb*. 1673).
May:
Jun: Turkey declares war on Poland.

C   Jul: Louis XIV makes series of treaties with Hanover, Osnabrück, Brunswick and the Palatinate (*–Dec*.).
Aug:
Sep: Vauban begins construction of forts in the Netherlands.

D   Oct:
Nov: 1st, Treaty of Neutrality between France and Emperor Leopold I who promises neutrality to France against Dutch provided Louis does not invade Spain or the Empire.
Dec: Spain makes a defensive treaty with Holland.

E   Philip of Orleans marries Liselotte, heiress to the Palatinate;
The Danes take St. Thomas;
The French Senegal company is founded.

F **Politics, Economics, Law and Education**
William Carter, *England's Interest by Trade Asserted*.
The English Crown resumes direct control of the customs system (farmed since 1605).

G **Science, Technology and Discovery**
Giovanni Cassini discovers the satellite Iapetus, the ninth in distance from Saturn.
G. W. von Leibniz adapts an adding-machine to facilitate multiplication.

H **Philosophy, Religion and Scholarship**
Jacques Bénigne Bossuet, *Exposition de la foi catholique*.
John Bunyan, *A Confession of My Faith, and A Reason of My Practice*.
Stephen Skinner, *Etymologicon linguae anglicanae*.
The Bible is printed in Arabic (in Rome).

J **Art, Sculpture, Fine Arts and Architecture**
Painting:
Sir Peter Lely, *Francis Mercury van Helmont*.
Adriaen van Ostade, *Travellers Resting*.
Architecture:
Christopher Wren, The Monument (–1677), to commemorate the Great Fire of 1666.
Lionel Bruant, Hôtel des Invalides, Paris (–1675).

K **Music**
Robert Cambert, *Pomone* (opera), first performed in Paris at the opening of the first
public opera house in France.

L **Literature (including Drama)**
Aphra Behn, *The Forced Marriage* (drama).
Sir Richard Fanshawe, *To Love Only for Love Sake* (dramatic romance translated and
adapted from Hurtado de Mendoza's *Querer por sólo querer* of 1623).
John Milton, *Paradise Regained; Samson Agonistes*.
Molière, *Les Fourberies de Scapin*, *La Comtesse d'Escarbagnas* (comedies).
Marie, Marquise de Sévigné, *Letters* (to her married daughter, Madame de Grignan),
first series.

M **Births and Deaths**
Feb. 26th Anthony Ashley Cooper, third Earl of Shaftesbury, b. (–1713).
Apr. 21st John Law b. (–1729).
May Edward Montagu, Earl of Manchester, d. (69).
June 15th John Ashburnham d. (68).
Nov. 6th Colley Cibber b. (–1757).
Nov. 12th Thomas, Lord Fairfax, d. (59).
— Rob Roy b. (–1734).
— Francesco Stradivari b. (–1743).

A Jan: 2nd, Stop of the Exchequer, whereby cash payments are suspended for 12 months;
many are made bankrupt and an economic council is organised with Shaftesbury as
President and Locke as Secretary.
Feb:
Mar: 15th, Charles II issues Declaration of Indulgence towards Roman Catholics and
Nonconformists (withdrawn 1673);
17th, Britain declares war on Holland and attacks Dutch ships in Atlantic and North
Sea; France subsequently declares war on the Dutch.

B Apr: 14th, alliance between French and Swedes against the Dutch.
May: 2nd, Great Elector concludes alliance with Dutch, promising an army of 22,000
which leads to the First Coalition against France;
28th, indecisive naval battle of Southwold Bay between British and Dutch.
Jun: 7th, Admiral de Ruyter's successful action against the combined English and French
fleets in Southwold Bay;
12th, the French army crosses the Rhine at Tolhoys;
15th, the Sluices are opened in Holland to save Amsterdam from the French;
23rd, alliance between Brandenburg and the Emperor Leopold I, to prevent extension
of French power;
29th, Louis XIV rejects Dutch terms for a peace.

C Jul: 4th, William of Orange, having been elected Stadtholder of Zeeland on 2nd, is elected
Stadtholder of Holland, and, 8th, becomes Captain and Admiral-General of the
Union.
Aug: 20th, the De Witt brothers, the leading republican statesmen, are assassinated at the
Hague.
Sep: 6th, William of Orange captures Naarden.

D Oct: 18th, Treaty of Buczacz follows Turkish attack on Poland which is forced to cede
Podolia and Ukraine;
27th, Dutch conclude treaty of alliance with the Emperor Leopold I at the Hague.
Nov: 17th, the Earl of Shaftesbury is appointed Lord Chancellor.
Dec: William of Orange is forced to raise the siege of Charleroi and withdraw to Amsterdam.

E Reconstruction of the English Royal Africa Company which obtains a monopoly of slave
trade, and English Guinea Company is merged with it;
The French occupy Pondicherry and Coromandel Coast in India.

M **Births and Deaths**
Jan 15th John Cosin d. (77).
Mar — Richard Steele b. (–1729).
May 1st Joseph Addison b. (–1719).
May 28th Edward Montagu, Earl of Sandwich, d. (47).
May 30th Peter the Great b. (–1725).
Aug. 20th John de Witt d. (47).
Sept. 16th Anne Bradstreet d. (c. 60).
Oct. 21st Ludovico Antonio Muratori b. (–1750).
— Jean Martinet d. (70).
— John Webb d. (60).

F Politics, Economics, Law and Education
  William Temple, *Observations upon the United Provinces of the Netherlands.*
  Jan. 2nd, the Stop of the Exchequer in London, which suspends payments for a year,
  causing many bankruptcies.
  Charles II grants a charter to the Royal Africa Company, which subsequently builds
  forts at Sekondi, Accra and Whydah and repairs Cape Coast Castle, Gold Coast.
  S. Pufendorf, *De jure naturae et gentium,* places international law on an ethical basis.
  The French postal services are farmed (–1790).
  Donneau de Vizé establishes *Mercure galant,* Paris.

G Science, Technology and Discovery
  Marcello Malpighi, *Anatome plantarum.*
  The medicinal root epecacuanha is introduced to Europe.
  Jan van der Heyde and his son make a flexible hose, by sewing together the edges of a
  strip of leather, for use in fighting fires.
  Jacques Marquette explores the country around Chicago, north of the R. Missouri
  (–1673).

H Philosophy, Religion and Scholarship
  Nicolas Antonio, *Bibliotheca Hispana Nova* (–1696).
  Joseph Alleine, *An Alarm to the Unconverted ; or The Sure Guide to Heaven* (posth.).
  Elias Ashmole, *Institution, Laws, Ceremonies of the Order of the Garter.*
  William Cave, *Primitive Christianity.*
  John Josselyn, *New-England Rarities Discovered.*
  The Declaration of Indulgence issued by Charles II.
  Synod of Jerusalem revives the *Confession of Faith* of the Greek Orthodox Church, re-
  futing Cyril Lucaris (–1629).

J Art, Sculpture, Fine Arts and Architecture
  Painting:
    Claude, *Aeneas at Delos.*
  Architecture:
    Christopher Wren, St. Stephen's Walbrook, London.
  Fine Arts:
    John Dwight sets up his pottery at Fulham.

K Music
  John Banister holds first public concerts in London at Whitefriars (–1678); seats 1/-
  each.
  Thomas Salomon, *An Essay toward the advancement of Music by Casting Away the . . .
  Cleffs* (answered by Matthew Locke in 1673).
  Académie Royale de Danse is enlarged to become the Académie Royale de Musique et
  de Danse.

L Literature (including Drama)
  John Dryden, *The Conquest of Granada, or Almanzor and Almahide* (heroic drama;
  burlesqued in *The Rehearsal,* see below).
  Molière, *Les Femmes Savantes.*
  Jean Racine, *Bajazet* (tragedy).
  George Villiers, 2nd Duke of Buckingham, *The Rehearsal* (burlesque).
  William Wycherley, *Love in a Wood* (comedy).
(*Continued opposite*)

A Jan:
Feb: Abrogation of French *Parlement*'s rights to object to Royal Edicts.
Mar: 8th, Charles II withdraws Declaration of Indulgence (of *Mar.* 1672);
    29th, the Test Act receives Royal Assent and excludes Roman Catholics from office in England.

B Apr: 10th, the Great Elector makes preliminary peace with Louis XIV (confirmed *June*), ending the First Coalition against Louis XIV.
May:
Jun: 6th, Peace of Vossem between Brandenburg and France; the Great Elector promises not to support any enemies of Louis XIV;
    12th, James, Duke of York, is forced by Test Act to retire as Lord High Admiral and is replaced by Prince Rupert (–*July* 9th when Charles assumes responsibility);
    19th, Sir Thomas Osborne succeeds Lord Clifford as Lord High Treasurer (–1673) and subsequently reforms finances;
    a peace conference opens at Cologne under Swedish mediation (–*June* 1674), but negotiations founder.

C Jul: 1st/11th, William of Orange signs a defensive alliance with Denmark.
Aug: 11th/21st, Rupert is defeated off Texel, and this marks the end of efforts to land troops in Holland and frees Dutch coast from blockade;
    30th, alliance of the Emperor Leopold I with Holland, which is joined by Spain and the Duke of Lorraine against France;
    Dutch capture New York.
Sep: 16th, Emperor Leopold I declares war against France;
    30th, Duke of York contracts to marry Maria d'Este of Modena.

D Oct:
Nov: 9th, Shaftesbury is removed from Chancellorship and Finch becomes Lord Keeper;
    10th, Michael, King of Poland, dies;
    11th, John Sobieski defeats Turks at Khorzim;
    12th, William of Orange captures Bonn, and relieves the danger to Utrecht. As a result Cologne and Münster sue for peace, while the Bishops of Trèves and Mainz join the Coalition.
Dec:

E The French take Chandarnaga, north of Calcutta, and send an expedition against Ceylon;
Marquette and Joliet descend Mississippi to Arkansas;
Frontenac, who arrived in Canada *Sept.* 12th, 1672, founds Fort Frontenac, with La Salle as commandant, and conciliates Iroquois.

F **Politics, Economics, Law and Education**
Richard Hoare founds Hoare's Bank, London.
Edmund Ludlow, the Parliamentary general, completes his *Memoirs*.

G **Science, Technology and Discovery**
C. Huygens, *Horologium oscillatorium*.

H **Philosophy, Religion and Scholarship**
Robert Clavel, *A Catalogue of all the Books Printed in England since the Dreadful Fire of London in 1666 to the end of Michaelmas Term, 1672*.

J **Art, Sculpture, Fine Arts and Architecture**
Painting:
Adriaen van Ostade, *The Violin Players*.
Willem van de Velde, *Three Ships in a Gale*.
Sculpture:
Caius Cibber, reliefs for The Monument, London (–1675).
Architecture:
Christopher Wren is knighted.

K **Music**
Matthew Locke, *Melothesia, or Certain Rules for Playing on a Continued Bass* . . .
J. B. Lully, *Cadmus and Hermonie*, first performed in Paris.
Buxtehude starts the Abendmusiken performances at Lubeck.

L **Literature (including Drama)**
Aphra Behn, *The Dutch Lover* (comedy).
John Dryden, *Marriage à la mode* (comedy). *Amboyna* (tragedy).
John Milton, *Poems Upon Various Occasions* (written since 1645).
Molière, *Le Malade imaginaire* (comedy).
Jean Racine, *Mithridate* (tragedy).
Thomas Shadwell, *Epsom Wells* (comedy).
William Wycherley, *The Gentleman Dancing-Master* (comedy).
Pedro Calderon de la Barca, *La vida es sueno* (tragi-comedy).

M **Births and Deaths**
Feb. 17th Molière d. (51).
Mar. 15th Salvator Rosa d. (*c.* 58).
Aug. — Thomas, Lord Clifford, d. (43).

1674   The French devastate the Palatinate—John Sobieski elected king of Poland

A Jan: Denmark joins the Coalition against France.

Feb: 9th/19th, Treaty of Westminster by which British withdraw from the Dutch War, and New Netherlands (New York) and New Sweden are definitely recognised as British. The peace party in England, led by Shaftesbury, forces Charles II's agreement.

Mar: The Elector Palatine joins the Coalition against France.

B Apr:

May: 21st, John Sobieski is elected King of Poland as John III;

28th, at the German Diet of Ratisbon, Emperor Leopold I declares war on France.

Jun: (*–Oct.*), French successes in Franche-Comté, Flanders and western Germany, under the direction of Vauban, while Turenne defeats the imperialists at Sinsheim.

C Jul: 1st, Triple Alliance of Emperor, Dutch and Spanish against French is formally concluded, and is joined later by the Pope and Elector of Brandenburg.

Aug: French troops devastate the Palatinate.

Sep: William of Orange takes Grave, but is unable to invade France.

D Oct:

Nov: Turenne begins his march across the Vosges from Lixheim in Lorraine to Belfort.

Dec:

E The States-General of the United Provinces declare the office of Stadtholder hereditary in the family of Orange;

French Guinea is organised;

Natives expel the French from Madagascar;

Sivaji, founder of the Mahratta State, concludes a treaty with Britain and declares himself independent of the Mogul Emperor Aurangzeb.

F **Politics, Economics, Law and Education**

G **Science, Technology and Discovery**
Thomas Willis, *Pharmaceutice rationalis*.
John Mayow in *Tractatus quinque medico-physici* propounds a theory on the nature of combustion.

H **Philosophy, Religion and Scholarship**
Nicolas Boileau, *L'Art poétique*.
Étienne Baluze, *Capitularia Regum Francorum* (edicts).
Henry Hammond, *Collected Works* (posth.).
Thomas Hobbes, translation of Homer's *Odyssey*.
Nicolas Malebranche, *De la recherche de la vérité* (Eng. trans. *The Search for Truth*, 1694).
Louis Moreri, *Le Grand dictionnaire historique; ou, Le Mélange curieux de l'histoire sainte et profane* (the first encyclopaedic reference work of its kind).
Thomas Rymer, *Reflections on Aristotle's Treatise of Poesie*, by René Rapin, translated.
Anthony à Wood, *Historia et Antiquitates Universitatis Oxoniensis*.

J **Art, Sculpture, Fine Arts and Architecture**
Painting:
Murillo, *St. Francis*.
Sculpture:
Grinling Gibbons, pedestal for Charles I's statue.

K **Music**
J. B. Lully, *Alceste* (opera).

L **Literature (including Drama)**
Giambattista Basile, *Il Pentamerone*.
Thomas Flatman, *Poems and Songs*.
John Milton, *Paradise Lost*, 2nd edition (in 12 books; –1667).
Jean Racine, *Iphigénie en Aulide*.
Theatre Royal, Drury Lane, London rebuilt (*Mar.* 26th) after the fire, and reopened.

M **Births and Deaths**
Jan. 7th Margaret Cavendish, Duchess of Newcastle, d. (50).
Jan. 12th Giacomo Carissimi d. (*c.* 70).
Jan. 13th Prosper Jolyot de Crébillon b. (–1762).
Feb. 22nd Jean Chapelain d. (78).
Feb. — Jean La Badie d. (64).
Mar. — Jethro Tull b. (–1741).
June — Nicholas Rowe b. (–1718).
July 17th Isaac Watts b. (–1748).
Sept. 27th Thomas Traherne d. (36).
Oct. 18th Richard ('Beau') Nash b. (–1762).
Oct. — Robert Herrick d. (83).
Nov. 8th John Milton d. (66).
Dec. 9th Edward Hyde, Earl of Clarendon, d. (65).
— Henry Sacheverell b. (–1724).
— Charles Townshend b. (–1738).

A Jan: 5th, Turenne defeats the Great Elector of Brandenburg at Colmar (or the battle of
       Turkheim);
       12th, left bank of R. Rhine is freed of Germans.
   Feb:
   Mar:

B Apr:
   May:
   Jun: 11th, alliance between France and Poland;
       12th, Victor Amadeus II becomes Duke of Savoy;
       25th, Great Elector defeats Swedes at Rathenow and decisively, 28th, at Fehrbellin.

C Jul: 27th, Turenne is killed at Sassbach, and his death marks the end of great French
       victories.
   Aug: French defeat Dutch and Spanish fleets in Bay of Palermo and take Sicily.
   Sep: Créquy capitulates to the Duke of Lorraine at Saarbrück;
       9th, New England Confederation declares war against Wampanoag Indians, for
       breaking truce (–Aug. 1676).

D Oct: War between Denmark and Sweden breaks out.
   Nov: 6th, Charles II of Spain attains his majority;
       22nd, bribed by Louis XIV, Charles II of England prorogues English Parliament for 15
       months.
   Dec:
       the Prince of Condé retires from military affairs.

E Duke George William, last Piast of Lower Silesia (Liegnitz line), dies and, despite the
       Elector of Brandenburg's claims, the Emperor seizes Leignitz, Brieg and Wohlau as a
       Bohemian fief;
   Guru Gobind Singh organises political power of Sikhs.

F Politics, Economics, Law and Education

Savary, *Le Parfait Négociant*.

The Green Ribbon Club is founded by Shaftesbury and Buckingham as the headquarters of the Whig faction.

G Science, Technology and Discovery

Greenwich Observatory is established, *Aug.*, under John Flamsteed as first astronomer
royal.

Olaus Römer discovers the finite velocity of light, estimating the sun's rays reach the
earth in 11 minutes.

Isaac Newton, *Opticks*.

Robert Boyle invents the hydrometer for determining the density of bodies.

G. W. von Leibniz discovers the differential and integral calculus.

Nicolas Lemery, *Cours de Chymie*.

H Philosophy, Religion and Scholarship

Sir William Dugdale, *The Baronage of England*.

Philipp Jakob Spener (founder of Pietism), *Pia Desideria*.

Thomas Traherne, *Christian Ethics*.

Philosophical Transactions of the Royal Society of London are initiated.

J Art, Sculpture, Fine Arts and Architecture

Architecture:

Sir Christopher Wren begins rebuilding St. Paul's Cathedral, London.

K Music

L Literature (including Drama)

William Wycherley, *The Country Wife* (comedy).

M Births and Deaths

Jan. 16th Louis de Rouvroy, Duc de Saint-Simon, b. (–1755).

July 27th Turenne d. (63).

July 28th Bulstrode Whitelocke d. (69).

Oct. 11th Samuel Clarke b. (–1729).

— John Erskine, Earl of Mar, b. (–1732).

— Bernard Lintot b. (–1736).

— Antonio Vivaldi b. (–1741).

1676   Bacon's Rebellion in Virginia—Peace of Zurawna

A   **Jan:** 29th, Theodore III, son of Alexis, becomes Tsar of Russia on death of his father (–1682).
Feb: 7th/17th, secret alliance between Charles II of Britain and Louis XIV whereby neither is to help the enemies of the other, and Charles is assured of his French pension.
Mar:

B   **Apr:** 22nd, Duquesne defeats De Ruyter at Catania, off Messina.
May: Louis XIV takes Bouchain.
Jun: A *coup d'état* in Spain leads to the overthrow of the Queen Mother; Don John, a natural son of Philip IV, pro-French, takes command.

C   **Jul:** 22nd, Pope Clement X dies, and is succeeded (*Sept.* 21st) by Innocent XI.
Aug: 3rd, Nathaniel Bacon's manifesto, 'Declaration of People of Virginia', gains support for rebellion against the authority of the Governor.
Sep: The Duke of Lorraine captures Philipsburg for the Emperor Leopold I.

D   **Oct:** 27th, Peace of Zurawna between Turkey and Poland; Podolia is divided between the parties and Turkey keeps only part of the Ukraine.
Nov: 3rd, Ahmad Kiuprili dies, and is succeeded by his brother-in-law, Kara Mustafa, as Grand Vizier of Turkey.
Dec: Charles XI of Sweden defeats the Danes at Lunden.

E   A demarcation line between East and West New Jersey is settled.

F Politics, Economics, Law and Education
   Serious 'flu epidemic in England.

G Science, Technology and Discovery
   Mariotte independently discovers 'Boyle's Law'.
   G. W. von Leibniz discovers the infinitesimal calculus.
   Nehemiah Grew in the 'Anatomy of Plants', describes to the Royal Society the functions of stamens and pistils (published 1682).
   Thomas Sydenham, *Observationes Medicae*, suggests cooling treatment for smallpox.
   Wiseman, *Seven Chirurgical Treatises*.

H Philosophy, Religion and Scholarship
   Noël Alexandre, *Selecta historiae ecclesiasticae capita* (–1686, 26 vols.).
   Gabriel de Foigny, *La Terre Australe Connue* (a utopia).
   Benjamin Thompson, *New England's Crisis*.
   Roger Williams, *George Fox Digg'd Out of his Burrowes* (against Quaker teachings).

J Art, Sculpture, Fine Arts and Architecture
   Painting:
      Godfrey Kneller, *Mr. Banks*.
   Architecture:
      Sir Christopher Wren, Trinity College Library, Cambridge (–1684).

K Music
   Thomas Mace, *Musical Grammarian*.

L Literature (including Drama)
   Charles Cotton, Walton's *Compleat Angler*, Part 2 (–1653).
   John Dryden, *Aureng-Zebe* (Dryden's last tragedy in rhymed verse).
   Sir George Etherege, *The Man of Mode* (comedy).
   Thomas Otway, *Don Carlos* (tragedy).

M Births and Deaths
   Mar. 11th Allart van Everdingen d. (54).
   Mar. 27th Francis II, Rákóczy, of Transylvania, b. (–1735).
   Apr. 29th Michael Adrianzoon de Ruyter d. (69).
   June 21st Anthony Collins b. (–1729).
   July 16th Marie, Marquise de Brinvilliers, d. (46).
   Aug. 17th Hans Jakob Christoffel von Grimmelshausen d. (*c.* 51).
   Aug. 26th Robert Walpole b. (–1745).
   Nov. 14th Benjamin Hoadly b. (–1761).
   Dec. 25th Matthew Hale d. (67).
   — Alexander Selkirk b. (–1721).
   — James Thornhill b. (–1734).

A **Jan:**

Feb: 15th, English Parliament meets (*–July* 1678); Charles II declares he has made an alliance with the Dutch against France;

—, Lords Shaftesbury, Buckingham, Salisbury and Wharton are imprisoned in the Tower for having argued in Opposition that the present Parliament is illegal.

Mar: Louis XIV takes Valenciennes and St. Omer.

Massachusetts buys most of Maine from the heirs of Sir Ferdinando Gorges.

B **Apr:** 11th, William of Orange is defeated at Cassel by the Duke of Orleans;

22nd, Dutch fight indecisive naval action against the French at Catania.

May:

Jun: 11th, a Swedish defeat at Öland by a combined Dutch-Danish fleet.

C **Jul:**

Aug: 1st, Great Elector begins siege of Stettin.

Sep:

D **Oct:**

Nov: 4th/14th, William of Orange marries Princess Mary, daughter of James, Duke of York;

the French take Freiburg.

Dec: 12th, Great Elector takes Stettin and (in 1678) Rugen and pursues the Swedes to Riga;

Christian V of Denmark is defeated by a Swedish force at Cassel.

E

F **Politics, Economics, Law and Education**
J. Houghton, *England's Great Happiness; or a Dialogue between Content and Complaint*.
Innsbruck University is founded.

G **Science, Technology and Discovery**

H **Philosophy, Religion and Scholarship**
William Cave, *History of Martyrdoms* (*Apostolici*).
Johann Jacob Hofmann, *Lexicon Universale*, 2 vols. (the first treatment of knowledge in the sciences and the arts in lexicon form).
Increase Mather, *The Troubles That Have Happened in New England*.
Robert Plot, *The Natural History of Oxfordshire*.
Benedict de Spinoza, *Ethics*.

J **Art, Sculpture, Fine Arts and Architecture**
Painting:
Pieter de Hooch, *Musical Party in a Courtyard*.
Godfrey Kneller, *Mr. Vernon*.

K **Music**

L **Literature (including Drama)**
Richard Head, *The Life and Death of Mother Shipton*.
Jean Racine, *Phèdre* (tragedy).
William Wycherley, *The Plain Dealer* (comedy).

M **Births and Deaths**
Feb. 21st Benedict Spinoza d. (44).
Mar. 20th George Digby, Earl of Bristol, d. (64).
Mar. 28th Wenceslaus Hollar d. (70).
May 4th Isaac Barrow d. (47).
July 13th William Berkeley d. (69).
Sept. 11th James Harrington d. (66).
Nov. 9th Gilbert Sheldon d. (79).
— George Farquhar b. (–1707).

A **Jan:**
Feb: The Earl of Shaftesbury is released from the Tower.
Mar: 2nd/12th, British sign an earlier treaty (of *Dec.* 31st/*Jan.* 10th) with the Dutch to force France to make peace, but this proves ineffectual;
Louis XIV captures Ghent and Ypres.

B **Apr:**
May: 17th, Charles II signs a secret treaty with Louis XIV, but refuses to ratify it.
Jun:

C **Jul:** 16th/26th, further Anglo-Dutch treaty to present an ultimatum to France.
Aug: 10th, Peace of Nijmegen between France and Holland; by its terms France restores Maestricht to Holland and Messina to Spain. The Dutch receive favourable commercial advantages in place of Colbert's hostile tariff; William of Orange is restored to his estates in the Spanish Netherlands, France, Franche-Comté and the Charolais. The Dutch cede Goree to France;
13th, the Popish Plot, in which it is alleged that the Pope has required the Jesuits to overthrow Charles II with French and Spanish aid, is brought to the King's notice;
14th, the battle of St. Denis is fought, after the Peace of Nijmegen is signed.
Sep: 6th, Titus Oates deposes his version of the Popish Plot before Sir Edmund Berry Godfrey, a London magistrate;
17th, Franco-Spanish peace Treaty of Nijmegen, by which Spain cedes Franche-Comté and 14 towns including Valenciennes, Cambrai and Ypres, comprising a line of fortifications stretching from the Marne to Dunkirk; France restores Charleroi, Ghent and other conquests in the Netherlands and Catalonia.

D **Oct:** 12th, the Great Elector conquers Stralsund from the Swedes;
17th, Sir Edmund Berry Godfrey is found murdered.
Nov: 5th, Greifswald, Sweden's last possession in Pomerania, falls to the Great Elector;
30th, following Louis XIV's disclosure of his last secret treaty with Charles II to the Opposition and the revelations of Titus Oates, Roman Catholics are excluded from both Houses of Parliament.
Dec: 21st, Thomas Osborne, Earl of Danby is impeached in the House of Commons for alleged negotiations with France (not proceeded with by the Lords).

E Emeric Tokoly becomes leader of the Hungarian rebels against the Hapsburgs;
Russo-Swedish war breaks out.

F Politics, Economics, Law and Education

G Science, Technology and Discovery
C. Huygens records his discovery of the polarisation of light in *Traité de la lumière* (published 1690).
Thomas Thatcher, *A Brief Rule . . . in Small Pocks or Measles* (first medical publication in America).
La Salle explores the Great Lakes of Canada (–1679).

H Philosophy, Religion and Scholarship
Robert Barclay, *An Apology for the True Christian Divinity Held by the Quakers* (Latin text in 1676).
Isaac Barrow, *Sermons On Various Occasions*.
John Bunyan, *The Pilgrim's Progress, part 1* (–1684).
David Calderwood, *History of the Kirk of Scotland* (1514–1625).
Ralph Cudworth, *The True Intellectual System of the Universe*.
Charles Du Fresne, Seigneur Du Cange, *Glossarium ad scriptores mediae et infirmae latinatis*, 3 vols.
Narcissus Luttrell, *A Brief Historicall Relation of State Affairs, 1678* (concluded 1714; not published until 1837).

J Art, Sculpture, Fine Arts and Architecture
Painting:
Murillo, *The Virgin and the Christ Child distributing bread to Pilgrims;* also *Immaculata de Soult* (Murillo paints 30 other pictures on the same theme).
Architecture:
Jules Hardouin-Mansart, Versailles, Marly Trianon, etc. (–1699).

K Music
Thomas Britton holds concerts (–1714) above his coalhouse in Clerkenwell, London (Handel and Pepusch later play there).
The first German opera house opens in Hamburg.

L Literature (including Drama)
Anne Bradsheet, *Contemplations*.
Samuel Butler, *Hudibras*, part 3 (–1662, 1663).
Thomas Corneille, *Le Comte d'Essex* (tragedy).
John Dryden, *All For Love* (tragedy).
Marie-Madeleine, Comtesse de La Fayette, *La Princesse de Clèves*.
Jean de La Fontaine, *Fables choisies, mises en vers* (continued —1668).
Izaak Walton, *The Life of Dr. Sanderson*.

M Births and Deaths
July 26th Emperor Joseph I b. (–1711).
July — Thomas Hearne b. (–1735).
Aug. 15th Andrew Marvell d. (57).
Oct. 1st Henry St. John, Viscount Bolingbroke, b. (–1751).
Oct. 8th Isaac Penington d. (62).
Oct. — Edmund Berry Godfrey d. (56).
— William Croft b. (–1727).
— George Farquhar b. (–1707).

A   Jan: 24th, the 'Cavalier Parliament' (sitting since 1661) is dissolved, due to Charles II's fear of passage of Exclusion Bill to exclude the Catholic James, Duke of York, from the succession; at the same time the Lords refuse to commit Danby who was dismissed in *Dec.* 1678 for alleged contract with France (although impeachment not carried, he is kept in the Tower until 1685).
Feb: 5th, Peace of Nijmegen between Emperor Leopold I and Louis XIV, who obtains Freiburg and Breisach, but restores Philipsburg;
20th, Earl of Sunderland is appointed a Secretary of State (–1631).
Mar: 4th, James, Duke of York, sails for Antwerp, to begin his banishment;
6th, third Parliament of Charles II meets (–*May* 27th); leading ministers are William Temple, Halifax, Essex, Sunderland and Shaftesbury.

B   Apr:
May: 3rd, Archbishop Sharp of St. Andrews is murdered by Fife lairds for his treatment of Covenanters;
26th, Habeas Corpus Amendment Act.
Jun: 1st, the Scottish Covenanters defeat Royal troops under Claverhouse at Drumclog;
22nd, the Duke of Monmouth subdues insurrection of Scottish Covenanters at Bothwell Bridge;
29th, Peace of St. Germain-en-Laye between Sweden and Brandenburg by which Brandenburg loses all of her conquests, except a strip on the right bank of the R. Oder.

C   Jul: 12th, Charles II dissolves Parliament for attempting to exclude the Duke of York from the throne.
Aug: Charles II of Spain marries Marie Louise of Orleans.
Sep: 18th, New Hampshire is created a separate province from Massachusetts;
26th, formal peace is signed between Denmark and Sweden by Treaty of Lund, following earlier peace at Fontainebleau (*June* 29th) by which the Danes lose all their conquests at the insistence of Louis XIV.

D   Oct: 7th, fourth Parliament of Charles II meets but is immediately prorogued over the Exclusion Bill, and does not meet again for a year; subsequently Shaftesbury is dismissed, William Temple, Essex and Halifax resign and they are replaced by the 'Chits', or 'Tory' ministry of Godolphin, Hyde and Sunderland. This begins the use of the terms Tory and Whig to describe the two parties;
12th, Peace of Nijmegen between Holland, Sweden and Spain is confirmed;
'Chambers of Reunion' meet at Metz, Breisach, Besançon and Tournai to adjudge for France certain towns on the left bank of the Rhine.
Nov:
Dec: 17th, the effective ruler of Spain, Don John, dies and the Queen Mother, Marie of Austria, regains power; Hapsburg influence is again established in Madrid.

E

F **Politics, Economics, Law and Education**
Sir William Petty, *A Treatise on Taxes and Contributions*.
Colbert requires French merchants to be examined in book-keeping and commercial law.
Louis XIV issues a stringent edict against duelling and secures the agreement of the French nobility that they will not engage in duels under any provocation.
Serious fire at Boston, Massachusetts, destroys the dockyard, warehouses and many dwellings.

G **Science, Technology and Discovery**
Edmund Halley, *Catalogus stellarum australium*.
Théophile Bonet, *Sepulcretum*, founds the study of morbid anatomy.
Denis Papin makes a 'stream digester', or engine for softening bones (paper read to the Royal Society, 1681).
J. Kunkel develops the manufacture of glass at Potsdam.

H **Philosophy, Religion and Scholarship**
Thomas Blount, *Ancient Tenures and Jocular Customs of Some Manors*.
Gilbert Burnet, *History of the Reformation of the Church of England*, vol. 1 (–1681, 1714).
Robert South, *Sermons* (–1715, 1717, 1744).

J **Art, Sculpture, Fine Arts and Architecture**
Painting:
Charles Le Brun, Décor, Versailles, Galérie des Glaces (–1684).

K **Music**

L **Literature (including Drama)**
Francis Beaumont and John Fletcher, *Fifty Comedies and Tragedies* (posth.).
Nathaniel Lee and John Dryden, *Oedipus* (tragedy).
P'U Sungling, *Liao Chai* (collection of short stories).
John Dryden is attacked by hired ruffians in Rose Alley, Covent Garden, London (*Dec.* 18th, the Earl of Rochester having attributed to him an anonymous *Essay on Satire*, actually written by John Sheffield, third Earl of Mulgrave, a patron of Dryden).
Govert Bidloo, *Karel, efprins van Spanje* (one of the first dramas in Dutch written in the French classical style, with ballets and interludes, by the playwright-lessee of the Amsterdam Theatre).

M **Births and Deaths**
Feb. 5th Joost van den Vondel d. (92).
May 3rd James Sharp d. (59).
Aug. 24th Cardinal de Retz d. (65).
Dec. 4th Thomas Hobbes d. (91).
Dec. 31st Giovanni Alfonso Borelli d. (69).
— Firman Abauzit b. (–1767).
— Charles Edouard Le Blond b. (–1719).
— Jan Steen d. (55).

A   Jan:

Feb: The Duke of Medina-Celi becomes First Minister in Spain (–1685).

Mar: 17th, the Dauphin marries a Bavarian princess;

22nd, Breisach *Parlement* adjudges French sovereignty in Alsace.

B   Apr:

May: Louis XIV wins over the Bishop of Strasburg with a pension.

Jun:

C   Jul: 11th, Maximilian II Emanuel becomes Elector of Bavaria (–1726).

Aug: The Breisach Chamber of Reunion claims Upper and Lower Alsace for France;

John George III, the new Elector of Saxony advocates that the German princes should arm to oppose Louis XIV.

Sep:

D   Oct: 21st, Charles II's fourth Parliament finally meets (summoned for *Oct.* 1679);

Charles XI of Sweden declares himself absolute.

Nov: 4th, first reading of second Exclusion Bill which not only bars James from the throne but also makes it treason for him to enter Britain (passes the Commons, 11th, but at the instigation of Lord Halifax, 15th, is rejected by House of Lords);

30th, Lord Stafford is tried for treason.

Dec: 29th, Lord Stafford is executed;

the Bishop of Münster signs a treaty of alliance with Louis XIV.

E   Tsunayoshi becomes Shōgun of Japan;

August de Saxe Weissensels, last Archbishop of Magdeburg, dies and the Great Elector incorporates the Archbishopric with Brandenburg;

First Brandenburg expedition to W. Africa;

French colonial empire from Quebec to the mouth of the R. Mississippi is organised;

A French factory is founded in Siam.

F **Politics, Economics, Law and Education**
Robert Filmer, *Patriarcha; or the Natural Power of Kings.*
Sir William Temple, *An Essay on Government;* and *A Survey of the Constitution.*
William Dockwra establishes a penny post in London (–1688).
George Dalgarno, *Didasculocophus; or the Deaf and Dumb Man's Tutor,* an exposition of the 'hard alphabet'.

G **Science, Technology and Discovery**
Robert Boyle obtains phosphorus by evaporating urine and distilling the residue with sand.
G. A. Borelli, *De motu animalium* (posth.), explaining functions on physical and mechanical principles.

H **Philosophy, Religion and Scholarship**
John Bunyan, *The Life and Death of Mr. Badman.*
François de Salignac de La Mothe-Fénelon, *Dialogues sur l'éloquence* (–1690, 1718).
Esprit Fléchier, *Oraisons funèbres.*
Sir Roger L'Estrange translates *Select Colloquies of Erasmus* (–1689).
César-Pierre Richelet, *Dictionnaire françois* (. . . les mots et les choses . . . remarques sur la langue françoise . . . prononciation, etc.).

J **Art, Sculpture, Fine Arts and Architecture**
Architecture:
Jules Hardouin-Mansart, Chapel des Invalides, Paris (–1719).
Sir Christopher Wren, St. Clement Dane's Church, London.

K **Music**
Henry Purcell is appointed organist of Westminster Abbey.
First musical entertainments are held at Sadler's Wells, Islington.
Stradivari makes his earliest known cello.

L **Literature (including Drama)**
Thomas Otway, *The Orphan* (tragedy).
La Comédie-Française formed by merging of the *Théâtre Guénéguad* and Players from the *Hôtel de Bourgogne* (*see* 1658).

M **Births and Deaths**
Feb. 17th Denzil, Lord Holles, d. (80).
Mar. 17th François, Duc de la Rochefoucauld, d. (67).
July 26th John Wilmot, Earl of Rochester, d. (33).
Sept. 25th Samuel Butler d. (68).
Oct. 30th Antoinette Bourignon d. (64).
Nov. 4th Joseph Glanvill d. (44).
— Peter Lely d. (63).
— Jean Louis Ligonier b. (–1770).

A   Jan: 11th, a defensive alliance is signed between Brandenburg and France;
18th, fourth Parliament of Charles II is dissolved.
Feb:
Mar: 4th, royal charter for Pennsylvania;
21st (–28th), fifth Parliament of Charles II meets at Oxford, but is dissolved when the Exclusion Bill is brought in.

B   Apr: Brandenburg forms a defensive alliance with Sweden by the Treaty of Finsterwalde.
May:
Jun:

C   Jul:
Aug:
Sep: 30th, French troops take Strasbourg and Casale in peacetime;
—, Hague Treaty of Guarantee between Holland and Sweden to maintain the Treaties of Westphalia and Nijmegen (leads to the League of Augsburg);
the Turks mass on the borders of Syria.

D   Oct: 30th, European Congress meets at Frankfurt-on-Main.
Nov: 9th, religious toleration is granted to Hungarian Protestants at Diet of Odenburg;
French begin siege of Luxemburg (–1682).
Dec: 23rd, Earl of Argyle is sentenced to death for treason, but has fled.

E   Large-scale emigration of Huguenots from northern and western France begins;
Tobago is established as a colony of James, Duke of Courland.

F Politics, Economics, Law and Education
James Dalrymple Stair, *Institutions of the Laws of Scotland*.
Sir Stephen Fox persuades Charles II to found Chelsea Hospital for wounded and dis-
charged soldiers.

G Science, Technology and Discovery
Canal du Midi, or Languedoc Canal, joining the Bay of Biscay to the Mediterranean
is completed on the scheme devised by Baron Paul Riquet de Bonrepos.

H Philosophy, Religion and Scholarship
Jacques-Bénigne Bossuet, *Discours sur l'histoire universelle*.
Thomas Burnet, *Telluris Theoria Sacra*.
Jean Mabillon, *De re diplomatica, libri sex* (−1704; on the study of certain medieval
charters, lays the foundation of modern historical criticism).

J Art, Sculpture, Fine Arts and Architecture
Architecture:
Sir Christopher Wren, Tom Tower, Christ Church, Oxford.

K Music
In Lully's ballet *The Triumph of Love* professional female dancers appear at the Paris
Opéra for the first time.

L Literature (including Drama)
John Dryden, *Absalom and Achitophel*, part 1 (part 2 −1682).
Andrew Marvell, *Miscellaneous Poems* (posth.).

M Births and Deaths
May 25th Pedro Calderón de la Barca d. (81).
June 9th William Lilly d. (79).
Nov. 28th Jean Cavalier b. (−1740).
— Georg Telemann b. (−1767).

A Jan:
  Feb: The Earl of Shaftesbury, sent to the Tower in *July* 1681 on a charge of treason, is
    discharged on bail (he leaves England for Holland *Oct.* 19th);
      Louis XIV promises the Count Palatine a pension by the Convention of Areillen;
      Louis' agents foment opposition to the government in Hungary, Poland and Sweden.
  Mar: The Assembly of the French Clergy endorse Louis XIV's Declaration of Four
    Articles to secure the independence of the Gallican Church: the Pope's power is
    declared to be limited to spiritual affairs; his opinion in questions of faith requires
    confirmation by the whole Church; General Councils of the Church are superior to
    the Pope; the independence of the Gallican Church is asserted.

B Apr: 9th, La Salle, claims the entire area of Louisiana for France.
  May: 15th (–18th), Revolt of the Streltsi in Russia.
  Jun: James, Duke of York, returns to England.

C Jul: 5th, on the death of Tsar Feodore, Tsaritza Sophia becomes Regent (–1689) for her
    infant brothers, Ivan and Peter, who are to rule jointly.
  Aug:
  Sep:

D Oct: Pennsylvania adopts a Constitution (the Great Charter), and Philadelphia is laid out.
  Nov:
  Dec: The Turks proclaim Emeric Tokoly King of Hungary.

E A Danish settlement is made on the Gold Coast;
  Sir John Child becomes Governor of Bombay (–1690).

F **Politics, Economics, Law and Education**
Sir William Petty, *Essay Concerning Multiplications of Mankind.*
Robert Cavalier, sieur de la Salle, takes possession of the Mississippi Valley for France
(Louisiana is first settled in 1699).
A weaving-mill with 100 looms is established at Amsterdam.

G **Science, Technology and Discovery**
P. Bayle, *Thoughts on the Comet of 1680*, ends the superstitious fear about comets.
Jan Schreyer first applies the hydrostatic test for determining live births.
Elias Ashmole founds the Ashmolean Museum, Oxford, on the collections of the
Tradescants.

H **Philosophy, Religion and Scholarship**
John Bunyan, *The Holy War.*
William Cave, *Ecclesiastici.*
François Eudes de Mézeray, *De l'origine des Français.*
John Milton, *A Brief History of Muscovia* (posth.).
Bulstrode Whitelocke, *Memorials of English Affairs* (from Charles I to the Restoration).
Acta Eruditorum starts in Germany (the first learned periodical; –1776).
Sir George MacKenzie founds the Advocates Library, Edinburgh (–1689).

J **Art, Sculpture, Fine Arts and Architecture**
Architecture:
Sir Christopher Wren, Chelsea Hospital (–1692).

K **Music**
Archangelo Corelli's concerti grossi played in Rome (published 1746).

L **Literature (including Drama)**
John Dryden, *The Medall; Religio Laici; Mac Flecknoe;* and *Absalom and Achitopel,*
part 2.
Thomas D'Urfey, *Wit and Mirth; or Pills to Purge Melancholy* (anthology).
Thomas Otway, *Venice Preserv'd* (tragedy).
Joost van den Vondel, *Poëzy of Verscheide gedichten* (posth.).

M **Births and Deaths**
Mar. 14th Jacob van Ruysdael d. (*c.* 57).
Apr. 3rd Esteban Murillo d. (65).
June 17th Charles XII of Sweden b. (–1718).
Oct. 19th Sir Thomas Browne d. (*c.* 77).
Nov. 23rd Claude of Lorraine (Claude Gelée) d. (82).
Nov. 29th Prince Rupert d. (62).
— James Gibbs b. (–1754).

A Jan: 21st, Shaftesbury dies in Holland having fled, *Nov.* 1682, on learning of his impending rearrest;

28th, Sunderland is appointed Secretary of State, North (–1684, then South until 1688).

Feb: League of the Hague by which the Emperor Leopold I and Charles II of Spain join Dutch-Swedish alliance of *Sept.* 1681 against France.

Mar: 31st, Polish alliance with Emperor against the Turks;

Louis XIV demands a 30-year truce with the Emperor and the German States, in which France may enjoy her fresh conquests.

B Apr:

May:

Jun: 12th, Rye House Plot, to assassinate King Charles II and his brother James, Duke of York, is discovered;

Algiers submits to French bombardment;

Turks begin siege of Vienna.

C Jun: 21st, William Russell is beheaded for his part in plotting against the King.

Aug:

Sep: 6th, on Colbert's death, Le Peletia becomes leading Finance Minister of France;

12th, John III of Poland and Charles of Lorraine raise Turkish siege of Vienna;

—, Peter (Pedro) II accedes to the throne of Portugal (–1706) on the death of his brother Alfonso VI.

D Oct: 4th, judgment is entered against the City of London for forfeiture of its charter after struggle by the Court to remove Whig supremacy in the city;

17th, Charter of franchises and liberties is drawn up in New York.

Nov:

Dec: 7th, Algernon Sydney is executed for plotting against Charles II;

25th, the Duke of Monmouth flees to Holland, following the discovery of the Rye House plot and the arrest of Whig leaders;

Spain declares war against France.

E Dutch traders are admitted at Canton;

Brandenburg East African Company builds fortresses of Grossfriedrichsburg on Guinea Coast;

Manchus conquer Isle of Formosa (which remains in Chinese possession until 1895).

F **Politics, Economics, Law and Education**
  William Penn, *A General Description of Pennsylvania*.
  Sir William Petty, *The Growth of the City of London*.
  Matthew Hale, *A Discourse touching provision for the Poor*.

G **Science, Technology and Discovery**
  John Brown, *Compleat Treatise of the Muscles*. . . . (illustrated).
  Kenelm Digby, *Chymical Secrets and Rare Experiments in Physick and Philosophy*.
  Dampier begins his voyage round the world.

H **Philosophy, Religion and Scholarship**
  Isaac Barrow, *Works*, ed. by John Tillotson (posth.) (–1687).
  François Charpentier, *L'Excellence de la langue française*.
  John Dryden's translation of Plutarch: *Parallel Lives* (with others).

J **Art, Sculpture, Fine Arts and Architecture**
  Painting:
      Godfrey Kneller, *Sir Charles Cotterell*.
      Charles Le Brun is made Director of the Académie Royale.
  Architecture:
      Sir Christopher Wren, St. James's Church, Piccadilly.

K **Music**
  Henry Purcell is appointed composer to Charles II.
  First St. Cecilia's Day festival is held, in London.

L **Literature (including Drama)**
  Edme Boursault, *Le Mercure galant* (satirical comedy).
  Bernard Le Bovier, Sieur de Fontenelle, *Dialogues des morts*.

M **Births and Deaths**
  Jan. 21st Anthony Ashley Cooper, Earl of Shaftesbury, d. (61).
  Mar. 1st Caroline of Ansbach b. (–1737).
  Apr. — Roger Williams (*c*. 80).
  May 20th Elijah Fenton b. (–1730).
  June 21st Lord William Russell d. (43).
  July — Edward Young b. (–1765).
  Aug. 24th John Owen d. (69).
  Sept. 6th Jean Baptiste Colbert d. (64).
  Sept. 22nd Jean Philippe Rameau b. (–1764).
  Oct. 25th William Scroggs d. (*c*. 60).
  Oct. 30th George II b. (–1760).
  Dec. 7th Algernon Sidney d. (61).
  Dec. 15th Izaak Walton d. (90).
  — Anne Oldfield b. (–1730).
  — René-Antoine Ferchault de Réaumur b. (–1757).

A Jan: 12th, Louis XIV marries Mme. de Maintenon, after death of Maria Theresa, his
first wife (in 1683).

Feb: The Great Elector offers a refuge in his dominions to French Huguenots.

Mar: 5th, Holy League of Linz between Empire, Poland and Venice, against the Turks.

B Apr: Louis XIV reopens the siege of Luxemburg.

May: James, Duke of York, is restored as Lord Admiral since Charles II has given him
dispensation from the Test Act;

work is begun on remodelling the charters of London and 65 cities under Whig control,
giving King power to veto election of officers including M.P.s (–*Jan.* 1685).

Jun: French take Trier, Courtrai, Oudenarde and Luxemburg.

C Jul:

Aug: 15th, Truce of Ratisbon between the Emperor Leopold I (who is pre-occupied
with the Turkish War) and Louis for 20 years, whereby the French retain all places in
the Spanish Netherlands assigned to them by the Chambers of Reunion;

24th, Earl of Middleton is appointed a Secretary of State (–1688).

Sep: The French bombard Genoa.

D Oct: Charter of Massachusetts is annulled by the English Court of Chancery.

Nov: 93 Jewish families are expelled from Bordeaux.

Dec: Arrival at Versailles of Embassy from Siam.

E British abandon Tangiers to the Moors.

F **Politics, Economics, Law and Education**
Marquess of Halifax writes *The Character of a Trimmer* (published 1688).
London streets are first lit.

G **Science, Technology and Discovery**
Giovanni Cassini, *Les Éléments de l'astronomie vérifiés*.
Edmund Halley persuades Isaac Newton to investigate the problem of gravitation.
Kämpfer travels to the Persian Gulf, Java and Japan.

H **Philosophy, Religion and Scholarship**
Jakob Abbadie, *Traité de la vérité de la religion Chrétienne*.
John Bunyan, *The Pilgrim's Progress*, part 2 (since 1678).
Thomas Burnet, *Sacred Theory of Earth* (trans. of his *Telluris Theoria Sacra* of 1681).
Increase Mather, *Remarkable Providences* (i.e. *An Essay for the Recording of Illustrious Providences*).
Alexander Olivier Esquemeling, *History of the Bucaniers of America*.
Antoine Furetière is expelled from the French Academy for compilation and attempted publication of a dictionary of his own, but issues his *Essai d'un dictionnaire universel* (–1690).
Pierre Bayle founds *Nouvelles de la République des Lettres* (literary review published in Rotterdam).

J **Art, Sculpture, Fine Arts and Architecture**
Painting:
Sir Godfrey Kneller, *The Duchess of Portsmouth*.

K **Music**

L **Literature (including Drama)**
François de Cortete, *Ramounet* and *Mirainounda* (comedies; posth.).
Takemoto Gidayu starts a Japanese puppet play theatre and company (Joruri) in Tokio.
Giovanni Paolo Marana, *L'Espion du Grand Seigneur* (Paris –1686), translated as *Letters Written by a Turkish Spy* (a new form in European literature; see *Lettres Persanes*, by Montesquieu –1721; and *Citizen of the World*, i.e. *Chinese Letters*, by Goldsmith –1760, for celebrated imitations).

M **Births and Deaths**
Apr. — William Pulteney, Earl of Bath, b. (–1764).
July — George Downing d. (*c.* 60).
Aug. 30th Marguerite Delaunay, Baronne de Staal, b. (–1750).
Oct. 1st Pierre Corneille d. (78).
Oct. 10th Antoine Watteau b. (–1721).
Nov. 12th Edward Vernon b. (–1757).
Dec. 3rd Ludvig Holberg b. (–1754).
— George Vertue b. (–1756).
— Adriaen van Ostade d. (74).

A Jan:
   Feb: 6th, Charles II dies and is succeeded by James II (–1688);
     16th, Halifax becomes Treasurer and, 18th, Lord President of the Council;
     20th, Henry Hyde, second Earl of Clarendon, becomes Keeper of Privy Seal.
   Mar: The Duke of Lorraine recaptures Neuhäusel from the Turks.

B Apr:
   May: 19th, English Parliament meets (–*Nov.* 20th);
     —, Earl of Danby is discharged from bail;
     —, James II's first Parliament meets (–*July* 2nd, 1687);
     20th, Titus Oates is flogged to Newgate from Aldgate and, 22nd, from Newgate to
     Tyburn;
     26th, Charles, Elector Palatine, dies and Louis XIV claims the electorate for his
     sister-in-law, Liselotte.
   Jun: 11th, outbreak of the Duke of Monmouth's rebellion;
     30th, the Earl of Argyle is executed.

C Jul: 6th, Monmouth is defeated at Sedgemoor;
     15th, Monmouth is beheaded.
   Aug:
   Sep: Judge Jeffreys conducts 'Bloody Assizes', sentencing adherents of Monmouth in
     West Country, and
     28th, is appointed Lord Chancellor.

D Oct: 18th, Louis XIV revokes Edict of Nantes; thousands of French Protestant refugees
     flee to Britain, Holland and Brandenburg. The revocation turns the Great Elector into
     an opponent of France;
     21st, Lord Halifax is struck off the Privy Council.
   Nov:
   Dec: 4th, Sunderland becomes Lord President;
     Morosini conquers parts of the Morea and Dalmatia for the Venetians.

E Count Oropesa becomes First Minister of Spain in succession to the Duke of Medina-
     Celi;
   K'ang-hsi opens all Chinese ports to foreign trade;
   Entail is introduced in Scotland;
   A French Embassy is sent to Siam.

F **Politics, Economics, Law and Education**

Massive emigration of Huguenots from France to Geneva, Holland, Brandenburg and England, following the Revocation of the Edict of Nantes.

G **Science, Technology and Discovery**

David Abercromby, *De pulsis Variatione;* and *Ars explorandi medicas facultates plantarum ex solo sapore.*

Menno, Baron von Coehoorn, *Nieuwe Vestingbouw* (a treatise on fortification).

H **Philosophy, Religion and Scholarship**

Adrien Baillet, *Jugements des savants sur les principaux ouvrages des auteurs* (–1686, 9 vols.).

Charles Cotton translates the *Essays* of Montaigne.

César de Rochefort, *Dictionnaire général et curieux* (les principaux mots et les plus usitez en la langue français).

William Shakespeare, *Fourth Folio* (posth.).

J **Art, Sculpture, Fine Arts and Architecture**

Painting:

Godfrey Kneller, *Philip, Earl of Leicester.*

K **Music**

L **Literature (including Drama)**

John Dryden, *Albion and Albanius* (dramatic opera).

Edmund Waller, *Divine Poems.*

M **Births and Deaths**

Jan. 17th Wentworth Dillon, Earl of Roscommon, d. (52).

Feb. 10th Aaron Hill b. (–1750).

Feb. 23rd George Frideric Handel b. (–1759).

Mar. 12th George Berkeley b. (–1753).

Mar. 21st Johann Sebastian Bach b. (–1750).

Apr. 16th Thomas Otway d. (33).

July 15th James, Duke of Monmouth, d. (36).

July 28th Henry Bennet, Earl of Arlington, d. (67).

Sept. 16th John Gay b. (–1732).

Oct. 1st Emperor Charles VI b. (–1740).

Oct. 26th Domenico Scarlatti b. (–1757).

Nov. 10th Duncan Forbes of Culloden b. (–1747).

Dec. 4th John Cotton b. (–1752).

— William Kent b. (–1748).

1686   The League of Augsberg is founded against Louis XIV—
          the Turks lose Buda

A Jan:
   Feb:
   Mar:

B **Apr:** 1st, alliance between Emperor Leopold I and the Great Elector who obtains
          Schweibus and a promise of East Friedland, and renounces claim to Silesia.
   May: James II forms Federation of New England in attempt to remodel colonies in
          North America.
   Jun: Following the pro-royalist judicial decision in Godden v. Hales, James II introduces
          Roman Catholics into the Church and the army.

C **Jul:** 9th, League of Augsburg is formed between the Emperor, Spain, Sweden, Saxony,
          the Palatinate and Brandenburg against Louis XIV; the Dutch are not signatories, but
          play a part in plans for alliance;
          a Court for ecclesiastical commissions is set up by James II.
   Aug: James II forms a camp of troops on Hounslow Heath.
   Sep: 2nd, Charles, Duke of Lorraine, takes Buda from the Turks after a lengthy siege
          (Buda had been in Turkish hands for 145 years).

D **Oct:** Russia declares war on Turkey, having secured possession of Kiev by a treaty with
          Poland.
   Nov:
   Dec: 11th, Prince of Condé dies.

E Second Siamese embassy is sent to France;
   The Duke of Savoy persecutes the Protestant Vaudois;
   Louis XIV proclaims annexation of Madagascar;
   Aurangzeb annexes the Kingdom of Bijapur.

F **Politics, Economics, Law and Education**
First European settlement is made in Arkansas by the French.
Maison de St. Cyr is founded as a convent school for daughters of poor gentlefolk by Louis XIV for Mme. de Maintenon, who directs it and draws up instructions for the girls' education.

G **Science, Technology and Discovery**
[J. Ray and] F. Willughby, *Historia Piscium*.

H **Philosophy, Religion and Scholarship**
Pierre Bayle, *Commentaire philosophique sur les paroles de Jésus-Christ*.
Bernard Le Bovier, Sieur de Fontenelle, *Entretiens sur la pluralité des mondes*.
Jean Le Clerc, *Bibliothèque universelle et historique* (25 vols. –1693).

J **Art, Sculpture, Fine Arts and Architecture**

K **Music**
J. B. Lully, *Armide and Renaud* (opera) performed.

L **Literature (including Drama)**
Sir Thomas Browne, *Works* collected in folio (posth.).
Chikamatsu Monzaemon, *Shusse Kagekiyo* (puppet play) produced in Tokio (*see* 1684 L).
The first Swedish theatre is opened in Stockholm.

M **Births and Deaths**
Feb. 10th William Dugdale d. (80).
Apr. 26th Arthur Annesley, Earl of Anglesey, d. (71).
May 14th Gabriel Daniel Fahrenheit b. (–1736).
July 10th John Fell d. (61).
Oct. 15th Allan Ramsay b. (–1758).
Dec. 11th Louis, Prince of Condé, d. (65).
— Jean Baptiste Oudry b. (–1755).

1687 Venetian bombardment of Athens—Hapsburg succession in Hungary

A Jan:
Feb: 17th, Richard Talbot, Earl of Tyrconnel is sworn in as Lord Deputy in Ireland.
Mar: 19th, La Salle is murdered by his colleagues.

B Apr: 4th, Declaration of Indulgence for Liberty of Conscience is issued by James II.
May:
Jun:

C Jul: 3rd, James II receives the Papal Nuncio;
4th, English Parliament, prorogued since *Nov.* 1685, is dissolved.
Aug: 12th, Duke of Lorraine and Louis of Baden defeat Turks under Suleiman Pacha at the Battle of Mohacs, thus subduing Croatia and Transylvania.
Sep: 26th, Venetians bombard Athens and destroy the Parthenon and Propyleiea and, 28th, Turks surrender the city; the Morea is subjugated.

D Oct: 11th, Hungarian Diet of Pressburg renounces rights of resistance and recognises the Crown as a hereditary possession of the male line of Hapsburgs (Leopold, Joseph's son is crowned King *Dec.* 9th).
Nov: 2nd, Mohammed IV is deposed in a revolution in Constantinople and succeeded by Suleiman III with Mustafa Kiuprili as Grand Vizier.
Dec:

E Dispute between Louis XIV and Pope;
James II interferes with the appointment of lords-lieutenants of English counties and endeavours to replace Protestants in Oxford and Cambridge Universities by Roman Catholics;
Arguin, Guinea, is established as a colony by the Elector of Brandenburg;
Aurangzeb conquers Golkonda;
The French build Fort Niagara to prevent British reaching the Upper lakes of Canada;
French Huguenots settle at the Cape of Good Hope.

F Politics, Economics, Law and Education
James II founds the Order of the Thistle in Scotland.
Samuel Pufendorf, *The Relation of Religions Liberty to Civilian Life*.
François de Salignac de la Mothe-Fénelon, *Traité de l'éducation des filles*.

G Science, Technology and Discovery
Isaac Newton *Principia Mathematica* (–1727)
Sir Hans Sloane visits Jamaica, beginning his botanical collections.

H Philosophy, Religion and Scholarship
Jacques Bénigne Bossuet, *Oraison funèbre du Grand Condé*.
Gerard Langbaine, *A New Catalogue of English Plays*.
Pasquier Quesnel, *Reflexions morales sur le Nouveau Testament* (–1713).
Christian Thomasius lectures on jurisprudence in Leipzig and Berlin, in German, not Latin, and is the first professor to do so in Germany.
John Wallis, *Institutio Logicae*.
William Winstanley, *Lives of the English Poets*.
Second *Declaration of Indulgence*, issued by James II.

J Art, Sculpture, Fine Arts and Architecture
Painting:
Godfrey Kneller, *The Chinese Convent*.
Architecture:
Figueroa, Hospital de Venerables Sacerdotes, Seville.
The Venetian bombardment of the Acropolis, Athens, causes a powder magazine to explode in the Parthenon, rending the building asunder.

K Music

L Literature (including Drama)
John Dryden, *The Hind and the Panther*, and *Song for St. Cecilia's Day*.

M Births and Deaths
Mar. 22nd Jean Baptiste Lully d. (*c.* 50).
Apr. 16th George Villiers, 2nd Duke of Buckingham, d. (59).
Sept. 1st Henry More d. (73).
Sept. 12th John Alden d. (88).
Oct. 21st Edmund Waller d. (81).
Nov. — Nell Gwyn d. (37).
Dec. 16th William Petty d. (64).

A Jan:
Feb: James II recalls to England the regiments serving in Holland since 1678.
Mar:

B Apr:
May: 4th, Declaration of Indulgence is reissued;
  9th, Frederick William, the Great Elector, dies and is succeeded by Frederick III
  (–1713);
  Leopold I signs a treaty with Transylvania, by which Turkish suzerainty is removed
  and Transylvania becomes a province under the King of Hungary.
Jun: 10th, birth of a son to James II—the 'Warming-pan Incident';
  29th (–30th), trial and acquittal of the Seven Bishops for opposing the Declaration of
  Indulgence;
  30th, seven Whig Lords, Devonshire, Shrewsbury, Danby, Compton, Sidney Lumley,
  and Robinson, invite William of Orange to England.

C Jul:
Aug:
Sep: 6th, Turks lose Belgrade to the Emperor Leopold I, and imperial forces subsequently occupy Bosnia, Servia and Wallachia;
  24th, Louis XIV begins war against the Empire, the War of the League of Augsburg;
  25th, Louis XIV invades the Palatinate, uniting the German Princes against him;
  30th, William of Orange accepts the Whig lords' invitation and issues Manifesto (Oct.
  1st).

D Oct: 24th, French take Heidelberg and, 29th, Philipsburg; Louis XIV seizes Avignon.
Nov: 5th, William lands at Torbay;
  26th, Louis declares war on Holland and subsequently quarrels with Duke of Savoy,
  who joins the League of Augsburg;
  the French occupy the Palatinate nominally for the Duchess of Orleans.
Dec: 11th, James II attempts to escape but is brought back to London from Sheerness;
  19th, William of Orange enters London;
  25th, James II escapes to France;
  29th, Convention Parliament is summoned to meet.

E Revolution in Siam against French influence;
French bomb Algiers and subsequently make treaty with the Bey.

F **Politics, Economics, Law and Education**
London underwriters begin to meet regularly in Lloyd's Coffee House.

G **Science, Technology and Discovery**
Plate glass is first cast.

H **Philosophy, Religion and Scholarship**
Adrien Baillet, *Des Enfants devenus célèbres par leurs études et par leurs écrits.*
Nicholas-Despréaux Boileau, *Dialogue des héros de roman* (satire against romances of the type written by Madeleine de Scudéry; written *c.* 1688; not published until 1713).
Jacques-Bénigne Boussuet, *Histoires des variations des églises protestantes.*
William Cave, *Scriptorum Ecclesiasticorum Historia Literaria.*
Jean de La Bruyère, *Caractères* (de Théophraste traduits du grec, avec les Caractères, ou les Moeurs de ce siècle).
Charles Perrault, *Parallèle des anciens et des modernes* (–1697).
George Savile, Marquess of Halifax, *The Character of a Trimmer.*
Cornelius a Beughen, *Incunabula typographicae* (Amsterdam; lists books printed in 'the cradle period', before 1500; early, perhaps first use of the term).

J **Art, Sculpture, Fine Arts and Architecture**

K **Music**

L **Literature (including Drama)**
Thomas Shadwell, *The Squire of Alsatia* (comedy). Shadwell is made Poet Laureate.

M **Births and Deaths**
Jan. 29th Emanuel Swedenborg b. (–1772).
Feb. 4th Pierre Carlet de Chamblain de Marivaux b. (–1763).
May 12th Joseph Nicolas Delisle b. (–1768).
May 21st Alexander Pope b. (–1744).
June 10th James Francis Edward Stuart (the Old Pretender) b. (–1766).
June 26th Ralph Cudworth d. (71).
July 21st James Butler, Duke of Ormonde, d. (77).
Aug. 15th Frederick William I of Prussia b. (–1740).
Aug. 31st John Bunyan d. (60).
Oct. 12th Henry Morgan d. (*c.* 53).
Oct. 23rd Charles du Fresne, Sieur du Cange, d. (77).
Nov. 26th Philippe Quinault d. (53).
— Laurence Eusden b. (–1730).

A   Jan: 22nd, Convention Parliament meets (–1690);
        28th, Parliament declares James II has abdicated;
        Melas devastates the Palatinate (–June).
    Feb: 12th, Declaration of Rights in England; making or suspension of laws without
        Parliament is illegal; William and Mary are proclaimed King and Queen for life;
        13th, Bill of Rights is drawn up by a Committee of Commons, embodying the Declara-
        tion of Rights (enacted July);
        the German Diet declares war against France, following the devastation of the Palati-
        nate.
    Mar: 5th, Nottingham becomes Secretary of State, Southern Department;
        12th, James arrives in Ireland (and May holds a Parliament in Dublin);
        14th, a Convention Parliament meets in Scotland and William and Mary are proclaimed
        King and Queen.

B   Apr: Coronation of William and Mary;
        15th, Louis XIV declares war on Spain;
        20th, siege of Londonderry (–July).
    May: 2nd/12th, Britain and Holland join the League of Augsburg, which is generally
        ratified and becomes the Grand Alliance;
        24th, Toleration Act;
        Leopold I makes treaties of alliance with Holland and Bavaria.
    Jun: The French burn Baden-Baden.

C   Jul: 1st, Episcopacy is abolished in Scotland;
        25th, Louis XIV declares war on Britain;
        27th, Scottish Jacobites under Claverhouse, Viscount Dundee defeat the Covenanters at
        Killiekrankie.
        Iroquis massacre French Canadian settlers at Lachine, near Montreal;
    Aug: 12th, Pope Innocent XI dies;
        21st, Covenanters defeat Scottish Jacobites at Dunkeld;
        Lewis of Baden defeats the Turks, takes Nissa, and occupies Bulgaria;
        the Irish are defeated at Newtown Butler.
    Sep:

D   Oct: 6th, Pope Alexander VIII elected;
        11th, Peter the Great becomes Tsar of Russia.
    Nov: Bonn is captured by Frederick, Elector of Brandenburg.
    Dec: Bill of Rights is amended.

E   Rising of Protestants in the Cevennes;
    Russia joins the war against Turkey;
    Natal becomes a Dutch colony;
    William and Mary recognise old charters of the English colonies (–1691);
    Louis XIV appoints de Frontenac Governor of Canada.

F Politics, Economics, Law and Education
John, Lord Somers, *A brief history of the succession to the Crown of England*.
John Locke, *Two Treatises on Civil Government*, the first answering Filmer's *Patriarcha* (1680), the second justifying the Glorious Revolution of 1688.
William III establishes Devonport dockyard.
The Dutch hold the first modern trade fair, at Leyden.

G Science, Technology and Discovery
Montaliche Erzählunger, a periodical devoted to natural science, is first issued.
Baron La Hontau first describes the Great Salt Lake, Utah.

H Philosophy, Religion and Scholarship
John Locke, *Letter Concerning Toleration* (the first; 2nd –1690; 3rd –1692).
Cotton Mather, *Memorable Providences relating to Witchcraft and Possessions*.
William Sherlock, *A Practical Discourse Concerning Death*.
Act of Toleration (for Dissenters; *May* 24th).
Advocates Library, Edinburgh, opened (founded 1682).

J Art, Sculpture, Fine Arts and Architecture
Painting:
Hobbema, *Avenue at Middleharris*.

K Music
Henry Purcell, *Dido and Aeneas* (opera) written for a boarding school for gentlewomen.

L Literature (including Drama)
Daniel Casper von Lohenstein, *Grossmüthiger Feldherr Arminius*, 2 vols. (posth.).
Andrew Marvell, *Poems of Affairs of State*.
Jean Racine, *Esther* (tragedy).
John Selden, *Table Talk* (posth.).
Anselm von Zigler, *Die asiatische Banise; oder, das bluthig-doch muthige Pegu* (German baroque novel).

M Births and Deaths
Jan 18th Charles Louis de Secondat, Baron de Montesquieu, b. (–1755).
Apr. 16th Mrs. Aphra Behn d. (49).
Apr. 18th Judge Jeffreys d. (41).
Apr. 19th ex-Queen Christina of Sweden d. (63).
May 3rd William Broome b. (–1745).
May 26th Lady Mary Wortley Montagu b. (–1762).
July 27th John Graham of Claverhouse, Viscount Dundee, d. (c. 40).
Dec. 29th Thomas Sydenham d. (65).
— Samuel Richardson b. (–1761).

1690   Battles of Beachy Head, the Boyne and Fleurus

A   Jan: 6th, Joseph I is elected King of the Romans.
Feb: 6th, Convention Parliament is dissolved in England;
    19th, Lord Halifax is dismissed as Lord Privy Seal.
Mar: 16th, Louis XIV sends troops to Ireland to fight for James II;
    20th, second Parliament of William and Mary meets (–*May* 3rd, 1695).

B   Apr: 18th, Charles, Duke of Lorraine, dies;
    Apasi, Prince of Transylvania, dies; the Estates recognise his son as Prince, but the Turks nominate Emeric Tokoly.
May: 20th, Act of Grace is passed in England;
    the French occupy Liège.
Jun: 2nd, Lord Shrewsbury resigns as a Secretary of State (his successor, Viscount Sydney, is not appointed until *Dec.* 26th);
    6th, Spain joins the Grand Alliance against France;
    11th, William III leaves for Ireland;
    30th/*June* 10th, French under Admiral Tourville defeat English and Dutch fleets at the battle of Beachy Head.

C   Jul: 1st, William III defeats James II at the battle of the Boyne, and James flees to France;
    —, French, under the Duke of Luxemburg, defeat the allies at Fleurus;
    30th, Londonderry is relieved after a siege of ~~150~~ days. ᴸᵉ 5
Aug: 18th, a French army under Catinat, defeats Victor Amadeus of Savoy at Staffarda;
    27th, William III fails to take Limerick.
Sep: 6th, William III returns to England.

D   Oct: 8th, the Turks reconquer Belgrade and reoccupy Bulgaria;
    28th, Savoy formally joins the Grand Alliance against France.
Nov:
Dec:

E   Louis XIV restores Avignon to the Pope (seized in 1663)
A British factory is established in Calcutta.

F **Politics, Economics, Law and Education**

Sir William Petty, *Political Arithmetic*, an essay in comparative statistics.
J. Child, *A Discourse about Trade*.
Job Charnock founds Calcutta (*Aug.* 24th).

G **Science, Technology and Discovery**

C. Huyghens propounds a theory of the undulation of light.
Paul Hermann coins the term 'Angiosperm' as one of the primary divisions of the plant kingdom.
Denis Papin devises a pump with a piston raised by steam.

H **Philosophy, Religion and Scholarship**

Antoine Furetière, *Dictionnaire universel*, 3 vols. (posth. publication in Rotterdam, 1684).
John Locke, *An Essay Concerning Human Understanding*.
Sébastien Le Nain de Tillemont, *Histoire des empereurs et des autres princes qui ont régné pendant les six premiers siècles de l'Eglise* (–1738).
Consolazium dell'olma Devoziusa: an anthology of religious lyrics compiled by the Benedictines in the Romansch dialect.
Accademia dell'Arcadia founded in Rome.

J **Art, Sculpture, Fine Arts and Architecture**

K **Music**

Henry Purcell, *Amphitryon* and *The Prophetess* (operas).

L **Literature (including Drama)**

Edme Boursault, *Esope à la ville* (comedy –1701).
John Dryden, *Amphitryon* (comedy). *Don Sebastian, King of Portugal* (tragi-comedy).
Nathaniel Lee, *The Massacre of Paris* (tragedy).
Edmund Waller, *Poems* (posth.).
The *Athenian Gazette* (later *Mercury*) starts the practice of answers to readers' letters in English journalism.

M **Births and Deaths**

Feb. 12th Charles le Brun d. (71).
Feb. 19th Alexis Petrovich b. (–1718).
Apr. 22nd John Carteret, Earl of Granville, b. (–1763).
July 1st Friedrich Hermann Schonberg d. (75).
July 1st George Walker d. (72).
Oct. 17th Marguerite Marie Alacoque d. (43).
Dec. 1st Philip Yorke, Earl of Hardwicke, b. (–1764).
— William Ged b. (–1749).

A Jan: 18th, William III leaves England for Holland; a congress of the allies meets at the
       Hague to plan for the defeat of France.
   Feb: 1st, Pope Alexander VIII dies.
   Mar: Catinat takes Nice.

B Apr: 9th, French capture Mons.
   May: The Duke of Savoy invades Dauphiné.
   Jun: 12th, Innocent XII elected Pope (in succession to Alexander VIII);
       Ahmad II succeeds Suleiman III as Sultan of Turkey (–1695).

C Jul: Capitulation of Limerick; many Irish enter the services of Louis XIV;
       22nd, Anglo-Dutch army defeats French at Aghrim.
   Aug: 19th, Louis of Baden defeats the Turks at Salem Kamen; Mustafa Kiuprili is
       killed in action.
   Sep: 17th, the colony of Massachusetts is given a new charter.

D Oct:
   Nov:
   Dec: 4th, with the re-conquest of Transylvania, the Hapsburgs are recognised as rulers.

E A society meets in London and ultimately becomes New East India Company.

F **Politics, Economics, Law and Education**

G **Science, Technology and Discovery**
    G. W. von Leibniz, *Protogaea*, a study of geology.

H **Philosophy, Religion and Scholarship**
    Adrien Baillet, *La Vie de Descartes.*
    Claude Fleury, *Histoire ecclésiastique* started (completed in 20 volumes, 1720; the first learned and complete history of the Church).
    Kaspar Stieler, *Teutsche Sprachschatz.*
    Henry Wharton, *Anglia Sacra*, 2 vols.
    Anthony à Wood, *Athenae Oxonienses* ('an exact history of all the Writers and Bishops who have had their education in the University of Oxford' from 1500 to 1690—with *The Fasti or Annals* of Oxford University), 2 vols.
    Christian Faith Society for the West Indies, founded in London.

J **Art, Sculpture, Fine Arts and Architecture**
    Architecture:
    Figueroa, Magdalene Church, Seville (–1709).

K **Music**
    Henry Purcell, *King Arthur* (opera).

L **Literature (including Drama)**
    Jean Racine, *Athalie* (tragedy).

M **Births and Deaths**
    Jan. 13th George Fox d. (66).
    Feb. 28th Edward Cave b. (–1754).
    May 29th Cornelius Van Tromp d. (61).
    July 16th François le Tellier, Marquis de Louvois, d. (50).
    Dec. 8th Richard Baxter d. (76).
    Dec. 30th Robert Boyle d. (64).
    — George Etherege d. (*c.* 56).
    — Edward Pococke d. (87).
    — Peter Scheemakers b. (–1770).

1692   Massacre of Glencoe—Battles of La Hogue and Steinkirke

A   Jan: 10th, Earl of Marlborough dismissed for allegedly communicating with the exiled James II.

Feb: 13th, massacre of Highlanders at Glencoe, after refusal of MacDonald to swear allegiance to William III.

Mar: 3rd, Nottingham again becomes sole Secretary of State;

7th, Lord Pembroke becomes Lord Privy Seal;

Maximilian, Elector of Bavaria, is installed as Governor and Captain-General of the Spanish Netherlands.

B   Apr: The Duke of Savoy again invades Dauphiny.

May: 5th, Marlborough is sent to the Tower of London;

19th/29th, British defeat French navy at La Hogue, ending the attempted invasion of England.

Jun: 5th, Louis of Baden, the new Imperial General, takes Grosswardein from Turks;

—, the French capture Namur, in Louis XIV's presence.

C   Jul:

Aug: 3rd, William III is defeated at Steinkirke by the Duke of Luxemburg.

Sep: Maximilian of Bavaria relieves Charleroi from French attack.

D   Oct:

Nov:

Dec: 19th, Duke Ernest Augustus of Hanover becomes the ninth Elector of the Holy Roman Empire, following Treaty of Perpetual Alliance (of *Mar.*) with Emperor Leopold I.

E   Beginning of trade between Russia and China.

F **Politics, Economics, Law and Education**
Queen Mary founds Greenwich Hospital for wounded sailors and pensioners.
William and Mary College, Virginia, is founded.

G **Science, Technology and Discovery**
Isaac Newton's papers are accidentally burnt.
Ijsbrand Iders explores the Gobi Desert (–1694).

H **Philosophy, Religion and Scholarship**
The Anglo-Saxon Chronicle, edited by Edmund Gibson.
Nahum Tate is appointed Poet Laureate and Thomas Rymer as Historiographer Royal.
Sir William Temple, *Of Ancient and Modern Learning* (revives the Phalaris controversy –1694, 1697), essay in vol. 2 of *Miscellanea*.

J **Art, Sculpture, Fine Arts and Architecture**
Painting:
  Hobbema, *The Watermill*.
Sculpture:
  Cibber, Hampton Court sculptures (–1694).

K **Music**
Henry Purcell, *The Fairy Queen* (opera).

L **Literature (including Drama)**
William Congreve, *Incognita* (novel).
Florent Carton Dancourt, *Les Bourgeoises à la mode* (comedy of manners).

M **Births and Deaths**
May 18th Elias Ashmole d. (75).
May 18th Joseph Butler b. (–1752).
Oct. 4th Charles Fleetwood d. (72).
Oct. 25th Elizabeth Farnese b. (–1766).
Nov. 21st Carlo Fragoni b. (–1768) and Thomas Shadwell d. (*c.* 50).
— Giuseppe Tartini b. (–1770).

A Jan:
Feb: The National Debt is established in England.
Mar: 14th, William III vetoes Bills to exclude 'Placemen' (office holders) from Parliament and to introduce triennial parliaments in England;
23rd, Lord Somers is appointed Lord Keeper, the head of the 'Whig' Junta.

B Apr: Charles XII of Sweden declares himself absolute.
May: 22nd, the French again destroy Heidelberg, and ravage the Rhineland.
Jun: 20th/30th, French defeat British merchant fleet from Smyrna at Battle of Lagos.

C Jul: 19th/29th, William III is defeated at Neerwinden by the Duke of Luxemburg.
Aug: Louis XIV fails to take Liège and never appears in the field with his troops again.
Sep:

D Oct: 4th, Catinat defeats Victor Amadeus of Savoy at the Battle of Marsaglia;
11th, the French take Charleroi;
a new charter is granted to the old East India Company.
Nov: The English bombard St. Malo;
7th, English Parliament meets (–*Apr.* 25th, 1694);
Earl of Nottingham is dismissed from Secretaryship of State.
Dec: Louis XIV puts out feelers for peace—the turning-point in his foreign policy.

E Leopold, Prince of Anhalt, organises Prussian army;
Carolina is divided into North and South Carolina;
Dutch take Pondicherry after siege;
The Gallican Church is reconciled with the Papacy;
Pope Innocent XII attempts to check the sale of offices in the papal court.

F **Politics, Economics, Law and Education**

Edmund Halley reads a paper on 'The degrees of mortality of mankind' to the Royal Society, containing important observations, based on records of deaths and baptisms at Breslau, about life insurance and the calculations of annuities.

William Penn, *An Essay on the Present and Future Peace of Europe*, suggests federation.

G. W. von Leibniz, *Codex juris gentium diplomaticus* (–1700), a treatise on positive law.

John Locke, *Thoughts Concerning Education*.

G **Science, Technology and Discovery**

J. Ray, *Synopsis Animalium*.

Edmund Halley compiles tables for calculating the distance from the sun.

H **Philosophy, Religion and Scholarship**

Cotton Mather, *Wonders of the Invisible World*.

[William Penn], *Fruits of Solitude*.

Sébastien Le Nain de Tillemont, *Mémoires pour servir à l'histoire ecclésiastique des six premiers siècles* (–1712).

Knights of the Apocalypse founded in Italy by Agostino Gabrino to defend the Church against antichrist (a secret society).

J **Art, Sculpture, Fine Arts and Architecture**

Painting:

Godfrey Kneller, *Dr. Burnet*.

K **Music**

L **Literature (including Drama)**

William Congreve, *The Old Bachelor* (comedy).

Jean de La Fontaine, *Fables*, vol. 3.

M **Births and Deaths**

Feb. 4th George Lillo b. (–1739).

June 1st Alexius Petrovich, Count Bestuzhev-Ryumm, b. (–1768).

Nov. 24th William Sancroft d. (77).

— Robert Dinwiddie b. (–1770).

— Thomas Pelham Holles, Duke of Newcastle, b. (–1768).

— Marie-Madeleine, Comtesse de La Fayette, d. (59).

— Nicholaes Maes d. (59).

A   **Jan:**
      Feb:
      Mar: 2nd, Earl of Shrewsbury appointed Secretary of State (–1695).

B   **Apr:** 10th, Duke Victor Amadeus of Savoy begins siege of Casale;
          25th, the Bank of England founded by William Paterson.
      May: The ministry in England is remodelled when William III dismisses Tories, except
          Godolphin and Danby, and introduces Whig Junta of Somers, Russell, Montague
          and Wharton.
      Jun: Noailles invades Spain. An English fleet is sent under Russell to prevent fall of
          Barcelona.

C   **Jul:** An English fleet bombards the Channel Ports of Dieppe, Havre and Dunkirk, but an
          expedition to Brest is defeated.
      Aug:
      Sep:

D   **Oct:** Admiral Russell winters his fleet at Cadiz.
      Nov:
      Dec: 3rd, Triennial Bill becomes law, providing for new Parliament to be elected every
          third year;
          20th, Frederick of Brandenburg restores Schweibus to Empire, thereby reviving his
          claims to Silesia;
          28th, Queen Mary II dies.

E   Accession of Augustus the Strong, Elector of Saxony (–1733);
      Accession of Hussain, Shah of Persia (–1721).

F **Politics, Economics, Law and Education**
The Bank of England is founded, *July* 27th.
Halle University is founded.

G **Science, Technology and Discovery**
Rudolf Camerarius discusses the reproductive organs of plants in *De sexu plantarum epistola*.

H **Philosophy, Religion and Scholarship**
William Burnaby translates the *Satyricon* of Petronius.
Dictionnaire de l'Académie française, 2 vols. Supplemented by *Dictionnaire des arts et des sciences*, 2 vols. prepared by Thomas Corneille.
George Fox, *Journal* (posth.), edited by Thomas Ellwood.
Louis XIV grants letters patent to Académie des Jeux floraux de Toulouse (founded –1323 probably by seven troubadours; the most ancient surviving academy in France).
William Wotton, *Reflections on Ancient and Modern Learning* (attacking Temple's essay, –1692, 1697).

J **Art, Sculpture, Fine Arts and Architecture**
Painting:
Godfrey Kneller begins painting the series of 'Hampton Court Beauties'.
Architecture:
Sir Christopher Wren, Greenwich Hospital.

K **Music**
Henry Purcell, *Timon of Athens;* and *Te Deum for St. Cecilia's Day.*

L **Literature (including Drama)**
William Congreve, *The Double Dealer* (comedy).

M **Births and Deaths**
June 4th François Quesnay b. (–1774).
Aug. 8th Francis Hutcheson b. (–1746).
Sept. 22nd Philip Dormer Stanhope, Earl of Chesterfield, b. (–1773).
Oct. 26th Samuel Pufendorf d. (62).
Nov. 21st Voltaire (François-Marie Arouet) b. (–1778).
Nov. 25th John Tillotson d. (64).
Dec. 2nd William Shirley b. (–1771).
— John Lambert d. (75).
— John Micheal Rysbrack b. (–1770).

A Jan: 4th, Marshal of France, the Duke of Luxemburg, dies and is succeeded as commander in the Netherlands campaign by the Duke of Villeroi;
27th, Mustafa II succeeds as Sultan of Turkey (–1703), on the death of Ahmad II;
William III becomes reconciled to his sister-in-law, the Princess Anne.
Feb:
Mar: 18th, Sir John Trevor, Speaker of the House of Commons, is expelled for accepting a bribe from the City of London.

B Apr: Government censorship of the Press is ended in England.
May: 3rd, an Act is passed to prevent bribery in Parliamentary elections;
6th, the Duke of Leeds (Thomas Osborne) is forced to retire as Lord President of the Council for accepting a bribe for the grant of a new charter to the East India Company;
9th, the Scottish Parliament meets and enquires into the massacre of Glencoe;
12th (–Oct. 10th), William III serves with the army in Holland.
Jun: A Polish army wins a striking victory over the Tartars.

C Jul: English fleet bombards St. Malo.
Aug: 13th (–15th), Villeroi bombards Brussels.
Sep: 1st, William III takes Namur.

D Oct:
Nov: 22nd, third Parliament of William III, staunchly Whig, meets (–July 5th, 1698);
—, Peter the Great returns to Moscow, after the failure of a campaign to take Azov.
Dec:

E

F **Politics, Economics, Law and Education**

William Lowndes, *An Essay for the Amendment of the Silver Coin*, recommending that the re-coined money should become current at a higher rate, but John Locke denies the price of silver has risen and in the re-coinage (of 1696) the denomination of the English currency remains unchanged.

Sieur de Boisguilbert, *Le Détail de la France, la cause de la dimunition de ses biens.*

Window Tax is enforced in England.

Berlin University is founded.

A model school for pauper children is opened in Halle.

G **Science, Technology and Discovery**

G. Amontons invents the pendant barometer.

N. Grew isolates magnesium sulphate ('Epsom Salts').

John Woodward, *An Essay toward a Natural History of the Earth and Terrestrial Bodies.*

H **Philosophy, Religion and Scholarship**

William Camden's *Britannia* translated by Edmund Gibson.

John Dryden translates *De arte graphica Liber*, by Charles-Alphonse Dufresnoy.

John Locke, *The Reasonableness of Christianity.*

J **Art, Sculpture, Fine Arts and Architecture**

K **Music**

Henry Purcell, *The Indian Queen* and *The Tempest* (operas) and 'Thou Knowest, Lord', an anthem for Queen Mary's funeral.

L **Literature (including Drama)**

William Congreve, *Love For Love* (comedy).

Nikolaes Heinsius, *Den Vermakelijkten Avonturier* (picaresque novel).

M **Births and Deaths**

Jan. 4th François-Henri de Montmorency-Bouteville, Duc de Luxemburg, d. (66).

Feb. 2nd William Borlase b. (–1772).

Apr. 5th George Saville, Marquess of Halifax, d. (61).

Apr. 13th Jean de la Fontaine d. (73).

Apr. 23rd Henry Vaughan d. (73).

June 8th Christiaan Huygens d. (66).

Nov. 21st Henry Purcell d. (37).

Nov. 29th Anthony à Wood d. (62).

Nov. 29th James, Viscount Stair d. (76).

— Edward Braddock d. (–1755).

— Richard Busby d. (89).

— Maurice Green b. (–1755).

— Dorothy Osborne, Lady Temple, d. (68).

— Henry Pelham b. (–1754).

— Louis François Roubiliac b. (–1762).

A Jan:

Feb: 14th, William III announces to Parliament the discovery of Sir John Fenwick's plot to assassinate him;

27th, the Oath of Association to defend William III and preserve the Protestant settlement is taken throughout England and Wales (*–May*);

the French prepare for an invasion of England.

Mar: 10th, William III vetoes a bill for a landed property qualification for members of Parliament but

27th, supports the Tory scheme for a Land Bank;

Commodore Benbow bombards Calais.

B Apr: 27th, Acts for regulating treason trials in England and for a new coinage.

May: 7th (*–Oct.* 8th), William III is in Holland campaigning against the French.

Jun: 17th, John III (John Sobieski), King of Poland, dies (the Elector Augustus of Saxony is elected successor, *June* 1697).

C Jul: 28th, de Croissy becomes chief Finance Minister in France on Colbert's death;

29th, Peter the Great takes Azov from the Turks;

—, Louis XIV signs a peace treaty with Victor Amadeus of Savoy, detaching him from the Grand Alliance; by its terms the Duke regains Savoy, Nice, Susa, Casale and Pignerolo, and his daughter is to be betrothed to the Duke of Burgundy.

Aug:

Sep: Russia conquers Kamchatka.

D Oct: 20th, Parliament meets (*–Apr.* 16th, 1697), and institutes proceedings against Sir John Fenwick and his collaborators for treason.

Nov:

Dec:

E Fort William, Calcutta, is built.

F Politics, Economics, Law and Education

J. Bellers, *Proposals for Raising a Colledge of Industry*, suggests the establishment of a self-sufficing community for educating children.

Re-coinage of British silver money is carried out under John Locke and Isaac Newton.

The Board of Trade and Plantations is founded in England.

The Journeymen hatters in England, who have formed a trade union, proclaim a strike.

Edward Lloyd starts a thrice-weekly paper, *Lloyd's News* (–1697).

G Science, Technology and Discovery

H Philosophy, Religion and Scholarship

Nicolas Antonio, *Bibliotheca Hispana vetus* (since 1672; a bibliography of all Spanish works from Augustus).

Nicholas Brady and Nahum Tate, *A 'New' Metrical Version of the Psalms*.

William Nicolson, *The English Historical Library; or* A Short view and character of most of the writers, 3 vols. (–1699).

J Art, Sculpture, Fine Arts and Architecture

K Music

L Literature (including Drama)

Jean-François Regnard, *Le Joueur* (comedy).

Christian Reuter, *Schelmuffsky* (comic novel).

Thomas Southerne, *Oroonoko* (tragedy).

M Births and Deaths

Apr. 17th Marie de Rabutin-Chantal, Marquise de Sévigné, d. (70).

May 10th Jean de la Bruyère d. (50).

June 17th John Sobieski d. (72).

Oct. 13th Jean Hervey b. (1743).

Oct. 28th Marshal Saxe b. (–1750).

— Giovanni Tiepolo b. (–1770).

A   Jan: Sir John Fenwick is executed for treason.
Feb:
Mar: 21st, Peter the Great visits Prussia, Holland, England and Vienna (–*Sept.* 1698) which prompts him to introduce reforms into Russia.

B   Apr: 15th, Charles XII of Sweden succeeds (–1718), on the death of Charles XI;
16th, Parliament ends the immunity from arrest hitherto enjoyed by inhabitants of the Savoy and Whitefriars;
22nd, Lord Somers is created Lord Chancellor;
the charter of the Bank of England is renewed (–1711).
May: 1st, the English ministry becomes wholly Whig in composition on the resignation of Lord Treasurer Godolphin;
24th, William III leaves for Holland.
Jun: 2nd, Augustus, the Elector of Saxony, announces his conversion to Roman Catholicism;
27th, the Elector Augustus of Saxony is elected King of Poland in succession to John III.

C   Jul:
Aug:
Sep: 11th, Prince Eugène defeats the Turks at Zenta;
10th/20th, the Treaty of Ryswick is signed between France, England, Holland and Spain, to end the war. France recognises William III as King of England and Princess Anne as heiress presumptive; Louis XIV undertakes he will not support any plot against William. France agrees to the chief fortresses in the Netherlands being garrisoned by Dutch troops. Mutual restoration of conquests in Europe since the Peace of Nijmegen. Overseas, Fort Albany is restored to the Hudson's Bay Company; France regains Pondicherry and Acadia; Spain is left with East San Domingo, Cuba and Porto Rico in the West Indies.

D   Oct: 30th, Peace of Ryswick between France and Austria. France restores the right bank of the Rhine, surrendering Philipsburg, Frieburg and Breisach. France restores Lorraine to the Duke, is compensated by cash payment for the claims of the Duchess of Orleans to the Palatinate, and abandons her support for a French candidate for the electorate of Cologne.
Nov: 10th, Robert Harley succeeds in bringing in a motion for the reduction of the strength of the British Army.
Dec: 4th, E. von Danckelman, Chancellor of Brandenburg, falls from power at the instigation of Queen Sophia, the Elector's second wife.

E   The French, under de Brue, attempt to establish a colonial empire in West Africa (–1702; 1714–20);
China conquers West Mongolia.

F **Politics, Economics, Law and Education**

Daniel Defoe, *An Essay upon Projects*, recommends income tax and the establishment of benefit societies, and urges the higher education of women.

G **Science, Technology and Discovery**

Abraham Demoivre's researches on the expansion of multinomials and other algebraic problems.

H **Philosophy, Religion and Scholarship**

Pierre Bayle, *Dictionnaire historique et critique*, 2 vols. (biographical).

Edward Bernard, *Catalogi librorum manuscriptorum Angliae et Hiberniae*.

John Dryden translates Virgil's *Pastorals*; *Georgics*; and the *Aeneid*.

François de Salignac de la Mothe-Fénelon, *Explication des maximes des saints sur la vie intérieure* (condemned 1698 by Pope Innocent XII).

Barthélemy d'Herbelot, *Bibliothèque orientale*.

William Wotton, *Reflections on Ancient and Modern Learning* (2nd. ed. –1694, with an introduction by Richard Bentley exposing the Phalaris forgery –1699).

J **Art, Sculpture, Fine Arts and Architecture**

K **Music**

John Blow, anthem for opening service of St. Paul's Cathedral, London.

L **Literature (including Drama)**

William Congreve, *The Mourning Bride* (tragedy).

Gunno Dahlshjern, *Kungaskald* (elegy on the death of Charles XI).

John Dryden, *Alexander's Feast*; or *The Power of Musique* (second ode for St. Cecilia's Day, see 1687).

Charles Perrault, *Contes de ma mère l'Oye* (see 1729 H).

Sir John Vanbrugh, *The Provok'd Wife*; *The Relapse, or Virtue in Danger* (comedies).

M **Births and Deaths**

Jan. 16th Richard Savage b. (–1743).

Jan. 28th John Fenwick d. (*c.* 52).

Apr. 1st Antoine François Prévost b. (–1763).

Apr. 23rd George Anson b. (–1762).

June — John Aubrey d. (71).

July 11th Jean-Baptiste Bouguignon d'Anville b. (–1782).

July 18th Antonio Vieira d. (89).

Oct. 18th Antonio Canale b. (–1768).

Nov. 18th William Hogarth b. (–1764).

— Joseph-François Dupleix b. (–1763).

A   Jan: Peter the Great arrives in England.
Feb: Marquis d'Harcourt, Marshal of France, arrives in Spain for negotiations on the future of the Spanish dominions.
Mar:

B   Apr: Marshall Tallard is sent from Vienna to London to negotiate a partition treaty.
May:
Jun: 17th, Peter the Great's foreign mercenaries scatter the Streltzy rebels in Moscow.

C   Jul:
Aug:
Sep: 5th, the New East India Company is granted a charter by William III;
Peter the Great executes the Streltzy rebels (–Oct.). He imposes a tax on beards in Russia.

D   Oct: 11th, first Partition Treaty for the division of Spanish possessions; Prince Joseph, son of the Elector of Bavaria, to receive Spain, the Spanish Netherlands, and the possessions in the New World; the Dauphin to receive Naples, Sicily and ports in Tuscany and Guispuscoa; the Archduke Charles to receive Milan;
the Earl of Marlborough is restored to favour by William III.
Nov: A Scottish colony is established in the Darien Isthmus (it fails, 1699).
Dec: 6th, the fourth Parliament of William III meets (Apr. 11th, 1700);
23rd, George Lewis succeeds as Elector of Hanover (the future George I of Great Britain), on the death of the Elector Ernest Augustus.

E   The Africa trade is opened to all English subjects;
The French establish a legation in China.

F **Politics, Economics, Law and Education**
   Algernon Sidney, *Discourses concerning Government* (posth.).
   White's Chocolate House becomes the London headquarters of the Tory Party.

G **Science, Technology and Discovery**
   The first Eddystone lighthouse is built.
   Savery patents a pumping-machine.

H **Philosophy, Religion and Scholarship**
   Jeremy Collier, *A Short View of the Immortality and Profaneness of the English Stage.*
   Gerard Langbaine and Charles Gildon, *The Lives and Characters of the English Dramatick Poets* (with 'an Account of All the Plays that were ever yet printed in the English Tongue').
   Edmund Ludlow, *Memoirs* (posth.).
   Dr. Thomas Bray founds in London *The Society for Promoting Christian Knowledge* (SPCK).
   Cardinal Casanatense founds the Bibliotheca Casanatense in Rome.

J **Art, Sculpture, Fine Arts and Architecture**
   Sculpture:
     Cibber, work in St. Paul's Cathedral (–1700).
   Architecture:
     Jules Hardouin-Mansart, Place Vendôme.
     Andreas Schlüter, Berlin Palace (–1706).
     Christopher Wren, Painted Hall, Greenwich.

K **Music**

L **Literature (including Drama)**

M **Births and Deaths**
   Jan. 13th Metastasio (Pietro Trapassi) b. (–1782).
   May 8th Henry Baker b. (–1774).
   May 15th Marie Champmeslé d. (56).
   June 28th James Radcliffe, Earl of Derwentwater, b. (–1716).
   Nov. 28th Louis de Buade, Comte de Frontenac et Palluan, d. (78).
   Dec. 24th William Warburton b. (–1779).

Peace of Karlowitz—Second Spanish Partition Treaty—French colonise Louisiana

A Jan: 26th, the Peace of Karlowitz is signed by Austria, Russia, Poland and Venice with Turkey; it cedes Hungary, Transylvania, Croatia and Slavonia to the Hapsburgs; Poland gains Podolia and the Ukraine; Venice gains the Morea; Russia retains its conquest of Azov.

Feb: 6th, Joseph, son of the Elector of Bavaria, and sole heir of Charles II of Spain, dies; the size of the British army is drastically reduced.

Mar:

B Apr: Admiral Benbow is sent to the West Indies to gain reparation from Spain for destruction to British ships at Darien.

May:

Jun: 1st/11th, second Partition Treaty is signed between France, England and Holland. The Archduke Charles to receive Spain and the Spanish possessions in South America; the Dauphin to receive the two Sicilies; the Tuscan Poerts, Guispuscoa and also the Milanese, which are to be exchanged for Lorraine; the two branches of the House of Hapsburg to be separated (the Treaty is ratified *Mar.* 1700).

C Jul:

Aug: 24th, Denmark and Russia sign a convention for mutual defence; Frederick IV accedes to the throne of Denmark (–1730) on the death of Christian V.

Sep: 25th, Denmark forms an alliance with Germany and Poland against Sweden.

D Oct:

Nov: 22nd, the Treaty of Preobrazhenskoe is signed between Denmark, Russia, Saxony and Poland for the partition of the Swedish empire.

Dec: The lavish grants by William III to his followers are attacked in Parliament; 20th, Peter the Great decrees that the New Year in Russia is to begin on *Jan.* 1st (instead of *Sept.* 1st), and introduces administrative reforms.

E

F **Politics, Economics, Law and Education**
  J. Child, *Observations Concerning Trade and Interest*.
  Samuel Garth, *The Dispensary* (satirical poem advocating free dispensaries).
  Pierre Lemoyne founds the first European settlement in Louisiana at Fort Maurepas.

G **Science, Technology and Discovery**
  Francisco Redi investigates maggots in meat.
  Dampier explores the north-west coast of Australia.

H **Philosophy, Religion and Scholarship**
  Richard Bentley, *Dissertation Upon the Epistles of Phalaris* (begins a new era in scholarship in Europe, and ends an old controversy).
  Gilbert Burnet, *Exposition of the XXXIX Articles*.

J **Art, Sculpture, Fine Arts and Architecture**
  Architecture:
    Figueroa, St. Luis Church, Seville (–1731).
    John Vanbrugh, Castle Howard (–1726).

K **Music**
  Feuillet, *Chorégraphie* (manual of dance notation).

L **Literature (including Drama)**
  John Dryden, *Fables, Ancient and Modern*.
  George Farquhar, *Love and a Bottle* (comedy).
  François de Salignac de la Mothe-Fénelon, *Télémaque* (suppressed; –1717).

M **Births and Deaths**
  Jan. 27th William Temple d. (71).
  Mar. 12th Count Peder Griffenfeld d. (63).
  Apr. 21st Jean Racine d. (60).
  June 22nd Josiah Child d. (69).
  — Robert Blair b. (–1746).
  — Jean Chardin b. (–1779).

1700   Death of Charles II of Spain—Outbreak of Great Northern War—Elector of Brandenburg becomes King of Prussia

A Jan:

Feb:

Mar: 14/25th, second Partition Treaty (of *June* 1699) is ratified.

B Apr: 17th, William III is forced to dismiss Somers as Lord Chancellor, to placate the Commons over the Act of Resumption of Irish grants (which was brought in as a bill on *Dec.* 15th, 1699).

May: The Partition Treaty is communicated to Charles of Spain and to the Emperor, both of whom reject it;

Saxon troops invade Livonia, which marks the start of the Great Northern War (–1721).

Jun:

C Jul: 4th, truce between Russia and Turkey, which cedes Azov;

30th, on the death of the Duke of Gloucester, the succession to the English throne passes to the Electress Sophia.

Aug: 18th, Charles XII enforces the peace of Travendal on Denmark which agrees to abstain from hostilities against Sweden.

D Oct: 3rd, Charles II of Spain appoints Philip of Anjou his heir and backdates his will to *Oct.* 2nd.

Nov: 1st, Charles II dies;

16th, Crown treaty between Emperor and Elector of Brandenburg, who is recognised as King of Prussia provided he will supply troops for the expected war against France, will support the Austrian Hapsburgs in future Imperial elections, and will vote in the Diet in support of the Hapsburgs;

23rd, Clement XI is elected Pope after the death of Innocent XII;

30th, Charles XII defeats Peter the Great at Narva.

Dec: 12th, Sidney Godolphin becomes Treasurer.

E Administrative reorganisation of Bengal under Sir Charles Eyre.

F **Politics, Economics, Law and Education**
Sewall, *The Selling of Joseph*, the first American protest against slavery.
English Royal African Company loses its monopoly of trade between the Gold Coast and Britain.
Great Fire of Edinburgh.
Approximate populations (in millions): France 19; Austrian Hapsburg dominions 7½; Great Britain and Ireland 7½; Spain 6.

G **Science, Technology and Discovery**
Berlin Academy of Science is founded, with Gottfried von Leibniz as president.
Edmund Halley compiles charts with lines of equal magnetic variation.
N. Lemery shows that a mixture of hydrogen and air detonates on the application of a light.
J. P. Tournefort discovers the composition of sal ammoniac (ammonia chloride).
Henry Winstanley completes Eddystone lighthouse (the tower is destroyed by gale, *Nov.* 20th, 1703).

H **Philosophy, Religion and Scholarship**
Thomas Hyde, *Historia religionis veterum Persarum*.
Peter Anthony Motteux translates *Don Quixote* from the Spanish of Cervantes.
Sir John Cotton bestows his grandfather's collection of books and manuscripts (Sir Robert Bruce Cotton's library) to the nation. Transferred to British Museum, 1753.
The *Gregorian Calendar* adopted by German Protestants.
George Whitefield starts a mission in America.
A Reading Room is established by Earl of Bellomont in the City Hall, New York (becomes the New York Society Library, 1754).
Académie des Sciences, Belles Lettres et Arts de Lyon founded.

J **Art, Sculpture, Fine Arts and Architecture**
Painting:
    Godfrey Kneller, *Matthew Pryor*. Kneller also begins series of portraits of Admirals at Greenwich.

K **Music**
W. Croft, *Courtship à la Mode* (stage music for).
Sauveur measures and explains musical vibrations.

L **Literature (including Drama)**
William Congreve, *The Way of the World* (comedy).
George Farquhar, *The Constant Couple, or A Trip to the Jubilee* (comedy) (–1701).
Matthew Pryor, *Carmen Saeculare*.
George Savile, 1st Marquess of Halifax, *Advice to a Daughter* and *The Character of a Trimmer* (written 1688; both published with other essays, maxims, etc., in *Miscellanies*).

M **Births and Deaths**
May 1st John Dryden d. (69).
Aug. 13th Henrich von Brühl b. (–1763).
Sept. 11th James Thomson b. (–1748).
Nov. 30th Armande Grésinde Bejart d. (55).
— Lambert Sigisbert Adam b. (–1759).
— Bartolomeo Rastrelli b. (–1771).

1701 War of Spanish Succession opens—Act of Settlement in England— Detroit founded

A Jan: 18th, Frederick III of Brandenburg is crowned Frederick I, King of Prussia.
   Feb: 6th (*–June* 24th), fifth Parliament of William III has a Tory majority, with Robert
   Harley as Speaker. The Tories impeach Lords Somers, Orford, Portland, and Halifax,
   leading Whigs, for their part in signing Partition Treaties, but they are subsequently
   discharged due to support by Lords and due to the increasing gravity of European
   situation;
   War of Spanish Succession begins; Philip of Anjou enters Madrid as Philip V of Spain
   while French troops also occupy Southern Spanish Netherlands.
   Mar: 9th, Electors of Bavaria and Cologne sign treaties of alliance with France.

B Apr:
   May:
   Jun: 12th, Act of Settlement, necessitated by death of Duke of Gloucester, provides for
   Protestant succession in Britain of House of Hanover by Sophia, Princess of Hanover,
   and grand-daughter of James I. In addition the Act prevents the removal of judges by
   the sovereign;
   17th, having invaded Livonia, Charles XII of Sweden relieves Riga from Russian occupation and subsequently invades Courland and Poland.

C Jul: 9th, Prince Eugène defeats the French in Lombardy at the battle of Carpi.
   Aug: 27th/*Sept.* 7th, the Treaty of the Hague, known as the Grand Alliance, is signed, by
   which Britain, Holland and the Emperor ally against France.
   Sep: 6th, James II dies and Louis XIV recognises the Old Pretender as James III (James
   Edward, son of James II);
   17th, Prince Eugène defeats the French at Chiara.

D Oct:
   Nov: 11th, English Parliament is dissolved.
   Dec: 30th (*–July* 2nd, 1702), sixth Parliament of William III.

E A fort and settlement at Detroit is founded by Antoine de la Mothe Cadillac to control the
   Illinois trade.

F **Politics, Economics, Law and Education**
Daniel Defoe, *The Villany of Stock-Jobbers Debated.*
Anon., *Considerations for the East India Trade.*
The French found Detroit.
William III's charters to weavers in Axminster and Wilton for making carpets.
Yale College, New Haven, Connecticut, founded and Yale Collegiate School founded
at Saybrook, Connecticut.
Capt. Kidd is hanged for piracy (*Feb.* 23rd).

G **Science, Technology and Discovery**
Jethro Tull invents a machine-drill for sowing crops in drills.
A terrestrial globe is made at Lyons showing the lakes of Africa.

H **Philosophy, Religion and Scholarship**
Académie des Inscriptions founded in France.
Jeremy Collier, *The Great Historical, Geographical, Genealogical and Poetical Dictionary*
(to 1688), 2 vols. (−1721).
John Dennis, *The Advancement and Reformation of Modern Poetry.*
Sir Richard Steele, *The Christian Hero; an argument.*
Society for Propagating the Gospel in Foreign Parts founded (SPG), London.
Father Francisco Ximénez collects and translates the *Popul Vah*, the sacred national
book of the Quiché Indians of Guatemala (−1721).
Benjamin Whichcote, *Several Discourses; Moral and Religious Aphorisms* (−1703; 1707).
Yale College Library opens.

J **Art, Sculpture, Fine Arts and Architecture**
Painting:
Hyacinthe Rigaud, *Louis XIV.*

K **Music**

L **Literature (including Drama)**
Edme Boursault, *Esope à la cour* (−1690).
Daniel Defoe, *The True-Born Englishman*: a satire.
John Dryden, *The Comedies, Tragedies and Operas, collected.* 2 vols. *Original Poems and
Translocations, collected* (posth.).
George Farquhar, *Sir Harry Wildair* (comedy), sequel to *The Constant Couple* (of 1700).
John Philips, *The Splendid Shilling*: an imitation of Milton.
Sir Richard Steele, *The Funeral; or, Grief à la Mode* (comedy).

M **Births and Deaths**
Feb. 23rd William Kidd d. (*c.* 56).
May 31st Alexander Cruden b. (−1770).
Aug. 30th Charles Sedley d. (*c.* 61).
Sept. 6th James II d. (67).
— Madeleine de Scudéry d. (94).

A Jan:
Feb: 1st, Prince Eugène raids Cremona;
20th, Act for the attainder of the Pretender;
24th, Act of Abjuration of the Pretender, making it obligatory to swear oath of fidelity to King and heirs according to Act of Settlement.
Mar: 8th/19th, William III dies and is succeeded by Queen Anne in Britain (–1714);
in Holland there is no Stadtholder and control of affairs is in the hands of the States-General under Heinsius;
24th, the Earl of Marlborough becomes Captain-General of the English armed forces.

B Apr: 23rd/*May* 4th, Britain, Holland and the Emperor declare war against France;
New Jersey is reunited as Royal Province when the Proprietors surrender their interest.
May: 8th, Sidney Godolphin again becomes Treasurer;
14th, Charles XII of Sweden takes Warsaw.
Jun:

C Jul: 19th, Charles XII defeats the Poles at Klissow and subsequently takes Cracow.
Aug: 4/15th (–*Sept.* 4/15th), British expedition to Cadiz fails.
Sep: 5/16th, Marlborough takes Venlo;
26th/*Oct.* 7th, Marlborough takes Ruremonde.

D Oct: 1/12th, Sir George Rooke seizes part of Spanish treasure fleet in Vigo Bay;
20th (–*Mar.* 14th, 1705), first Parliament of Queen Anne with Robert Harley as Speaker;
12/23rd, Marlborough captures Liège;
16/27th, British plunder St. Augustus in Florida in the war with Spain.
Nov:
Dec:

E Rebellion of Camisards Protestant peasants, in Cévennes;
Frederick I of Prussia acquires countships of Lingen and Mors.

F **Politics, Economics, Law and Education**
   The Daily Courant, the first daily paper is issued in London (*Mar.* 2nd to 1735).
   The 'Moscow Gazette' (*Moskovskya Viedomosti*) is issued by order of Peter the Great
   (*Dec.* 16th).
   The Asiento Company is founded to transport negroes to Spanish America.

G **Science, Technology and Discovery**
   Wilhelm Homberg first prepares boric acid.

H **Philosophy, Religion and Scholarship**
   Abel Boyer, *Anglo-French and Franco-English Dictionary* (compiled by a Huguenot
   settler in England).
   Edward Bysshe, *The Art of English Poetry*.
   Edward Hyde, the Earl of Clarendon, *The History of the Rebellion* (posth.).
   Daniel Defoe, *The Shortest Way With Dissenters*.
   Laurence Echard, *A General Ecclesiastical History* (from the Nativity to Constantine).
   John Kersey, *A New English Dictionary*.
   William King, *De Origine Mali* (trans. 1729).
   Thomas Madox, *Formulare Anglicanum*: Charters and Instruments (from the Conquest
   to the end of the reign of Henry VIII).
   Cotton Mather, *Magnalia Christi Americana* (an ecclesiastical history of New England).
   Peter Mechitar (or Mekhitar) founds in Constantinople the Mechitharist Congregation
   of Armenian Monks, in communion with Rome (–1717).

J **Art, Sculpture, Fine Arts and Architecture**
   Painting:
      Godfrey Kneller, 'Kit Cat' series of portraits (–1717).

K **Music**
   W. Croft. *The Funeral* (stage music for).

L **Literature (including Drama)**
   George Farquhar, *The Inconstant* and *The Twin Rivals* (comedies).

M **Births and Deaths**
   Mar. 8th William III d. (52).
   June 2nd Cenon de Sonodevilla, Marquess de la Ensenada b. (–1781).
   June 26th Philip Doddridge b. (–1751).
   Sept. 28th Robert Spencer, Earl of Sunderland d. (62).
   Nov. 4th John Benbow d. (49).
   Dec. — Jack Sheppard b. (–1724).
   — Thomas Arthur, Comte de Lally, Baron de Tollendal, b. (–1766).

A **Jan:** Delaware becomes a separate colony from Pennsylvania; a separation is approved by
   Privy Council.
   Feb:
   Mar:

B **Apr:** 21st/*May* 2nd, Portugal concludes treaty with Britain and joins Grand Alliance.
   May: 1st, Charles XII of Sweden defeats Peter the Great at Rultusk;
   the Chushingura Incident in Japan when Kiva Yoshinaka is murdered by supporters of
   the dead Lord of Ako;
   Duke of Villars threatens Vienna;
   7/18th, Marlborough occupies the Electorate of Cologne and subsequently takes Bonn,
   Limburg, Huy and Guelders, while Prince Eugène also conducts a vigorous campaign
   in Rhineland and Southern Germany.
   Jun:

C **Jul:**
   Aug:
   Sep: 12th, Archduke Charles is proclaimed King of Spain in Madrid;
   20th, French victory at Hochstadt.

D **Oct:**
   Nov: 4th, Savoy joins the Grand Alliance;
   Queen Anne's Bounty constitutes grant of the first fruits and tenths which Henry VIII
   had confiscated for the Crown, in trust to increase the incomes of small benefices.
   Dec: 16th/27th, Methuen Treaty between Britain and Portugal is signed, whereby the
   latter is to import all her woollen goods from Britain who, in turn, agrees to import
   Portuguese wines at a third less duty than French wines.

E Hungarians, supported by the French, revolt against Emperor.

F **Politics, Economics, Law and Education**

Following the reduction of duties on port, brought about by the Methuen Treaty with Portugal, port becomes popular in England compared with the heavier taxed French and German wines.

Peter the Great lays the foundations of St. Petersburg (*June*).

G **Science, Technology and Discovery**

Guillaume Amontons publishes papers on thermometers.

John Adair, *Description of the Sea Coasts and Islands of Scotland.*

H **Philosophy, Religion and Scholarship**

George Hickes, *Thesaurus* ('Thesaurus Grammaticocriticus et archaeologicus'; (in 1735 translated).

Thomas Hearne, *Reliquiae Bodleianae.*

Jean Le Clerc, *Bibliothèque choisie* (28 vols. –1713).

Universal, Historical, Geographical, Chronological and Classical Dictionary (the first A–Z treatment of knowledge in an English publication).

Ellis Wyn, o Lasynys, *Gweledigaethan y Bardd Cwsc.*

J **Art, Sculpture, Fine Arts and Architecture**

Painting:

Hyacinthe Rigaud, *Marquis de Chamilly.*

K **Music**

W. Croft, *The Twin Rivals* (stage music for).

L **Literature (including Drama)**

Richard Steele, *The Lying Lover* (comedy).

M **Births and Deaths**

May 16th Charles Perrault d. (75).

May 25th Samuel Pepys d. (70).

June 17th John Wesley b. (–1791).

June 23rd Marie Leszczynska b. (–1768).

Oct. 5th Jonathan Edwards b. (–1758).

Oct. 28th John Wallis d. (86).

— François Boucher b. (–1770).

— 'The Man in the Iron Mask' d. (—).

A Jan: Augustus II of Poland is deposed.
   Feb:
   Mar:

B Apr: 20th, Henry St. John, a moderate Tory, joins the English Ministry as Secretary at
        War and
        22nd, Nottingham, Secretary of State, Southern Department is dismissed;
        the French ally with the Indians and massacre inhabitants of Deerfield, in the Connecti-
        cut Valley.
   May: 18th, Robert Harley, a moderate Tory, becomes Secretary of State, Northern
        Department;
        8th/19th, Duke of Marlborough leaves Bedburg, near Juliers, to begin his march to
        the Danube;
        30th/*June* 10th, Marlborough meets Prince Eugène at Mandelsheim; they are joined
   Jun: 2nd/13th, by Prince of Baden, and they arrive
        12th/23rd, near Ulm;
        21st/*July* 2nd, Marlborough is victorious at Donauwörth.

C Jul: 24th/*Aug.* 4th, British, under Sir George Rooke, take Gibraltar;
        Stanislaus Lesczcynski is elected King of Poland as Stanislaus I (–1709) at Charles
        XII's instigation.
   Aug: 2nd/13th, Marlborough and Prince Eugène defeat the French and Bavarians at
        Blenheim;
        4th, Peter the Great takes Dorpat;
        31st, Peter takes Narva.
   Sep:

D Oct: 7th, the Convention of Ilbersheim, by which the lands of the Elector of Bavaria are
        placed under control of the Emperor.
   Nov:
   Dec:

E Peter the Great fortifies Kronstadt to protect St. Petersburg.

F **Politics, Economics, Law and Education**
Beau Nash becomes master of ceremonies at Bath.
Daniel Defoe starts weekly newspaper *The Review* (–1713).
Boston News-Letter, the first newspaper in America is issued weekly from *Apr.* 24th.
A Registry of Deeds is statutorily established for the West Riding of Yorkshire.

G **Science, Technology and Discovery**
Isaac Newton, *Optics*, defends the emission theory of light.
John Harris, *Lexicon Technicum*, the first scientific encyclopaedia.

H **Philosophy, Religion and Scholarship**
Antoine Galland, translates into French *The Arabian Nights Entertainment* (–1708;
  being the first translation into any Western language).
Thomas Rymer, *Feodera* (–1735).
The earliest German Subscription Library opens in Berlin.
The Jesuits' *Dictionnaire de Trévoux* (a universal French and Latin dictionary of terms
  used in the sciences and arts, published at Trévoux; based on the posthumous work of
  Furetière, in 1690).

J **Art, Sculpture, Fine Arts and Architecture**
Architecture:
  Thomas Archer, North Front, Chatsworth (–1705).

K **Music**
J. S. Bach writes his first cantata.
W. Croft, *The Dying Lover* (stage music for).

L **Literature (including Drama)**
Jonathan Swift, *A Tale of a Tub* and *The Battle of the Books*.
George Farquhar (with P. A. Motteux), *The Stage Coach* (comedy).
William Wycherley, *Miscellany Poems*.

M **Births and Deaths**
Apr. 12th Jacques-Bénigne Bossuet d. (76).
July 15th August Gottlieb Spangenberg b. (–1792).
Sept. 4th Roger L'Estrange d. (88).
Oct. 28th John Locke d. (72).
— John Byng b. (–1757).
— John Kay b. (–1764).
— John Wood the elder b. (–1754).

1705   Death of Emperor Leopold I

A Jan:
Feb:
Mar:

B Apr:
May: 5th, Emperor Leopold I dies and is succeeded by Joseph I (–1711).
Jun: 16th, Swedish victory at Gemaurhof.

C Jul: Revolution in Russia at Astrakhan, against Peter's westernisation.
Aug: 28th, George William, Duke of Luneburg-Celle, dies and his lands are united with Hanover.
Sep:

D Oct: 4th/15th, British navy, under Lord Peterborough, takes Barcelona;
Charles III, Archduke of Austria, is recognised in Catalonia, Valencia and Aragon;
11th, Lord Cowper is appointed Lord Chancellor;
25th, Queen Anne's second Parliament meets with a Whig majority.
Nov:
Dec:

E Husseinite dynasty of Beys becomes ruler of Tunis and throws off Turkish suzerainty.

F **Politics, Economics, Law and Education**
Thomasius, *Fundamenta Juris Naturalis et Gentium*.

G **Science, Technology and Discovery**
Edmund Halley conjectures that a comet seen in 1682 was identical with comets observed in 1607, 1531 and earlier; he correctly predicts its return in 1758.
Berlin Royal Observatory is founded.
John Ray, *Methodus Insectorum* (posth.).
Thomas Newcomen improves the steam-engine by devising a vacuum under the piston.

H **Philosophy, Religion and Scholarship**
Samuel Clarke, *The Being and Attributes of God :* the Boyle Lectures.
Bernard de Mandeville, *The Grumbling Hive* (–1714).

J **Art, Sculpture, Fine Arts and Architecture**
Architecture:
John Vanbrugh, Blenheim Palace.

K **Music**
J. S. Bach walks 200 miles to Lubeck to hear the Abendmusiken, directed by Buxtehude.
G. F. Handel, *Almira* (opera) produced (*Jan.* 8th) in Hamburg.

L **Literature (including Drama)**
Colley Cibber, *The Careless Husband* (comedy).
Prosper Jolyot Crébillon (*père*), *Idoménée* (tragedy).
Charles de Saint-Denis, Seigneur de Saint-Évremond, *Conversation du maréchal d'Hocquincourt avec le père Canaye* (posth.).
Sir Richard Steele, *The Tender Husband* (comedy).
Sir John Vanbrugh, *The Confederacy* (comedy; adapted from Dancourt's *Les Bourgeoises à la mode*).

M **Births and Deaths**
Jan. 12th Luca Giordano d. (73).
Jan. 17th John Ray d. (76).
Mar. 2nd William Murray, Earl of Mansfield, b. (–1793).
July 12th Titus Oates d. (56).
Aug. 16th Jacques Bernoulli d. (50).
Nov. 23rd Thomas Birch b. (–1766).
Dec. 31st Catherine of Braganza d. (66).
— Edward Hawke b. (–1781).
— Ninon de Lenclos d. (90).
— Farinell (Carlo Broschi) b. (–1782).

A   Jan:
Feb: 13th, Charles XII of Sweden defeats the Russians and Saxons at Fraustadt.
Mar:

B   Apr: 29th, Electors of Bavaria and Cologne are outlawed by the Emperor.
May: 11th/22nd, British raise siege of Barcelona by French;
      12th/23rd, Marlborough defeats French at Ramillies and conquers Spanish Netherlands.
Jun: British and Portuguese enter Madrid.

C   Jul:
Aug: 21st/*Sept.* 1st, successful defence of Charleston, S.C., against French and Spaniards;
      first negotiations for peace are opened by Louis XIV but are rejected by the allies (in
      Oct.).
Sep: 7th, Prince Eugène defeats the French at Turin and French troops subsequently
      leave Piedmont;
      24th, Peace of Altrandstadt between Sweden and Saxony; Augustus renounces Polish
      throne and recognises Stanislaus Lesczcynski, the pro-Swedish nominee.

D   Oct:
Nov:
Dec: 3rd, Lord Sunderland is appointed Secretary of State, Southern Department.

E   Riots in Scotland over proposed union with England.

F **Politics, Economics, Law and Education**
The Evening Post is issued in London, the first evening paper.
Christopher Semler founds a Real-Schule at Halle for the study of mathematics and applied science.
The Sun Fire Office is founded in London.

G **Science, Technology and Discovery**
O. Römer's catalogue of astronomic observations.
Giovanni Morgagni, *Adversaria anatomica*.

H **Philosophy, Religion and Scholarship**
Matthew Tindal, *Rights of the Christian Church* (Asserted Against the Romish and all other Priests).
James Watson, *Choice Collection of Scottish Poems*.
Isaac Watts, *Horae Lyricae*.

J **Art, Sculpture, Fine Arts and Architecture**
Painting:
Hyacinthe Rigaud, self-portrait.

K **Music**

L **Literature (including Drama)**
Daniel Defoe, *The Apparition of One Mrs. Veal*.
George Farquhar, *The Recruiting Officer* (comedy).
Sir John Vanbrugh, *The Mistake* (comedy).

M **Births and Deaths**
Jan. 17th Benjamin Franklin b. (–1790).
Jan. 28th John Baskerville b. (–1775).
Feb. 27th John Evelyn d. (85).
June 10th John Dollond b. (–1761).
July 2nd John Methuen d. (56).
Dec. 28th Pierre Bayle d. (59).
— Dick Turpin b. (–1739).

A Jan: 1st, John V succeeds in Portugal (–1750) on death of Peter II;
   4th, Louis of Baden dies;
   16th, Act of Security by Scottish Parliament finally receives Royal assent and is designed
   to protect the Protestant religion and the Presbyterian Church of Scotland.
Feb:
Mar: 3rd, Aurangzeb dies in India and is succeeded by Bahadur, but his Empire falls
   apart;
   13th, having taken Naples, the Emperor agrees to the Convention of Milan, whereby
   French troops are to leave northern Italy.

B Apr: 14th/25th, British are defeated at Almanza.
May: 1st, Union between England and Scotland under the name of Great Britain which
   provides for: (a) the Hanoverian succession; (b) one Parliament, to which Scotland is
   to send members; (c) Churches to remain as before; and (d) adoption of one flag, the
   Union Jack.
Jun: British expedition against Acadia lands.

C Jul:
Aug: 11th/22nd, unsuccessful siege of Toulon by allies is abandoned by Prince Eugène;
   'Perpetual' Alliance between Prussia and Sweden is signed, guaranteeing military
   support to each other in event of attack by third party;
   Prussia acquires Neuchatel, Tecklenburg and Valengrin.
Sep:

D Oct: Revival of Queen Anne's second Parliament as first Parliament of Great Britain.
Nov:
Dec:

E

F   Politics, Economics, Law and Education

Vauban in *Dîme Royal* attacks exemptions from taxation in France and pleads for uniform land and income taxes; it is burnt on Louis XIV's orders.

G   Science, Technology and Discovery

Georg Stahl, *Theoria Medica Vera*.

John Floyer introduces the practice of counting the rate of pulse-beats of patients.

M. B. Valentin prepares 'magnesia alba'.

Denis Papin invents the high-pressure boiler.

H   Philosophy, Religion and Scholarship

Issac Watts, *Hymns and Spiritual Songs*.

Refoundation of the Society of Antiquaries, London (*see* 1572, 1751).

J   Art, Sculpture, Fine Arts and Architecture

Architecture:

     John Vanbrugh, Kimbolton.

K   Music

L   Literature (including Drama)

George Farquhar, *The Beaux' Stratagem* (comedy).

Alain-René Lesage, *Le Diable boiteux* (translated sometimes as *Asmodeus; or The Devil Upon Two Sticks*). *Crispin rival de son maître* (comedy).

M   Births and Deaths

Jan. 10th Philibert, Comte de Gramont, d. (86).

Jan. 20th Frederick, later Prince of Wales ('Poor Fred'), b. (–1751).

Feb. 25th Carlo Goldoni b. (–1793).

Mar. 3rd Aurangzeb, Emperor of Hindustan, d. (89).

Mar. 30th Sébastien Vauban d. (74).

Apr. 6th Willem Van de velde the younger d. (74).

Apr. 15th Leonhard Euler b. (–1783).

Apr. 22nd Henry Fielding b. (–1754).

Apr. 29th George Farquhar d. (30).

May 9th Dietrich Buxtehude d. (70).

May 23rd Carl von Linné (Linnaeus) b. (–1778).

May 27th Marquis de Montespan d. (66).

June. 19th William Sherlock d. (66).

Aug. 4th Johann August Ernesti b. (–1781).

Aug. 18th William Cavendish, Duke of Devonshire, d. (67).

Aug. 24th Selina, Countess of Huntingdon, b. (–1791).

Sept. 7th Georges-Louis Leclerc, Comte de Buffon, b. (–1788).

Dec. 18th Charles Wesley b. (–1788).

Dec. 26th Jean Mabillon d. (75).

A   Jan:
    Feb: 13th, Robert Harley is dismissed as Secretary of State, Northern Department;
        25th, Robert Walpole is appointed Secretary at War.
    Mar: 23rd, the Old Pretender arrives at Firth of Forth but, 27th, returns to Dunkirk.

B   Apr:
    May:
    Jun: 30th/*July* 11th, Duke of Marlborough and Prince Eugène defeat French at Oudenarde.

C   Jul: 4th, Charles XII defeats Russians at Holowczyn;
        5th, Emperor claims reversion of Duchy of Mantua on death of Duke.
    Aug: 18th/29th, British capture Minorca;
        British take Sardinia.
    Sep: 29th, British East India Co. and New East India Co. are merged;
        Swedes are routed at Lysema.

D   Oct: 10th/21st, allies take Lille but fail to capture the citadel until *Dec.*;
        28th, Prince Consort, George of Denmark, dies;
        Charles XII takes Mohilev and invades Ukraine (*–Feb.* 1709).
    Nov: 16th, third Parliament of Anne, with a Whig majority, meets.
    Dec:

E   Russia is divided into eight governments for administrative purposes;
    War of Emboabas in Brazil between Portuguese and Paulistas (Portuguese slave-raiding
        parties); the former are ultimately successful, in 1711.

F **Politics, Economics, Law and Education**
A Professorship of Poetry is founded at Oxford University.

G **Science, Technology and Discovery**
Hermann Boerhaave, *Institutiones medicae* develops theories of inflammation, obstruction and plethora in the human body.
The first accurate map of China is made as a result of surveys by Jesuit missionaries.

H **Philosophy, Religion and Scholarship**
Jeremy Collier, *The Ecclesiastical History of Great Britain* (–1714).
Gian Vincenzo Gravina, *Della Ragion Poetica*.
Matthew Henry, *Exposition of the Old and New Testaments*.
John Locke, *Some Familiar Letters* (between Mr. Locke and Several of his Friends posth.).
Bernard de Montfaucon, *Palaeographia Graeca*.
Simon Ockley, *The Conquest of Syria, Persia and Egypt by the Saracens* (–1757).
Rabelais translated (complete) by Peter Anthony Motteux and Sir Thomas Urquhart (*see* 1653, 1693).
Vienna: the first Austrian theatre opens.
Andrew Mack of Swartzenau founds the German Baptist Brethren (the Dunkers; –1719, 1732).

J **Art, Sculpture, Fine Arts and Architecture**
Painting:
James Thornhill, Painted Hall, Greenwich.

K **Music**

L **Literature (including Drama)**
Prosper Jolyot, Sieur de Crébillon, *père*, *Électre* (tragedy).
Jean-François Regnard, *Le Légataire universel* (comedy).

M **Births and Deaths**
Aug. — Petter Dass d. (66).
Oct. 1st John Blow d. (60).
Oct. 16th Albrecht von Haller b. (–1777).
Oct. 28th Prince George of Denmark d. (53).
Nov. 15th William Pitt, Earl of Chatham, b. (–1778).
Dec. 8th Emperor Francis I b. (–1765).
— Lavinia Fenton b. (–1760).
— Francis Hayman b. (–1776).
— Jules Mansart d. (62).

A Jan:
Feb: The Hague Conference for peace negotiations is opened.
Mar:

B Apr:
May: 11th, Charles XII of Sweden lays siege to Poltava;
Louis XIV rejects peace preliminaries;
first mass emigration of Germans from the Palatinate to North America.
Jun: Louis XIV makes direct appeal to French nation over rejection of peace negotiations.

C Jul: 8th, Peter I of Russia defeats Charles XII at Poltava;
19th/30th, Duke of Marlborough and Prince Eugène take Tournai.
Aug: 31st/*Sept.* 11th, Marlborough and Prince Eugène defeat the French at Malplaquet,
with very heavy casualties. Tories nickname Marlborough the 'Butcher'.
Sep:

D Oct: 9th/20th, Marlborough and Prince Eugène take Mons;
18th/29th, first Dutch Barrier Treaty is negotiated by Townshend; under this the
United Provinces acquire the right to garrison nine fortified places in the Spanish
Netherlands, together with 10 others should they be retaken from the French.
Nov:
Dec:

E First Russian prisoners are sent to Siberia;
Ienobe becomes Shōgun in Japan;
Rising of Afghans at Kandahar under Mir Vais.

F **Politics, Economics, Law and Education**
First Copyright Act in Britain, to operate from *Apr.* 1st, 1710.
The Tatler, edited by Richard Steele with Addison's help, is issued (*Apr.* 12th–*Jan.* 1711).

G **Science, Technology and Discovery**
George Berkeley, *New Theory of Vision* maintains that the eye only conveys sensations of colour and that perceptions of form are gathered by touch.
Francis Hawksbee makes first accurate observations of the capillary action of tubes and glass plates.
Abraham Darby constructs first successful experiment, at Colbrookdale, Shropshire, for using coke in a blast-furnace to smelt iron.
Japanese magnolias are introduced to England.

H **Philosophy, Religion and Scholarship**
Arthur Collins, *The Peerage of England*, vol. 1 (–1735, 1756).
Nicholas Rowe, *The Works of Mr. William Shakespeare*, Revised and Corrected, 6 vols. (–1714).
John Strype, *Annals of the Reformation* (–1731).
Remaining Port-Royalists forcibly removed and the buildings destroyed.

J **Art, Sculpture, Fine Arts and Architecture**

K **Music**
'For he's a Jolly Good Fellow' improvised after the Battle of Malplaquet.
Bartolomeo Cristofori makes the first pianoforte, called *gravicembalo col piano e forte*. Two of his instruments still survive, made in 1726 and 1720.

L **Literature (including Drama)**
Alain-René Lesage, *Turcaret; ou, Le financier* (satirical comedy).
Alexander Pope, *Pastorals* (in Tonson's *Poetical Miscellanies*, sixth part).
Matthew Prior, *Poems on Several Occasions*.

M **Births and Deaths**
Jan. 24th George Rooke d. (59).
July 5th Étienne de Silhouette b. (–1767).
Sept. 18th Samuel Johnson b. (–1784).
Nov. 23rd William Bentinck, Earl of Portland, d. (64).
Dec. 1st Abraham a Sancta Clara d. (73).
Dec. 18th Elizabeth (Petrovina), Empress of Russia, b. (–1762).

1710   Peace negotiations opened at Gertruydenberg

A   Jan: 27th, first budget in Russia.
    Feb: Negotiations to bring about peace in Europe are opened at Gertruydenberg.
    Mar: 20th, trial of Dr. Sacheverell (which began on *Feb.* 27th) ends, and, 23rd, he is
        sentenced to be suspended from preaching for 3 years, for having preached ultra-
        Tory sermons.

B   Apr:
    May:
    Jun: 14th, Sunderland is dismissed.

C   Jul: 16th/27th, British victory at Alminara.
    Aug: 8th, fall of Whig Ministry; Robert Harley and Henry St. John form Tory Ministry;
        9th/20th, allied victory at Saragosa.
    Sep: 21st, Parliament is dissolved;
        Charles III enters Madrid but soon retires to Catalonia.

D   Oct: 2nd/13th, British take Port Royal (Annapolis) in Acadia.
    Nov: 25th, Parliament, Anne's fourth, meets with Tory majority; St. John is Secretary of
        State, Northern Department (and Harley later becomes Treasurer);
        30th, Turkey declares war against Russia at the instigation of Charles XII;
        30th/*Dec.* 10th, British troops are defeated at Brihuega.
    Dec: 10th, the French defeat Imperial troops at Villa Viciosa.

E   Mauritius, which was formerly part of Dutch East Indies, becomes French;
    War of Mascates between Portuguese and Brazilian Indians begins, and Indians are sub-
        sequently defeated.

F **Politics, Economics, Law and Education**
Fénélon, in a tract for his pupil the Duke of Burgundy, recommends the summoning of the States-General in France.
The Examiner, started by William King, Jonathan Swift, Matthew Prior, Mrs. Mary Manley, and others (from *Aug.* 3rd–*July* 26th, 1714).
J. A. de la Gibonnais, *Intérêt et Profit*, a criticism of commercial morality.
English South Sea Company is founded.

G **Science, Technology and Discovery**
The dye, Prussian blue, is first made.
Theodore Krump publishes an account of his travels to Abyssinia (1700–2).

H **Philosophy, Religion and Scholarship**
Bayle's *Dictionary* (1696) translated into English.
George Berkeley, *A Treatise Concerning the Principles of Human Knowledge*.
Thomas Hearne's edition of *The Itinerary of John Leland the Antiquary*, 9 vols. (–1712).
William King, *An Historical Account of the Heathen Gods and Heroes*.
Gottfried Wilhelm von Leibniz, *Théodicée*.
Cotton Mather, *Essays to Do Good*.
Edward Stillingfleet, *Works* (with a Life by Richard Bentley), 6 vols.

J **Art, Sculpture, Fine Arts and Architecture**
Architecture:
Gabriel Boffrand, Hôtel Amelot, Paris.
Christopher Wren, Marlborough House, Westminster.

K **Music**
Handel visits England.

L **Literature (including Drama)**
William Congreve, *Collected Works*, 3 vols.

M **Births and Deaths**
Jan. 3rd Giovanni Battista Pergolesi b. (–1736).
Feb. 7th William Boyce b. (–1779).
Feb. 15th Louis XV b. (–1774).
Feb. 16th Esprit Fléchier d. (77).
Mar. 5th John Holt d. (67).
Mar. 12th Thomas Arne b. (–1778).
Apr. 15th Marie Anne de Cupis de Camargo b. (–1770).
Apr. 26th Thomas Reid b. (–1796).
Apr. 28th Thomas Betterton d. (75).
— John Snetzler b. (—).

A Jan:
   Feb: 16th, Landed Property Qualification bill is brought into the House of Lords and is passed on 22nd;
   Administrative Senate is formed in Russia to rule in the absence of Peter the Great.
   Mar: 19th, war is proclaimed between Russia and Turkey;
   29th, Robert Harley becomes Lord Treasurer.

B Apr: 14th, the Dauphin dies;
   17th, Joseph I dies and is ultimately succeeded by his brother, Charles III of Spain, as the Emperor Charles VI, but he does not leave Spain until September.
   May: 1st, Peace of Szathmar, an agreement between the Hungarian rebels and the Emperor is signed. Charles VI promises to respect the Hungarian Constitution;
   23rd, Harley is created Earl of Oxford.
   Jun: 12th, Toleration Act (Scotland) receives royal assent and restores lay patronage in the Church of Scotland which had been repealed in 1690.

C Jul:
   Aug: 1st, Peter I, surrounded by Turks at the Pruth, makes peace and restores Azov; in addition, he allows Charles XII to return to Sweden.
   Sep: 12th, the French enter the Bay of Rio de Janiero;
   22nd, Rio de Janiero captured by the French;
   —, the Tuscarura War in North Carolina breaks out when Indians massacre 200 settlers, but they are defeated (–1712).

D Oct:
   Nov:
   Dec: 15th, Occasional Conformity Act is brought in by Nottingham;
   plague in Copenhagen;
   31st, Duke of Marlborough is dismissed as Commander-in-Chief.

E Newspaper Act places tax on newspapers and pamphlets (repealed 1855), and on advertisements (repealed 1853).

F **Politics, Economics, Law and Education**

G **Science, Technology and Discovery**
 A machine for raising water is constructed at Wolverhampton.

H **Philosophy, Religion and Scholarship**
 Francis Atterbury, *Representation of the State of Religion*.
 Thomas Madox, *The History and Antiquities of the Exchequer*.
 Anthony Ashley Cooper (3rd Earl of Shaftesbury), *Characteristics of Men, Manners, Opinions and Times*, 3 vols.
 John Dennis, *On the Genius and Writings of Shakespeare*.
 William Whiston, *Primitive Christianity Revived*.
 Berlin Academy started, under the Presidency of Leibniz.
 London Academy of Arts opened.

J **Art, Sculpture, Fine Arts and Architecture**
 Architecture:
  Thomas Archer, Pavillion, Wrest Park (–1712).
  John Vanbrugh, King's Weston.

K **Music**
 G. F. Handel, *Rinaldo* (opera) first performed in London (words by Aaron Hill).
 Johann Adolf Hasse introduces the clarinet into the orchestra in his opera *Croesus*.
 John Shore invents the tuning fork.

L **Literature (including Drama)**
 Joseph Addison and Richard Steele, *The Spectator*, started *Mar.* 1st (*–Dec.* 6th, 1712).
 Prosper Jolyot de Crébillon, *Rhadamiste et Zénobie* (tragedy).
 [Alexander Pope], *Essay on Criticism*.
 Jonathan Swift, *The Conduct of the Allies*.

M **Births and Deaths**
 Jan. 24th Jean Bérain d. (73).
 Feb. 2nd Anton, Prince von Kaunitz-Rietburg b. (–1794).
 Mar. 13th Nicolas Boileau-Despréaux d. (74).
 Mar. 19th Thomas Ken d. (74).
 Apr. 26th David Hume b. (–1776).
 Aug. 19th Edward Boscawen b. (–1761).
 Aug. 22nd Louis François, Duc de Boufflers, d. (65).
 — Kitty Clive b. (–1785).
 — Arthur Devis b. (–1787).

A Jan: 1st/12th, Peace Congress opens at Utrecht;
     17th, Robert Walpole is sent to the Tower of London for alleged corruption as Secretary at War in dealing with Scottish affairs.
   Feb: 18th, Louis, Duke of Burgundy, heir to the French throne, dies;
     8th, Duke of Brittany, second son of the late Duke of Burgundy and next heir to the French throne, dies.

B Apr:
   May:
   Jun:

C Jul: 7th, Henry St. John is created Viscount Bolingbroke;
     8th/19th, Anglo-French truce;
     24th, the Dutch are defeated by Villars at Denain and join the truce;
     25th, Battle of Villmergen between Catholic and Protestant Swiss Cantons is won by the Protestant Berne.
   Aug: 11th, the Treaty of Aarau ends the Swiss war, guaranteeing the domination of Protestants over 5 Catholic cantons.
   Sep: 7th, the Danes occupy Bremen, including Stade, and together with Russian troops defeat Swedes in Baltic and Scandinavia;
     15th, Sidney Godolphin dies.

D Oct:
   Nov: 15th, Philip of Spain renounces claim to the French throne and the Dukes of Berry and of Orleans subsequently renounce claims to the Spanish throne.
   Dec: 20th, the Swedes defeat the Danes at Gadebusch.

E War of Succession between Bahadur's four sons in India;
   Crozat obtains a monopoly of the Illinois trade, including that of Louisiana, for 15 years.

F **Politics, Economics, Law and Education**
The Stamp Act in England imposes a tax of ½d. on pages of half a sheet and of 1d. on a whole sheet, from *Aug.* 1st.
The last execution for witchcraft in England.

G **Science, Technology and Discovery**

H **Philosophy, Religion and Scholarship**
Don Quixote of Cervantes, translated by Peter Motteux.
Jonathan Swift, *A Proposal for Correcting the English Language.*
Académie des Sciences, Belles Lettres et Arts, Bordeaux, founded.
Biblioteca National, Madrid, founded.

J **Art, Sculpture, Fine Arts and Architecture**
Architecture:
Thomas Archer, St. Paul's Church, Deptford (–1730).
Gabriel Boffrand, Hôtel de Montmorency, Paris.
Nicholas Hawksmoor, St. Anne's Church, Limehouse (–1724).
John James, St. George's Church, Hanover Square, London (–1725).

K **Music**
G. F. Handel, festal *Te Deum*, for the Peace of Utrecht.

L **Literature (including Drama)**
John Arbuthnot, *The History of John Bull* (5 pamphlets collected).
Alexander Pope, *The Rape of the Lock.*

M **Births and Deaths**
Feb. 28th Louis, Marquis Montcalm de Saint Veran, b. (–1759).
Mar. 22nd Edward Moore b. (–1757).
May 13th Johann Hartwig, Count von Bernstorff, b. (–1772).
June 11th Louis, Duc de Vendôme, d. (58).
June 28th Jean-Jacques Rousseau b. (–1778).
July 12th Richard Cromwell d. (85).
July 26th Thomas Osborne, Marquess of Carmarthen, d. (80).
Sept. 11th Giovanni Dominico Cassini d. (87).
Sept. 15th Pierre Simon Fournier b. (–1768).
Sept. 15th Sidney, Earl Godolphin, d. (*c.* 67).
Oct. 14th George Grenville b. (–1770).
Dec. 12th Alexander Selkirk d. (36).
Dec. 25th William King d. (49).
— Francesco Guardi b. (–1793).
— John Christopher Smith b. (–1795).

A Jan: 30th/*Feb*. 10th, second Dutch Barrier Treaty, similar to the first, but certain places which have passed into French hands are omitted.

Feb: 25th, Frederick I of Prussia dies and is succeeded by Frederick William I (–1740); Charles XII of Sweden, who has been encamped since 1709 at Bender in Moldavia, which is part of Turkish Empire, is taken prisoner by the Sultan (until *Sept*. 1714).

Mar: 16th/27th, Spain agrees at Utrecht to cede Gibraltar and Minorca to Britain and to grant the Assiento or monopoly of importing Negroes to Spanish America, to the Royal African Company;

31st/*Apr*. 11th, Peace of Utrecht between France, Britain, Holland, Savoy, Portugal and Prussia. France agrees to dismantle Dunkirk, to recognise the Protestant Succession in Britain and to cede Newfoundland, Acadia and Hudson Bay to Britain, but gains fortresses on the Canadian frontier. Spain cedes San Sacramento north of the River Plate to Portugal, cedes the Spanish Netherlands to Holland which are to be given to Emperor once Holland has established a barrier against France. Philip V, a Bourbon, is recognised as King of Spain, but Spain and France are never to be united under one king. Sicily is to be united under Savoy as a kingdom; Prussia gains Neuchatel and Upper Gelderland.

B Apr: 19th, the Emperor Charles VI issues the Pragmatic Sanction setting out female rights of succession to Hapsburg domains.

May: 6th, the Swedes capitulate at Oldensworth (Oldenburg).

Jun:

C Jul: 16th, Queen Anne's fourth Parliament is dissolved;
27th, the Peace of Adrianople between Turkey and Russia.

Aug:

Sep:

D Oct:

Nov:

Dec:

E Infant Ietsugu becomes Shogun of Japan.

F **Politics, Economics, Law and Education**
Abbé Saint Pierre, *Projet pour la Paix Perpétuelle*.
Gravina, *Origines Juris Civilis*.
Clarendon Building is erected at Oxford to house the University printer, financed from the profits of Clarendon's *History of the Rebellion*.

G **Science, Technology and Discovery**
Roger Cotes edits a revised edition of Isaac Newton's *Principia*.
A Board of Longitude is established in England.

H **Philosophy, Religion and Scholarship**
George Berkeley, *Dialogues between Hylas and Philonous*.
Arthur Collier, *Clavis Universalis; or A New Enquiry after Truth*.
François de Salignac de la Mothe-Fénelon, *Traité de l'existence et des attributs de Dieu*.
Anthony Hamilton, *Mémoires du comte de Grammont* (trans. –1714).
Papal condemnation by Clement XI of 101 propositions in Pasquier Quesnel's *Réflexions* (of 1687).
The Scriblerus Club founded in London (by Alexander Pope, Jonathan Swift, William Congreve, John Gay and others).
The Royal Spanish Academy, Madrid, founded.

J **Art, Sculpture, Fine Arts and Architecture**
Painting:
Desportes, *Spaniels with dead game*.
Architecture:
Gabriel Boffrand, Hôtel de Seigneley, Paris.

K **Music**
The School of Dance is established at the Paris Opéra.

L **Literature (including Drama)**
Joseph Addison, *Cato*.
Alexander Pope, *Windsor Forest; Ode on St. Cecilia's Day*.

M **Births and Deaths**
Jan. 2nd Marie Françoise Dumesnil b. (–1803).
Feb. 14th Anthony Ashley Cooper, 3rd Earl of Shaftesbury, d. (42).
May 25th John Stuart, Earl of Bute, b. (–1792).
June 13th Arcangelo Corelli d. (60).
July 10th Thomas Rymer d. (72).
Oct. 4th Francis Child d. (61).
Oct. 8th Alison Cockburn b. (–1794).
Oct. 15th Denis Diderot b. (–1784).
Nov. 24th Laurence Sterne b. (–1768).
— Allan Ramsay b. (–1784).
— Jacques Louis Soufflot b. (–1780).
— Charles Stanley b. (–1786).

A   Jan:
Feb: 16th, fifth Parliament of Queen Anne (–*Aug.* 25th) in Britain.
Mar: 7th, the Peace of Rastatt between France and Emperor, by which France recognises
Hapsburg's possessions in Italy, the Electors of Bavaria and Cologne are restored and
the Empire takes possession of the Spanish Netherlands;
13th, Battle of Storkyro leads to Russian domination of Finland.

B   Apr: 4th, Charles, Duke of Berry, next heir to the French throne, dies;
12th, a bill is introduced into the House of Commons to forbid anyone to keep a private
school unless he is a member of the Church of England and is licensed by a Bishop;
this later forms part of the Schism Act.
May:
Jun: 26th, Peace of Utrecht between Spain and Holland, which is recognised as a 'most
favoured nation' for trade, apart from the Assiento, which is a British monopoly.

C   Jul: 27th, the Earl of Oxford is dismissed, and
30th, the Earl of Shrewsbury becomes Lord Treasurer.
Aug: 1st, Queen Anne dies and is succeeded by George Lewis, Elector of Hanover, as
George I (–1727) (the Electress Sophia had died *May* 28th).
Sep: 7th, France signs the Peace of Baden with Emperor, whereby France keeps Alsace
and Strasbourg;
11th, Duke of Berwick, leading a combined Spanish and French force, storms Barcelona,
the last stronghold of the supporters of Charles (III);
16th, Philip V of Spain, following the death of his first wife, Marie Louise of Savoy,
marries Elizabeth Farnese and Cardinal Alberoni becomes the leading minister in
Spain;
17th, in Britain Townshend becomes Secretary of State, Northern Department, and
the Whig Ministry includes Robert Walpole, and the Earls of Sunderland, Orford
and Halifax, while the Duke of Marlborough returns as Commander-in-Chief;
18th, King George I lands in England.

D   Oct:
Nov: 22nd, Charles XII of Sweden arrives at Stralsund, having ended his Turkish
captivity in *Sept.*
Dec:

E   Tripoli under Ahmad Bey, becomes independent from Turkey.

F **Politics, Economics, Law and Education**

Böhmer in *Jus Ecclesiasticum Protestantium* discusses the modifications of Canon Law caused by the Reformation.

Worcester College, Oxford, founded.

G **Science, Technology and Discovery**

Dominique Anel invents a fine-pointed syringe which he uses for successful surgical treatment of cases of *fistula lacrymalis*.

Jethro Tull introduces the horse-hoe to England from France.

Henry Mill takes out a patent for a typewriter.

H **Philosophy, Religion and Scholarship**

Gottfried Arnold, *Unpartheyische Kirchen und Ketzerhistorie* (*An Impartial History of Church and Heresy*), 3 vols.

Thomas Ellwood, *History of the Life of Thomas Ellwood* (written by his own hand).

Jean Le Clerc, *Bibliothèque ancienne et moderne* (29 vols. –1726).

Gottfried Wilhelm von Leibniz, *Monadologie*.

John Locke, *Collected Works* (posth.).

Nicholas Rowe edits his *Stage Edition of the Works of William Shakespeare* (9 vols. –1709).

The Spanish Academy of Science, Madrid, founded.

J **Art, Sculpture, Fine Arts and Architecture**

Architecture:

Thomas Archer, St. John's Church, Smith Square, Westminister (–1728).

Gabrielle Boffrand, Hôtel de Torcy, Paris.

James Gibbs, St. Mary-le-Strand Church, London (–1717).

K **Music**

L **Literature (including Drama)**

Joseph Addison, *The Spectator*, collected.

John Gay, *The Shepherd's Week*.

Nicholas Rowe, *Jane Shore* (drama).

M **Births and Deaths**

Feb. 22nd Louis Georges Oudard Feudrix de Bréquigny b. (–1795).

Feb. 25th René Nicolas Maupeon b. (–1792).

Feb. 26th James Hervey b. (–1758).

Mar. 14th Karl Philipp Emanuel Bach b. (–1788).

July 2nd Christoph Willibald von Gluck b. (–1787).

Aug. 1st Richard Wilson b. (–1782).

Nov. 1st John Radcliffe d. (64).

Nov. 6th Charles Davenant d. (58).

Dec. 16th George Whitefield b. (–1770).

— Jean Baptiste Pigalle b. (–1785).

— Charles Pratt, Earl of Camden, b. (–1794).

A **Jan:**

Feb: 6th, the Peace of Utrecht ends the war between Spain and Portugal (ratified by Portugal *Mar.* 9th).

Mar: 17th, first Parliament of George I has a Whig majority;

27th, Lord Bolingbroke, fearing arrest for his part in the secret negotiations with France before the Treaty of Utrecht in 1713, flees to France.

B **Apr:** 15th, rising of Yamassees and other Indian tribes in S. Carolina takes place, but they are subsequently defeated and driven across the Spanish border into Florida;

Prussia, Saxony, Poland, Hanover and Denmark form an alliance against Sweden and war is declared. As part of this pact, Denmark agrees to sell Duchies of Bremen and Verden to Hanover.

May:

Jun: 10th, Bolingbroke is impeached.

C **Jul:** 9th, Robert Harley, Earl of Oxford, is imprisoned in the Tower of London for his part in negotiations with the French;

—, British Parliament passes Riot Act because of fear of Jacobitism and

12th, suspends the Habeas Corpus Act;

23rd, Bolingbroke joins the exiled James III as his adviser.

Aug: 18th, an Act of Attainder is passed against Bolingbroke.

Sep: 1st, Louis XIV dies and is succeeded by Louis XV, (–1774), his 5-year-old great-grandson, under the regency of the Duc d'Orleans, his nephew, until 1723, although Louis had decreed that power was to be shared between Orleans and the Duc de Maine, his illegitimate son; Philip V of Spain, the rightful heir to the French throne, had previously surrendered his right of succession;

6th, Jacobite rising, known as 'The Fifteen', begins at Braemar in Scotland, under the Earl of Mar.

D **Oct:** 12th, Robert Walpole becomes First Lord of the Treasury and Chancellor of the Exchequer.

Nov: 13th, the Jacobites are defeated at Sheriffmuir and separate;

13th (–14th), at the Battle of Preston the Jacobites are also defeated;

15th, Barrier Treaty is signed between Holland and the Empire, which obtains Spanish Netherlands, while the Dutch occupy eight fortresses against possible French attack.

Dec: 3rd/14th, commercial treaty between Britain and Spain;

22nd, James III, the 'Pretender', arrives at Peterhead having sailed from France;

24th, Prussians take Stralsund from Sweden and Charles XII attacks Norway.

E Mir Abdullah becomes ruler of Kandahar;

Venetians are expelled from the Morea by Turks;

Large-scale German and Scots-Irish immigrations to N. America begins, with settlements made in the Piedmont and other interior regions avoided by previous settlers.

F **Politics, Economics, Law and Education**
Doggett's Coat and Badge, a prize for annual rowing race for Thames Waterman, is founded by Thomas Doggett.

G **Science, Technology and Discovery**
Brook Taylor in *Methodus Incrementorum Directa et Inversa* invents the calculus of finite differences.
John Lethbridge devises a water-tight suit for diving.

H **Philosophy, Religion and Scholarship**
Dimitrie Cantemir, *Descriptio Moldaviae*.
Gian Vincenzo Gravina, *Della Tragedia*.
Giacomo Leoni translates Palladio's *Four Books of Architecture* (published in Venice in 1570).
Alexander Pope's verse translation of Homer's *Iliad*, vol. 1 (–1720).
Isaac Watts, *Divine Songs for Children*.
Gallia Christiana (–1765).

J **Art, Sculpture, Fine Arts and Architecture**
Painting:
Hyacinthe Rigaud publishes *The Theory of Painting*.
James Thornhill, decorations for Hampton Court Palace, and (–1717) for the dome of St. Paul's Cathedral.
Giovanni Tiepolo, *Sacrifice of Isaac*.
Architecture:
Colin Campbell, Wanstead House; Campbell also publishes *Vitruvius Britannicus*.

K **Music**
Handel writes the *Water Music*.

L **Literature (including Drama)**
Alain-René Lesage, *Gil Blas de Santillane* (–1735).
Nicholas Rowe, *Lady Jane Grey* (drama).
James Quin, from Dublin, has his London début at Drury Lane, as Bajazet, in Rowe's *Tamerlane* (Nov. 8th).

M **Births and Deaths**
Jan. 7th François de la Mothe-Fénelon d. (64).
Jan — Charles Adrien Helvétius b. (–1771).
Mar. 7th Ewald Christian von Kleist b. (–1759).
Mar. 17th Gilbert Burnet d. (71).
Mar. 19th Charles Montague, Earl of Halifax, d. (52).
Mar. — William Dampier d. (62).
Jun. 24th John Partridge d. (69).
July 4th Christian Gellert b. (–1769).
Aug. 12th Nahum Tate d. (63).
Sept. 30th Étienne Bonnot de Condillac b. (–1780).

1716   Jacobite Rebellion is Suppressed

A **Jan:** 26th/*Feb.* 6th, commercial treaty between England and Dutch renews former treaties of alliance and commerce.
Feb: 10th, James III, the Pretender, lands in France, having left Britain, and subsequently dismisses Bolingbroke from his service.
Mar:

B **Apr:** 13th, the Emperor declares war on Turkey;
26th, British Parliament passes the Septennial Act, in the aftermath of the Jacobite Rebellion, extending the life of Parliament from 3 to 7 years.
May: 25th/*June* 5th, Treaty of Westminster is signed between England and the Emperor for mutual defence;
15th/26th, Anglo-Spanish commercial treaty amplifies treaty of *Dec.* 3rd/14th, 1715, and removes certain restrictions on Britain's trade and also facilitates the Empire's trade;
John Law sets up a joint-stock Banque Générale in Paris.
Jun:

C **Jul:**
Aug: 5th, Prince Eugène defeats the Turks at Peterwardein (Petrovaradine).
Sep: 28th/*Oct.* 9th, Treaty of Hanover between England (Hanover) and France forms basis of the Triple Alliance of *Dec.*

D **Oct:** 13th, Temesvar, the last Turkish possession in Hungary, falls;
Russians leave Denmark and occupy Mecklenburg.
Nov:
Dec: 15th, Townshend is dismissed as Secretary of State for the Northern Department over disagreement on foreign policy, particularly over opposition towards French alliance, and is appointed Lord Lieutenant of Ireland;
24th/*Jan.* 4th, 1717, Triple Alliance of England France and Holland against intrigues of the Pretender, Charles XII of Sweden and Alberoni, the Parmesan Minister at Madrid. The French promise support against Jacobites and English agree to support Orleans against Philip of Spain.

E Tsar Peter's second visit to Western Europe;
Yoshimune becomes Shōgun of Japan;
Moldavia and Wallachia obtain Phanariot governors.

F **Politics, Economics, Law and Education**
     John Law establishes the Banque Générale in France (it becomes the Banque Royale in 1718).
     Diario di Roma, first Italian newspaper, is issued.
     The *Historical Register* started (quarterly –1738), 'containing an impartial relation of all transactions, foreign and domestic'.

G **Science, Technology and Discovery**
     The scientific collection of Albert Seba in Amsterdam is purchased by Peter the Great and removed to St. Petersburg.
     De Moivre, *Doctrine of the Chances*.

H **Philosophy, Religion and Scholarship**
     François de la Mothe-Fénelon, *Lettre sur les occupations de l'Académie* (posth.).
     Thomas Hearne starts his collection of *Old English Chronicles* (–1735).

J **Art, Sculpture, Fine Arts and Architecture**
     Painting:
         Antoine Watteau, *La leçon d'amour*.
     Architecture:
         Nicholas Hawksmoor, Church of St. Mary, Woolnoth, London.

K **Music**
     François Couperin, *L'Art de toucher le clavecin*.

L **Literature (including Drama)**
     John Gay, *Trivia*.
     Matias Pereira da Silva edits *Fénix Renascida* (an anthology of Portuguese poetry).

M **Births and Deaths**
     Jan. 1st William Wycherley d. (*c.* 76).
     Jan. 20th Jean Jacques Barthélemy b. (–1795).
     Feb. 24th James Radclyffe, Earl of Derwentwater, d. (27).
     May 29th Louis Jean Marie Daubenton b. (–1800).
     Sept. — Fletcher of Saltoun (Andrew Fletcher) d. (61).
     Oct. 3rd Giovanni Battista Beccaria b. (–1781).
     Nov. 14th Gottfried Wilhelm von Leibniz d. (70).
     Dec. 26th Thomas Gray b. (–1771).
     Dec. 26th Jean François de Saint-Lambert b. (–1803).
     — James Brindley b. (–1772).
     — Lancelot ('Capability') Brown b. (–1783).
     — Étienne-Maurice Falconet b. (–1791).

A **Jan:** Governor Spotswood of Virginia, having led an expedition to the Shenandoah Valley, makes a speech favouring the settlement of various areas including Lake Erie;

Gyllenborg, the Swedish Ambassador in London, is arrested in connexion with the alleged plot of Goertz, the Swedish Minister at the Hague, with Spain to aid the Pretender to invade England again.

Feb: The Polish Diet accepts the Saxon settlement;

James III, the Pretender, is forced to leave France because of the Triple Alliance, and flees to the Papacy.

Mar:

B **Apr:** 9th, Townshend, never having gone to Ireland, resigns as Lord Lieutenant, and this leads to

10th, Walpole's resignation as First Lord of Treasury and Chancellor of Exchequer and he is succeeded, 15th, by Stanhope.

May: 17th, Maria Theresa of Austria is born;

Peter the Great stays in Paris (until middle of *June*).

Jun:

C **Jul:** 1st, Robert Harley, Earl of Oxford is acquitted of the charge of secretly negotiating with the French;

12th, Alberoni is created a Cardinal;

Gyllenborg is released.

Aug: 16th, Prince Eugène defeats the Turks at Belgrade, which he subsequently occupies;

17th, by the Convention of Amsterdam, France, Russia and Prussia agree to maintain the Treaties of Utrecht and Baden; France is allowed to act as mediator in the north, and Russian troops are to leave Mecklenburg;

22nd, Spain attacks Sardinia under the pretext that some Spanish subjects had been arrested in Italy, and it is taken by the end of *Nov.*;

John Law's Mississippi Company is given the monopoly of trade with Louisiana.

Sep: 24th, Dubois, the former tutor of the Duc d'Orleans, becomes French Foreign Secretary.

D **Oct:**
Nov:
Dec:

E The Act of Grace provides for the release of the Jacobite rebels in British prisons;

Stanhope puts into force Walpole's Sinking Fund to reduce the national debt by annual instalments;

The fund itself is set up from the surplus obtained by reducing the interest on national securities;

Lhasa is seized by western Mongols;

Russian expedition to Khiva fails;

The British Government closes Convocation;

Mir Abdullah is succeeded by Mir Mahmud in Kandahar, but Abdalis of Herat leads a revolt and sets up a separate Afghan state.

F Politics, Economics, Law and Education

John Wise, *Vindication of the Government of New England Churches*.

G Science, Technology and Discovery

John Bernouilli declares that the principle of virtual displacement is applicable to all cases of equilibrium.

Gravesande lectures at Leyden on Newton's discoveries.

H Philosophy, Religion and Scholarship

Claude Buffier, *Traité des vérités premières*.

Benjamin Hoadly, *The Nature of the Kingdom or Church of Christ*: sermon preached before the King; answered by William Law (in *Letters to the Bishop of Bangor*).

The Bangorian Controversy (arising from Bishop Hoadly's sermon, above –1720), which led to the indefinite prorogation of Convocation.

The Mechitharist Congregation of Armenian Monks, confirmed by the Pope in 1712, finally settles on the island of San Lazzaro, near Venice.

Joseph Simon Assemani sent by the Pope to Egypt and Syria to search for manuscripts.

J Art, Sculpture, Fine Arts and Architecture

Painting:

Antoine Watteau, *Embarkation for the Isle of Cytheria*.

Architecture:

Earl of Burlington, The Bagno, Chiswick House, Middlesex.

Colin Campbell remodels Burlington House, London (–1719).

K Music

G. F. Handel, first performance of *Water Music* suite of 21 pieces, by a band of 50 musicians in a barge alongside King George's barge at a water concert on the Thames.

John Weaver produces *The Loves of Mars and Venus* (ballet) in London.

L Literature (including Drama)

François de la Mothe-Fénelon, *Télémaque* (continuing, as a satirical story, criticising the court of Louis XIV, Book IV of Homer's *Odyssey* –1699).

Alexander Pope, *Collected Works* (–1742).

Adrienne Lecouvreur makes her début in Paris at the *Comédie-Française* in *Electre*, by Crébillon *père* (–1708).

M Births and Deaths

Jan. 29th Jeffrey Amherst b. (–1797).

Feb. 2nd Ernst Gideon Loudon b. (–1790).

Feb. 19th David Garrick b. (–1779).

Mar. 19th John Campbell, Earl of Breadalbane, d. (80).

May 17th Maria Theresa b. (–1780).

Sept. 24th Horace Walpole b. (–1797).

Nov. — Jean le Rond d'Alembert b. (–1783).

Dec. 9th Johann Joachim Winckelmann b. (–1768).

Dec. 16th Elizabeth Carter b. (–1806).

Dec. 20th Charles Gravier, Comte de Vergennes, b. (–1787).

1718   Peace of Passarowitz—Quadruple Alliance against Spain—Death of Charles XII of Sweden

A   **Jan:** 7th, repeal of Schism Act and of Act of Occasional Conformity in Britain.
Feb:
Mar: 21st, Earl of Sunderland reconstructs Cabinet with Stanhope as Secretary of State for the Northern Department.

B   **Apr:** 26th/*May* 7th, Mary Beatrix, widow of James II, dies in France.
May:
Jun: Spanish army sails for Sicily, which is conquered by *July*.

C   **Jul:** 7th, Alexis, heir to Peter the Great of Russia, is murdered at the instigation of his father;
21st, the Peace of Passarowitz, signed through British mediation, ends the war between the Empire and Turkey; the Empire retains Belgrade, thus completing the possession of Hungary, and also keeps the Banat of Temesvar and part of Serbia; Turkey keeps the Morea; Venice retains Corfu and her conquests in Albania and Dalmatia; the parties agree to adhere to this agreement for at least 25 years;
22nd/*Aug.* 2nd, the Quadruple Alliance is signed between France, the Emperor, England and Holland (the latter in name only) against Spain, after the Spanish seizure of Sicily and a plot by Cardinal Alberoni for a Swedish attack on Scotland, a combined Russo-Swedish attack on Hanover and a Spanish invasion of England. The Emperor and Philip of Spain are to renounce claims to each other's possessions, Savoy is to exchange Sicily for Sardinia, and the succession to Tuscany and Parma is to be secured by the children of Philip's second marriage; war will be declared if necessary to secure Spain's acquiescence;
31st/*Aug.* 11th, Admiral Byng defeats Spain off Cape Passaro after Philip's rejection of the terms of the Quadruple Alliance.
Aug:
Sep:

D   **Oct:**
Nov: The King of Sicily surrenders his title and becomes King of Sardinia at command of Quadruple Alliance.
Dec: 11th, Charles XII of Sweden is killed at Frederikshall in an expedition against Norway and is succeeded, after a revolution, by his sister Ulrica Eleanor (–1720); the treaty with Russia is annulled;
17th, England declares war on Spain;
25th/*Jan.* 5th, 1719, Alliance of Vienna between England, Hanover, Saxony, Poland and the Emperor against Russia and Prussia, to force Russians from Mecklenburg and Poland and to guarantee Poland's frontiers.

E   New Orleans is founded by John Law's Mississippi Company;
Spain founds Pensacola, Florida;
Chinese troops are annihilated by the western Mongols in an attempt to obtain Lhasa.

F **Politics, Economics, Law and Education**
  Abbé Charles Saint-Pierre, *Discours sur la Polysynodie*, recommends a system of conciliar government and attacks Louis XIV's reputation. He is expelled from the Academy and forms an independent political club 'Entre sol' (suppressed in 1731). *The Leeds Mercury* issued.

G **Science, Technology and Discovery**
  Edmund Halley discovers that certain fixed stars have 'proper motions'.
  Etienne Geoffroy presents to the French Academy tables of affinities (*tables des rapports*).
  Thomas Lombe's patent (*Sept.* 9th) for introducing to England a machine to make thrown silk.

H **Philosophy, Religion and Scholarship**
  Philibert-Joseph Le Roux, *Dictionnaire comique, satyrique, critique, burlesque, libre et proverbial.*
  Academia de Scienze, Lettere ed Arti founded at Palermo, Sicily.

J **Art, Sculpture, Fine Arts and Architecture**
  Painting:
  Sir Godfrey Kneller, portraits of the *Duke of Newcastle* and of the *Earl of Lincoln*.
  Antoine Watteau, *Park Fête.*

K **Music**

L **Literature (including Drama)**
  Colley Cibber, *The Non-Juror* (comedy).

M **Births and Deaths**
  Jan. 18th Peter Anthony Motteux d. (58).
  Feb. 19th George Brydges Rodney b. (-1792).
  May 7th Mary of Modena d. (59).
  May 16th Maria Gaetana Agnesi b. (-1799).
  May 23rd William Hunter b. (1783).
  June 21st Alexius Petrovich d. (28).
  July 28th Étienne Baluze d. (87).
  July 30th William Penn d. (73).
  Dec. 6th Nicholas Rowe d. (44).
  — John Roebuck b. (-1794).

A   Jan: 9th, France declares war on Spain.
    Feb:
    Mar:

B   Apr: 28th, British Peerage Bill, to close House of Lords, is rejected by Commons. The
    Bill was introduced by Sunderland who feared the creation of a larger number of peers
    by a Tory Ministry and required that the number of existing peers, 178, was not to be
    increased by more than six, apart from members of the Royal family;
    French army enters Spain and subsequently seizes Fuentarrabia.
    May: 27th, Emperor Charles VI founds Oriental Company in Vienna to compete with
    Dutch trade in Orient.
    Jun: 10th, Spanish invaders are defeated at Glenshiels and surrender on 11th, the main
    fleet having previously been scattered by storms;
    Emperor Charles VI expels Spaniards from Sicily.

C   Jul:
    Aug:
    Sep: 23rd, Lichtenstein becomes an independent Principality of the Empire.

D   Oct:
    Nov: 20th, Peace of Stockholm is finalised between Sweden and Hanover, which buys
    Bremen and Verden for 1,000,000 thalers.
    Dec: 15th, Cardinal Alberoni falls in Spain and is banished by Philip V.

E   Mohammed Shah, grandson of Bahadur, Great Mogul (–1748);
    Ireland is declared inseparable from England by statute.

F **Politics, Economics, Law and Education**
The Boston Gazette is founded by William Brooker (*Dec.* 21st) and *The American Mercury* is issued in Philadelphia (*Dec.* 22nd).
The Daily Post started (*Oct.* 3rd–*Feb.* 14th, 1746), edited by Daniel Defoe.

G **Science, Technology and Discovery**
D. Lemmaire, French consul at Cairo, sends the French Academy an account of the Egyptian method of manufacturing sal ammoniac.

H **Philosophy, Religion and Scholarship**

J **Art, Sculpture, Fine Arts and Architecture**
Painting:
William Kent, decorations for Burlington House, London.

K **Music**
Dimitrie Cantemir, *Tratat de musica turceasca*, first book on Turkish music, published in Russia.

L **Literature (including Drama)**
Daniel Defoe, *Robinson Crusoe* (and *The Further Adventures of Robinson Crusoe*).
Baron Ludvig Holberg, *Pedar Paars* (mock heroic poem; the first Danish classic).

M **Births and Deaths**
Jan. 22nd William Paterson d. (60).
Jan. 28th Sir Samuel Garth d. (58).
Feb. 20th Joseph Bellamy b. (–1790).
Mar. 30th John Hawkins b. (–1789).
Apr. 15th Françoise D'Aubigné, Marquise de Maintenon, d. (83).
June 28th Étienne-François, Duc de Choiseul, b. (–1785).
June 17th Joseph Addison d. (47).
Aug. 1st Pedro de Bolea, Count d'Aranda, b. (–1798).
Sept. — John Harris d. (52).
Nov. 23rd Spranger Barry b. (–1777).
Dec. 2nd Pasquier Quesnel d. (85).
Dec. 31st John Flamsteed d. (73).
— Leopold Mozart b. (–1787).

1720 Peace between the Quadruple Alliance and Spain—The 'South Sea Bubble'

A Jan:
Feb: 1st, Treaty of Stockholm between Sweden and Prussia, which obtains Pomerania between the Oder and Peene, which includes Stettin, for two million thalers. Prussia agrees to help Sweden in the event of a Russian attack;

6th/17th, Peace treaty is signed between the Quadruple Alliance and Spain; the Emperor Charles VI gives up his claim to Spain while Philip V renounces his claim to Italy, provided the Emperor allows Charles, Philip and Elizabeth Farnese's son, to succeed to the thrones of Parma, Piacenza and Tuscany. Savoy obtains Sardinia from the Emperor in exchange for Sicily and the Duke of Savoy becomes King of Sardinia;

29th, Ulrica, Queen of Sweden abdicates in favour of her husband, Frederick I, Prince of Hesse-Cassel (–1751).
Mar:

B Apr:
May: 21st, John Law's 'Edict' states that there is too much money in circulation.
Jun: 11th, Charles Townshend returns to office as Lord President of the Council with Robert Walpole as Paymaster-General.

C Jul: 3rd, Treaty of Frederiksborg between Sweden and Denmark; Sweden's exemption from the Sound toll is abolished and she recognises the Danish annexation of Schleswig.
Aug:
Sep:

D Oct: The 'South Sea Bubble' begins to burst. The company had offered in *Jan.* to take over the National Debt and this had led to financial speculation, especially in *Aug.*, resulting in disastrous panic, ruining thousands of people by *Dec.*
Nov:
Dec: 31st, Prince Charles Edward, the Young Pretender, is born;
John Law flees from France after his financial schemes, in particular those of his Mississippi Company, lead to a wave of speculation resulting in national bankruptcy.

E Spain occupies Texas (–1722) under Marquis of Aguayo, after fighting between Spain and France in Texas and Florida since 1718;
William Burnet, Governor of New York, begins his efforts to prevent the French from isolating the English colonies in the west and extends trade with the Indians to prevent French influence among the tribes;
The Pragmatic Sanction is formally recognised by Estates of Upper and Lower Austria;
A proposal is made to the Emperor Charles VI for the formation of a chartered company, based at Ostend, to trade with the East Indies.

F **Politics, Economics, Law and Education**

Vico, *De Uno Universi Juris Principis*.

The French government establishes a body of technical civil servants to oversee roads and bridges.

The Elector Palatine moves his court from Heidelberg to Mannheim.

G **Science, Technology and Discovery**

Fahrenheit uses mercury in a thermometer.

H **Philosophy, Religion and Scholarship**

Dom Augustin Calmet, *Dictionnaire historique, critique, chronologique, géographique et littéraire de la Bible*, 4 vols. (–1721).

Arthur Collins, *Baronetage of England* (an historical and genealogical account), 2 vols.

Edward Hyde, Earl of Clarendon, *History of the Rebellion and Civil Wars in Ireland* (–1702).

Thomas Hearne edits *Robert of Gloucester's Chronicle*, the first scholarly edition of a Middle-English text.

John Stow, *Survey of London* (of 1598) revised and enlarged edition by John Strype, 2 vols.

Bernard de Montfaucon, *L'Antiquité Expliquée* (–1724, 15 vols.).

Christian Freiherr von Wolff, *Rational Thoughts on God, the World, and the Human Soul*.

J **Art, Sculpture, Fine Arts and Architecture**

Painting:

Giovanni Tiepolo, *Martyrdom of St. Bartholomew*.

Architecture:

James Gibbs, Ditchley House (–1725) and the Octagon, Orleans House, Twickenham, Middlesex.

Nicholas Hawksmoor, Church of St. George's, Bloomsbury, London (–1730).

Pedro de Ribera, Montserrat Church, Madrid.

K **Music**

G. F. Handel composes 5th Harpsicord Suite, containing 'Harmonious Blacksmith', and also *The Chandos Te Deum*.

L **Literature (including Drama)**

Daniel Defoe, *Memoirs of a Cavalier. Captain Singleton. Duncan Campbell.*

John Gay, *Collected Poems*.

M **Births and Deaths**

Jan. 27th Samuel Foote b. (–1777).

Mar. 13th Charles Bonnet b. (–1793).

Apr. 20th George Gordon, Earl of Aberdeen, d. (82).

July 18th Gilbert White b. (–1793).

July 31st Emmanuel, Duc d'Aigullon, b. (–1782).

Oct. 10th Charles Antoine Coysevox d. (80).

Dec. 31st Charles Edward Stuart ('the Young Pretender') b. (–1788).

A   Jan:
Feb: 5th, James, Earl of Stanhope, dies after a fit;
10th, Charles Townshend becomes Secretary of State for Northern Department.
Mar: 9th, John Aislabie, Chancellor of the Exchequer at time of the South Sea Bubble, is
sent to the Tower of London for fraud;
27th, Treaty of Madrid between Spain and France for mutual defence and guarantee;
it also deals with the question of the Italian duchies and Spain's right to Gibraltar,
which is supported by France.

B   Apr: 3rd, Robert Walpole becomes First Lord of the Treasury and Chancellor of the
Exchequer (–1742); he subsequently helps to restore public credit by transferring the
South Sea Company's stock in equal parts to the East India Company and to the
Bank of England.
May: 8th, Pope Innocent XIII (–1724) elected, on death of Clement XI.
Jun: 2nd/13th, England joins the Treaty of Madrid of *Mar.*;
20th/*July* 1st, Defensive Alliance between England, Spain and France. Louis is be-
trothed to Phillip V's daughter by Dubois;
21st, Charles Townshend resigns as Lord President of Council.

C   Jul: Dubois becomes a Cardinal by bribery.
Aug:
Sep: 10th, Treaty of Ŗystad is signed between Sweden and Russia; the latter acquires
Livonia, Estonia, Ingria and East Karelia, the best part of Sweden's Baltic Provinces,
but restores Finland.

D   Oct:
Nov: 2nd, Peter I is proclaimed Emperor of All the Russias, and the sovereign is now
allowed to name his successor.
Dec: 29th, the French occupy Mauritius and call it Île de France.

E   China suppresses a revolution in Formosa.

F Politics, Economics, Law and Education

G Science, Technology and Discovery
Lady Mary Wortley Montague introduces the practice of inoculation for smallpox into England; the inoculation of the Princess of Wales makes it fashionable.

H Philosophy, Religion and Scholarship
Nathaniel Bailey, *An Universal Etymological English Dictionary* (–1731). The first English dictionary to have accentual marks; used by Dr. Johnson as the basis of his work.
John Strype, *Ecclesiastical Memorials . . . under Henry VIII, Edward VI and Queen Mary*, 3 vols.

J Art, Sculpture, Fine Arts and Architecture
Architecture:
Colin Campbell, Houghton Hall.

K Music
J. S. Bach completes *The Brandenburg Concertos*.
G. F. Handel, *Acis and Galatea* (opera).

L Literature (including Drama)
Joseph Addison, *Collected Works*.
Charles de Secondat, Baron de la Brede et de Montesquieu, *Lettres Persanes*.
Alain-René Lesage writes a play to be performed by puppets.

M Births and Deaths
Mar. — Tobias Smollett b. (–1771).
Apr. 15th William Augustus, Duke of Cumberland, b. (–1765).
July 18th Antoine Watteau d. (37).
Aug. 3rd Grinling Gibbons d. (73).
Sept. 18th Nathaniel Crew d. (88).
Sept. 18th Matthew Prior d. (56).
Sept. 19th William Robertson b. (–1793).
Dec. 25th William Collins b. (–1759).
Dec. 29th Jeanne D'Étoiles, Marquise de Pompadour, b. (–1764).
— Nicholas Desmaretz d. (73).
— John Manners, Marquess of Granby, b. (–1770).
— Elihu Yale d. (73).

A Jan:
   Feb:
   Mar: 8th, Mir Mahmud of Afghanistan begins war against Persia (which capitulates by
       Sept., and he becomes Shah);
       10th, George I's first Parliament is dissolved.

B Apr:
   May:
   Jun: 16th, John, Duke of Marlborough, dies;
       30th, the Hungarian Diet rejects the Pragmatic Sanction.

C Jul:
   Aug:
   Sep: 12th, Russians take Baku and Derbent on the Caspian Sea from Persia, which is
       unable to prevent this on account of the Afghan invasion;
       24th, Atterbury, Bishop of Rochester, is arrested for contacting the Pretender.

D Oct: 3rd, second Parliament of George I;
       13th, William Wood obtains from the Duchess of Kendal the Treasury's concession to
       issue new copper coinage in Ireland and the affair is known as 'Wood's Halfpence';
       17th, Habeas Corpus Act is suspended after discovery of Atterbury's plot, which was
       designed to proclaim 'James III' as King.
   Nov:
   Dec:

E Emperor Charles VI grants a charter for the formation of the Austrian East India
       Company to compete with the Dutch and English in trade with the Indies, China and
       Africa;
   Yung Cheng dynasty in China with the accession of Shih Tsung (–1735).

F Politics, Economics, Law and Education
Vossische Zeitung is issued in Berlin (–1933).
British Parliament resolves that journalists shall not report debates.

G Science, Technology and Discovery
F. Hoffmann announces that the base of alum is an individual substance.
Réaumur in *L'Art de couvertir le fer forgé en acier et l'art d'adoucir le fer fondu* first describes the process of making iron, and discusses ferrous metals.

H Philosophy, Religion and Scholarship

J Art, Sculpture, Fine Arts and Architecture
Painting:
Hyacinthe Rigaud, *Chevalier Lucas Schout ;* Rigaud also publishes his 'Grand Tour' handbook.
Architecture:
Richard, Earl of Burlington, Dormitory, Westminster School.
James Gibbs, Senate House, Cambridge, and Church of St. Martin-in-the-Fields, London (–1726).
Pedro de Ribera, Doorway, Hospice St. Ferdando, Madrid.

K Music
J. S. Bach, *Das Wohltemperierte Clavier*, pt. I, being 'Clavierbuechlein fuer Anna Magdalena Bach'.
Jean-Philippe Rameau, *Traité de l'harmonie*.

L Literature (including Drama)
Daniel Defoe, *A Journal of the Plague Year. Colonel Jacque. Moll Flanders* ('The Fortunes and Misfortunes of the Famous Moll Flanders').
Richard Steele, *The Conscious Lovers* (comedy).

M Births and Deaths
Apr. 12th Christopher Smart b. (–1771).
June 16th John Churchill, Duke of Marlborough, d. (72).
Sept. 27th Samuel Adams b. (–1803).
— John Burgoyne b. (–1792).
— Flora MacDonald b. (–1790).

A Jan:
Feb: 16th, Louis XV attains his majority.
Mar:

B Apr:
May:
Jun: Lord Bolingbroke returns from exile, having been pardoned in *May*, but is forbidden to sit in the House of Lords.

C Jul:
Aug: 10th, Dubois, Louis XV's First Minister, dies and is succeeded by Duke of Orleans, with the Comte de Morville as Foreign Minister.
Sep: 29th/*Oct.* 10th, Treaty of Charlottenburg between England and Prussia, by which George I's grandson is to marry a Prussian princess and Prince Frederick of Prussia is to marry the daughter of the Prince of Wales. In addition, there is to be a military alliance to combine English sea power with the might of Prussia's armies, but various difficulties prevent the enactment of the treaty.

D Oct:
Nov: 1st, the Grand Duke of Tuscany dies.
Dec: 2nd, Duke of Orleans dies and Louis XV becomes greatly influenced by the Duke of Bourbon.

E Revolt of Abraham Davel in the Vaud against the oppressive rule of Berne, but he is soon captured and subsequently executed;
Prussia establishes a General Directory of War, Finance and Domains.

F Politics, Economics, Law and Education

G Science, Technology and Discovery
    M. A. Capeller, *Prodromus Crystallographie*, the earliest treatise on crystallography.

H Philosophy, Religion and Scholarship
    Gilbert Burnet, *History of My Own Time*, vol. I (–1734; posth.).
    Pietro Giannoni, *Storia civile del regno di Napoli*, the first work of 'constitutional history' proper (publication resulted in the banishment from Naples of the author).
    Ludovico Antonio Muratori edits first vols. of a vast collection of mediaeval chronicles, poems, inscriptions, and letters, known as *Rerum italicarum scriptores* (–1738; vol. 28 –1751).
    Christian Thomasius, *Gedanken und Erinnerungen* (–1726).
    T' U Shu Chi Ch'éng—a Chinese Encyclopaedia, compiled by Imperial Mandate (–1736).

J Art, Sculpture, Fine Arts and Architecture
    Painting:
        William Kent, decorations to Kensington Palace.
        Godfrey Kneller, *Alexander Pope*.
    Architecture:
        George Dance, Guy's Hospital, London.
        Nicholas Hawksmoor, Christ Church, Spitalfields (–1739).
        Pedro de Ribiera, Toledo Bridge (–1724).

K Music
    J. S. Bach, *Magnificat*.

L Literature (including Drama)
    Baron Ludvig Holberg. *Comoedier* (3 vols. –1725).
    Sir Richard Steele, *The Conscious Lovers* (comedy).
    John Thurmond, *Harlequin Dr. Faustus* (a pantomime, produced at Drury Lane Theatre, London).
    Voltaire, *La Henriade* (first published as *La Ligue*).

M Births and Deaths
    Feb. 23rd Richard Price b. (–1791).
    Apr. 30th Mathurin Jacques Brisson b. (–1806).
    June 5th Adam Smith b. (–1790).
    June 20th Adam Ferguson b. (–1816).
    July 10th William Blackstone b. (–1780).
    July 16th Joshua Reynolds b. (–1792).
    Aug. 10th Guillaume Dubois d. (67).
    Aug. 23rd Increase Mather d. (84).
    Nov. 7th Godfrey Kneller d. (*c.* 75).
    — William Chambers b. (–1796).
    — Christopher Wren d. (90).

A   Jan: 14th, Philip V of Spain abdicates, during a fit of religious mania, in favour of Don
     Luis, as Luis I (*–Aug.*).
     Feb: 22nd, Treaty of Stockholm between Sweden and Russia for mutual assistance.
     Mar: 7th, Pope Innocent III dies.

B   Apr: 1st, Swift's first *Drapier's Letters* attacking Wood's 'Halfpence' for debasing Irish
     currency and as an example of English dictation over Ireland;
        3rd, John, Lord Carteret, a Stanhope supporter and rival to Robert Walpole and
        Charles Townshend, is dismissed over a dispute concerning Walpole's French
        alliance, from his position as Secretary of State, Southern Department and is suc-
        ceeded
        6th, by Duke of Newcastle, Thomas Pelham-Holles, whose brother, Henry Pelham
        becomes Secretary of State for War.
     May: 29th, Benedict XIII is elected Pope.
     Jun: 23rd, Treaty of Constantinople between Russia and Turkey, directed against
     Persia to secure Erivan for the Sultan.

C   Jul:
     Aug: 31st, Luis I of Spain dies and Philip V returns as King.
     Sep:

D   Oct: 13th, last of Swift's *Drapiers Letters*;
        John, Lord Carteret becomes Lord Lieutenant of Ireland.
     Nov:
     Dec:

E   The Afghan ruler Mahmud becomes insane and orders the massacre of the Persian
     nobility and royal family;
     Congress of Cambrai meets throughout the year, at which France and England undertake
     to support Spain against the Emperor Charles VI but the results are inconclusive;
     The Austrian Netherlands agree to the Pragmatic Sanction.

F **Politics, Economics, Law and Education**
Jonas Alströmer establishes first woollen factory in Sweden.
George I founds professorships of modern history and languages at Oxford and Cambridge.

G **Science, Technology and Discovery**
Hermann Boerhaave, *Elementa chemicae*.
J. F. Riccati propounds his equation.
Cotton Mather, *Angel of Bethesda* (treatise on medicine in America).

H **Philosophy, Religion and Scholarship**
Daniel Defoe, *A Tour Through the Whole Island of Great Britain* (–1727).
John Oldmixon, *A Critical History of England* (–1726; critical of Clarendon's *History of the Rebellion*, 1702; with *The Essay on Criticism* as a preface).
William Stukeley, *Itinerarium Curiosum* ('an account of the antiquities . . . observed in Great Britain').

J **Art, Sculpture, Fine Arts and Architecture**
Architecture:
Leonardo de Figueroa, West Entrance, St. Telmo Church, Seville.
James Gibbs, Fellows' Building, King's College, Cambrige (–1749).

K **Music**
J. S. Bach, *St. John Passion* (oratorio).
François Couperin, *Le Parnasse ou L'Apothéose de Corelli*, and *L'Apothéose de Lully* (programme sonatas).
The Three Choirs Festival is founded for choirs in Gloucester, Hereford and Worcester.

L **Literature (including Drama)**
Daniel Defoe, *Roxana, The Fortunate Mistress*.
Charles Johnson, *General History of the Robberies and Murders of the Most Notorious Pyrates*.
Jonathan Swift, *Drapier's Letters* ('A Letter to the Whole People of Ireland, by M. B. Drapier').

M **Births and Deaths**
Apr. 22nd Immanuel Kant b. (–1804).
May 21st Robert Harley, Earl of Oxford, d. (63).
June 5th Henry Sacheverell d. (50).
June 8th John Smeaton b. (–1792).
July 2nd Gottlieb Fredrich Klopstock b. (–1803).
Aug. 21st Noël Alexandre d. (84).
Sept. 3rd Guy Carleton b. (–1808).
Nov. 16th Jack Sheppard d. (21).
Dec. 12th Samuel Hood b. (–1816).
Dec. 13th Franz Aepinus b. (–1802).
Dec. 27th Thomas Guy d. (80).
— George Stubbs b. (–1806).

1725   Alliance of Spain and the Empire and Counter-Alliance of England, France and Prussia—Death of Peter the Great

A   **Jan:**

Feb: 8th, Peter the Great of Russia dies and is succeeded by his wife, Catherine (–1727), who is influenced by Prince Menshikoff and Andrei Ostermann;

Louis XV dismisses the Spanish Infanta who was due to marry him, which angers Spain. As a result Spain draws nearer to the Emperor.

Mar:

B   **Apr:** 30th, the influence of John, Baron de Ripperda results in the Treaty of Vienna between the Emperor and Spain, which guarantees the Pragmatic Sanction, and the Emperor's Italian provinces, and is a reconciliation of the two powers.

May: 1st, Supplementary Treaty of Vienna by which the Emperor Charles VI agrees to help Spain regain Gibraltar and Spain offers protection for the Ostend Company. Both treaties are setbacks for French and English discussions at Cambrai.

Jun:

C   **Jul:**

Aug: 23rd/*Sept.* 3rd, Treaty of Herrenhausen (or Hanover) between England, France and Prussia guarantees Prussia's claim to Jülich-Berg and is designed to counteract the Spanish alliance with the Emperor.

Sep: 5th, Louis XV marries Maria Lesczcyinski of Poland.

D   **Oct:**

Nov: 5th, further secret treaty between the Empire and Spain, allowing for marriages between the two royal families and providing for their respective shares of captured French territory in the event of war.

Dec:

E   Holland, having purchased the last of the Prussian factories in Africa, occupies Gross-Fredericksburg and renames it Fort Hollandia;

Ashraf Shah, an Afghan, succeeds Mahmud in Persia.

F **Politics, Economics, Law and Education**
George I founds the Order of the Bath.
Office-holders and witnesses in Pennsylvania are permitted to subscribe to a form of attestation without any reference to God.
Demoivre, *Treatise on Annuities.*
Guy's Hospital, founded by Thomas Guy in 1721, is opened.
The New York Gazette is issued.

G **Science, Technology and Discovery**
John Flamsteed, *Historia coelestis* (posth.).
George Graham graduates an 8-ft. mural circle for Greenwich Observatory.
St. Petersburg Academy of Science founded.

H **Philosophy, Religion and Scholarship**
Francis Hutcheson, *An Inquiry into the Original of Our Ideas of Beauty and Virtue.*
Alexander Pope, *The Odyssey of Homer* translated. *The Works of Shakespeare*, edited by Alexander Pope, in 6 vols.
Giambattista Vico, *Scienza nuova intorno alla natura* (revised 1730, 1744).

J **Art, Sculpture, Fine Arts and Architecture**
Painting:
Antonio Canaletto, Four views of Venice, for Stefano Conti of Lucca.
Architecture:
Richard, Earl of Burlington, Villa, Chiswick House, Middlesex.

K **Music**
Joseph Fux, *Gradus ad Parnassum* (treatise on counterpoint) published in Vienna.

L **Literature (including Drama)**
'Sir John Mandeville', *Travels* (*The Voyage of Sir John Mandeville* ; authorship doubtful). first full English text; *see* 1496 L
Allan Ramsay, *The Gentle Shepherd.*

M **Births and Deaths**
Feb. 5th James Otis b. (–1783).
Apr. 25th Augustus Keppell b. (–1786).
May 24th Jonathan Wild d. (*c.* 43).
Aug. 21st Jean Baptiste Greuze b. (–1805).
Sept. 2nd Ewald von Hertzberg b. (–1795).
Sept. 16th Nicolas Desmarest b. (–1815).
Sept. 29th Robert Clive b. (–1774).
Oct. 24th Alessandro Scarlatti d. (66).
— Robert Bakewell b. (–1795).
— Giovanni Casanova de Seingalt ('Casanova') b. (–1798).

1726   Fleury comes to power in France—Close relations between Austria and Russia

A   Jan:
     Feb:
     Mar:

B   Apr:
     May: Fall of John de Ripperda in Spain, who is succeeded by Patiño.
     Jun: 11th, Cardinal Fleury becomes Chief Minister in France, after the dismissal of Duc de Bourbon.

C   Jul:
     Aug: 6th, the Empire and Russia conclude a military alliance against Turkey, with a guarantee of mutual aid for 30 years;
     the Empire and Palatinate agree, by treaty, on the succession of the Elector to Jülich and Berg. This treaty marks the establishment of close relations between Vienna and St. Petersburg.
     Sep:

D   Oct: 17th, by the Treaty of Wusterhausen with the Empire, Prussia leaves the alliance of Herrenhausen (of *Aug.* 1725), and guarantees the Pragmatic Sanction. Prussia undertakes to aid Austria in any war with 10,000 troops, while Charles VI gives vague assurance about the succession in Jülich, Berg and Ravenstein.
     Nov: 24th, Bolingbroke and Pulteney edit a journal, *The Craftsman*, to attack the government of Walpole.
     Dec:

E   Admiral Hosier blockades Porto Bello;
     Voltaire is banished from France and visits England.

F Politics, Economics, Law and Education
Edward Lloyd issues *Lloyd's List* (twice weekly).
General George Wade begins building military roads in Scottish Highlands.

G Science, Technology and Discovery
John Harrison invents a compensating balance for clocks, a gridiron pendulum which maintains its length despite variations of temperature.

H Philosophy, Religion and Scholarship
Joseph Butler, *Fifteen Sermons*.
Pierre-François Guyot, l'abbé Desfontaines, *Dictionnaire néologique, à l'usage des beaux esprits du siècle* (satirical).
Johann Lorenz von Mosheim, *Institutiones Historiae Ecclesiasticae*.
Lewis Theobald, *Shakespeare Restored* (criticising Alexander Pope's edition of 1725).
May: Voltaire lands in England on liberation from the Bastille (returns to France 1729).
Dec. 27th. Canonisation of St. John of the Cross.
First Circulating Library opened by Allan Ramsay in Edinburgh.
Académie des Sciences, Belles Lettres et Arts, Marseilles, founded.
Real Academia Espanola, Madrid (–1714, publishes vol. 1 of a *Diccionario* –1739).

J Art, Sculpture, Fine Arts and Architecture
Painting:
　Giovanni Tiepolo, frescoes in the Bishop's Palace, Udine (–1728).
Architecture:
　Colin Campbell, Compton Place, Eastbourne, Sussex.

K Music
Marie-Anne de Camargo makes her début at the Paris Opéra. She is the first woman to perform an *entre chat quatre*.
G. F. Handel becomes a British subject by Act of Naturalisation.
G. F. Handel, *Scipio* (opera); the march from this opera has been used by the Grenadier Guards for parade ever since.
Jean-Philippe Rameau, *Nouveau système de musique théorique*.

L Literature (including Drama)
Daniel Defoe, *The Four Voyages of Capt. George Roberts*.
Jonathan Swift, *Gulliver's Travels*.
James Thomson, *Winter* (part 1 of *The Seasons* –1727, 1728, 1730).

M Births and Deaths
Mar. 8th Richard Howe b. (–1799).
Mar. 11th Louis Florence d'Epinay b. (–1783).
Mar. 26th John Vanbrugh d. (62).
Apr. 12th Charles Burney b. (–1814).
Apr. 26th Jeremy Collier d. (75).
May 20th Nicholas Brady d. (66).
June 3rd James Hutton b. (–1797).
Aug. 7th James Bowdoin b. (–1790).
Sept. 2nd John Howard b. (–1790).
Sept. 25th Angelo Maria Bandini b. (–1800).
— Eyre Coote b. (–1783).

1727   Anglo-Spanish War

A **Jan:**

Feb: Without a formal declaration, war begins between England and Spain by the latter's siege of Gibraltar. In addition Spain issues commissions for attacks against British islands and against British shipping.

Mar:

B **Apr:** 5th/-6th, the Hanoverian Alliance is joined by Denmark.

May: 20th/31st, at the Preliminaries of Paris, with France, England and the States-General of Holland, the Emperor Charles VI agrees to suspend the trade of the Austrian East India Company for 7 years;

29th, Peter II, grandson of Peter I and son of Alexis, becomes Tsar of Russia (–1730).

Jun: 2nd/13th, on the death of Catherine I, Spain, who has no minister in Paris, accedes to the peace preliminaries at Vienna;

11th, George I dies and is succeeded by his son George II (–1760).

C **Jul:** 17th, formal dissolution of the second Parliament of George I.

Aug:

Sep: 20th, Prince Menshikoff, one of the leading ministers, is ousted from power by the Dolgoruki family and exiled from Russia.

D **Oct:** Chauvelin, head of the anti-British party, succeeds the Comte de Morville, French Foreign Secretary, and draws France nearer to Spain.

Nov: 12th, Secret Treaty of 1714, between France and Bavaria is renewed, and France undertakes to support the claims of the Elector to the Hapsburg inheritance.

Dec:

E England first engages Hessian mercenaries for the defence of Hanover.

476

F Politics, Economics, Law and Education
Daniel Defoe, *The Complete English Tradesman.*
The decision in Curl's Case in England, that an obscene libel is a misdemeanour at common law and cannot be punished in an ecclesiastical court.
Comte de Boulainvilliers investigates the history of local government in France to support his demand that the nobility be given greater power.

G Science, Technology and Discovery
Stephen Hales obtains oxygen by heating minimum, but fails to recognise he has discovered a new element. His *Statical Essays* explain the nutrition of plants and describe numerous experiments in plant physiology.
J. A. de Peyssonel discovers the animal nature of red coral.

H Philosophy, Religion and Scholarship
John Balguy, *The Foundation of Moral Goodness* (–1728).
Francesco Scipione Maffei, *Istoria diplomatica.*

J Art, Sculpture, Fine Arts and Architecture
Sculpture:
John Michael Rysbrack, *George I.*
Architecture:
William Kent publishes *Designs of Inigo Jones.*
John Wood, the elder, *Plans for Bath.*

K Music

L Literature (including Drama)
Philippe Destouches, *Le Philosophe marié* (comedy).
John Dyer, *Grongar Hill.*
John Gay, *Fables* (1st series –1750).
James Thomson, *Summer* (–1730).

M Births and Deaths
Jan. 2nd James Wolfe b. (–1759).
Feb. 8th Jean André Deluc b. (–1817).
Mar. 20th Isaac Newton d. (74).
Apr. 7th Michel Adanson b. (–1806).
May 10th Anne Robert Jacques Turgot b. (–1781).
Oct. 9th Étienne de Loméric de Brienne b. (–1794).
Oct. 17th John Wilkes b. (–1797).
Oct. 27th Hester Chapone b. (–1791).
— Giovanni Battista Cipriani b. (–1785).
— Thomas Gainsborough b. (- 1788).
— Alexander Hood b. (–1814).

1728   End of Anglo-Spanish War—Treaty between Emperor and Prussia

A   Jan: 23rd, first Parliament of George II.
     Feb: 24th/*Mar*. 6th, Convention of the Pardo ends the Anglo-Spanish war;
          26th, publication of Parliamentary debates is considered a breach of privilege in
          England.
     Mar: Spain raises the siege of Gibraltar.

B   Apr:
     May:
     Jun: 14th, the Congress of Soissons meets, attended by the main powers, including
          Russia (–1729).

C   Jul:
     Aug:
     Sep:

D   Oct:
     Nov:
     Dec: 23rd, Treaty of Berlin between the Emperor Charles VI and Frederick William of
          Prussia, by which the Emperor recognises Prussia's claim to Berg and Ravenstein,
          while Prussia guarantees the Pragmatic Sanction.

E   A Foreign Ministry is established in Prussia.

Oct. 7th Charles Geneviève d'Eon de Beaumont ('Le Chevalier d'Eon') b. (–1810).
Oct. 28th James Cook b. (–1779).
Nov. 10th Oliver Goldsmith b. (–1774).
Dec. 2nd Ferdinando Galiani b. (–1787).
— Joseph Black b. (–1799).
— Antony Raphael Mengs b. (–1779).

F **Politics, Economics, Law and Education**

William Byrd, *History of the Dividing Line* (between Britain and the American Colonies).

Arthur Onslow is elected Speaker of the House of Commons (–1761).

G **Science, Technology and Discovery**

J. B. Labat, *Nouvelle relation de l'Afrique Occidentale* (a description of West African coast from Senegal to Sierra Leone).

James Bradley discovers the annual shifting of the stars is due to the aberration of light.

Fauchard, *Le Chirugien Dentiste ou traité des dents*.

Payn and Hanbury constructs a rolling-mill for sheet iron.

Vitus Behring discovers Behring Strait.

H **Philosophy, Religion and Scholarship**

Ephraim Chambers, *Cyclopaedia; or An Universal Dictionary of Arts and Sciences*, 2 folio vols.

Thomas Hearne edits 'The Black Book of the Exchequer' (*Liber niger scaccarii*).

Francis Hutcheson, *An Essay on the Nature and Conduct of the Passions and the Affections*.

William Law, *A Serious Call to Devout and Holy Life*.

Jonathan Swift, *A Short View of the State of Ireland*.

J **Art, Sculpture, Fine Arts and Architecture**

Painting:

J. B. S. Chardin, *The Rain*.

J. F. de Troy, *The Continence of Scipio*.

Architecture:

James Gibbs publishes *Book of Architecture*.

K **Music**

John Gay, *Beggar's Opera*, first performed in Lincoln's Inn Fields Theatre, London (book by Gay, music by Pepusch).

L **Literature (including Drama)**

Léonor-J.-C. Soulas D'Allainval, *L'École des bourgeois* (a comedy of manners).

Colly Cibber, *The Provok'd Husband* (comedy left unfinished by Vanbrugh).

Daniel Defoe, *Augusta Triumphans, or the Way to make London the Most Flourishing City in the Universe*.

Henry Fielding, *Love in Several Masques* (comedy).

Alexander Pope, *The Dunciad*, bks. 1–3.

Allan Ramsay, *Poems*.

Richard Savage, *The Bastard*.

James Thomson, *Spring* (–1730).

William Wycherley, *Posthumous Works*.

M **Births and Deaths**

Jan. 9th Thomas Warton b. (–1790).

Jan. 16th Niccola Piccinni b. (–1800).

Feb. 13th John Hunter, b. (–1793).

Feb. 13th Cotton Mather d. (65).

Apr. 13th Paolo Frisi b. (–1784).

July 3rd Robert Adam b. (1792).

Sept. 3rd Matthew Boulton b. (–1809).

(*Continued opposite*)

16*

A Jan:
   Feb:
   Mar:

B Apr:
   May: 2nd, Sophia Augusta Frederica, Princess of Anhalt-Zerbst, is born at Stettin.
   Jun:

C Jul: The Congress of Soissons is dissolved.
   Aug:
   Sep: Birth of the Dauphin.

D Oct: 29th/*Nov.* 9th, Treaty of Seville between Spain, France and England weans Spain
       from her alliance with the Empire; it provides for the suppression of the Austrian
       East India Company and for the accession of Don Carlos to Parma and Tuscany, and
       is subsequently joined by Holland.
   Nov: 10th/21st, Holland joins Treaty of Seville;
       Portugal loses Mombassa to the Muscat Arabs.
   Dec:

E Baltimore is founded;
   Corsica becomes independent of Genoa after a series of revolutions (–1732);
   North and South Carolina become Crown colonies when their charter is forfeited due to
       the misrule by the Lord's Proprietors.

Oct. — Sir Richard Blackmore d. (—).
Nov. 11th Louis Antoine de Bougainville b. (–1811).
Nov. 12th Alexander Danilovich, Prince Menshikov, d. (*c.* 66).
Dec. 13th Anthony Collins d. (53).
— Thomas Newcomen d. (68).
— Clara Reve b. (–1807).

F **Politics, Economics, Law and Education**

Act of Parliament requires attornies to serve a 5-year apprenticeship under formal 'articles'.

The Emperor Yung Cheng prohibits opium smoking in China.

James and Benjamin Franklin publish *The Pennsylvania Gazette* (–1765).

G **Science, Technology and Discovery**

Stephen Gray discovers that some bodies are conductors and others non-conductors of electricity.

Sir Isaac Newton's *Principia* is translated into English by Andrew Motte.

H **Philosophy, Religion and Scholarship**

Charles Perrault, *Contes*, of 1697, translated into English by Robert Samber.

Thomas Sherlock, *A Tryal of the Witnesses of the Resurrection of Jesus.*

Dr. William's Library, London, is founded in memory of the nonconformist minister, Daniel Williams, for students of religion and philosophy.

Academia de Beunas Letras, Barcelona, founded.

J **Art, Sculpture, Fine Arts and Architecture**

Painting:

Desportes, *Still life with Oysters.*

J. F. de Troy, *Rape of the Sabines*; also *Birth of Romulus and Remus.*

Architecture:

Nicolas Hawksmoor, quadrangle and hall, All Souls, Oxford; and Castle Howard.

John Wood, Queen's Square, Bath (–1736).

K **Music**

J. S. Bach, *St. Matthew Passion* (oratorio).

L **Literature (including Drama)**

Henry Carey, *Poems on Several Occasions* (–1713; this enlarged edition contained *Sally in Our Alley*).

Henry Fielding, *The Author's Farce*, presented at the Haymarket Theatre, London, with a Puppet Show (including Mr. Punch) called *The Pleasures of the Town.*

John Gay, *Polly* (ballad opera).

Albrecht von Haller, *Die Alpen* (a descriptive poem on The Alps).

Richard Savage, *The Wanderer.*

Jonathan Swift, *A Modest Proposal* (for Preventing the Children of the Poor People from being a Burthen to the Parents).

M **Births and Deaths**

Jan. 10th Lazaro Spallanzani b. (–1799).

Jan. 12th Edmund Burke b. (–1797).

Jan. 19th William Congreve d. (59).

Jan. 22nd Gotthold Ephraim Lessing b. (–1781).

Mar. 21st John Law d. (58).

Apr. 13th Thomas Percy b. (–1811).

May 2nd Catherine the Great b. (–1796).

May 17th Samuel Clarke d. (53).

July 17th Pierre-André de Suffren Saint Tropez b. (–1788).

Sept. 1st Richard Steele d. (57).

Sept. 6th Moses Mendelssohn b. (–1786).

(*Continued opposite*)

A Jan:

Feb: 11th, Peter II of Russia dies and is succeeded by Anne, daughter of Ivan V (–1740); 21st, Pope Benedict XIII dies.

Mar:

B Apr:

May: 15th, Robert Walpole quarrels with Charles Townshend, who resigns as Secretary of State for the Northern Department.

Jun:

C Jul: 12th, Clement XII is elected Pope (–1740).

Aug: 4th, Frederick, Crown Prince of Prussia, tries to flee to England but is imprisoned by his father.

Sep: 17th, Ahmad XII is deposed and succeeded by Mahmoud I in Turkey (–1754); 30th, Victor Amadeus XI of Savoy abdicates and is succeeded by Charles Emanuel III (–1773);

King of France orders the Paris *Parlement* not to meddle in politics on its refusal to accept the Bull 'Unigenitus'.

D Oct: 12th, Christian VI becomes King of Denmark on death of Frederick IV (–1746).

Nov:

Dec:

E Kuli Khan expels Afghans from Persia; Ashraf is murdered. Khan subsequently extends his personal influence in the country.

F **Politics, Economics, Law and Education**
   The Daily Advertiser started in London (–1807). Because of its dependence on adver-
   tisements this may be regarded as the first modern newspaper.
   Grub Street Journal started (–1737).
   Martin Wright, *Introduction to the Law of Tenures*, a scientific study of English land
   law.

G **Science, Technology and Discovery**
   De Moivre propounds theorems of trigonometry concerning imaginary quantities.
   James Stirling, *Methodus differentiais sive tractatus summatione et interpolatione
   serierum infinitarum.*
   Townshend introduces a four-course system of husbandry in Norfolk, cultivating
   clover and turnips.
   Zinc-smelting is first practised in England.

H **Philosophy, Religion and Scholarship**
   Sir Francis Bacon, Lord Verulam, *Works*, edited by John Blackbourne, 4 vols. (the first
   collected edition of *Opera omnia* (–1740)).
   César Chesneau, Sieur du Marsais, *Principes des grammaire.*
   Matthew Tindal, *Christianity as Old as the Creation* ('the Deist's Bible').

J **Art, Sculpture, Fine Arts and Architecture**
   Painting:
   William Hogarth, *Before and After.*
   Architecture:
   William Kent completes Holkham Hall, Norfolk.

K **Music**
   Concerts popularly known as the 'Gardens' Vauxhall (1720–1859), Ranelagh (1742–
   1803), Marylebone (1650–1776) in London.

L **Literature (including Drama)**
   Henry Fielding, *Rape Upon Rape* (comedy; modern title *Lock Up Your Daughters*).
   Tom Thumb (revised—1731, as *The Tragedy of Tragedies; or, The Life and Death of
   Tom Thumb the Great*, a burlesque comedy).
   Pierre Carlet de Chamblain de Marivaux, *Le Jeu de l'amour et du hasard* (comedy).
   James Thomson, *The Seasons* (collected edition, with *Autumn* –1726, –27, –28).

M **Births and Deaths**
   Mar. 19th Charles Watson Wentworth, Marquess of Rockingham, b. (–1782).
   July 12th Josiah Wedgwood b. (–1795).
   July 13th Elijah Fenton d. (47).
   Sept. 27th Laurence Eusden d. (42).
   Oct. 23rd Anne Oldfield d. (47).
   Dec. 14th James Bruce b. (–1794).
   — Leonardo de Figueroa d. (80).

1731   Treaty of Vienna averts a European War over the Italian Duchies

A Jan: 10th, the direct Farnese line becomes extinct in Parma and Piacenza; Charles, son of
Elizabeth Farnese succeeds, in accordance with the Treaty of Seville (*Nov.* 1729). The
Emperor Charles VI subsequently seizes the territories, but France and England re-
fuse to aid Spain to expel him.

Feb:

Mar:

B Apr:

May:

Jun:

C Jul: 11th/22nd, a general war over the Italian duchies is averted by the Treaty of Vienna
between England, Holland, Spain and the Emperor by which the Maritime Powers
guarantee the Pragmatic Sanction, Spain obtains Parma and Piacenza, and the
Austria East India Company is to be finally abolished (originally the treaty was
drafted in *Mar.* but Spain refused to sign). By a secret clause England insists that Maria
shall not marry a Bourbon.

Aug:

Sep: Paris *Parlement* declares the temporal power independent of all other powers and
places the clergy under the jurisdiction of the Crown. Fleury has the decree annulled.

D Oct: 31st, the expulsion of thousands of Protestants from Salzburg begins, at the instigation of Archbishop Firmian.

Nov:

Dec: The Empire, Russia and Prussia agree to act together to oppose Stanislaus I in
Poland.

E The French fortify Crown Point on Lake Champlain;

Spanish *guarda-costas* mutilate Jenkins, an English captain, for trading in defiance of
their monopoly.

F **Politics, Economics, Law and Education**
Officials of the Charitable Corporation, founded in England in 1707, absconds with
£570,000 of the capital.

G **Science, Technology and Discovery**
John Arbuthnot, *An Essay concerning the Nature of Ailments*.
René-Antoine Ferchault de Réaumur invents alcohol thermometer and temperature
scale in which the freezing point of water is 0° and the boiling point 80°.
Stahl in *Observationes Chemicae* propounds new theory of the composition of com-
pounds and of chemical action.
Jethro Tull publishes *Horse-Hoeing Husbandry*.
Hadley invents the quadrant for use at sea.

H **Philosophy, Religion and Scholarship**
Ralph Cudworth, *Treatise Concerning Eternal and Immutable Morality*.
Benjamin Franklin founds a Subscription Library in Pennsylvania.
The Cottonian Library, then in Ashburnham House, Westminster, is partly burned
(*see also* 1753).
The Gentleman's Magazine started by Edward Cave (*Apr.* 26th; monthly –1907).

J **Art, Sculpture, Fine Arts and Architecture**
Painting:
   William Hogarth, *Harlot's Progress* (–1732).
Sculpture:
   L. F. Roubiliac, *Lady Elizabeth Nightingale*.
Architecture:
   Richard, Earl of Burlington, Assembly Rooms, York.

K **Music**
J. S. Bach, *Claviervebung*, Pt. 1.
Lodovico Giustini di Pistoia composes 12 sonatas for *cimbalo di piano e forte*, probably
the first works written specially for piano.
First known public concerts are held in America at Boston, Massachusetts, and at
Charleston, South Carolina.

L **Literature (including Drama)**
George Lillo, *The London Merchant;* or *The History of George Barnewell* (domestic
drama).
De Hellevart von Doktor Ioan Faust.
Pierre Carlet de Chamblain de Marivaux, *La Vie de Marianne* (–1741).

M **Births and Deaths**
Feb. — Charles Churchill b. (–1764).
Apr. 26th Daniel Defoe d. (70).
July 1st Adam Duncan b. (–1804).
Oct. 16th Henry Cavendish b. (–1810).
Oct. 18th John Dunning, Lord Ashburton, b. (–1783).
Nov. 15th William Cowper b. (–1800).
Dec. 7th Abraham Hyacinthe Anquetil Duperron b. (–1805).
Dec. 12th Erasmus Darwin b. (–1802).
Dec. 18th Girolamo Tiraboschi b. (–1794).

1732   Expulsion of Members of Paris Parlement

A   Jan: 21st, by the Treaty of Riascha, Russia gives up her claim to certain Persian terri-
    tories;
       the Emperor Charles VI obtains recognition of the Pragmatic Sanction by the Diet of
       German princes at Ratisbon, but the Electors of Saxony, Bavaria and the Palatine
       refuse to guarantee it.
    Feb:
    Mar: Don Carlos arrives in Florence.

B   Apr: Villars and Chauvelin urge Louis XV to make an alliance with Spain against
       England (leads to a treaty of *Nov.* 1733).
    May:
    Jun: James Oglethorpe is granted a charter to establish a colony in Georgia.

C   Jul: 139 members of the Paris *Parlement* are exiled by order of the King, but are eventu-
       ally triumphant over the Crown, and secure their recall in *Dec.*
    Aug:
    Sep:

D   Oct:
    Nov:
    Dec:

E   20,000 Salzburg Protestants settle in E. Prussia;
    Genoa regains Corsica.

Oct. 6th Nevil Maskelyne b. (−1811).
Nov. 8th John Dickinson b. (−1808).
Nov. 9th Jeanne Julie de Lespinasse b. (−1776).
Dec. 4th John Gay d. (47).
Dec. 6th Warren Hastings b. (−1818).
Dec. 23rd Richard Arkwright b. (−1792).
— André Charles Boulle d. (90).
— John Broadwood b. (−1812).
— Henry Flood b. (−1791).

F **Politics, Economics, Law and Education**
  J. J. Moser, *Foundations of International Law.*

G **Science, Technology and Discovery**
  H. Boerhaave, *Elements of Chemistry*, a pioneer study of organic chemistry.
  Improvements to the navigation of the R. Weaver are completed.

H **Philosophy, Religion and Scholarship**
  George Berkeley, *Alciphron; or The Minute Philosopher.*
  Johan Christoph Gottsched, *Versuch einer kritischen Dichtkunst.*
  Francesco Scipione Maffei, *Verona illustrata*, 4 vols.
  Danial Neal, *The History of the Puritans or Protestant Nonconformists* (from the Reformation to the Act of Toleration; 4 vols. –1738).
  Johann Heinrich Zedler, *Universal-Lexicon* (64 vols. –1750).
  Conrad Beissel founds the Ephrata Community, known as Seventh Day Baptists (Dunkers), in Germantown, Pennsylvania, after the schism with the first congregation (*see* 1708, 1719).
  Moravian Brethren, a Christian sect, start missionary work.

J **Art, Sculpture, Fine Arts and Architecture**
  Painting:
  J. B. S. Chardin, *Kitchen table with shoulder of mutton.*
  Architecture:
  Salvi, The Trevi Fountain, Rome.

K **Music**
  Covent Garden Theatre is opened in London; the present Royal Opera House is the third on this site.
  G. F. Handel, *Acis and Galatea* (opera) first performed London.
  Handel reconstructs his masque *Haman and Mordicai* as *Esther*, his first English oratorio.

L **Literature (including Drama)**
  Philippe Néricault Destouches, *Le Glorieux* (comedy).
  Benjamin Franklin, *Poor Richard's Almanack* started (–1757).
  The London Magazine started (*Apr.* 'Gentleman's Monthly Intelligencer' –1785).
  Olof von Dalin starts the first satirical weekly in Sweden: *Then Svänska Argus* (–*Dec.* 1734), modelled on Addison's *Spectator.*
  A London theatrical company gives the first dramatic performance of London players in Pearl Street, New York.

M **Births and Deaths**
  Jan. 20th Richard Henry Lee b. (–1794).
  Jan. 24th Pierre-Augustin Caron de Beaumarchais b. (–1799).
  Feb. 11th/22nd George Washington b. (–1799).
  Feb. 22nd Francis Atterbury d. (70).
  Mar. 31st Franz Joseph Haydn b. (–1809).
  Apr. 5th Jean-Honoré Fragonard b. (–1806).
  Apr. 13th Frederick North (Lord North) b. (–1792).
  Sept. 3rd Jacques Necker b. (–1804).

(*Continued opposite*)

1733   War of Polish Succession—First Family Compact of France and Spain

A Jan:
   Feb: 1st, Augustus II of Poland (and Saxony) dies. Subsequently non-Catholics are ex-
        cluded from office by Potocki, the Primate and supporter of Stanislaus Lesczcyinski.
   Mar:

B Apr: 11th, defeat of Walpole's Excise Bill is the first real victory for his Parliamentary
        opponents.
   May:
   Jun: St. Crois (Santa Cruz) in the West Indies, comes under Danish control.

C Jul:
   Aug: 14th, outbreak of War of Polish Succession in which Russia and the Emperor
        Charles VI recognise the Elector Augustus III of Saxony as ruler whereas France
        supports the claim of Stanislaus Lesczcyinski.
   Sep: 26th, the League of Turin is signed between France, Spain and Sardinia against the
        Emperor, by which France is to obtain Savoy; Sardinia is to be recompensed with
        Milan; Don Carlos is to renounce Parma and the succession to Tuscany in favour of
        his brother, in return for Naples, Sicily and Presidi.

D Oct: 10th, France declares war on the Emperor Charles VI, for aiding the Elector
        Augustus III of Saxony;
        siege of Danzig (–June 1734).
   Nov: 7th, by the Treaty of Escurial, France and Spain are to guarantee each other's
        possessions and form an alliance against England; France will help Spain recover
        Gibraltar and will withdraw the trade concessions given to England by the Treaty of
        Utrecht; the Union of the two branches of the Bourbon family is declared indivisible
        and this forms the first Family Compact.
   Dec:

E Conscription is introduced in Prussia;
   James Oglethorpe founds Savannah.

F **Politics, Economics, Law and Education**

The practice of proceedings in English courts of law being written in Latin and in court hand is abolished.

James Oglethorpe makes first settlement in Georgia, at Savannah, following a charter to establish this, the last of the English colonies in North America.

The New York Weekly Journal, a popular paper edited by Peter Zenger, is first issued.

G **Science, Technology and Discovery**

John Kay patents his Flying Shuttle (*May* 26th).

The great bell at Moscow 'Tsar Kolokol', of c. 180 tons, is cast.

H **Philosophy, Religion and Scholarship**

Corporation for the Propagation of the Gospel in New England founded.

Society of Dilettanti, London, founded to encourage the study of antiquities.

J **Art, Sculpture, Fine Arts and Architecture**

Painting:

J. F. de Troy, *Le Temps de Voile la Vérité*.

Fine Arts:

Oudry is appointed director of the Beauvais tapestry factory.

Landscape Gardening:

The Serpentine Lake, Hyde Park, London, is laid out for Queen Caroline.

K **Music**

J. S. Bach presents *B Minor Mass* to Elector of Saxony in a shorter version, with petition for the post of court composer (full version 1738).

G. Pergolese, *The Servant as Mistress* (one of the first opera buffa) first performed Naples.

J. P. Rameau, *Hippolytus and Aricio* (opera), first performed Paris.

L **Literature (including Drama)**

Alexander Pope, *Essay on Man*.

Antoine François Prévost, *Manon Lescaut* (vol. 7 of *Mémoires et aventures d'un homme de qualité*).

Voltaire, *English Letters*.

M **Births and Deaths**

Jan. 17th George Byng, Viscount Torrington, d. (70).

Mar. 13th Mlle. Aïssé d. (39).

Mar. 13th Joseph Priestley b. (–1804).

Mar. 18th Christoph Friedrich Nicolai b. (–1811).

May 23rd Franz Anton Mesmer b. (–1815).

Aug. 22nd Jean François Ducis b. (–1816).

Sept. 5th Christoph Martin Wieland b. (–1813).

Sept. 12th François Couperin d. (65).

— Johann Zoffany b. (–1810).

1734 Defeat of Emperor Charles VI's forces in Italy

A Jan:
Feb: Turko-Persian war (–1735).
Mar: 14th, Prince of Orange-Nassau marries Marie Anne, daughter of George II of Britain.

B Apr: 16th, the first Parliament of George II is dissolved.
May: The Spanish army, under Don Carlos, which crossed the Neapolitan border in *Mar.*, conquers Naples;
25th, the Spanish army wins the battle of Bitonto; subsequently the Emperor's forces are defeated throughout Italy;
the French occupy Lorraine and the Electorate of Trèves.
Jun: 17th, French troops take Philipsburg, but the Duke of Berwick is killed in the siege;
30th, Russian troops take Danzig, after the failure of a French expedition to relieve the city; which had been besieged since *Oct.* 1733;
Franco-Spanish troops defeat the Austrians at Parma.

C Jul: 2nd, Stanislaus is expelled from Poland and takes refuge in Prussia.
Aug:
Sep: Austrian army is defeated at Guastella.

D Oct: Risings of Servian and Hungarian peasants are put down with ruthlessness.
Nov:
Dec: 2nd/13th, Anglo-Russian treaty of commerce (which is ratified by Russia *Feb.* 17th/28th, 1735).

E 8,000 Protestants from Salzburg settle in Georgia;
Lord Bolingbroke gives up his struggle in opposition to Robert Walpole and retires to France.

F **Politics, Economics, Law and Education**

Peter Zenger is arrested for libel for printing criticisms of the New York administration in his *Weekly Journal* (he is found not guilty in 1735).

Mme. de Lambert, *Avis d'une Mère à sa Fille* advocates that women should study the classics and philosophy.

First horse-race in America, at Charleston Neck, South Carolina (a Jockey Club is founded at Charleston in 1735).

The Boston Weekly Post-Boy.

G **Science, Technology and Discovery**

H **Philosophy, Religion and Scholarship**

Francis Atterbury, *Sermons*, 2 vols.

Johann Albrecht Bengel, edits a notable edition of the Greek New Testament.

La Fontaine's *Fables* translated into English (anon.).

George Sale translates *The Koran* into English.

Charles-Louis de Secondat, Baron ... de Montesquieu, *Considérations sur la cause de la grandeur des Romains et de leur décadence.*

The Works of Shakespeare (collated with the oldest copies), with notes, 7 vols, edited by Lewis Theobald.

The Capitoline Museum of Antiquities, Rome, acquires the Albani Collection.

J **Art, Sculpture, Fine Arts and Architecture**

Painting:

François Boucher, illustrations for editions of Molière.

J. F. de Troy, *Jupiter and Callisto* and *Diane Surprise par Achaeon.*

Architecture:

Nicholas Hawksmoor, West Towers, Westminster Abbey.

William Kent, The Treasury, Whitehall.

K **Music**

J. S. Bach, *Christmas Oratorio.*

L **Literature (including Drama)**

Charles Johnson, *The Lives and Adventures of the Most Famous Highwaymen.*

M **Births and Deaths**

Jan. 6th John Dennis d. (77).

Feb. 18th Jean Marie Roland b. (–1793).

May 4th James Thornhill d. (58).

June 12th James, Duke of Berwick d. (63).

June 17th Claude, Duc de Villars, d. (80).

Oct. 7th Ralph Abercromby b. (–1801).

Oct. 23rd Nicholas Edme Restif de la Bretonne b. (–1806).

Nov. 14th Louise de Kéroualle, Duchess of Portsmouth, d. (85).

Dec. 26th George Romney b. (–1802).

Dec. 28th 'Rob Roy' d. (64).

— Jean Louis Rodolphe Agassiz b. (–1807).

— Charles-Alexandre de Calonne b. (–1802).

A **Jan:** 14th, second Parliament of George II meets.
   Feb:
   Mar: Spanish troops take Orbitello in Tuscany.

B **Apr:** Imperial force under Seckendorf defeat French at Klaussen.
   May: Spaniards lay siege to Mantua.
   Jun:

C **Jul:**
   Aug: A Russian army reaches the Rhine; Fleury in alarm hastens his peace overtures.
   Sep:

D **Oct:** 3rd, by the peace preliminaries at Vienna, the Emperor Charles VI receives Parma
   and Piacenza; Don Carlos is to succeed as Charles III to Naples and Sicily which are,
   however, not to be united under one crown with Spain; Charles Emannuel III of
   Savoy is to hold Novara and Tortona; France guarantees the Pragmatic Sanction;
   Stanislaus renounces his claims to Poland and is to receive Lorraine when the Grand
   Duke of Tuscany dies (which is to revert to France on Stanislaus' death); the Duke of
   Lorraine is to receive Tuscany and Bar when the Grand Duke dies (confirmed by the
   definitive Treaty of Vienna, *Nov.* 1738);
   the Turko-Persian War ends.
   Nov:
   Dec:

E Chien Lung becomes Emperor of China.

Oct. 25th Charles Mordaunt, Earl of Peterborough and Monmouth, d. (*c.* 77).
Oct. 30th John Adams b. (–1826).
Dec. 29th Thomas Banks b. (–1805).
— Johann Christian Bach b. (–1782).

F **Politics, Economics, Law and Education**
French families settle at Vincennes, Indiana.
The Boston Evening Post is issued.
John Rich establishes The Sublime Society of Steaks at Covent Garden Theatre, London.
The Colony of Georgia forbids the sale of spirits (in force to 1742).

G **Science, Technology and Discovery**
Linnaeus, *Systema Naturae*.
Benoît de Maillet in *Telliamed* puts forward the evolutional hypothesis.
A French scientific expedition under Charles de la Condamine is sent to South America to explore the R. Amazon.

H **Philosophy, Religion and Scholarship**
Arthur Collins, *Peerage of England* completed, 3 vols. (begun 1709).
Bernardo Gomes de Brito edits *História Trágico-Maritima* (2 vols. of narratives of Portuguese shipwrecks, written by survivors).
Dr. Samuel Johnson translates (anonymously) Father Lobo's *Voyage to Abyssinia*.
The *Holy Bible* translated complete, into Lithuanian.
John Wesley, *Journals*, started (–1790).
The Wesleys (Charles and John) start their Methodist Revival in Georgia, America (–1738).

J **Art, Sculpture, Fine Arts and Architecture**
Painting:
  Giovanni Tiepolo, frescoes in Verolanvora Church (–1740).
  William Hogarth, *Rake's Progress*. Hogarth is also instrumental in securing the passage of the Copyright Act for the protection of painters and engravers.

K **Music**
G. F. Handel *Alcina* (opera) is first performed London.
J. S. Bach, *Claviervebung*, Pt. II.
Rameau, *Les Indes Galantes* (ballet).

L **Literature (including Drama)**
Pierre-Claude Nivelle de La Chaussée, *Le Préjugé à la mode* (*comédie larmoyante*).
Marivaux, *Le Paysan parvenu*.
William Somerville, *The Chace*.
Jonathan Swift, *Collected Works*, 4 vols. (the first collection, and published in Dublin; 20 vols. –1772).

M **Births and Deaths**
Jan. 1st Paul Revere b. (–1818).
Jan. 8th John Carroll b. (–1815).
Jan. 9th John Jervis, Earl of St. Vincent, b. (–1823).
Mar. 15th Cesare Beccaria-Bonesana b. (–1794).
Mar. 20th Torbern Olof Bergman b. (–1784).
June 10th Thomas Hearne d. (57).
Sept. 14th Robert Raikes b. (–1811).
Oct. 6th Jesse Ramsden b. (–1800).
Oct. 9th Karl Wilhelm, Duke of Brunswick, b. (–1806).
Oct. 25th James Beattie b. (–1803).
(*Continued opposite*)

A   Jan: 26th, Stanislaus I formally abdicates as King of Poland.
    Feb: 12th, Maria Theresa marries Stephen, Duke of Lorraine;
        Nadir Shah becomes King of Persia (–1747).
    Mar:

B   Apr: 15th, Baron Theodore of Neuhof is elected King of Corsica;
        21st, Prince Eugène dies; henceforth Bartenstein directs imperial policy.
    May: 18th, Spain accedes to the preliminary Treaty of Vienna of 1735;
        English statutes of witchcraft is repealed;
        Russia, with the support of the Emperor Charles VI, attacks Turkey in order to regain
        Azov (the war lasts till 1739).
    Jun:

C   Jul: Russian successes in the Crimea.
    Aug:
    Sep: 7th, Porteous Riots in Edinburgh, when Porteus, the captain of the town guard,
        orders troops to fire on a mob demonstrating at the arrest of smugglers. He is subse-
        quently sentenced to death by Edinburgh magistrates for murder and although he is
        reprieved by Queen Caroline, the sentence is still carried out.

D   Oct:
    Nov: Laquadra becomes Chief Minister in Spain on the death of José Patrino (3rd.).
    Dec:

E

F Politics, Economics, Law and Education
   Matthew Bacon, *Abridgment of English Laws*.
   English Statutes against witchcraft are repealed.
   Pope Clement XII condemns freemasonry.
   The Gentlemen's Magazine begins printing lengthy reports of British Parliamentary
   proceedings, giving the first and last letters of speakers' names.
   Voltaire's *Le Mondain* defends luxury.
   Thomas Carte, *Life of James, Duke of Ormonde*.

G Science, Technology and Discovery
   The French Academy sponsors an expedition to Lapland under Andreas Celsius to
   measure the arc of meridian.
   Euler founds the study of analytical mechanics.
   Guiseppe Briati begins to manufacture glass in Venice in imitation of the new
   'Bohemian' fashion.

H Philosophy, Religion and Scholarship
   Robert Ainsworth, *Latin-English; English-Latin Dictionary*.
   Joseph Butler, *Analogy of Religion*.
   Gabriel Girard, *Synonymes françois, leurs significations, et le choix qu'il en faut faire pour
   parler avec justesse*.
   William Warburton, *The Alliance Between Church and State*.

J Art, Sculpture, Fine Arts and Architecture
   Painting:
      William Hogarth, *Good Samaritan*.
   Architecture:
      Gabriel Boffrand, Pavillion for Hôtel de Soubise, Paris.

K Music
   J. S. Bach, *Easter Oratorio*.
   G. Pergolese, *Stabat Mater* (oratorio).
   The first public concert is given in New York.

L Literature (including Drama)

M Births and Deaths
   Jan. 8th Jean le Clerk d. (78).
   Jan. 19th James Watt b. (–1819).
   Jan. 25th Joseph Louis Lagrange b. (–1813).
   Feb. 3rd Bernard Lintot d. (61).
   Feb. 29th Ann Lee b. (–1784).
   Mar. 17th Giovanni Battista Pergolese d. (26).
   Mar. 25th Nicholas Hawksmoor d. (75).
   Apr. 2nd Jacob Tonson the elder d. (80).
   Apr. 21st Prince Eugène d. (82).
   May 21st Francis Egerton, Duke of Bridgwater, b. (–1803).
   May 29th Patrick Henry b. (–1799).
   June 14th Charles Augustin Coulomb b. (–1806),
   June 25th John Horne Tooke b. (–1812).
   Sept. 5th Jean-Sylvain Bailly b. (–1793).
   Sept. 16th Gabriel Daniel Fahrenheit d. (50).
   Oct. 27th James Macpherson b. (–1796).

1737   Disgrace of Chauvelin

A **Jan:**
Feb: 20th, Chauvelin, the French Foreign Secretary, is suddenly disgraced and dismissed through antagonism with Fleury over relations with Spain.
Mar: Russians, under Count Münnich, take Ochàkov from the Turks (conquest abandoned *May* 1738).

B **Apr:** William Byrd founds Richmond, Virginia.
May: 4th, the last of the Kettler line, rulers of Courland, dies and Ernst Biron, through influence of Queen Anne of Russia, becomes Duke of this Polish fief, and promotes Russia's interests.
Jun:

C **Jul:** 9th, on the death of the Grand Duke of Tuscany, the last of the Medici, Stephen, Duke of Lorraine, receives Tuscany and Stanislaus acquires Lorraine (as agreed at the preliminaries of Vienna *–Oct.* 1735);
31st, Frederick, Prince of Wales quarrels with his father, George II, taking his wife away from the royal household at Hampton Court. The incident leaves the Prince as the unacknowledged leader of the Opposition.
Aug:
Sep:

D **Oct:**
Nov: 20th, Queen Caroline dies.
Dec:

E Turkish army defeats Maria Theresa's forces which are supporting the Russians; Seckendorf, Austrian Field Marshal, is recalled and imprisoned until 1740.

Aug. 11th Joseph Nollekens b. (–1823).
Sept. 9th Luigi Galvani b. (–1798).
Sept. 19th Charles Carroll b. (–1832).
Nov. 20th Queen Caroline d. (54).
Dec. 11th John Strype d. (93).
— Francis Abington b. (–1815).
— Johann Michael Hayden b. (–1806).
— Francis Hopkinson b. (–1791).

F **Politics, Economics, Law and Education**
   J. J. Moser, *German Law.*
   Gottingen University founded by George II with John Lorenz Mosheim (1693–1755)
   as first chancellor.

G **Science, Technology and Discovery**
   René Réaumur, *History of Insects.*
   Thomas Simpson, *Treatise on Fluxions.*
   J. Swammerdam, *Biblia naturae.*

H **Philosophy, Religion and Scholarship**
   Alexander Cruden, *Concordance of the Holy Scriptures.*
   Jonathan Edwards, *The Surprising Work of God in the Conversion of Many Hundred*
   Souls ('a Faithful narrative').
   William Oldys, *The British Librarian.*
   David Wilkins, *Concilia Magnae Britanniae et Hiberniae,* 446–1717.
   John Wesley, *Psalms and Hymns* (published in Charleston).
   Moravian missionaries under George Schmidt arrive in Cape Town.
   Vincent de Paul is canonised by Pope Clement XII.
   The Radcliffe Camera, Oxford, is founded.

J **Art, Sculpture, Fine Arts and Architecture**
   Painting:
   J. B. S. Chardin, *The Draughtsman.*
   Sculpture:
   L. F. Roubiliac, *G. F. Handel.*
   Fine Arts:
   F. Boucher, Designs for Beauvais tapestry factory.
   Architecture:
   James Gibbs, Radcliffe Camera, Oxford (–1749).

K **Music**
   J. P. Rameau, *Castor and Pollux* (opera) first performed Paris.
   William Boyce conducts the Three Choirs Festival (–1745).

L **Literature (including Drama)**
   Matthew Green, *The Spleen.*
   William Shenstone, *Poems on Various Occasions* (including *The Schoolmistress,* revised
   –1742).
   A Licensing Act restricts the number of playhouses in London.
   Dr. Samuel Johnson, accompanied by David Garrick, leaves Lichfield for London
   (*Mar.* 2nd).
   The 'reformation' of the German theatre by Johann Christoph Gottsched with the
   abolition of clowns on the stage.

M **Births and Deaths**
   Jan. 19th Jacques-Henri Bernadin de Saint-Pierre b. (–1814).
   Jan. 23rd John Hancock b. (–1793).
   Jan. 24th William Wake d. (79).
   Jan. 29th Thomas Paine b. (–1809).
   Apr. 27th Edward Gibbon b. (–1794).
   May 20th William Petty Fitzmaurice, Earl of Sherburne, b. (–1805).
(*Continued opposite*)

1738   'Jenkins' Ear'

A **Jan:**

Feb: 4th, William Pitt joins the opposition to Robert Walpole;
26th, Cocceji becomes Prussian Minister of Justice.

Mar: 28th, debate in Parliament urging war on Spain becomes known as the debate on 'Jenkins' Ear', due to Spaniards pillaging Captain Jenkins' ship in 1731, setting it adrift and cutting off his ear (Walpole delays a declaration of war until *Oct.* 1739).

B **Apr:**

May: 9th, British Parliament orders reinforcement of the Mediterranean fleet and Admiral Haddock's squadron sails to patrol the coast of southern Spain. In addition ships are sent to the West Indies, and troops to Georgia, where there is a border dispute with Spain;
27th, Turks take Orsova, the Russians abandon Ochakov and the Emperor Charles VI's troops are subsequently driven back to Belgrade.

Jun:

C **Jul:**

Aug: Fleury offers French mediation to the Emperor Charles VI in his war with Turkey, hoping to detach Austria from her Russian alliance.

Sep:

D **Oct:** The War Party in Sweden, known as the 'Hats', oust Horn's 'Caps', the Peace Party, and Gyllenborg, the new Chancellor, forms an alliance with France.

Nov: 18th, France recognises the Pragmatic Sanction at the definitive Peace Treaty of Vienna (for terms, see the preliminaries of *Oct.* 1735).

Dec:

E The *Corvée*, a system of using forced labour to construct and repair main roads, is organised in France by Orry, the Controller-General;
Persia attacks Afghanistan.

F **Politics, Economics, Law and Education**

G **Science, Technology and Discovery**
Peter Artedi, *Bibliotheca Ichthyologia* (posth.).
Daniel Bernoulli in *Hydrodynamica* studies the pressure and velocities of fluids.
Voltaire introduces Newtonian ideas to France.

H **Philosophy, Religion and Scholarship**
Ludovico Antonio Muratori, *Antiquitates Italicae* (6 vols. –1742).
Voltaire, *Discours sur l'homme*.
John Wesley's evangelical conversion (*May.* 24th).
George Whitefield follows John Wesley to Georgia as 'Leader of the Great Awakening'.
Bernard de Montfaucon edits the works of St. John Chrysostom.
Papal Bull against Freemasonry: *In Eminenti*.
Louis de Beaufort attacks the credibility of early Roman history, much of which he concludes is mythical.
Excavation of Herculaneum begins under Colonel D. Rocco de Alcubierre.
Don Martin Bouquet, *Recueil des Historiens des Gaules et de la France*, vol. 1.

J **Art, Sculpture, Fine Arts and Architecture**
Painting:
J. B. S. Chardin, *La Gouvernante*.
Sculpture:
L. F. Roubiliac, *Alexander Pope*.

K **Music**
G. F. Handel, *Israel in Egypt* (oratorio) and *Saul* (oratorio), including the 'Dead March'.
Imperial Ballet School is founded in St. Petersburg.

L **Literature (including Drama)**
Olof von Dalin, *The Envious Man* (tragedy).
Samuel Johnson, *London* (a poem in imitation of Juvenal).
Alexis Piron, *La Métromanie* (comedy).
Jonathan Swift, *A Complete Collection of Genteel and Ingenious Conversation*.

M **Births and Deaths**
Apr. 14th William Henry Cavendish Bentinck, Duke of Portland, b. (–1809).
May 28th Joseph Guillotin b. (–1814).
June 4th George III b. (–1820).
June 21st Charles, Viscount Townshend, d. (64).
June 22nd Jacques Delille b. (–1813).
July 3rd John Singleton Copley b. (–1815).
Oct. 10th Benjamin West b. (–1820).
Nov. 15th Frederick William Herschel b. (–1822).
Dec. 25th Claude Michel ('Claudion') b. (–1814).
Dec. 31st Charles, Marquess of Cornwallis, b. (–1805).
— John Wolcot ('Peter Pindar') b. (–1819).
— William Selby b. (–1798).

A **Jan:** 3rd/14th, Convention of the Pardo to settle Anglo-Spanish disputes over the Assiento trade and maritime quarrels: Spain agrees to pay certain damages but refuses to give up her right to search English vessels for smuggled goods and also demands unpaid royalties from the South Sea Company. The English representative agrees to recall the fleet from Spanish waters but subsequently this order is revoked, causing consternation in Spain;

by a secret treaty with the Emperor, France agrees to the occupation of Jülich-Berg by the Sulzbach line of the House of Wittelsbach, on the death of the Elector Palatine.

Feb:
Mar:

B **Apr:** 5th, France concludes a secret treaty with Prussia, whereby on the death of Charles Philip, the Elector Palatine, the duchies of Jülich-Berg are to be shared between the Sulzbach line and Prussia (thus France is contradicting the secret agreement with the Emperor);

21st, Spain joins the Treaty of Vienna, of *Nov.* 1738, and Naples subsequently joins.

May:
Jun:

C **Jul:** 22nd, Turks defeat Emperor's troops at Crocyka and threaten Belgrade.

Aug:
Sep: 18th, Peace of Belgrade between the Emperor Charles VI and Turkey, by which Austria cedes Orsova, Belgrade and Serbia, which she had gained by the Treaty of Passarowitz;

23rd, Treaty of Belgrade between Russia and Turkey by which the Tsar restores all conquests except Azov, which is to be dismantled as a military garrison, and he agrees not to maintain vessels in the Black Sea or the Sea of Azov.

D **Oct:** 8th/19th, England declares war against Spain after Spain refuses to adhere to the Convention of Pardo (of *Jan.*).

Nov: 21st, Admiral Vernon captures Porto Bello.
Dec:

E The Vice-Royalty of New Grenada is separated from Peru;

Nadir Shah of Persia sacks Delhi and conquers the Punjab.

F **Politics, Economics, Law and Education**
The Foundling Hospital, London, is founded.

G **Science, Technology and Discovery**
J. F. Gronovius, *Flora Virginica*.
Jean d'Alembert, *Mémoire sur le calcul intégral*.
John Winthrop IV, *Notes on Sunspots*.

H **Philosophy, Religion and Scholarship**
David Hume, *A Treatise on Human Nature* (–1740).
Bernard de Montfaucon compiles *Bibliotheca Bibliothecarum*, a catalogue of manuscripts in European libraries.
Thomas Wentworth, Earl of Strafford, *Letters and Despatches*, 1611–1640, edited by W. Knowler, with a short life by Sir George Radcliffe.
Moravian Church in America founded by Bishop August Gottlieb Spangenberg.

J **Art, Sculpture, Fine Arts and Architecture**
Painting:
    J. B. S. Chardin, *Saying Grace*.
    Oudry, *Hyena attacked by two Dogs*.
    Allan Ramsay, *The Artist's first wife, Anne Bayne*.
Architecture:
    George Dance, Mansion House, London (–1752).

K **Music**
G. F. Handel's oratorios *Saul* and *Israel in Egypt* are first performed.
J. P. Rameau, *Dardanus* (opera) first performed Paris.

L **Literature (including Drama)**
Jonathan Swift, *Verses on the Death of Dr. Swift*.

M **Births and Deaths**
Jan. 10th Ethan Allen b. (–1789).
Apr. 7th Dick Turpin d. (33).
July 26th George Clinton b. (–1812).
Sept. 3rd George Lillo d. (46).
Sept. 14th Pierre Samuel Du Pont de Nemours b. (–1817).
Nov. 2nd Karl Ditters von Dittersdorf b. (–1799).
Nov. 20th Jean François de la Harpe b. (–1803).
— Charles François Dumouriez b. (–1823).
— Prince Grigory Aleksandrovich Potemkin b. (–1791).
— John Walter b. (–1812).

A Jan:
   Feb: 6th, Pope Clement XII dies and is succeeded by Prospero Lambertini as Benedict
       XIV (–1758).
   Mar:

B Apr:
   May: 31st, Frederick William I of Prussia dies and is succeeded by Frederick II ('the
       Great'–1786).
   Jun:

C Jul:
   Aug:
   Sep: 18th, George Anson sets out on voyage around the world (*–June* 15th, 1744).

D Oct: 20th, Charles VI, the last Hapsburg Emperor, dies and is succeeded by his daughter
       Maria Theresa, Queen of Bohemia and Hungary and Archduchess of Austria (–1780).
       The succession is disputed (i) by Charles Albert, Elector of Bavaria, who is the husband
       of Joseph I's daughter and is claimant by will of Ferdinand I; (ii) by Frederick
       Augustus II of Saxony through his wife, the eldest daughter of Joseph I; (iii) by
       Philip V of Spain, as heir of the Spanish Hapsburgs, who is particularly interested in
       the Italian provinces. England and Holland support Maria Theresa while Russia re-
       mains neutral. In France the party led by Belleisle, is eager for war;
       28th, Anne, daughter of Peter the Great, dies and is succeeded by Ivan VI (–1741),
       grandson of Anne's sister Catherine. Ivan's mother acts as Regent, but power is in the
       hands of Count Münnich, who succeeds in banishing Ernst Biron, Duke of Courland,
       from Russia.
   Nov: Maria Theresa appoints John Palffy Governor of Hungary.
   Dec: 16th, Frederick II of Prussia enters Silesia and begins the first Silesian War.

E Frederick II abolishes torture and introduces liberty of the Press and freedom of worship
   in Prussia;
   Bengal becomes independent under Alivardi Khan;
   Nadir Shar extends his influence in Balkh and Bokhara.

May 31st Frederick William I of Prussia d. (61).
May — Jean Cavalier d. (58).
Sept. 17th John Cartwright b. (–1824).
Oct. 29th James Boswell b. (–1795).
Nov. 24th John Bacon b. (–1799).
— Pierre Couthière b. (–1860).
— Augustus Toplady b. (–1778).

F **Politics, Economics, Law and Education**
>   Frederick the Great publishes *Anti-Machiave*, and founds the Berlin Academy of
>   Science.

G **Science, Technology and Discovery**
>   Louis Castel, *Optique des couleurs*.
>   Pierre Bouguer's experiments on the gravity of the earth.
>   Thomas Simpson, *Treatise on the Nature and Laws of Chance*.
>   Henry Hindley constructs a dividing-engine for cutting the teeth of clock wheels.
>   Benjamin Huntsman improves the 'crucible' process for smelting steel.
>   J. H. Potts experiments concerning manganese.
>   The dye 'Saxony blue' (Indigo extract) is made.
>   Anson's voyage round the world in *Centurion*.

H **Philosophy, Religion and Scholarship**
>   Sir Francis Bacon (Baron Verulam), *Works*, collected and again edited with a *Life* by
>   David Mallet (–1730).
>   Johann Jakob Bodmer, *Kritische Abhandlung von dem Wunderbaren in der Poesie*.
>   William Stukeley, *Stonehenge*.

J **Art, Sculpture, Fine Arts and Architecture**
>   Painting:
>   Antonio Canaletto, *Return of the Bucintoro*.
>   François Boucher, *Morning Toilet*.
>   Francis Hayman, decor of Vauxhall Gardens (–1750).
>   Oudry, *Le Cygne*.
>   Arthur Devis, *The Bull family*.
>   William Hogarth, *Captain Coram*.

K **Music**
>   T. Arne, *Alfred* (masque, with words by James Thomson) first performed, containing
>   the song 'Rule Britannia'.
>   Haydn enters the choir school of St. Stephen's, Vienna.
>   Domenico Scarlatti visits London and Dublin.
>   Johann Adolf Scheibe, *Der critische Musicus*.
>   John Snetzler, German organ builder, establishes himself in England; among his
>   surviving instruments are those at Snettisham, Norfolk, and St. Martin's, Leicester.

L **Literature (including Drama)**
>   Colley Cibber, *An Apology for the Life of Mr. Colley Cibber, Comedian*.
>   Johann Christoph Gottsched, *Die deutsche Schaubühne* (6 vols. –1745) provides for the
>   German stage a classical repertory, chiefly of translations from the French.
>   Samuel Richardson, *Pamela; or Virtue Rewarded*.
>   Louis de Rouvroy, Duc de Saint-Simon, *Memoirs* (–1752).

M **Births and Deaths**
>   Feb. 4th Carl Michael Bellman b. (–1795).
>   Feb. 16th Giambattista Bodini b. (–1813).
>   Feb. 17th Horace Bénédict de Saussure b. (–1791).
>   Mar. 18th Jean Antoine Houdon b. (–1828).
>   May 15th Ephraim Chambers d. (*c.* 60).

(*Continued opposite*)

1741   War of Austrian Succession

A Jan:
   Feb:
   Mar: Count Münnich falls from power in Russia.

B Apr: 10th, Frederick II defeats Maria Theresa's forces at Mollwitz and conquers
        Silesia. During the engagement his cavalry is routed and he flees, but his infantry
        defeats the Austrians;
        25th, George II's second Parliament is dissolved.
   May: 4th, Frederick II captures Brieg;
        8th, by Treaty of Nymphenburg between France and Bavaria, assistance is promised
        for Charles Albert of Bavaria's claim to the Empire;
        28th, treaty between Spain and Bavaria to partition the Hapsburg lands.
   Jun: 5th, Treaty of Breslau is signed between France and Prussia, to partition the Empire,
        following the breakdown of Frederick's negotiations with Maria Theresa; Prussia is to
        receive Breslau and Lower Silesia and, in return, to recognise Charles Albert as
        Emperor and to recognise the Sulzbachs in the whole of Jülich-Berg;
        25th, Maria Theresa accepts the Crown of Hungary.

C Jul:
   Aug: 10th, Frederick II takes Breslau;
        15th, French troops cross Rhine in order to invade south Germany, Austria and Bohemia,
        without a formal declaration of war.
   Sep: 7th-8th, England attempts to mediate between Austria and Prussia;
        George II secures the neutrality of Hanover, by a treaty with France;
        14th, Franco-Bavarian army takes Linz;
        19th, Saxony joins France against Maria Theresa;
        21st, the Hungarian Diet accepts the Grand Duke Francis as co-Regent, following the
        'Insurrection' decree of *Sept.* 11th.

D Oct: 9th, Frederick II and Maria Theresa conclude the secret Treaty of Klein Schnellen-
        dorf, promising the cession of Lower Silesia to Prussia (Prussia breaks the treaty in
        Nov.).
   Nov: 1st, Frederick II breaks agreement of Klein Schnellendorf by entering Neisse and
        signing a treaty with Saxony and Bavaria for the partition of the Empire;
        26th, French, Bavarian and Saxon troops take Prague.
   Dec: 1st, third Parliament of George II (after prorogation since *June* 25th);
        Uhlfeld becomes Minister of State in Austria;
        18th, Glatz falls to the Prussians;
        27th, Prussians take Olmütz;
        Elizabeth becomes Empress of Russia after a bloodless revolution (–1762);
        Spanish troops land in Tuscany.

E Russian expedition to Alaska opens fur trade under Behring;
   English attack on Carthagena and Cuba fails.

F **Politics, Economics, Law and Education**
Benjamin Franklin founds *The General Magazine* in Philadelphia.

G **Science, Technology and Discovery**
Linnaeus founds a botanical garden in Upsala.

H **Philosophy, Religion and Scholarship**
Jonathan Edwards, *Sinners in the Hands of an Angry God*: sermon delivered at Enfield,
Massachusetts and published (a notable event in 'The Great Awakening').
David Hume, *Essays: Moral and Political* (–1742).
Shakespeare's *Julius Caesar*, translated into German by Caspar Wilhelm von Borck
(Alexandrines)—the first German translation of a Shakespeare play to be printed.

J **Art, Sculpture, Fine Arts and Architecture**
Painting:
François Boucher, *Autumn*.
Architecture:
Bartolomeo Rastrelli, Summer Palace, St. Petersburg.
Jacques-Louis Soufflot, Hôtel-Dieu, Lyons.

K **Music**
Gluck, *Artaserse* (opera) performed in Milan.
G. F. Handel, *Messiah*. Note on his score in his own hand 'composed between
22 August and 12th September 1741'.
Rameau, *Pièces de clavecin en concert* (written 10 to 20 years earlier).

L **Literature (including Drama)**
Thomas Betterton, *A History of the English Stage* (by a number of authors probably
using the material collected by Betterton).
Robert Dodsley, *The Blind Beggar of Bethnal Green* (play).
[Henry Fielding], *Shamela* (a satirical story parodying Samuel Richardson's *Pamela*
–1740, now attributed with near-certainty to Fielding).
Pierre Claude Nivelle de La Chaussée, *Mélanide* (*comédie larmoyante*).
Samuel Richardson, *Familiar Letters*.
David Garrick's début at Ipswich as Aboan in Southerne's *Oroonoko*; début in London,
as Richard III, produced at Goodman's Fields (*Oct.* 19th).

M **Births and Deaths**
Jan. 14th Benedict Arnold b. (–1801).
Jan. 16th Hester Lynch Piozzi b. (–1821).
Feb. 7th Henry Fuseli b. (–1825).
Feb. 8th André Grétry b. (–1813).
Feb. 13th Johann Joseph Fux d. (81).
Feb. 21st Jethro Tull d. (66).
Mar. 13th Joseph II b. (–1790).
Apr. 16th Charles Willson Peale b. (–1826).
Apr. 17th Samuel Chase b. (–1811).
May 9th Giovanni Paisiello b. (–1816).
Sept. 11th Arthur Young b. (–1820).
Sept. 22nd Peter Simon Pallas b. (–1811).
Oct. 4th Edmund Malone b. (–1812).
Oct. 11th James Barry b. (–1806).
Oct. 18th Pierre Choderlos de Laclos b. (–1803).
Oct. 30th Angelica Kauffman b. (–1807).

A   Jan: 24th, Charles Albert, Elector of Bavaria, is elected Emperor.
    Feb: 1st, Charles Emanuel of Sardinia rejects alliance with France and Spain and signs
      a convention with Maria Theresa for the defence of Lombardy against Spain;
    3rd, English Parliament is adjourned;
    9th, Robert Walpole becomes Earl of Orford and
    11th, resigns his offices;
    12th, Charles Albert is crowned, Emperor Charles VII;
    16th, the Earl of Wilmington becomes Prime Minister and Carteret returns as Secretary
      of State for the Northern Department, with the intention of mediating a peace be-
      tween Prussia and Austria.
    Mar:

B   Apr: Prussians lose Olmütz as Frederick II's Moravian campaign fails.
    May: 17th, Frederick II defeats the Austrians at Chotusitz.
    Jun: Preliminary Peace of Breslau results in

C   Jul: 28th, Peace of Berlin between Maria Theresa and Prussia, which ends first Silesian
      War. Prussia obtains Silesia and Glatz and takes over the Silesian debt to England and
      Holland. Prussia and Poland withdraw from the coalition against Maria Theresa.
    Aug: English navy commanding the Mediterranean prevents Neapolitans and Spaniards
      from taking Lombardy.
    Sep: Uhlfeld becomes Chancellor of Austria, following Count Zinzendorf's death.

D   Oct:
    Nov: 7th/18th, Anglo-Prussian defensive alliance, aimed at France.
    Dec: 11th/22nd, England secures the neutrality of Russia;
    12th, the French evacuate Prague and return to France.

E   Dupleix becomes Governor-General of French possessions in India.

F **Politics, Economics, Law and Education**
  Charles Viner, *Legal Encyclopedia* (–1753; 23 vols.).
  Place Act in Britain nominates eight Crown stewardships, including the Stewardship of
  the Chiltern Hundreds, which cannot be held by a Member of Parliament.

G **Science, Technology and Discovery**
  Anders Celsius invents the centigrade (or Celsius) thermometer.
  Colin Maclaurin, *Treatise on Fluxions*.
  Royal Society of Denmark is founded.

H **Philosophy, Religion and Scholarship**
  John Campbell, *Lives of the Admirals* (–1744).
  Colley Cibber, *Letters to Mr. Pope*.
  Étienne Fourmont, *Grammatica Sinica*.
  John Thurloe, *Collection of State Papers*, ed. in 7 vols. by Thomas Birch, with a *Life*.

J **Art, Sculpture, Fine Arts and Architecture**
  Painting:
    François Boucher, *Bath of Diana* and *La Toilette*.
    William Hogarth, *The Graham Children*.
    Oudry, *The Gardens at Arcueil* (–1747).
  Fine Art:
    François Boucher, *La Pêche Chinoise*, series of nine tableautins—cartoons for
    Beauvais tapestry factory. Sets are made for Louis XV, Mme. de Pompadour and
    the Emperor of China.
    J. F. de Troy, seven designs of Jason and Medea for Gobelins tapestry (produced
    1746).
  Architecture:
    William Kent, 44 Berkeley Square, London (–1744).

K **Music**
  Handel's *Messiah* first performed in Dublin (*Apr.* 8th).

L **Literature (including Drama)**
  William Collins, *Persian Eclogues*.
  Henry Fielding, *Joseph Andrews*.
  Edward Young, *The Complaint, or Night Thoughts on Life, Death and Immortality*
  (–1745).

M **Births and Deaths**
  Jan. 14th Edmund Halley d. (85).
  May 18th Lionel Lukin b. (–1834).
  June 27th Nathaniel Bailey d. (*c.* 67).
  July 1st Georg Christoph Lichtenberg (–1799).
  Jul. 9th John Oldmixon d. (69).
  July 14th Richard Bentley d. (80).
  July 29th William Somerville d. (67).
  Aug. 7th Nathanael Greene b. (–1786).
  Sept. 14th James Wilson b. (–1798).
  Dec. 16th Gebhard von Blücher b. (–1819).
  Dec. 19th Karl Wilhelm Scheele b. (–1786).
  — George Chalmers b. (–1825).

1743   Second Family Compact

A **Jan:** 29th, the death of Fleury marks the beginning of an aggressive policy in French foreign relations.
  Feb:
  Mar:

B **Apr:** Maria Theresa is crowned at Prague.
  May:
  Jun: 16th/27th, George II defeats French at Dettingen but plans to invade France are not carried out;
    27th, by the Convention of Niederschönfeld, Bavaria, except for Ingolstadt, is handed over to Austria until the end of the war.

C **Jul:** 2nd, the Earl of Wilmington dies and is succeeded by Henry Pelham as First Lord of Treasury (*Aug.* 27th).
  Aug: 17th, Peace of Åbö between Russia and Sweden, which cedes South Finland as far as the R. Kiümen, ends the war.
  Sep: 2nd/13th, Treaty of Worms between Maria Theresa, Britain and Sardinia, to expel the Bourbons from Italy, to obtain part of Milan for Sardinia, and guaranteeing English subsidies to her allies.

D **Oct:** 25th, Second Family Compact between France and Spain is established by the offensive and defensive alliance of Fontainebleau; Gibraltar and Port Mahon to be wrested from Britain; Charles Emmanuel III of Sardinia to surrender his recent acquisitions in Italy; and Milan, Parma and Piacenza to pass to Don Philip.
  Nov:
  Dec: Austria and Saxony sign an alliance.

E War between Turkey and Persia resumes;
  The Orange Party in Holland control the States-General and press for France to be opposed.

F **Politics, Economics, Law and Education**
Erlangen University, Germany, founded.

G **Science, Technology and Discovery**
J. N. Delisle devises a method for observing the transits of Mercury and of Venus by instants of contacts.
Sevington Savary invents a chronometer for measurement by double image (the 'heliometer').
The American Philosophical Society founded.
Jean d'Anville's map of Italy.

H **Philosophy, Religion and Scholarship**
Philip Francis translates *The Odes, Epodes and Carmen Seculare* of Horace (–1746).
Sir Thomas Hanmer edits *The Works of Shakespeare* (carefully revised and corrected), 6 vols.
John Milton's *Letters and Papers of State* (addressed to Oliver Cromwell) edited by John Nicholls.
William Oldys, *Catalogus Bibliothecae Harleianae* (–1744).
George Whitefield's meeting at Wadford, Glamorgan, at which the Welsh Calvinistic Methodists form the first Methodist Association (*Jan.* 5th/6th).

J **Art, Sculpture, Fine Arts and Architecture**
Painting:
Arthur Devis, *Miss Fenton*.
William Hogarth, *Marriage à la Mode*.
Oudry, *Octave Alexandre Nédonchel as a Huntsman*.

K **Music**
G. F. Handel *Dettingen Te Deum* written to celebrate George II's victory at Dettingen.

L **Literature (including Drama)**
Robert Blair, *The Grave*.
Henry Fielding, *Jonathan Wild the Great*; *A Journey from this World to the Next* (both contained in a volume of *Miscellanies*).
Alexander Pope, *The Dunciad* (the final edition in Pope's lifetime).
Voltaire, *Mérope* (drama).

M **Births and Deaths**
Jan. 21st John Fitch b. (–1798).
Jan. 29th André-Hercule de Fleury d. (89).
Feb. 13th Joseph Banks b. (–1820).
Feb. 19th Luigi Boccherini b. (–1805).
Apr. 13th Thomas Jefferson b. (–1826).
Apr. 24th Edmund Cartwright b. (–1823).
May 24th Jean-Paul Marat b. (–1793).
June 8th Alessandro, Count Cagliostro, b. (–1795).
June 13th Francis Dana b. (–1811).
June 17th John Lowell b. (–1802).
Aug. 1st Richard Savage d. (46).
Aug. 14th John, Lord Hervey of Ickworth, d. (46).
Aug. 26th Antoine Laurent Lavoisier b. (–1794).
Sept. 17th Marie Jean Caritat, Marquis de Condorcet, b. (–1794).
Nov. 18th Johannes Ewald b. (–1781).
— Thomas Archer d. (75).
— William Paley b. (–1805).

A Jan:
   Feb: 11th/22nd, undecided naval Battle of Toulon between England and combined Franco–Spanish fleet.
   Mar: 4th/15th, France declares war on England.

B Apr: 26th, France declares war on Maria Theresa.
   May: 25th, Prussia acquires East Friesland on death of last prince, Charles Edward;
        Austrian troops invade Alsace, but (in *Aug.*) are allowed by the French to withdraw into Bohemia;
        Union of Frankfurt between Frederick of Prussia, Charles of Bavaria, the Elector Palatine, and the Landgrave of Hesse, to force Maria Theresa to restore Bavaria, make peace and restore the constitution of the Empire.
   Jun: 6th, France allies with Prussia against Maria Theresa, and guarantees the Union of Frankfurt;
        15th, Sir George Anson completes voyage round the world.

C Jul: Elizabeth of Russia's nephew and heir, Charles Peter, marries Catherine of Anhalt-Zerbst.
   Aug: 15th, second Silesian War begins with Frederick II's invasion of Saxony;
        Louis XV is dangerously ill at Metz.
   Sep: 16th, Frederick II takes Prague but, as he is deserted by the French, is driven back into Saxony.

D Oct:
   Nov: 24th, fall of John Carteret (now Earl Granville), Secretary of State for the Northern Department; the Cabinet is reconstructed to include all shades of Whig opinion, with William, Earl of Harrington, Secretary of State;
        D'Argenson becomes French Foreign Minister, in succession to Amelot.
   Dec: Clive arrives in Madras;
        28th/*Jan.* 8th, Quadruple Alliance, between Great Britain, Maria Theresa, Saxony-Poland and Holland against Prussia;
        Adolphus Frederick, heir to the Swedish Crown, marries Ulrica, Frederick the Great's daughter.

E French take Annapolis, Nova Scotia, but withdraw.

June 4th Jeremy Belknap b. (–1798).
Aug. 1st Jean-Baptiste de Monet, Chevalier de Lamarck, b. (–1829).
Aug. 25th Johann Gottfried von Herder b. (–1803).
Oct. 18th Sarah, Duchess of Marlborough, d. (84).

F **Politics, Economics, Law and Education**
  Matthew Decker, *Essay on the Causes of the Decline of the Foreign Trade, consequently of the Value of the Lands in Britain, and on the means to restore both.*
  First ascent of the peak Titlis in the Alps.

G **Science, Technology and Discovery**
  Jean d'Alembert, *Traité de l'équilibre et du mouvement des fluides.*
  S. E. Martin's imitation of Japanese lacquer.
  Eruption of Mount Cotopaxi in S. America.

H **Philosophy, Religion and Scholarship**
  George Berkeley, *A Chain of Philosophical Reflexions and Inquiries* (later revision entitled *Siris*), on the virtues of tar-water.
  Benjamin Franklin prints and sells in Philadelphia, Cicero's *Cato Major; or His Discourse of Old-Age*, with explanatory notes (an example of the finest American printing of the Colonial era).
  The Harleian Miscellany, vols. 1–2, edited by William Oldys, with intro. by Samuel Johnson (vols. 3–6, –1745).
  Ludovico Antonio Muratori, *Annali d'Italia* (12 vols. –1749).
  Hermann Samuel Reimarus, *Wolfenbüttelsche Fragmente eines Ungenannten* (published by Lessing, 1774–8).
  George Whitefield's second tour in New England (–1748).
  William Kenrick delivers the first public lecture on Shakespeare. Admission 2/0, at the *Devil Tavern*, Temple Bar, London (*Jan.* 19th at 7 p.m.).

J **Art, Sculpture, Fine Arts and Architecture**
  Painting:
  Francis Hayman, illustrations for an edition of Shakespeare.
  Oudry, illustrations for *Une Histoire pour le Jardin Botanique* (–1747).
  Sculpture:
  J. M. Rysbrack, *Dr. Radcliffe* (Oxford).
  Architecture:
  Bartolomeo Rastrelli, Anichkon Palace, St. Petersburg.

K **Music**
  J. S. Bach, *Das Wohltemperiete Clavier*, Pt. 2.
  Gluck, *Iphigenie en Aulide* (opera) performed in Paris.

L **Literature (including Drama)**
  Mark Akenside, *The Pleasures of Imagination.*
  Robert Dodsley, *A Select Collection of Old Plays*, 12 vols.
  Samuel Johnson, *Life of Mr. Richard Savage* (subsequently included in the *Lives of the Poets*).
  John Newbery publishes *A Little Pretty Pocket-Book*, for children.

M **Births and Deaths**
  Jan. 20th Giovanni Battista Vico d. (75).
  Feb. 6th Pierre Joseph Desault b. (–1795).
  Feb. 10th William Mitford b. (–1827).
  Feb. 20th William Cornwallis b. (–1819).
  Feb. 23rd Josiah Quincy b. (–1775).
  May 30th Alexander Pope d. (66).

(Continued opposite)

A Jan: 20th, Emperor Charles VII dies; his son Maximilian Joseph of Bavaria subsequently agrees to support the candidature of the Grand Duke Francis, Maria Theresa's husband, as Emperor.
Feb:
Mar: 18th, Walpole dies.

B Apr: 2nd/13th, England undertakes to pay subsidies to Maria Theresa;
22nd, Peace of Füssen between Maria Theresa and Bavaria, which renounces its claim to the Empire and Maria Theresa restores all her conquests in Bavaria to Maximilian Joseph;
30th/*May* 11th, French under Marshal Saxe defeat English led by the Duke of Cumberland at Fontenoy, and conquer the Austrian Netherlands.
May: 21st/*June* 1st, England's agreement with Maria Theresa (of 2nd/*Apr.* 13th) is extended to provide troops;
Austria and Saxony sign the Treaty of Warsaw for the partition of Prussia.
Jun: 4th, Frederick defeats Maria Theresa, who is invading Silesia at Hohenfriedberg;
16th, British take Cape Breton Island and subsequently Louisburg, at mouth of St. Lawrence.

C Jul: 23rd, Charles Edward, the Young Pretender, lands on Eriskay Island, Scotland and crosses to the Moidart Peninsula, 25th. English troops are recalled from the Netherlands.
Aug: 15th/26th, by the Convention of Hanover with Prussia, George II deserts Maria Theresa and promises to negotiate a peace settlement.
Sep: 11th, Jacobites enter Edinburgh;
12th, Francis Stephen, husband of Maria Theresa is elected Holy Roman Emperor (–1765), the first of the Lorraine-Tuscany line;
Austrians are defeated at Basignano in Italy by a Franco-Spanish army;
Frederick II defeats the Austrians at Sohr;
21st, Charles Edward defeats English army under General Cope at Prestonpans;
Mme. de Pompadour is installed at Versailles as Louis XV's recognised mistress;
France, unwilling to support Austria in regaining Silesia, breaks off negotiations for an alliance with Maria Theresa.

D Oct:
Nov: Frederick II defeats the Austrians at Hennersdorf.
Dec: 4th, Charles Edward advances as far south as Derby but
6th, is forced to retreat;
15th, Prussian army under Leopold von Dessau defeats Saxons at Kesseldorf;
18th, Jacobite victory at Penrith;
25th, by the Peace of Dresden with Maria Theresa and Saxony, Prussia retains Silesia and in return recognises the Pragmatic Sanction and Francis I as Emperor.

E Franco-Spanish troops take Milan;
Machault D'Arronville becomes French Controller for Finances (–1754);
Ishege becomes Shōgun of Japan.

Dec. 10th Thomas Holcroft b. (–1809).
Dec. 12th John Jay b. (–1829).
— Charles Dibden b. (–1814).
— Henry Holland b. (–1806).

F **Politics, Economics, Law and Education**

The True Patriot, an organ of the British government is edited by Henry Fielding (–1746).

Taxation of glass by weight in Britain checks the manufacture of heavy crystal glass.

Earliest meeting of an Oddfellows Lodge in England (at the Globe Tavern, Hatton Garden, London).

Van Smieten, a Dutch physician, begins to reform education in Vienna.

Yale College, Connecticut receives a new royal charter.

G **Science, Technology and Discovery**

E. G. von Kleist invents the Leyden jar, a condenser which accumulates and preserves electricity. (Next year P. von Musschenbroek and Cunaeus both independently make the same discovery.)

Charles Bonnet, *Traité d'insectologie*.

R. Bakewell begins to reform stock-breeding in Leicestershire.

H **Philosophy, Religion and Scholarship**

Philip Doddridge, *The Rise and Progress of Religion in the Soul*.

Samuel Johnson, *Observations on the Tragedy of Macbeth* (with *Proposals for a New Edition of Shakespeare*, with a Specimen).

Julien Offroy de Lammettrie, *L'Histoire naturelle de l'âme* (published and burnt in public in France).

J **Art, Sculpture, Fine Arts and Architecture**

Painting:

J. F. de Troy, *Lot and his daughters*.

Francis Hayman, *The Gascoigne Family* and *The Grant Family*.

William Hogarth, self-portrait; also *Lord George Graham in his Cabin*.

Oudry, *Gazelle with White Dogs* and *Still Life of Pheasants*.

Giovanni Tiepolo, frescoes on the theme of Antony and Cleopatra for Labia Palace, Venice; also begins painting 137 etchings of Rome.

K **Music**

Gluck, *Ippolita* (opera) performed in Milan.

'The Campbells are Coming', Scottish tune is published.

J. J. Rousseau, *Les Muses Galantis* (opera).

L **Literature (including Drama)**

Mark Akenside, *Odes*.

Claude-Prosper Jolyot de Crébillon, *fils*, *Le Sopha*.

Jean-Baptiste Louis Gresset, *Le Méchant*; and *Sidney*.

Jonathan Swift, *Directions to Servants in General*.

James Thomson, *Tancred and Sigismunda* (tragedy).

M **Births and Deaths**

Feb. 2nd Hannah More b. (–1833).

Feb. 18th Alessandro Volta b. (–1827).

Feb. 27th John Arbuthnot d. (87).

Mar. 18th Robert Walpole, Earl of Orford, d. (68).

Aug. 26th Henry MacKenzie b. (–1831).

Oct. 10th Jonathan Swift d. (87).

Nov. 16th William Broome d. (56).

(*Continued opposite*)

1746 Jacobites are defeated at Culloden—Saxe overruns Austrian Netherlands

A Jan: 4th, Charles Emanuel of Sardinia, on learning of the Peace of Dresden (*Dec.* 1745), vigorously supports Austria;

16th, Prince Charles Edward is victorious at Falkirk.

Feb: 10th, upon the King's refusal to admit William Pitt into the Cabinet as Secretary at War, the Pelham Ministry resigns but Bath and Granville are unable to form an administration so that

14th, Pelham and his colleagues return and, 22nd, Pitt is made Joint Vice-Treasurer for Ireland;

20th, Brussels falls to Marshal Saxe, after a siege since the end of *Jan.*

Mar: Charles Emanuel recovers Milan, and proceeds to overrun Piedmont and Lombardy (*–June*).

B Apr: 16th, the final defeat of the Jacobites at Culloden by the Duke of Cumberland, who subsequently abolishes the Clan organisation, earning the nickname 'Butcher' for his ruthlessness.

May: 6th, William Pitt becomes Paymaster-General for the forces and Henry Fox subsequently becomes Secretary at War.

Jun: 2nd, Maria Theresa concludes an alliance with Russia against Prussia, for the restoration of Silesia;

16th, victorious at the Battle of Piacenza, Maria Theresa and Sardinia are able to expel the French and Spanish forces from Lombardy and Sardinia;

Antwerp falls to Marshal Saxe.

C Jul: 9th, Ferdinand VI becomes King of Spain on the death of Philip V (*–1759*);

French fleet under Labourdonnais arrives at Pondicherry.

Aug: 6th, Christian VI of Denmark dies and is succeeded by Frederick V (*–1766*).

Sep: 10th/21st, the French, under Labourdonnais and Dupleix, conquer Madras after a short siege;

20th, with the help of Flora MacDonald the Young Pretender escapes to France;

Genoa surrenders to Maria Theresa's and Sardinian forces, the French and Spanish troops having withdrawn.

D Oct: 11th, the French, under Marshal Saxe, are victorious at Raucoux and Maria Theresa loses the Austrian Netherlands.

Nov:

Dec: Genoese people revolt against Maria Theresa's forces.

E Prussia frees herself from jurisdiction of the Imperial Courts;

Persecution of Christians in China.

F Politics, Economics, Law and Education
    The College of New Jersey is founded (*Oct.* 22nd; becomes Princeton University in 1896).

G Science, Technology and Discovery
    Albert von Haller, *Disputationes Anatomicae Selectiones*, a pioneer work of anatomy, which includes his discovery of the contraction of muscles.
    Jean Étienne Guettard makes first geological map (of France).
    John Roebuck introduces leaden condensing-chambers for the manufacture of sulphuric acid.

H Philosophy, Religion and Scholarship
    Étienne Bonnot, Abbé de Condillac, *Essai sur l'origine des connaissances humaines.*
    Jonathan Edwards, *A Treatise Concerning the Religious Affections.*
    James Hervey, *Meditations and Contemplations*, vol. 1 (–1747).
    John Upton, *Critical Observations on Shakespeare.*
    The *Satires, Epistles* and *The Art of Poetry*, of Horace, translated by Philip Francis.
    The Museum started by Robert Dodsley (–1747).

J Art, Sculpture, Fine Arts and Architecture
    Painting:
        F. Boucher, *The Milliners.*
        Antonio Canaletto works in England (–1755); he paints Whitehall from Richmond House.
        Joshua Reynolds, *The Eliot Family.*

K Music
    Gluck, *Artamene* (opera) performed in London.
    G. F. Handel, *Judas Maccabaeus* (oratorio).

L Literature (including Drama)
    Christian Furchtegott Gellert, *Fabeln und Erzählungen.*

M Births and Deaths
    Jan. 12th Johann Heinrich Pestalozzi b. (–1827).
    Jan. 25th Stéphanié-Félicité du Crest de St. Aubyn, Comtesse de Genlis, b. (–1830).
    Feb. 4th Robert Blair d. (47).
    Mar. 30th Francisco José de Goya y Lucientes b. (–1828).
    May 22nd Thomas Southerne d. (86).
    July 3rd Henry Grattan b. (–1820).
    Aug. 3rd James Wyatt b. (–1813).
    Aug. 19th Marie Jeanne Bécu, Comtesse du Barry, b. (–1793).
    Sept. 28th William Jones b. (–1794).
    Nov. 1st Francis Hutcheson d. (52).
    — William Billings b. (–1800).
    — James Hook b. (–1827).

A Jan: Puysieulx succeeds D'Argenson as French Foreign Minister.
Feb:
Mar:

B Apr:
May: 4th, William IV of Orange-Nassau, grand-nephew of William III, is elected hereditary Stadtholder, Captain and Admiral-General of the seven provinces of Holland
(–1751);
29th, Prusso-Swedish Alliance of Stockholm for mutual defence, providing for military aid if either is attacked by a third party.
Jun: 17th, George II's third Parliament is dissolved;
21st/*July* 2nd, British army under the Duke of Cumberland is defeated by the French,
led by Saxe, at Lauffeldt near Maestricht, after the French invasion of Holland.
Marshal Saxe advances to take Bergen-op-Zoom;
Anglo-Russian alliance is signed, but Britain refuses to aid Russia in her war with
Sweden.

C Jul: 6th, France and Spain, having tried to relieve Genoa since *Feb.*, finally break the
combined blockade of the English fleet and troops of Maria Theresa;
19th, French force invading Piedmont is defeated at the battle of Exilles.
Aug:
Sep:

D Oct:
Nov: 10th, fourth Parliament of George II.
Dec: 10th/21st, by the Convention of St. Petersburg between Britain, Holland and Russia
the Tsar's troops are allowed to pass through Germany and Britain gives subsidies for
30,000 men (after an earlier convention of *June* 12th/23rd).

E After the murder of Nadir Shah, Ahmad Shah proclaims himself King of Afghanistan
which becomes independent of Persia.

F **Politics, Economics, Law and Education**
Benjamin Franklin, _Plain Truth_.

G **Science, Technology and Discovery**
Jean d'Alembert, _Réflexion sur la cause générale des vents_.
B. Robins first expounds, to the Royal Society, the physics of a spinning projectile.
Bradley's discoveries relating to the earth's axis.

H **Philosophy, Religion and Scholarship**
Thomas Birch, _Lives_ (-1752).
Thomas Carte, _History of England to 1654_ (-1755), 4 vols.
Étienne Fourmont, _Réflexions sur l'origine, l'histoire des anciennes peuples Chaldéens Hébreux_.
Samuel Johnson, _Plan of a Dictionary of the English Language_.
William Warburton's edition of Shakespeare 'with notes'.
Gilbert West, _Observations on the Resurrection_.
George Whitefield, _God's Dealings with George Whitefield_ (-1740).
Biographia Britannica (-1766).
Biblioteca Nazionale founded in Florence in memory of Antonio Magliabecch (d. 1714), who bequeathed his library of 30,000 volumes to the Grand Duke of Tuscany.
National Library, Warsaw, opens.

J **Art, Sculpture, Fine Arts and Architecture**
Architecture:
Bartolomeo Rastrelli reconstructs Peterhof Palace, St. Petersburg (begun by Blond; -1767).
Horace Walpole purchases Strawberry Hill.

K **Music**

L **Literature (including Drama)**
Charles Collé, _La Vérité dans le vin_ (comedy of manners; public performance prohibited).
William Collins, _Odes_ (_Odes to a Lady; Ode to Evening; How Sleep the Brave_).
David Garrick, _Miss in Her Teens; or The Medley of Lovers_ (comedy).
Christian Fürchtegott Gellert, _Die kranke Frau_ (comedy).
Thomas Gray, _Ode on Eton College_.
Samuel Johnson, _Prologue and Epilogue_ (at the opening of the Theatre in Drury Lane).
Henry Fielding's _The Jacobite's Journal_ (-1748).

M **Births and Deaths**
Jan. 19th Johann Elert Bode b. (-1826).
May 5th Leopold III b. (-1792).
Apr. 9th Simon Fraser, Lord Lovat, d. (_c._ 80).
July 6th John Paul Jones b. (-1792).
Nov. 17th Alain-René Le Sage d. (78).
Dec. 10th Duncan Forbes of Culloden d. (61).
— François Tourte b. (-1835).
— Francis Wheatley b. (-1801).

1748   Peace of Aix-la-Chapelle ends War of Austrian Succession

A   Jan: 26th, following the breakdown of preliminary peace negotiations the allies make a new treaty, for containing France.
Feb: Russian troops pass through Bohemia *en route* for the Rhine.
Mar:

B   Apr: 19th/30th, preliminary peace is signed between France and the maritime powers at a Conference at Aix-la-Chapelle.
May:
Jun: Turkey and Russia sign a treaty of neutrality.

C   Jul:
Aug:
Sep:

D   Oct: 6th/17th, French raise English siege of Pondicherry;
7th/18th, by the Peace of Aix-la-Chapelle there is a general recognition of the Pragmatic Sanction and Francis I as Holy Roman Emperor and of Frederick II's conquest of Silesia. The French evacuate the Austrian Netherlands, recognise George II as King of Great Britain and transfer Madras to England in exchange for Louisburg (Cape Breton Island). The Spanish Bourbons achieve the ambitions of their mother, Elizabeth Farnese, for Don Philip acquires Parma, Piacenza and Guastella, while Charles Emanuel III of Sardinia receives the Upper Novara and Vigevano in Milan. All other conquests are restored. France emerges from the war considerably wealthier than in 1741;
9th/20th, Spain accedes to the Treaty.
Nov: Maria Theresa and Sardinia sign treaty confirming the Peace.
Dec:

E   Shah Rukh, grandson of Nadir Shah, becomes ruler of Persia and, despite being blinded by a rival, immediately establishes his rule.

Friedrich Gottlieb Klopstock, *The Messiah* (–1773).
Samuel Richardson, *Clarissa; or The History of a Young Lady*, 7 vols. (i.e. *Clarissa Harlowe*).
Tobias George Smollett, *The Adventures of Roderick Random*, 2 vols.
James Thomson, *The Castle of Indolence*.
Marie-Thérèse Geoffrin (*née* Rodet) opens her *salon* as a literary rendezvous for the *philosophes* and the *encyclopaedistes*, other men of letters and artists of Paris.

M   **Births and Deaths**
Jan. 1st Gottfried August Bürger b. (–1794).
Feb. 15th Jeremy Bentham b. (–1832).
Mar. 11th Christian Ditley, Count Reventlow, b. (–1827).
Apr. 12th William Kent d. (63).
Apr. 13th Joseph Bramah b. (–1814).
Apr. 30th Jacques Louis David b. (–1825).
May 3rd Emmanuel-Joseph Sieyès b. (–1836).
Aug. 27th James Thomson d. (47).
Nov. 25th Isaac Watts d. (74).
Dec. 9th Claude-Louis Berthollet b. (–1822).
— Anne Bracegirdle d. (74).
— William Marshall b. (–1833).

F **Politics, Economics, Law and Education**
  [Montesquieu], *De l'esprit des lois.*
  The abolition of heritable jurisdiction in Scotland reduces the powers of Highland chiefs.

G **Science, Technology and Discovery**
  George Anson, *A Voyage Round the World*, compiled for the explorer by R. Walter.
  L. Euler's *Analysis Infinitorum*, an introduction to pure analytical mathematics.
  Thomas Lowndes founds a chair of astronomy at Cambridge University.
  John Fothergill, *Account of the Sore Throat, attended with Ulcers*, an early description of diphtheria.
  The Apothecaries' Company charter empowers them to licence apothecaries to sell medicines within seven miles of London.
  William Lewis makes a scientific investigation of the composition of ink.
  Daniel Bourn invents water-powered rollers.
  Lewis Paul invents a hand machine for wool-carding.
  Jared Eliot, *Essays on Field Husbandry in New England* (–1759).

H **Philosophy, Religion and Scholarship**
  Maria Gaetana Agnesi, *Instituzioni Analitiche.*
  Johann Jakob Bodmer, *Minnesänger.*
  Archibald Bower, *History of the Popes* (from the foundation of the See of Rome), 7 vols. (–1766).
  Thomas Edwards, *Canons of Criticism.*
  David Hume, *Philosophical Essays Concerning Human Understanding* (–1753).
  André-Joseph Panckouche, *Dictionnaire des proverbes françois et des façons de parler comiques burlesques et familières.*
  Somers Tracts ('A collection of scarce and valuable Tracts selected' from public and private libraries, 4 vols.).
  Thomas Tanner, *Bibliotheca Britannico-Hibernica.*
  Peter Whalley, *An Enquiry into the Learning of Shakespeare.*
  George Whitefield appointed Methodist chaplain by Selina, Countess of Huntingdon.
  Excavations begin at Pompeii.
  Subscription library is founded in Charleston, S. Carolina.

J **Art, Sculpture, Fine Arts and Architecture**
  Painting:
    J. F. de Troy, *Susanna and the Elders.*
    Thomas Gainsborough, *Cornard Wood.*
    William Hogarth, *Calais Gate.*

K **Music**
  The Holywell Music Room, Oxford, is opened. It is the oldest remaining music room in Europe still in regular use.

L **Literature (including Drama)**
  Robert Dodsley, *A Collection of Poems by Several Hands*, 3 vols.
  Christian Fürchtegott Gellert, *Leben der schwedischen Gräfin von G–* (a popular novel in the style of Samuel Richardson).
  Carlo Gozzi (Count), *Turandot* (drama).
  Thomas Gray, *Odes* (*On the Spring; On the Death of a Favourite Cat;* in Dodsley's *Collections*, above).

(Continued opposite)

A Jan:
   Feb:
   Mar: Prince Kaunitz, who represented Maria Theresa at Aix-la-Chapelle, further extends his influence in the Empire by proposing an alliance with France and Russia for the recovery of Silesia from Prussia.

B Apr:
   May: 11th, Consolidation Act of British Navy for the improvement of the service;
       14th, by an administrative reform Maria Theresa unites the Austrian and Bohemian Chanceries (following the death of Kinsky, the Bohemian Chancellor, in 1748).
   Jun:

C Jul: Having achieved the ambitions of the Spanish Bourbons in the Italian duchies by the Peace of Aix-la-Chapelle, Ferdinand VI of Spain severs himself from the Family Compact with France.
   Sep: Machault D'Arnnouville attempts to reform the levying of direct taxes in France.

D Oct: 22nd/*Nov*. 2nd, the first settlement is founded by the Ohio Co. (which received a royal charter in *Mar*.).
   Nov:
   Dec:

E Halifax, Nova Scotia, named after the President of the Board of Trade, the Earl of Halifax, is established as a fortress and leads to dispute with France over the respective boundaries;
   Dupleix secures French control of the Carnatic after the battle of Ambur in a war of succession in the Deccan by replacing the Nawab by his own nominee.

May 17th Edward Jenner b. (–1823).
June 19th Ambrose Philips d. (74).
Aug. 28th Johann Wolfgang von Goethe b. (–1832).
Sept. 19th Jean-Baptiste Joseph Delambre b. (–1822).
Oct. 19th William Ged d. (59).
Dec. 17th Domenico Cimarosa b. (–1801).
— Georg Voghler ('Abbé Vogler') b. (–1814).

F Politics, Economics, Law and Education

François Philidor, *Analyse des échecs*, a study of chess.

Gottfried Achenwall (1719–72), *Staatsverfassung der europäischen Reiche*, a political and statistical survey of Europe.

Giacobbo Rodriguez Pereire invents a sign language for deaf-mutes, and presents a pupil to the Paris Academy of Sciences in proof of the practical value of his method.

G Science, Technology and Discovery

G. L. L. de Buffon, *Theory of the Earth*.

Pierre Bouguer, *Figure de la terre déterminée*, an account of his ten-year operations in measuring to a degree the meridian near the equator.

Denis Diderot, *Lettre sur les aveugles à l'usage de ceux qui voient*, gives expression to the doctrine of relativity, for which he is imprisoned.

H Philosophy, Religion and Scholarship

Joseph Ames, *Typographical Antiquities*.

Henry St. John (Viscount Bolingbroke), *Idea of a Patriot King. On the Spirit of Patriotism. On the State of the Parties at the Accession of George I.*

Étienne Bonnet, Abbé de Condillac, *Traité des systèmes*.

David Hartley, *Observations on Man*.

Le Sage, *Gil Blas*, translated by Smollett.

Conyers Middleton, *A Free Inquiry into the Miraculous Powers*.

Pindar's *Odes*, translated by Gilbert West.

J Art, Sculpture, Fine Arts and Architecture

Painting:

Thomas Gainsborough, *Mr. and Mrs. Robert Andrews*.

Sculpture:

J.-B.-Pigalle, *Madame de Pompadour;* and *Children with a Bird-Cage* (marble).

Architecture:

Peter Harrison, Redwood Library, Newport, Rhode Island (–1758) and King's Chapel, Boston, Mass. (–1758).

Bartolmeo Rastrelli, Great Palace, Tsarkoie Selo (–1756).

K Music

G. F. Handel, *Music for Royal Fireworks* is performed in Green Park, London, to celebrate the Peace of Aix-la-Chapelle, by a band of 100 performers.

J. S. Bach, *Die Kunst der Fuge*.

L Literature (including Drama)

William Chetwood, *A General History of the Stage*.

Henry Fielding, *The History of Tom Jones, A Foundling*.

Samuel Johnson, *Irene* (tragedy); and *The Vanity of Human Wishes*.

Ewald Christian von Kleist, *Der Frühling* (descriptive poem influenced by James Thomson's poems –1728).

M Births and Deaths

Jan. 17th Vittorio Alfieri b. (–1803).

Jan. 24th Charles James Fox b. (–1806).

Mar. 9th Honoré Gabriel Riqueti, Comte de Mirabeau, b. (–1791).

Mar. 28th Pierre Simon, Marquis de Laplace, b. (–1827).

May 4th Charlotte Smith b. (–1806).

(Continued opposite)

A Jan:
Feb: Russian intrigues in Sweden alarm Frederick II of Prussia.
Mar:

B Apr: Anglo-French discussions on the boundary between Canada and Nova Scotia.
May:
Jun:

C Jul: 31st, Joseph I succeeds as King of Portugal on the death of John V (–1777).
Aug:
Sep: 24th/*Oct*. 5th, by treaty with Spain, England renounces the Assiento trade in return for confirmation of her other commercial rights.

D Oct: 30th/*Nov*. 10th, England accedes to Russian-Empire alliance.
Nov:
Dec:

E Spain and Portugal conclude a treaty relating to South America and in particular to exchange colonies in Paraguay and San Sacramento, which leads to a war in Paraguay lasting six years; the treaty is abrogated in 1761.

Jan. 23rd Ludovico Antonio Muratori d. (77).
Feb. 8th Aaron Hill d. (64).
May 31st Karl August von Hardenberg b. (–1822).
June 15th Marguerite De Launay, Baronne Staal, d. (65).
July 25th Henry Knox b. (–1806).
July 30th Johann Sebastian Bach d. (65).
Sept. 25th Abraham Gottlob Werner b. (–1817).
Sept. 26th Cuthbert Collingwood b. (–1810).
Nov. 30th Marshal Saxe d. (54).
— Henry William Bunbury b. (–1811).
— Richard Payne Knight b. (–1824).
— Antonio Salieri b. (–1825).
— Joanna Southcott b. (–1814).
— John Stafford Smith b. (–1836).

F **Politics, Economics, Law and Education**

Ferdinando Galiani, *Trattato della moneta*, a Mercantilist tract.

The population of Europe reaches 140,000,000.

Lord Chancellor Hardwicke tries the case Penn *v.* Baltimore, concerning the boundaries between Pennsylvania and Maryland.

The English Jockey Club is founded.

Hambledon Cricket Club is founded, playing on Broad Halfpenny Down, Hampshire.

G **Science, Technology and Discovery**

Nicolas de Lacaille leads French expedition to the Cape of Good Hope to observe 10,000 stars in the southern heavens and determines the lunar and solar parallax.

John Pringle, *Observations on the Nature and Cure of Hospital and Jayl Fevers.*

John Canton's proposals for making artificial magnets.

William Watson first describes platinum.

Stockholm Academy of Sciences and Observatory is founded.

G. Gist leads expedition to explore the Ohio River.

H **Philosophy, Religion and Scholarship**

Benedictines of Saint-Maur, *Dictionnaire de l'art de vérifier les dates des faits historiques* ('et des chartes, des chroniques et autres anciens monuments depuis la naissance de Notre-Seigneur, jusqu'à l'année 1750, par le moyen d'une table chronologique').

Frederick the Great, *Oeuvres du Philosophe de Sanssouci.*

Thomas Hobbes, *Works*, edited by J. Campbell.

L'Abbé Prevost, *Manuel lexique ; ou, Dictionnaire portatif des mots françois.*

J. J. Rousseau, *Discours sur les lettres : Sur les arts et les sciences.*

'Blue-Stocking' evening parties first held at the house of Mrs. Montagu and other literary ladies of London society.

J **Art, Sculpture, Fine Arts and Architecture**

Sculpture:

L. F. Roubiliac works in Chelsea china factory.

Landscape Gardening:

Lancelot ('Capability') Brown lays out Warwick Castle Gardens.

Architecture:

William Kent, The Horse Guards, Whitehall (–1758).

K **Music**

G. Pergolese, *The Servant as Mistress* (opera) is first performed in London (in Naples in 1777).

Johann Breitkopf first uses moveable type for printing music, in Leipzig.

L **Literature (including Drama)**

John Cleland, *The Memoirs of a Woman of Pleasure.*

Samuel Johnson, *The Rambler* started, *Mar.* 20th (–1752).

James Thomson, *Poems on Several Occasions; Works*, 4 vols. ed. by Lord Lyttelton.

First playhouse opened in New York.

Rival performances in London of Shakespeare's *Romeo and Juliet.* David Garrick's at Drury Lane; Spranger Barry's at Covent Garden.

M **Births and Deaths**

Jan. 7th Robert Anderson b. (–1830).

Jan. 10th Thomas Erskine b. (–1823).

(Continued opposite)

A Jan:
   Feb:
   Mar: 20th, Frederick Lewis, Prince of Wales, dies;
      the Calendar in Britain is altered by Act of Parliament to bring it 11 days forward (in
      Sept. 1752); henceforth *Jan.* 1st is to be the beginning of the New Year.

B Apr: 5th, Frederick II of Sweden dies and is succeeded by Adolphus Frederick, of
      Holstein-Gottorp, his brother-in-law (–1771).
   May: Pombal curbs power of the Inquisition in Portugal by decreeing that no *auto da fé*
      takes place without government approval.
   Jun: 17th, English Cabinet is reconstructed with John Carteret, Earl Granville, as Lord
      President of the Council (–1763) and Earl Holdernesse as Secretary of State.

C Jul:
   Aug: 31st, Robert Clive takes Arcot, defeating the plans of Dupleix.
   Sep: Clive defeats Dupleix at Arni and, *Nov.*, at Coveripack, relieves French pressure on
      Trichinopoly;
      13th, England joins Austro-Russian alliance of *June* 1746, aimed against Prussia.

D Oct: 22nd, on death of William IV of Holland, his widow Anne, sister of George II,
      acts as Regent for the infant heir.
   Nov:
   Dec: 12th, Lord Bolingbroke dies.

E China invades Tibet.

June 2nd John Bampton d. (61).
June 4th John Scott, later Earl of Eldon, b. (–1838).
Oct. 26th Philip Doddridge d. (49).
Oct. 30th Richard Brindsley Sheridan b. (–1816).
Dec. 12th Henry St. John, Viscount Bolingbroke, d. (73).
Dec. 26th Lord George Gordon b. (–1793).
— John André b. (–1780).
— Thomas Sheraton b. (–1806).
— Muzio Clementi b. (–1832).
— Johann H. Voss b. (–1826).

F **Politics, Economics, Law and Education**
Disorderly Houses Act in England.
Code Fredéric, drawn up by Cocceji, replaces Roman law in Prussia.
The Halifax Gazette, the first English newspaper in Canada, is issued.
École Supérieure de Guerre, an officer's training school, is founded in Paris.
Göttingen Society of Sciences is founded.
Frederick the Great, *Mémoires pour servir à l'histoire de la maison de Brandenbourg* (down to 1740).
Pennsylvania Academy founded by Benjamin Franklin (becomes College of Philadelphia, 1755, at the University in 1741).

G **Science, Technology and Discovery**
Carl Linné (Linnaeus), *Philosophia Botanica.*
J. A. von Segner discusses the idea of the surface tensions of liquids.
A. F. Cronstedt isolates nickel from niccolite.
Benjamin Franklin's experiments on electricity at Philadelphia.
Cadwallader Colden, *The Principles of Action in Matter.*

H **Philosophy, Religion and Scholarship**
Denis Diderot and Jean le Rond d'Alembert, *Encyclopédie; ou Dictionnaire Raisonné des Sciences, des Arts et des Métiers, par une société de gens de lettres,* Paris.
David Hume, *Enquiry Concerning the Principles of Morals.*
Henry Home (Lord Kames), *Essays on the Principles of Morality and Natural Religion.*
Alexander Pope, *Works,* edited by William Warburton, 9 vols. (–1757).
Society of Antiquaries, London, granted a royal charter (*Nov.* 2nd; refounded 1707).
Thomas Holles, Duke of Newcastle, as Chancellor of Cambridge University, initiates an Award of a Medal for Classical Scholarship.
James Stuart and Nicholas Revett explore the topography of Athens.
Real Academia Sevillana de Beunas Letras founded.

J **Art, Sculpture, Fine Arts and Architecture**
Painting:
François Boucher, *Toilet of Venus;* also *Recumbent Girl.*
Antonio Canaletto, the Rotunda at Ranelagh.
Arthur Devis, *Sir George and Lady Strickland.*
George Stubbs, illustrations for a textbook on midwifery; also eight panels *Fowling and Horticulture* (–1755).
Landscape Gardening:
Lancelot ('Capability') Brown, Croom Court Gardens and House.

K **Music**
Germiniani, *The Art of Playing on the Yiolin.*
G. F. Handel, *Jephtha* (oratorio).

L **Literature (including Drama)**
Henry Fielding, *Inquiry Into the Increase of Robbers.*
Thomas Gray, *An Elegy Wrote in a Country Churchyard.*
Robert Paltock, *The Life and Adventures of Peter Wilkins, a Cornish Man.*
Tobias Smollett, *The Adventures of Peregrine Pickle,* 4 vols.
Gotthold Ephraim Lessing becomes literary critic of *Vossiche Zeitung.*

M **Births and Deaths**
Mar. 29th Thomas Coram d. (*c.* 83).
May 11th Ralph Earle b. (–1801).
(*Continued opposite*)

A Jan:

Feb:

Mar: 17th, Bill to provide that Scottish estates forfeited in the '45 are to be bestowed on the Crown and the revenue is to be used for improvement of Highlands, passes the Lords, and subsequently becomes law.

B Apr: Count de Broglie is sent as French ambassador to Poland to counter influences of Austria and Russia.

May: Georgia becomes Crown province upon surrender of Charter by Trustees.

Jun: 9th, the French, before Trichinopoly, under John Law, surrender to Clive and Lawrence;

14th, the Treaty of Aranjuez between Spain and Empire to provide for mutual guarantee for their European possessions (is later joined by Sardinia, Naples and Parma).

C Jul:

Aug:

Sep: 14th, Britain adopts the Gregorian Calendar (the days *Sept.* 3rd–13th are omitted).

D Oct:

Nov:

Dec:

E The *Parlement* of Paris seizes the temporal possessions of the Archbishop of Paris.

F **Politics, Economics, Law and Education**
Manchester Royal Infirmary is founded.
David Hume, *Political Discourses*.

G **Science, Technology and Discovery**
Benjamin Franklin's lightning conductor.

H **Philosophy, Religion and Scholarship**
William Dodd, *Beauties of Shakespeare*.
Jonathan Edwards, *Misrepresentations Corrected and Truth Vindicated*.
Jean-Baptiste Ladvocat, *Dictionnaire historique portatif* (abridged from Moreri's work of 1674).
R. P. Croiset, *Reflexions Chrétiennes*.
William Law, *The Way to Divine Knowledge*.

J **Art, Sculpture, Fine Arts and Architecture**
Painting:
François Boucher, chalk portraits of Mme. de Pompadour.

K **Music**
Charles Avison 'Essay on Musical Expression' marks the beginning of musical criticism by professional musicians about their fellows.
Gluck completes his opera *La Clemenza de Tito*.
J. J. Rousseau, *The Village Soothsayer* is first performed at Fontainebleau.

L **Literature (including Drama)**
Henry Fielding, *Amelia*, 4 vols.
Henry St. John (Viscount Bolingbroke) *Letters on the Study and Uses of History*, 2 vols. (posth.).
Charlotte Lennox, *The Female Quixote*.
Christopher Smart, *Poems on Several Occasions* (including *The Hop Garden*).
The Adventurer started (*Nov.* 7th) by John Hawkesworth (contributors include Samuel Johnson and James Boswell –*Mar*. 9th, 1754).
Henry Fielding starts *The Covent Garden Journal*.

M **Births and Deaths**
Jan. 31st Gouverneur Morris b. (–1816).
Apr. 5th Sébastien Erard b. (–1831).
June 13th Fanny Burney (Frances D'Arblay) b. (–1840).
June 16th Guilio Alberoni d. (90).
July 5th Luke Hansard b. (–1828).
July 7th Joseph Marie Jacquard b. (–1834).
Aug. 18th Gaetano Filangieri b. (–1788).
Oct. 16th Johann Gottfried Eichhorn b. (–1827).
Nov. 20th Thomas Chatterton b. (–1770).
— John Nash b. (–1835).

1753   Duquesne seizes the Ohio Valley

A Jan: 11th, Ferdinand VI of Spain makes a Concordat with Pope Benedict XIV, who recognises the King's rights to patronage and appointments.
Feb:
Mar: 8th, George II assents to a land tax at the rate of 2s. in the £ in England and Wales.

B Apr:
May: Frederick the Great learns of the secret articles of the Russo-Austrian treaty of *June* 1746. Britain refuses to aid Russia and possibly prevents the incident from leading to a war. France informs Britain that if Prussia is attacked, she will be bound, under the treaty of *June* 1741, to aid Frederick the Great.
Jun: 2nd/13th, ratification of a secret convention for mutual defence between Austria, Britain and the Duchy of Modena.

C Jul: 7th, Act for the naturalisation of Jews in England, and Lord Hardwicke's Act for preventing clandestine marriages.
Aug: Duquesne, French Governor of Canada, seizes the Ohio Valley (and builds Fort Duquesne in 1754).
Sep: 18th, Board of Trade instructs governors of colonies in North America to confer with the Iroquois Indians to retain their allegiance to Britain in the face of the coming war against France.

D Oct:
Nov: Archbishop Andrew Stone of Dublin prorogues the Irish Parliament when the Opposition secures the rejection of the Money Bill. There is a public outcry against Stone and the Duke of Dorset, the Lord Lieutenant of Ireland, who is subsequently removed from office.
Dec: Dupleix holds a conference at Sadras with English representatives to reach a settlement, but he insists on being recognised as ruler of the Carnatic.

E France faces bankruptcy;
Louis XV supports the Archbishop of Paris and exiles the Paris *Parlement* in the dispute over ecclesiastical causes. The provincial *Parlements* support the Paris *Parlement*.

F **Politics, Economics, Law and Education**
Lord Hardwicke's Marriage Act in Britain ends 'Fleet Prison' and other weddings by unlicensed ministers and requires notice to be given by the calling of banns.
A private member's bill to provide for an annual census in England passes the Commons but is thrown out of the Lords.
The Jockey Club establishes a permanent race-course at Newmarket.

G **Science, Technology and Discovery**
Claude Geoffray discusses the properties of bismuth.
Carl Linné (Linnaeus), *Species Planatarum*.

H **Philosophy, Religion and Scholarship**
Georges-Louis Leclerc, Comte de Buffon, *Discours sur le style* (delivered on admission to the Académie Française).
David Hume, *Essays and Treatises on Several Subjects* (4 vols. –1756).
William Law, *Collected Works*.
Robert Lowth, *De Sacra Poesi Hebraeorum*.
Voltaire, *Essai sur les moeurs*.
The Villa dei Papiri is discovered at Herculaneum, and scrolls there are found (–1738).
Joseph Warton, Verse translation of the *Eclogues* and *Georgics*, with an edition of Virgil, edited by several hands.
British Museum Foundation Charter granted (*Apr.* 5th; *see also* 1757, 1759).
Sir Robert Bruce Cotton's Library transferred to the British Museum Library (–1700).

J **Art, Sculpture, Fine Arts and Architecture**
Painting:
William Hogarth publishes *The Analysis of Beauty* (essay).
Oudry, *The White Duck*.
Joshua Reynolds, *Commodore Keppel*.
Fine Arts:
François Boucher, 'Lever du Sol' and 'Coucher du Sol', designs for Gobelins tapestries.
Sculpture:
J.-B.-Pigalle, Tomb Maréchal de Saxe, Strasburg (–1776).

K **Music**
Haydn's Quintet 'Cassatio' in G is completed.

L **Literature (including Drama)**
Samuel Richardson, *Sir Charles Grandison*, vols. 1–4 (–1754).
Tobias George Smollett, *Ferdinand Count Fathom*.

M **Births and Deaths**
Jan. 11th Sir Hans Sloane d. (92).
Jan. 14th George Berkeley d. (67).
Mar. 9th Jean Baptiste Kléber b. (–1800).
Mar. 26th Benjamin Thompson, later Count Rumford, b. (–1814).
Mar. 27th Andrew Bell b. (–1832).
May 13th Lazare Nicolas Marguerite Carnot b. (–1823).
Aug. 12th Thomas Bewick b. (–1828).
Aug. 17th Joseph Dobrovsky b. (–1829).
Sept. 10th Sir John Soane b. (–1837).
Oct. 15th Elizabeth Inchbald b. (–1821).
Oct. 18th Jean-Jacques Régis de Cambacérès, Duke of Parma, b. (–1824).
— Tippoo of Mysore b. (–1799).
— Giovanni Viotti b. (–1824).

A Jan:
   Feb:
   Mar: 6th, Henry Pelham dies;
        18th, Pelham is succeeded as Prime Minister by the Duke of Newcastle, his brother;
        Henry Legge is appointed Chancellor of the Exchequer (*Apr*. 6th).

B Apr: 6th, George II's fourth Parliament is dissolved;
        8th, on the death of Don José Carvajal, the Marquis of Ensenada, leader of the pro-
        French faction, becomes Chief Minister in Spain (*–July*).
   May: 31st, fifth Parliament of George II meets (*–Mar*. 1761).
   Jun: 19th, Delegates from New England colonies, New York, Pennsylvania and Mary-
        land attend Albany Congress which accepts Benjamin Franklin's scheme for American
        Union; the scheme is later rejected by colonial and home governments.
        Anglo-French war breaks out in North America when a force under George Washington
        skirmishes with French troops near Fort Duquesne.

C Jul: To end the disputes on ecclesiastical affairs, which brings Paris to the verge of Civil
        War, Louis XV recalls the *Parlement*;
        the Marquis of Ensenada is dismissed in Spain, following the discovery of his intrigues
        with France.
   Aug: 3rd, Louis XVI is born;
        Anglo-French discussions in Paris (*–Dec*.) on colonial boundaries in North America.
   Sep:

D Oct:
   Nov:
   Dec: 26th, Godeheu, Director of the French East India Company, who succeeds
        Dupleix in India, abandons schemes for further French conquests.

E

Jan. 28th Ludvig Holberg d. (70).
Jan. — Jacques Pierre Brissot b. (–1793).
Feb. 13th Charles Maurice de Talleyrand-Périgord b. (–1838).
Mar. 17th Manon Jeanne Philopon (Madame Roland) b. (–1793).
Mar. 24th Joel Barlow b. (–1812).
Apr. 1st Joseph de Maistre b. (1821).
Apr. 2nd Thomas Carte d. (68).
May 6th Thomas William Coke, Earl of Leicester, b. (–1842).
May 10th Sir John Sinclair b. (–1835).
July 11th Thomas Bowdler b. (–1825).
Aug. 21st William Murdock b. (–1839).
Aug. 23rd Louis XVI b. (–1793).
Oct. 2nd Louis Gabriel Ambroise, Vicomte de Bonald, b. (–1840).
Oct. 8th Henry Fielding d. (47).
Dec. 24th George Crabbe b. (–1832).
— William Bligh b. (–1817).
— Gabriel Boffrand d. (86).
— John Wood the elder d. (50).

F **Politics, Economics, Law and Education**

Roumer, *Origine de l'Inégalité*.

John Woolman, *Some Considerations on the Keeping of Negroes*.

Society for the Encouragement of Arts and Manufactures is founded in England.

King's College, New York, founded (in 1784 becomes Columbia College).

Noel François de Wailly, *Principes généraux de la langue française* (revolutionises methods of teaching grammar in France).

Samuel Heinicke begins his school at Dresden for the deaf and dumb (removes to Leipzig 1778).

St. Andrews Royal and Ancient Golf Club founded.

G **Science, Technology and Discovery**

The Royal Society tests the arithmetical memory of Jedediah Buxton and presents him with a gratuity.

Joseph Black discovers carbonic acid gas by heating limestone, and shows that lime and magnesium, hitherto confused, are different substances.

Anton Büsching, *Erdebeschreibung* (–1761).

Charles Bonnet, *Essai de psychologue*.

H **Philosophy, Religion and Scholarship**

Thomas Birch, *Memoirs of the Reign of Queen Elizabeth*.

Étienne Bonnot, Abbé de Condillac, *Traité des sensations*.

Jonathan Edwards, *Inquiry into Freedom of the Will*.

Zachary Grey, *Notes on Shakespeare*, 2 vols.

David Hume, *History of Great Britain* (Vol. 1; only 45 copies are sold in the first year).

J. J. Rousseau, *L'inégalité parmi les hommes : discours* (–1755).

Thomas Warton, *Observations on 'The Faerie Queene'*.

J **Art, Sculpture, Fine Arts and Architecture**

Painting:

François Boucher, *Judgement of Paris* series at Hôtel de l'Arsenal for Mme. de Pompadour.

William Hogarth, *The Election*.

Sculpture:

E. M. Falconet, *Milo of Croton*.

Fine Arts:

Thomas Chippendale publishes *The Gentleman and Cabinetmaker's Directory*.

Architecture:

Bartolomeo Rastrelli, Winter Palace, St. Petersburg.

K **Music**

L **Literature (including Drama)**

Henry St. John (Viscount Bolingbroke), *Collected Works* (posth.).

Prosper Jolyot de Crébillon, *père*, *Le Triumvirat* (drama).

Salomon Gessner, *Daphnis*.

Antoine de Léris, *Dictionnaire portatif historique et littéraire des théâtres contenant l'origine des différents théâtres de Paris*.

M **Births and Deaths**

Jan. 10th Edward Cave d. (62).

Jan. 20th John Erskine, Earl of Mar, d. (57).

(Continued opposite)

A Jan: Renewed negotiations for an alliance between England and Austria (–*Aug*.).
Feb:
Mar:

B Apr: Pasquale de' Paoli is elected a general in Corsica and subsequently leads revolt against Genoa (–1769).
May:
Jun: The Landgrave of Hesse undertakes to supply Hessian mercenaries to fight for England in the defence of Hanover.

C Jul: 9th, British army under General Braddock is crushed by French near Fort Duquesne; 15th, the French ambassador is recalled from London following Boscawen's action at mouth of the St. Lawrence.
Aug: Britain ends alliance with Austria;
19th, the Austrian ambassador in Paris opens negotiations for a treaty with France.
Sep: 8th, French defeated at Lake George;
19th, Anglo-Russian Convention of St. Petersburg by which Russia is to supply troops in return for annual subsidies (ratified *Feb.* 1756).

D Oct: 20th, Russia declares she will aid any power against Prussia.
Nov: 1st, Lisbon earthquake kills 30,000 inhabitants. The British government sends a donation of £100,000;
14th, reconstruction of Newcastle's ministry with Fox as Secretary of State Southern Department and Leader in the House of Commons;
20th, Pitt is dismissed as Paymaster-General and Legge and Grenville, Treasurer for Navy, also leave ministry for opposition to Russian subsidies for the protection of Hanover.
Dec:

E

Mar. 2nd Louis, Duc de Saint-Simon, d. (80).
Mar. 6th Jean Pierre Claris de Florian b. (–1794).
Apr. 10th Samuel Christian Friedrich Hahnemann b. (–1843).
June 30th Paul François Nicolas Barras b. (–1829).
July 5th Sarah Kemble (Mrs. Siddons) b. (–1831).
July 6th John Flaxman b. (–1826).
July 13th Edward Braddock d. (60).
Aug. 4th Nicolas Jacques Conté b. (–1805).
Sept. 24th John Marshall b. (–1835).
Nov. 2nd Marie Antoinette b. (–1793).
Nov. 17th Louis XVIII b. (–1824).
Dec. 1st Maurice Greene d. (60).
— Jean Baptiste ('Anacharsis') Cloots b. (–1794).
— Joseph de Maistre b. (–1821).

F **Politics, Economics, Law and Education**

Brissot, *Recherches sur la propriété*.

R. Cantillon, *Essai sur la nature du commerce en général* founds Physiocratic School of French economists.

Benjamin Franklin, *Observations concerning the Increase of Mankind, Peopling of Countries, etc.*

Cogers Hall, a London tavern debating society founded at the White Bear Inn, Fleet Street.

Aloung P'Houra Alompra founds Rangoon.

Richard Burn, *Justice of the Peace*.

The Lisbon earthquake.

The Monitor newspaper attacks corruption at the British court.

Moscow University founded.

G **Science, Technology and Discovery**

Joseph Black, *Experiments upon Magnesia, quicklime and other alkaline substances*, gives impetus to the study of chemistry.

Menghini publishes a study of the action of camphor on various animals.

Charles Perry, *Mechanical Account and explication of the hysterical passion and of all other nervous disorders incident to the sex, with an appendix on cancers.*

Immanuel Kant, *On the Causes of Earthquakes.*

Charles Weisenthal invents a double-pointed needle, a precursor of the sewing-machine.

H **Philosophy, Religion and Scholarship**

Philip Doddridge, *Hymns*.

Francis Hutcheson, *A System of Moral Philosophy* (with a *Life*).

Samuel Johnson, *Dictionary of the English Language* (revised –1773).

Tobias George Smollett, Cervantes' *Don Quixote* translated.

Immanuel Kant presents his doctoral thesis on *The True Measure of Forces.*

Johann Joachim Winckelmann, *Gedanken über die Nachahmung der griechischen Werke.*

Library of Writers to the Signet, Edinburgh, founded.

J **Art, Sculpture, Fine Arts and Architecture**

Painting:

François Boucher, *Arninte* series.

Thomas Gainsborough, *Milkmaid and a Wood-cutter;* also *The Artist's Daughter chasing a Butterfly* (–1756).

Allan Ramsay, *The Artist's Second Wife.*

Fine Arts:

François Boucher, *La Noble Pastorale*, six designs for Beauvais tapestry.

K **Music**

David Garrick appoints Noverre ballet master at Drury Lane.

Haydn composes his first string quartet.

L **Literature (including Drama)**

Henry Fielding, *Journal of a Voyage to Lisbon* (posth.).

Gotthold Ephraim Lessing, *Miss Sara Sampson* (first domestic tragedy in German drama).

M **Births and Deaths**

Feb. 10th Charles Louis, Baron de Montesquieu, d. (66).

Feb. 16th Friedrich von Bülow, Count of Dennewitz, b. (–1816).

(*Continued opposite*)

533

A **Jan:** 16th, Treaty of Westminster between Britain and Prussia by which Frederick II guarantees neutrality of Hanover, which is designed to frustrate French attempts to seize George II's German provinces. This precipitates the Franco-Austrian *rapprochement*.
Feb: England demands a contingent of 6,000 troops from Holland.
Mar: Carvalho becomes First Minister in Portugal.

B **Apr:** Russia proposes to Austria the partition of Prussia.
May: 1st, Alliance of Versailles between France and Austria constitutes the Diplomatic Revolution, achieved by the Austrian Chancellor, Kaunitz; the Empire is to be neutral in an Anglo-French war but either party to aid the other if attacked by Prussia. In addition France is to recognise the Austrian Netherlands and to aid Austria if the latter is attacked by Turkey;
17th, Britain declares war on France;
the French take Minorca.
Jun: 4th, end of the Quaker supremacy in Pennsylvania, when six leading Quakers resign from the Assembly;
20th, Black Hole of Calcutta, in which over 120 British soldiers are imprisoned and die.

C **Jul:**
Aug: 14th, Montcalm, French commander, takes Oswego, builds forts in Illinois and drives British from the Great Lakes;
29th, Frederick II invades Saxony, on the pretext of having learnt of the Franco-Austrian alliance and subsequently takes Dresden. This marks the outbreak of the Seven Years' War. Holland and Sweden decide to remain neutral.
Sep:

D **Oct:** 1st, Frederick II fights indecisive engagement against troops at Lobositz, in Bohemia, near the Saxon border;
15th, Saxon army capitulates to Prussia at Pirna and approximately 19,000 troops are taken prisoner;
16th, Robert Clive and Admiral Watson set out towards Calcutta against the Nawab of Bengal.
Nov: 13th, fall of Newcastle ministry after Fox resigns as Secretary of State, Southern Department;
16th, the Duke of Devonshire forms ministry and
Dec: 4th, Pitt becomes Secretary of State, Southern Department;
6th, Robert Clive takes Fulta and relieves the English fugitives;
31st, Russia accedes to the Treaty of Versailles (*May*).

E

Mar. 4th Henry Raeburn b. (–1823).
Mar. 7th André Michaux b. (–1802).
Apr. — William Gifford b. (–1826).
May 6th André Masséna b. (–1817).
June 6th John Trumbull b. (–1843).
July 24th George Vertue d. (72).
July — Thomas Rowlandson b. (–1827).
Sept. 7th Willem Bilderdijk b. (–1831).
Sept. 21st John Loudon McAdam b. (–1836).
Nov. 12th Gerhard Johann von Scharnhorst b. (–1813).

F **Politics, Economics, Law and Education**
Victor, Marquis de Mirabeau, *Ami des hommes ou traité de la population*.
Burroughs *Law Reports* introduce new standards to reporting cases.
The Society of Arts stages an exhibition in London, with prizes for improvements in the manufactures of tapestry, carpets and porcelain.
Anon, *La Noblesse Commerçante*.

G **Science, Technology and Discovery**
Tobias Mayer of Göttingen draws up a catalogue of 1,000 zodiacal stars and deduces the proper motions of 80 stars for comparison with O. Römer's observations made in 1706.
M. Brisson, *Le Règne animal*.
Vienna Imperial Observatory and the Royal Society of Naples are founded.
T. Birch's *History of the Royal Society of London* (-1757).
Charles de Brosses, *Histoire des navigations aux terres australes*.
John Smeaton builds a tower on the Eddystone Lighthouse; he is the first to use dove-tailed joints for the stones.

H **Philosophy, Religion and Scholarship**
Edmund Burke, *Origin of Our Ideas of the Sublime and Beautiful* (-1757); *Vindication of Natural Society*.
Alban Butler, *Lives of the Saints*, vol. 1 (-1757-9).
Arthur Collins, *The Peerage of England* completed (since 1709).
Voltaire completes *Siècle de Louis XIV* (begun in 1735).
Samuel Johnson, *Proposals for Printing by Subscription the Dramatic Works of Shakespeare*.
Sainte-Palaye, Jean-Baptiste de la Curne de, *Projet d'un glossaire de l'ancienne langue française*.
Joseph Warton, *Essay on the Genius and Writings of Pope*, vol. 1 (-1782).

J **Art, Sculpture, Fine Arts and Architecture**
Painting:
Joshua Reynolds, *Admiral Holbourne and his Son*; also *Mrs. Francis Beckford*.
George Stubbs works on the anatomy of the horse (-1760).
Sculpture:
J. Rysbrack, *Hercules*.

K **Music**
Gluck, *Antigono* (opera) performed in Rome.
Haydn writes his Concerto in C for clavier or organ.
Leopold Mozart, *Violonschule*.

L **Literature (including Drama)**
Robert and James Dodsley, *Theatrical Records*.
Salomon Gessner, *Idyls*; and *Unkel und Yariko*.
William Mason, *Odes*.
Voltaire, *Désastre de Lisbonne*.

M **Births and Deaths**
Jan. 27th Wolfgang Amadeus Mozart b. (-1791).
Feb. 6th Aaron Burr b. (-1836).
Mar. 3rd Françoise Saucerotte (Mlle. Raucourt) b. (-1815).
Mar. 3rd William Godwin b. (-1836).
(*Continued opposite*)

18+C.E.W.

A Jan: 2nd, Clive retakes Calcutta and the Nawab subsequently concludes alliance with British;

5th, J.-F. Damiens attempts to assassinate Louis XV and is subsequently executed;

17th, Empire declares war on Prussia (and is subsequently joined by Russia, Poland and Sweden).

Feb: Russia and the Empire make a new alliance; neither to make peace until Silesia and Glatz are conquered.

Mar: 14th, Admiral Byng is shot for neglect of duty resulting in loss of Minorca (*May 1756*).

B Apr: 5th, fall of Devonshire-Pitt ministry in England;

6th, Pitt resigns, on the grounds that Cumberland refuses to take over command of the army in Germany unless Pitt resigns, as he is afraid he will not get the necessary military and financial support from him.

May: 1st, second Treaty of Versailles between France and Empire, by which Prussia is to be partitioned, losing Silesia and Glatz to the Empire and Louis XV agrees to increase annual subsidies to Maria Theresa; the Netherlands to be granted to Don Philip;

6th, Frederick II, who has invaded Bohemia, defeats Charles of Lorraine (Emperor Francis I's brother) at Prague.

Jun: 18th, Emperor's forces defeat Frederick II at Kollin and he loses 13,000 of his 33,000 troops;

23rd, Clive takes Plassey, after the Nawab breaks alliance, and recovers Calcutta;

29th, Coalition of Newcastle, First Lord of Treasury, and Pitt, Secretary of State, Southern Department.

C Jul: 26th, French, under D'Estrées, defeat British, under Cumberland, at Hastenbeck.

Aug: 9th, Montcalm takes Fort William Henry;

30th, Russian victory over Prussians at Gross Jägerndorf; Russian troops subsequently occupy East Prussia but, surprisingly, withdraw;

the Imperial army joins forces with the French under Soubise.

Sep: 8th, British under the Duke of Cumberland capitulate at Kloster Seven to Richelieu, the new French commander, and surrender Hanover and Brunswick. George II replaces Cumberland by Ferdinand of Brunswick and refuses to ratify the Convention of Kloster Seven.

D Oct: Pitt's influence increases and he subsequently rejects terms of Kloster Seven.

Nov: 5th, Frederick II defeats French and Imperial troops at Rossbach by skilful use of his cavalry;

22nd, Prince Charles of Lorraine defeats small Prussian force at Breslau.

Dec: 5th, Frederick II defeats Imperial troops at Leuthen, due mainly to deliberate flight of Württemburg battalions supporting the Emperor.

E Militia Act reduces militia in Britain to 32,340 troops.

Oct. 30th Edward Vernon d. (72).

Nov. 1st Antonio Canova b. (–1822).

Nov. 15th Jacques René Hébert ('Père Duchesne') b. (–1794).

Nov. 28th William Blake b. (–1827).

Dec. 12th Colley Cibber d. (86).

— James Gillray b. (–1815).

— Ignaz Playel b. (–1831).

— René-Antoine Ferchault de Réaumur d. (74).

— Domenico Scarlatti d. (72).

F **Politics, Economics, Law and Education**
The London Chronicle is started.
John Baskerville prints first volume in his new type at Birmingham.

G **Science, Technology and Discovery**
Roger Boscovich in *Theoris philosophiae naturalis redacta ad unicam legem virium in natura existentium* propounds an atomic theory.
Haller, *Elementa Physiologiae*.
M. Adanson, *Histoire naturelle du Sénégal*.
Dollond makes achromatic lenses.

H **Philosophy, Religion and Scholarship**
Johann Jakob Bodmer, edits *Nibelungenlied*.
Denis Diderot, *Entretiens sur Le Fils naturel*.
David Hume, Four Dissertations (including *The Natural History of Religion*); *History of Great Britain*, vol. 2.
Richard Price, *Review of the Principal Questions in Morals*.
The Royal Library is transferred to the British Museum Library (*see also* 1753, 1759).
Horace Walpole starts his Strawberry Hill Press.

J **Art, Sculpture, Fine Arts and Architecture**
Painting:
　Thomas Gainsborough, *The Artist's Daughter with a Cat* (–1758).
　J. B. S. Greuze, *La Paresseuse Italienne*; *Jeune homme accordant une Guitare*; and *Silence!*
Architecture:
　William Chambers, Casino Marino, Dublin (–1769) and The Pagoda, Kew (–1762).
　Jacques Soufflot, St. Geneviève (The Panthenon), Paris.

K **Music**
First concert is given in Philadelphia, Pennsylvania.

L **Literature (including Drama)**
John Dyer, *The Fleece*.
Christian Fürchtegott Gellert, *Geistliche Oden und Lieder*.
Thomas Gray, *Odes*.
John Home, *Douglas* (tragedy).
Friedrich Gottlieb Klopstock, *Der Tod Adams* (tragedy).
Charles Bertram forges a 14th-century English Chronicle.

M **Births and Deaths**
Jan. 9th Bernard le Bovier de Fontenelle d. (99).
Jan. 11th Alexander Hamilton b. (–1804).
Feb. 1st John Philip Kemble b. (–1823).
Feb. 28th Edward Moore d. (44).
Mar. 1st Samuel Romilly b. (–1818).
Mar. 14th John Byng d. (53).
Apr. 19th Edward Pellew, later Viscount Exmouth, b. (–1823).
May 30th Henry Addington b. (–1844).
June 5th Pierre Jean George Cabanis b. (–1808).
Aug. 9th Thomas Telford b. (–1834).
Sept. 6th Marie Joseph de Montier, Marquis de La Fayette, b. (–1834).
Oct. 26th Heinrich Friedrich Karl von Stein b. (–1831).

(*Continued opposite*)

A Jan: Russians retake East Prussia which has been left defenceless as Prussian army is required elsewhere for winter campaign.
Feb:
Mar:

B Apr: 11th, London Convention, by which Britain grants annual subsidy to Prussia of £670,000 and a British army is to be maintained in Germany.
May: 3rd, Pope Benedict XIV dies and is succeeded by Clement XIII (–1769);
   8th, Frederick the Great invests Olmütz, but is forced to abandon the siege.
Jun: 23rd, the French are defeated at Crefeld by Ferdinand of Brunswick;
   30th, Prussian blockade of Olmütz since *May* 8th is ended after defeat of Prussian convoys by Imperial troops at Domstadtl.

C Jul: 8th, Abercromby is defeated in an attempt on Ticonderoga;
   26th, British, under James Wolfe and Jeffrey Amherst, take Louisburg.
Aug: 14th, 8,500 English troops join Ferdinand of Brunswick;
   25th, undecided battle of Zorndorf between Prussians, led by Frederick the Great, and Russian troops under Fermor, but
   27th, Russian troops withdraw.
Sep: 3rd, revolution in Portugal, led by Marquis of Tavora and his wife, who wound King Joseph, but plotters soon arrested.

D Oct: 5th, Austrians begin siege of Neisse (relieved by Frederick the Great, *Nov.*);
   14th, Austrian victory at Hochkirch against Prussia, in a fog.
Nov: 25th, John Forbes and George Washington take Fort Duquesne, which is subsequently renamed Pittsburg;
   the Duke of Choiseul becomes French Foreign Secretary, in succession to Cardinal Bernis;
   British conquer French Senegal.
Dec: 30th and 31st, Secret Treaty of Paris whereby France is to continue to maintain troops in Germany and to subsidise Empire until Emperor regains Silesia and Glatz; Lally advances against Madras.

E Robert Clive becomes Governor of Bengal, as President of ruling council of 10 members;
The Dutch capitulate to Clive at Chinsura;
China occupies East Turkestan.

F **Politics, Economics, Law and Education**
Quesnai, *Tableau Économique.*
Emerich de Vattel, *Le Droit des gens.*
The various Sergeants' Inns of Court in London are amalgamated to form Serjeants
Inn (–1877).
Sir William Blackstone is appointed first Vinerian Professor of Law at Oxford.

G **Science, Technology and Discovery**
Jedediah Strutt invents a ribbing-machine for the manufacture of hose.

H **Philosophy, Religion and Scholarship**
Elizabeth Carter's translation of *Epictetus.*
Claude Adrien Helvétius, *De l'esprit* (published, condemned, publicly burnt but
'everybody read it').

J **Art, Sculpture, Fine Arts and Architecture**
Painting:
François Boucher, *The Mill at Charenton*; also *Jesus and St. John.*
Allan Ramsay, *Dr. William Hunter.*
Sculpture:
J.-B. Pigalle, *Love and Friendship.*
Architecture:
John and Robert Adam, Harewood House (–1771).

K **Music**

L **Literature (including Drama)**
Denis Diderot, *Le père de famille* (drama).
Salomon Gessner, *Tod Abels.*
Samuel Johnson, *The Idler* (Universal Chronicle; weekly; –1760; 2 vols. collected
1761).
Jonathan Swift, *The History of the Four Last Years of the Queen.*

M **Births and Deaths**
Jan. 7th Allan Ramsay d. (71).
Mar. 9th Franz Joseph Gall b. (–1828).
Mar. 22nd Jonathan Edwards d. (54).
Apr. 4th John Hoppner b. (1810).
Apr. 28th James Monroe b. (–1831).
May 6th Maximilien François Robespierre b. (–1794).
Sept. 29th Horatio Nelson b. (–1805).
Oct. 11th Heinrich Wilhelm Matthias Olbers b. (–1840).
Oct. 15th Johann Heinrich von Dannecker b. (–1841).
Oct. 16th Noah Webster b. (–1843).
Nov. 25th John Armstrong b. (–1843).
Dec. 25th James Hervey d. (44).
— Samuel Whitbread b. (–1815).

A Jan: 13th, the Marquis of Tavora and his wife are executed in Portugal.
Feb: French, under Lally, abandon siege of Madras (since *Dec.* 1758) on arrival of
British fleet.
Mar:

B Apr: 8th, English take Masulipatam;
13th, French victory at Bergen near Frankfurt.
May:
Jun:

C Jul: 23rd, Russians under Saltikóv defeat Prussians at Kay and one quarter of Prussian
army of 27,000 is lost.
Aug: 1st, French are decisively defeated at Minden by Ferdinand of Brunswick;
10th, Ferdinand VI of Spain dies and is succeeded by Charles III (formerly Charles IV
of Naples, which passes to his nine-year-old son Ferdinand);
12th, Russian and Austrian troops, led by Laudon, defeat Frederick II at Kunersdorf,
and Dresden falls into Austrian hands;
17th, Boscawen defeats French off Cape St. Vincent.
Sep: 3rd, expulsion of Jesuits begins in Portugal as a result of the conspiracy of 1758;
the Russians retire into Poland;
18th, British victory at Quebec, but both Montcalm and Wolfe (who scaled the Heights
of Abraham, 13th) are killed.

D Oct:
Nov: 20th, Royal Navy under Admiral Hawke defeats French at Quiberon Bay;
21st, Prussian army of von Finck capitulates at Maxen.
Dec: Dublin riots by Protestants who, on learning of rumour of union with Britain, sack
the Parliament House.

E Eyre Coote succeeds Stringer Lawrence as British Commander in Madras.

M Births and Deaths
Jan. 25th Robert Burns b. (–1796).
Apr. 14th George Frederick Handel d. (74).
Apr. 19th August Wilhelm Iffland b. (–1814).
Apr. 27th Mary Wollstonecraft Godwin b. (–1797).
May 6th François Guillaume Andrieux b. (–1833).
May 28th William Pitt b. (–1806).
June 12th William Collins d. (38).
Aug. 12th Ewald Kleist d. (44).
Aug. 24th William Wilberforce b. (–1833).
Sept. 13th James Wolfe d. (32).
Sept. 14th Louis Joseph, Marquis Montcalm de Saint Veram, d. (46).
Oct. 22nd Thomas Cooper (b. –1840).
Oct. 25th William Wyndham Grenville b. (–1834).
Oct. 26th Georges Jacques Danton b. (–1794).
Nov. 10th Johann Christoph Friedrich von Schiller b. (–1805).
Dec. 25th Richard Porson b. (–1808).
— Friedrich August Wolf b. (–1824).

F **Politics, Economics, Law and Education**

The Annual Register is first issued, edited by Robert Dodsley and Edmund Burke (remains under Burke's control to 1788).

Étienne de Silhouette, French Controller-General of Finances, is forced to resign through public outcry at his land tax; his surname becomes synonymous for a figure reduced to its simplest form.

Giovanni, Count of Carli-Rubbi, *Ragionamento sopra i bilanci economici delle nazioni*.

The Public Ledger, a daily paper, is issued in London.

G **Science, Technology and Discovery**

Alexis Clairault and Jean Bailly calculate the perihelion of Halley's comet. Observations of the return of the comet verify Newton's law.

John Winthrop IV, *Lectures on Comets*.

Franz Aepinus, *Tentamen Theoriae Electricitatis et Magnetesmi* (St. Petersburg).

C. F. Wolff, *Theoria generationis*.

Bavarian Academy of Science is founded.

H **Philosophy, Religion and Scholarship**

Thomas Francklin, translation of the *Tragedies* of Sophocles.

Alexander Gerard, *An Essay on Taste*.

Oliver Goldsmith, *An Enquiry into the Present State of Polite Learning in Europe*.

David Hume, *History of Great Britain*, vols. 3 and 4.

Richard Hurd, *Moral and Political Dialogues*.

Gotthold Ephraim Lessing, *Die Litteraturbriefe* (–1765).

Charles-Louis Richard, *Dictionnaire universel dogmatique, canonique, historique, géographique and chronologique des sciences ecclesiastiques*, 5 vols. (–1765).

William Robertson, *The History of Scotland, 1542–1603*.

Adam Smith, *Theory of Moral Sentiments*.

Edward Young, *Conjectures on Original Composition*.

British Museum opened (*Jan.* 16th).

J **Art, Sculpture, Fine Arts and Architecture**

Painting:

J. B. Greuze, *Portrait of the Bookseller, François Babuti*.

William Hogarth, *Sigismunda*.

Joshua Reynolds, *James 7th earl of Lauderdale*.

Architecture:

John and Robert Adams, Interiors, Kedleston Hall.

Peter Harrison, Synogogue, Newport, Rhode Island (–1763).

William Chambers publishes, *Treatise on Civil Architecture*.

K **Music**

L **Literature (including Drama)**

Thomas Godfrey, *The Prince of Parthia* (tragedy) written.

Edward Hyde, Earl of Clarendon, *Life* (by himself) (posth.).

Samuel Johnson, *Rasselas*.

Gotthold Ephraim Lessing, *Philotas* (tragedy).

Voltaire, *Candide*.

Thomas Wilkes, *A General View of the Stage*.

Oliver Goldsmith, *The Bee*, numbers 1–8 (*Oct.* 6th–*Nov.* 24th).

(*Continued opposite*)

A   Jan: 22nd, French are defeated by Eyre Coote at Wandewash.
Feb: 25th, Robert Clive leaves India, to return to England.
Mar:

B   Apr: 1st, treaty between Austria and Russia, to provide for assistance in continuation of
war against Prussia.
May:
Jun: 23rd, Prussian army at Landshut, guarding the passes into Silesia, suffers crushing
defeat.

C   Jul: 26th, Laudon takes the Silesian fortress of Glatz from the Prussians.
Aug: 15th, Frederick II, against all odds, defeats Austrian forces at Leignitz.
Sep: 8th, British troops under Jeffrey Amherst take Montreal, and control Canada;
Russian and Swedish troops ravage Pomerania, while Imperial troops occupy Saxony
and Halle.

D   Oct: 9th–13th, Russians burn Berlin which is occupied by them, together with Imperial
troops, until Frederick's advance from Silesia, but he is forced to allow them to retreat
unmolested;
25th, George II dies and is succeeded by his grandson George III (–1820), then aged 22.
Nov: 3rd, Frederick II defeats Austrian troops under Daun at Torgau, and the Austrians
evacuate all Saxony except Dresden.
Dec:

E   Jacobus Coetsee leads a party of Hottentots beyond the Orange River;
Secret treaty between English East India Company and Mir Kassem, who becomes Nawab
of Bengal.

Sept. 14th Maria Luigi Cherubini b. (–1842).
Sept. 29th William Beckford b. (–1844).
Oct. 21st Hokusai b. (–1849).
— Marie Tussaud b. (–1850).

F Politics, Economics, Law and Education

Lawrence Shirley, 4th Earl of Ferrers, is the last nobleman in England to suffer a felon's death for murder (*May* 5th).

Portsmouth dockyard is destroyed by fire.

Thomas Braidwood opens in Edinburgh the first school in Britain for teaching the deaf and dumb (visited by Dr. Johnson, –1773; later transferred to Hackney, London).

G Science, Technology and Discovery

M. Brisson, *Ornithologie*.

P. Lyonnet's monograph on the goat-moth caterpillar.

John Smeaton devises a cylindrical cast-iron bellows for smelting iron.

William Oliver first makes 'Bath Oliver' biscuits.

The silk hat is invented in Florence.

H Philosophy, Religion and Scholarship

Giuseppe Baretti (friend of Dr. Johnson), *Italian and English Dictionary*.

Francis Fawkes, *The Works of Anacreon, Sappho, Bion, Moschus and Musaeus*, translated.

J Art, Sculpture, Fine Arts and Architecture

Painting:

Thomas Gainsborough, *Mrs. Philip Thicknesse*.

Angelica Kauffman, *Allegory, Music and Painting*.

Joshua Reynolds, *Georgiana, Countess of Spencer and her daughters*.

Saint-Aubin, *La Parade de Boulevarde*; and *Le Boulevarde*.

Architecture:

Robert Adam, Interior, Syon House (–1769).

Peter Harrison, Christchurch, Cambridge, Mass.

K Music

W. Boyce publishes his collection of Cathedral Music (–1778).

Haydn composes his symphonies No. 2 in C, No. 3 in G, No. 4 in D and No. 5 in A about this time.

Noverre, *Letters on Dancing and Ballets*. Noverre is appointed ballet master at Stuttgart.

L Literature (including Drama)

Denis Diderot writes *La Religieuse* (not published until 1790).

Oliver Goldsmith, *Citizen of the World* (in *The Public Ledger*, from *Jan.* 24th to *Aug.* 14th, 1761; –1762).

Charles Johnstone, *Chrystal; or, The Adventures of a Guinea*.

George, 1st Baron Lyttelton, *Dialogues of the Dead*.

James Macpherson ('Ossian'), *Fragments of Ancient Poetry* (–1762).

Laurence Sterne, *Sermons* (of 'Mr. Yorick') (–1769); *Tristram Shandy* (vols. 1 and 2) (–1767).

M Births and Deaths

Jan. 24th Lavinia Fenton d. (52).

Mar. 2nd Lucie Camille Desmoulins b. (–1794).

Mar. 28th Pegg Woffington d. (*c*. 46).

Mar. 28th Thomas Clarkson b. (–1846).

Apr. 13th Thomas Beddoes b. (–1808).

May 16th Claude Joseph Rouget de Lisle b. (–1836).

May 12th John Bannister b. (–1836).

(Continued opposite)

A Jan: 7th, Afghans defeat Mahrattas at Paniput;
   16th, Eyre Coote takes Pondicherry after a siege (since *Sept.* 1760) and this marks the
   end of French dominion in India.
Feb:
Mar: 19th, formal dissolution of George II's fifth Parliament;
   25th, the Earl of Bute is appointed Secretary of State, Northern Department, as successor to the Earl of Holdernesse.

B Apr:
May:
Jun: Henrik Hop leads a further expedition beyond Orange River.

C Jul:
Aug: 15th, third Family Compact between France and Spain guaranteeing the possessions of the Bourbon powers. Spain is to declare war if no peace is concluded by *May*
   1st, 1762; any enemy of one party is the enemy of the other; additional clauses relate
   to commerce.
Sep: Choiseul opens peace negotiations, 17th (–19th);
   Pitt fails to carry the Cabinet in continuing the war.

D Oct: 5th, Pitt resigns as Secretary of State, Southern Department, because of the opposi-
   tion of George III, a supporter of Bute. He is succeeded by Charles Wyndham, Earl of
   Egremont;
   Austrian troops under Laudon take Schweidnitz and blockade Frederick II at Bunzel-
   witz.
Nov: 3rd (–*Mar.* 10th, 1768), first Parliament of George III meets.
Dec: 16th, Russians take Kolberg, thus gaining a harbour which enables them to keep a
   fleet in communication with Russia and with the arms depôt at Pillau.

E Ieharu becomes Shōgun in Japan;
   Whiteboys societies founded in Ireland, due to discontent caused by evictions, after value
   of pasture land has soared because of murrain of cattle in England and on the Continent.

J.-J. Rousseau, *Julie; ou La Nouvelle Héloïse* started (–1765).
Benjamin Victor, *History of the Theatres of London and Dublin.*
In *May* Oliver Goldsmith moves to Fleet Street and is visited there by Dr. Johnson.

M **Births and Deaths**
   Jan. 10th Edward Boscawen d. (49).
   Jan. 29th Albert Gallatin b. (–1849).
   Feb. 9th Johann Ludwig Dussek b. (–1812).
   Feb. 16th Charles Pichegru b. (–1804).
   Apr. 9th William Law d. (75).
   Apr. 17th Benjamin Hoadly d. (84).
   May 3rd August von Kotzebue b. (–1819).
   May — John Opie b. (–1807).
   June 7th John Rennie b. (–1821).
   June 18th Nicholas Anselme Baptiste b. (–1830).
   July 4th Samuel Richardson d. (72).
   July 18th Thomas Sherlock d. (83).
   Aug. 17th William Carey b. (–1834).
   Nov. 13th Sir John Moore b. (–1809).
   Nov. 30th John Dollond d. (55).

F **Politics, Economics, Law and Education**
J. P. Süssmilch makes pioneer study of the science of statistics.
Robinet, *De La Nature*.
The Society of Arts stages an exhibition of agricultural machinery in London.
New York Assembly insists that judges in the colony should hold office during good behaviour, instead of during pleasure.

G **Science, Technology and Discovery**
Leopold Avenbrugger in *Inventum novum* describes his method of recognising diseases of the chest by percussion.
The French government found a veterinary school at Lyons.
Canton shows the compressibility of water.
James Brindley completes the Duke of Bridgwater's Canal between Manchester and the Worsley collieries.
Duhamel du Monceau first issues a catalogue of new manufactures and inventions approved by the French Academy of Sciences (–1788).
The Danish government sponsors an expedition under C. Niebuhr to explore Arabia (–1763).

H **Philosophy, Religion and Scholarship**
Paul Heinrich Dietrich, Baron d'Holbach, *Le Christianisme dévoilé* (wrongly attributed in some translations to Nicholas Antoine Boulanger).
Henry Home (Lord Kames), *An Introduction to the Art of Thinking*.
Samuel Johnson's edition of *The English Works of Roger Ascham* (with Johnson's *Life of Ascham*).
Voltaire, *Works*, translated by Smollett and others (–1774).

J **Art, Sculpture, Fine Arts and Architecture**
Painting:
François Boucher, *A Girl and a Bird-catcher*.
Anton Mengs, Parnassus; Villa Albani, Rome.
George Stubbs, *The 2nd Duke and Duchess of Richmond watching horses exercising*.
Sculpture:
L. F. Roubiliac, *Religion*.
J. Rysbrack, *Flora*.
Architecture:
Robert Adams, Interior, Osterley Park (–1780).
Peter Harrison, Brick Market, Newport, Rhode Island (–1772).
Landscape Gardening:
Lancelot ('Capability') Brown, Bowood gardens.

K **Music**
Peal of 'Plain Bob Major', 40,320 changes, is rung at Leeds, Kent, by 14 men in 27 hours, the record for tower bells.
Angiolini produces Gluck's *Don Juan* (ballet) in Vienna.
T. Arne, *Judith* (oratorio) is performed in London.
Haydn probably completes his symphonies No. 6 in D ('Le Matin'), No. 7 in C ('Le Midi') and No. 8 in G ('Le soir et la tempeste').
Haydn is engaged as second kapellmeister to Paul Esterházy of Galántha on *May* 1st.

L **Literature (including Drama)**
Charles Churchill, *The Rosciad*.
George Colman, *The Jealous Wife* (comedy).
Carlo Goldoni, *Una delle ultime sere di Carnevale* (comedy).
Samuel Johnson, *The Idler*, 2 vols. (since 1758).
(*Continued opposite*)

1762　Peace preliminaries at Fontainebleau

A　Jan: 4th, Britain declares war against Spain and Naples;
　　5th, Tsarina Elizabeth of Russia dies and is succeeded by Peter III (*–July*), who aims at peace.
　　Feb:
　　Mar:

B　Apr: Britain ceases to subsidise Prussia.
　　May: 5th, Treaty of St. Petersburg between Russia and Prussia, whereby Russia restores all conquests and forms a defensive and offensive alliance;
　　22nd, peace between Sweden and Prussia by Treaty of Hamburg;
　　26th, the Duke of Newcastle resigns and the Earl of Bute becomes First Lord of the Treasury;
　　Spanish invasion of Portugal, after Portuguese refuse to accept Franco-Spanish note ordering them to close ports to British ships and to remain neutral in war. The Spanish subsequently take Braganza and Almeida.
　　Jun: 8th, Russo-Prussian alliance against Austria is formally concluded.

C　Jul: 17th, Peter III is assassinated and is succeeded by Catherine II (–1796). Panin becomes Chief Minister;
　　21st, Frederick II defeats Austrian forces at Burkersdorf.
　　Aug:
　　Sep:

D　Oct: 29th, battle of Freiburg, in which Austrian troops are defeated by Prince Henry—the only battle won by Prussia without the personal command of Frederick II.
　　Nov: 1st, the French capitulate at Cassel and evacuate the right bank of the Rhine;
　　3rd, peace preliminaries of Fontainebleau are signed between France, Spain and Britain. Under its terms (1) Britain secures Canada, Nova Scotia, Cape Breton, St. Vincent, Tobago, Dominica, Grenada, Senegal and Minorca from France, and Florida from Spain; (2) France regains Martinique, Guadeloupe, St. Lucia and Goree and is guaranteed fishing rights off Newfoundland; (3) the French settlements in India are restored, but no fortifications are to be built there; (4) Spain acquires Louisiana from France, exchanges Florida for Havana and recovers Manila and the Philippines; France retains New Orleans (confirmed by the Peace of Paris, *Feb.* 10th, 1763);
　　24th, truce between Prussia, Saxony and Empire.
　　Dec: 9th, Pitt attacks the terms of the Peace in the Commons.

E　During the year Britain captures the following colonies: St. Vincent, by General Monkton, Martinique (*Feb.* 12th), Grenada (*Mar.* 10th), Havana (*Aug.* 14th) and Manila (*Oct.* 6th).

F **Politics, Economics, Law and Education**

J.-J. Rousseau, *Du Contrat Social; ou principes du droit politique*.
[Gouttes and Turgot], *La Théorie de l'Intérêt de l'Argent*.
First British settlement in New Brunswick, at Maugerville on the St. John River.
Matthew Boulton opens Soho Engineering works at Handsworth Heath, Birmingham.
The 'Cock Lane Ghost' hoaxes Londoners.
Robert Lowth, *Introduction to English Grammar*.
The Briton, ed. Tobias Smollett (–1763).
The North Briton, ed. by John Wilkes and Charles Churchill (–1763).

G **Science, Technology and Discovery**

John Roebuck devises method for converting cast iron into malleable iron at his Carron ironworks in Stirlingshire.
John Harrison claims the Board of Longitude's prize for an accurate chronometer for use at sea which determines the longitude within 18′ (he is paid £20,000 in 1773).

H **Philosophy, Religion and Scholarship**

George Campbell, *Dissertation on Miracles*.
Henry Home (Lord Kames), *The Elements of Criticism*.
David Hume, *History of Great Britain* (to 1688) 6 vols. (–1778).
Richard Hurd, *Letters of Chivalry and Romance*.
John Parkhurst, *Hebrew and English Lexicon*.
James Stuart and N. Revett, *The Antiquities of Athens, measured and delineated*.
C. M. Wieland, Seventeen Plays of Shakespeare, translated into German (–1766; the first German version).
The Library of the Sorbonne, Paris, founded; Annapolis Circulating Library opened.
Samuel Johnson is granted a Crown civil list pension of £300 a year.

J **Art, Sculpture, Fine Arts and Architecture**

Painting:
　　François Boucher, *A Sleeping Girl and a Gardener*; also *A Girl and a Shepherd*.
　　Joshua Reynolds, *Garrick between Comedy and Tragedy*.
　　George Stubbs, *Mares and Foals*.
　　Giovanni Tieppolo, frescoes in Madrid Palace.
　　Johann Zoffany, *Garrick in 'The Farmer's Return'*.

K **Music**

C. Gluck, *Orpheus and Eurydice* (opera) is first performed in Vienna in Italian.
St. Cecilia Society (founded in Charleston, South Carolina, –1912).
W. A. Mozart and his sister (aged 6 and 10) begin touring Europe giving keyboard concerts.
T. Arne, *Artaxerxes* (opera), is performed in London.
J. J. Rousseau, *Pygmalion* (opera; performed in 1770).

L **Literature (including Drama)**

Count Gustaf Philip Creutz, *Atis och Camilla* (Swedish idyll).
Denis Diderot, *Le Neveu de Rameau* (–1773).
William Falconer, *The Shipwreck*.
Henry Fielding, *Works*, ed. by Arthur Murphy, 4 vols.
Carlo Goldoni, *Le Baruffe chiozzotte* (comedy of the lower classes).
Oliver Goldsmith, *The Citizen of the World*, 2 vols. (–1760).
James Macpherson ('Ossian'), *Fingal*.
Tobias George Smollett, *Sir Launcelot Greaves*, 2 vols.
Edward Young, *Resignation*.

Rousseau, Du Contrat Social—Child's Orphan and Daughter

A Politics, Economics, Law and Education

J.-J. Rousseau, Du Contrat Social, on treatise on state politics.

Catherine II (—1796), czarina of Russia.

First turnpike erected in New Brunswick, or Maidenville in the Sir John Rivett

Mathew lindon pays Soho engineering works at Handsworth Heath, Birmingham.

The Cock Lane Ghost delves mademania.

Robert Lowth, Introduction to English Grammar.

Tom Brown, ed., Tobias Smollett (—1763).

The North Briton, ed. by John Wilkes and Charles Churchill (—1763).

C Science, Technology and Discovery

John Roebuck devises method for converting cast iron into malleable iron at his Carron

ironworks in Stirlingshire.

John Harrison, Clock, the H and the Longitude's prize for an accurate chronometer

that measures which determines the longitude within of the is position correctly.

D Philosophy, Religion and Scholarship

Gaspar Campbell, Observations on Miracles.

Henry Home (Lord Kames), The Elements of Criticism

Lord Home, History of Great Britain (to 1688) (1 vols.) (—1763).

Richard Hurd, Letters on Chivalry and Romance.

John Perkins, Liturgy and English Litanies.

Imm. Kant and Rousseau, Observations of the Beautiful and Sublime.

Al. Ireland, Seventeen Days of Shakespeare, translated into German (—1766, the

first German version).

The Library of the Sorbonne, Paris, founded; Annapolis Circulating Library opened;

Samuel Johnson is granted a Crown civil list pension of £300 a year.

E Art, Sculpture, Fine Arts and Architecture

Painting

Frances Boucher, Shoofor, Oise and Cytheris; plan of Earl Curton's Shepherd.

Indian Reynolds, portrait of Lady Sarah Bunbury and Treasury.

Horace Stubbs, Mares and Foals.

Grosvenor Tiepolo, frescoes in Madrid Palace.

Johann Zoffany, Cazariel and The Farmer's Return.

F Music

J.C. Gluck, Orpheus und Eurydice (Orfeo), a first performance first opera in Italian.

S. Cecilia Society founded in Charleston, South Carolina—1710.

W. A. Mozart and his sister (aged 6 and 10) begin touring Europe as five keyboard

wonders.

T. Arne, Artaxerxes (opera), is performed in London.

J.-J. Rousseau, Pygmalion (opera) performed in 1762.

G Literature (including Drama)

Giambattista Philip Crevitz, the late Canelia (Swedish idyll).

Denis Diderot, Le Neveu de Rameau (pr.).

William Falconer, The Shipwreck.

Henry Fielding, Works, ed. by Arthur Murphy, 5 vols.

Carlo Goldoni, Baruffe chiozzotte (comedy of the lower class).

Oliver Goldsmith, The Citizen of the World, 2 vols. (—1760).

James Macpherson (?), Poems, Fingal.

Franz Grillparzkalet, Sir Launcelot Greaves, 4 vols.

Edward Young, Resignation.

M **Births and Deaths**

Jan. 5th Elizabeth, Empress of Russia d. (52).
Jan. 11th Louis François Roubiliac d. (57).
Feb. 3rd Richard ('Beau') Nash d. (87).
Mar. 9th William Cobbett b. (–1835).
Apr. 10th Giovanni Aldini b. (–1834).
Apr. 29th Jean Baptiste Jourdan b. (–1833).
May 19th Johann Gottlieb Fichte b. (–1814).
June 6th George Anson d. (65).
June 17th Prosper Jolyot de Crébillon d. (80).
July 13th James Bradley d. (69).
July 28th George Bubb Doddingdon d. (71).
Aug. 3rd Stanislas Pontiatowski d. (85).
Aug. 21st Lady Mary Wortley Montagu d. (73).
Sept. 24th William Lisle Bowles b. (–1850).
Oct. 15th Samuel Holyoke b. (–1820).
Oct. 30th André de Chenier b. (–1794).
Nov. 1st Spencer Perceval b. (–1812).

INDEX

The scheme of this Index is described in the Introduction, pp. ix, x. Attention is drawn here to the main series of Subject Entries, in some cases running to several pages.

Nationalities of Persons are abbreviated as follows:

Am. American
Aus. Austrian
Da. Danish
Du. Dutch
E. English
F. French
Flem. Flemish
G. German
Ir. Irish
It. Italian

Pol. Polish
Port. Portuguese
R. Russian
Sc. Scottish
Sp. Spanish
Swe. Swedish
Swi. Swiss
Turk. Turkish
We. Welsh.

INDEX

A

Aachen (Aix-la-Chapelle), W. Germany, 1502 B, 1520 D, 1614 C, 1656 C; Protestants expelled from, 1560 A; Protestants control, 1582 C; Catholicism re-introduced, 1598 B
Aaran, Treaty of, 1712 C
Abauzit, Firman, F. philosopher and natural scientist (1679–1767), 1679 M
Abbadie, Jakob, Swi. theologian (1654–1727), 1684 H
Abbas I, Shah of Persia (1586–1629), 1586 E, 1590 E
Abbas II, Shah of Persia (1642–67), 1642 E
Abbaye of the Holy Ghost, The (Rolle), 1496 H
Abbott, George, E. churchman, Archbishop of Canterbury (1562–1633), 1611 A, 1618 C, 1621 B, 1633 C, M
Abdalis, ruler of Herat, 1717 E
Abdullah, Mir, ruler of Kandahar, 1715 E, 1717 E
Abdullah II, Uzbek ruler, 1590 E
Abencerraje y de la Hermosa Jarifa, 1565 L
Abercromby, David, Sc. physician, 1685 G
Abercromby, Sir Ralph, E. soldier (1734–1801), 1734 M
Aberdeen, Scotland, 1494 F, 1605 C
Aberdeen, Earl of. *See* Gordon
Abington, Frances, E. actress (1737–1815), 1737 M
Åbo (later Tunku), Finland, university, 1640 F
Abrabanel, Isaac, Jewish philosopher (1437–1508), 1508 M
Abraham, Heights of, Canada, 1759 D
Abrégé chronologique (de Mézeray), 1667 H
Abridgement of English Laws (M. Bacon), 1736 F
Abridgement of the Year Books (Fitzherbert), 1516 F
Abruzzi, Italy, 1500 D
Absalom and Achitophel (Dryden), 1681 L, 1682 L
Abyssinia, travels to, 1710 G
Academies, etc.
America, American Philosophical Society, 1743 G
Denmark, Royal Society of Denmark, 1742 G
England. *See* Royal Society, The
France, Académie de Poésie et de Musique, 1570H
Académie des Inscriptions, 1701 H
Académie des Inscriptions et Belles Lettres, Paris, 1663 H
Académie des Jeux floraux de Toulouse, 1694 H
Académie des Sciences, Paris, 1666 G
manufactures approved by, 1761 G
Académie des Sciences, Belles Lettres et Arts, de Bordeaux, 1712 H

Académie des Sciences, Belles Lettres et Arts, de Lyon, 1700 H
Académie des Sciences, Belles Lettres et Arts, de Marseilles, 1726 H
Académie du Palais, Paris, 1576 H
Académie Française, 1635 F
expulsion from, 1718 G
reports to, 1719 G
sponsors expedition to Lapland, 1736 G
Académie Nationale de Musique, Paris, 1669 K
Académie Royale, 1683 J
Académie Royale de Danse, Paris, 1661 K
Germany, Academy of Science, Berlin, 1700 G, 1740 F
Academy of Science, Göttingen, 1751 F
Bavarian Academy of Science, 1759 G
Naturae Curiosi, 1652 G
Holland, Academy of Rhetoric (Egelantier), Amsterdam, 1578 H, 1617 H
Italy, Accademia degli Innominati, Padua, 1550 F
Accademia del Cimento, Florence, 1657 G
Accademia della Crusca, Florence, 1582 H, 1612 H
Accademia dell'Arcadia, Rome, 1690 H
Accademia de Scienze, Lettere ed Arti, Palermo, 1718 H
Accademia di Scienze, Lettere ed Arti, Lucca, 1584 H
Accademia Nazionale dei Lincei, Rome, 1603 G
Academy of Fine Arts, Florence, 1550 J
Royal Society, Naples, 1756 G
Scientific Academy, Naples, 1560 G
Russia, Academy, Kiev, 1589 F
Spain, Academia, Barcelona, 1729 H
Academia, Sevillana, 1751 H
Academia, Valencia, 1592 H
Royal Spanish Academy, Madrid, 1613 E
Sweden, Academy of Science, Stockholm, 1750 G
Acadia (later Nova Scotia), French settlement in, 1604 F; 1613 E; Scottish settlements in fail, 1632 E; England acquires, 1667 C; France recovers, 1697 C; ceded to Britain, 1713 A
Acadia Island, Nova Scotia, expedition to, 1707 B
Accesi, The (Commedia dell'arte), 1590 L
Accoramboni, Vittoria, It. adventuress (1557–85), 1557 M, 1585 M
Account of the Sore Throat, attended by Ulcers (Fothergill), 1748 G
Accra, Gold Coast, forts at, 1672 F
Achenwall, Gottfried, G. political economist (1719–72), 1749 F

553

B

Baptiste, Nicolas Anselme, F. actor (1761–1835), 1761 M
Baptism of Christ (Bellini), 1501 J
Baptism of Christ (El Greco), 1612 J
Baptism of Christ (Reni), 1623 J
Baptists. *See* Religious Denominations
Bar, in Podolia, Russia, 1735 D
Baracoa, Cuba, 1514 F
Barbados: claimed by England, 1605 E; settlements in, 1624 E, 1625 F
Barbar, Mogul Emperor of India (1482–1530), 1526 B, 1530 M; invades Punjab, 1525 E; defeats Hindu Confederacy, 1527 A
Barbarossa, Turkish corsair, 1534 B, 1535 B, 1538 E, 1544 B
Barbary States, of Tunis and Algiers, founded, 1518 E. *See also under* Piracy
Barberini, Maffeo, It. Pope Urban VIII (1568–1644), 1568 M, 1644 M; election, 1623 C
Barbour, John, Sc. poet (?1316–95), 1570 L
Barcelona, Spain: revolts in, 1533 C, 1640 B; aid to prevent fall of, 1694 B; British take, 1705 D; siege raised, 1706 B; French and Spaniards storm, 1714 C; Academy founded, 1729 H
Barcelona, Treaties of, 1493 A, 1529 B
Barclay, Alexander, Sc. poet and translator (1476–1552), 1509 H, 1520 H, 1552 M
Barclay, John, Sc. satirist (1582–1621), 1582 M, 1621 M
Barclay, Robert, Sc. apologist for Quakers (1648–90), 1678 H
Bardi, Count, It. patron of music, 1581 K
'Barebones Parliament', 1653 C
Barents, William, Du. navigator (*c.* 1547–97), 1596 G, 1597 M
Baretti, Giuseppe, Marc Antonio, It. author and critic (1719–89), 1760 H
Barium sulphide, discovered, 1602 G
Barletta, Italy, siege of, 1502 D
Bar lines in music, 1523 K
Barlow, Joel, Am. poet and politician (1754–1812), 1754 M
Barnard, John, E. musician, 1641 K
Barnfield, Richard, E. poet (1524–1627), 1574 M, 1627 M
Barometer, The:
Torricelli's, 1642 G
pendant, 1695 G
Baronage of England, The (Dugdale), 1675 H
Baronetage, the, founded, 1611 F
Baronetage of England, The (Collins), 1720 H
Baronius, Cesare, It. church historian, cardinal and Vatican librarian (1538–1607), 1588 H, 1596 H
Barras, Paul François Nicolas, F. politician (1755–1829), 1755 M
Barrel-organ-player by a Cottage (van Ostade), 1640 J
Barros, João de, Port. historian (1496–1570), 1552 H, 1570 M
Barrowe, Henry, E. Puritan (*c.* 1550–93), 1589 H, 1593 A, M
Barrow, Isaac, E. mathematician and divine (1630–77), 1630 M, 1677 M, 1678 H, 1683 H
Barry, James, E. artist (1741–1806), 1741 M
Barry, Marie Jeanne Béan, Comtesse du, F. adventuress (1746–93), 1746 M
Barry, Spranger, Ir. actor (1719–77), 1719 M, 1750 L
Bartas, Du. F. poet (1544–90), 1578 L, 1605 H
Bartenstein, Johann Christoph, Aus. chancellor (1689–1767), 1736 B
Barthélemy, Jean Jacques, F. author and numismatist (1716–95), 1716 M

Bartholomew Fayre (Jonson), 1614 L, 1631 L
Barton, Elizabeth ('The Maid of Kent'), E. nun (1506–28), 1528 M, 1534 B
Barwalde, Treaty of, 1631 A
Bashful Lover, The (Massinger), 1655 L
Basil III, Tsar of Russia (1504–33), 1504 E, 1514 B, 1533 E
Basil IV, Tsar of Russia, 1505 E
Basile, Giambattista, It. poet and authority on folklore (?1575–1632), 1632 L
Basilikon Doron (James VI), 1599 F
Basing House, Hampshire, England, seige, 1645 D
Baskerville, John, E. typographer (1706–75), 1706 M, 1757 F
Basle, Switzerland, 1513 J, 1572 G; joins Swiss Confederation, 1501 E; University, 1527 G
Basle, Peace of, 1499 C
Bastard, The (Savage), 1728 L
Bastidas, de, Sp. explorer, 1501 G
Bastwick, John, E. physician (1593–1654), 1637 B, F
Batavia (now Jakarta, Indonesia): founded, 1619 F; Tasman's voyage from, 1642 G
Bate, John, E. merchant, 1606 F, 1610 A
Bath, Somerset, England: Beau Nash at, 1704 F; Queen's Square, 1729 J; Wood's plans for, 1727 J
Bath, Earl of. *See* Pulteney, W.
Bath of Diana (Boucher), 1742 J
'Bath Oliver' biscuits, 1760 G
Báthory, Andrew, of Moldavia, deposed, 1599 E
Báthory, Gabriel, Prince of Transylvania, 1613 D
Báthory, Sigismund, Prince of Transylvania (1572–1613), 1613 M
Báthory, Stephen, Prince of Transylvania, 1571 A; as King of Poland, 1575 D
Batrachomyomachia (trans. Chapman), 1624 H
Battle of Alcazar (Peele), 1594 L
Battle of Alexander (Altdorfer), 1529 J
Battle of Carnival (Breughel), 1559 J
Battle of the Books (Swift), 1704 L
Battle of the Frogs and Mice, 1624 H
Bauer, George. *See* Agricola
Bauhin, Jean, F. botanist, 1650 G
Bavaria: joins Schmalkaldic League, 1531 D; accession of Duke William, 1579 D; church in, Concordat with Papacy, 1583 E; William V governs with his son Maximilian, 1591 D; accession of Maximilian I, 1597 E; elector is outlawed, 1706 B; restoration of elector, 1714 A
Bavarian Royal Library, 1558 H
Baxter, Richard, E. Puritan (1615–91), 1615 M, 1650 H, 1657 H, 1691 M
Bayard, Pierre ('the Chevalier Bayard'), F. soldier (1473–1524), 1524 B, M
Bayazid II, Sultan of Turkey (1447–1512), 1512 B, M
Bayazid, son of Sultan Suleiman I, 1559 B
Bayerische Chronik (Aventinus), 1566 H
Bayeux, France, 1589 D
Bayle, Pierre, F. philosopher, lexicographer and theologian (1647–1706), 1647 M, 1682 G, 1684 H, 1686 H, 1697 H, 1706 M, 1717 H
Bayonne, France, 1523 D, 1565 B, 1638 B
Bay Psalm Book (Eliot), 1640 H
Beachy Head, Sussex, England, battle off, 1690 B
Béarn, France, 1620 D; Spanish designs on, 1585 A; annexed to French Crown, 1592 E; restoration of Roman Catholicism, 1617 B; Louis XIII enters, 1620 C
Beaton, David, Sc. cardinal, Regent and Archbishop of St. Andrews (1494–1546), 1494 M, 1524 C, 1538 D, 1539 A, D, 1543 C; deposed from Regency, 1543 A; burns Wishart, 1546 A; assassinated, 1546 B, M

Bower, Archibald, Sc. theologian (1686–1766), 1748 M

Bowes, Sir George, E. administrator (1517–66), Warden of the East March, 1542 C

Bowles, William Lisle, E. poet (1762–1850), 1762 M

Bowman, Christopher, E. coffee-house owner, 1652 F

Bowood, Wiltshire, England, gardens, 1761 J

Boyars, in Russia, 1564 B

Boyce, William, E. musician (1710–79), 1710 M, 1737 M

Boyer, Abel, F. Huguenot (1667–1729), 1702 H

Boyle, Richard, Earl of Cork, E. politician (1566–1643), 1566 M, 1643 M

Boyle, Robert, E. natural philosopher (1627–91), 1627 M, 1645 G, 1659 G, 1662 G, 1663 G, 1665 G, 1675 G, 1680 G, 1691 M

Boyle, Roger, Earl of Orrery, E. novelist and dramatist (1621–79), 1668 L

Boyle's Law, independent discovery of, 1676 G

Boyne, Ireland, Battle of, 1690 C

Bracegirdle, Anne, E. actress, 1748 M

Bracton, Henry de, E. jurist (d. 1268), 1569 H

Braddock, Edward, E. soldier (1695–1755), 1695 M, 1755 M; defeated near Fort Duquesne, 1755 C

Bradford, Yorkshire, England, Cavaliers lose, 1643 A

Bradford, William, E. colonial governor and historian (1590–1657), 1590 M, 1657 M; as Governor of Plymouth Colony, 1621 B

Bradley, James, E. astronomer (1693–1762), 1693 M, 1728 G, 1747 M, 1762 M

Bradshaw, Henry, E. Benedictine monk of Chester (1450–1513), 1513 M, 1521 H

Bradshaw, John, E. regicide (1602–59), 1602 M, 1659 M

Bradstreet, Anne, E. author, 1650 L, 1678 L

Brady, Nicholas, E. cleric and author (1659–1726), 1659 M, 1696 H, 1726 M

Braemar, Aberdeenshire, Scotland, Jacobite rising at, 1715 C

Braganza, Catherine of. See Catherine of Braganza

Brahe, Tycho, Dan. astronomer (1546–1601), 1546 M, 1569 G, 1575 G, 1598 G, 1601 M, 1602 G

Braidwood, Thomas, Sc. educationalist, 1760 F

Bramah, Joseph, E. engineer (1748–1814), 1748 M

Bramante, Donato d'Augnolo, It. architect and artist (1444–1514), 1492 J, 1503 J, 1506 J, 1514 M, 1546 J

Brandenburg, Germany: becomes a Lutheran state, 1524 A; secularization of the duchy under Polish suzerainty, 1525 B; accession of Joachim II, 1535 C; Joachim II becomes a Protestant, 1539 A; war with Turkey, 1542 B; treaties for succession in, 1563 D, 1571 C; accession of Joachim Frederick, 1598 A; agreement of Hohenzollerns for succession in electorate and margravate, 1599 B; John Sigmund becomes a Calvinist, 1613 D; Capital is removed to Konigsberg, 1678 C; finances expedition to West Africa, 1680 E

Brandon, Charles, Duke of Suffolk (c. 1484–1545), E. soldier and politician 1530 A, 1536 D; marries Mary, sister of Henry VIII, 1515 A; ravages Normandy and Picardy, 1522 C, 1523 C, D

Brandt, Sebastian, G. satirical poet (1458–1521), 1494 L

'Bras-de-fer'. See Noue, F. de la

Braunsberg, Sweden, 1629 C

Bray, Thomas, E. divine and philanthropist (1656–1730), 1698 F

Brazil: coastline, explored, 1499 G, 1500 G, 1531 G; hereditary captaincies in, 1533 F; revolt in, 1645 E; Dutch driven from, 1654 F; Dutch-Portuguese war, 1657 E; retained by Portugal, 1661 E

Breadalbane, Earl of. See Campbell, J.

Brecht, Lewin, Du. Jesuit and dramatist, 1555 L

Breda, Holland, 1624 A; falls to Maurice of Nassau, 1590 A; Spinola takes, 1625 B; Dutch re-capture, 1637 D

Breda, Compromise, of, 1566 B

Breda, Conference of, 1575 B

Breda, Declaration of, 1660 B

Brederode, Henry, Count of, Du. leader, 1566 B

'Breeches' Bible, 1560 E

Breisach, Bad.-Württemberg, West Germany: Saxe-Weimar takes, 1638 D; France obtains, 1648 D; surrender of, 1654 A; Louis XIV obtains from Empire, 1679 A; Chamber of Reunion meets, 1679 D; Parliament at, 1680 A; Chamber of Reunion claims Alsace for France, 1680 C; France surrenders, 1697 D

Breisgau, Bad.-Württemberg, West Germany, 1631 C, 1638 B

Breitenfeld, Saxony, West Germany, battle, 1642 D

Bremen, West Germany, 1530 D, 1629 A, 1648 D; rising in, 1530 E; Danes occupy, 1712 C; Duchy to be sold by Denmark to Hanover, 1715 B; Hanover purchases, 1719 D

Brenner Pass, on Austro-Italian border of Alps, 1551 B

Brentford, Middlesex, England, 1642 D

Bréquigny, Louis Georges Oudard Fendrix de, F. scholar (1714–95), 1714 M

Brescia, Lombardy, Italy: French capture, 1512 A; Imperialist claims to, 1516 C; Ursuline Order in, 1535 F; music in, 1562 K

Breslau, Poland, 1527 B, 1693 F; University, 1695 F; Prussia to receive, 1741 B; Frederick II takes, 1741 C; battle at, 1757 D

Breslau, Treaties of, 1741 B, 1742 A

Bresse, France, French gain, 1601 A

Brest, France: naval action off, 1512 C; Spanish loose hold on, 1594 D; defeat of British expedition to, 1694 C

Brevarium Romanum, 1568 H

Breviate of the Prelates intolerable Usurpations (Prynne), 1637 H

Brewster, William, Am. colonial leader (1566–1644), 1644 M

Briati, Giuseppe, It. manufacturer of glass, 1736 G

Bribery, in English elections, 1695 A, B

Bridges, notable:
  London, 1581 G
  Purana Pul, 1593 G
  Rialto, Venice, 1587 G

Bridges, overseers of French, 1720 F

Bridgwater, Somerset, 1645 C

Bridgwater, Duke of. See Egerton, F.

Bridgwater, Duke of, Canal, 1761 F

Briefe and True Report of . . . Virginia (Hariot), 1588 G

Brief Historicall Relation of State Affairs (Luttrell), 1678 H

Brief History of Muscovia (Milton), 1682 H

Brief History of the Succession to the Crown of England (Somers), 1689 F

Brief Observations Concerning Trade and the Interest of Money (Child), 1668 F

Brief Rule . . . in Small Pocks or Measles (Thatcher), 1678 G

Brieg, Germany, 1675 E, 1741 B

Brienne, Étienne. See Loménie de Brienne

Brieven der Heilighe Maeghden (Vondel), 1642 L

Briggs, Henry, E. mathematician (1561–1630), 1624 G

Bright, Timothy, E. author (c. 1551–1615), 1588 F

Brill, Holland, 1585 C; Beggars of the Sea capture, 1572 B; England restores to Holland, 1616 B

Brindisi, Italy, Ferdinand I captures, 1509 B
Brindley, James, E. engineer (1716–72), 1716 M, 1761 G
Brinvilliers, Marie, Marquise de, F. poisoner (c. 1630–76), 1676 M
Brisson, Mathurin Jacques, F. zoologist (1723–1806), 1723 M, 1756 G, 1760 G
Brissot, Jacques Pierre, F. politician (1754–93), 1754 M
Brissot de Warville, Jan Pierre, F. economist, 1755 F
Bristol, Somerset, 1497 G; Prince Rupert takes, 1643 C; surrenders to Fairfax, 1645 C
Bristol, Earl of. *See* Digby
Bristol, Treaty of, 1574 C
Britannia (Camden), 1586 H, 1610 H, 1695 H
Britania's Pastorals (Browne), 1613 L, 1616 L
Britannicus (Racine), 1669 L
British Librarian, The (Oldys), 1737 H
British Museum, London, 1753 H, 1759 H. *See also under* London
Brittany, France, 1492 D, 1493 A, 1504 C, 1506 B; is united with Crown of France, 1547 E
Britton, Thomas, E. concert-promoter, 1678 K
Broad Halfpenny Down, Hampshire, England, cricket on, 1750 F
Broglie, Victor François, Duke of, F. soldier (1718–1804), 1752 B
Broken Heart, The (Ford), 1633 L
Brombery, Treaty of, 1657 D
Brome, Richard, E. dramatist (d. 1652), 1640 L, 1659 L
Brömsebro, Peace of, 1645 C
Brömsebro, Treaty of, 1570 D
Bronzino, Angelo (*alias* Agnolo Allori), It. artist (1503–72), 1503 M, 1525 J, 1503 J, 1545 J, 1572 M
Brooke, Sir Fulke Greville, first baron. *See under* Greville
Brooke, Henry, Lord Cobham, E. conspirator (d., 1619), 1603 C
Broome, William, E. scholar and poet (1689–1745), 1689 M, 1745 M
Brosse, Salomon de, F. architect (c. 1562–1626), 1613 J, 1615 J, 1616 J, 1618 J, 1619 J
Brosses, Charles de, F. navigator, 1756 G
Brother Paravicino (El Greco), 1609 J
Brown, John, Sc. chemists (d. 1736), 1683 G
Brown, Lancelot ('Capability'), E. landscape-gardener (1716–83), 1716 M, 1750 J, 1751 J, 1761 J
Browne, Robert, E. puritan, founder of the Brownists (c. 1550–1633), 1580 H, 1604 H, 1633 M
Browne, Sir Thomas, E. physician and author (1605–82), 1605 M, 1643 L, 1646 L, 1658 F, L, 1682 M, 1686 L
Browne, William, E. poet (?1590–1645), 1613 L, 1616 L
Bruant, Liberal, F. architect (d. 1697), 1671 J
Bruce, James, Sc. explorer (1730–94), 1730 M
Brue, André de, F. colonial explorer, 1697 E
Brueghel, Jan, Du. artist (1668–1725), 1668 M
Brueghel, Pieter, Du. artist (1525–69), 1525 M, 1559 J, 1560 J, 1562 J, 1563 J, 1564 J, 1565 J, 1566 J, 1567 J, 1568 J
Bruges, Belgium, 1584 B, 1615 D
  canal to Dunkirk, 1622 G
  cathedral, art in, 1502 J
Bruges, Treaty of, 1521 C
Brühl, Heinrich, Count von, G. statesman (1700–63), 1700 M
Brun, Charles Le, F. architect (1619–90), 1662 J, 1679 J, 1683 J, 1690 M

Brunei, Borneo, Portuguese at, 1522 G
Brunkeberg, Germany, 1497 D
Bruno, Giordano, It. philosopher and author (c. 1548–1600), 1583 H, 1584 H, 1585 H, 1591 H, 1600 M
Brunschwig, Jerome, G. scientist, 1500 G
Brunswick, W. Germany, 1531 A; duchy is sequestered by Schmalkaldic League, 1542 C; Duke Henry is restored, 1547 C; Tilly joins Wallenstein at, 1626 C; Technical College, 1745 F; British surrender, 1757 C
Brunswick–Luneburg, Duke of, G. prince, becomes a Lutheran, 1524 A
Brus, The (Barbour), 1570 L
Brussels, Belgium, 1566 B, 1577 B, C, D, 1631 E, 1632 C, 1633 D; postal services in, 1505 F; Charles V resigns government to Philip of Spain at, 1555 D; Archduke Ernest arrives at, 1594 A; rising in, suppressed, 1633 D; bombardment of, 1695 C; surrender of, 1746 A
Brussels, Treaties of, 1516 A, 1522 A
Brutus (Michelangelo), 1540 J
Bry, Theodorus ('Dirk') de, G. engraver and publisher (1528–98), 1528 M, 1598 M
Bruyère, Jean de la, F. essayist and novelist (1645–96), 1645 M, 1688 H, 1696 M
Buade, Louis de. *See* Frontenac
Bucaniers of America, History of (Esquemeling), 1684 H
Bucer, Martin, G. religious reformer (1491–1551), 1524 E, 1551 M
Buch von der deutschen Poeterey (Opitz), 1624 H
Buchanan, George, Sc. humanist (1506–82), 1506 M, 1582 H, M
Buckhurst, Lord. *See* Sackville, T.
Buckingham, Duke of. *See* Villiers, G.
Bucquoy, Count de, Aus. soldier, 1618 C
Budapest (Buda), Hungary, 1529 D, 1541 C, 1544 B; Imperial Diet at, 1527 D; taken by Charles of Lorraine, 1686 C
Budé, Guillaume (Budaeus), F. humanist and philologist (1467–1540), 1508 H, 1529 H, 1540 M, 1547 F
Buenos Aires, Argentina, founded, 1536 G
Buffier, Claude, F. philosopher and educationalist (1661–1737), 1661 M, 1717 H, 1737 M
Buffon, George Louis, Comte de, F. naturalist (1707–88), 1707 M, 1749 G, 1753 H
Bugey, France, 1601 A
Bulgaria: Louis of Baden occupies, 1689 C; Turks reoccupy, 1690 D
Bull, John, E. musician (1563–1623), 1563 M, 1610 K, 1611 K, 1628 M
Bulls, Papal:
  Council of Trent, to summon, 1544 D
    for resumption of, 1550 D
  Cum ad nihil, 1531 D
  Cum ex apostolatus, 1559 A
  Detestabilis, forbids usury, 1586 F
  Exsurge, is burnt by Luther, 1520 D
  Inter cetera, 1493 B
  Regimini militantis ecclesiae, 1540 C
  Regnans in excelsis, 1570 E
  Unigenitus, causes rift in France, 1730 C
  Zelo domus dei, 1648 D
Bulls, Papal, forbidden to be brought into England, 1571 B
Bullinger, Heinrich, Swi. religious reformer (1504–75), 1504 M, 1536 H, 1566 H, 1575 M
Bülow, Friedrich Wilhelm von, Count of Dennewitz, Pruss. general (1755–1816), 1755 M
Bunch of Violets (Dürer), 1502 J

Bunyan, John, E. religious leader and author (1628–88), 1628 M, 1656 H, 1665 H, 1666 H, 1671 H, 1678 H, 1680 H, 1682 H, 1684 H, 1688 M

Bunzelintz, Poland, Frederick II blockaded at, 1761 D

Buoncompagno, Ugo, It. churchman (1502–85), Pope Gregory XIII, 1502 M, 1585 M; elected Pope, 1572 B

Burbage, James, E. actor and theatre-builder (c. 1530–97), 1576 L, 1597 L

Burbage, Richard, E. actor (1567–1619), 1567 M, 1619 M

Buren, Maximilian van, Count of Egmont, Flem. soldier (d. 1548), 1546 C

Burford, Oxfordshire, England, Levellers at, 1649 B

Bunbury, Henry William, E. caricaturist (1750–1811), 1750 M

Bürger, Gottfried August, G. poet (1748–94), 1748 M

Burghley, Lord. See Cecil, W.

Burgi (—), It. mathematician, 1611 G

Burgos, Spain, 1506 C, 1528 A; cathedral, 1519 J

Burgoyne, John, E. general and dramatist (1722–92), 1722 M

Burgundy, France, 1506 B, 1521 C; Francis I promises to surrender to Charles V, 1526 A; revolt in, 1595 B

Burke, Edmund, E. author and politician (1729–97), 1729 M, 1756 H, 1759 F, H

Burkesdorf, E. Germany, battle, 1762 C

Burial of Count Orgaz (El Greco), 1586 J

Burlador de Sevilla y convidado de Piedra, El (de Molina), 1630 L

Burlington, Richard Boyle, Earl of, E. architect (1694–1753), 1717 J, 1722 J, 1725 J, 1731 J

Burman, Pieter, the elder, Du. classical scholar (1668–1741), 1668 M, 1741 M

Burn, Richard, E. legal writer (1709–85), 1755 F

Burnaby, William, E. dramatist and translator (?1672–1706), 1694 H

Burnet, Gilbert, E. churchman, historian and Tory politician, Bishop of Salisbury (1643–1715), 1643 M, 1679 H, 1693 J, 1699 H, 1715 M, 1723 H, 1724 H

Burnet, Thomas, E. theologian and writer on cosmology (1635–1715), 1631 H, 1683 H

Burnet, William, E. Governor of New York colony (d. 1729), 1720 E

Burney, Charles, E. musicologist (1726–1814), 1726 M

Burney, Frances (Madame D'Arblay), E. novelist and diarist (1752–1840), 1752 M

Burning of Books. See under Persecution

Burns, Robert, Sc. poet (1759–96), 1759 M

Burr, Aaron, Am. politician (1756–1836), 1756 M

Burrough, Stephen, E. merchant, 1556 G

Burrows, Sir John, E. seaman (c. 1559–1620), 1592 C

Burton, Henry, E. Independent (1578–1648), 1637 B, F

Burton, Robert, E. author (1577–1640), 1621 H, 1640 M

Busby, Richard, E. schoolmaster (1606–95), 1606 M, 1695 M

Büsching, Anton, Aus. scientist, 1754 G

Bussy D'Ambois (Chapman), 1607 L

Bussy-Rabutin, Roger, Comte de, F. author (1618–93), 1665 L

Bute, Earl of. See Stuart, J.

Butler, Alban, E. Catholic hagiographer (1710–73), 1756 H

Butler, Charles (d. 1647), E. naturalist, 1609 G

Butler, James, Earl of Ormonde, Ir. politician (1610–88), 1610 M, 1649 A, 1688 M

Butler, Joseph, E. divine and moral philosopher (1692–1752), 1692 M, 1726 H, 1736 H, 1752 M

Butler, Samuel, E. satirist (1612–80), 1612 M, 1662 L, 1663 L, 1678 L, 1680 M

Butter, Nathaniel, E. journalist, 1638 F

Buxtehude, Dietrich, Da. musician (1637–1707), 1637 M, 1673 K, 1705 K, 1707 M

Buxton, Jedediah, E. prodigy (1707–72), 1754 G

Buyazid II, Sultan of Turkey (1481–1512), abdicates, 1512 B

Buys, Paul, Du. lawyer, Advocate of Holland (1531–94), 1572 C

Byng, George, Viscount Torrington, E. admiral (1663–1733), 1733 D; defeats Spanish fleet off Cape Passaro, 1718 C

Byng, John, E. admiral (1704–57), 1704 M, 1757 A, M

Byrd, William, E. musician and poet (1543–1623), 1543 M, 1563 K, 1572 K, 1575 K, 1588 K, 1589 K, 1607 K, 1610 K, 1611 K, 1623 M, 1641 K

Byrd, William, Am. (1674–1744), 1728 F, 1737 B

Bysshe, Edward, E. anthologist, 1702 H

C

Cabal Ministry, 1667 C

Cabanis, Pierre Jean George, F. physiologist (1757–1808), 1757 M

Cabbalah, The (Reuchlin), 1494 H, 1517 H

Cabinet-making, directory of (Chippendale), 1754 J

Cabot, John, It. navigator (1450–98), 1498 M; commissioned by Henry VII, 1496 A; discovers Newfoundland, 1497 G

Cabot, Sebastian, E. navigator (1474–1557), 1496 A, 1526 G, 1527 F

Cabral, Perálvarez, Port. explorer, 1500 G

Caccini, Giulio, It. musician, 1602 K

Cadamosto, Alvise, Port. navigator, 1507 G

Cadillac, Antoine de la Mothe, sieur, F. colonial governor of Louisiana (1656–1730), founds Detroit, 1701 E

Cadiz, Spain, 1656 C, 1694 D; Drake sacks, 1587 B; expeditions to, 1596 B, 1625 D; failure of British expedition to, 1702 C

Caedmon, Anglo-Saxon poet (d. ?680), edition of extant mss. of, 1655 H

Caerwys, Wales, Eisteddfod at, 1568 F

Caesar, Sir Julius, E. politician and judge (1558–1636), Chancellor of Exchequer, 1612 B

Cagliostro, Alessandro, Count, It. alchemist and impostor (1743–95), 1743 M

Cairo, Egypt, 1517 A, 1719 G

Caius, John, E. physician (1510–73), 1510 M, 1555 G, 1573 M

Cajetano, de Plaisance, It., Cardinal, 1494 H

Calabria, S. Italy, 1500 D; taken by Spanish, 1501 C

Calais, France, 1518 D; English wool staple at, 1493 C, 1528 A; Lisle's arrest at, 1540 B; French capture, 1558 A; to remain in French hands, 1559 B; England renounces claim to, 1564 B; Spanish Armada at Calais Roads, 1588 C; Spanish capture, 1596 B; restored to France, 1598 B; is bombarded, 1696 A

Calais, Conference of, 1521 C

Calais, Treaty of, 1570 C

Calais Gate (Hogarth), 1748 J

Calamy, Edmund, E. Puritan (1600–66), 1600 M, 1666 M

Calandria, La (Dovizi), 1513 L

Calasanza, Joseph, It. Catholic educationalist, 1607 H

Calculation, manuals on, 1522 F, 1537 F

Carter, Elizabeth, E. translator and blue-stocking (1717–1806), 1717 M, 1758 H

Carter, William, E. author of commercial tracts, 1671 F

Cartaret, John, Earl of Granville, E. statesman (1690–1763), 1690 M; dismissed from secretaryship of state, 1724 B; appointed lord lieutenant of Ireland, 1724 D; re-appointed secretary of state, 1742 A; falls from office, 1744 D; is unable to form administration, 1746 A; appointed lord president of council, 1751 B

Carthage, North Africa, 1534 B

Cartier, Jacques, F. explorer and navigator (1491–1557), 1534 G, 1535 G, 1557 M

Cartography, trigonometrical triangulation for, 1617 G; charts with lines of equal magnetic variation, 1700 G. See also Maps, Notable

Cartoon, Political, earliest, 1499 G

Cartwright, Edmund, E. inventor of power loom (1743–1823), 1743 M

Cartwright, John, E. Parliamentary reformer (1740–1824), 1740 M

Cartwright, Thomas, E. Puritan minister (c. 1535–1603), 1603 M

Cartwright, William, E. cleric and dramatist (1611–43), 1639 L, 1651 L

Carvajal, Luis de ('El Mozo'), Mexican Jew (1567–96), 1596 H

Carvalho, Marquis de. See Pombal

Carver, John, E. Pilgrim Father, first Governor of Plymouth Colony (c. 1575–1621), 1620 D, 1621 B, M

Cary, Lucius, Viscount Falkland, E. soldier (c.1610–43), 1643 M

Casa Contratacion, founded in Spain, 1503 A

Casale, Italy: under seige, 1629 E, 1694 B; French take, 1681 C; Savoy regains, 1696 C

Casanatense, Cardinal, It., 1698 H

'Casanova' (Giovanni Jacopo Casanova de Seingalt), It. adventurer (1725–98), 1725 M

Casas, Bartolomé de Las, Sp. churchman ('Apostle of the Indies', 1566–91), 1566 M

Casaubon, Isaac, F. (naturalised E.) classical scholar and theologian (1559–1614), 1559 M, 1587 H, 1614 M

Casaubon, Méric, E. divine and scholar (1599–1671), 1634 H

Cascarido, Vincenzio, It. chemist, 1602 G

Case is Altered, The (Jonson), 1609 L

Casimir IV, of Poland (1447–92), 1492 B

Casimir, John. See John Casmir

Casket Letters, The, 1567 B, 1568 D

Caslon, William, E. printer and type-founder (1692–1766), 1734 H

Cassandre (de la Calprenède), 1642 L

Cassel, W. Germany, battles, 1677 D, 1762 D

Cassini, Giovanni Dominico, It. astronomer (1625–1712), 1625 M, 1665 G, 1667 G, 1671 G, 1684 G, 1712 M

Castagna, Giovanni Battista, It. (1521–90), elected Pope Urban VII (1521–90), 1521 M, 1590 C, M

Castel, Louis, F. scientist and mathematician (1688–1757), 1740 G

Castel Gandolfo, Italy, church, 1658 J

Castel of Love, The (trans. Berners), 1540 H

Castell, Edmund, E. orientalist (1606–85), 1669 H

Castelleto, Italy, 1528 D

Castellion, Sebastian, F. humanist (1515–63), 1542 F, 1554 H

Castiglione, Baldassare, Count, It. diplomat and author (1478–1529), 1528 F, 1561 H

Castille, Spain, 1523 C; death of Queen Isabella,

1504 D; Spanish Navarre is annexed, 1515 C; revolt in, 1520 C

Cast-iron, Roebuck's method for, 1762 G

Castle Howard, Yorkshire, England, 1699 J, 1729 J

Castle of Indolence, The (Thomson), 1748 L

Castle of Knowledge, The (Recorde), 1551 G

Castro, War of, 1644 A

Castro, John de, Viceroy of Portuguese India, 1545 E

Catacombs, in Rome, 1578 H

Catalogi librorum manuscriptorum Angliae et Hiberniae (Bernard), 1697 H

Catalogue of English Books (Maunsell), 1595 H

Catalogue (of Most Vendible Books in England) (London), 1658 H

Catalogus stellarum australium (Halley), 1679 G

Catalonia, Spain: revolts in, 1640 B, 1652 E; French retire to, 1643 D; French conquests are restored to Spain, 1678 C

Catania, Sicily, battles, 1676 B, 1677 B

Catch as Catch Can (Hilton), 1652 K

Cateau–Cambrésis, Peace Conference and Treaty, 1559 A, B

Caterpillars, study of, 1760 G

Catesby, Robert, E. conspirator (1573–1605), 1605 D

Cathay, the search for, 1603 G. See also North-West Passage

Catherine I, Empress of Russia (1725–7), 1725 A, 1727 B

Catherine II ('The Great'), Empress of Russia (1762–96), 1729 B, M, 1762 C

Catherine de' Medici, Queen consort of Henry II of France (d. 1589), 1562 D, 1569 A, 1589 A; marries Henry, Duke of Orleans, 1531 B, D; tours France, 1564 A; meets Alva, 1565 B; issues Moulins Ordinances, 1566 D; provokes massacre of St. Bartholomew, 1572 C; acts as Regent, 1574 B; meets Henry of Navarre, 1586 D

Catherine of Aragon, Queen consort of Henry VIII of England (d. 1536), 1531 C, 1536 A; betrothal to Prince Arthur, 1497 C, 1498 A; marries Prince Arthur, 1501 D; betrothal to Prince Henry, 1503 B, D; marries Henry VIII, 1509 B; Henry VIII's proceedings for divorce from, 1527 B, D, 1528 A, B, D, 1531 B; marriage to Henry VIII declared null, 1533 B; Clement VII declares the marriage valid, 1534 A

Catherine of Braganza, Port. Queen consort of Charles II of England (1638–1705), 1638 M, 1662 B, 1705 M

Catherine Howard, Queen consort of Henry VIII (d. 1542), 1540 C, 1541 D, 1542 A

Catherine Parr, Queen consort of Henry VIII of England (1512–48), 1543 C, 1548 M

Catherine Sforza, It. ruler (1460–1503), 1500 A

Catiline (Jonson), 1611 L

Catiline Conspiracy, The (Sallust; trans.), 1608 H

Catinat de la Fauconnerie, Nicholas de, F. general (1637–1712), marshal of France, defeats Victor Amadeus at Staffade, 1690 C; takes Nice, 1691 A; defeats Victor Amadeus at Marsaglia, 1693 D

Cato (Addison), 1713 L

Cats, Jacob, Du. poet and humanist (1577–1660), 1577 M, 1620 L, 1623 L, 1660 M

Cattle near a building (A. van de Velde), 1663 J

Causes of Wealth (Serra), 1613 F

Cautio Criminalis (von Langenfeld), 1631 H

Cavalier, Jean, F. chief of the Camisards (1681–1740), 1681 M, 1740 M

Cavalier, Robert, sieur de la Salle, F. explorer, 1682 F

Cavalieri, Emilio de, It. musician, composer of first extant opera, 1600 K

Cavaliers, The. *See under* Civil Wars, English

Cavalli, Francesco, It. musician, 1660 K

Cave, Edward ('Sylvanus Urban'), E. journalist and printer (1691–1754), 1691 M, 1731 H, 1754 M

Cave, William, E. church historian (1637–1713), 1672 H, 1677 H, 1682 H, 1688 H

Cavendish, George, E. biographer (1500–61), 1557 H, 1667 L

Cavendish, Henry, E. scientist and eccentric (1731–1810), 1731 M

Cavendish, Margaret, Duchess of Newcastle, E. author (1624–74), 1624 M, 1674 M

Cavendish, Thomas, E. circumnavigator (*c.* 1555–92), 1586 G, 1592 M

Cavendish, William, Duke of Devonshire, E. politician (1641–1707), 1707 M

Cavendish, William, Duke of Devonshire, E. politician (1720–64), prime minister, 1756 D; resigns, 1757 B

Cawdrey, Robert, E. lexicographer, 1604 H

Cayenne, F. Guiana, French occupy, 1625 E

Cecil, James, Earl of Salisbury, E. politician (*c.* 1646–83), imprisoned, 1677 A

Cecil, Robert, Earl of Salisbury, E. statesman (1563–1612), James I retains as Secretary of State, 1603 A; adopts anti-Spanish policy, 1610 B; death, 1612 B, M

Cecil, Sir William, Lord Burghley, E. statesman (1520–98), 1520 M, 1598 M; as secretary of state, 1550 C; Elizabeth I re-appoints, 1558 D; reforms currency, 1560 F; plots to oust, 1569 A; created Lord Burghley, 1571 A; appointed Lord Treasurer, 1572 C; in disgrace, 1587 A

Celebes, Indonesia, discovered, 1512 G

Celestial fire, 1551 G

Celestina, the Spanish Bawd (de Rojas), 1501 L; trans., 1631 H

Cellini, Benvenuto, It. artist, connoisseur and author (1500–71), 1500 M, 1543 J, 1545 J, 1571 M

'Cells', Hooke uses term, 1665 G

Celsius, Anders, Swe. astronomer and inventor (1701–44), 1736 G, 1742 G

Celtes, Konrad, G. humanist (1459–1508), 1508 M

Cena de le ceneri, La (Bruno), 1584 H

Cenci, Beatrice, It. heroine (1577–99), 1577 M, 1599 M

Cenci, Francesco, It. politician, tried, 1595 F

Censorship of Books and the Press:
  in America, attempted in New York, 1734 F
  in England, 1587 F, 1632 F
    ended, 1641 F
    Milton's plea for freedom, 1644 F
    L'Estrange as licenser of press, 1663 F
    ended, 1695 B
  in France, 1615 F, 1626 F, 1707 F

Censures des théologiens de Paris (Estienne), 1552 H

Census:
  in Canada, taken in Quebec, 1665 F
  in England, annual, proposed, 1753 G

Centigrade thermometer, the, invented, 1742 G

Cerdagne (Cerdaña), France and Spain, 1493 A; France obtains, 1659 D

Cerignola, Italy, Spaniards are driven from, 1502 C

Cerisolo, Italy, 1544 B

Ceritosa, Italy, 1522 J

Cervantes Saavedra, Miguel de, Sp. novelist (1547–1616), 1547 M, 1585 L, 1605 L, 1612 H, 1613 L, 1614 L, 1615 L, 1616 M; translations of works of, 1620 H, 1640 H, 1700 H, 1712 H, 1755 H

Cervini, Marcello, It. Pope Marcellus II (1501–55), 1501 M, 1555 M

Cessi, Bernard, It. (1581–1630), 1603 G

Ceulen, Ludolph von, G. mathematician (1540–1610), 1596 G

Cevennes, France: Protestant rising, 1689 E; revolt of Camisards, 1702 E

Ceylon: settled by Dutch, 1636 E; Dutch retain, 1661 C; French expeditions against, 1673 E

Chablis, France, 1564 C

Chace, The (Somerville), 1735 L

Chain of Philosophical Reflections (on Tar Water) (Berkeley), 1744 H

Chalais, Henri, Comte de, F. conspirator, 1626 C

Chalgrove Field, Oxfordshire, England, battle, 1643 B

Chalmers, George, Sc. antiquarian (1742–1825), 1742 M

Chalons, René of, F. soldier, 1540 B

Chambord, Treaty of, 1552 C

Chamberlen, P., E. author, 1649 F

Chamber music, 1753 K

Chambers, Ephraim, E. lexicographer (?1680–1740), 1728 H, 1740 M

Chambers, Sir William, E. architect (1723–96), 1723 M, 1757 J, 1759 J

Chambery, France, 1600 C

Champagne, France, 1594 B

Champaigne, Philippe de, Flem. artist (1602–74), 1630 J, 1635 J, 1650 J, 1662 J

Champfleury (Tory), 1529 H

Champlain, Samuel de, F. explorer and Lieutenant of Canada (1567–1635), 1603 G, 1604 F, 1608 F, 1609 G, 1613 G

Champlain, Lake, Canada, discovered, 1609 G

Champmeslé, Marie, F. actress (1642–98), 1642 M, 1698 M

Chancellor, Sir Richard, E. navigator (d. 1556), 1553 G, 1556 M

Chandernagore, Bengal, India, taken by French, 1673 E

Changeling, The (Middleton), 1653 L

Chantries, dissolution of, 1545 D, 1548 D

Chapeau de Paille (Rubens), 1620 J

Chapelain, Jean, F. poet and critic (1595–1674), 1595 M, 1656 L, 1674 M

Chapman, George, E. poet, dramatist and translator (1559–1634), 1559 M, 1598 H, 1605 L, 1606 L, 1607 L, 1608 L, 1611 H, 1613 L, 1614 H, 1615 H, 1616 H, 1618 H, 1624 H, 1634 M, 1654 L

Chapone, Hester (née Muslo), E. essayist (1727–91), 1727 M

Character Essays:
  Hall, 1608 L
  Overbury, 1614 L
  Earle, 1628 L
  Halifax, 1684 F, 1688 L

Character of a Trimmer, The (Halifax), 1684 F, 1688 L

Characteristics of Men, Manners, Opinions and Times (Shaftesbury), 1711 H

Chardin, Jean Baptiste Siméon, F. artist (1699–1779), 1728 J, 1732 J, 1737 J, 1738 J, 1739 J

Charité, La, France, 1570 C, 1577 B

Charity (Pontormo), 1525 J

Charleroi, Belgium: William of Orange is forced to raise siege, 1672 D; France restores to Spain, 1678 C; Maximilian of Bavaria relieves, 1692 L; French capture, 1693 D

Charles V, Holy Roman Emperor (1519–56), 1500 A, 1501 C, 1518 F, 1521 F, 1529 G, 1531 A, B, F, 1533 E, 1536 C, 1539 A, 1540 D, 1543 B, C
  treaty to marry Mary Tudor, 1502 D, 1508 D
  as governor of Netherlands, 1515 A
  succeeds as King of Spain, 1516 A
  agrees to marry Louise of France, 1516 C
  arrives in Spain, 1517 C
  enters Valladolid, 1517 D

Chemistry:
first text book on, 1610 G
treatise on, 1675 G
pioneer study of organic chemistry, 1732 G
Black's studies, 1755 G
Chemnitz, Martin, G. Lutheran theologian and librarian (1522–86), 1567 H, 1577 H
Chemnitz, Philip Bogeslav de, G. author (1605–78), 1647 F
Chemnitz, E. Germany, battle, 1639 B
Chenier, Marie André, F. poet (1762–94), 1762 M
Cherasco, Treaty of, 1631 B
Cherubini, Marcia Luigi Carlo Zenobio Salvatore, It. musician (1760–1842), 1760 M
Cherubinischer Wandersmann (Silesius), 1657 H
Chesne, André du, F. geographer (1584–1640), 1584 M, 1640 M
Chesneau, César, F. philologist (1676–1756), 1730 H
Chess, study of, 1749 F
Chester, Cheshire, England, rising in, 1659 C
Chesterfield, Earl of. *See* Stanhope, Philip Dormer
Chetham, Humfrey, E. manufacturer (1580–1653), 1653 H
Chetwood, William, E. dramatic historian (d. 1766), 1749 L
Chiabrera, Gabriello, It. poet (1552–1637), 1552 M, 1637 M
Chiampel, Durich, Raeto-Romansch poet and humanist (*c.* 1510–82), 1554 L
Chiari, Italy, battle, 1701 C
Chiaroscuro, discovered, 1514 J
Chicago, Illinois, US, exploration near, 1672 G
Chien Lung, Emperor of China (1723–35), 1735 E
Chievra, William de Croy, Seigneur de, Sp. minister, 1517 D
Chigi, Fabio, It. Pope Alexander VII (1599–1667), 1599 M, 1667 M; *q.v.*
Child, Sir Francis, E. economist and banker (1642–1713), 1642 M, 1713 M
Child, Sir John, E. Governor of Bombay (d. 1690), 1682 E
Child, Sir Josiah, E. merchant and banker (1630–99), 1630 M, 1668 F, 1690 F, 1699 F, M
Children's Literature:
first picture book, 1654 F
John Newbery, 1744 L
Children with a bird-cage (Pigalle), 1749 J
Chile, Spanish Conquest, epic on, 1569 L
Chillingworth, William, E. theologian, Cambridge Platonist (1602–44), 1602 M, 1638 H, 1644 M
Chiltern Hundreds, stewardship of, 1742 F
China: Portuguese settlement in, 1520 E; Portuguese expelled from, 1523 E; tea from China reaches Europe, 1609 F; Manchus proclaim Ch'ing dynasty at Mukden, 1636 E; trade with Russia, 1692 E; French legate at, 1698 E; invasion of Tibet, 1751 E; occupation of E. Turkestan, 1758 E
China and Porcelain, 1750 J
Chinchou, Countess of, 1639 G
Chinese Convent, The (Kneller), 1687 J
Ch'ing dynasty in China, 1636 E, 1644 E
Ching P'ing Mei (Hsu Wei), 1560 L
Chinsura, India, Clive defeats Dutch at, 1758 E
Chios, Isle of, Aegean, Turks capture island from Genoa, 1566 E
Chippendale, Thomas, E. furniture designer (1718–79), 1754 J
Chirugien Dentiste ou traité des dents (Fauchard), 1728 G
Chiswick House, Middlesex, England, 1717 J, 1725 J

Chocolate: in slab form, 1520 F; drinking, first sold in London, 1657 F; houses for sale of, 1698 F
Choderlos de Laclos, Pierre, F. novelist and politician (1741–1803), 1741 M
Choiseul, Étienne François Duc de, F. statesman (1719–85), 1719 M; appointed foreign secretary, 1758 D; opens peace negotiations, 1761 C
Chorégraphie (Feuillet), 1699 K
Chotusitz, Poland, battle, 1742 B
Christ and the Woman taken in Adultery (Lotto), 1529 J
Christ at Emmaus (Pontormo), 1525 J
Christ before Pilate (Honthorst), 1618 J
Christ carrying the Cross (Bruegel) 1564 J
Christ's Nativity (Milton), 1645 L
Christ washing the Disciples' Feet (Tintoretto), 1555 J
Christening Feast, The (Steen), 1664 J
Christian II of Denmark and Norway (1513–23), 1522 C, 1531 D, 1535 D; accession, 1513 A; defeats Swedes, 1520 A; crowned King of Sweden, 1520 D; massacres Eric Vasa, 1520 D; Danish swing against, 1522 D; deposition and exile, 1523 A
Christian III of Denmark and Norway (1535–59), 1536 B, 1559 A; accession, 1535 B; establishes authority, 1536 C; reforms Danish church, 1537 C
Christian IV of Denmark and Norway (1588–1648), 1625 B, D, 1648 A, M; accession of 1588 B; war with Sweden, 1611 B, 1612 C; defeated at Lutter, 1626 C; withdraws to Denmark, 1627 D; signs Peace of Lübeck, 1629 B
Christian V of Denmark (1670–99), 1699 C; accession, 1670 E; defeated at Cassel, 1677 D
Christian VI of Denmark (1730–46), 1730 D, 1746 C
Christian, Prince of Anhalt, G. (1568–1630), 1591 A; as leading German Calvinist, 1603 E; leads Protestant Union, 1608 B; defeated at battle of White Mountain, 1620 D; placed under ban of Empire, 1621 A
Christian of Brunswick (1611–33), G. ruler and soldier, bishop of Minden, defeated at Hochst, 1622 B; defeated at Stadtlohn, 1623 C
Christian of Halberstadt, G. prince (d. 1626), 1626 B
Christian I, Elector of Saxony (d. 1591), 1586 A, 1590 B, 1591 A, C
Christian II, Elector of Saxony (1591–1611), 1591 C, 1611 C
Christian Ethics (Traherne), 1675 H
Christian Faith Society, in London, 1691 H
Christian Fathers, 1645 H
Christian Hero, The (Steele), 1701 H
Christianae Religionis Institutio (Calvin; original edition), 1536 H. For later editions *see under* Calvin
Christianismi Restitutio (Servetus), 1553 G, H
Christianisme dévoilé, Le (Holbach), 1761 H
Christianity as Old as the Creation (Tindal), 1730 H
Christianopolis (Andreae), 1619 H
Christina, Queen, of Sweden (1626–89), daughter of the Elector of Brandenburg, 1626 M, 1689 M; accession, 1632 D; personal rule, 1644 D; forms Protestant rule, 1651 A; abdicates, 1654 B
Chronicles:
Schedel: Nuremburg, 1493 H
Arnold: London, 1502 H
Fabyan: England and France, 1516 H
Froissart: England and France, trans. 1523 H
Polydore Vergil: Anglicae Historiae, 1534 H
Edward Halle: England (Lancaster and York), 1550 H
Grafton: England, 1562 H
Aventinus: Bavaria, 1566 H
Holinshed: England, 1577 H, 1587 F
Stow: England, 1580 H

Baker: Kings of England, 1643 H
See also under Annals
Chronicles, medieval, editions of, 1571 H, 1720 H
Chronologia (Mercator), 1569 G
Chronology:
ecclesiastical, 1759 H
history, 1498 H, 1583 H, 1606 H, 1658 H, 1667 H, 1720 H, 1750 H, 1752 H
printing, 1749 H
theatres, 1754 H
Chronometers:
clock-wheels, machine for cutting teeth of, 1740 G
for measurement by double-image, 1743 G
Harrison's, 1762 G
See also Clocks; Watches
Chrysal (Johnstone), 1760 L
Church Music, notable:
Barnard's collection, 1641 K
Blow, 1697 K
Byrd, 1575 K, 1607 K, 1611 K
Clifford's collection, 1663 K
Gibbons, 1611 K, 1622 K
de Lassus, Masses, 1556 K
Monteverdi, Great Mass, 1632 K
Palestrina, Masses, 1554 K
des Prés, Masses, 1512 K, 1513 K
Purcell, 1694 K, 1695 K
Schütz, 1625 K, 1648 K
Tomkins, 1668 K
Churchill, Charles, E. poet and satirist (1731–64), 1731 M, 1761 L, 1762 F, L
Churchill, John, Duke of Marlborough, E. general (1650–1722), 1650 M, 1722 B, M; dismissal, 1692 A; sent to Tower, 1692 B; restored to favour, 1698 D; appointed captain-general of armed forces, 1702 A; takes Venlo, 1702 C; takes Liège, 1702 D; occupies Cologne, 1703 B; takes Bonn and Guelders, 1703 B; begins march to Danube, 1704 B; victory at Donauwörth, 1704 B; victory at Blenheim, 1704 C; defeats French at Ramillies, 1706 B; at Oudenarde, 1708 C; at Tournai, 1709 C; battle of Malplaquet, 1709 C; nicknamed 'Butcher', 1709 C; helps take Mons, 1709 D; dismissed, 1711 D; re-appointed commander-in-chief, 1714 C
Churchill, Sarah (née Jennings), Duchess of Marlborough (d. 1744), 1744 M
Churchyard, Thomas, E. versifier (c. 1520–1604), 1604 M
Chushingura Incident, 1703 B
Chymical Secrets (Digby), 1683 G
Chymische Hochzeit Christiani Rosenkreutz (Andreae), 1616 H
Cibber, Caius Gabriel, E. sculptor (1630–1700), 1630 M, 1673 J, 1692 J, 1698 J, 1700 M
Cibber, Colley, E. actor, dramatist and poet laureate (1671–1757), 1671 M, 1718 L, 1728 L, 1740 L, 1742 H, 1757 M
Cicero, Marcus Tullius, Rom. statesman, orator and author (106 B.C.–43 B.C.), works of, 1537 H, 1550 H
Ciceronianus (Erasmus), 1528 H
Cid, Le (Corneille), 1636 L; trans. Rutter, 1637 H
Cimarosa, Domenico, It. musician (1749–1801), 1749 M
Cinna (Corneille), 1639 L
Cinq-Mars, Henri, Marquis of (1620–42), F. courtier, 1620 M, 1642 C, M
Cipriani, Giovanni Battista, It. artist and engraver (1727–85), 1727 M
Circle of Commerce, The (Misselden), 1623 F
Circulation of the blood, 1553 G, 1619 G, 1628 G

Circumnavigation of the globe, voyages of: Magellan, 1519 G; Drake, 1577 D, 1580 D, G; Cavendish, 1586 G; Dampier, 1683 G; Anson, 1740 G
Cisnéros, Jimenez de, Sp. statesman, 1516 A
Citizen of the World (Goldsmith), 1760 L
City Madam, The (Massinger), 1632 L
City of the Sun, The (Campanella), 1623 H
Civil Conversations (Guazzo), trans., 1581 H
Civil Service, in France, 1634 E, 1720 F
Civil Wars:
in Denmark, 1523 A
'War of the Counts', 1533 B
in England, Parliament v. Charles I
Royalist standard raised at Nottingham, 1642 C
Battle of Powicke Bridge, 1642 C
Battle of Edgehill, 1642 D
opposing armies at Brentford, 1642 D
Royalists take Marlborough, 1642 D
Parliamentarians take Winchester, 1642 D
Royalists lose Bradford, 1643 A
Charles I meets Commissioners, 1643 A
Essex takes Reading, 1643 B
Battles of Grantham and Stratton, 1643 B
Parliamentarians take Wakefield, 1643 B
arrest of Royalist plotters, 1643 B
Hampden's death, 1643 B
Battle of Atherton Moor, 1643 B
Battle of Roundaway Down, 1643 C
Prince Rupert takes Bristol, 1643 C
Cromwell takes Gainsborough, 1643 C
Essex relieves Colchester, 1643 C
first Battle of Newbury, 1643 C
Parliament signs Solemn League and Covenant with the Scots, 1643 C
Charles I seeks Irish aid, 1643 C
Charles I holds Oxford Parliament, 1644 A
Battle of Nantwich, 1644 A
Scots invade England, 1644 A
Battle of Copredy Bridge, 1644 B
Battle of Marston Moor, 1644 C
Henrietta Maria flees to France, 1644 C
York surrenders, 1644 C
surrender of Essex's army, 1644 C
Newcastle surrenders, 1644 D
second Battle of Newbury, 1644 D
execution of Laud, 1645 A
Lords reject Self-Denying Ordinance, 1645 A
Fairfax supplants Essex, 1645 A
Battle of Inverlocky, 1645 A
failure of Uxbridge negotiations, 1645 A
Self-Denying Ordinance is passed, 1645 B
Parliament creates New Model Army, 1645 B
Cromwell appointed general of New Model, 1645 B
Battle of Naseby, 1645 B
Royalists lose Carlisle, 1645 B
Battle of Langport, 1645 C
Bristol surrenders, 1645 C
Royalists lose Winchester, 1645 C
siege of Basing House, 1645 C
Glamorgan's Irish Treaty, 1645 A
Charles I surrenders at Newark, 1646 B
surrender of Oxford, marks virtual end of operations, 1646 B
Levellers' 'Remonstrance', 1646 C
Newcastle Propositions, 1646 C
Charles I attempts escape, 1646 D
Scots agree to sell Charles I to Parliament, 1647 A
Commons vote to disband army, 1647 B
Cromwell flees, 1647 B

Cockaine, William, E. merchant and lord mayor of London (d. 1626), 1615 A
Cockburn, Alison, Sc. poet (1713–94), 1713 M
Codes of Law:
in England, codification proposed, 1650 F
in France, Code Louis, 1667 F
Codex juris gentium diplomaticus (Leibniz), 1693 F
Codex Theodosianus (ed. Godefroy), 1665 H
Coehoorn, Menno, Baron von, Du. military engineer (1641–1704), 1685 G
Coen, Jan Pieters, Du. colonist and explorer (1587–1630), 1619 F
Coetsee, Jacobus, Du. explorer, 1760 E
Coffee: is brought to Europe, 1517 F; is drunk in Paris, 1643 F; first coffee-house in London, 1652 F
Cogers Hall Debating Society, 1755 F
Cognac, France, 1570 C, 1586 D
Cognac, League of, 1526 B
Coinage:
decimal system for, advocated, 1585 G
Empire, Ferdinand I standardises, 1559 F
England, milled coins introduced, 1562 F
copper coins introduced, 1613 F
silver pennies, discontinued, 1662 F
gold guineas, 1663 F
recoinage, 1695 F, 1696 B, F
Spain, changes in, 1596 D, 1598 F
See also Currency
Coke, used in blast-furnaces, 1709 G
Coke, Sir Edward, E. lawyer and politician (1552–1634), 1552 M, 1600 F, 1634 M; dismissed from office, 1616 D; imprisoned, 1621 D; drafts Petition of Right, 1628 B, F
Coke, Thomas William, Earl of Leicester, E. agri-culturalist (1754–1842), 1754 M
Colbert, Jean Bapiste, F. statesman (1619–83), 1619 M, 1679 F, 1683 C, M; becomes leading finance minister, 1661 C; reforms colonial and commercial system, 1663 E; abolishes internal duties, 1664 F; founds Académie des Sciences, 1666 G; encourages fine arts, 1666 J, 1667 F
Colbert de Croissy, Charles, marquis de, F. diploma-tist (1625–96), 1696 C
Colchester, Essex, England: abbey, Abbot of, 1539 D; Fairfax takes, 1648 C
Colden, Cadwallader, Am. botanist and loyalist (1688–1776), 1751 G
Coldstream, Northumberland, England, 1640 C
Colet, John, E. scholar and humanist (c. 1467–1519), 1496 F, 1505 H, 1510 F, 1519 M
Coligny, Gaspard de, F. Huguenot leader and statesman, Admiral of France (1519–72), 1519 M, 1561 A, 1562 E, 1569 A; defeated by Anjou, 1569 D; becomes powerful at court, 1570 C; is reconciled with Charles IX, 1571 C; aids Dutch, 1572 C; assassination, 1572 C, M
Colin Clouts Come Home Again (Spenser), 1595 L
Collé, Charles, F. dramatist (1709–83), 1747 L
Collegium Germanicum, Rome, 1552 H
Collier, Arthur, E. philosopher (1680–1732), 1713 H
Collier, Jeremy, E. non-juror and author (1650–1726), 1650 M, 1698 H, 1701 H, 1708 H, 1726 M
Collingwood, Cuthbert, Lord Collingwood, E. admiral (1750–1810), 1750 M
Collins, Anthony, E. deist (1676–1729) 1676 M, 1729 M
Collins, Arthur, E. historian (1690–1760), 1709 H, 1720 H, 1735 H
Collins, William, E. poet (1721–59), 1721 M, 1742 L, 1747 L, 1759 M
Colloquies (Erasmus), 1519 H, 1524 H

Colloquim Heptaplomeres (Bodin), 1592 H
Colman, George, the elder, E. dramatist (1732–94), 1761 L
Colmar, France (form. Germany), 1639 C, 1675 A
Cologne, West Germany, 1697 D
diet at, 1512 D
Archbishop von Wied deposed, 1543 B
resigns, 1547 A
Archbishop Gebhard is opposed, 1583 A, B
retires, 1589 E
peace negotiations at, 1638 D
peace conference at, 1673 B, D
English army occupies, 1703 B
Elector of, outlawed, 1706 B
Elector of, restored, 1714 A
Colombo, Ceylon: Portuguese factory at, 1517 F; Dutch capture, 1656 E
Colonel Jacque (Defoe), 1722 L
Colonna, Italy, 1504 D, 1506 J
Colonna family, feud with Orsini, 1498 A
Colonna, Francesco, It. Dominican friar (c. 1432–1527), 1499 H
Colonna, Pompeo, It. cardinal (d. 1532), 1526 C
Colonna, Prosper, It. soldier (d. 1523), 1521 D, 1523 D
Colonna, Vittoria, marchioness of Pesara, It. poet (1490–1547), 1533 H, 1547 M
Columbus, Christopher (Cristobal Colón), Sp. navigator (1451–1506), 1506 M; first voyage to America, 1492 B, C, D, G, 1493 A, G; second voyage to America, 1493 G; third voyage, 1498 G; final voyage, 1502 G
Colvile, George, E. translator, 1556 H
Combustion, nature of, discussed, 1674 G
Comedias (de Vega), 1604 L
Comédie-Française, 1680 L
Comedy of Errors (Shakespeare), 1593 L
Comenius, John Amos (Komenský), Moravian educationalist (1592–1671), 1630 H, 1654 F, 1657 F
Comets:
Bayle's tract on, 1682 G
Halley's, 1705 G
perihelion of, calculated, 1759 G
Winthrop's lectures on, 1759 G
See also Astronomy
Comical Revenge, The (Etherege), 1664 L
Comines, Philippe de, F. historian (1445–1511), 1511 M, 1524 H, 1545 L
Commedia dell'arte, 1590 L
Commentaire philosophique (Bayle), 1686 H
Commentaries on Roman Law (Cujas), 1578 F
Commentaries on . . . the reign of Charles V (Sleidan), 1545 F
Commentarii in Organum Logicum Aristotelis (Balfour), 1618 H
Commentariorum de statu religionis et reipublicae (de Serres), 1572 F
Commentarios de la guerra de Alemana (Zuniga), 1548 F
Commentary on the Epistle to the Romans (Calvin), 1539 H
Commercial and Financial Crises:
Anglo-Spanish, 1528 A, B, 1568 D, 1571 E, 1574 C
English, 1612 B, 1672 F
French, 1557 E, F, 1720 D, 1753 E
Italian, 1607 C
Spanish, 1557 E, 1575 E, 1596 E, 1598 D
Commercial Tracts, notable, 1601 F, 1615 F, 1621 F, 1622 F, 1623 F, 1662 F, 1664 F, 1668 F, 1671 F, 1690 F, 1699 F
Common land. *See* Enclosures
Commons, House of. *See* Parliaments etc., England

Constantinople, Treaties of, 1540 B, 1573 A, 1724 B
Constitutions:
  for Carolina, 1670 F
  for Germany, discussed, 1647 F
  for Hungary, 1514 E
  for Poland, 1504 E
  for Venice, amended, 1582 E
Constitutional history, first study of, 1723 H
Consuetudo vel Lex Mercatoria (de Malynes), 1622 F
Conté, Nicolas Jacques, F. engineer and chemist (1755–1805), 1755 M
Contemplations (Bradstreet), 1678 L
Contemplations (Hall), 1626 H
Contention of Ajax and Ulysses, The (Shirley), 1659 L
Contes (Perrault), 1697 L
Contes et nouvelles en vers (Fontaine), 1665 L
Conti, Stefano, of Lucca, It., 1725 J
Continence of Scipio, The (Troy), 1728 J
Contraction of muscles, discovered, 1746 G
Contrat Social (Rousseau), 1762 H
Conventions, International:
  Amsterdam (France, Russia and Prussia), 1717 C
  Areillen (France and Palatinate), 1682 A
  Ilkersheim (Austrian control of Bavaria), 1704 D
  Leipzig (German Protestant Princes), 1631 A
  London (England and Prussia), 1758 B
  Milan (Holy Roman Empire and France), 1707 A
  Niederschonfeld (Bavarian army capitulates), 1743 B
  Pardo (England and Spain), 1728 A, 1739 A, D
Conversation du Marechal d'Hocquincourt avec le père Canaye (St. Évremond), 1705 L
Conversion of St. Paul (Bruegel), 1567 J
Conversion of St. Paul (Caravaggio), 1601 J
Convocations of English Clergy: last meet, independently of Crown, 1532 B; separate taxation of clergy, 1664 F; closed by government, 1717 E
Conway, Sir Edward, lord Conway (d. 1631), E. politician, secretary of state, 1623 A
Cook, The (Vermeer), 1660 J
Cook, James, E. navigator and explorer (1728–79), 1728 M
Cooper, Anthony Ashley, first Earl of Shaftesbury (1621–83), E. politician and author, 1621 M; 1682 A, 1683 A, M; member of the Cabal, 1667 C; president of Economic Council, 1672 A; Lord Chancellor, 1672 D; dismissed, 1673 D; forces Charles II to agree to Treaty of Westminister, 1674 A; imprisoned, 1677 A; released, 1678 A; Lord President of Council, 1679 A; dismissed, 1679 D; writings, 1675 F
Cooper, Anthony Ashley, third Earl of Shaftesbury, E. moral philosopher (1671–1713), 1711 H, 1713 M
Cooper, Thomas, Am. educationalist and philosopher (1759–1840), 1759 M
Cooper, Thomas, E. scholar (c. 1517–94), 1565 H, 1588 H
Cooper's Hill (Denham), 1642 L
Coote, Sir Eyre, E. soldier (1726–83), 1726 M; commander in Madras, 1759 E; defeats French at Wanderwash, 1760 A; takes Pondicherry, 1761 A
Cope, Sir John, E. soldier (d. 1760), defeated at Prestonpans, 1745 C
Copenhagen, Denmark: surrenders to Christian III, 1536 C; besieged by Charles X, 1658 C; press in, 1663 F; plague in, 1711 E
Copenhagen, Peace of, 1660 B
Copernicus, Nicolaus, Pol. astronomer (1473–1543), 1543 G, M, 1551 G
Copernican system, 1543 G
  Galileo is forbidden to teach, 1616 G

Copland, William, E. translator, 1528 H
Copley, John Singleton, the elder, Am. artist (1738–1815), 1738 M
Copper, mining of, 1561 C
Copper coins, 1599 F, 1613 F
Copredy Bridge, Oxon, England, battle, 1644 B
Copyright Acts in Britain, 1709 F, 1735 J
Coral, red, nature of, discovered, 1727 G
Coram, Thomas, E. philanthropist (c. 1668–1751), 1751 M
Córdoba, Francisco Hernández de, Sp. navigator, 1517 G
Córdoba, Gonzalo Fernandez de, Sp. general and statesman (1443–1515), 1495 C, 1497 B, 1502 A, D, 1503 B, D, 1515 M
Corelli, Archangelo, It. virtuoso violinist and composer (1653–1713), 1653 M, 1682 K, 1713 M
Corfu, Ionian Islands, 1537 A
  Turks retain, 1718 C
Coriolanus (Shakespeare), 1608 L
Cork, vesicular nature of, 1665 G
Cork, Eire, Warbeck at, 1497 C
Cork, Earl of. *See* Boyle, R.
Cornard Wood (Gainsborough), 1748 J
Corneille, Pierre, F. tragic dramatist (1606–84), 1606 M, 1629 L, 1630 L, 1634 L, 1635 L, 1636 L, 1637 L, 1639 L, 1640 L, 1641 L, 1642 L, 1645 L, 1646 L, 1650 L, 1652 L, 1655 H, 1659 L, 1660 L, 1670 L, 1684 M
Corneille, Thomas, F. dramatist and lexicographer (1625–1709), 1678 L, 1694 H
Cornucopiae (Calepino), 1502 H
Cornwall, England, rebellions in, 1497 B, 1549 B
Cornwall, Survey of (Carew), 1602 H
Cornwallis, Charles, first marquess of Cornwallis, E. soldier and colonial administrator (1738–1805), 1738 M
Cornwallis, Sir William, E. admiral (1744–1819), 1744 M
Coromandel Coast, south east India, French occupy, 1672 E
Coronado, Francisco Vasquez de, Sp. explorer (c. 1500–45), 1541 G
Coronation of the Virgin (Raphael), 1502 J
Coronations:
  imperial, the last, 1530 A
  first tsar to assume crown formally, 1547 A
  of Charles II at Scone, 1651 A
Corporation Act, in England, 1661 D
Corpuscles, red, discovered, 1668 G
Corpus doctrinae Prutenicum (Chemnitz), 1567 H
Corral (Spanish Yard Play), 1568 L
Correggio, Antonio Allegri da, It. artist (1494–1534), 1494 M, 1514 J, 1518 J, 1530 J, 1534 M
Corrichie, Aberdeenshire, Scotland, 1562 D
Corsica, Island of, Mediterranean: rebellion in, 1553 E; revolts against Genoa, 1729 E, 1755 B; independence recognised, 1732 E; election of King, 1736 B
Corte-Real, Gaspar de, Port. explorer, 1500 G
Cortegiano, Il (Castiglione), 1528 F; trans. Hoby, 1561 H
Cortes, Hernando, Sp. explorer and soldier (1485–1547), 1533 E, 1547 M; enters Mexico, 1519 D; takes control of Mexico, 1521 C; appointed governor of Mexico (New Spain), 1522 D
Cortete, François de, F. Provençal poet (1571–1655), 1684 L
Cortona, Pietro da (Pietro Berettini), It. architect, (1596–1669), 1635 J, 1668 J
Corunna, Spain, English attack on, 1589 B
Corvée, establishment of, in France, 1738 E

Crébillon, Prosper Jolyot de, *fils*, F. novelist (1707–77), 1745 L
Crefeld, E. Germany, battle, 1758 B
Cremation, advocated, 1658 F
Cremona, Italy, 1526 C, 1572 K, 1702 A
Crépy, Peace of, 1544 C
Créquy, France, 1675 C
Crete, Island of, Mediterranean: Turks attack, 1645 E; Turks conquer, 1669 C
Creutz, Gustaf Philip, Count, Swe. politician and poet (1731–85), 1762 L
Crew, Nathaniel, E. churchman, Bishop of Durham (1633–1721), 1633 M, 1721 M
Cribbage, invented, 1630 F
Crichton, James ('Admirable'), Sc. lawyer, lord advocate (c. 1560–85), 1585 M
Cricket, 1750 F
Crimea, Russia, 1736 C
Crispin, rival de son maître (Lesage), 1707 L
Cristofori, Bartolomeo, It. maker of pianofortes, 1709 K
Critical History of England, A (Oldmixon), 1724 H
Criticón, El (y Morales), 1651 L
Critische Musicus, Der (Scheibe), 1740 K
Crivelli, Carlo, It. artist (d. 1495), 1492 J
Croatia, Yugoslavia: Turks invade, 1493 E, 1532 C; Usbeks settled in, 1617 C; ceded to Austria, 1699 A
Crocyka, Turkey, battle, 1739 C
Croiset, R. P., F. philosopher, 1752 H
Croissy. *See* Colbert de Croissy
Crojon, Brittany, France, 1594 C
Crompton, Richard, E. lawyer (d. 1599), 1594 F
Cromwell, Oliver, E. statesman, general, Lord protector (1599–1658), 1599 M, 1643 B, C, 1646 C, 1655 D, 1657 F
    enters Parliament, 1628 A
    appointed general of New Model Army, 1645 B
    defeats Royalists at Naseby, 1645 B
    at Langport, 1645 C
    flees, 1647 B
    speech against Charles I, 1648 A
    defeats Scots at Preston, 1648 C
    sacks Drogheda, 1648 C
    sacks Wexford, 1648 D
    forms economic council, 1650 C
    defeats Scots at Dunbar, 1650 C
    takes Edinburgh Castle, 1650 D
    takes Perth, 1651 C
    defeats Charles II at Worcester, 1651 C
    expels Long Parliament, 1653 B
    appoints Council of Ten, 1653 B
    is established as Protector, 1653 D
    excludes extremist Republicans, 1654 C
    appoints 'triers and ejectors', 1654 H
    dissolves Parliament, 1655 A
    appoints major generals, 1655 C
    rejects title of King, 1657 A
    power increased, 1657 B
    re-installed as Protector, 1657 B
    dissolves Parliament, 1658 A
    death, 1658 C, M
    portrait, 1653 J
    papers relating to, 1742 H, 1743 H
Cromwell, Richard, E. Protector (1626–1712), 1626 M, 1658 C, 1659 B, 1712 M
Cromwell, Thomas, Earl of Essex, E. statesman (c. 1485–1540), defends Wolsey, 1529 D; visits Religious houses, 1535 A; Injunctions as Vicar General, 1535 F, 1538 C; Lord Privy Seal, 1536 B; arranges Cleves marriage, 1539 D;

created Earl of Essex, 1540 B; fall, 1540 B; execution, 1540 B, M
Cronstedt, Axel Frederick, Swe., chemist (1722–65), 1751 G
Croom Court, Worcs., England, 1751 J
Crowley, Robert, E. religious and social reformer (c. 1518–88), 1550 F, 1588 M
Crown Point, Lake Champlain, US, 1731 E
Crowning with Thorns (Titian), 1570 J
Crucible process for steel, 1740 G
Crucifixion, The (Cranach), 1500 J
Cruden, Alexander, Sc. bookseller and compiler of Biblical concordance (1701–70), 1701 M, 1737 H
Crudities (Coryate), 1611 L
Cryptography, 1518 H
Crystallography, treatise on, 1723 G
Crystals, quartz, angles of, determined, 1669 G
Cuba, West Indies: discovered, 1492 G; is circumnavigated, 1508 G; is occupied, 1511 F; Spain annexes, 1539 E; Spain retains, 1697 C; failure of British attack on, 1741 E
Cudworth, Ralph, E. philosopher, Cambridge Platonist (1617–88), 1617 M, 1678 H, 1688 M, 1731 H
Cujas, Jacques, F. jurist (1522–90), 1578 F
Culloden, Inverness-shire, Scotland, battle, 1746 B
Culmbach, West Germany, succession in, 1599 B
Culpeper, Nicholas, E. writer on astrology (1616–54), 1616 M
Culverwell, Nathanael, E. philosopher (d. 1651), 1652 H
Cumberland, Duke of. *See* William Augustus
Cunaeus, Pierre, Du. author, 1745 G
Cuneiform signs, discovered, 1621 H
Cunha, Tristão da, Port. explorer (c. 1460–1540), 1506 G
Cunitz, Maria, Silesian astronomer (c. 1610–64), 1650 G
Cupid Carving his Bow (Parmigianino), 1531 J
Curaçao, Netherlands Antilles, Dutch capture, 1634 E
Cure of the Diseased in Remote Regions, The, 1598 G
Currency:
    English, debased, 1551 F
        reformed, 1558 F, 1560 F
        copper coins, 1613 F
        reformed, 1696 F
    Swedish, 1658 F
    See also Coinage
Cusanus, Nicolaus, Cardinal (Nicolaus of Cusa), G. ecclesiastic (1401–64), 1514 H
Customs Systems, English, 1605 F, 1672 F. *See also* Taxation
Cutter of Coleman Street, The (Cowley), 1663 L
Cuzco, Peru, 1533 E
Cycloid, solutions of, 1658 G
Cyclopaedia, or An Universal Dictionary of Arts and Sciences (Chambers), 1728 H
Cygne, Le (Oudry), 1740 J
Cylindrical projection, Mercator's, 1568 G
    mathematical basis of, 1599 G
Cymbeline (Shakespeare), 1610 L
Cypress Grove, A (Drummond), 1623 H
Cyprianus Anglicanus (Heylyn), 1668 H
Cyprus, Mediterranean: Venice refuses to surrender, 1570 C; Turks attack, 1571 C, 1572 B; Venice cedes to Turks, 1573 A
Cyrano de Bergerac, Savinien, F. author and duellist (1620–55), 1620 M, 1654 L, 1655 M
Cyropaedia (Xenophon), 1632 H

D

Dacre, Leonard, Lord Dacre, E. rebel (d. 1573), 1570 A

Dave, William, Lord Dacre of Gilsland, E. politician (1500–63), 1534 C

Dacres, Edward, E. translator, 1640 H

Dafne (Peri), the first opera, 1597 K

Dahlshjern, Gunno, Swe. poet (1661–1709), 1697 L

Daille, Jean, F. religious controversialist, 1632 H

Dalgarno, George, E., pioneer of tuition for deaf and dumb, 1680 F

Dalin, Olof von, Swe. author (1708–63), 1732 L, 1738 L

Dallam, Thomas, E. organ-builder, 1594 K

Dalmatia, Yugoslavia, 1685 D; Turks invade, 1493 E, 1499 C; Turks retain conquests, 1718 C

Dalrymple, James, Viscount Stair, Sc. lawyer and statesman (1619–95), 1619 M, 1695 M

Damiano de Goes, Port. historian (1501–73), 1539 H

Damiens, Robert François F. conspirator (1714–57), 1757 A

Damon and Pithias (Edwards), 1571 L

Dampier, William, E. navigator and buccaneer (1652–1715), 1652 M, 1683 G, 1699 G, 1715 M

Damville, Marquis de, Marshal of France, 1574 D

Dana, Francis, Am. jurist (1743–1811), 1743 M

Danae (Rembrandt), 1636 J

Danae (Titian), 1553 J

Danby, Earl of. *See* Osborne, T.

Dance, George, E. architect (1700–68), 1723 J, 1739 J

Dance of Death, The, Holbein's illustrations for, 1523 J

Danckelmann, Ernst von, G. politician, chancellor of Brandenburg, 1697 D

Dancourt, Florent Carton, F. dramatist (1661–1725), 1692 L, 1705 L

Dangan Hill, Eire, battle, 1647 C

Dangon, Claude, F. engineer, 1697 D

Daniel, Samuel, E. poet (1562–1619), 1592 L, 1603 H, 1605 L, 1619 M

Danish Ballads, 1591 L

Dannecker, Johann Heinrich von, G. sculptor (1758–1841), 1758 M

Danton, George Jacques, F. revolutionary leader (1759–94), 1759 M

Danube, River, Czechoslovakia, 1619 D, 1632 B

Danzig, Poland, 1629 C; surrenders to Stephen Báthory, 1577 D; sieges of, 1627 D, 1733 D; Russians take, 1734 B

Darby, Abraham, E. engineer (1677–1717), 1709 G

Darcy, Thomas, Lord Darcy, E. traitor (1467–1537), 1537 C

Dare, Virginia (b. 1587), first infant born in Raleigh's Roanoke Colony, 1587 M

Darien, Panamá, 1699 B; Balboa at, 1513 G; failure of Scottish colony at, 1698 D

Darnley, Henry, Lord Darnley, consort of Mary Queen of Scots (1545–67); marries Mary, 1565 C; share in Rizzio's murder, 1566 A; murdered, 1567 A

Daphnaida (Spenser), 1591 L

Daphnis and Chloe, translated, 1587 H, 1657 H

Darnell, Thomas, E. patriot (d. 1640), 1627 D

Darwin, Erasmus, E. scientist and poet (1731–1802), 1731 M

Dās Tutsī, Hindu poet (1532–1623), 1532 M, 1623 M

Dass, Petter, Norw. poet (?1648–1708), 1708 M

Daubenton, Louis Jean Marie, F. naturalist (1716–1800), 1716 M

Daun, Leopold, Count von, Aus. general (1705–66), defeated at Torgau, 1760 D

Dauphiné, France: peasant rising in, 1644 E; Savoy invades, 1691 B, 1692 B

Davel, Jean Abraham, Swi. rebel (d. 1724), 1723 E

Davenant, Charles, E. economist (1656–1714), 1656 M, 1714 M

Davenant (or D'Avenant), Sir William, E. poet and dramatist (1606–68), 1606 M, 1651 L, 1656 K, L, 1663 L, 1668 M

David, Gerard, Flem. artist (c. 1450–1523), 1502 J, 1509 J

David, Jacques Louis, F. artist (1748–1825), 1748 M

David (Bernini), 1623 J

David (Michelangelo), 1501 J

David and Bethsabe (Peele), 1599 L

Davidson, William, E. secretary of state (c. 1541–1608), 1587 A

Davies, Sir John, E. philosopher and poet (1569–1626), 1569 M, 1612 F, 1626 M

Davies, John of Mallwyd, We. scholar and lexicographer (c. 1570–1644), 1632 H

Davies, John of Hereford, E. schoolmaster, 1636 F

Davies, John, E. translator (c. 1627–93), 1656 H

Davila y Padilla, Augustin, Sp. historian (1562–1604), 1596 M

Davis, John, E. navigator (c. 1550–1605), 1585 G

Davis Strait, between Greenland and Baffin Island, 1585 G, 1616 G

Day, Angel, E. translator, 1587 H

Day, John, E. printer (1522–84), 1522 M, 1567 H, 1584 M

Day, John, E. dramatist (1574–1640), 1659 L

Day of Doom, The (Wigglesworth), 1662 H

'Day of Dupes', 1630 D

'Day of the Barricades', 1588 B

Deaf and Dumb:
  schools for, 1680 F, 1760 F
  sign language for, 1749 F

Deal, Kent, England, 1495 C

De Alpibus Commentarius (Simler), 1574 G

De Amicitia (Cicero, trans. Harington), 1550 H

Deane, Henry, E. churchman, Archbishop of Canterbury (1501–3), 1503 B

De Antiquitate Britannicae Ecclesiae (Parker), 1572 H

De Aquatilibus (Belon), 1553 G

De arte combinatoria (Leibniz), 1666 G

De arte graphica Liber (Dufresnoy), 1695 H

De arte supputandi (Tunstall), 1522 F

Death and the Woman (Baldung), 1514 J

Death of Saul (Bruegel), 1562 J

Death's Duell (Donne), 1632 H

Debating Society, 1755 F

De bello Belgico (Strada), 1632 F

Decades (Martyr), 1516 G

Decades de Orbe Nova (Martyr), 1530 F

Decades of the New World (Eden), 1555 G

Decades of the Portuguese in Asia (Barros), 1552 H

De Causis Errorum (Ld. Herbert), 1645 H

Deccan, The, India: Akbar's operations in, 1599 E; War of Succession in, 1749 E

Decimals: used to extend whole number rules to fractions, 1530 G; decimal fractions, 1576 G; Stevin advocates decimal system, 1585 G; decimal point first used, 1612 G

De Cive (Hobbes), 1642 F, 1651 F

Decker, Sir Matthew, E. political economist (1679–1749), 1744 F

Declaration of Indulgence, issued in England, 1672 H, 1687 B, H, 1688 B

Declaration of the People of Virginia, 1676 C

Declaration of Rights, in England, 1689 A

De

Derwentwater, Earls of. *See* Raddclyffe.
De Sacramento Matrimonii (Sanchez), 1592 H
De Sacra Poesi Hebraeorum (Lowth), 1753 H
Désastre de Lisbonne (Voltaire), 1756 L
Desault, Pierre Joseph, F. anatomist (1744–95), 1744 M
Descartes, René. F. philosopher (1596–1650), 1596 M, 1628 H, 1637 G, H, 1641 H, 1644 G, H, 1649 H, 1650 H, M, 1691 H
    Cartesian method used for study of conic sections, 1655 G
Descent from the Cross (Rubens), 1611 J
Descent from the Cross (Tintoretto), 1560 J
Descriptio Moldaviae (Cantemir), 1715 H
Description of England (Harrison), 1577 G
Description of New England, A (Smith), 1616 F
Description of the Country of Scotland (Howell), 1649 H
Description of the Sea Coasts and Islands of Scotland (Adair), 1703 H
De sexu planatarum epistola (Camerarius), 1694 G
Desfontaines, Pierre-François Guyot, Abbé, F. satirist and translator (1685–1745), 1726 H
De signatura rerum (Boehme), 1622 H
Desmarest, Nicolas, F. geologist (1725–1815), 1725 M
Desmarets, Jean de Saint-Sorlin, F. novelist and poet (1595–1676), 1637 L
Desmaretz, Nicolas, F. statesman (1648–1721), 1648 M, 1721 M
Desmond, Earl of. *See* Fitzgerald
Desmoulins, Lucie Simplice Camille Benoist, F. journalist and revolutionary (1760–94), 1760 M
Desportes, François, F. artist (1661–1743), 1713 J, 1729 J
Dessau, East Germany: Catholic League founded at, 1525 C; battle, 1676 B
De Statu Reipublicae Germanicae (Pufendorf), 1667 F
De Statu Religionis et Reipublicae Carlo V Caesare (Sleidanus), 1555 H
Destouches, Philippe Néricault, F. dramatist (1680–1754), 1727 L, 1732 L
Destruction of Troy (Denham), 1656 H
De subtilitate rerum (Cardan), 1551 H
Détail de la France, Le (Boisguilbert), 1695 F
De Thiende (Stevin), 1585 H
De Trinitatis Erroribus (Servetus), 1531 H
Detroit, Michigan, US, 1701 E, F
Dettingen, Bavaria, West Germany, battle of, 1743 B
De Uno Universi Juris Principis (Vico), 1720 F
Deutsche Schaubühne, Die (Gottsched), 1740 L
Deux dialogues de langage français italianisé (Estienne), 1578 F
De Varietate Rerum (Cardan), 1554 H
Deventer, Holland, 1591 B
De vera et falsa religione (Zwingli), 1525 H
De verbo mirifico (Reuchlin), 1494 H
Devereux, Robert, E. second Earl of Essex (1566–1601), 1566 M, 1591 C, 1592 A, 1598 C, 1599 F; at Cadiz, 1596 B; on Islands Voyage, 1597 C; appointed lord lieutenant of Ireland, 1599 A; signs truce with Tyrone, 1599 C; returns home and is arrested, 1599 C; trial, 1600 B; rebellion, 1601 A; execution, 1601 A, M
Devereux, Robert, E. third Earl of Essex (1591–1646), 1613 C; commands Parliamentary Army, 1642 C; at Edgehill, 1642 D; faces Charles I at Brentford, 1642 D; takes Reading, 1643 B; relieves Gloucester, 1643 C; escapes, 1644 C; deprived of office, 1645 A
De Veritate (Lord Herbert), 1624 H
Devil Is an Asse, The (Jonson), 1631 L
Devil's Law Case, The (Webster), 1623 L

Devil Upon Two Sticks, The. See Diable Boiteux, Le
Devis, Arthur, E. artist (1711–87), 1740 J, 1743 J, 1751 J
Devon, Earl of. *See* Courtenay, E.
Devonport, Devon, dockyard, 1689 F
Devonshire, Duke of. *See* Cavendish, William
Devotions Upon Emergent Occasions (Donne), 1624 H
Deza, Bishop, Sp. ecclesiastic, 1568 D
De Zeeuwsche Nachtegaal (Cats and others), 1623 L
Diable Boiteux, Le (Lesage), 1707 L
Diablo Conjuelo (de Guevara), 1641 L
Diall of Princes, The (North), 1557 H
Dialoge of Comfort Against Tribulacion (More), 1553 H
Dialogo de la musica antiqua e della moderna (Galilei), 1581 K
Dialogo de Medallas y Inscriciones (Agustino), 1587 F
Dialogo de Mercurio y Caron (Valdez), 1528 F
Dialogo sopra i due massimi sistema del mondo (Galileo), 1632 K
Dialogue des héros de romans (Boileau-Despréaux), 1688 H
Dialogues between Hylas and Philonous (Berkeley), 1713 H
Dialogues des Morts (Fontenelle), 1683 L
Dialogues of the Dead (Lyttelton), 1760 L
Dialogues Sacrés (Castellio), 1542 F
Dialogues Sur l'éloquence (Mothe-Fénelon), 1680 H
Diana (Constable), 1592 L
Diana, La (Montemayor), 1559 L
Diana and Calliste (Titian), 1559 J
Diana and a Stag (Goujon), 1560 J
Diane surprise par Achaeon (de Troy), 1734 J
Diaz de Novaes, Bartholomew, Port. explorer (1430–1500), 1500 G, M
Dickinson, John, Am. politician (1732–1808), 1732 M
Dictionaries (including Lexicons and Encyclopaedias):
    Reisch, *Margarita philosophia*, 1496 H
    Calepino, 1502 H
    Reuchlin, Hebrew, 1512 H
    Aleandro, 1512 H
    Estienne, Lat.–Fr., 1532 H
    van Ringelberg, 1541 H
    Aztec, 1555 H
    Scalich de Lika, *Encyclopaedia*, 1559 H
    Florio, It.–Eng., 1598 H
    Cawdrey, *Table Alphabetical*, 1604 H
    Cotgrave, Fr.–Eng., 1611 H
    Vocabolario, Italian, 1612 H
    Minsheu, *Guide to Tongues*, 1617 H
    Alsted, *Encyclopaedia*, 1620 H
    Spelman, *Glossarium*, 1626 H
    Académie Française, 1639 H
    Manwayring, *The Seaman's*, 1644 G
    Gilles Ménage, *Origines de la langue française*, 1650 H
    Borel, *Termes du vieux françois*, 1655 H
    Saunier, *L'Encyclopédie des beaux esprits*, 1657 H
    Lancelot, *Racines grecques*, 1657 H
    Phillips, *New World of Words*, 1658 H
    Somner, *Saxonico-Latino-Anglicum*, 1659 H
    Howell, *Lexicon Tetraglotten*, 1660 H
    Somaize, *Dict. des Prétieuses*, 1660 H
    Castell, *Heptaglotten*, 1669 H
    Moreri, *Dict. historique*, 1674 H
    Hofmann, *Universale*, 1677 H
    Du Cange, *Glossarium ad scriptores*, 1678 H
    Richelet, *Dict. françoise*, 1680 H
    Funetière, *Essais d'un dict. universel*, 1684 H, 1690 H
    Rochefort, *Dict. général et curieux*, 1685
    Corneille, *Dict. de l'Académie française*, 1694 H

Dictionaries

F

Bristol, 1645 C; Commons vote to retain as commander, 1647 B; takes Colchester, 1648 C
Fair Quarrel, A. (Middleton and Rowley), 1617 L
Faithful Farrier, The (Markham), 1629 H
Faithful Shepherdess, The (Fletcher), 1610 L
Falconer, William, Sc. poet (1732–69), 1762 L
Falconet, Étienne Maurice, F. sculptor (1716–91), 1716 M, 1754 J
Falkirk, Stirlingshire, Scotland, battle, 1746 A
Fall of Princes, The (Lydgate), 1494 L
Fall of the Rebel Angels (Bruegel), 1562 J
Fallopius, Gabriello, It. anatomist (*c.* 1523–62), 1561 G
Famagusta, Cyprus, falls to Turks, 1571 C
Family Compacts, between France and Spain:
First, by Treaty of Escorial, 1733 D
Second, 1743 D
Ferdinand VI of Spain severs himself from, 1749 C
Third, 1761 C
'Family of Love, The', sect, 1539 H
Famines, etc.:
in England, scarcity of corn, 1586 F
in France, at Paris, 1590 B
in India, 1661 E
in Italy, at Siena, 1555 B
at Florence, 1497, A
Fano, Italy, 1514 H
Fanshawe, Sir Richard, E. diplomat, translator and poet (1608–66), 1608 M, 1647 H, 1655 H, 1666 M, 1671 L
Fantazies of Three Parts (Gibbons), 1608 K
Fanzola, Italy, Villa Emo at, 1556 J
Farewell to Folly (Lyly), 1591 L
Farnaby, Thomas, E. schoolmaster, of Goldsmiths' Rents, Cripplegate, London (d. 1647), 1647 M
Farnese, Alessandro. *See under* Parma
Farnese, Elizabeth, Queen of Spain (1692–1766), 1692 M; marries Philip V of Spain, 1714 C; ambitions of, achieved, 1748 D
Farnese, Ottavio, It. soldier, 1550 D, 1551 B, 1552 B
Farnese, Pierluigi, Duke of Parma (1490–1547), 1545 C
Farnese, House of, extinction of, 1731 A
Farquhar, George, Ir. dramatist (1678–1707), 1678 M, 1699 L, 1700 L, 1701 L, 1702 L, 1704 L, 1706 L, 1707 L, M
Farrant, Richard, E. musician (1532–82), 1582 M
Farsas y églogas (Fernández), 1514 L
Faubourg St. Antoine, Paris, battle of, 1652 C
Fauchard, F. dentist, 1728 G
Faust Legend, The, 1587 L, 1731 L
Fawkes, Francis, E. cleric, scholar and poet (1721–77), 1760 H
Fawkes, Guy, E. conspirator (1570–1606), 1570 M; arrested, 1605 D; tried, 1606 A; executed, 1606 M
Fayette, Marie Joseph du Motier, Marquis de, F. politician (1757–1834), 1757 M
Fayette, Marie-Madeleine Pioche de la Vergne, Comtesse de, F. novelist (1634–93), 1634 M, 1670 L, 1678 L, 1693 M
Fayrfax, Robert, E. musician (d. 1529), 1520 K
Federation, Penn suggests, 1693 F
Fehrbellin, E. Germany, battle, 1675 B
Félibien, André, F. author (1619–95), 1666 J
Felicini Madonna (Francia), 1494 J
Fell, John, E. divine (1625–86), 1625 M, 1686 M
Felltham, Owen, E. essayist (?1602–68), 1623 H
Felton, John, E. Catholic layman (d. 1570), 1570 A
Felton, John, E. assassin (*c.* 1596–1628), 1628 C, M
Female Quixote, The (Lennex), 1752 L
Feminine Monarchie, The; or a treatise concerning bees (Butler), 1609 G

Femmes Savantes, Les (Molière), 1672 L
Fencing, manual on, 1535 F
Fénelon, François de Salignac de la Mothe, F. religious writer, polemicist, and Archbishop of Cambrai (1651–1715), 1651 M, 1680 H, 1687 F, 1697 H, 1699 L, 1710 F, 1713 H, 1715 M, 1716 H, 1717 L
Fénix Renascida (da Silva), 1716 L
Fens, The, East Anglia, drainage of, 1621 G; history of, 1662 G
Fenton, Sir Geoffrey, E. translator (1539–1608), 1579 H
Fenton, Elijah, E. poet (1683–1730), 1683 M, 1730 M
Fenton, Lavinia, E. actress, duchess of Bolton (1708–60), 1708 M, 1760 M
Fenton, Roger, E. divine (1565–1616), 1612 F, 1653 F
Fenwick, Sir John, E. conspirator (*c.* 1645–97), 1696 A, D, 1697 A, M
Feodore III, Tsar of Russia (1676–82), *see* Theodore III
Fer, Jambe de, F. musician, 1556 K
Ferdinand I, Holy Roman Emperor (1558–64), grandson of Maximilian I and son of Philip the Handsome, 1522 A, 1564 C
as Archduke of Austria, betrothed to Anne of Hungary, 1506 A, 1515 C
granted lands by Charles V, 1521 B
marries Anne of Hungary, 1521 B
plans to reform Church, 1524 B
as King of Bohemia, 1527 A, B, 1538 A, B, 1540 C
election, 1526 D
defeats John Zápolya, 1527 C
regains western Hungary, 1547 B
right to succession in Hungary and Transylvania, 1551 C
as King of Romans, election, 1531 A
opposition to, 1532 B
Hapsburg family compact for succession to Empire, 1551 A
opens diet of Augsburg, 1555 A
as Emperor, Charles V resigns government to, 1556 C
assumes title of Emperor, 1558 A
truce with Turks, 1562 B
Ferdinand II, Holy Roman Emperor (1619–37), 1578 M, 1631 A, 1632 B, 1633 B, 1637 A, M
as archduke of Styria, 1590 C, 1617 C
support for imperial claim, 1616 E
recognised as heir to Bohemian Crown, 1617 B
crowned King of Hungary, 1618 C
assumes Crown of Bohemia, 1619 A
elected Emperor, 1619 C
deposed by Bohemian Diet, 1619 C
signs treaty with Maximilian of Bavaria, 1619 D
gains armed support for Catholic League, 1619 D
captures Lower Austria, 1620 C
places Frederick V of Palatinate under ban of Empire, 1621 A
signs peace with Bethlen Gabor, 1622 A, 1626 D
holds Heidelberg, 1622 D
grants Upper Palatinate to Maximilian of Bavaria 1623 A
confiscates Jagerndorf, 1623 A
appoints Wallenstein imperial general, 1625 B
creates Wallenstein Duke of Friedland, 1625 B
signs treaty with Turks, 1627 C
disputes succession to Mantua, 1627 D, 1630 C
places Mecklenburg under ban of Empire, 1628 B
signs Peace of Lubeck, 1629 B
Promises to dismiss Wallenstein, 1630 C
reinstates Wallenstein, 1632 B
suspects Wallenstein of treachery 1633 D

Fitzjames, James, Duke of Berwick, E. soldier (1670–1734), 1670 M, 1714 C, 1734 B, M
Fitzmaurice, William Petty, Earl of Shelburne, E. statesman, prime minister (1737–1805), 1737 M
Fitzroy, Henry, Duke of Richmond (1519–36), natural son of Henry VIII, 1525 B, 1536 B
Fitzwilliam Virginal-Book (ed. Tregian), 1619 K
Flacius, Matthias, G. Protestant scholar and controversialist (1520–75), 1559 H, 1560 H
Flageolet, the, 1581 K
Flags, national, 1606 B
Flamsteed, John, E. astronomer (1646–1719), 1646 M, 1675 G, 1719 M, 1725 G
Flatman, Thomas, E. miniaturist and poet (1637–88), 1674 L
Flaxman, John, E. sculptor (1755–1826), 1755 M
Fléchier, Esprit, F. churchman and author, bishop of Nîmes (1632–1710), 1632 M, 1680 H, 1710 M
Fleece, The (Dyer), 1757 L
Fleetwood, Charles, E. Parliamentary general (d. 1692), 1692 M
Fleix, Treaty of, 1580 D
Fletcher, Andrew, Sc. patriot (1655–1716), 1655 M, 1716 M
Fletcher, John, E. dramatist (1579–1625), 1579 M, 1610 L, 1619 L, 1621 L, 1625 M, 1634 L, 1647 L, 1679 L
Fletcher, Phineas, E. poet (1582–1650), 1582 M, 1633 L, 1650 M
Fleurian, Charles-Jean-Baptiste, F. politician, 1723 C
Fleurus, Belgium, battle, 1690 C
Fleury, André Hercule de, F. cardinal and statesman (1653–1743), 1653 M, 1735 C, 1738 C, 1743 A, M; becomes chief minister, 1726 B; annuls decree on temporalities, 1731 C; relations with Chauvelin, 1737 A
Fleury, Claude, F. church historian (1640–1723), 1691 H
Flintlock, perfection of, 1630 G
Floating Island, The (Strode), 1655 L
Flodden, Northumberland, England, battle, 1513 C
Flöhhaz, Die (Fischart), 1573 L
Flood, Henry, Ir. statesman (1732–91), 1732 M
Flora (Rysbrack), 1761 J
Flora (Titian), 1515 J
Flora Virginica (Grovonius), 1739 G
Florence, Italy, 1492 B, 1760 G
  alliance with Naples, 1492 D
  famine, 1497 A
  joins French alliance, 1499 A
  militia formed, 1506 D, F
  takes Pisa, 1509 B ..
  at mercy of Holy League, 1512 B
  becomes Republic, 1527 B
  Charles V undertakes to restore Medici, 1529 B
  opposition to Medici, 1529 D
  restoration of Medici, 1530 C
  accession of Cosimo de Medici, 1537 A
  plague in, 1575 H
  places in:
    Biblioteca Laurenziana, 1524 J
    Fine Arts Academy, 1550 J
    Florentine Camerata, 1581 K
    frescoes in, 1496 J
    Medici Palace, 1521 J
    Medici tombs, 1521 J
    Michelangelo's fortifications, 1528 J
    Pallazzo Pandolfini, 1520 J
    porcelain manufacture in, 1575 G
    S. Lorenziana, 1513 J, 1526 J
      Medici chapel in, 1520 J

  statues in, 1594 J
  music in, 1592 K
Florence, Guicciardini's *History*, 1536 F
Florentine History (Machiavelli), 1525 H; trans. 1595 H
Flores, in Azores, 1591 C, 1592 C
Flores Historicum (ed. Parker), 1570 H
Florian, Jean Pierre Claris de, F. poet (1755–94), 1755 M
Florida, US: discovered, 1513 G; exploration of, 1519 G, 1524 G, 1539 G; Huguenot claims to, 1562 E; Indians driven into, 1715 B; exchanged by Spain for Havana, 1762 D; Britain secures, 1762 D
Florio, John, E. humanist and translator (?1553–1625), 1598 H, 1603 H
'Floris', Cornelius (de Vriendt), Flem. architect (1520–70), 1561 J
Floures for Latine Speaking (Udall), 1553 H
Flowres of Sion (Drummond), 1623 L
Floyd, Edward, E. lawyer and Roman Catholic (c. d. 1648), 1621 A
Floyer, Sir John, E. physician (1649–1734), 1707 G
Fludd, Robert, E. experimental philosopher (1574–1637), 1633 G
Fluids, pressure of, 1738 G
Flushing, Holland, 1585 C, 1625 A; sold by English to Dutch, 1616 B
Fluxions, notation of, 1666 G
  treaties on, 1737 G, 1742 G
Flying-machine, designed, 1492 J
'Flying Shuttle', Kay's, 1733 G
Foedera (ed. Rymer), 1704 H
Foigny, Gabriel de, F. philosopher (c. 1640–c. 92), 1676 H
Foix, France, annexed to French crown, 1591 E
Folastries, Les (Ronsard, 1553 L
Folembray, Decrees of, 1596 A
Folengo, Teofilo, It. poet (c. 1496–1544), It. macaronic poet, 1517 L, 1544 M
Foliot, Henry, E. soldier, 1608 C
Folkstone, Kent, England, 1652 B
Fontaine, Jean de la, F. poet (1621–95), 1621 M, 1664 L, 1665 L, 1668 L, 1678 L, 1693 L, 1695 M, 1734 M
Fontainebleau, France, 1602 B
Fontainebleau, Edict of, 1540 B
Fontainebleau, Treaties of, 1631 B, 1679 C
Fontana, Domenico, It. architect (1543–1607), 1588 J
Fontenelle, Bernard le Bovier, sieur de, F. author (1657–1757), 1657 M, 1683 L, 1686 H, 1757 M
Fontenoy, Belgium, battle, 1745 B
Fool's Paradise (Bruegel), 1567 J
Foote, Samuel, E. dramatist and actor (1720–77), 1720 M
Forbes, Duncan, of Culloden, Sc. statesman (1685–1747), 1685 M, 1747 M
Forced Marriage, The (Behn), 1671 L
Ford, John, E. dramatist (1586–c. 1640), 1586 M, 1629 L, 1633 L, 1634 L, 1638 L, 1640 M, 1656 L
Forgeries, Literary:
  Annius of Viterbo, 1498 H
  Bertram, 1757 H
  Macpherson, 1760 L, 1762 L
Forgery, made a capital offence in England, 1634 F
Forli, Italy, 1500 A
Forli, Countess of. *See* Sforza, Caterina
Forli, Melozzo da, It. artist (c. 1438–94), 1494 M
Formosa (Taiwan), China: Dutch occupy, 1635 E; China wrests from Dutch, 1662 E; Manchus conquer, 1683 E; revolution in, suppressed, 1721 E

Gotha, League of, 1526 A

Gotland, Sweden, succession to, 1534 B

Göttingen, Lower Saxony, West Germany: Tilly takes, 1626 C; University, 1737 F; Society of Sciences in, 1751 F

Gottsched, Johann Christoph, G. dramatist and critic (1700–66), 1700 M, 1732 H, 1737 L, 1740 L

Gotz, Count Sigismund von, G. soldier, 1636 D

Goujon, Jean, F. artist (*fl.* 1540–62), 1560 J

Gouttes, Jean Louis, F. prelate and economist (1740–94), 1762 F

Gouthière, Pierre, F. metal-worker (1740–1806), 1740 M

Gouvernante, La (Chardin), 1738 J

Gowanns Bay, Rhode Island, US, 1636 F

Gowrie conspiracy, 1600 C

Gowrie, Earls of. *See* Ruthven

Gowrie raiders, 1582 C, 1583 B

Goya y Lucientes, Francisco ('Goya'), Sp. artist (1746–1828), 1746 M

Goyen, Jan van, Du. artist (1596–1656), 1641 J, 1646 J, 1650 J, 1653 J, 1659 J

Gozzi, Count Carlo, It. author (1720–1806), 1748 L

Grace Abounding to the Chief of Sinners (Bunyan), 1666 H

Gracián y Morales, Baltasar, Sp. Jesuit (1584–1658), 1647 H

Gradualia (Byrd), 1607 K

Gradus ad parnassum (Fux), 1725 K

Grafton, Richard, E. chronicler (d. 1572), 1562 H

Graham, George, E. mathematician (1673–1751), 1725 G

Graham, James, Marquess of Montrose, Sc. soldier (1612–50), 1612 M, 1645 B; defeats Covenanters, 1644 C; victory at Inverlocky, 1645 A; victory at Auldearn, 1645 B; defeat at Philiphaugh, 1645 C; execution, 1650 B, M

Graham, John, of Claverhouse, Viscount Dundee, Sc. soldier (1649–89), 1649 M, 1689 M; defeated at Drumclog, 1679 B; at Killiecrankie, 1689 C

Grammatica Sinica (Fourmont), 1742 H

Gramont, Philibert, Comte de, F. courtier and libertine (1621–1707), 1621 M, 1707 M, 1713 H

Granada, Spain: Spanish conquest, 1492 A; persecution of Moors, 1499 A; Moorish revolts, 1500 B, 1501 A, 1568 D, 1569 E; declared a Christian state, 1501 C; Cathedral, 1528 J; University, 1531 F

Granada, Treaty of, 1500 D

Granby, Marquess of. *See* Manners, John

Grand Canyon, Arizona, US, discovered, 1540 G

Grand Cyrus, Le (de Scudéry), 1649 L, 1653 L

Grand Dictionnaire des Prétieuses; ou, la Clef de la langue des ruelles, Le (Bandeau), 1660 H

Grand dictionnaire historique; ou, le Mélange curieux de l'histoire sainte et profane (Moreri), 1674 H

Grandes Misères de la Guerre, Les (Callot), 1632 J

Grandeur des Romains et leur Décadence (Montesquien), 1734 H

Grandjean, Philippe, F. printer, 1702 H

Grand Mystery of Godliness (More), 1660 H

Grand Tour, handbook on, 1722 J

Gran Quivira region, US, search for, 1541 G

Grantham, Lincolnshire, England: parish library, 1598 H; battle, 1643 B

Granville, Earl. *See* Carteret, John

Grasslands, irrigation of, 1610 G

Gratton, Henry, Ir. statesman (1746–1820), 1746 M

Graunt, John, E. statistician (1620–74), 1661 F

Grave, Belgium, 1674 C

Grave, The (Blair), 1743 L

Gravelines, France, 1520 B, C, 1657 A; English victory at, 1558 C; Armada defeated at, 1588 C;

French capture, 1644 B; Spanish capture, 1652 B; Spanish defeated at, 1658 C

Granvella, Cardinal. *See* Perrenot, Antoine

Gravesande, William Jacob, Du. scientist (1688–1742), 1717 G

Gravièr, Charles. *See* Vergennes, Comte de

Gravina, Gian Vincenzo, It. critic and dramatist (1664–1718), 1708 H, 1713 F, 1715 H

Gravity, experiments on, 1684 G, 1740 G

Gray, Stephen, E. scientist (d. 1736), 1729 G

Gray, Thomas, E. poet (1716–71), 1716 M, 1747 L, 1748 L, 1751 L, 1757 L

Graz, Styria, south Austria, university, 1585 F

Great Contract, The, 1610 B, 1611 A

Great Duke of Florence, The (Massinger), 1636 L

Great Elector, The. *See* Frederick William I of Brandenburg

Great Improvement of Lands by Clover, The (Yarranton), 1663 G

Great Lakes, Canada, explored by La Salle, 1678 G

Great Passion (Dürer), 1498 J

Greco, El (Dominico Theotocopuli), Cretan artist (d. 1614), 1577 J, 1586 J, 1597 J, 1598 J, 1608 J, 1609 J, 1610 J, 1612 J, 1614 J, M

Greek, Classical, study of, 1518 H, 1529 F, 1533 F printing press, 1513 H

Greek Language Commentaries (Budé), 1529 H

Green, Matthew, E. poet and Quaker (1696–1737), 1737 L

Greene, Maurice, E. musician (1695–1755), 1695 M, 1755 M

Greene, Nathanael, Am. general (1742–86), 1742 M

Greene, Robert, E. dramatist and pamphleteer (1558–92), 1558 M, 1589 L, 1591 L, 1592 L, M, 1594 L

Greenland, exploration of, 1500 G, 1585 G

Greensleeves, the tune, 1580 K

Greenwich, Kent, England, 1579 C
  Queen's House, 1616 J, 1666 J
  Hospital, 1692 F, 1694 J
    painted hall, 1698 J, 1708 J
  Observatory, 1675 G, 1725 G

Greenwich, Treaties of, 1526 B, 1543 C

Gregorian Calendar. *See under* Calendar

Gregory XIII, Pope (Ugo Buoncompagno), It. (1502–85), 1502 M, 1585 B, M; election, 1572 B; mediates Russo-Polish peace, 1582 A; reforms Calendar, 1582 D; concordat with Bavaria, 1583 E

Gregory XIV, Pope (Nicolo Sfondrato), It. (1535–91), 1535 M, 1591 A, 1591 D, M; election, 1590 D

Gregory XV, Pope (Alessandro Ludovisi), It. (1554–1623), 1621 A, 1623 C, 1628 H

Greifswald, Rostock, East Germany, Great Elector conquers, 1678 D

Grembloux, Holland, 1578 A

Grenada, West Indies, Britain obtains, 1762 D, E

Grenada, Nicaragua, founded, 1524 F

Grenoble, France, 1590 D

Grenville, George, E. statesman (1712–70), 1712 M, 1755 D

Grenville, Sir Richard, E. naval commander (*c.* 1541–91), 1585 C, 1591 C, M

Grenville, William Wyndham, baron Grenville, E. statesman (1759–1834), 1759 M

Gresham, Sir Thomas, E. economist and financier (1519–79), 1519 M, 1558 F, 1565 F, 1579 M

Gresham's Law, 1558 F

Gresset, Jean-Baptiste Louis, F. poet and dramatist (1709–77), 1745 L

Grétry, André, F. musician (1741–1813), 1741 M

Greuze, Jean-Baptiste, F. artist (1725–1805), 1725 M, 1757 J, 1759 J

Greville, Fulke, Lord Brooke, E. author (1554–1628), 1554 M, 1628 M, 1652 L

Grew, Nehemiah, E. botanist (1641–1712), 1676 G, 1695 G

Grey, Henry, Duke of Suffolk, E. soldier and politician (d. 1554), 1554 A

Grey, Henry, E. Parliamentary general (?1599–1673), 1643 B

Grey, Lady Jane. See Jane

Grey, Leonard, Lord Grey, E. traitor (d. 1541), 1541 B

Grey, Thomas, Marquess of Dorset, E. soldier (1477–1530), 1512 B

Grey, Thomas, Baron of Wilton (d. 1614), E. politician, 1603 C

Grey, Zachary, E. scholar (1688–1766), 1754 H

Griffenfeldt, Count Peder ('Peder Schumacher'), Dan. statesman (1635–99), 1635 M, 1699 M

Grijalva, Juan de, Sp. explorer, 1518 G

Grimald, Nicholas, E. churchman, translator and anthologist (1519–62), 1557 L

Grimaldi, Francis, It. scientist (1618–63), 1665 G

Grimmelshausen, Hans Jacob Christoffel von, G. novelist (c. 1625–76), 1668 L, 1676 M

Grimestone, Edward, E. historian, 1608 H

Grindal, Edmund, E. churchman, archbishop of Canterbury (c. 1519–83), 1583 C; election, 1575 D; sequestration, 1577 B

Grisons, Canton, south east Switzerland: League with Valtelline, 1620 B; Austrian power in, 1622 C; independence confirmed, 1626 A; Jenatsch assassinated, 1639 A; obtains Valtelline, 1639 C

Groatsworth of Wit (Greene), 1592 L

Grobianus (Dedekind), 1552 H

Grolier de Servier, Jean, Viscomte d'Aguisy, F. bibliophile (1475–1565), 1565 M

Grongar Hill (Dyer), 1727 L

Groningen, Holland, University, 1614 F

Gronovius, Jean Frederick, G. naturalist (1611–71), 1739 G

Gross-Fredericksburg. See Fort Hollandia

Gross Jagerndorf, East Germany, battle, 1757 C

Grossmüthiger Feldherr Arminius (von Lohenstein), 1689 L

Grosswardein (now Orádea Mare), Roumania: surrenders to Turks, 1660 C; Louis of Baden takes, 1692 B

Grosswardein, Treaty of, 1538 A

Grotius, Hugo, Du. publicist and statesman (1583–1645), 1583 M, 1619 B, 1625 F, 1645 M

Growth of the City of London, The (Petty), 1683 F

Grumbling Hive, The (Fable of the Bees) (de Mandeville), 1705 H, 1714 H

Grünewald, Mathis, G. artist (c. 1470–1528), 1509 J, 1520 J

Gruter, Janus, Du. classical scholar (1560–1627), 1603 H

Gryphius, Andreas, G. poet and dramatist (1616–64), 1616 M, 1649 L, 1650 L, 1657 L, 1663 L, 1664 M

Guadeloupe, West Indies: French occupy, 1635 E; France retains, 1762 D

Guardi, Francesco, It. artist (1712–93), 1712 M

Guardian, The (Massinger), 1655 L

Gueraino, It., Stefano (1591–1666), 1591 M, 1666 M

Guarini, Giovanni Battista, It. diplomat, poet and dramatist (1537–1612), 1537 M, 1612 M, 1647 H

Guastella, Italy, 1734 C, 1748 D

Guatemala: Spanish capture, 1522 E; settlement of, 1537 F

Guazzo, Stefano, It. diplomat and author (1530–93), 1581 H

Guebriant, Jean Baptiste Budes, Comte de, marshal of France (1602–43), 1641 B, 1642 A

Guelders. See Gelders

Guericke, Otto von, G. scientist (1602–86), 1650 G, 1654 G, 1663 G

Guettard, Jean Étienne, F. geologist (1715–86), 1746 G

Guevara, Antonio de, Sp. bishop and author (1490–1545), 1529 L, 1557 H

Guevara, Luiz Vélez de, Sp. dramatist (c. 1572–1644), 1641 L

Guiana, British, company is chartered, 1627 B
Dutch, 1598 E, 1667 C
French, 1674 E

Guicciardini, Francesco, It. statesman and historian (1483–1540), 1536 F, 1540 M, 1567 H, 1579 H

Guide des arts et sciences (Mareschal), 1598 H

Guide to Tongues (Minsheu), 1617 H

Guide to Truth (Pázmány), 1613 H

Guidobaldi, Duke of Urbino, 1503 D

Guido Reni, It. artist (1575–1642), 1575 M, 1642 M

Guinne, south west France, 1511 D, 1621 D; English expedition to, 1512 B; civil war in, 1615 C; revolt in, 1637 B

Guilds, Craft, regulations of:
in England, 1504 F, 1563 F
in France, 1561 F

Guilford, Earl of. See North, Frederick

Guillotine, Joseph, F. physician and inventor (1738–1814), 1738 M

Guilio, Romano, It. artist and architect (c. 1492–1546), 1492 M, 1546 M

Guinea, West Africa, 1616 A
slave trading expeditions to, 1562 F, 1593 E
English Guinea Company, 1588 F
merges with Royal Africa Company, 1672 E

Guinegate, France, battle ('the Spurs'), 1513 C

Giupúzcoa, north Spain, to be retained by Dauphin, 1698 D

Guise, north France, duchy, occupation of, 1536 C

Guise, Charles of, Cardinal of Lorraine, F. churchman and politician (1525–1574), 1525 M, 1561 C, 1562 A, 1574 D, M

Guise, Charles, fourth Duke of, F. soldier and politician (1571–1640), 1594 B, 1596 A

Guise, Francis of Lorraine, second Duke of, F. politician and soldier (1519–63), 1552 D, 1556 D, 1557 C, 1560 A, 1561 A, 1562 A, 1563 A

Guise, Henry, third Duke of, F. politician and soldier (1550–88); Coligny eclipses, 1570 C; expulsion from France demanded, 1574 D; Henry III allies himself to, by marriage, 1575 A; forces Huguenot army to withdraw, 1575 D; forms Catholic League, 1576 B; controls elections to Estates General, 1576 D; develops Catholic League to oppose Navarre, 1584 B; supports Catholic enterprise against England, 1584 D; arranges treaty of Joinville with Spain, 1585 A; Henry III capitulates to demands of, 1585 C; supported by The Sixteen in Paris, 1586 D; operations near Chartres, 1587 D; forbidden to enter Paris, 1587 D; becomes master of Paris, 1588 B; assassinated at Blois, 1588 D

Guise, Henry, fifth Duke (1614–64), formerly archbishop of Rheims, 1647 D

Guise, Louis, Cardinal of, F. churchman, assassinated, 1588 D

Gulberg, Sweden, 1612 A, B

Gulliver's Travels (Swift), 1726 L

Guls Horne-booke (Dekker), 1609 L

Gunshot wounds, treatment for, 1545 G

Gunter, Edmund, E. mathematician (1581–1626), 1620 G, 1622 G

Charles VII (1742–5)
Francis I (1745–65)
See also under Hapsburg, house of; Wars
Holyroodhouse, Edinburgh, Scotland, 1566 A
Holy State, The (Fuller), 1642 H
Holy War, The (Bunyan), 1682 H
Homberg, William, Du. chemist (1652–1715), 1702 G
Home, Henry, Sc. philosopher (1696–1782), 1751 H, 1761 H, 1762 H
Home, John, Sc. clergyman and dramatist (1722–1808), 1757 L
Homer, works of, translations:
 Chapman, 1598 H, 1611 H, 1614 H, 1616 H, 1624 H
 Hobbes, 1674 H
 Ogilby, 1660 H
 Pope, 1715 H, 1725 H
Hondschoote, Belgium, riots in, 1566 C
Honduras, Cen. America, Columbus visits, 1502 G
Hontau, baron de la, F. explorer, 1689 G
Honthorst, Gerard von, Du. artist (1590–1656), 1618 J, 1620 J, 1622 J, 1623 J, 1628 J
Honwaerd, Baptista, Du. poet (c. 1550–1600), 1583 L
Hooch, Pieter de, Du. artist (1629–c. 85), 1654 J, 1658 J, 1663 J, 1664 J, 1677 J
Hood, Alexander, Viscount Bridport, E. admiral (1727–1814), 1727 M
Hood, Samuel, Viscount Hood, E. admiral (1724–1816), 1724 M
Hooke, Robert, E. scientist (1635–1703), 1665 G, 1668 G
Hooker, Richard, E. theologian (1554–1600), 1554 M, 1594 H, 1600 M, 1648 H, 1665 L
Hooper, John, E. churchman, reformer and Bishop of Gloucester (d. 1555), 1555 A, M
Hoorn, Philip de Montmorency, Count of, Du. patriot (d. 1568), 1567 C, 1568 B
Hop Garden, The (Smart), 1752 L
Hôpital, Michel de l', F. statesman, Constable of France (c. 1505–73), 1560 B, 1561 A, 1562 A, 1573 A, M; dismissed, 1568 A; supports Huguenots, 1572 C
Hops, introduced to England, 1525 G
Hoppner, John, E. artist (1758–1810), 1758 M
Horace, works of, translated, 1743 H, 1746 H
Horace (Corneille), 1639 L
Horae Lyricae (Watts), 1706 H
Horn, Count Arvid Bernhard, Swe. statesman (1664–1742), 1738 D
Horologium Oscillatorium (Huygens), 1673 G
Horribilicribrifax (Gryphius), 1663 L
Horrocks, Jeremiah, E. astronomer (c. 1617–41), 1639 G
Horse-hoe, 1714 G
Horse-hoeing Husbandry (Tull), 1731 G
Horse-racing:
 in England, Jockey Club founded, 1750 F
  Newmarket race-course, 1753 F
 in America, first races, 1734 F
  Jockey Club founded, 1734 F
Hortus medicus (Camerarius), 1588 G
Hose, flexible, for fire-fighting, 1672 G
Hose, stocking, ribbing-machine for making, 1758 G
Hospitals:
 in England, dissolution of medieval, 1545 D
  Chelsea, for soldiers, 1681 F, 1682 J
  Foundling Hospital, London, 1739 F
  Greenwich, for seamen, 1692 F, 1694 J
  Guy's, London, 1725 F
  Manchester Royal Infirmary, 1752 F
  St. Bartholomew's, London, 1544 F
   Harvey's lectures at, 1619 G
 dispensaries advocated, 1699 F

in France, Renaudot's plans for free medical treatment, 1641 F
Hotman, François, F. political author (1524–90), 1524 M, 1573 M, 1590 M
Hottentots, party of, travels beyond Orange River, 1760 E
Houdon, Jean Antoine, F. sculptor (1740–1828), 1740 M
Houghton, John, E. author on agriculture and trade (d. 1705), 1677 F
Houghton Hall, Yorks, England, 1721 J
Hounslow Heath, Middlesex, England, army camps at, 1686 C
Howard, Charles, Lord Howard of Effingham, Earl of Nottingham, E. admiral (1536–1624), 1536 M, 1588 C, 1596 B, 1624 M
Howard, Sir Edward, E. admiral (c. 1477–1513), 1512 C
Howard, Lady Francis, E., successively Countess of Essex and of Somerset, 1613 C, D
Howard, Henry, Earl of Surrey, E. poet and soldier (1517–47), 1517 M, 1546 A; downfall, 1546 D; execution, 1547 A, M; works, 1557 H, L
Howard, Henry, Earl of Northampton, E. politician (1540–1614), first Lord of Treasury, 1612 B
Howard, John, E. reformer of prisons (1726–90), 1726 M
Howard, Philip, Earl of Arundel, E. Catholic layman (1557–95), 1557 M, 1595 M
Howard, Thomas, third Duke of Norfolk, E. soldier and politician (1473–1554), 1538 J; at Flodden, 1513 C; harries Scots, 1523 A, C; puts down Pilgrimage of Grace, 1536 D; opposes Cromwell, 1540 B; invades Scotland, 1542 D; downfall of, 1546 D
Howard, Thomas, fourth Duke of Norfolk, E. politician (1536–72), 1562 J, 1569 A, D; sent to Tower, 1571 C; trial, 1572 A
Howard, Thomas, Earl of Suffolk, E. admiral and statesman (1561–1626), lord treasurer, 1614 C
Howard, William, Viscount Stafford, E. politician (1614–80), treason of, 1680 D
Howe, Richard, Earl Howe, E. admiral (1726–99), 1726 M
Howell, James, We. pamphleteer and letter-writer (c. 1594–1666), 1640 H, 1642 H, 1645 H, 1649 H, 1660 H
Hsu Wei, Chin. novelist, 1560 L
Hudibras (Butler), 1662 L, 1663 L, 1678 L
Hudson Bay, Canada, discovered, 1610 G; ceded by France to Britain, 1713 A
Hudson River, New York, US, discovered, 1524 G, 1609 G
Hudson, Henry, E. navigator (d. 1611), 1609 G, 1610 G, 1611 M
Huguenots. *See* Religious Denominations
Humayum, Mogul Emperor of India (d. 1556), 1545 E, 1547 E, 1556 D
Humble Petition and Advice, 1657 A, B
Hume, David, Sc. historian, philosopher and economist (1711–76), 1711 M, 1739 H, 1741 H, 1748 H, 1751 H, 1752 F, 1753 H, 1754 H, 1757 H, 1759 H, 1762 H
Human Understanding (Hume), 1748 H
Hundredth Good Pointes of Husbandrie, A (Tusser), 1557 G
Hungary:
 Peasants' revolt, 1514 C
 Louis II succeeds Ladislas II, 1516 B
 Louis II is killed at Mohacs, 1526 C
 John Zápolya crowned King, 1526 D
 Ferdinand of Bohemia defeats Zápolya, 1527 C

Imola, North Italy, revolt in, 1503 D
Importante, suppressed, in France, 1643 C
Impositions, royal, in England, 1606 F. *See also*
  Taxation, in England
Inchbald, Elizabeth, E. author (1753–1821), 1753 M
Inclosures thrown open; or Depopulation depopulated
  (Halhead), 1650 F
Incognita (Congreve), 1691 L
Inconstant and the Twin Rivals, The (Farquhar),
  1702 L
Incunabula typographicae (a Beughen), 1688 H
Index Librorum Prohibitorum, 1543 H, 1557 H, 1559 H,
  1564 H, 1595 H
India:
  Barbar defeats Hindu Confederacy, 1527 A
  Portuguese in, History of, 1539 H
  Afghan emperor rules at Delhi, 1540 C
  John de Castro as Portuguese viceroy, 1545 E
  Akbar defeats Afghans, 1556 D
  Akbar conquers Rajput Kingdom, 1560 E
  first English settler, 1579 H
  expeditions to, 1583 G
  English East India Company, chartered, 1600 F
    See also under East India Company
  first skirmishes between English and Dutch, 1610 D
  English settlements, 1611 F
  Anglo–Dutch commercial rivalry regulated by
    treaty, 1619 B
  English settlement at Cochin, 1634 F
    at Madras, 1640 F
  French settlements in, restored, 1762 D
  See also East India Companies; Wars
Indians, North American:
  Frontenac conciliates Iroquois, 1673 C
  Iroquois, massacre of French-Canadian settlers at
    Lachine by, 1689 C
    treaty with, 1753 C
  Tuscarura massacre white settlers, 1711 C
  Wampanrag attack British, 1675 C
Indies, West. *See* West Indies
Indivisibles, method of, 1658 G
Industion (Sackville), 1559 L, 1563 L
Indulgences, for rebuilding St. Peter's Rome, 1507 H,
  1517 F, H
Inégalité parmi des hommes, L' (Rousseau), 1754 H
Inflammation, theory of, 1708 G
Ingoldstadt, Bavaria, West Germany: university,
  1563 H; Swedish siege raised, 1632 B; Wallenstein
  withdraws to, 1632 C
Ingria, Sweden: Sweden obtains, 1617 A; Sweden
  cedes to Russia, 1721 C
Inigo extract, 1740 C
Ink, composition of, 1748 G
Inkel and Yariko (Gessner), 1756 L
Innocency with her Open Face (Penn), 1669 H
Innocent VIII, Pope (Giovanni Battista Cibo), It.
  (1432–92), 1492 B
Innocent IX, Pope (Giovanni Antonio Fachinetti),
  It. (1519–91), 1519 M, 1591 M
Innocent X, Pope (Giovanni Battista Pamfili), It.
  (1574–1655), 1574 M, 1655 M; election, 1644 C;
  condemns Treaty of Westphalia, 1648 D, H
Innocent XI, Pope (Benedetto Odescalchi), It. (1611–
  89), 1676 C, 1689 C
Innocent XII, Pope (Antonio Pignatelli), It. (1615–
  1700), 1691 B, 1693 E, 1700 D
Innocent XIII, Pope (Michele Angelo Conti), It.
  (1655–1724), 1721 B, 1724 A
Innsbruck, Austria, 1552 B; university, 1677 F
Inoculation for small pox, 1721 G
In Praise of Folly (Erasmus), 1511 H
Inquiry into Freedom of the Will (Edwards), 1754 H

Inquiry into Increase of Robbers (Fielding), 1751 L
*Inquiry into the Original of our Ideas of Beauty and
  Virtue* (Hutcheson), 1725 H
Inquisition, The:
  in France, 1557 B
  in Italy, at Rome, established, 1542 C, H
    calls Veronese to account, 1573 J
    threatens Galileo, 1616 G
  in Netherlands, withdrawal of, 1566 B, C
  in Portugal, founded, 1531 D
    at Lisbon, 1547 E
    Pombal curbs, 1751 B
Inscriptiones antiquiae totius orbis Romanorum
  (Gruter), 1603 H
Inspiration of the Poet, The (Poussin), 1640 J
Instauratio Magna : novum organum (Bacon), 1620 H
Institutes, The (Calvin), 1539 H, 1560 H, 1561 H
Institutio Christiani Principis (Erasmus), 1510 F
Institutio Logicae (Wallis), 1687 H
Institutiones Historiae Ecclesiasticae (Mosheim),
  1726 H
Institutiones Medicae (Boerhaave), 1708 G
Institutions of the Laws of Scotland (Stair), 1681 F
Instituzioni Analitiche (Agnesi), 1748 H
Instructions for Foreign Travel (Howell), 1642 H
Instructions sur le Faict de la Guerre (Fourquevaux),
  1548 F
Instrument of Government, The, 1653 D
Insurance:
  fire, 1706 F
  life, first policy in England, 1583 F
    statistical information for, 1661 F, 1693 F
  marine, 1523 F
Intendant, office of, in France, reformed, 1634 E
Intérêt et Profit (Gibonais), 1710 F
Interpreter, The (Cornell), 1607 F, 1610 A
Introductio in geographiam universam (Cluver), 1624 G
Introductio in Ptolemaei Cosmographiam (Stobnicza),
  1512 G
Introductio Universalis in omnes Respublicas (Werden-
  hagen), 1632 F
Introduction à la vie dévote (de Sales), 1608 H, 1609 H
Introduction to English Grammar (Lowth), 1762 F
Introduction to the Laws of Tenure (Wright), 1730 F
Inventaire genéral de l'histoire de France (de Serres),
  1597 F
Inventum novum (Avenbrugger), 1761 G
Inverlocky, Inverness-shire, Scotland, 1645 A
Ionian Islands, 1503 A
Iphigénie en Aulide (Racine), 1674 L
Ipswich, Suffolk, England, Wolsey's college at, 1528 E
Ireland:
  Poynings Act, making Irish Parliament dependent
    on English, 1494 F
  Kildare accused of treason, 1534 A
  assassination of Archbishop Allen, 1534 C
  treason of Lord Grey, 1541 B
  Henry VIII takes title of King of Ireland, 1542 A
  Shane O'Neill's rebellion, 1562 A, B
  Tyrone defeats the MacDonnells, 1565 B
  assassination of Tyrone, 1567 B
  Fitzmaurice's rebellion, 1573 A
  Fitzgerald's rebellion, 1579 B, C
  estates granted to English adventurers, 1583 D
  Plantation of Munster, 1586 C, 1589 E
  O'Rourke's treachery, 1591 D
  Tyrone's rebellion, 1594 C, 1595 B
  Pacification signed, 1596 B
  Spanish expedition to, wrecked, 1596 D
  Tyrone renews rebellion, 1598 C, 1600 A, B
  Essex as lord deputy, 1598 C, 1599 A, C
  Mountjoy as lord deputy, 1599 D

prorogues Parliament, 1604 C
undertakes to mediate between Spain and Holland, 1604 C
proclaimed King of Great Britain and Ireland, etc., 1604 D
writes *Counterblaste to Tobacco*, 1604 F
second Parliament, 1610 B, C
negotiations for Great Contract, 1610 B, 1611 A
negotiations for daughter's marriage, 1611 A, 1612 B
dissolves Parliament, 1611 A
ennobles Carr, 1611 A, 1613 D
institutes baronetage, 1611 F
becomes own secretary of state, 1612 B
financial problems, 1612 B
endangers relations with Spain, 1612 C
Howard faction's hold over, 1613 D
dissolves Addled Parliament, 1614 B
imprisons M.P.s, 1614 B
negotiations for Prince Charles to marry Infanta of Spain, 1616 C
sells peerages, 1616 C
revisits Scotland, 1617 B
meets Scottish Parliament, 1617 B
imposes Articles of Religion in Scotland, 1618 C
offers to mediate in Bohemia, 1618 C
executes Raleigh, 1618 D
issues Book of Sports, 1618 F
refuses aid to Frederick V of Palatinate, 1619 C
forbids discussion of state affairs, 1620 D
attempts to mediate between Palatinate and Empire, 1621 B
Commons petition to declare war on Spain, 1621 D
Commons Protestation against, 1621 D
imprisons Coke, 1621 D
arrests Pym, 1622 A
dissolves Parliament, 1622 A
further negotiations for Prince Charles to marry Infanta, 1622 A, C, 1623 D
meets last Parliament, 1624 A
James II King of Great Britain and Ireland (1633–1701), 1633 M
as Duke of York resigns offices after Test Act, 1673 B
contracts to marry Mary of Modena, 1673 C
Bill to exclude from succession, 1679 A
sails for Antwerp, 1679 A
returns, 1682 B
restored to office of lord high admiral, 1684 B
accession, 1685 A
meets first Parliament, 1685 B
forms Federation of New England, 1686 B
encamps troops on Hounslow Heath, 1686 C
receives Papal Nuncio, 1687 C
places Catholics in high office, 1687 E
founds Order of Thistle, 1687 F
recalls regiments from Holland, 1688 A
birth of 'Old Pretender', 1688 B
escapes to France, 1688 D
Parliament declares he has abdicated, 1689 A
holds Parliament in Dublin, 1689 A
aided by French troops in Ireland, 1690 A
defeated at the Boyne, 1690 C
flees to France, 1690 C
death, 1701 C, M
James Edward, Prince of Wales, the 'Old Pretender', E. (1688–1766), 1688 B; recognised as 'James III' by France, 1701 C; Acts of Attainder and Abjuration, 1702 A; lands in Scotland, 1708 A; returns to France, 1708 A; lands in Scotland, 1715 D; returns to France, 1716 A; Spain and Sweden plot to establish him in England, 1717 A; flees to Papacy, 1717 A

James, Duke of Courland (1610–82), obtains Gambia, 1654 E; obtains Tobago, 1681 E
James, John, E. architect (d. 1746), 1712 J
Jamestown, Virginia, US: founded, 1607 B, F; assembly at, 1619 C
Jameses, History of the Five (Drummond), 1655 H
Jambonitz, Poland, battle, 1645 A
Jam-Zapolski, Treaty of, 1582 A
Jane, Queen of England (Lady Jane Grey (1537–54); marries Guildford Dudley, 1553 B; succession on, 1553 B; deposed, 1553 C; executed, 1554 A
Jane Seymour, Queen Consort of Henry VIII of England (1509–37), 1536 B, 1537 D, J
Jane Shore (Rowe), 1714 L
Janissaries, Turkish, become a hereditary caste, 1566 C
Jannequin, Clément, F. musician, 1559 K
Jansen, Cornelius, Flem. ecclesiastic and theologian, Bishop of Ypres and father of Jansenism (1585–1638), 1585 M, 1635 F, 1638 M, 1640 H, 1642 D, H, 1665 H
Jansen, Zacharias, Flem. scientist, 1590 G
Jansenism, 1642 D, 1665 H
Japan: first European reaches, 1542 G; Europeans in, 1543 E; Hideyoshi appointed dictator, 1585 E; missionaries banished, 1587 E; Korean invasion, 1597 E; Shogunate restored, 1598 E; Ieyasu defeats rivals, 1600 E; Spanish traders in, 1602 E; Dutch obtain trading monopoly, 1642 E; travels to, 1684 G
Japanese lacquer, imitation of, 1744 G
Japanese theatre and puppet plays, 1684 L, 1686 L
Jardin des racines grecques (Lancelot), 1657 H
Jargean, France, battle, 1652 A
Jarnac, France, battle, 1569 A
Jassy, France, battle, 1620 C
Java: Dutch occupation, 1628 E; travels to, 1684 G
Jay, John, Am. statesman (1745–1829), 1745 M
Jealous Wife, The (Colman), 1761 L
Jeanne d'Albret, Queen of Navare (1528–72), 1540 C
Jedburgh, Roxburghshire, Scotland, burnt, 1523 C
Jefferson, Thomas, Am. statesman, third president of US (1743–1826), 1743 M
Jeffreys, George, Lord Jeffreys, E. judge (1648–89), 1648 M, 1689 M; holds 'Bloody Assizes', 1685 C; appointed Lord Chancellor, 1685 C
Jehangir, Mogul Emperor of India, 1605 D
Jemmingen, Holland, 1568 C
Jena, E. Germany, university, 1558 F
Jenatsch, George, Swi. Grisons leader (d. 1639), 1639 A
Jenkins, Robert, E. seaman, 1731 E, 1738 A
'Jenkins Ear', debate on, 1738 A. *See also under* Wars
Jenkinson, Anthony, E. traveller and merchant (d. 1611), 1558 G
Jenner, Edward, E. physician (1749–1823), 1749 M
Jennings, Sarah, Duchess of Marlborough (1660–1744), 1660 M, 1744 M
Jephta (Vondel), 1659 L
Jersey, State of, US, Colony divided into East and West, 1676 E
Jerusalem Delivered (Tasso), 1581 L; trans., 1594 H, 1600 H
Jervaulx, Yorkshire, England, Abbey, abbot of, 1537 C
Jervis, John, Earl of St. Vincent, E. admiral (1735–1823), 1735 M
Jesuiterhütlein, Das (Fischart), 1580 F
Jesuits. *See* Religious Orders
Jesus and St. John (Boucher), 1758 J
Jesus, Society of. *See* Religious Orders
Jeu de l'amour et du Hasard, Le (Marivaux), 1730 L

Jeune homme accordant une Guitare (Greuze), 1757 J
Jeux floraux de Toulouse, 1694 H
Jewel, John, E. churchman (1522–71), 1522 M, 1559 H, 1562 H, 1571 M
Jewish Bride, The (Rembrandt), 1665 J
Jew of Malta, The (Marlowe), 1633 L
Jews, The:
 re-admitted into England, 1655 H
 expelled from Bordeaux, 1684 D
 naturalisation, in Britain, 1753 B
Jeyasu, Jap. ruler, 1598 E, 1600 E
Jimenez de Cisnéros, Sp. administrator and soldier. *See* Ximenes
Joachim I, elector of Brandenburg (1499–1535), G. Catholic ruler, 1525 C, 1527 B, 1533 D, 1535 C
Joachim II, elector of Brandenburg (1535–71), 1535 C, 1537 D, 1542 B; becomes a Protestant, 1539 A
Joachim Frederick, elector of Brandenburg, G. Calvinist (1598–1608), 1582 C, 1598 A, 1608 C
Joanna of Austria, Regent of Portugal, 1557 B, 1562 C
Joanna of Castille ('Mad Joanna'), 1500 A, B, 1504 D, 1505 D; marries Philip of Burgundy, 1496 D; in England, 1505 A; insanity of, 1506 C
Joanna, Queen consort of Louis XII (daughter of Louis XI), divorce from Louis XII, 1498 C, 1499 D
Job (Reni), 1622 J
Jocasta (Gascoigne), 1566 L, 1575 L
Jockey Clubs, 1750 F, 1753 F
Jodelet; ou, le maître Valet (Scarron), 1645 L
Jodelle, Étienne, F. poet and dramatist (1532–73), 1552 L
John I, King of Denmark and Norway (1481–1513), 1497 D, 1513 A
John I, King of Poland (1492–1501), 1492 B, 1500 C
John II (Casimir), King of Poland (1648–68), 1648 E, 1655 C; defeated by Charles X, 1655 C; defeated at Warsaw, 1656 C; abdicates, 1668 C
John III (Sobieski), King of Poland (1674–96), 1696 M; defeats Kiuprili at Khoczim, 1673 D; elected King, 1674 B
John II ('the Perfect'), King of Portugal (1481–95), 1495 D
John III, King of Portugal (1521–57), 1521 D, 1557 B
John IV, King of Portugal (1640–56), 1640 D, 1656 E
John V, King of Portugal (1707–50), 1707 A, 1750 C
John III, King of Sweden (1568–92), 1568 C, 1592 D; becomes a Catholic, 1578 E
John, Don, of Austria, Aus. general (1545–78), 1545 M, 1572 B, 1578 M; subdues Moors, 1508 D, 1569 E, 1570 E; defeats Turks at Lepanto, 1571 C, D; appointed governor of Netherlands, 1576 A; issues Perpetual Edict, 1577 A; troops of, to leave Netherlands by land route, 1577 A; enters Brussels, 1577 B; threatens England, 1577 A, C; seizes Namur, 1577 C; deposed by States General, 1577 C; defeats Dutch at Grembloux, 1578 A; Secretary of, assassinated, 1578 A, 1584 C
John, Don, of Austria, the younger, Sp. soldier, natural son of Philip IV (1629–79), 1647 D, 1679 D; restores Spanish rule in Naples, 1648 B; suppresses Catalonian revolt, 1652 E; takes command in Spain, 1676 B
John, Prince of Moldavia ('The Terrible') (d. 1574), 1574 E
John, 'the Steadfast', elector of Saxony (1525–32), 1525 B, 1526 A, 1532 C; alliance with Philip of Hesse, 1525 D; forms League of Torgau, 1526 B; makes Alliance of Weimar, 1528 A; signs Schmalkaldic League, 1530 D

John, Infante of Spain (d. 1497), 1497 D; marries Margaret of Austria, 1497 B
John Casimir of the Palatinate (d. 1592), G. soldier, Protestant, 1576 A, 1588 C, 1590 B, 1593 A; aids French Huguenots, 1567 D; treaty with Huguenots, 1575 C; pensioned by Henry III, 1576 B; Elizabeth I pays subsidy to, 1577 A; holds Ghent, 1578 D; operations in S. Netherlands, 1580 D; signs alliance with Henry of Navarre, 1587 A; joins League of Torgau, 1591 A
John Frederick I ('the Magnanimous'), elector of Saxony (1532–54), 1532 C, 1542 C, 1554 A; placed under imperial ban, 1546 C; deprived of electorate, 1546 D; imprisoned, 1547 B
John Frederick, Duke of Saxony (1529–95), Lutheran, 1558 F
John George, Elector of Brandenburg (d. 1598), 1591 C, 1598 A
John George I, elector of Saxony (1611–56), 1611 C; supports Ferdinand of Styria, 1617 C; applies to join Protestant Union, 1618 B; placed under imperial ban, 1623 A; appeals to Ferdinand II, 1631 A; signs treaty with Gustavus Adolphus, 1631 C; enters Prague, 1632 B; negotiations with Wallenstein, 1633 B; signs Peace of Prague with Ferdinand II, 1635 B; prepares army to fight for Emperor against Sweden, 1636 A; defeated by Swedes at Wittstock, 1636 D
John George II, elector of Saxony (1656–80), 1680 C
John Sigismund, Elector of Brandenburg, becomes a Calvinist, 1613 D
John Sigismund Zápolya, Prince of Transylvania (1540–71), 1540 C, 1570 C, 1571 A
John William, Duke of Julich-Cleves (d. 1609), 1609 A
John Zápolya, Prince of Transylvania, King of Hungary (1526–40), 1527 C, 1529 D, 1531 A, 1538, 1540 C; crowned King of Hungary, 1526 D; invades Bohemia, 1527 A; treaty with Suleiman I, 1528 A; truce with Ferdinand of Bohemia, 1531 A
John Bull, History of (Arbuthnot), 1712 L
John of the Cross, St. (Juan de Yepez y Alvarez), Sp. Carmelite, poet and mystic (1542–91), 1542 M, 1591 M, 1726 M
Johnson, Charles, 'Captain', E. author, 1724 L, 1734 L
Johnson, Edward, Am. chronicler (1598–1672), 1654 H
Johnson, Francis, E. theological controversialist, 1604 H
Johnson, Samuel, Dr., E. lexicographer, poet and critic (1709–84), 1709 M, 1735 H, 1737 L, 1738 L, 1744 L, 1745 H, 1747 H, L, 1749 L, 1750 L, 1755 H, 1756 H, 1758 L, 1759 L, 1760 F, 1761 L, 1762 H, 1763 L
Johnstone, Charles, Ir. journalist and novelist (c. 1719–1800), 1760 L
Joinville, Treaty of, 1585 A
Joinville, Charles, Duke of, F. (d. 1588), 1588 D
Joliet, Louis, F. explorer (1645–1700), 1673 E
Jonathan Wild (Fielding), 1743 L
Jones, Inigo, E. architect (1573–1651), 1573 M, 1616 J, 1619 J, 1623 J, 1625 J, 1651 M, 1727 J
Jones, John Paul, Am. seaman (1747–92), 1747 M
Jones, Robert, E. poet, 1610 L
Jones, Sir William, E. orientalist (1746–94), 1746 M
Jonson, Ben, E. poet and dramatist (1572–1637), 1572 M, 1600 L, 1601 L, 1602 L, 1605 L, 1607 L, 1609 L, 1610 L, 1611 L, 1614 L, 1616 L, 1631 L, 1637 H, M, 1640 L, 1641 L
Jonsonus Virbius (Duppa), 1637 H

Limerick, Eire: Siege of, 1651 B, D; William III fails to take, 1690 C; capitulates, 1691 C

Limning, treatise on, 1600 J

Linacre, Thomas, E. humanist and physician (c. 1460–1524), 1518 G, 1524 M

Lincoln, Lincs., England, 1536 D

Lindsay, Alexander, Earl of Balcarres, Sc. politician (1618–59), 1618 M, 1659 M

Lindsay, Sir David, Sc. courtier and poet (1490–1555), 1535 F, 1540 L, 1554 F, 1602 L

Lindschoten (—), Du. cartographer, 1598 G

Lingen, West Germany, 1702 E

Linlithgow, Linlithgowshire, Scotland, 1543 C, 1570 A

Linné, Carl von (Linnaeus), Swe. botanist (1707–78), 1707 M, 1735 G, 1741 G, 1751 G, 1753 G

Linnet, The (Fabritius), 1654 J

Linz, Austria: Maurice of Saxony takes, 1552 B; assembly of Hapsburg estates at, 1614 C; Maximilian occupies, 1620 C; Holy League of, 1684 A; Franco-Bavarian army takes, 1741 C

Lion Hunt, The (Rubens), 1616 J

Lionne, Hugues de, Marquis de Berry, F. diplomat (1611–71), 1658 C

Lippershey, Johann, Du. scientist, 1608 G

Lippi, Filippino, It. artist (1458–1504), 1497 J, 1501 J

Lipsius, Justus, F. classical scholar, jurist and political philosopher (1547–1606), 1574 H, 1589 F, 1605 F

Lisabetha (Sachs), 1546 L

Lisbon, Portugal: Inquisition in, 1531 D, 1547 E; university of, transferred to Coimbra, 1537 F; fever epidemic, 1569 F; spice market at, closed, 1594 E; Spanish expedition leaves, 1596 D; earthquake, 1755 D, F

Liselotte, Duchess of Orleans, heiress to Palatinate (1652–1722); marries Philip of Orleans, 1671 E; Louis XIV claims Palatinate for, 1685 B

Lisle, Lord. *See* Plantagenet

Literaturbriefe, Die (Lessing), 1759 H

Lithuania: Russia invades, 1501 E; Union with Poland and Lublin, 1569 C; Treaty of peace with Sweden, 1595 D

Little Harbor, New Hampshire, US, 1623 F

Little Passion (Dürer), 1509 J

Lives (Birch), 1747 H

Lives of the Artists (Vasari), 1550 J

Livonia: Russians invade, 1557 E; transfers allegiance to Poland, 1561 E; Poland acquires, 1582 A; Russians withdraw claim to, 1617 A; Sweden retains conquests, 1629 C; settlement in, 1660 B; Saxons invade, 1700 B; Swedes invade, 1701 B; ceded by Sweden to Russia, 1721 C

Livre des marchands, Le (la Planche), 1565 F

Livy (Titus Livius), Roman historian (59 B.C.–17 A.D.), works of, 1600 H

Lixheim, France, Turenne's march across Vosges from, 1674 D

Lloyd, Edward, E. coffee-house-keeper, 1696 F, 1726 F

Lobo, Father Jeronimo, Port. traveller (1593–1678), 1735 H

Lobositz, Poland, battle, 1756 D

Locarno, Switzerland, 1512 C

Loches, France, 1539 D

Lochleven, Fifeshire, Scotland, 1567 B, 1568 B

Loci Communes (Melanchthon), 1521 H

Locke, John, E. philosopher (1632–1704), 1632 M, 1704 M; secretary of economic council, 1672 A; draws of constitutions for Carolina, 1669 C; political works, 1689 F, 1695 F, 1696 F;

philosophical works, 1690 H, 1695 H, 1708 H, 1714 H

Locke, Matthew, E. musician (c. 1630–77), 1653 K, 1656 K, 1661 K, 1669 K, 1672 K, 1673 K

Lock Up Your Daughters (Fielding), 1730 L

Lodge, Thomas, E. dramatist and author of romances (1558–1625), 1558 M, 1579 L, 1590 L, 1625 M

Lodi, Italy, 1524 D

Logan, Friedrich von, G. epigrammatist (1604–55), 1654 L

Logarithms:
Napier's Tables, 1614 G
Gunter discusses, 1620 G
Briggs' Tables, 1624 G
See also under Mathematics

Lohenstein, Daniel Casper von, G. poet and novelist (1635–83), 1689 L

Lombardy, Italy: operations in, 1501 B, 1522 B; Savoyards overrun, 1746 A

Lombe, Sir Thomas, E. inventor (1685–1739), 1718 G

Loménie de Brienne, Étienne Charles de, F. politician and ecclesiastic (1727–94), 1727 M

London, England:
events:
rebels march on, 1497 B
anti-clericalism in, 1514 D
May Day riots, 1517 B
legatine court at Blackfriars, 1529 B
heretics burnt, 1546 C
poor rate levied in, 1547 E
Protestants burnt at Smithfield, 1555 A
first Russian envoy to, 1557 A
plague in, 1563 F
Anabaptists burnt at, 1575 C
growth of, restricted, 1580 C
water supply for, 1582 G, 1613 F
plague in, 1592 F
Hanseatic Steelyard closed, 1598 C
Essex's revolt, 1601 A
heretics burnt in, 1612 A
City is fined by Charles I, 1632 E, 1633 A
arrest of Royalist plotters, 1643 B
army marches into, 1647 C
unrest of apprentices in, 1649 F
Monck's army enters, 1660 A
Great Plague, 1665 C, F, 1666 F
Great Fire, 1666 C, F
end commemorated by Monument, 1671 J
Stop on the Exchequer, 1672 F
Charter forfeited, 1683 D
growth of, 1683 F
Charter remodelled, 1684 B
streets, lighting of, 1684 F
immunity from arrest in liberty of Savoy, etc., ended, 1697 B
Exhibition of Manufactures in, 1756 F
Exhibition of agricultural machinery in, 1761 F
Cock Lane ghost, hoax of, 1762 F
places in or near:
Academy of Arts, 1711 H
Apothecaries' Company, 1748 G
Banqueting House, Whitehall, 1619 J, 1635 J
Blackfriars Theatre, 1597 L, 1608 L
British Museum opened, 1759 F
Burlington House, 1717 J, 1719 J
Charterhouse, The, 1535 B
Chelsea China factory, 1750 J
Chelsea Hospital, 1681 F, 1682 J
Christ's Hospital, 1552 F
Covent Garden Church, 1625 J
Covent Garden Theatre Club, 1735 F

exchange for Cape Breton Island, 1748 D; siege of, 1758 D, 1759 A

Madrid, Spain, 1623 C, 1703 C; becomes capital, 1560 E; College of Doña Maria de Arragon, 1590 F; capital transferred from, 1601 A; Philip of Anjou enters, 1701 A; British and Portuguese enter, 1706 B; Montserrat Church, 1720 J; Hospice St. Ferdando, 1722 J; Palace, frescoes in, 1762 J

Madrid, Peace Treaties of, 1526 A, 1530 E, 1617 C, 1630 D, 1721 A

Madrigals, collections of, published, 1533 K, 1588 K, 1601K, 1620K

Maes, Nicolaes, Du. artist (1634–93), 1634 M, 1655 J, 1666 J, 1693 M

Maestricht, Holland: falls to Spanish, 1579 C; Dutch take, 1632 C; restored to Dutch, 1678 C

Maffei, Francesco Scipione, It. scholar and palaeographer (1675–1755), 1727 H, 1732 H

Magdalen, The (Titian), 1531 J

Magdalene with the Lamp (Tour), 1630 J

Magdeburg, E. Germany, 1530 D, 1629 A, 1648 D: joins League of Torgau, 1526 B; under ban of empire, 1548 B; besieged, 1550 C, D; capitulates, 1551 D; disputed rule in bishopric, 1582 C; siege, 1631 A, B; Saxony obtains, 1635 B; incorporated with Brandenburg, 1680 E

Magdeburg, Centuries, The (M. Flacius, etc.), 1560 H, 1588 H

Magdeburg hemispheres, 1654 G

Magellan, Ferdinand, Port. navigator (c. 1480–1521), 1519 G, 1520 G, 1521 M

Magellan Straits, S. China, 1520 G

Maggots in meat, investigated, 1699 G

Magia Naturalis (B. Porta), 1560 G, 1589 G

Magic lantern, 1600 G

Magiore, Count La, It. politician, conspiracy against Cesare Borgia, 1502 D

Magliabechi, Antonio, It. bibliophile and librarian (1633–1714), 1747 H

Magnalia Christi Americana (Mather), 1702 H

Magnesia alba, 1707 G

Magnesium sulphate, 1695 G

Magnetic 'dip', 1576 G

Magnetic Needle, Gunter's discovery of declination of, 1622 G

Magnetic Pole, Mercator's discovery of, 1546 G

Magnetic Variation, charts with lines of equal, 1700 G

Magnetism, studies in, 1581 G. See also Electricity

Magnets, proposals for making, 1750 G

Magnificence (Skelton), 1533 L

Magnolias, introduced to England, 1709 G

Magnum Opus Musicum (di Lasso), 1604 K

Mahmoud I, Sultan of Turkey (1730–54), 1730 C

Mahmud, Mir, Shah of Persia (1722–5), 1717 E, 1719 E, 1722 A, 1724 E, 1725 E

Mahomet III, Sultan of Turkey (1595–1603), 1603 D

Mahrattas, defeated at Panipat, 1761 A

Maiden's Dream, The (Lotto), 1505 J

Maid of Honour, The (Massinger), 1632 L

Maid's Tragedy, The (Beaumont and Fletcher), 1619 L

Maillet, Benoît de, F. scientist (1656–1738), 1735 G

Maine, State, US: English settlement at, 1623 E; accepts authority of Massachusetts, 1653 E; restored to heirs of Sir Ferdinando Gorges, 1665 E; government of, resumed by Massachusetts, 1668 E; purchased by Massachusetts, 1677 A

Maine, Cuthbert, E. seminary priest (d. 1577), 1577 D

Maine, duke of. See Louis Auguste de Bourbon

Maintenon, Françoise d'Aubigné, marquise de, F. adventurer and author (1635–1714), 1635 M, 1686 F, 1719 M; marries Louis XIV, 1684 A

Mainz, W. Germany, archbishopric, 1525 C, 1538 B: Swedes occupy, 1631 D; French take, 1644 C; withdraws from Thirty Years' War, 1647 B; bishop joins coalition against France, 1673 D

Mairet, Jean, F. dramatist (1604–86), 1634 L

Maistre, Joseph de, F. diplomat and author (1754–1821), 1754 M

Maitland, John, earl, later duke, of Lauderdale, Sc. politician (1616–82): ostracism of, 1662 F; appointed a member of the Cabal, 1667 C

Maitland, William, of Lethington, Sc. politician (1528–73), 1528 M, 1570 A, 1573 A, B, M

Major (or Maior), John, Sc. historian (c. 1470–1550), 1521 H

Majorca, Island, 1521 E

Malabar Coast, India, explored, 1498 G

Malacca, Malaya: Portuguese capture, 1511 E, G; occupied by Dutch, 1628 E; Dutch destroy, 1640 F; Portuguese surrender, 1641 A

Malade imaginaire, Le (Molière), 1673 L

Malar, Lake, Sweden, 1606 G

Malay Peninsula, Lancaster rounds, 1592 G

Malcontent, The (Marston), 1604 L

Malebranche, Nicolas, F. theologian, scientist and philosopher (1638–1715), 1624 H

Malherbe, François de, F. poet and critic (1555–1628), 1555 M, 1628 M, 1630 L

Mallet, David, Sc. poet (c. 1705–65), 1740 H, L

Malmö, Sweden, 1536 B

Malmö, Peace of, 1512 E

Malone, Edmund, E. Shakespearian scholar (1741–1812), 1741 M

Malpighi, Marcello, It. anatomist (1628–94), 1669 G, 1672 G

Malplaquet, France, battle, 1709 C

Malta: Knights Hospitallers in, 1530 E; Turkish attack on, 1551 C; defence of, against Turks, 1565 B, C

'Malus Intercursus', 1506 B, 1507 D

Malyues, Gerard de, E. economist (d. 1641), 1601 F, 1622 F

Man clasping a hand (Hilliarde), 1588 J

Man in Armour (Tintonetto), 1560 J

Man of Mode, The (Etherege), 1676 L

Mananiello, (–), It., assassinated, 1647 C

Mannasseh ben Israel, Du. Jewish controversialist and scholar (1604–1657), 1656 H

Manchester, Lancs., England, 1642 C: Royal Infirmary, 1752 F; Duke of Bridgwater's Canal to, 1761 G

Manchester, Earl of. See Montagu, E.

Manchu Dynasty, in China, 1644 E

Mandelsheim, W. Germany, 1704 B

Mander, Karel van, G. historian of art, 1604 J

Mandeville, Bernard de, Du. satirist (writing in English; c. 1620–1733), 1705 H, 1714 H

Mandeville, Sir John (pseud.) ? Ir. traveller (d. 1372), works of, 1496 L, 1725 L

Mandragola, La (Machiavelli), 1513 L

Manganese, experiments on, 1740 G

Manganita philosophia (Reisch), 1496 H

Manhattan, Island, New York, US, Dutch settlement in, 1612 E

Manière de traitez les plaies (Paré), 1545 G

Manifestos:

the Levellers', in England, 1647 F

Damville's, in France, calling for religious toleration, 1574 D

Tassoni's, in Italy, 1627 F

Maurice, elector of Saxony, G. ruler (1521–53), 1521 M, 1541 B; aids Charles V, 1546 B; invested with Saxon electorate, 1546 D, 1547 B; takes Magdeburg, 1551 D; signs treaty with France, 1552 A; secedes from Charles V, 1552 B; nearly captures Charles V, 1552 B; holds Passau Conference, 1552 C; killed, 1553 C, M

Maurists, congregation of Benedictine Order, 1621 H, 1630 H, 1645 H

Mauritius: Dutch take, 1598 E; Dutch settlement in, 1644 E; French acquisition of, 1710 E; name changed to Ile de France, 1721 D

Maxen, E. Germany, Prussians capitulate at, 1759 D

Maximes (La Rochefoucould), 1665 L

Maximilian I, Holy Roman Emperor (1493–1519), 1493 A, 1494 B, 1499 A, 1502 F, 1504 L, 1506 A, 1508 A, F, 1513 B, D, 1515 C, 1519 A:
elected Emperor, 1493 C
marries Blanche Sforza, 1494 A
appeals to Diet of Worms, 1495 A
leads army against French in Italy, 1496 C
leaves Italy, 1496 D
at Diet of Augsburg, 1580 B
summons princes to a crusade, 1502 A
pronounces ban on Rupert of Palatinate, 1504 B
at battle of Regensburg, 1504 C
takes Kufstein, 1504 D
meets Diet at Cologne, 1505 A
attacks Venice, 1508 A
signs truce with Venice, 1508 A
appoints Maragaret of Austria regent in Netherlands, 1509 A
fails to take Padua, 1509 C
joins Holy League, 1512 B, 1513 A
at battle of the Spurs, 1513 C
signs truce with Louis XII, 1514 A
Italian expedition fails, 1516 B
makes alliance with Henry VIII, 1516 D
signs Peace of Brussels, 1516 D

Maximilian II, Holy Roman Emperor (1564–76), 1555 C, 1567 C, 1570 C, 1571 A, 1576 B: succession to Bohemia recognised, 1549 A; succeeds as King of Bohemia, 1562 C; becomes King of the Romans, 1562 C; elected King of Hungary, 1563 C; accession as Emperor, 1564 C; forced to grant concessions in Lower Austria, 1568 C; asked to intervene in Netherlands, 1568 C; advocates toleration in France, 1574 B; as candidate for Polish throne, 1575 D; death, 1576 D

Maximilian, Archduke of Austria (d. 1618), 1596 D, 1618 D: imprisoned, 1588 A; renounces claims to Poland, 1589 A; renounces claim to Empire, 1616 E

Maximilian I, elector of Bavaria (1597–1651), 1591 D, 1597 E: occupies Donauwörth, 1607 D; heads Catholic League, 1609 C; signs Treaty of Munich, 1619 D; obtains support of Catholic League against Bohemia, 1619 D; occupies Linz, 1620 C; gains the Palatinate, 1621 A; confirmation of grant of Palatinate, 1623 A; signs Treaty of Fontainebleau, 1631 B; Bavarian electorate confirmed, 1648 D

Maximilian II, Emmanuel, elector of Bavaria (1679–1726), 1680 C: installed as governor of Spanish Netherlands, 1692 A; relieves Charleroi, 1692 C

Maximilian III, Joseph, elector of Bavaria (1745–77), 1745 A, B

May, Thomas, E. author and translator (1595–1650), 1627 H, 1647 F

Mayas, in Mexico, rising of, 1546 E

Mayence, France, 1514 D

Mayenne, Charles of Lorraine, duke of, F. general of Catholic League (1554–1611), 1577 B, 1588 D, 1589 A, C, 1590 A, 1594 A: routed at Ivry, 1590 A; truce with Henry IV, 1595 B; submits to Henry IV, 1596 A

Mayenne, Henry of Lorraine, duke of, F. politician (d. 1623): rebellions of, 1614 A, 1620 B

Mayer, Tobias, G. astronomer (1723–62), 1756 G

Mayflower, The, 1620 C

Mayflower Compact, The, 1620 D

Maying or Disport of Chaucer, The, 1508 L

Mayow, John, E. scientist (1640–79), 1674 G

Mazarin, Jules, F. cardinal and statesman (1602–61), 1602 M, 1647 C, 1648 A: elected cardinal, 1641 D; becomes chief minister, 1642 D; confirmed in power, 1643 B; as a book collector, 1643 H, 1651 H; forced to reduce taxation, 1644 E; is victorious over Paris Parlement, 1645 C; alliance with old Fronde, 1650 A; flees from Paris, 1651 A; leaves France, 1652 C; is recalled, 1652 D, 1653 A; reconciled with Orleans, 1656 C; death, 1661 A, M

Mazzochi, Vergilio, It. musician (1597–1646), 1639 K

Measles, cure for, 1678 G

Measure for Measure (Shakespeare), 1604 L

Measurement: by double image, 1743 G; of the meridian, 1747 G

Meaux, France: preachers of, trial of, 1525 A; Protestant congregation in, 1546 D; Huguenot conspiracy at, 1567 C

Mecca, Sherif of, 1517 A

Méchant, Le (Gresset), 1745 L

Mechanical Account ... of the Hysterical Passion and of all the Nervous Disorders (Perry), 1755 G

Mechanics, Analytical, study of, founded, 1736 G

Mechithar, Peter (or Mekhitar), Am. Catholic priest (1676–1749), 1702 H, 1717 H

Mechlin, Treaty of, 1513 B

Meklenburg, East Germany, duchy, 1550 A, C: seized by Wallenstein, 1628 A; under imperial ban, 1628 B; Wallenstein created duke of, 1629 B; Russians occupy, 1716 D, 1717 C; treaty for evacuation of Russian and Prussian troops from, 1718 D

Médailles sur les évènements du règne de Louis-le-Grand, 1702 H

Medall, The (Dryden), 1682 L

Médicin malgré lui (Molière), 1666 L

Medée (Corneille), 1635 L

Medical Schools, 1518 G

Medical treatment, free, advocated, 1699 F

Medici, Alessandro de', It. ruler (d. 1537), 1529 B, 1530 D, 1537 A

Medici, Alexander, It. churchman (1535–1605), elected Pope Leo XI, 1605 B

Medici, Catherine de', Queen Mother of France (1519–89). *See under* Catherine de' Medici

Medici, Cosimo de', It. ruler (1519–74), Grand Duke of Tuscany. *See under* Cosimo I

Medici, Cardinal Ferdinand de', It. churchman, 1587 D

Medici, Francesco de'. *See* Francesco de Medici

Medici, Giovanni Angelo, It. churchman (1499–1565), elected Pope Pius IV, 1559 D

Medici, Giovanni de', It. churchman (1475–1521), elected Pope Leo X, 1513 A

Medici, Lorenzo de', It. statesman (c. 1449–92), 1492 M

Medici, Marie de', Queen Consort of France. *See under* Marie de Medici

Medici cycle of paintings (Rubens), 1622 J

Medici family, death of last member of, in Tuscany, 1737 C

Mexico, History of (Padilla), 1596 H
Mey, Cornelius Jacobsen, Du. navigator, 1614 G
Mézeray, François Eudes de, F. historian (1610–83), 1643 H, 1667 H, 1682 H
Michael I, King of Poland (1669–73), Michael Wisniowiecki, 1673 D
Michael I, Tsar of Russia (1613–45), Michael Romanov, 1613 A, 1617 A, 1645 M
Michael 'the Brave', Prince of Wallachia (d. 1601), 1593 B, 1599 E, 1601 C
Michaux, André, F. botanist (1756–1802), 1756 M
Michel, Claud ('Claudion'), F. sculptor (1738–1814), 1738 M
Michelangelo (Michelangelo Buonarroti), It. artist, architect and sculptor (1475–1564), 1498 J, 1501 J, 1513 J, 1519 J, 1524 J, 1533 J, 1534 J, 1542 J, 1546 J, 1555 J, 1561 J, 1564 M:
　as architect, 1513 J, 1514 J, 1520 J, 1526 J
　Bacchus, 1497 J
　Bologna statue, 1511 B
　Brutus, 1540 J
　fortifications by, 1528 J
　Last Judgment, 1536 J
　Madonna and Child, 1500 J, 1504 J
　Medici tombs, 1521 J
　Moses, 1513 J
　replans Capitol, 1536 J
　self-portrait, 1550 J
　works on Sistine Chapel, 1508 J
Micrographia (Hooke), 1665 G
Micrometer, the, invented, 1639 G
Microcosmographie (Earle), 1628 L
Microscope, the, 1590 G, 1608 G, 1665 G
Midas (Lylly), 1592 L
Middleburg, Holland, 1608 G
Middle-English studies, 1720 H
Middleton, Charles, Earl of Middleton and of Monmouth (c. 1640–1719), Sc. politician, 1662 F: Secretary of State, 1684 C
Middleton, Conyers, E. theologian (1683–1750), 1749 H
Middleton, Thomas, E. dramatist (1570–1627), 1570 M, 1608 L, 1611 L, 1617 L, 1624 L, 1625 L, 1627 M, 1630 L, 1653 L, 1657 L
Midsummer Night's Dream, A (Shakespeare), 1600 L
Milan, Italy, 1511 C, 1512 C, 1515 C, 1516 C, 1521 B, C, 1636 B: S. Maria della Grazie, 1492 J; Louis XIII's alliance with Venice for recovery, 1513 A; French invasion, 1513 B; siege, 1523 D; French expelled from, 1524 B; Spaniards surrender to French, 1524 D; blockade, 1526 D; granted to Francesco Sforza, 1529 C; end of house of Sforza, 1535 D, Charles V occupies, 1535 D; Philip of Spain is invested with, 1540 D, 1542 C; Le Gracie Church, 1542 J; plague in, 1575 F; disposal of, under Partition treaties, 1698 D, 1700 A; convention at 1707 A; disposal of, under Franco-Spanish second Family Compact, 1743 D; Franco–Spanish troops take, 1745 D; is recovered by Charles Emmanuel, 1746 A; music in, 1741 K, 1745 K
Milan, Peace of, 1639 C
Mildmay, Sir Walter, E. administrator and benefactor (c. 1520–89), 1584 F
Melitz, Charles von, G. theologian, 1519 A
Milkmaid and a Wood-cutter (Gainsborough), 1755 J
Mill at Charenton, The (Boucher), 1758 J
Mills:
　rolling, for sheet iron, 1728 G
　weaving, 1682 F
　See under Machines
Milliners, The (Boucher), 1746 J

Milton, John, E. poet and political author (1608–74), 1608 M, 1674 M, 1682 H: poems, 1637 L, 1638 L, 1645 L, 1667 L, 1671 L, 1673 L; political works, 1640 H, 1642 H, 1643 F, 1649 F, 1651 F, 1654 F, 1659 F, 1660 F, 1670 H; pleads for unlicensed printing, 1644 F
Minden, West Germany, 1547 A, 1648 D: French defeated at, 1759 C
Mineralogy, studies in, 1530 H, 1556 G. *See also* Geology
Mines:
　coal, 1590 F
　copper, 1561 C
　lead, 1561 C
　silver, 1545 F, 1548 F
Mines, explosive, 1503 G
Ming dynasty, ends, 1644 E
Miniatures, notable, 1588 J, 1590 J, 1593 J, 1596 J, 1605 J, 1616 J
Minnesänger (Bodmer), 1748 H
Minorca: British capture, 1708 C; Spain cedes to Britain, 1713 A; French capture, 1756 B; Britain secures, 1762 D
Minsheu, John, E. lexicographer, 1617 H
Mirabeau, Honoré Gabriel Riquetti, Comte de, F. statesman (1749–91), 1749 M
Mirabeau, Victor-Riquetti, Marquis de (1715–89), 1756 F
Miracle of San Diego, The (Murillo), 1646 J
Miracle Plays, Dutch, 1500 L
Miracles (Campbell), 1762 H
Miracles of St. Fillipo (del Sarto), 1509 J
Miracles of St. Zenobius (Botticelli), 1500 J
Mirainoundo (Cortete), 1684 L
Mirandola, Italy, 1538 A: taken by Pope Julius II, 1511 A; recaptured, 1511 A
Mirifici Logarithmorum Canonis Descriptio (Napier), 1614 G
Mirror for Magistrates, The (Baldwin), 1559 H; collection similar to, 1563 L
Misrepresentations Corrected and Truth Vindicated (Edwards), 1752 H
Missa Papae Marcelli (Palestrina), 1565 K
Miss in Her Teens (Garrick), 1747 L
Miss Sarah Sampson (Lessing), 1755 L
Misselden, Edward, E. economist (d. 1654), 1623 F
Missionaries:
　in China, 1582 H
　in Goa, 1542 H
　in Japan, 1548 H
　in Macao, 1610 H, 1737 H
　in Mexico, 1529 H
　See also under Religious Denominations; Religious Orders
Mississippi R., US: discovered, 1541 G; descent of 1673 E
Mississippi Valley, Louisiana, French occupy, 1682 F
Missouri R., US, exploration near, 1672 G
Mistake, The (Vanbrugh), 1706 L
Mistress, The (Cowley), 1647 L
Mitchell, Francis, E. politician, commissioner for monopolies, 1621 A
Mitford, William, E. historian of Greece (1744–1827), 1744 M
Mithridate (Racine), 1673 L
Modèles de Caractères (Fournier), 1736 H
Modena, Italy, 1510 B, 1597 K: Ferrara seizes, 1527 B; awarded to Duke of Ferrara, 1531 B
Modest Proposal for Preventing the Children of the Poor People from being a Burden to the Parents (Swift), 1729 L
Mogul dynasty, established in Delhi, 1526 B

Montferrat, Italy, 1615 B: assigned to Duke of Mantua, 1533 E; Savoy, obtains part of, 1631 B
Montigny, Baron, Du. leader, assassinated, 1570 D
Montmélion, France, 1600 C, D
Montmorency, Anne, Duke of, constable of France (1493–1567), 1541 A, 1561 A, 1562 A, D
Montmorency, François, Duke of (1530–79), 1575 D
Montmorency, Henry, Duke of, F. (1595–1632), governor of Languedoc, 1632 D
Montmorency-Bouteville, François de. See Luxemburg, Duke of
Montmidi, Luxemburg, French take, 1657 C
Montpelier, Treaty of, 1622 C
Montpensier, Louis, Duke of, F. (1513–82), 1575 B
Montreal, Canada: site of, 1535 G; British take, 1760 C
Montreuil, France, siege of, 1544 C
Montrose, marquess of. See Graham, James
Montserrat, W. Indies, 1667 C: English settlement of, 1632 E; French capture, 1667 A
Monzon, Treaty of, 1626 A
Mookden Heath, Holland, battle, 1574 A
Moon, The:
  libration of, in longitude, 1647 G
  orbit of, measured, 1666 G
Moore, Edward, E. dramatist (1712–57), 1712 M, 1757 M
Moore, Sir John, E. soldier (1761–1809), 1761 M
Moors, The:
  found Empire of Morocco, 1519 F
  in Spain (Moriscos), massacred, 1568 D
    subdued in Granada, 1569 E
    subdued in Andalusia, 1570 C
  control Tangier, 1684 E
Moral and Political Dialogues (Hurd), 1759 H
Moral Fables of Aesop, The (Henryson), 1670 L
Moral Philosophy: anthology (Baldwin), 1547 H
Morales, Battasar Gracian y, Sp. author, 1651 L
Morales, Cristóbal de, Sp. musician (c. 1500–53), 1538 K
Moralities: Everyman, 1495 L, 1520 L
Morals (Plutarch), trans., 1603 H
Moravian Brethren. See under Religious Denominations
Moray, Earl of. See Stewart, J.
Mordaunt, Charles, Earl of Peterborough and Monmouth, E. soldier and politician (c. 1658–1735), 1735 M: takes Barcelona, 1705 D
More, Hannah, E. novelist and dramatist (1745–1833), 1745 M
More, Henry, E. Neo-Platonist philosopher (1614–87), 1614 M, 1647 L, 1659 H, 1660 H, 1667 H, 1668 H, 1687 M
More, Sir Thomas, E. humanist and lawyer (1478–1535), 1527 J, 1534 B, D: writings, 1510 H, 1516 F, 1529 F, 1535 H, 1543 H, 1551 H, 1553 H, 1557 H, 1588 H; elected Speaker, 1523 A; appointed Lord Chancellor, 1529 D; resigns, 1532 B; trial and execution, 1535 C, D, M
Morea, The, Greece: Turks capture, 1538 E; Morosini's victory in, 1685 D; subjugation of, 1687 C; Venice 'gains, 1699 A; Turks expel Venetians, 1715 E; Turks retain, 1718 C
Moreri, Louis, F. lexicographer (1643–80), 1674 H
Morgagni, Giovanni, It. anatomist (1682–1771), 1706 G
Morgan, Sir Henry, We. buccaneer (c. 1635–88), 1671 A, 1688 M
Morgan, William, We. biblical scholar, 1588 H
Morley, Thomas, E. musician (1553–1603), 1553 M, 1597 K, 1600 K, 1601 K, 1603 M

Mornay, Philippe de, seigneur du Plessis-Mornay, F. Protestant leader (1549–1623), 1549 M, 1623 M
Morning Toilet (Boucher), 1740 J
Moro, Antonio (Sir Anthonis Mor), Flem. artist (c. 1517–77), 1554 J
Morocco: Moorish Empire founded, 1519 F; Portuguese invasion, 1578 C; treaty with France, 1671 C
Morone, Girolamo, It. ruler of Milan, 1525 C
Morosini, Francisco, It. soldier, 1685 D
Morris, Gouverneur, Am. statesman (1752–1816), 1752 M
Mörs, West Germany, 1702 E
Mort de Pompée, La (Corneille), 1641 L
Mortality, bills of, analysis of, 1661 F
Morton, Earl of. See Douglas, J.
Morville, Charles Jean Baptiste Fleurian, comte de, F. diplomat (1686–1732), 1727 D
Moscherosch, Johann Michael, G. satirist and moral philosopher (1601–69), 1643 L
Moscow, Russia, 1547 A, 1695 D: patriarch of, 1511 H; fire of, 1547 F; Chancellor reaches, 1553 G; Ivan IV driven from, 1564 B; Dmitri advances on, 1608 E; risings in, 1647 E, 1648 E; 'Tsar Kolokol' bell, 1733 G; University, 1755 H
Moser, Johann Jakob, G. jurist (1701–85), 1732 F, 1737 F
Moses saved from the waters (Veronese), 1575 J
Moses Striking the Rock (Tintoretto), 1570 J
Mosheim, Johann Lorenz von, G. Protestant theologian (1694–1755), 1726 H
Mota, Antonio da, Sp. explorer, 1542 G
Mother Bombie (Lyly), 1594 L
Motier, Marie Joseph du. See Lafayette, Marquis de
Motion of falling bodies, Galileo investigates, 1638 G
Motte, Andrew, E. mathematician (d. 1730), 1729 G
Motteux, Peter Anthony, F. dramatist and translator (1660–1718), 1660 M, 1700 H, 1704 L, 1708 H, 1712 H, 1718 M
Moulins, France, 1576 A, 1639 D
Moulins Ordinances, 1566 D
Mount Popocatepetl, Mexico, 1522 G
Mountaineering:
  ascent of Mont Aiguille, 1492 G
  ascent of Mount Popocatepetl, 1522 G
  exploration beyond Himalayas, 1624 G
  ascent of Titlis, 1744 F
Mountjoy, Lord. See Blount, Charles
Mount of Olives, The (Vaughan), 1652 H
Mourning Bride, The (Congreve), 1697 L
Mousehold Heath, near Norwich, England, 1549 C
Mozambique, coastline of, explored, 1498 G
Mozart, Leopold, Aus. musician (1719–87), 1756 K
Mozart, Wolfgang Amadeus, Aus. musician (1756–91), 1756 M
Much Ado About Nothing (Shakespeare), 1600 L
Mühlberg, East Germany, battle, 1547 B
Muhlhausen, East Germany, 1620 A
Mulcaster, Richard, E. schoolmaster and author (c. 1530–1611), 1581 F
Mulheim, West Germany, 1614 C
Munn, Thomas, E. economist (1571–1641), 1621 F, 1664 F
Munday, Anthony, E. translator (1553–1633), 1590 H
Munich, Bavaria, West Germany: Catholic League founded at, 1609 C; entered by Swedes, 1632 B
Munich, Treaty of, 1619 D
Münnich, Burkhard Christoph, Count, R. politician (1683–1767), 1737 A, 1740 D, 1741 A
Münster, in Westphalia, West Germany: Anabaptists in, 1533 E, 1534 A, C, H, 1535 B; peace conference at, 1643 C, 1644 B, 1645 B, 1648 A; joins

N

Nice, France: French and Turkish fleets take, 1543 C; Catinat takes, 1691 A; Savoy regains, 1696 C

Nice, Truce of, 1538 B

Nickel, is isolated from niccolite, 1751 G

Nicolai, Christoph Friedrich, G. author (1733–1811), 1733 M

Nicolson, William, E. antiquary (c. 1655–1726), 1696 H

Nicomède (Corneille), 1652 L

Nicosia, Cyprus, Turks sack, 1570 C

Nicot, Jean, F. diplomat (1530–1600), 1558 F

Niebuhr, Carstens, Da. explorer (1733–1815), 1761 G

Niederschönfeld, Covention of, 1743 B

Nieuport, Holland, 1600 C

Nieuville, Comte de la, F. politician, 1621 D, 1624 C

Nieuwe Vestingsbouw (Coehoorn), 1685 G

Night Thoughts (Young), 1742 L

Night-Watch, The (Rembrandt), 1642 J

Nightingale of Wittenberg, The (Sachs), 1523 H

Nijmegen, Holland, 1591 D

Nijmegen, Treaties of, 1678 C, 1679 A, C, D

Nil Volentibus Arduum, 1669 H

Nimes, France, Huguenots in, 1572 C, 1573 C, 1629 B

Nimphidia (Drayton), 1627 L

Nine Daies Wonder (Kemp), 1600 L

Nissan, France, 1689 C

No Cross, No Crown (Penn), 1669 H

No Me Mueve, Mi Dios, Para Querete, 1628 H

No Wit Like a Woman's (Middleton), 1657 L

Noailles, Adrien Maurice, Duke of, F. general (1678–1766), 1694 B

Noble Numbers (Herrick), 1648 L

Noble Sciences des Jouers d'épée, 1535 F

Noblesse Commerçante, La, 1756 F

Nobunaga, Jap. ruler (1567–82), 1567 E, 1582 E

Nollekens, Joseph, E. sculptor (1737–1823), 1737 M

Nombre de Dios, Cen. America, 1502 G

Nominalism, defence, of, 1663 H

Noue, François de la ('Bras-de-fer'), F. soldier, Huguenot and author, 1580 F

Norden, John, E. surveyor and cartographer (1548–1625), 1593 G, 1607 G

Nördlingen, West Germany, battles, 1634 C, 1645 C

Norman, Robert, E. scientist, 1576 G, 1581 G

Normandy, France, 1522 C: peasants' revolt in, 1644 E. *See also under* Havre, Le

Norris, Sir John, E. soldier (c. 1547–97), 1586 D, 1589 B, 1592 B, 1595 B

North, Council in the, 1537 D

North, Frederick, Lord North, Earl of Guilford, E. politician, prime minister (1732–92), 1732 M

North, Sir Thomas, E. translator and classical scholar (1535–1601), 1535 M, 1557 H, 1579 H, 1601 M

Northampton, Earl of. *See* Howard, H.

North-East Passage to China, search for, 1553 G

Northumberland, Earl of. *See* Percy

North-West Passage, search for, 1616 G

Norton, Thomas, E. politician and poet (1532–84), 1561 H, 1562 L

Norway: invasion attempted, 1531 D; Sweden surrenders claim to, 1570 D

Norwich, Norfolk, England, Kett's rebellion in, 1549 C

Nostradamus (Michel de Notredame), F. astrologer (1503–66), 1503 M, 1566 M

Nôtre, André le, F. landscape gardener (1613–1700), 1613 M, 1656 J, 1662 J

Nottingham, Nottinghamshire, England, 1642 C

Nottingham, Earls of. *See* Finch, D. and H.; Howard, C.

Nouveau Système de musique theorique (Rameau), 1722 K

Nouvelle Heloïse, La. See Julie

Nouvelle relation de l'Afrique Occidentale (Labat), 1728 G

Nouvelles de la République des Lettres (Bayle), 1684 H

Nova, João, Port. navigator, 1502 G

Nova Methodus discendique juris (Leibniz), 1667 H

Nova Scientia, La (Tartaglia), 1537 G

Nova Scotia, Canada: coastline explored, 1524 G; French settlement in, 1604 F; French prevent English from colonising, 1613 E; discussions on boundaries, 1750 B; Britain secures, 1762 D. *See also* Acadia

Nova Stereometria Doliorum (Kepler), 1615 G

Novara, Italy: French capitulate at, 1495 C, 1500 A; battle at, 1513 B; French retreat to, 1524 A; Charles Emmanuel II to acquire, 1735 D, 1748 D

Novaya Zemlya, Russia, 1556 G

Novelas Ejemplares (Cervantes), 1613 L

Novelle, Le (Bandello), 1554 L

Noverre, Jean-Georges, F. choreographer (1727–1810), 1755 K, 1760 K

Novgorod, Russia, surrendered by Sweden, 1617 A

Novum Organum (Bacon), 1620 H

Nowell, Alexander, E. churchman, dean of St. Paul's (c. 1507–1602), 1568 G, 1602 M

Noyon, Picardy, France, 1591 C

Noyon, Peace of, 1516 C

Numbering the People (Bruegel), 1566 J

Numismatics, study of, 1587 F. *See also under* Coinage

Nun, The. See Religieuse, La

Nuñez, Pedro, Port. astronomer (1492–1577), 1537 G

Nuovo Musiche (Caccini), 1602 K

Nuremberg, West Germany, 1492 G, 1499 A, 1517 C, 1533 B, 1632 C: Diets at, 1523 A, 1524 A; postal services in, 1570 F; imperial electors at, 1611 D; Gustavus Adolphus takes, 1632 A

Nuremberg, Peace of, 1532 C

Nuremberg, Treaty of, 1650 B

Nuremberg Chronicle, The (Schedel), 1493 H

'Nuremberg Egg, The' (or watch), invented, 1509 G

Nymphenberg, Treaty of, 1741 B

Nymph Galatea (Raphael), 1514 J

Nymph of Fontainebleau (Cellini), 1543 J

Nystad 1721 C

O

Oates, Titus, E. demagogue (1649–1705), 1649 M, 1678 C, 1685 B, 1705 M

Oath of Association, 1588 D, 1696 A

Obedience of a Christian Man (Tyndale), 1528 H

Oberammergau Passion Play, 1634 L, 1662 L

Oboes, 1655 K

Obscene libel, 1727 F

Observationes anatomicae (Fallopius), 1561 G

Observationes chemicae (Stahl), 1731 G

Observationes medicae (Sydenham), 1676 G

Observations concerning the Increase of Mankind … (Franklin), 1755 F

Observations concerning Trade and Interest (Child), 1699 F

Otis, James, Am. patriot (1725–83), 1725 M
Otranto, Italy, 1509 B
Ottawa R., Canada, explored, 1613 G
Otway, Thomas, E. dramatist (1652–85), 1652 M, 1676 L, 1680 L, 1682 L, 1685 M
Oudenarde, Belgium, 1539 C: Parma takes, 1582 C; French take, 1668 B, 1684 B; battle, 1708 C
Oudenburg, Belgium, 1600 B
Oudry, Jean Baptiste, F. artist (1686–1755), 1733 J, 1739 J, 1740 J, 1742 J, 1743 J, 1744 J, 1745 J, 1753 J
Outcry of the Young Men and Apprentices of London, 1649 F
Overbury, Sir Thomas, E. politician (1581–1613), 1581 M, 1613 C, M, 1614 L, 1615 D
Ovid (Publius Ovidius Naso), Latin poet (43 B.C.–A.D. 17): works of, trans., 1565 H, 1626 H
Owen, John, E. Nonconformist minister (1616–83), 1616 M, 1683 M
Oxenstjerna, Axel, Count (Axel Gustafsson), Swe. statesman (c. 1575–1654), 1611 D, 1632 C, D, 1635 B, 1636 B, 1654 M
Oxford, England, 1643 A: surrenders to Parliament, 1646 C; court moves to, 1665 F; Parliament at, 1681 A
Oxford University:
    favours Henry VIII's divorce, 1530 B
    disputation at, 1554 B
    Ashmolean Museum, 1682 G
    Bodleian Library, 1598 H, 1602 H
    Botanic Gardens, 1632 G
    Clarendon Building, 1713 F
    Colleges:
        All Souls, Hawksmoor's buildings at, 1729 J
        Brase Nose, 1509 F
        Cardinal (Wolsey's), 1525 F, 1528 E
        Christ Church, 1545 F
            Tom Tower at, 1681 F
        Corpus Christi, 1517 F
        Pembroke, 1624 F
        Trinity, 1555 F
        St. John's, Laud's presidency, 1611 B
        Wadham, 1612 F
        Worcester, 1714 F
    degrees, in music, 1499 K
    histories of, 1674 H, 1691 H
    lectures, notable, 1496 F, 1547 H
    Parliamentary representation, 1604 F
    professorships:
        Heather, of music, 1626 K
        Lady Margaret, of divinity, 1502 F
        Regius, of divinity, Greek, Hebrew, 1540 F
            of modern history, 1724 F
        vinerian, of law, Blackstone as, 1758 F
    Radcliffe Camera, 1737 H, J
    scientific discussions at, 1645 G
    Sheldonian Theatre, 1664 K
    University printer, 1713 F
    visitation of, 1647 F
    See also Universities
Oxford, Earl of. *See* Harley, R.
Oxygen, obtained by heating minium, 1727 G

P

Pace, Richard, E. diplomat and author (c. 1482–1536), 1517 H, 1519 B
Pacific Ocean, Balboa discovers, 1513 G: search for passage to, 1516 G

Pacioli, Luca, It. mathematician, 1494 G
Packe, Christopher, E. translator and scholar, 1662 H
Padrilla, Juan de la, Sp. soldier, 1520 C
Padua, Italy, 1509 D: botanical gardens in, 1545 G; anatomical theatre in, 1549 G; Accademia degli Innominati, 1550 J
Paget, Sir William, Lord Paget, E. politician (1505–63), secretary of state, 1543 B, 1548 B
Paine, Thomas, E. author (1737–1809), 1737 M
Painter, William, E. translator (c. 1540–94), 1566 L
Paisiello, Giovanni, It. musician (1741–1816), 1741 M
Palace of Pleasure, The (Painter), 1566 L
Palace of the Maidens, The (Honwaerd), 1583 L
Palaeographia Graeca (Montfaucon), 1708 H
Palaeography, studies in, 1681 H
Palatinate, The, electorate, West Germany:
    becomes Protestant, 1545 E
    accession of Frederick II, 1559 B
        Lewis VI (1576–83), 1576 B
        Frederick IV (1583–92), 1592 A
        Frederick V, 1592 A
    for operations in, 1618–48. *See under* Wars, Thirty Years' War
    Restored to Charles Louis, 1648 D
    French attack, 1673 B
    devastated by Frency, 1674 C
    French occupation, 1688 C, D
    mass emigration to America from, 1709 B
Palermo, Sicily, Academy, 1718 H
Palestrina, Giovanni Pierluigi da, It. musician (1526–94), 1526 M, 1554 K, 1565 K, 1571 K, 1594 M; appointed to St. Peter's Rome, 1551 K
Paley, William, E. divine (1743–1805), 1743 M
Palffy, John, governor of Hungary, 1704 D
Palissy, Bernard, G. geologist (c. 1510–90), 1580 G
Palladio, Andrea, It. architect (1508–80), 1508 M, 1538 J, 1545 J, 1549 J, 1550 J, 1553 J, 1554 J, 1556 J, 1560 J, 1561 J, 1565 J, 1570 J, 1571 J, 1576 J, 1579 J, 1580 M, 1715 H
Palladis Tamia (Meres), 1598 H
Pallas, Peter Simon, G. naturalist and traveller (1741–1811), 1741 M
Pallavicino, Pietro, It. cardinal, 1656 H
Palma, Italy, 1496 C: Cathedral, 1522 J, 1525 J, 1530 J; St. Paul's convent, 1518 J
Palma, Vecchio, It. artist (1480–1528), 1512 J, *Palmedes* (Vondel), 1514 J, 1525 J, 1625 L
Palmistry, 1661 F
Palmstruck, Johann, Swe. financier, 1656 F, 1658 F
Palos, Majorca, 1492 C, G, 1493 A
Paltock, Robert, E. novelist (1697–1767), 1751 L
Palyce of Honour (Douglas), 1553 L
Pamela (Richardson), 1740 L
Pamfili, Giovanni Battista, It. churchman (1574–1655): elected Pope Innocent X, 1644 C
Pammelia (Ravenscroft), 1609 K
Panama, Cen. America, 1532 D: coastline, explored, 1501 G; Columbus visits, 1502 G; Isthmus, Balboa crosses, 1513 G; Morgan destroys, 1671 A
Panckoucke, André-Joseph, B. publisher and lexicographer (1700–53), 1748 H
Panin, Nikita Ivanovitch, Count, R. politician (1718–83), 1762 C
Panipat, India, battles at, 1526 B, 1556 D, 1761 A
Pantagruel (Rabelais), 1532 G, L, 1534 L
Pantomime, 1636 L, 1723 L
Panuco R., near Yucatán, Mexico, 1518 G
Paoli, Pasquale, Corsican leader (1725–1807), 1755 B

Peter III, Tsar of Russia (1762), marries Catherine, 1744 C: accession, 1762 A; assassination, 1762 C
'Peter Pindar'. *See* Wolcot, J.
Peter Wilkins (Paltock), 1751 L
Peterborough and Monmouth, Earl of. *See* Mordaunt, C.
Peterwardein, Russia, battle, 1716 C
Peterhead, Aberdeenshire, Scotland, 1715 D
Petite Pallace of Pettie (Pettie), 1576 L
Petitions, Notable:
　Millenary Petition, 1603 B
　Petition of Right, 1628 B; interpretation of, 1637 F
　Root and Branch, 1640 D
　Humble Petition and Advice, 1657 A, B
　Derby Petition, 1659 B
Petri, Olaus, Swe. divine (c. 1493-1552), 1541 H, 1550 L
Petronius, Arbiter Gaius, Latin satirical poet, works of, trans., 1694 H
Petrucci, Ottaviano de, It. printer, 1501 K, 1512 K, 1513 K
Pettie, George, E. author (1548-89), 1576 L, 1581 H
Petty, Sir William, E. economist (1623-87), 1623 M 1645 G, 1662 F, 1679 F, 1682 F, 1683 F, 1687 M, 1690 F
Peyssonel, Charles, Count of, F. author (1700-57), 1727 G
Pfyffer, Colonel, Swi. politician, 1586 B
Phaer, Thomas, We. translator (d. 1560), 1558 H
Phalaris Controversy, The, 1692 H, 1694 H, 1697 H, 1699 H
Phanariot governors in Moldavia and Wallachia, 1716 E
Pharamond (La Caprenède), 1661 L
Pharmaceutice rationalis (Willis), 1674 G
Pharmacopeia Londinensis, 1618 G
Pharsalia, The (Lucan), trans., 1593 H, 1600 H, 1614 H, 1627 H
Phèdre (Racine), 1677 L
Philadelphia, Pennsylvania, US: laid out, 1682 D; university founded, 1751 F; the press in, 1719 F, 1741 F
Philibert Emmanuel, Duke of Savoy (d. 1580), 1580 A, C
Philidor, François, F. student of chess, 1749 F
Philip of Anjou. *See* Philip V of Spain
Philip I ('The Handsome'), King of Spain (1506), Archduke of Austria, 1499 E, 1504 C, 1506 C, M: marries Joanna, Infanta of Spain, 1496 D; visits England, 1506 A, B; signs Treaty of Windsor, 1506 A; meets Cortes, 1506 C; signs Treaty of Villafavila, 1506 C
Philip II, King of Spain (1556-98), 1527 M, 1551 J, 1555 B, 1568 D, J, 1584 C, D, 1587 B, 1592 D, 1593 C, 1598 B, M
　invested with Duchy of Milan, 1540 D, 1542 C
　opposition to, in Germany, 1553 A
　treaty to marry Mary, 1553 D
　marries Mary, 1554 C
　renounces claim to Empire, 1555 C
　coronation in England, opposed, 1555 D
　begins to rule in the Netherlands, Milan and Naples, 1555 D
　Charles V resigns Spain to, 1556 A
　returns to England, 1557 A
　hopes of succession in England fade, 1558 A
　aims to marry Elizabeth, 1559 A
　builds Escorial, 1563 J
　recalls Granvelle from Netherlands, 1564 A
　Egmont seeks concessions from, 1565 A
　establishes archives at Simancas, 1567 F
　orders Montigny's death, 1570 D

　marries Anne of Austria, 1570 D
　asked to recall Alva, 1573 C
　suspends payments, 1575 E
　appoints Don John of Austria governor of Netherlands, 1576 A
　asked to recall troops from Netherlands, 1576 D
　southern Netherlands, reconciliation with, 1579 A, B
　claims throne of Portugal, 1580 A
　Portuguese Cortes submits to, 1581 B
　Northern provinces of Netherlands renounce allegiance to, 1581 C
　'Enterprise against England', 1584 D, 1587 C
　supports French Catholic League, 1585 A, 1590 A
　Mary Queen of Scots recognises as her heir, 1586 B
　sends Armada, 1588 B, C
　claims French throne for Infanta Isabel, 1589 C
　suppresses liberties of Aragon, 1591 D
　plans for Infanta Isabel, 1592 D, 1593 A
　is openly at war with France, 1595 A
　aids Tyrone's rebellion, 1595 B
　prevented from sending Armada, 1596 B
　peace negotiations with Henry IV, 1597 D, 1598 B
　resigns claim to French throne, 1598 B
　assigns Netherlands to Archduke Albert and Infanta Isabel, 1598 B
Philip III, King of Spain (1598-1621), 1598 D, 1621 A: accession, 1598 C; marries Margaret of Austria, 1598 D; aspires to marry Princess Elizabeth Stuart, 1612 C; abandons designs against England, 1613 A
Philip IV, King of Spain (1621-65), 1612 C, 1622 C, 1623 C, 1649 J, 1665 C: marries Elizabeth Bourbon, 1615 D; accession, 1621 B
Philip V, King of Spain (1700-46), 1700 A, D, 1715 C, 1716 D, 1746 C: proclaimed king, 1701 A; renounces claim to French throne, 1712 D; recognised as King of Spain, 1713 A; marries Elizabeth Farnese, 1714 C; attacks Sardinia, 1717 C; abdicates, 1724 A; resumes crown, 1724 C; claimant to Empire, 1740 D
Philip, Don, Sp. Prince, 1743 D, 1757 B: acquires Piacenza, 1748 D
Philip, landgrave of Hesse, G. Protestant ruler (1504-67), 1524 A, 1526 A: alliance with John of Saxony, 1525 D; forms League of Torgau, 1526 B; alarmed at Catholic Princes, 1527 B; founds Marburg University, 1527 F; makes alliance of Weimar, 1528 A; attempts reconciliation between Luther and Zwingli, 1529 C; signs Schmalkaldic League, 1530 D; leaves Schmalkaldic League, 1532 D; defeats Ferdinand of Austria, 1534 B; bigamous marriage, 1540 A; comes to terms with Charles V, 1541 B; invades Brunswick, 1542 C; under ban of Empire, 1546 C; imprisoned, 1547 B
Philip William, Prince of Orange (d. 1618), 1618 A
Philiphaugh, Scotland, battle, 1645 C
Philipon, Manon Jeanne. *See* Roland, Madame
Philippines, The, Pacific: Magellan reaches, 1520 G; Spanish possessions in, 1668 A; Spain recovers, 1762 D
Philips, Ambrose, E. poet (1675-1749), 1749 M
Philips, John, E. poet (1676-1709), 1701 L
Phillips, Edward, E. lexicographer (1630-96), 1658 H
Phillippsburg, West Germany: captured, 1635 A, 1644 C; Duke of Lorraine takes, 1676 C; Louis XIV restores, 1679 A; French recapture, 1688 D; French surrender, 1697 D; French recapture, 1734 B
Philomela (Lyly), 1591 L
Philosophe de Sanssouci, Le : Oeuvres (Frederick the Great), 1750 H

Q

R

Rebellions

Maurice of Nassau and Vere defeat Spanish at
Nieuport, 1600 C
fall of Sluys, 1604 B
fall of Ostend, 1604 C
Twelve Years' Truce signed, 1609 B
account of, 1595 F
rising in Brussels, 1633 D
independence of United Provinces recognised,
1648 D
in Portugal, 1640 D, 1667 D, 1758 C
in Russia, of Boyars, 1564 B
in the 'Time of the Troubles', 1604 B, 1613 A
in Moscow, 1647 E, 1648 E
of the Streltsy (soldiers of the Moscow garrison),
1682 B, 1698 B
in Astrahkan, 1705 C
'the bloodless' revolution, 1741 D, E
in Scotland, by Huntley, 1562 D. *See also under*
Scotland
in Siam, 1688 E
in Spain, of Moors in Grenada, 1500 B, 1501 A
in Toledo and Castille, 1520 C, 1521 B
in Barcelona, 1533 C
of Moors, 1568 D
in Barcelona, 1640 B
in Catalonia, 1652 E
in Madrid, 1676 B
in Sweden, 1520 D, 1521 A, 1522 C, 1523 B
in Switzerland, by Peasants in Berne, 1653 E
in Berne, 1723 E
in Turkey, at Constantinople, 1687 D
See also under Civil Wars; Riots and Risings
Recherches de la France (Pasquier), 1560 H, 1611 F
Recherches sur la propriété (Brissot), 1755 F
Recorde, Robert, E. mathematician (*c.* 1510–58),
1537 F, 1551 G, 1557 G
Recruiting Officer, The (Farquhar), 1706 L
Recumbent Girl (Boucher), 1751 J
Rederijckkunst, 1587 L
Redi, Francisco, It. scientist, 1699 G
Reeve, Clara, E. novelist (1729–1807), 1729 M
Réflexions (Quesnel), 1713 H
Réflexions Chrétiennes (Croiset), 1752 H
Réflexions Morales sur le Nouveau Testament (Quesnel),
1687 H
Réflexions sur la cause générale des vents (d'Alembert),
1747 G
Réflexions sur la poétique d'Aristote (Rapin), 1674 H
Réflexions sur les divers génies du peuple romain
(St.-Évremond), 1663 H
*Réflexions sur l'origine, l'histoire des anciennes peuples
Chaldéens, Hébreux* (Fourmont), 1747 H
Reformation, The:
Plans for reform within the Church, 1524 B
in Denmark, episcopacy ended, 1536 D
Church ordinance, 1537 C
in England, Henry VIII's divorce proceedings,
attacked, 1530 F. *See also* Henry VIII
proceedings against entire clergy, 1530 D
Henry VIII recognised as Supreme Head of
Church, 1531 A, H
clergy pardoned, 1531 A
Supplication of the Ordinaries, 1532 A
Henry VIII confiscates Annates, 1532 A
Submission of the Clergy, 1532 B, H
royal supremacy is urged, 1532 F
restraint on Appeals to Rome, 1533 A
Henry VIII is excommunicated, 1533 C
severance from Rome, 1534 A
Act of Supremacy, 1534 D, H
Henry VIII as Supreme Head, 1535 A
Clergy abjure Pope's authority, 1535 A

Cromwell's visitation, 1535 A
execution of Carthusians, 1535 B
execution of Fisher and More, 1535 H, M
The Ten Articles, 1536 C, H
Pope's authority declared void, 1536 C
Cromwell's Injunctions, 1536 C, H
English Bible, 1536 C
Tyndale executed, 1536 H
Dissolution of Lesser Monasteries, 1536 H
Pilgrimage of Grace, 1536 D, 1537 A, B, C
Visitation of Greater Monasteries, 1538 A
Greater Monasteries surrender, 1539 B
Act of Six Articles, 1539 B
execution of abbots, 1539 D
Repeal of Act of Six Articles, 1547 D
Act of Uniformity, 1549 A
Prayer Book, 1549 A, B, C
Act of Uniformity, 1552 A
Second Prayer Book, 1552 A
Protestants leave for continent, 1553 C
Roman Catholicism re-established, 1554 D
Smithfield burnings, 1555 A, 1557 E
Cranmer's trial, 1555 C
Protestant exiles return, 1558 D
Elizabethan Acts of Supremacy and Uniformity,
1559 A
Prayer Book, 1559 B
Pius V excommunicates Elizabeth I, 1570 A
39 Articles, 1571 B
Anabaptists burnt, 1575 C
Puritans plan to reform church, 1576 A
execution of seminary priests, 1577 D
legislation against Catholics, 1581 A
expulsion of Jesuits, 1584 D
legislation against Puritans, 1593 A
See also under Religious Denominations, England
in France, Lutherans, trial of, 1525 A, 1528 B
Calvin lays foundation of French Protestantism,
1532 H
movement gains ground, 1533 H
placards provoke persecution, 1534 D
Calvin's *Institutes*, 1536 H
freedom of conscience promised, 1536 A
persecution of Protestants, 1538 D, 1540 B,
1546 C, D, H, 1547 D, 1557 D
Huguenots plot at Amboise, 1560 A
persecution suspended, 1561 A
Poissy Conference, 1561 C
Edict of St. Germain recognises Huguenots,
1562 A
massacre of Vassy, 1562 A
concessions to Huguenots during Wars of
Religion (*q.v.*), 1563 A, 1568 A, 1570 C
Massacre of St. Bartholomew, 1573 C
concessions to Huguenots, 1573 C, 1575 D,
1576 B, 1577 C
Guise forms Catholic League, 1576 B
toleration for Huguenots revoked, 1585 C
Henry III is pressed to persecute Huguenots,
1588 A
Henry IV becomes a Roman Catholic, 1593 C
Jesuits expelled, 1594 D
Huguenots demand securities, 1594 E
Edict of Nantes grants Huguenots limited free-
dom of worship, 1598 B
in Germany, Luther's Theses, 1517 D, H
the Leipzig Disputation, 1519 H
Luther's Address to the German Nation, 1520 H
Luther is declared a heretic, 1520 H
Luther burns the papal bull, 1520 H
Melanchthon on the Protestant dogma, 1521 H

Reformation

Reve, Clara, E. novelist (1729–1807), 1729 M
Revenge for Honour (Chapman), 1654 L
Revenge of Bussy D'Ambois, The (Chapman), 1613 L
Revenger is Tragedy, The (Towneur), 1607 L
Revere, Paul, Am. patriot (1735–1818), 1735 M
Reventlow, Christian Ditlev Frederick, Count, Dan. statesman (1748–1827), 1748 M
Revett, Nicholas, E. author (1720–1804), 1762 H
Reynolds, Sir Joshua, E. artist (1723–92), 1723 M, 1746 J, 1753 J, 1756 J, 1759 J, 1760 J
Rhadamiste et Zénobie (Crébillon, *père*), 1711 L
Rhé, Isle of, France, expedition to, 1627 C
Rheims, France, 1575 A: English College, 1578 H; Louis XIV's coronation, 1654 B
Rheinfelden, West Germany, 1638 A
Rhenish League, 1658 C
Rheticus, George, Swi. mathematician (1514–76), 1596 G
Rhine, R., Europe: French army crosses, 1672 B; left bank is freed from Germans, 1675 A; right bank is restored to France, 1697 D; Russian army reaches, 1735 C; Russians march towards, 1748 A; French evacuate right bank, 1762 D
Rhineland, West Germany, ravaged by French, 1693 B
Rhode Island, State, US, 1636 B: Williams settles at Providence, 1636 F; Anne Hutchinson settles in, 1638 H; royal charter, 1663 C
Rhodes, Dodecanese Isles, Aegean, Turks take, 1522 D
Riascha, Treaty of, 1732 A
Ribault, Jean, F. colonist (c. 1520–65), 1562 E
Ribbing-machine, 1758 G
Ribera, José, Sp. artist (1591–1652), 1630 J, 1641 J, 1644 J, 1646 J, 1647 J, 1648 J
Ribera, Pedro de, Sp. architect, 1720 J, 1722 J, 1723 J
Riccati, Jacopo Francesco, Count, It. mathematician (1676–1754), 1724 G
Ricci, Matteo, It. missionary to China (1552–1610), 1552 M, 1610 M
Rich, John, E. father of British pantomime (c. 1682–1761), 1735 F, 1761 M
Rich, Penelope, E. author and beauty (c. 1562–1607), 1607 M
Richard, Charles-Louis, F. Dominican (1711–94), 1759 H
Richard II (Shakespeare), 1597 L
Richard III (Shakespeare), 1597 L
Richard III, History of (More), 1543 H
Richardson, Samuel, E. novelist (1689–1761), 1689 M, 1740 L, 1741 L, 1748 L, 1753 L, 1761 M
Richelet, César-Pierre, F. grammarian and lexicographer (1631–98), 1680 H
Richelieu, Armand Jean du Plessis de, F. statesman and cardinal (1585–1642), 1585 M, 1619 C, 1627 B, C, 1631 B, 1632 D, 1634 A, 1635 D, J, 1642 M:
appointed minister for war and foreign affairs, 1616 D
supports Marie de' Medici, 1617 B
is exiled, 1618 B
recalled, 1619 A
negotiates peace between factions, 1620 C
resumes offices, 1622 A
created a cardinal, 1622 C
appointed first minister, 1624 C
suppresses conspiracy, 1626 C
increases his power, 1626 C
summons notables, 1626 D
imposes rigid censorship, 1626

appointed superintendent of commerce and navigation, 1627 A
founds French Companies for Canada and Senegal, 1628 E, 1629 F
anti-Hapsburg policy, 1629 C
supports Savoy, 1629 E
demands Wallenstein's dismissal, 1630 A
plot against, 1630 C
overthrows conspirators in 'Day of Dupes', 1630 D
intrigues against, 1631 E
reforms administration, 1634 E
forms League of Rivoli, 1635 B
attacked by Jansen for indifference to Catholic interests, 1635 F
arrests pretender to Palatinate, 1639 D
uncovers conspiracy of Cinque-Mars, 1642 C
Richmond, Duke of. *See* Fitzroy, H.
Richmond, Margaret, Countess of ('The Lady Margaret'), mother of Henry VII (1441–1509). *See under* Beaufort
Richmond, Virginia, US, founded, 1737 B
Rickets, treatise on, 1650 G
Ridley, Nicholas, E. churchman, Protestant martyr and author (c. 1500–55), 1554 B, 1555 C, M
Ridolfi, Roberto di, It. conspirator (1531–1612), 1531 M, 1571 A, C, D, 1572 A, 1612 M
Rifling on firearms, 1520 G
Riga, Latvia: Great Elector reaches, 1677 D; Charles XII relieves, 1701 B
Rigaud, Hyacinthe, F. artist (1659–1743), 1659 M, 1701 J, 1703 J, 1706 J, 1715 J, 1722 J, 1743 M
Rights of the Christian Church (Tindal), 1706 H
Rijn, Rembrandt Harmens van. *See* Rembrandt
Rimas várias, Flores do Lima (Bernardes), 1597 L
Rimini, Italy: Cesare Borgia takes, 1500 D; Pope annexes, 1509 B
Ringelberg, J. D. van, Flem. humanist, 1541 H
Rio de Janiero, Brazil: French colony at, 1555 E; French conquest, 1711 C
Rio de la Plata, Argentina, 1516 G: exploration of, 1519 G, 1526 G. *See also under* Argentina
Riots and Risings:
in Afghanistan, 1709 E
in Austria, by peasants, 1595 D
in England, Cornish, 1497 B
'Evil May Day Riots', London, 1517 B
Weavers, against Wolsey, 1528 A
in Lincolnshire against dissolution of monasteries, 1536 C. *See also under* Rebellions, England, Pilgrimage of Grace
in Midlands, 1607 B
Penruddock's, in Wiltshire, 1655 A
Booth's, in Cheshire, 1659 C
Jacobite. *See under* Scotland
in France, by peasants, 1493 E
in Languedoc, 1583 C
in Cevennes, by Protestants, 1689 E
in Germany, at Speyer, by peasants, 1502 E
in Black Forest, by peasants, 1513 E
in Württemberg, by peasants, 1513 E
in Hungary, by peasants, 1514 E
in Ireland, by Protestants in Dublin, 1759 D
in Italy, at Genoa, against nobility, 1506 B
in Mexico, by Maya, 1546 E
in Netherlands, by extreme sectaries, 1566 C
in Scotland, by Covenanters, 1666 D, 1706 E
Porteous Riots, 1736 C
Jacobites, 1745 C, D, 1746 A, B, C
in Switzerland, in Geneva, 1555 E
in Transylvania, 1551 C
See also under Rebellions and Revolutions
Ripon, Yorkshire, England, rebels at, 1569 D

S

Savoy, duchy, Italy:
  French conquer, 1536 A
  Emmanuel Philibert's accession, 1553 D
  duchy restored to duke, 1559 B
  French garrisons in, 1562 D
  Turin becomes capital, 1562 D
  accession of Charles Emmanuel I, 1580 C
  Protestant Swiss Cantons oppose, 1584 E
  attack on Geneva, 1589 B
  Henry IV's war with, 1600 C, D
  accession of Victor Amadeus I, 1630
  accession of Emmanuel II, 1638
  massacre of Waldenses, 1655 H
  accession of Victor Amadeus II, 1675 B
  joins League of Augsburg, 1688 D, 1690 D
  duchy regained by Victor Amadeus II, 1696 C
  joins grand Alliance, 1703 D
  obtains Sicily, 1713 A
  agreement to exchange Sicily for Sardinia, 1718 C
  Victor Amadeus II becomes King of Sardinia, 1720 A
  plans for cession to France, 1733 C
  See also under Sardinia
Saw, mechanical, 1592 G
Saxe, Hermann Maurice, Count, G., Marshal (1696–1750), 1696 M, 1750 M: at Fontenoy, 1745 B; takes Brussels, 1746 A; takes Antwerp, 1746 B
Saxe-Weimar, Duke of, 1591 C
Saxony, East Germany: accession of Duke John the Steadfast, 1525 B; accession of Duke Maurice, 1541 B; Charles V assigns Saxon electorate to Duke Maurice, 1546 D, 1547 B; Charles V invades, 1547 B; imprisonment of elector John Frederick, 1547 B; accession of Duke Augustus, 1553 C; electorate united in Albertine branch, 1553 C; accession of Christian I, 1586 A; accession of Christian II, 1591 C; Calvinism in, uprooted, 1591 C; accession of elector George, 1611 C. *See* Wars, Thirty Years' War (1618–48); invasion of, 1756 C; Imperial troops occupy, 1760 C, D
Saxony blue, the dye, 1740 G
Saxton, Christopher, E. cartographer (d. 1596), 1575 G
Saybrook, Connecticut, US: settlement at, 1635 E; united with Connecticut, 1644 E; Yale collegiate school at, 1701 F
Saye, Lord. *See* Fiennes, W.
Saying Grace (Chardin), 1739 J
Scale of Perfection, The (Hylton), 1494 H
Scalich de Lika, Count Paul, Croatian scholar, 1559 H
Scaliger, Joseph Justus, F. scholar (1540–1609), 1540 M, 1583 H, 1606 H, 1609 M
Scaliger, Julius Caesar, It. humanist, philosopher and scientist (1484–1558), 1561 H, 1558 M
Scarlatti, Alessandro, It. musician (1659–1725), 1725 M
Scarlatti, Domenico, It. musician (1685–1757), 1685 M, 1740 K, 1757 M
Scarlet 'Bow' dye, 1620 G
Scarron, Paul, F. poet and dramatist (1610–60), 1610 M, 1645 L, 1651 L, 1660 M
Sceptical Chemist, The (Boyle), 1662 G
Schafthausen, Germany, 1501 E
Scharnhorst, Gerhard Johann David von, Pruss. general (1756–1813), 1756 M
Schärtlin, Sebastian, G. soldier, 1546 C
Schedel, Hartmann, G. historian (1440–1514), 1493 H
Scheele, Karl Wilhelm, Swe. chemist (1742–86), 1742 M

Scheemakers, Peter, Flem. sculptor (1691–1770), 1691 M
Scheffler, Johann. *See* Angelus Silesius
Scheibe, Johann Adolf, G. musician, 1740 K
Schelmuffsky (Reuter), 1696 L
Schenck, Martin von, G. soldier, 1587 D
Scherpe Resolution, in Holland, 1618 C
Schiller, Johann Christoph Friedrich von, G. poet, dramatist and philosopher (1759–1805), 1759 M
Schleswig, duchy: becomes a Lutheran state, 1524 D; reduced by Tilly and Wallenstein, 1622 D; Sweden recognises Denmark's annexation of, 1720 C
Schlick, Arnold, G. organ-builder, 1511 K
Schlüter, Andreas, G. architect (1664–1714), 1698 J
Schmalkalden, Germany, Protestant Princes meet at, 1530 D
Schmalkaldic War. *See under* Civil Wars, Germany. survey of, 1548 F
Schoole of Abuse (Gosson), 1579 L
Schoole of Musicke (Robinson), 1603 K
Schoolmistress, The (Shenstone), 1737 L
Schonberg, Friedrich Hermann, Duke of, F. (later E.), soldier (d. 1690), 1690 M
Schönborn, Georg von, G. author (d. 1637), 1637 M
Schreyer, Jan, Du. physician, 1682 G
'Schumacher, Peder'. *See* Griffenfeldt, Count Peder
Schütz, Heinrich, G. musician (1585–1672), 1585 M, 1617 K, 1625 K, 1627 K, 1629 K, 1645 K, 1648 K
Schwank: *Till*, 1500 L; *Fortunatus*, 1509 L; *Das Rollwagenbüchlein*, 1555 L
Schwarzart, East Germany, 1554 B
Schweibus, East Germany: Great Elector obtains, 1686 B; Brandenburg restores, 1694 D
Schweidnitz, East Germany: battle, 1642 B; Imperialists take, 1761 D
Science Fiction, early example of, R. Paltock, 1751 L
Scienza Mechanica (Galileo), 1592 G
Scienza Nuova intorno alla natura (Vico), 1725 H
Scolemaster, The (Ascham), 1570 F
Scone, Scotland, coronation of Charles II at, 1651 A
Scotland:
  Battle of Flodden, 1513 C
  accession of James V, 1513 C
  James V marries Mary of Guise, 1538 B
  Beaton becomes chief adviser to James V, 1539 A
  Battle of Hadden Rigg, 1542 C
  Battle of Solway Moss, 1542 D
  accession of Mary Queen of Scots, 1542 D
  Beaton's regency, 1542 D
  Arran's regency, 1543 A, C
  peace with England, 1543 C
  Parliament repudiates Treaty of Greenwich, 1543 D
  Somerset invades, 1547 C
  Battle of Pinkie, 1547 C
  Union with England, discussed, 1548 A
  Mary of Guise becomes Regent, 1554 B
  Knox returns, 1555 B
  Scots invade England, 1557 C
  first Covenant, 1557 D, H
  Regent deposed, 1559 D
  Treaty of Berwick, 1560 A
  Treaty of Edinburgh, ends 'Auld Alliance', 1560 C
  Mary returns, 1561 C
  Huntley's rebellion, 1562 D
  Mary marries Darnley, 1566
  Darnley's murder, 1567 A
  Bothwell marries Mary, 1567 B
  Battle of Carberry Hill, 1567 B
  Mary imprisoned, 1567 B

Scotland—*contd.*
 Mary abdicates, 1567 C
 Moray as regent, 1567 C
 Mary escapes from Lochleven, 1568 B
 Battle of Langside, 1568 B
 Mary takes refuge in England, 1568 B
 Moray's assassination, 1570 A
 civil war in, 1570 A
 Marians' *coup* at Stirling, 1571 C
 death of Regent Lennox, 1571 C
 Mar succeeds as Regent, 1571 C
 Morton succeeds as Regent, 1572 D
 war with Marians ends, 1573 A
 Morton resigns regency, 1578 A
 James VI begins personal rule, 1578 A
 Second Confession of Faith, 1581 A
 Marians' plots, 1581 C
 Ruthven Raid, 1582 C
 James VI escapes, 1583 B
 League of Amity with England, 1586 C
 Gowrie Conspiracy, 1600 C
 James VI leaves for England, 1603 B
 Case of the *Post Nati*, 1608 F
 James VI revisits Scotland, 1617
 Charles I's coronation, 1626 C
 Episcopacy forced on Scotland, 1637 B, H, 1639 H
 Bishops' wars, 1639 A, B, 1640 B, C, D
 Scots army crosses Tweed, 1644 A
  See Civil Wars, England
 Charles II crowned, 1650 B
 Battle of Dunbar, 1650 B
 Scottish Covenanters rise, 1666 C, D, 1679 B
 Massacre of Glencoe, 1692 A
 Union with England, 1707 B
 James Edward lands, 1708 A
 Jacobite Risings, 1715 C, D, 1716 A, 1745 C, D, 1746 A, B
 Battle of Culloden, 1746 B
 heritable jurisdictions abolished, 1748 F
Scotland, borders of, English harry, 1541 C, 1542 C, 1545 A, 1570 A
Scotland, Description of (Howell), 1649 L
Scotland, Histories of:
 Boece, 1526 H
 Buchanan, 1582 H
 Robertson, 1759 H
Scott, James, Duke of Monmouth (1649–85), E. rebel, 1649 M, 1685 M: captain general of army, 1670 A; defeats Covenanters, 1679 B; exiled, 1683 D; rebellion, 1685 C; defeated at Sedgemoor, 1685 C; execution, 1685 C
Scott, John, Earl of Eldon, B. lawyer and Tory politician (1751–1838), 1751 M
Scott, Reginald, E. author (c. 1538–99), 1584 F
Scourge of Villainy (Marston), 1598 L
Scourging of St. Andrew (Domenichino), 1608 J
Scriblerus Club, 1713 H
Scriptorum Ecclesiasticorum Historia Literaria (Cave), 1688 H
Scroggs, Sir William, E. judge (c. 1623–83), 1683 M
Scrooby, Nottinghamshire, England, 1620 C
Scudéry, Madeleine de, F. novelist (1607–1701), 1607 M, 1641 L, 1649 L, 1653 L, 1654 L, 1656 H, 1660 L, 1701 M
Seamans Dictionary, The (Manwayring), 1644 G
Search for Truth, The (Malebranche), 1674 H
Seasons, The (Thomson), 1730 L
Seaweed, soda ash from, 1574 G
Seba, Albert, Du. scientist (1665–1736), 1716 G
Sebastian I, King of Portugal (1557–78), 1557 B, 1578 C

Sebastian, King of Fez (d. 1578), 1578 A
Sebastiano del Piombo, It. artist (c. 1485–1547), 1510 J, 1517 J, 1520 J, 1547 M
Secchia rapita (Tassoni), 1622 L
Seckendorf, Frederick Henry, Count of, G. soldier (1673–1737): defeats French, 1735 B; imprisoned, 1737 E
Second Helvetian Confession (Bullinger), 1566 H
Secondat, Charles de. *See* Montesquieu, Baron de
Secret Society: Knights of the Apocalypse, in Italy, 1693 H
Secretaries of State, first appointed in England, 1540 A
Secrets of Angling, The (Dennys), 1613 G
Sedan, France, 1576 A, 1606 A
Sedeno, Antonio de, Sp. explorer, 1530 E
Sedgemoor, Somerset, England, battle, 1685 C
Sedley, Charles, E. author (c. 1640–1701), 1701 M
Segner, Johann Andreas von, G. physicist (1704–77), 1751 G
Sejanus, His Fall (Jonson), 1605 L
Sekigahara, Japan, battle, 1600 E
Selden, John, E. jurist and antiquary (1584–1654), 1584 M, 1654 M: helps frame Petitition of Right, 1628 B; sent to Tower, 1629 B; works, 1614 H, 1616 F, 1618 H, 1632 F, 1635 H, 1640 F, 1689 L
Select Colloquies of Erasmus (L'Estrange), 1680 H
Selecta historiae ecclesiasticae capita (Alexander), 1676 H
Selenographia (Hevel), 1647 F
Self-Denying Ordinance, 1645 B
Selfstrijt (Cats), 1620 L
Selim I, Sultan of Turkey (1512–20), 1512 B, 1520 C: marches on Turkey, 1514 B; defeats Persians, 1514 C; conquers Kurdistan, 1515 E; annexes Syria, 1516 C; captures Cairo, 1517 A
Selim II, Sultan of Turkey ('The Sot', 1566–74), 1566 C, 1568 A, 1574 D
Selkirk, Alexander, Scot. adventurer (1676–1721), 1676 M, 1721 M
Selling of Joseph, The (Sewall), 1700 F
Sellondi, West Africa, 1672 F
Semaine, La (du Bartas), 1578 L; trans., 1605 H
Semler, Christoph, G. educationalist (1669–1739), 1706 F
Sendomir, Consensus, 1570 B
Senegal (now Mali Republic):
 French Company founded, 1628 E
  reformed, 1671 E, 1673 E
 British secure lands in, 1758 D, 1762 D
Senegal R., West Africa, French settlements in, 1626 F, 1637 E
Senlis, Treaties of, 1493 B, 1498 C
Sennheim, West Germany, battle, 1638 D
Sens, France, Archbishop of, 1528 B
Sentences:
 boiling to death, 1531 F
 burning, 1525 A
  execution for heresy, last in England, 1612 F
  for publishing works against religion or the state, 1626 F
 for witchcraft, last in England, 1712 F
 felon's death, last nobleman to suffer, for murder, 1760 F
 mutilation, for seditious writings, 1637 F
 transportation to colonies, 1597 F
Septem horae canonicae, 1514 H
Sepulcretum (Bonet), 1679 G
Servia (now Yugoslavia): occupied by imperialists, 1688 C; empire retains part of, 1718 C; to be ceded to Turkey, 1739 C
Sergius (Reuchlin), 1496 L

Serlio, Sebastian, It. architect (1475–1552), 1537 J
Sermons, notable:
Lancelot Andrewes, 1629 H
Francis Attenbury, 1734 H
Isaac Barrow, 1678 H
Joseph Butler, 1726 H
John Donne, 1626 H, 1632 H, 1640 H, 1649 H, 1660 H
John Fisher, 1521 H
Hugh Latimer, 1548 H, 1571 H
William Laud, 1651 H
Robert South, 1679 H
Serious Call to a Devout and Holy Life, A (Law), 1728 H
Serra (or Serres), Oliver de, F. economist (1539–1619), 1613 F
Serres, Jean de, F. historian, Huguenot, 1572 F, 1597 F
Servetus, Michael, Sp. theologian and physician (1511–53), 1531 H, 1553 G, H, M
Sesia R., Italy, 1524 A
Seufl, Ludwig, G. musician (1492–c. 1556), 1492 M
Seven Bookes on the Art of War (Machiavelli), 1521 F
Seven Chirurgical Treatises (Wiseman), 1676 G
Seven Deadly Sinnes of London, The (Dekker), 1606 L
Seven Penitential Psalms, The, Fyssher, 1509 H
Seven Sacraments (Poussin), 1641 J, 1644 J
Sévigné, Marie de Rabutin-Chantal, Marquise de, F. letter-writer (1626–96), 1626 M, 1671 L, 1696 M
Seville, Spain: Hospital de Venerables Sacerdotes, 1687 J; Magdalene Church, 1691 J; St. Luis Church, 1699 J; Telmo Church, 1724 J; Academy 1751 H
Seville, Treaty of, 1729 D
Sèvre, Jacques de, F. New Testament scholar (d. 1525), 1525 A
Sewall, Samuel, Am. author and judge (1652–1730), 1700 F
sewing-machine, precursor of, 1755 G
Seymour, Edward, Earl of Hertford, Duke of Somerset, E. statesman (1500–52), 1500 M, 1549 B: campaigns in Scotland, 1545 C; as commander in France, 1546 A; secures downfall of Norfolk, 1546 D; appointed Lord Protector, 1547 A; created Duke of Somerset, 1547 A; invades Scotland, 1547 C; builds Somerset House, 1547 J; Scottish negotiations, 1548 A, C; fall, 1549 D; submission, 1549 D; execution, 1552 A, M; failure of policy of, tract on, 1550 F
Seymour, Thomas, Lord Seymour of Sudeley, E. admiral (1508–49), 1508 M, 1549 A, M
Seymour, William, Earl of Hertford (1588–1660), husband of Arabella Stuart, 1610 B, 1611 B
Sfondrato, Nicolo, It. churchman (1531–91), Pope Gregory XIV, 1535 M, 1591 M: election, 1590 D
Sforza, Ascanio, 1492 C
Sforza, Bianca Maria (Blanche), It., marries Emperor Maximilian I, 1494 A
Sforza, Caterina, Countess of Forli, It. ruler (1509–46), 1509 M, 1546 M
Sforza, Francesco, It. ruler (d. 1535), is granted Duchy of Milan for life, 1529 E; death, 1535 D, M
Sforza, Giovanni, It., Lord of Pesaro: marries Lucretia Borgia, 1493 B; divorces Lucretia Borgia, 1497 A
Sforza, Ludovico, It. ruler (d. 1505), 1493 A, 1505 B: flees from Milan, 1499 C; recovers Milan, 1500 A; imprisoned, 1500 B
Sganarelle (Molière), 1660 L
Shaftesbury, Earl of. *See* Cooper, Anthony Ashley

Shadwell, Thomas, E. dramatist and satirist (c. 1642–92), 1673 L, 1688 L, 1692 M
Shakespeare, William, E. poet and playwright (1564–1616), 1564 M, 1616 M:
Dates of plays as produced or printed; quartos; folios; and dates of the Sonnets and Poems:
1591 L, 1592 L, 1593 L, 1594 L, 1597 L, 1598 L, 1599 L, 1600 L, 1601 L, 1602 L, 1603 L, 1604 L, 1605 L, 1607 L, 1608 L, 1609 L, 1610 L, 1613 L, 1622 L, *First Folio*, 1623 L, *Second Folio*, 1632 L, 1634 L, *Third Folio*, 1663 L, *Fourth Folio*, 1685 H
Shakespearean Scholarship and Criticism:
Nicolas Rowe, 1709 H, 1714 H
Alexander Pope, 1725 H, 1726 H
Lewis Theobald, 1734 H, 1741 H
Sir Thomas Hanmer, 1743 H
First public lecture on W.S., 1744 H
Hayman's edition, 1744 J
Dr. Samuel Johnson's *Proposals*, 1745 H, 1756 H
John Upton, 1746 H
Wm. Warburton, 1747 H
Thomas Edwards; *Canons*, 1748 H
Wm. Dodd: *Beauties of S.*, 1752 H
Zachary Grey, 1754 H
C. M. Wieland, trans. into German, 1762 H
Shamela (Fielding), 1741 L
Sharp, James, Sc. divine, Archbishop of St. Andrews (1618–79), 1618 M, 1679 B, M
Shaxton, Nicholas, E. bishop of Salisbury (c. 1485–1556), 1539 C
Sheen Palace, Richmond, Surrey, England, 1497 D
Sheep-farming, in England, size of flocks limited, 1534 F. *See also* Enclosures
Sheerness, Kent, England, James II at, 1688 D
Shelburne, Earl of. *See* Fitzmaurice, William
Sheldon, Gilbert, E. churchman, Archbishop of Canterbury (1593–1677), 1664 F, 1677 M
Shelton, Thomas, E. translator, 1612 H, 1620 H
Shenandoah Valley, Virginia, US, Spottswood's expedition to, 1717 A
Shenstone, William, E. poet (1714–63), 1737 L
Shepheards Calendar, The (Spenser), 1579 L
Shepherd's Week, The (Gray), 1714 L
Sheppard, Jack, E. criminal (1702–24), 1702 M, 1724 M
Sheppard, William, E. lawyer (d. 1675), 1641 F
Sheraton, Thomas, E. cabinet maker (1751–1806), 1751 M
Sheridan, Richard Brinsley, Ir. author and politician (1751–1816), 1751 M
Sheriff, Lawrence, E. benefactor, founder of Rugby School (d. 1567), 1567 F
Sheriffmuir, Perthshire, Scotland, battle, 1715 D
Sherley, Sir Thomas, E. diplomat (1564–1630), 1604 A, 1611 E
Sherlock, Thomas, E. divine, bishop of London (1678–1761), 1729 H, 1761 M
Sherlock, William, E. theologian, dean of St. Paul's (c. 1641–1707), 1689 H, 1707 M
Sher Shah, Emperor of Delhi, 1540 E
She Wou'd If She Cou'd (Etherege), 1668 L
Shih Tsung, Emperor of China of the Chia Ching Reign (1522–66), 1522 E
Shih Tsung, Emperor of China of the Yung Cheng Reign (1722–35), 1722 E
Ship Money, 1634 D, 1635 C, F, 1636 D, F, 1637 F, 1640 D
Ship of Fools, The (Bosch), 1500 J
Ship of Fools, The (Brandt), 1494 L; trans., 1509 H
Shipping, *Lloyd's List* of, 1726 F
Ship's course, calculations about, 1537 G
Shipton, Mother (Head), 1677 L

Stanley, Sir William, E. politician (d. 1495), executed, 1495 A

Stanyhurst, Richard, E. translator (1547–1618), 1582 H

Staple of Newes, The (Jonson), 1631 L

Stapleton, Thomas, E. Catholic scholar (1535–98), 1588 H

Star Chamber, Court of: proceedings against authors and printers, 1586 H, 1588 H, 1634 A, B, 1637 F; proceedings against those refusing benevolence, 1614 B; sentence of mutilation by, 1637 B, F; abolition, 1641 C, F

State of the Parties, The (Bolingbroke), 1749 H

State Papers, 1618–48 (ed. Rushworth), 1659 H

Stationers' Company of London, 1557 H

Statical Essays (Hales), 1727 G

Statistics, studies in, 1749 F, 1761 F

Statistics, comparative, studies in, 1690 F

Steam engines:
  'steam digester', 1679 G
  Newcomen's, 1705 G
  high-pressure boiler, 1707 G

Stearne, John, E. controversionalist (1624–69), 1648 F

Steel, crucible process for, 1740 G

Steele, Sir Richard, Ir. essayist, dramatist and journalist (1672–1729), 1672 M, 1701 H, L, 1703 L, 1705 L, 1709 F, L, 1711 L, 1722 L, 1723 L, 1729 M

Steen, Jan, Du. artist (1626–79), 1626 M, 1660 J, 1661 J, 1664 J, 1665 J, 1679 M

Stein, Heinrich Friedrich Karl, Baron von, Pruss. statesman (1757–1831), 1757 M

Steinau, West Germany, battle, 1633 D

Steinkirke, Belgium, 1692 C

Stenay, France, 1654 C

Steno, Nicolaus, G. scientist, 1669 G

Stephen Báthory, King of Poland (1575–86), 1586 D: election, 1575 C, 1576 B; opposition to, ends, 1577 D; invades Russia, 1581 B

Stephens, Thomas, E. Jesuit (*c.* 1549–1619), settles in Goa, 1579 H

Steps to the Temple (Crashaw), 1646 L

Sterne, Laurence, E. novelist (1713–68), 1713 M, 1760 L

Sternhold, Thomas, E. author (*c.* 1510–49), 1551 H, 1562 H

Steterburg, West Germany, 1553 C

Stettin (Szczecin), Poland, form. Germany: siege of, 1677 C; Great Elector takes, 1677 D; Prussia obtains, 1720 A

Stettin, Peace of, 1570 D

Steuchus, Augustinus, G. Catholic theologian, 1540 H

Stevin, Simon, Du. mathematician (1548–1620), 1585 G

Stewart, Esmé, seigneur d'Aubigny and Earl, later Duke, of Lennox, Sc. politician (1542–83), 1579 C, 1582 C

Stewart, Dugald, Sc. philosopher (1753–1828), 1753 M

Stewart, Lord James, Earl of Mar and of Moray, Sc. politician, natural son of James V, half-brother of Mary Queen of Scots (*c.* 1531–70), 1562 D, 1570 A

Stewart, John, Duke of Albany, Sc. Regent (1481–1536), 1515 B, C, 1517 B, 1518 C, 1521 C, 1522 C, D, 1523 C, 1524 B, 1525 B

Stewart, Matthew, Earl of Lennox, Sc. Regent (1516–71), 1544 B, 1545 D, 1570 A, C, 1571 C *See also* Stuart

Stieler, Kaspar, G. poet and grammarian (1632–1707), 1691 H

Stiernhielm, Georg, Swe. poet, philosopher and lawyer (1598–1672), 1658 L

Still Life of Pheasants (Oudry), 1745 J

Stillingfleet, Edward, E. churchman and theologian (1635–99), 1662 H, 1710 H

Stirling, Scotland, 1571 C: Warbeck at, 1495 D; Covenanters take, 1639 B

Stirling, James, Sc. mathematician (1692–1770), 1730 G

Stobnicza, G. geographer, 1512 G

Stock-breeding, reform of, 1745 G

Stockholm, Sweden: 'bloodbath', 1520 D; the press in, 1645 F; Academy of Sciences, 1750 G; Observatory, 1750 G

Stockholm, Treaties of, 1719 D, 1720 A, 1724 A, 1747 B

Stocking-frame, invented, 1589 G

Stokesley, John, E. churchman, bishop of London (*c.* 1475–1539), 1530 H

Stolbova, Peace of, 1617 A

Stone, Andrew, E. politician (1703–73), prorogues Irish Parliament, 1753 D

Stonehenge (Stukeley), 1740 H

Stoning of St. Stephen (Giulio), 1523 J

Stop of the Exchequer, 1672 A

Storia civile del regno di Napoli (Giannoni), 1723 H

Storia d'Italia (Guicciardini), 1567 H, 1579 H

Storkyro, Finland, battle, 1714 A

Stormy Days (Bruegel), 1565 J

Story of Joseph, The (del Sarto), 1520 J

Stow, John, E. chronicler and antiquary (*c.* 1525–1605), 1525 M, 1565 H, 1580 H, 1598 H, 1605 M, 1618 H, 1631 H, 1720 H

Strada, Famianus, Flem. author, 1632 F

Stradivari, Antonio, It. violin-maker (1644–1737), 1680 K

Strafford, Earl of. *See* Wentworth, T.

Stralsund, East Germany: treaty concerning, 1628 B; siege of, 1628 B, C; Brandenburg conquers, 1678 D; Charles XII arrives at, 1714 D; Prussians take, 1715 D

Strasbourg, France, 1753 J: Bucer at, 1524 E; Calvin at, 1538 B; clock in, 1574 G; Louis XIV pensions bishop of, 1680 B; French take, 1681 C; France retains, 1714 C

Stratagemata Satanae (Aconzio), 1565 H

Stratton, Warwickshire, England, 1643 B

Strawberry Hill, Surrey, England, 1747 J: private press at, 1757 H

Street-fighting, 1580 B

Street-lighting, 1684 F

Streltsi, revolt in Russia, 1682 B, 1698 B, C

Strike, of hatters, 1696 F

Strode, William E. politician (*c.* 1599–1645), 1642 A

Strode, William, E. poet and dramatist (1602–45), 1655 L

Strozzi, Piero, It. soldier, 1554 C

Strutt, Jedediah, E. inventor (1726–97), 1758 G

Strype, John, E. ecclesiastical historian (1643–1737), 1643 M, 1709 H, 1721 H, 1721 H, 1737 M

Stuart, Henry, Lord Darnley, E. consort of Mary Queen of Scots (1545–67), 1545 M, 1563 J, 1566 B, 1567 A, M

Stuart, James, E. antiquarian ('Athenian Stuart') (1713–88), 1762 H

Stuart, John, third Earl of Bute, E. politician, Tory prime minister (1713–92), 1713 M: forces Pitt to resign, 1761 D; first lord of Treasury, 1762 B. *See also* Stewart

Stubbs, George, E. artists (1724–1806), 1724 M, 1751 J, 1756 J, 1761 J, 1762 J

Stubbs, John, E. Puritan (*c.* 1543–91), 1581 D

Treaties

Ulm, between Catholic League and Protestant Union in Germany, 1620 C

Venice with Florence and the Papacy, against France, 1524 D

Venice with Grissons, 1603 E

Venice with Savoy, 1623 A

France accedes to, 1624 D

Versailles, between France and H.R. Empire, 1756 B, 1757 B

Viborg, between Russia and Sweden, 1609 A

Vienna, between Britain, Hanover, Saxony, Poland and H.R. Empire, against Russia and Prussia, 1718 D

Vienna, between H.R. Empire and Spain, 1725 B

Villafavila, between Ferdinand of Aragon and Joanna of Castille, 1506 C

Vilna, between Russia and Poland, 1656 D

Warsaw, between Austria and Saxony, against Prussia

Wehlan, between Poland and Brandenburg, 1657 C

Weimar, between Hesse and Saxony, 1528 A

Westminster, between Britain and H.R. Empire, 1716 B

Windsor, between England and Spain, 1506 A, 1522 B

Wismar, between France and Sweden, 1636 B

Worms, between Austria, Britain and Sardinia, 1743 C

Wursterhausen, between H.R. Empire and Prussia, 1726 D

Treaties of Commerce:

English East India Company with Bengal, 1760 E

England with Denmark, 1654 D

England with France, 1494 B, 1604 D

England with Holland, 1619 A, 1716 A

England with H.R. Empire and Spain, 1520 C

England with Persia, 1611 E

England with Portugal, 1703 D, F

England with Russia, 1557 A, 1734 D

England with Spain, 1515 D, 1715 D, 1716 B, 1750 C

England with Sweden, 1654 B, 1656 B

England with Turkey, 1580 D

France with Russia, 1629 C

France with Sweden and Portugal, 1641 C

France with Turkey, 1535 A

Holland with Persia, 1623 E

'Magnus Intercursus', England with Flanders, 1496 A

'Malus Intercursus', England with Flanders, 1506 B, 1507 D

Methuen Treaty, Britain with Portugal, 1703 D, F

Conventions:

Amsterdam, between France, Russia and Prussia, 1717 C

Areillen, between France and Palatinate, 1682 A

Denmark with Russia, 1699 C

Hanover, between Britain and Prussia, 1745 C

H.R. Empire with Britain and Modena, 1753 B

Ilbersheim, between Bavaria and H.R. Empire, 1704 D

Klein Schellendorf, secret, between Prussia and H.R. Empire, 1741 D

Milan, between H.R. Empire and France, 1707 A

Pardo, between England and Spain, 1728 A, 1739 A

St. Petersburg, between Russia, Britain and Holland, 1747 D

St. Petersburg, between Russia and Britain, 1755 C

Sardinia with Austria, 1742 A

Sweden with Brandenburg, 1631 B

Treaties of Marriage:

England with France, 1518 D, 1520 B, 1624 D

England with Scotland, 1502 A

England with Spain, 1620 B

broken off, 1623 C, D

France with Spain (Toledo), 1539 C

Treaties of Peace:

Aarau, between Swiss Cantons, 1712 C

Åbo, between Russia and Sweden, 1743 C

Adrianople, between Turkey and Russia, 1713 C

Aix-la-Chapelle, between France and Spain, 1668 B

Aix-la-Chapelle, general treaty, 1748 D

Alais, between Louis XIII with Huguenots, 1629 B

Altmark, between Sweden and Poland, 1629 C

Altrandstadt, between Sweden and Saxony, 1706 C

Amboise, between French Crown and Huguenots, 1563 A

confirmed, 1568 A

Andrussor, Truce of, between Russia and Poland, 1667 A

Angoulême, between Louis XIII and Marie de' Medici, 1619 B

Andres, between France and England, 1546 B

Arras, reconciles S. Netherlands to Philip II, 1579 B

Asti, between Savoy and Lombardy, 1615 B

Augsburg, settlement of Germany, 1555 C

Baden, between France and H.R. Empire, 1714 C

to be maintained by Amsterdam Convention, 1717 C

Barcelona, between France and Spain, 1493 A

Basle, between Switzerland and Swabian League, 1499 C

Belgrade, between H.R. Empire and Turkey, 1739 C

Belgrade, between Russia and Turkey, 1739 C

Benten, settling Polish succession, 1589 A

Bergerac, between French Crown and Huguenots, 1577 C

Berlin, between Austria and Prussia, 1742 C

Berwick, Pacification of, between England and Scotland, 1639 B

Bologna, between Papacy and France, 1515 D

Bordeaux, between French Crown and rebels, 1650 C

Brandenburg with France, 1673 B

Breda, between Britain, Holland and France, 1667 C

Breslau, Preliminaries, between Austria and Prussia, 1742 B

Bristol, England with Spain, 1574 C

Brömsebo (of 1541), confirmed, 1570 D

Brussels, between H.R. Empire and France, 1516 D

Buczacz, between Turkey and Poland, 1672 D

Cambrai, between H.R. Empire and France, 1529 C

England accedes to, 1529 C

violated, 1537 A

Cardan, 1534 B

Cherasco, ends war of Mantuan succession 1631 B

Constantinople, between Turkey and H.R. Empire, 1540 B

Constantinople, between Turkey and Venice, 1573 A

Copenhagen, between Denmark and Sweden, 1660 B

Crépy, between France and H.R. Empire, 1544 C

23*

Treaties

U

Unitarians, 1558 H, 1605 H. *See also under* Religious Denominations
United Provinces. *See under* Holland
United Provinces of the Netherlands, Observations Upon the (Temple), 1672 H
Universa Medicina (Fernel), 1554 G
Universities:
in America, Harvard, 1636 F, 1641 F, 1650 F, 1665 F
  King's College, New York (later Columbia University), 1754 F
  New Jersey College (later Princeton University), 1746 F
  Pennsylvania, 1751 F
  William and Mary College, 1692 F
  Yale College, Connecticut, 1701 F, 1745 F
in Austria, Graz, 1585 F
  Innsbruck, 1677 F
  Salzburg, 1622 F
in Belgium, Louvain, 1517 F
in England, Parliamentary representation, 1604 F
  James II's Catholic appointments, 1687 E
  Cambridge, colleges:
    Christ's, 1505 F
    Emmanuel, 1584 F
    Gonville and Caius, 1557 F
    Jesus, 1496 F
    Magdalene, 1542 F
    St. John's, 1509 F
    Sidney Sussex, 1589 F
    Trinity, 1545 F
    professorships:
      astronomy, 1748 G
      divinity, 1502 F
      regius, 1540 F, 1724 F
  Durham, college, 1657 F
  Oxford, colleges:
    Brase Nose, 1509 F
    Cardinal, 1525 F
    Christ Church, 1545 F
    Corpus Christi, 1517 F
    Pembroke, 1624 F
    St. John's, 1611 B
    Trinity, 1555 F
    Wadham, 1612 F
    lectures, Colet's, 1496 F
      Martyr's, 1547 H
    professorships, divinity, 1502 F
      law, 1758 F
      music, 1626 K
      poetry, 1708 F
      regius, 1540 F, 1724 F
in Finland, Åbo, 1640 F
in France, Collège de France, 1529 F
  Paris, 1598 F
in Germany, Breslau, 1695 F
  Dillingen, Bavaria, 1554 F
  Duisburg, 1654 F
  Frankfort on Oder, 1506 F
  Geissen, Hesse, 1605 F
  Göttingen, 1737 F
  Halle, 1694 F
  Helmstadt, Brunswick, 1567 F, 1576 F
  Ingoldstadt, Bavaria, 1563 H
  Jena, Saxony, 1558 F
  Königsberg, Prussia, 1544 F
  Marburg, Hesse, 1527, 1605 F
  Wittenberg, Halle, 1502 F, 1518 H
in Holland, Groningen, 1614 F
  Leyden, 1575 F, 1658 G
  Utrecht, 1634 F
in Hungary, Tyrnau (Budapest), 1635 F

in Ireland, Trinity College, Dublin, 1591 F
in Italy, Messina, 1548 F
in Peru, Lima, 1553 F
in Poland, Warsaw, 1576 F
in Portugal, Lisbon, 1537 F
in Russia, Moscow, 1755 F
in Scotland, Aberdeen, King's College, 1494 F
  Edinburgh, 1582 F
in Spain, Alcala, 1499 F
  Granada, 1531 F
  Madrid, 1590 F
  Santiago de Compostela, 1504 F
in Sweden, Lund, 1668 F
  Uppsala, 1620 H
in Switzerland, Basle, 1527 G
Unloveliness of Love-Locks, The (Prynne), 1628 F
Unnatural Combat, The (Massinger), 1639 L
Unpartheyische Kirchen und Ketzerhistorie (Arnold), 1714 H
Upper Niger, 1590 E
Uppingham School, Rutland, England, 1584 F
Uppsala, Sweden: surrender of, 1521 A; university library, 1620 H; botanical garden, 1741 G
Uppsala, Convention of, 1593 D
Upton, John, E. critic (1707-60), 1746 H
Urana propitia (Cunitz), 1650 G
Urban VII, Pope (Giovanni Battista Castagna), It. (1590), 1521 M, 1590 C, M
Urban VIII, Pope (Maffeo Barberini), It. (1623-1644), 1568 M, 1644 A: election, 1623 C; annexes Urbino, 1631 C; condemns Jansen's *Augustinius*, 1642 D
Urbino, Italy: Borgia takes, 1502 D; operations of duke, 1526 C, D; court at, 1528 F; duchy bequeathed to Pope, 1626 E; annexed by Pope, 1631 C
Urbino Venus, The (Titian), 1538 J
Urfé, Honoré d', F. novelist (1567-1625), 1607 L
Urfey, Thomas d', E. dramatist and satirist (1653-1723), 1682 L
Urne-Buriall (Browne), 1658 L
Urquhart, Sir Thomas, Sc. translator (1611-60), 1611 M, 1653 H, 1660 M, 1708 H
Ursulines, Order of, 1535 H
Usbeks: driven from Khorasan, 1510 F; Persians defeat, 1597 E; settle in Carniola and Croatia, 1617 C
Ussher, James, Ir. churchman and scholar, Archbishop of Armagh (1581-1656), 1581 M, 1650 H, 1656 M, 1658 H
Usury: defended by Eck, 1574 F; forbidden by Sixtus V, 1586 F; tract on, 1612 F; discussion of, 1653 F
Utopia (More), 1516 F; trans., 1551 H
Utopias:
  Sir Thomas More's (Latin text), 1516 H; trans., 1551 H
  Antonio Francesco Doni's *I Mondi*, 1552 H
  Johann V. Andreae's *Christianopolis*, 1619 H
  Campanella's *City of the Sun*, 1623 H, 1652 H
  Gerrard Winstanley's 1652 H
  James Harrington's *Oceana*, 1656 H
  Gabriel de Foigny's *La Terre Australe connue*, 1676 H
Utrecht, Holland: Union of, 1579 A; library, 1582 H; University, 1634 F; relieved, 1673 D; peace congress at, 1712 A, 1713 A
Utrecht, Treaty of, 1713 A, 1714 B, 1715 A
Utrecht, Union of, 1579 A
Uxbridge, Middlesex, 1645 A

V

Venice Preserv'd (Otway), 1682 L

Venlo, Holland, 1586 C: siege of, 1511 D; Churchill takes, 1702 C

Venus, planet: rotation of, 1665 G; transit of, observed, 1639 G

Venus and Adonis (Shakespeare), 1593 L

Venus and Adonis (Titian), 1554 J

Venus and Cupid (Mabuse), 1521 J

Venus, The Rokeby (Velazquez), 1661 J

Vera Cruz, Mexico, coastline explored, 1519 J

Vera Cruz, Tierra de. *See* Brazil

Verböczy, Stephen, Hung. politician, 1514 E

Vercelli, Italy, Spanish take, 1638 A

Vercelli, Treaty of, 1495 D

Verdadera Inforacam des terras do Preste Joam (Alvarez), 1540 G

Verdelot, Phippe, F. musician, 1533 K

Verden, West Germany, Duchy: sale by Denmark to Hanover agreed, 1715 B; purchased by Hanover, 1719 D

Verdun, France: French occupy bishopric, 1552 A; French retain bishopric, 1553 A, 1559 B, 1648 D

Vere, Sir Francis, E. soldier (1560–1609), 1597 A, 1600 C

Vergennes, Charles Gravier, Comte de, F. statesman (1717–87), 1717 M

Vergil, Polydore, It. ecclesiastic and historian resident in England (c. 1470–1555), 1507 H, 1525 H, 1534 F, 1553 H, 1582 H

Véritable Saint Genest, Le (de Rotrou), 1646 L

Vérité dans le vin (Collé), 1747 L

Vermakelijkten Avonturier, Den (Heinsius), 1695 L

Vermeer, Jan, Du. artist (1632–75), 1632 M, 1656 J, 1660 J, 1664 J, 1665 J, 1670 J, 1675 M

Vermigli, Pietro Martine. *See* Martyr, Peter

Vermuyden, Sir Cornelius, Du. engineer resident in England (c. 1595–1683), 1621 G

Vernon, Sir Edward, E. admiral (1684–1757), 1684 M, 1757 M: captures Porto Bello, 1739 D

Verona, Italy, 1493 B, 1509 B, 1516 C, D: Palazzo Canossa, 1529 J; fortifications at, 1530 J

Verona illustrata (Maffei), 1732 H

Veronese, Paolo (Paoli Caliari), It. artist (1528–88), 1528 M, 1553 J, 1560 J, 1562 J, 1571 J, 1573 J, 1575 J, 1588 M

Verrazano, Giovanni de, Sp. explorer, 1524 G

Vers Lyriques (du Bellay), 1549 L

Versailles, France: palace is begun, 1662 J; Le Vau remodels, 1669 J; gardens, 1662 J; Galerie des glaces, 1679 J; Marly Trianon, 1678 J; Siamese embassies at, 1684 D, 1686 E

Versailles, Treaty of, 1756 B

Verses on the Death of Dr. Swift (Swift), 1739 L

Versuch einer Kritischen Dichkunst (Gottsched), 1732 H

Vertue, George, E. engraver (1684–1756), 1684 M, 1756 M

Verulam, Lord. *See* Bacon, F.

Vervins, Peace of, 1598 B

Very Woman, A (Massinger), 1655 L

Verzellini, Jacob, It. scientist, 1574 G

Vesalius, Andreas, Flem. anatomist (1514–64), 1542 G

Vesc, Étienne de, F. favourite, 1492 A

Vespucci, Amerigo, Sp. explorer (1451–1512), 1499 G, 1501 G, 1512 M

Vesteras, Swe., 1521 A

Vete, M., It. hymnologist, 1537 M

Veterinerary science, manuals on, 1566 G, 1598 G

Veuve, La (Corneille), 1634 L

Viborg, Denmark, assembly at, 1523 A

Viborg, Treaty of, 1609 A

Vibrations, musical, explained, 1700 K

Vicente, Gil, Port. author, 1511 L

Vicenza, Italy, 1509 B: ravaged, 1499 C; Basilica, 1549 J; Casa Civena, 1540 J; Loggia del Capitaniato, 1571 J; Palazzo Thiere, 1545 J; Palazzo Barbarano, 1570 J; Teatro Olimpico, 1579 J

Vico, Giovanni Battista, It. jurist and philosopher (1668–1744), 1668 M, 1720 F, 1725 H, 1744 M

Victor Amadeus I, Duke of Savoy (1630–7), 1635 B 1637 A

Victor Amadeus II, Duke of Savoy (1675–1730), King of Sardinia: accession, 1675 B; defeated at Staffade, 1690 C; defeated at Marsaglia, 1693 D; begins siege of Casale, 1694 B; signs peace with France, 1696 C; betrothed, 1696 C; exchanges Sicily for Sardinia, 1720 E

Victor, Benjamin, E. theatrical historian (d. 1778), 1761 L

Victory, The (Michelangelo), 1519 J

Vida del Buscón, La (Quevedo), 1603 L

Vida es sueño (Calderón de la Barca), 1635 L, 1673 L

Vie de Marienne, La (Marivaux), 1731 L

Vieira, Antonio, Port. Jesuit, noted preacher (1608–97), 1608 M, 1697 M

Vienna, Austria, 1574 B, 1619 B, D, 1621 B, 1626 D: postal services in, 1505 F; Turkish siege, 1529 C, D; Turks threaten, 1532 B; religious revival, 1669 H; Turkish siege, 1683 B, C; French threaten, 1703 B; reform of education in, 1745 F; Observatory, 1756 G; music in, 1761 K, 1762 K

Vienna, Congress of, 1515 C

Vienna, Treaties of, 1606 B, 1725 B, 1731 C, 1735 D, 1738 D, 1739 B

Vienza, Italy, 1550 J

Viète, François, F. mathematician, 1576 G

View of Delft (Fabritius), 1652 J

View of the Present State of Ireland (Spenser), 1633 H

View of the Rhine (Goyen), 1653 J

View of Toledo (El Greco), 1608 J

Vigevano, Italy: French retire from, 1524 A; Savoy obtains, 1748 D

Vigo Bay, Spain, treasure fleet seized in, 1702 D

Villach, Carinthia, Austria, 1552 B

Villafavila, Treaty of, 1506 C

Village Feast (Teniers), 1651 J

Villainy of Stock-Jobbers Detected, The (Defoe), 1701 F

Villalar, Spain, battle, 1521 B

Villanelle, first, 1541 K

Villars, Comte de, F. governor of Rouen, 1594 A

Villars, Claude Louis Hector de, Prince de Martignes, Duke of Villars, F. general (1853–1734), 1653 M, 1703 B, 1712 C, 1732 B, 1734 M

Villa Viciosa, Spain, Battles of, 1665 B, 1710 D

Villegas, Francisco Quevedo, Sp. author, 1645 M

Villeroi, François de Neufville, Duke of, F. general (1644–1730), 1695 A, C

Villiers, George, first Duke of Buckingham, E. minister (1592–1628), 1592 M, 1616 A: created Earl, 1617 A; accompanies Prince Charles to Spain, 1623 A, C; opposition to, in Commons, 1625 B; impeachment, 1626 A, B; Charles I refuses to dismiss, 1625 B; expedition to Isle of Rhé, 1627 B, C, D; dismissal is demanded, 1628 B; assassination, 1628 C, M

Villiers, George, second Duke of Buckingham (1628–87), E. politician: member of Cabal, 1667 C; imprisonment, 1677 A

Villmergen, Belgium, Battles of, 1656 A, 1712 C

Vilna, Confederation of, 1599 C

Vilna, Treaty of, 1656 D

Vincennes, Indiana, US, French settlement at, 1735 F

W

French take Montserrat, 1667 A
secret Anglo-French treaty, 1667 A
de Ruyter raids Chatham, 1667 B
Peace of Breda, 1667 B
Third War opens, 1672 A
France joins England, 1672 A
Franco-Swedish treaty, 1672 B
Brandenburg supports Holland, 1672 B
Battle of Southwold Bay, 1672 B
French cross R. Rhine, 1672 B
Dutch open Amsterdam sluices, 1672 B
France rejects Dutch peace terms, 1672 B
William of Orange appointed Stadtholder
  and captain general, 1672 C
de Witt brothers assassinated, 1672 C
Orange captures Naarden, 1672 C
Dutch alliance with Empire, 1672 D
Orange retires to Amsterdam, 1672 D
Brandenburg signs peace with France,
  1673 B
Cologne Peace Conference, 1673 B
Dutch alliance with Denmark, 1673 C
Battle of Texel, 1673 C
Dutch alliance with Empire, Spain and
  Lorraine, 1673 C
Dutch capture New York, 1673 C
French expedition to Ceylon, 1673 E
French capture Chandernagore, 1673 E
Peace of Westminster, 1674 A
England against Scotland:
James IV invades Northumberland, 1496 C
truce, 1497 A
Border warfare, 1497 C, 1513 C
James IV attacks Norham, 1513 C
Battle of Flodden, 1513 C
war renewed, 1522 B
siege of Carlisle, 1522 C
truce, 1522 D
English burn Jedburgh, 1523 C
peace is signed, 1534 B
war renewed, 1542 C, D, 1544 B, 1545 A
Battle of Ancrum Moor, 1545 A
Seymour's campaign, 1545 C
English invasion, 1547 C
Battle of Pinkie, 1547 C
English seize Haddington, 1548 B
war ended, 1550 A
border warfare, 1557 C
operations against French in Scotland, 1559 D,
  1560 A, B, C
Bishops' War, First, opens, 1639 A
  Covenanters take Edinburgh, Dunbarton and
    Stirling, 1639 A
  Battle of Turriff, 1639 B
  Pacification of Berwick, 1639 B
Bishops' War, Second, opens, 1640 C
  Scots victorious at Newburn, 1640 C
  Scots take Newcastle, 1640 C
  Great Council at York, 1640 C
  Treaty of Ripon, 1640 D
See also Civil Wars, England
England against Spain:
English shipping confiscated, 1585 B
English aid for Dutch rebels, 1585 C
Leicester's command in Netherlands, 1585 D
Drake sacks Cadiz, 1587 B
preparations to repel invasion, 1588 C
defeat of Armada, 1588 C
expedition to Portugal, 1589 B
expedition to Spain, failure of, 1590 D
capture of *The Revenge*, 1591 C
capture of *Madre de Dios*, 1592 C

Spaniards land in Cornwall, 1595 C
Drake's last voyage to Spanish Main, 1595 C
expedition to Cadiz, 1596 B
Islands Voyage, 1597 C
further Armadas fail, 1597 D, 1599 E
Peace negotiations, 1599 D, 1600 B
Spanish force in Ireland, 1601 C, 1602 A
peace treaty, 1604 C
See also under Civil Wars, France
War declared, 1624 A
expedition to Cadiz, 1625 D
Peace of Madrid, 1630 D
Spain declares war, 1656 A
treasure ships captured, 1656 C
Treaty of Paris, 1657 C
War of 1718–20. See under Quadruple Alliance
war breaks out, 1727 A, 1728 A
War of Jenkins' Ear, origins of, 1738 A, B, 1739 A
  declaration of war, 1739 D
  Vernon takes Porto Bello, 1739 D
  expedition to Cathagena and Cuba, 1741 E
  for later operations see Austrian Succession
  Peace of Aix-la-Chapelle, 1748 D
France against Spain. *See under* Hapsburg-Valois;
  and under Civil Wars, France (1588–98)
Peace signed, 1598 B
war breaks out, 1635 B
League of Rivoli, 1635 B
Spanish defeated in Valtelline, 1635 B
invasion of N.E. France, 1636 B
French invade Franche-Comté, 1636 B
Battle of Tornavento, 1636 B
Spaniards advance to Corbie, 1636 C
Battle of St. Jean-de-Losne, 1636 D
Spanish invasion of Languedoc, 1637 B
French conquest of Artois, 1637 B
French mutiny in Valtelline, 1637 B
Spanish take Vercelli, 1638 B
Condé is checked at Fontarabia, 1638 B
Spanish raise siege of Thiouville, 1639 B
Hesdin surrenders to French, 1639 B
defence of Roussillon, 1639 C
Turenne's victories in northern Italy, 1639 D
Spanish conspiracy with Cinque Mars, 1642 C
French occupy Roussillon, 1642 E
French retreat to Catalonia, 1643 D
French take Gravelines, 1643 B
French driven from Aragon, 1644 E
Battle of Orbitello, 1645 B
Harcourt's victory over Spanish, 1645 B
French capture Treves, 1645 D
French capture Courtrai, 1646 A
French fail at Orbitello, 1646 B
French take Dunkirk, 1646 D
French raise siege of Lerida, 1646 D
French alliance with Modena, 1647 C
French campaign in Netherlands fails, 1647 C
French take Tortosa, 1648 C
Battle of Lens, 1648 C
Spanish alliance with French rebels, 1650 B
French victories in Netherlands, 1655 C
Anglo-French alliance, 1655 D
Spain declares war on England, 1656 A
Spanish treasure ships captured, 1656 C
Turenne takes La Capella, 1656 C
Treaty of Paris with England, 1657 A
French take Montmidi, 1657 C
French take Mardyke, 1657 D
Battle of the Dunes, 1658 D
Spanish lose Dunkirk, 1658 B
Spanish defeat at Gravelines, 1658 C
Peace of Pyrenees, 1659 D

Wars

Wars

Britain joins Austro-Russian alliance, 1751 C
Prussia learns of secret articles of Russo-
Austrian treaty of 1746, 1753 A
Anglo-French rivalry in North America,
1754 B, C
Battle of Fort Duquesne, 1755 C
French ambassador recalled from London,
1755 C
Battle of Lake George, 1755 C
Britain demands troops from Holland, 1756 A
Franco-Imperial alliance, 1756 B
Russia proposes to Austria the partition of
Prussia, 1756 B
Britain declares war on France, 1756 B
French take Minorca, 1756 B
British driven from Great Lakes, 1756 C
Frederick II invades Saxony, 1756 C
Neutrality of Holland and Sweden, 1756 C
Battle of Lobositz, 1756 D
capitulation of Pirna, 1756 D
British march on Calcutta, 1756 D
Clive takes Fulta, 1756 D
Russia accedes to Franco-Austrian treaty,
1756 D
Clive recaptures Calcutta, 1757 A
H.R. Empire declares war on Prussia, 1757 A
Russia, Poland and Sweden declare war on
Prussia, 1757 A
Russo-Imperial alliance, 1757 A
Treaty of Versailles, 1757 B
Battles of Prague and Kolin, 1757 B
Battle of Hastenbeck, 1757 C
Montcalm takes Fort William Henry, 1757 C
Battle of Gross Jägerndorf, 1757 C
British capitulate at Kloster Zevern, 1757 C
British surrender Hanover and Brunswick,
1757 C
Battles of Rossbach, Breslau and Leuthen,
1757 D
Russians recapture E. Prussia, 1758 A
London Convention, 1758 A
blockade of Olmutz ends, 1758 B
Battle of Crefeld, 1758 B
Battle of Ticonderoga, 1758 C
British take Louisburg, 1758 C
British troops join Ferdinand of Brunswick,
1758 C
Battle of Zorndorf, 1758 C
siege of Neisse, 1758 D
Battle of Hochkirk, 1758 D
Washington takes Fort Duquesne, 1758 D
British conquer French Senegal, 1758 D
Treaty of Paris, 1758 D
French march on Madras, 1758 D, 1759 A
British take Masulipatam, 1759 B
Battle of Bergen, 1759 B
Battle of Kay, 1759 C
Battle of Minden, 1759 C
Battle of Kunersdorf, 1759 C
Battle of Cape St. Vincent, 1759 C
Russians withdraw to Poland, 1759 C
Wolfe scales Heights of Abraham, 1759 C
Battle of Quebec, 1759 C
Battle of Quiberon Bay, 1759 D
Prussians capitulate at Maxen, 1759 D
Battle of Wandewash, 1760 A
Russian treaty with H.R. Empire, 1760 B
Battle of Landshut, 1760 B
Prussians capitulate at Glatz, 1760 C
Battle of Liegnitz, 1760 C
British take Montreal, 1760 C
Russians and Swedes ravage Pomerania, 1760 C

Imperial forces occupy Saxony and Halle,
1760 C
Russians burn Berlin, 1760 D
Battle of Torgau, 1760 D
Coote takes Pondicherry, 1761 A
Third Family Compact, France with Spain,
1761 C
peace negotiations open, 1761 C
Austrians take Schweidnitz, 1761 D
Russians take Kolberg, 1761 D
Britain declares war on Spain and Naples,
1762 A
Britain ceases subsidies to Prussia, 1762 B
Russia restores conquests, 1762 B
Treaty of Hamburg, between Sweden and
Prussia, 1762 B
Spanish invade Portugal, 1762 B
Russo-Prussian treaty, 1762 B
Austrian defeat at Burkersdorf, 1762 C
Battle of Freiburg, 1762 D
French capitulate at Cassel, 1762 D
British take St. Vincent, Martinque and
Grenada, 1762 E
French evacuate right bank of Rhine, 1762 D
peace preliminaries of Fontainebleu, 1762 D
truce between Prussia, Saxony and H.R. Empire,
1762 D
Spain against France, 1683 D
siege of Luxembourg, 1684 B
French take Trier, Courtrai, Oudenarde and
Luxembourg, 1684 B
French bombard Genoa, 1684 C
Truce of Ratisbon, 1684 C
Spain against Holland, *for* Revolt of the Nether-
lands to 1609 *see* Rebellions and Revolutions,
Netherlands
Twelve Years' Truce, 1609 B
War renewed, 1621 C
relief of Bergen-op-Zoom, 1622 C
Spinola takes Breda, 1625 B
French aid Holland, 1629 C
fall of Maestricht, 1632 C
Spanish seek peace, 1632 C
Dutch recapture Breda, 1637 D
defeat of Spanish fleet, 1639 D
Peace of Münster, 1648 A
study of, 1632 F
Spanish Succession, opens, 1701 A
Philip of Anjou enters Madrid, 1701 A
French occupy Spanish Netherlands, 1701 A
Bavaria and Cologne ally with France, 1701 A
Battle of Carpi, 1701 C
Treaty of the Hague forms Grand Alliance,
1701 C
Louis XIV recognises Old Pretender as James
III, 1701 C
Battle of Chiara, 1701 C
raid on Cremona, 1702 A
Britain, Holland and H.R. Empire declare war
against France, 1702 B
British expedition to Cadiz, 1702 C
British take Venlo and Ruremonde, 1702 C
British capture Spanish fleet in Vigo Bay,
1702 D
British take Liège, 1702 D
British plunder St. Augustine, Florida, 1702 D
Portugal joins Grand Alliance, 1703 B
Allied successes in Germany and Netherlands,
1703 B
French threaten Venice, 1703 B
Archduke Charles proclaimed King of Spain,
1703 C

Wars—*contd.*
Spanish Succession—*contd.*
Battle of Hochstadt, 1703 C
Savoy joins Grand Alliance, 1703 D
France supports Hungarian rebels, 1703 E
French surprise Deerfield, Ohio Valley, 1704 B
Marlborough's march to Danube, 1704 B
Marlborough's juncture with Eugène, 1704 B
allied armies at Ulm, 1704 B
Battle of Donauwörth, 1704 B
Rooke takes Gibraltar, 1704 C
Battle of Blenheim, 1704 C
British fleet takes Barcelona, 1705 D
Archduke Charles is recognised in Catalonia, Aragon and Valencia, 1705 D
H. R. Emperor outlaws electors of Bavaria and Cologne, 1706 B
siege of Barcelona raised, 1706 B
Battle of Ramillies, 1706 B
British and Portuguese enter Madrid, 1706 B
defence of Charleston, 1706 C
peace negotiations open, 1706 C
Battle of Turin, 1706 C
French leave Piedmont, 1706 C
Emperor takes Naples, 1707 A
Convention of Milan, 1707 A
Battle of Almanza, 1707 B
British expedition against Acadia, 1707 B
siege of Toulon, 1707 C
Battle of Oudenarde, 1708 C
British take Minorca and Sardinia, 1708 C
Allies take Lille, 1708 D
Hague peace preliminaries, rejected by France, 1709 A, B
Allies take Tournai, 1709 C
Battle of Malplaquet, 1709 C
Allies take Mons, 1709 D
First Dutch Barrier Treaty, 1709 D
Gertruydenberg negotiations, 1710 A
British victory at Almínara, 1710 C
Allied victory at Saragosa, 1710 C
Charles III enters Madrid, but retires, 1710 C
British take Port Royal, 1710 D
Battle of Brihuega, 1710 D
Battle of Villa Viciosa, 1710 D
French obtain Mauritius, 1710 E
French capture Rio de Janeiro, 1711 C
Utrecht peace conference, 1712 A, 1713 A
Anglo-French truce, 1712 C
Battle of Denain, 1712 C
Dutch accede to truce, 1712 C
Philip V of Spain renounces claims to French throne, 1712 D
Dukes of Berry and Orleans renounce claims to Spanish throne, 1712 D
Second Dutch Barrier Treaty, 1713 A
Peace of Utrecht, 1713 A, 1714 B, 1715 A
Peace of Rastadt, 1714 A
Peace of Baden, 1714 C
storming of Barcelona, 1714 C
Swabian League against Swiss League, 1499 A, C
ended by Peace of Basle, 1499 C
Sweden against Poland. *See under* Northern Wars
Thirty Years' War:
opens, 1618 B
provisional government in Prague, 1618 B
reduction of Budweis, 1618 B
Mansfeld aids Bohemian rebels, 1618 B
Ferdinand crowned King of Hungary, 1618 C
Palatinate refuses passage for imperial troops, 1618 C

Emperor Matthias sends army against Bohemians, 1618 C
James I offers to mediate, 1618 C, 1621 B, 1622 D
occupation of Pilsen, 1618 D
death of Emperor Matthias, 1619 A
Thurn's march on Vienna, 1619 B
deposition of Ferdinand, 1619 C
election of Frederick V of Palatinate as King of Bohemia, 1619 C
Ferdinand II elected H.R. Emperor, 1619 C
Gabor's invasion of Hungary, 1619 C
Treaty of Munich, 1619 D
Gabor takes Pressburg, 1619 D
agreement of Mulhausen, 1620 A
agreement of Ulm, 1620 C
occupation of Linz, 1620 C
Lower Austria submits to Ferdinand II, 1620 C
Spanish troops invade Palatinate, 1620 C
Battle of White Mountain, 1620 D
suppression of Bohemian rebels, 1620 D
Frederick V under imperial ban, 1621 A
Maximilian of Bavaria gains Palatinate, 1621 A, 1623 A
Christian of Anhalt under imperial ban, 1621 A
Peace between H.R. Empire and Transylvania, 1622 A
Battle of Wiesloch, 1622 B
Battle of Wimpfen, 1622 B
Battle of Hochst, 1622 B
surrender of Heidelberg, 1622 D
surrender of Mannheim, 1622 D
Saxony gains Lusatia, 1623 A
Battle of Stadtlohn, 1623 C
Gabor resumes war, 1623 C
Mansfeld's expedition fails, 1624 A, 1625 A
Protestant Army is formed, 1625 A
English subsidies for Protestant army, 1625 B
Tilly invades Lower Saxony, 1625 C
Treaty of the Hague, 1625 D
Battle of Dessau, 1626 B
Tilly takes Göttingen, 1626 C
Tilly joins Wallenstein, 1626 C
Tilly defeats Christian IV at Lutter, 1626 C
death of Mansfeld, 1626 D
Treaty of Pressburg, 1626 D
Tilly enters Lauenburg, 1627 B
Turkish treaty with H.R. Empire, 1627 C
Tilly and Wallenstein subdue Holstein, Schleswig and Jutland, 1627 D
surrender of Wolfenbüttel, 1627 D
Wallenstein seizes Mecklenburg, 1628 A
Sweden enters War, 1628 A
siege of Stralsund, 1628 B, C
Mecklenburg placed under imperial ban, 1628 B
Tilly fails to take Gluckstadt, 1628 A
Wallenstein enforces Edict of Restitution, 1629 A
Peace of Lubeck, 1629 B
France demands Wallenstein's dismissal, 1630 B
Gustavus Adolphus marches into Germany, 1630 C
Tilly replaces Wallenstein, 1630 C
Treaty of Barwalde, 1631 A
Saxony demands revocation of Edict of Restitution, 1631 A
Convention of Leipzig, 1631 A
Tilly destroys New Brandenburg, 1631 A
siege of Magdeburg, 1631 A
Gustavus Adolphus takes Frankfurt-on-Oder, 1631 B
Swedish convention with Brandenburg, 1631 B
Tilly sacks Magdeburg, 1631 B
Tilly burns Halle, 1631 B

Battle of Werben, 1631 C
Tilly invades Saxony, 1631 C
Saxony's alliance with Sweden, 1631 C
Battle of Breitenfeld, 1631 C
Saxon invasion of Bohemia, 1631 D
Swedes advance on R. Rhine, 1631 D
Wallenstein forms army to oppose Swedes and Saxons, 1631 D
Saxons take Prague, 1631 D
Swedes take Würzburg and Mainz, 1631 D
Gustavus Adolphus takes Nuremburg, 1632 A
Wallenstein is reinstated, 1632 B
Battle of Lech, 1632 B
death of Tilly, 1632 B
siege of Ingoldstadt is raised, 1632 B
Swedes enter Munich, 1632 B
Saxons enter Prague, 1632 B
Battle of Alta Vesta, 1632 C
Wallenstein withdraws to Saxony, 1632 C
Gustavus Adolphus dies at Battle of Lützen, 1632 D
Bernhard of Saxe-Weimar commands Swedes, 1632 D
Wallenstein invades Silesia, 1633 A
Swedes return to Palatinate, 1633 A
League of Heilbronn, 1633 B
Wallenstein's negotiations with Saxony and Sweden, 1633 B
Wallenstein loses favour with Ferdinand II, 1633 C, D
Battle of Steinau, 1633 D
Regensburg falls to Swedes, 1633 D
Wallenstein is secretly replaced by Gallas, 1634 A
French secretly subsidise Swedes, 1634 B
Battle of Nordlingen, 1634 C
French enter Palatinate, 1634 C
Imperial reconquest of Württemburg and Franconia, 1634 D
French raise siege of Heidelburg, 1634 D
Imperialists recapture Phillipsburg, 1635 A
Franco-Swedish alliance, 1635 B
Peace of Prague, 1635 B
Treaty of St. Germain-en-Laye, 1635 D
Saxon army is formed to aid Empire against Sweden, 1636 A
Battle of Wittstock, 1636 D
Archduke Ferdinand elected King of Romans, 1636 D
accession of Ferdinand III as Holy Roman Emperor, 1637 A
Swedes take Rheinfelden, 1638 B
renewal of Franco-Swedish alliance, 1638 A
French army joins Swedes at Rheinfelden, 1638 B
Swedes take Freiburg, 1638 B
Battle of Sennheim, 1638 D
peace negotiations in Cologne and Hamburg, 1638 D, 1641 D
Imperialists fail to take Laufenburg, 1638 D
Swedes take Breisach, 1638 D
Battle of Chemnitz, 1639 B
siege of Prague, 1639 B
death of Bernhard of Saxe-Weimar, 1639 C
Swedes swear fidelity to France, 1639 D
French occupy Alsace, 1639 D, 1640 A
Swedes withdraw from Bohemia, 1640 B
Báner attacks Regensburg, 1641 A
Báner succeeded by Torstensen, 1641 B
Battle of Wolfenbüttel 1641 B
Swedish Treaty of Neutrality with Brandenburg, 1641 C

Battle of Kempten, 1642 A
Turks sign peace with Empire, 1642 A
Battle of Sweidnitz, 1642 B
second Battle of Breitenfeld, 1642 D
Peace conference at Münster, 1642 D, 1643 C, 1644 B, 1645 B
Peace conference at Osnabrück, 1643 C, 1645 B
French occupy Rhineland, 1644 C
French capture Phillipsburg, Mainz, Mannheim, Speyer and Worms, 1644 C
Battle of Herbsthausen, 1645 B
Battle of Nordlingen, 1645 C
Sweden abandons plans to attack Venice, 1645 C
Swedes surrender Prague, 1646 B
French and Swedes invade Bavaria, 1646 C
Treaty of Ulm, 1647 A
Mainz and Hesse withdraw from war, 1647 B
Treaty of Pilsen, 1647 C
further intervention of Bavaria and Cologne, 1647 D
Battle of Zusmarshausen, 1648 B
Peace of Westphalia, 1648 D
Turin, League of, against H.R. Empire, League formed, 1733 C
France declares war, 1733 D
Spanish conquer Naples, 1734 B
Battle of Bitonto, 1734 B
French occupy Lorraine and Treves, 1734 B
Battle of Philippsburg, 1734 B
Battle of Parma, 1734 B
imperialists defeated, 1734 C
Spanish take Orbitello, 1735 A
Battle of Klaussen, 1735 A
Spanish siege of Mantua, 1735 B
peace preliminaries of Vienna, 1735 D
Spain accedes to Peace of Vienna, 1736 B
definitive Peace of Vienna, 1738 D
Turkey against Holy Roman Empire, 1525 E
Battle of Mohacs, 1526 C
Buda surrenders, 1526 C
siege of Vienna, 1529 C, D
operations, 1532 B, C
peace signed, 1533 B
war resumed, 1533 B, 1534 B, 1542 C, 1544 A
Hungarian crown jewels seized, 1544 B
truce signed, 1545 D
Turks occupy Moldavia, 1546 E
truce signed, 1547 B
further campaigns, 1551 C, 1552 A, 1553 E
Spanish fleet routed, 1560 A
truce signed, 1562 B
Turks fail at Oran, 1563 C
attack on Malta, 1565 B, C
attack on Hungary renewed, 1566 B
peace treaty with Empire, 1568 A
Spain aids Venice, 1570 B, 1581 E
Turkish fleet harries shipping in Adriatic, 1571 C
Turks defeated at Lepanto, 1571 D
Peace of Constantinople ends war with Venice, 1573 A
Moldavia ravaged, 1574 E
Tunis falls to Turks, 1574 E
war with Empire resumed, 1593 B, 1594 B, 1594 E
Báthory defeats Turks and subdues Wallachia, 1595 D
imperialists defeated at Keresztres, 1596 D
Peace of Zsitva-Torok, 1606 D
Peace of Tyrnau, 1615 B
Battle of Jassy, 1620 C
War with Empire resumed, 1663 B
Battle of St. Gotthard-on-the-Raab, 1664 C

X

Y